MW01253342

Philosophical Perspectives 26, 2012
Philosophy of Mind

PHILOSOPHICAL PERSPECTIVES
Edited by John Hawthorne and Jason Turner

EDITORIAL ADVISORY BOARD
David Albert (Columbia University)
David Chalmers (Australasian National University)
Stewart Cohen (Arizona State University)
Cian Dorr (University of Oxford)
James Drier (Brown University)
Dorothy Edgington (University of Oxford)
Hartry Field (New York University)
Kit Fine (New York University)
Elizabeth Fricker (University of Oxford)
Delia Graff Fara (Princeton University)
Alan Hàjek (Australasian National University)
Rae Langton (Massachusetts Institute of Technology)
Penelope Maddy (University of California, Irvine)
Philip Pettit (Princeton University)
Paul Pietroski (University of Maryland)
Nathan Salmon (University of California, Santa Barbara)
Theodore Sider (Cornell University)
Michael Smith (Princeton University)
Scott Soames (University of Southern California)
Jason Stanley (Rutgers University)
Peter van Inwagen (University of Notre Dame)
Ralph Wedgewood (University of Southern California)
Timothy Williamson (University of Oxford)
Stephen Yablo (Massachusetts Institute of Technology)
Dean Zimmerman (Rutgers University)

Philosophical Perspectives 26, 2012
Philosophy of Mind

Edited by
JOHN HAWTHORNE and JASON TURNER

GUELPH HUMBER LIBRARY
205 Humber College Blvd
Toronto, ON   M9W 5L7

Copyright © 2012 by Wiley Periodicals, Inc.

Wiley Periodicals, Inc.
350 Main Street
Malden, MA 02148 USA

Wiley Periodicals, Inc.
108 Cowley Road
Oxford OX4 1JF
United Kingdom

All rights reserved. Except for the quotation of short passages for the purpose of criticism and review, no part of this publication may be reproduced, stored in a retrieval system or transmitted, in any form or byany means, electronic, mechanical, photocopying, recording or otherwise without the prior permission ofthe publisher.

Cataloging-in-Publication Data has been applied for, and is available at the Library of Congress.

ISBN 978 1 1183 3085 2
ISSN 1520-8583

Philosophical Perspectives, 26, Philosophy of Mind, 2012

Contents

Call for Papers

Philosophical Perspectives invites submissions for these upcoming volumes:

Volume 27, Philosophy of Language (submissions due March 1, 2013)

Volume 28, Ethics (submissions due March 1, 2014)

Up to a third of the papers in each volume will be drawn from submissions. We prefer electronic submissions, in either .pdf or Word .doc form, sent to the editors at:

eds.philosophicalperspectives@gmail.com

Philosophical Perspectives, 26, Philosophy of Mind, 2012

THE USES AND ABUSES OF THE PERSONAL/SUBPERSONAL DISTINCTION

Zoe Drayson
University of Stirling

1. Introduction

It is a commonplace assumption throughout contemporary philosophy of mind that there is a distinction to be made between *personal* and *subpersonal*. What it distinguishes, however, is a matter of confusion: one finds the terms 'personal' and 'subpersonal' predicated of states, facts, explanations, events, and levels, to name a few. Opinions on the grounds of the distinction are just as wide-ranging. As a result, the personal/subpersonal distinction has prompted confusion; philosophers confess to "not grasping exactly how this distinction is to be drawn" (Rey 2001, 105), describe it as a "somewhat obscure distinction" (Machery 2009, 25), or complain that it "isn't very often made clear" (Boghossian 2008, 133). This befuddlement has not prevented the personal/subpersonal distinction being adopted beyond contemporary philosophy of mind: one finds it in metaethics, legal theory, psychiatry, and economics,[1] and being used to reinterpret the work of past thinkers including Descartes, Kant, and Nietzsche.[2] The aim of this paper is to clarify what the personal/subpersonal distinction is and is not, and to caution against the common confusions that surround it.

In this paper, I claim that the personal/subpersonal distinction is first and foremost a distinction between two kinds of psychological theory or explanation: it is only in this form that we can understand why the distinction was first introduced, and how it continues to earn its keep. I go on to examine the different ontological commitments that might lead us from the primary distinction between personal and subpersonal *explanations* to a derivative distinction between personal and subpersonal *states*. I argue that on one of the most common metaphysical interpretations of the explanatory distinction, talk of a distinction between personal and subpersonal states simply makes no sense. When people insist on applying the personal/subpersonal terminology to psychological states, I allow that they are often making a genuine distinction, but one that it is best understood in terms of Stich's (1978) distinction between doxastic and subdoxastic states. I end the paper by considering some other common misinterpretations of the personal/subpersonal distinction, such as those involving consciousness, normativity, or autonomy.

2. Personal and Subpersonal Explanation

2.1 Horizontal and Vertical Explanation

The personal/subpersonal distinction is best understood as a distinction between two types of psychological explanation. The distinction is an instance of a more general distinction — not particular to psychology — between so-called 'vertical' and 'horizontal' approaches to explanation. The practise of separating vertical and horizontal explanation can be found in our everyday explanations as well as in many domains of scientific explanation.[3]

Horizontal explanations are singular and dated: the *explanandum* is a particular event, and the *explanans* cites temporally antecedent events, usually of a causal nature. Calling these 'horizontal' explanations reflects the standard practice whereby "we usually represent diachronic causal relations on a horizontal line, from past (left) to present (right)" (Kim 2005, 36). When we explain why a window broke by citing a sequence of events involving the throwing of a stone, for example, we are giving a horizontal explanation.

Vertical explanations focus on accounting for the features of an event rather than its occurrence. Instead of explaining why this particular window broke when it did, a vertical explanation might focus on why the glass shatters in this particular way: what is it about the glass itself that could account for this phenomenon? The *explanandum* of a vertical explanation is often thought of in terms of a thing's capacities or dispositions, and the *explanans* tends to cite the thing's parts or components, e.g. the molecular structure of the glass. 'Vertical' explanation is so-called "to reflect the usual practice of picturing micro-macro levels in a vertical array" (Kim 2005, 36).

In summary: horizontal explanations attempt to account for an event's occurrence by citing a sequence of preceding events, while vertical explanations attempt to account for a thing's features by citing its components. Notice that the distinction, as I have introduced it, is between explanations considered as semantically evaluable. In other words, it is a distinction between two types of *account*, two *approaches* one can take, or two kinds of explanatory *story* or *theory*. This leaves it open whether the explanations are true or not, and how horizontal and vertical explanations relate to each other. The distinction between horizontal and vertical explanations is therefore a more metaphysically-neutral version of such distinctions as Salmon's (1984) distinction between etiological and constitutive explanations and Schaffer's (forthcoming) distinction between causal and grounding explanations. Like the neutral horizontal/vertical framework, the personal/subpersonal distinction in psychology is primarily between the explanatory accounts themselves rather than between their truthmakers. Similarly, the practice of distinguishing between personal and subpersonal explanations does not rely on any claims about one providing the grounds of the other, or any sort of competition between the two.

2.2 Psychological Explanation

What happens when we apply the vertical/horizontal distinction to psychological explanation? It is clear to see that our everyday "folk" psychological explanations are horizontal: when we explain a person's behaviour, we cite the sequence of mental events that preceded the behaviour, primarily in terms of propositional attitudes such as the person's beliefs and desires. Horizontal psychological explanation of this sort is our default method of accounting for the actions of other people, and is often termed 'personal' explanation.

The idea of vertical psychological explanation has traditionally been considered problematic, because it is not clear how an explanation could be both vertical and psychological. To give a vertical account of a person's psychological features would require citing features of the person's components, but the obvious way to think about such components is in physiological terms: brain regions, cells, or neurotransmitters. While these sorts of physiological components might account for a person's physiological features like movements or reflexes, it's hard to see how they could account for a person's *psychological* features: their ability to learn a language, for example, or their capacity for mental arithmetic. Accounting for psychological features in terms of the features of physiological components seems to leave an explanatory gap. One might take this merely as evidence that we don't currently know how to give a satisfying physiological account of human psychology, but some philosophers have made a stronger claim: following in the tradition of Wittgenstein and Ryle, it is suggested that to use non-psychological concepts to account for psychological concepts is to change the subject or make a category mistake.

Does this mean there can't be vertical psychological explanations? The alternative approach would be to ascribe *psychological* instead of physiological predicates to a person's components: this would seem to count as genuinely psychological vertical explanation. Here, however, vertical psychological explanation can be accused of committing the *mereological fallacy*: ascribing to a part of something a predicate that can only correctly be ascribed to the whole thing. In this case, the fallacy would be to ascribe a psychological predicate to a person's component part, where that psychological predicate can only be ascribed correctly to the whole person. Worries about the mereological fallacy can be found in the work of Wittgenstein and followers:

> It comes to this: Only of a human being and what resembles (behaves like) a living human being can one say: it has sensations; it sees, is blind; hears, is deaf; is conscious or unconscious. (Wittgenstein 1953, para.281)

> It makes no sense to ascribe psychological predicates (or their negations) to the brain [...] Psychological predicates are predicates that apply essentially to the whole living animal, not to its parts. (Hacker and Bennett 2003, 72)

By the 1960s, however, psychologists were often to be found ascribing psychological predicates to parts of persons. The justification for such ascriptions was based on the observation that parts of persons — parts of their brains — behaved in ways sufficiently similar to whole persons that there was no fallacy involved. In the above quotation, notice that even Wittgenstein allowed that psychological predicates can be ascribed to what *resembles* or *behaves like* a person. When researchers in psychology, robotics, and computer science began to notice that parts of intelligent systems often seem to function in ways similar to the intelligent systems themselves, it looked like this similarity was "sufficient to warrant an adjusted use of psychological vocabulary to characterize that behavior" (Dennett 2007, 78).

2.3 Functional Analysis and Subpersons

Ascribing psychological predicates to parts of persons was the result of psychologists adopting the approach of *functional analysis*. Functional analysis is an approach to understanding complex systems, both biological and non-biological, in which we attempt to explain how a system works by understanding the functional contributions of its components. It involves singling out the functional phenomenon that we want to comprehend, and analysing it into a number of simpler functions. Each of these subfunctions can, if needed, be decomposed into further sub-subfunctions. The functional analysis ends when we can explain the lowest level of functions by appealing to natural laws such as mechanical or biological principles.[4] Many complex systems can be understood in this way, such as the fuel-injection system of a car or the digestive system of a cow.

In psychology, the adoption of functional analysis began with psychologists Deutsch (1960) and Attneave (1961). In opposition to the behaviourist trend of the time, Deutsch realized that functional analysis could provide a way of thinking about psychological states as internal states, without descending to the level of neuroscience:

> An event is explained by being deduced as the property of a structure, system or mechanism and not as an instance of events in its own class. [...] The precise properties of the parts do not matter; it is only their general relationships to each

other which give the machine as a whole its behavioural properties. (Deutsch 1960, 1)

The early of work of Fodor (1965, 1968) was also influential in emphasising the view that psychological theories work by providing descriptions of psychological *functions*.[5]

So how does functional analysis in psychology work? It explains complex psychological capacities, such as depth perception or language acquisition, by breaking them down into simpler subcapacities that combine to produce the complex phenomena. The following quotations illustrate how functional analysis works when applied to the science of psychology:

> [A] large part of the psychologist's job is to explain how the complex behavioral capacities of organisms are acquired and how they are exercised. Both goals are greatly facilitated by analysis of the capacities in question, for the acquisition of the analyzed capacity resolves itself into acquisition of the analyzing capacities and the requisite organization, and the problem of performance resolves itself into the problem of how the analyzing capacities are exercised. (Cummins 1975, 761)

> [T]he psychologist will first explain the behaviour and behavioural capacities of the whole person in terms of the joint behaviour and capacities of the person's immediately subpersonal departments, and if deeper and more detailed explanation is desired, the psychologist will explain the behaviour of the departments in terms of the joint behaviour and capacities of their own components, and so on down as far as anyone might care to go. (Lycan 1988, 5)

Functional analysis in psychology involves a particular kind of decomposition: the decomposition of the person into *subpersons* to whom we ascribe the sorts of psychological predicates that can explain the personal-level capacities. The ascription of subcapacities to subpersons is thought to avoid committing the mereological fallacy because the component parts of persons appear to function like persons themselves:

> It is an empirical fact, and a surprising one, that our brains — more particularly, parts of our brains — engage in processes that are strikingly like guessing, deciding, believing, jumping to conclusions, etc. And it is enough like these personal level behaviors to warrant stretching ordinary usage to cover it. (Dennett 2007, 86)

2.4 Subpersons and Homunculi

Functional analysis in psychology purports to offer vertical psychological explanation that is genuinely psychological, while avoiding the mereological fallacy. All this talk of subpersons or subagents, however, should worry us: it looks like we are trying to explain intelligent beings by positing internal intelligent beings. Worries about such 'homunculi' had earlier been problematic for introspectionist psychology, and were one of the motivations behind behaviourist psychology. As a result, behaviourist psychologists like Skinner (1964) were very suspicious of any attempt to reintroduce psychological predicates into vertical explanations.

> Skinner sees — or almost sees — that there is a special way that questions can be begged in psychology, and this way is akin to introducing a homunculus. Since psychology's task is to account for the intelligence or rationality of men and animals, it cannot fulfil its task if anywhere along the line it presupposes intelligence or rationality. (Dennett 1978, 58)

The homunculus fallacy is closely related to Ryle's (1949) worry about regress: if our explanations of intelligent mental states or activities require positing further intellectual mental states or activities, then the explanation will lead to an infinite regress. If we have to posit an internal learner or thinker or decider in order to explain a person's capacity to learn, think, or decide, then we have merely postponed the problem rather than solved it.

(Notice that the homunculus fallacy differs from the mereological fallacy. The latter concerns the correct use of our concepts, while the former concerns our explanatory practices. Even if we establish a case for ascribing psychological predicates to parts of persons, the question still remains regarding the explanatory work that can be done this way.)

Psychologist Attneave (1961) was the first to point out that as long as homunculi were used the right way, there was nothing either ghostly or regressive about them. Homunculi are only problematic if we posit an internal agent's psychological capacity to explain that same psychological capacity of the person. If, on the other hand, we posit *several* less-intelligent agents with a *range of capacities* to account for a more-intelligent agent's capacity, it looks like less of a problem.

> It was Attneave's insight that homunculi can after all be useful posits, so long as their appointed functions do not simply parrot the intelligent capacities being explained. For a subjects's intelligent performance can be explained as being the joint product of several constituent performances, individually less demanding, by subagencies of the subject acting in concert. We account for the subject's intelligent activity, not by idly positing a single homunculus within that subject whose job it simply is to perform that activity, but by reference to a collaborative team of homunculi, whose members are individually more specialized and less talented. (Lycan 1991, 259)

One of the important points to remember about functional analysis is that it bottoms out: at some point the functions are subsumed under basic laws. In the case of psychological functional analysis, this means that when the person's capacities are understood in terms of the subcapacities of various subpersons, each of these is further analysed into the subsubcapacities of various subsubpersons, getting progressively less intelligent at each level of decomposition. Eventually, we reach a level where we don't need to ascribe psychological predicates to the components at all: we can understand them in terms of mechanical or biological laws.

> The AI researcher *starts* with an intentionally characterized problem (e.g., how can I get a computer to *understand* questions of English?), breaks it down into sub-problems that are also intentionally characterized (e.g., how do I get the computer to *recognize* questions, *distinguish* subjects from predicates, *ignore* irrelevant parsings?) and then breaks these problems down still further until finally he reaches problem or task descriptions that are obviously mechanistic. (Dennett 1978, 80)

Any worries about homuncular regress are taken care of by this idea that the intelligent components become progressively less intelligent until they can be explained without the need for any psychological predicates at all. This leaves us with a notion of vertical explanation which is genuinely psychological, in virtue of decomposing the person into subpersons, without invoking a regress. This is what is meant by subpersonal explanation.

2.5 The Personal/Subpersonal Distinction

We are now in a position to see what subpersonal explanations are, why there are important to the science of psychology, and why it matters that we distinguish them from personal explanations.

The point of the personal/subpersonal distinction is to emphasise that there is a type of psychological explanation which is not folk-psychological: it is not horizontal, and it does not consist in ascribing psychological predicates to whole persons. In addition to our everyday 'personal' psychological explanations, there are 'subpersonal' psychological explanations that use functional analysis to understand the person in terms of their components, where these components function sufficiently like persons to be thought of as subpersons.

> Sub-personal theories proceed by analyzing a person into an organization of subsystems [...] and attempting to explain the behaviour of the whole person as the outcome of the interaction of these subsystems. (Dennett 1978, 154)

The practice of offering such psychological theories began with Deutsch (1960) and Attneave (1961), but the term 'subpersonal' was first coined by Dennett (1969) in his distinction between "personal and subpersonal *levels of explanation*" (Dennett 1969, 93). Dennett pointed out that while horizontal explanations in psychology focus on "the explanatory level of people and their sensations and activities", there was a second kind of psychological explanation, vertical explanation, which focused on "the sub-personal level of brains and events in the nervous system" (Dennett 1969, 93).

Subpersonal explanation offered an alternative to personal explanation that was still genuinely psychological, which in turn allowed the birth of cognitive science: explaining intelligence with intelligence became a reputable approach once it was clear how the mereological and homunculus fallacies are avoided. And it was in this sense that the personal/subpersonal distinction can be understood as being "instrumental in the development and flourishing of the cognitive sciences" (Kriegel 2012, 77). Subpersonal psychology allows us to give vertical explanations of psychological capacities without requiring detailed knowledge of neural factors, thereby providing "precisely the enabling move that lets us see how on earth to get whole wonderful persons out of brute mechanical parts" (Dennett 2007, 89). The introduction of a distinctively subpersonal level of psychological explanation provides an additional way to understand people, supplementing our traditional folk-psychological explanations and the theories of neural circuitry.

The personal/subpersonal distinction not only allows us to distinguish between vertical and horizontal psychological explanations in general, but also enables us to clarify individual instances of psychological predicate ascription. Since both horizontal and vertical explanations in psychology use the same terminology of mental states and intentionally specified capacities, it's important that we can distinguish the ascription of a particular psychological predicate to a part of person from the ascription of the same psychological predicate to a whole person. The personal/subpersonal distinction is what allows us to avoid confusion.

As should now be apparent, the personal/subpersonal distinction is first and foremost a distinction between kinds of psychological *explanation* or *theory*. When Dennett (1969) first introduces the distinction, he also talks of personal and subpersonal "stories" (78), "accounts" (92), and "points of view" (69) — all of which emphasise that the distinction is between semantically-evaluable entities. Dennett's distinction has become widely used throughout philosophy of mind and beyond, but it is no longer confined to explanation. In some of the more recent literature, the personal/subpersonal distinction is applied to entities such as events (Hurley 1998), processes (Rowlands 2006), states (Machery 2009), contents (McGinn 1988), mechanisms (Metzinger 2003), and facts (Hornsby 2001). In the following section, I focus on the concept of personal and subpersonal *states* to explore how the original distinction might be developed in such a way as to account for the contemporary usage.

3. Personal and Subpersonal States

3.1 What is a Personal State?

It is not obvious that we should expect a distinction between explanatory accounts to correspond to a distinction between other entities. First, notice that we might be anti-realist about explanation in general, and we might hold that an account is an explanation in virtue of its internal structure rather than in virtue of its relation to external states of affairs. And in order to be an explanation, recall that the account doesn't have to be true: 'how-possibly' explanation still count as explanations on this view. One might think that explanations can be instrumental, and that their terms can fail to refer. But even if we focus our attention on referential explanations, there's no one clear answer to what sort of states they posit. In the case of *personal* explanation, for example, notice that terms like 'belief' and 'desire' don't necessarily pick out internal states of the person. Following Steward, for example, we might think that "the 'ontological commitments' of folk psychology are usually best understood as commitments to abstract entities, not unobservable concrete ones" (Steward 1997, 242). On this view, to be in a mental state is to instantiate a certain relation to a proposition, rather than to possess an internal state: "Subjects are in mental states, not vice versa" (Williamson 2009, 331).[6]

On an alternative construal of folk psychology, one might think that we instantiate a relation to a proposition in virtue of having an internal representation: an internal state that bears the content of the proposition. This representational theory of mind involves a three-place relation rather than a two-place relation: the relation between people and the content of their thoughts is mediated by internal representations. But even on this view, we are not committed to any particular view of the nature of mental representations.

Merely to indulge in the practise of personal psychological explanation, therefore, is not to be committed to any particular notion of a 'personal state'. What about subpersonal explanations: do they posit a certain kind of 'subpersonal state'?

3.2 What is a Subpersonal State?

Subpersonal explanations, just like personal explanations, need not be referential. Some philosophers and scientists treat subpersonal psychological explanations as *heuristics* to help identify the underlying physiological explanations of behaviour, while denying the existence of subpersonal psychological states. Bickle (2003), for example, holds that subpersonal psychological explanations merely serve as methodological tools to help us locate the "real neurobiological explanations" (Bickle 2003, 110) that don't cite mental states:

> They tell us where in the brain to look [...] But that is all they do, and all they can do. When they've exhausted this descriptive and methodological function they fall away, much like Wittgenstein's ladder (Bickle 2003, 130)

Bechtel and McCauley (1999) hold a similar view called 'heuristic identity theory'.

If we reject such instrumentalist views of subpersonal explanations and claim that subpersonal explanations are more than mere heuristics, we can ask what sorts of states these explanations posit. As we saw, the standard method of subpersonal psychological explanation takes the form of functional analysis, which posits functional components of the persons that combine to account for the psychological capacities of the person. But notice that a commitment to subpersonal components is not a commitment to any particular relationship between those subpersonal components and the states (whatever they might be) posited by personal explanation.

Thus far, I have said nothing about computational states. The practice of functional analysis is logically independent of computation: the traditional view of functional analysis proceeds by specifying component types and their functions "without specifying the precise state types and state transitions that must occur within the analyzed system" (Piccinini 2004, 818). In practice, however, the project of functional analysis in psychology is often supplemented with computational theory. Computational theory can help us to understand how basic low-level capacities can result in more complex capacities in the way that functional analysis describes: it "supplies us with extremely powerful techniques for constructing diverse analyses of very sophisticated tasks into very unsophisticated tasks" (Cummins 1975, 764). In addition to psychological capacities and activities, computation adds the postulation of discrete internal psychological states. In order to explain the capacities of the subpersonal components, the computational states themselves have psychological predicates ascribed to them. In other words, computational states are understood as representational states.[7] And notice that thinking about subpersonal psychological explanations as computational is not to be committed to any particular view of the relation between personal and subpersonal psychological theories.

All of this serves to highlight that there is no definitive notion of a 'subpersonal state' that comes out of the distinction between personal and subpersonal explanations. The distinction between personal and subpersonal psychological explanations does not licence any particular commitment to personal or subpersonal states, without further metaphysical claims.

3.3 Personal/Subpersonal Relations

The existence of personal and subpersonal psychological explanations does not directly result in a commitment to personal and subpersonal psychological states: for that, one needs to supplement the claim about our explanatory accounts with some metaphysical claims. One way to do this is to combine the subpersonal explanatory strategy of functional analysis with personal explanation, and claim that the mental states posited by personal explanations correspond to the functional components posited by subpersonal explanation. An example of this approach is Lycan's 'homuncular functionalism':

I propose to type-identify a mental state with the property of having such-and-such an institutionally characterized state of affairs obtaining in one (or more) of one's appropriate homunctional departments or subagencies. (Lycan 1987, 41)

Lycan makes it clear that his metaphysical position of homuncular functionalism does not follow merely from the practise of giving subpersonal psychological explanations. He describes his position as "a metaphysics inspired by an epistemology" (Lycan 1991, 259), where the epistemological aspect is the explanatory approach of functional decomposition used in psychology.

This metaphysical position can be adapted to take into account the computational approach to subpersonal psychology. In this case, the beliefs and desires posited by personal explanation correspond to the computational states posited by subpersonal theories. In Fodor's words, "having a particular propositional attitude is being in some computational relation to an internal representation" (Fodor 1975, 198).[8] On this view, the computational state carries the content that we ascribe to the propositional attitude: we ascribe the same content to the mental state posited in personal explanation and to the computational state posited in subpersonal explanation.[9]

> We can begin from the assumption that *personal-level events of conscious thought* are underpinned by occurrences of physical configurations belonging to types that figure in the science of information-processing psychology. These physical configurations can be assigned the contents of the thoughts that they underpin. So we assume that, if a person consciously or occurrently thinks that p, then there is a state that has the representational content that p and is of a type that can figure in *subpersonal-level psychological structures and processes*. (Davies 2005, 370, my italics)

Notice that when we identify the posits of personal and subpersonal explanations, whether or not computational theory is involved, we lose any notion of a distinction between personal and subpersonal *states*: the terms of personal and subpersonal explanations refer to the same entities. So not only does the original personal/subpersonal distinction fail to licence *any clear distinction* between personal and subpersonal states, personal and subpersonal states become *indistinguishable* when common metaphysical claims are combined with the explanatory form of the personal/subpersonal distinction. This should make us very wary of some philosophers' tendencies to switch from talking of personal and subpersonal explanations to talking of the 'corresponding' personal and subpersonal states.

And although Lycan is clear on the difference between adopting the explanatory practice of psychology and using it to provide a metaphysics of mental states, not everyone keeps the distinction in mind. Fodor later acknowledged that some his own work may have contributed to what he calls "the widespread failure to distinguish the computational program in psychology from the functionalist program in metaphysics" (Fodor 2000, 105). Partly as a result of this failure, the distinction between personal and subpersonal psychological explanations has been entangled with talk of personal and subpersonal states. What's particularly troubling is that even those people who (like Lycan and Fodor) identify propositional attitudes with functional or computational states persist in drawing a distinction between what they call 'personal' and 'subpersonal' states — despite having a metaphysical position that prevents any such distinction. How should we understand this?

3.4 Doxastic and Subdoxastic States

Once the personal/subpersonal distinction is adapted into a metaphysical claim about the relation between the two types of explanation, as in the Fodor and Lycan examples above, something interesting happens. Each propositional attitude posited by personal explanation is identified with a functional or computational state posited by a subpersonal theory, but not every functional or computational state is identified with a propositional attitude. This is a result of how functional analysis works, and in particular the way it avoids committing the homunculus fallacy. Each intelligent capacity is analysed into less intelligent subcapacities, which are further analysed into even less intelligent sub-subcapacities. While the higher-level capacities might be identified with folk-psychological mental states, the lower-level capacities might play important roles in psychological explanation despite not corresponding to any of our standard 'mental states'. The two most often-cited examples of these lower-level capacities involve language-learning and visual processing. In the first of these, psychological theories of children's linguistic competence posit the existence of internal grammar states: stored information that allows children to become competent speakers despite having insufficient input from their environments. The second example concerns the early stages of visual processing: how does our sparse retinal data lead to a rich and detailed conscious percept? Vision psychologists propose that we have computational processes converting information about reflectance properties and light intensity into information about surfaces and edges, for example. Such capacities as these don't correspond to anything that we find in personal explanation: we don't have *beliefs* about the complex mathematical equations that convert luminosity values into edges; we can't *experience* the contents of our stored grammatical rules, or use the information to draw inferences, for example. So even if we identify some of the functions or computations posited by subpersonal explanations with states posited by personal explanations, there will remain other functions or computations that don't correspond to anything posited by personal explanation.

This observation was first made by Stich (1978), who labelled these lower-level states 'subdoxastic', in contrast to doxastic states like belief. He noticed that our subdoxastic states are isolated, in the sense that we can't use the information they carry in our reasoning or speech, and that we have no conscious access to them. Stich concluded that "[s]ubdoxastic states occur in a variety of separate, special purpose cognitive subsystems" (Stich 1978, 508). Our doxastic states, on the other hand, "form a consciously accessible, inferentially integrated cognitive subsystem" (Stich 1978, 508). This talk of cognitive subsystems makes it clear that Stich is drawing a distinction between two kinds of functional component that appear in subpersonal psychological explanations. His distinction is between those components that map onto everyday mental states, and those components that don't.

Stich's distinction does not appear to be used frequently in the current literature, at least if we look for the terminological indications. But the distinction itself, between those functional or computational states that correspond to our folk psychological states and those that don't, is still alive and well. But more often than not, the distinction is labelled as between 'personal' and 'subpersonal' states rather than 'doxastic' and 'subdoxastic' states.

Fodor (1983), for example, endorsed Stich's distinction in its original form. But a few years later, we find him describing the computational components of his metaphysical view as follows:

> At the very top are states which may well correspond to propositional attitudes that common sense is prepared to acknowledge [...] But at the bottom and middle levels there are bound to be lots of symbol processing operations that correspond to nothing that people – as opposed to their nervous systems – ever do. These are the operations of what Dennett has called "sub-personal" computational systems (Fodor 1987, 24)

The distinction that Fodor is drawing here is not Dennett's distinction between personal and subpersonal explanations: the computational hierarchy he describes is found in subpersonal rather than personal explanations. He is instead drawing a distinction between two types of computational component, on the basis of whether or not they correspond to propositional attitudes. This is quite clearly a reference to Stich's distinction rather than Dennett's distinction.

A more recent example of the confusion between the two distinctions can be found in Kriegel's (2012) discussion of the 'two visual systems' hypothesis. This is the suggestion that there are two computational pathways in the brain which process visual input in different ways: the dorsal stream leads to conscious perception, while the ventral stream guides fine-grained hand movements in the absence of conscious control. Kriegel makes the claim that "online, on-the-fly visually guided action turns out to be determined by dorsal stream (sub-personal) representations, not ventral stream (potentially personal) ones" (Kriegel 2012, 84). But the computational theories he is discussing are subpersonal psychological theories, which attempt to account for our psychological capacities in terms of subcapacities of our psychological components. Kriegel cannot be referring to the distinction between personal and subpersonal psychological explanations, because only the subpersonal explanations are relevant here. The distinction he seems to be drawing is between those computational states that correspond to the states posited in personal explanation (conscious perception, in this case) and those computational states that don't correspond in this way. If this interpretation is correct, then the distinction Kriegel is in fact using is Stich's distinction between doxastic and subdoxastic states.

Similar ways of using the terms 'personal' and 'subpersonal' can be found throughout philosophy of mind. The term 'subpersonal' is almost always used to refer to the states of the early visual system, or to the grammatical information in the language system, and almost never to refer to functional or computational states that correspond to our everyday mental states. This suggests that 'subpersonal' is being used instead of 'subdoxastic' to make Stich's (1978) distinction. Notice that in the following quotation, Burge cannot be using 'subpersonal level' to refer to the subpersonal level of explanation:

> I take the subpersonal level to be a level that is not only not conscious, but is not accessible to introspective or reflective consciousness and must be gotten at only theoretically. This is true of the basic grammatical structures underlying our linguistic competence and the information-processing structures underlying our perceptual experience. (Burge 2003, 384)

The subpersonal level of explanation can posit conscious states, accessible to introspection. The most charitable reading of Burge would interpret him as meaning 'subdoxastic' by 'subpersonal'.

4. What the Personal/Subpersonal Distinction Isn't

In the first part of this paper, I showed what the personal/subpersonal distinction *is*: a distinction between two kinds of psychological explanation, one horizontal and the other vertical. I also showed why this is an important distinction: the very introduction of subpersonal psychology, via the method of functional analysis, allows us to form psychological explanations that are genuinely vertical, i.e. distinct from our folk psychological horizontal explanations. This is turn allows us to bridge the explanatory gap between folk psychology and neural circuitry.

The remainder of the paper has been concerned with the abuses, rather than the uses, of the personal/subpersonal distinction. I showed that merely having a distinction between personal and subpersonal psychological explanations does not involve a commitment to any particular kind of psychological state: the explanatory distinction is consistent with a number of ways of thinking about the sorts of states referred to. Talk of personal and subpersonal psychological *states* only makes sense, therefore, within an established framework of metaphysical commitments. But on one of the most common metaphysical frameworks, personal and subpersonal explanations pick out the same set of psychological states: on this view, there is no distinction between personal and subpersonal states, only between the explanations that posit them. I suggest, therefore, that using the personal/subpersonal distinction as if it coincided with or licenced a distinction between two types of psychological states constitutes an abuse of the original distinction. Furthermore, I argued that in many instances where people take themselves to be implementing the personal/subpersonal distinction, they are in fact using Stich's distinction between doxastic and subdoxastic states. This abuse of the personal/subpersonal terminology has resulted in much confusion in philosophy of mind and beyond.

Any way of using the personal/subpersonal distinction that takes it to be a distinction between ontological categories is misleading. The personal/subpersonal distinction should not be understood as a distinction between the mental and physical, for example: the whole point of subpersonal explanations is that they involve the ascription of mental states, just as personal explanations do. Similarly, it is wrong to portray the personal/subpersonal distinction as equivalent to the distinction between intentional and mechanistic explanations. Even where subpersonal explanations posit mechanisms, they are intentionally described.

One common misinterpretation of the personal/subpersonal distinction involves taking it to distinguish what is conscious from what is unconscious. This is a misinterpretation whether we're talking about the cognitive unconscious or a Freudian notion of the unconscious. If we're interested in the cognitive unconscious, then Stich's distinction would be more suitable, for reasons already discussed. And if we're interested in the Freudian unconscious, then it's not clear that subpersonal explanations come into play at all: psychoanalytic theories tend to involve personal explanations in terms of beliefs, desires, and so on. These may be unconscious mental states, but they arguably account for behaviour by giving a horizontal explanation rather than a vertical explanation.[10]

One of the most pervasive misinterpretations of the personal/subpersonal distinction uses the distinction to support the Sellarsian idea that there are two distinct realms, the space of reasons and the space of causes. Proponents of this view, including Hurley (1998) and Hornsby (2001), take personal explanations to be essentially normative and reason-giving, and subpersonal explanations to be non-normative and mechanistic or causal. On this view, the point of the distinction is to emphasise the autonomy (irreducibility) of propositional attitude explanations that results from the normative constraints on them. This sort of position requires further argument, and cannot be derived from the personal/subpersonal distinction alone.

Acknowledgements

Versions of this paper have been presented at the University of Bristol, the University of Edinburgh, the Australian National University, and Macquarie University, and it was also presented at 'The Personal and Subpersonal' conference at the Institute of Philosophy in London in May 2012. Many thanks to everyone involved. Particular thanks are due to Kathleen Akins, David Chalmers, Andy Clark, John Collins, Tim Crane, Daniel Dennett, Anthony Everett, Patrick Greenough, Frank Jackson, Peter Menzies, Michelle Montague, Daniel Nolan, Matthew Nudds, Barry Smith, Mark Sprevak, Daniel Stoljar, and Tillman Vierkant.

Notes

1. Ferrero (2009) questions whether the principle constitutive of agency operate at the personal or subpersonal level; Moore (2010) includes the notion of 'subpersonal intentions' in his theory of criminal law; Hughes (2011) distinguishes understanding the dementia patient as a person from understanding the subpersonal causes of the dementia; Ross (2007) discusses various attempts to model an economics of the subpersonal.
2. See, for example, Sorell's *Descartes Reinvented* (2005), Brook's *Kant and the Mind* (1994), and Janaway's *Willing and Nothingness* (1998).
3. Further discussion on the notion of horizontal and vertical explanations can be found in Hoffman (1997), Bermúdez (2005), Gaukroger (2010), and Dear (2012).
4. See Cummins (1983) for a detailed treatment of functional analysis.
5. Piccinini (2004) contains an extended discussion of the birth of functional analysis in psychological theorizing.
6. See also Thau (2007) on the distinction between internal and instantial states.
7. Notice that this still leaves us with more than one way of cashing out the notion of a computational state. One might think, like Cummins (1989), that the attribution of mentalistic terms to computational states is just a matter of interpretation. Alternatively, one might have a semantic view of computation, according to which computational states are essentially representational: see Fodor (1975), for example.
8. Fodor remains neutral on the precise relation (e.g. identity, supervenience) between tokens of propositional attitudes and tokens of computational states. In his later work he claims that he is "by no means convinced that such issues have much substance" (Fodor 2008, 6).
9. It is possible to use computational theory to give subpersonal psychological explanations without first adopting the programme of functional analysis: a capacity can be analysed into a list of instructions for a sequence of operations without having first to be analysed into subcapacities of functional components (see Piccinini 2004). But most approaches to computational psychology, including Fodor's own, begin by analysing the person's psychological capacities into functional subcapacities. (Fodor's modularity view is a clear example of functional decomposition.) When Fodor identifies propositional attitudes with relations to computational states, those computational states are understood as the states of a *subsystem*. Even thought that subsystem is labelled as the 'central

system' or the 'general reasoner', it is still a functional *component* of the overall system.
10. Garvey (2008) also suggests the explanations in cognitive science are subpersonal whereas explanations in psychoanalysis are personal.

References

Attneave F. (1961). In defense of homunculi. In *Sensory Communication*, Rosenblith WA, (ed.), pp. 777–782. New York, NJ: MIT Press and John Wiley.

Bechtel, W. P. & McCauley, R. N. (1999). Heuristic identity theory (or back to the future): The mind-body problem against the background of research strategies in cognitive neuroscience. In Martin Hahn & S. C. Stoness (eds.), *Proceedings of the 21st Annual Meeting of the Cognitive Science Society*. Lawrence Erlbaum.

Bermúdez, J. L. (2005). *Philosophy of Psychology: A Contemporary Introduction*. Routledge.

Bickle, J. (2003). *Philosophy and Neuroscience: A Ruthlessly Reductive Account*. Kluwer Academic Publishers.

Boghossian, P. A. (2008). *Content and Justification: Philosophical Papers*. Oxford University Press.

Brook, A. (1994). *Kant and the Mind*. Cambridge University Press.

Burge, T. (2003). Concepts, conceptions, reflective understanding: Reply to Peacocke. In Martin Hahn & B. Ramberg (eds.), *Reflections and Replies: Essays on the Philosophy of Tyler Burge*. MIT Press.

Cummins, R. C. (1975). Functional Analysis. *Journal of Philosophy* 72 (November): 741–64.

Cummins, R. C. (1983). *The Nature of Psychological Explanation*. MIT Press.

Cummins, R. C. (1989). *Meaning and Mental Representation*. MIT Press.

Davies, M. (2005). Cognitive science. In F. Jackson & M. Smith (eds.), *The Oxford Handbook of Contemporary Philosophy*. Oxford University Press.

Dear, P. (2012). Horizontal explanations in the Enlightenment. *Studies in History and Philosophy of Science Part A* 43 (1): 221–223.

Dennett, D. C. (1969). *Content and Consciousness*. Routledge and Kegan Paul.

Dennett, D. C. (1978). *Brainstorms*. MIT Press.

Dennett, D. C. (2007). Philosophy as naïve anthropology: comment on Bennett and Hacker. In Bennett, M., Dennett, D. C., Hacker, P. M. S. & Searle, J. R. (eds.) *Neuroscience and Philosophy: Brain, Mind, and Language*. Columbia University Press.

Deutsch, J. A. (1960). *The structural basis of behavior*. Cambridge: Cambridge University Press.

Ferrero, L. (2009). Constitutivism and the inescapability of agency, *Oxford Studies in Metaethics* 4: 303–333.

Fodor, J. A. (1965). Explanations in psychology. In M. Black (Ed.), *Philosophy in America*. London: Routledge and Kegan Paul.

Fodor, J. A. (1968). *Psychological explanation*. New York: Random House.

Fodor, J. A. (1975). *The Language of Thought*. Harvard University Press.

Fodor, J. A. (1983). *The Modularity of Mind*. MIT Press.

Fodor, J. A. (1987). *Psychosemantics: The problem of meaning in the philosophy of mind*. MIT Press.

Fodor, J. A. (2000). *The Mind Doesn't Work That Way: The Scope and Limits of Computational Psychology*. MIT Press.

Fodor, J. A. (2008). *LOT2: The Language of Thought Revisited*. OUP.

Garvey, B. (2008). Quasi-beliefs and crazy beliefs: Subdoxastic states and the 'special characteristics' of the unconscious. In C. Kerslake and R. Brassier (eds.), *Origins and Ends of the Psyche: Philosophical Essays on Psychoanalysis*, Leuven University Press.

Gaukroger, S. (2010). *The Collapse of Mechanism and the Rise of Sensibility: Science and the Shaping of Modernity, 1680–1760*. OUP Oxford.

Hacker, P. M. S. & Bennett, M. R. (2003). *Philosophical Foundations of Neuroscience*. Malden MA: Blackwell Publishing.

Hoffmann, R. (1997). *The Same and Not the Same*, New York: Columbia University Press.

Hornsby, J. (2001). *Simple Mindedness: In Defense of Naive Naturalism in the Philosophy of Mind*. Harvard University Press.

Hughes, J. C. (2011). *Thinking Through Dementia*. Oxford University Press.

Hurley, S. L. (1998). *Consciousness in Action*. Harvard University Press.

Janaway, C. (1998). *Willing and Nothingness: Schopenhauer as Nietzsche's Educator*. Oxford University Press.

Kim, J. (2005). *Physicalism, or Something Near Enough*. Princeton University Press.

Kriegel, U. (2012). Personal-level representation. *Protosociology*. 28: 77–114.

Lycan, W. G. (1987). *Consciousness*. MIT Press.

Lycan, W. G. (1988). *Judgement and Justification*. Cambridge University Press.

Lycan, W. G. (1991). Homuncular functionalism meets PDP. In William Ramsey, Stephen P. Stich & D. Rumelhart (eds.), *Philosophy and Connectionist Theory*. Lawrence Erlbaum.

Machery, E. (2009). *Doing Without Concepts*. Oxford University Press.

McGinn, C. (1988). Consciousness and content. Proceedings of the British Academy 74: 219–39.

Metzinger, T. (2003). *Being No One: The Self-Model Theory of Subjectivity*. MIT Press.

Moore, M. A. (2010). *Placing Blame: a theory of the criminal law*. Oxford University Press.

Piccinini, G. (2004). Functionalism, Computationalism, and Mental States. *Studies in the History and Philosophy of Science* 35 (4): 811–833.

Rey, G. (2001). Physicalism and psychology: a plea for a substantive philosophy of mind. In C. Gillett & B. M. Loewer (eds.), *Physicalism and its Discontents*. Cambridge University Press.

Ross, D. (2007). The economics of the sub-personal: two research programs, In B. Montero and M.D. White (eds.), *Economics and the Mind*, 41–57. Taylor & Francis.

Ryle, G. (1949). *The Concept of Mind*. Hutchinson and Co.

Rowlands, Mark (2006). *Body Language: Representation in Action*. Cambridge MA: Bradford Book/MIT Press.

Salmon, W. (1984). *Scientific Explanation and the Causal Structure of the World*. Princeton University Press.

Schaffer, J. (forthcoming). Grounding, transitivity, and contrastivity. In Correia and Schnieder (eds.), *Grounding and Explanation*. CUP.

Skinner, B. F. (1964). Behaviorism at fifty. In T. Wann (ed.), *Behaviorism and Phenomenology: Contrasting Bases for Modern Psychology*. University of Chicago Press.

Sorell, T. (2005). *Descartes Reinvented*. Cambridge University Press.

Steward, H. (1997). *The Ontology of Mind: Events, Processes, and States*. Oxford University Press.

Stich, S. P. (1978). Beliefs and subdoxastic states. *Philosophy of Science* 45: 499–518.

Thau, M. (2007). Response to Jackson. *Philosophical Studies* 132 (3): 607–623.

Williamson, T. (2009). Replies to Critics. In D. Pritchard and P. Greenough (eds.) *Williamson on Knowledge*, 279–384. Oxford University Press.

Wittgenstein, L. (1953). *Philosophical Investigations*. G.E.M. Anscombe and R. Rhees (eds.), G.E.M. Anscombe (trans.), Oxford: Blackwell.

Philosophical Perspectives, 26, Philosophy of Mind, 2012

PERCEPTION WITHOUT PROPOSITIONS

Christopher Gauker
University of Cincinnati

1. Introduction

In recent years, many philosophers have claimed that perceptual representations bear some kind of propositional content. If the baby in the stroller looks unhappy, then I have a visual perception of the baby that says, "The baby is unhappy". If the tree on the left looks further away than the tree on the right, then I have a visual perception that says, "The tree on the left is further away than the tree on the right".

There are basically three motivations for this claim. The first is that perceptions can be correct or incorrect. The hypothesis that they bear propositional contents explains this, because on that hypothesis the correctness of a perception can be identified with the truth of the proposition it bears. The second has to do with the phenomenon of seeing-as. It is tempting to suppose that when one sees the duck-rabbit as a duck, one's perception says, "That's a duck". The third is the assumption that perceptions justify beliefs in much the way that beliefs justify other beliefs. On that assumption, it is argued that perceptions must bear propositional contents just as beliefs do.[1]

In the first half of this paper I will clear a space for an alternative account of perceptual representation by raising some doubts about the third of these motives. First, I will question an argument that is often given for the assumption that perceptions justify beliefs. Then I will argue that anyone committed to the view that perceptions justify beliefs is committed as well to the claim that the belief-justifying aspects of the propositional contents of perceptions are accessible to the perceiving subject without empirical research. Finally, I will argue, on the basis of that assumption, that the position that perceptions justify beliefs faces a basic dilemma. Either the concepts that make up the belief-justifying aspects of the propositions that perceptions bear are "general" concepts, comprising a range of determinate species, or, instead, the concepts that make up the belief-justifying aspects of the propositions that perceptions bear are maximally determinate. Neither of these options withstands scrutiny.

In the second half of the paper, I will propose an alternative theory of perceptual representation grounded in the concept of a *perceptual similarity space* and a mapping of points in that space into an *objective quality space*. The objects of perception have various gradable qualities, such as size, shape, color, and many others that do not so readily come to mind, such as jerkiness of motion. (The motion of a squirrel is jerkier than the motion of a cat.) Some of these variations are perceptible. An object's location in objective quality space is a measure of its location on a large number of such dimensions of perceptible variation. In addition, each mind contains a perceptual similarity space having dimensions to which dimensions of objective quality space correspond. When an object or scenario is perceived, a *mark* is placed in perceptual similarity space recording that object's or scenario's location in objective quality space.

A perceptual representation may be modeled as such a mark in perceptual similarity space. My perception of the baby is a mark in perceptual similarity space that is closer to other marks in perceptual similarity space representing unhappy children than it is to other marks in perceptual similarity space representing happy children. My perception of the trees is a mark in perceptual similarity space that is closer to other marks representing scenarios in which something on the left is further away than something on the right than it is to other marks representing scenarios in which that is not the case. Each point in perceptual similarity space will be, in a sense to be defined, *mapped into* a point in objective quality space; however, the point that that mark is mapped into may or not be the same as the point in objective quality space that the object or scenario is actually at.

In these terms, we can accommodate the two remaining motivations for attributing propositional contents to perceptions, but without attributing propositional contents. Instead of treating the correctness of a perception as the truth of the propositional content that it bears, we may define correctness as a kind of *accuracy* and define accuracy as a relation between the point in objective quality space that an object or scenario actually occupies and the point in objective quality space that the mark in perceptual similarity space is mapped into. Further, we can explain the phenomenon of seeing-as. Seeing something *as* of some kind will turn out to be, not a matter of infusing a perceptual representation with a concept; it will be instead a matter of perceiving a similarity relation between the object of perception and other objects that belong to that kind and then conceptualizing them on that basis. We cannot, in these terms, corroborate the first of the three motivations, the assumption that perceptions justify beliefs in the way that beliefs justify beliefs. But I will show that we can nonetheless account for the fact that perceptions may *guide* judgment.

The issue that I am addressing cuts across the issue whether perceptions represent only low-level properties such as colors and shapes or may also represent high-level kinds such as dogs and houses. Since I deny that perceptions have propositional content at all, I am certainly not siding with propositions about low-level properties and kinds against propositions about high-level properties and kinds. But since, as we will see, perceptual similarity space may include dimensions measuring similarity to a prototypical dog or similarity to a prototypical house, I allow that instances of high-level properties and kinds, such as dogs and houses, may have relevance to perception as well as colors and shapes.

2. Nonconceptual Content

It will be fair to characterize my theory as attributing to perceptions *nonconceptual* content. However, so many authors have said so many different things about "nonconceptual content" that at this point one cannot use the term without inviting confusion. So I will begin by highlighting some of the various things authors have meant by this term, so that it will be clearer how my own view differs from some of these others.

Propositions may be conceived as entities in terms of which we can characterize what two thoughts, in two different thinkers (or in a single thinker at different times), have in common. A propositional content is something that two thoughts have in common when in thinking those thoughts the two thinkers *think the same*. In particular, if two thoughts are the same with respect to propositional content, then the two thoughts have the same truth value when evaluated with respect to any arbitrarily chosen possible world (or, on some accounts, world-*cum*-time). Traditionally, propositions, or judgments, have been thought of as composed of *concepts* or *ideas*.[2] So the propositional content of the thought that *some mammals lays eggs* contains the concept *mammal* and the concept *egg*.

In recent decades, it has been common to suppose that the building blocks of propositions are individuals, properties, and kinds. So the propositional content of the thought that some mammals lay eggs contains the kind *mammal* and the kind *egg*. We can retain the traditional vocabulary if, when we are thinking of individuals, properties and kinds as components of propositions, we allow that they are also concepts. That equation strikes the contemporary philosophical ear as a bit odd, since concepts are supposed to be mind-dependent and many properties are supposed to be mind-independent. But it will simplify discussion and will do no harm, so long as we confine ourselves to calling properties "concepts" only when we are thinking of them as components of propositions. So I will ask those who think of propositions as composed of individuals and properties to live with that oddity.

One thing that may be meant in saying that the contents of perceptual representations are nonconceptual is just that they are not propositional contents — not the sort of contents that may be conceived of as built up from concepts in the manner of propositions. For instance, Christopher Peacocke (1992a, 1992b) has proposed that the contents of perceptions may be, roughly, *oriented ways of filling space*, where those are quite different sorts of things from propositions. My view will be like Peacocke's in denying that the contents of perceptions are propositions. But I do not adopt Peacocke's view, because I think it suffers from one major failing. Peacocke has nothing to say about what makes it the case that a particular perceptual representation has a particular oriented way of filling space as its content. Suppose someone misrepresents a certain surface as facing down (so that the top side is visible) when in fact it is facing up (so that the bottom side is visible). Why should we say that her representation represents such a way of filling space rather than the way of filling space in which the objects before her actually fill it? Peacocke has nothing to say about this (as others before me have noted, e.g., Millar 1996, p. 85n), and I do not know what answer one could give on his behalf.

Quite a few authors characterize nonconceptual content in a manner that is not as easy to grasp. They will say some or other variation of the following: A representation has nonconceptual content if and only if the content of the representation is such that the bearer of the representation need not *possess* the concepts that *characterize* the content.[3] We will get a variety of different theories out of this depending on how we understand the expressions "possess a concept" and "characterize a content", as I will now explain.

There are various things one could mean by *possessing a concept*. At one extreme, one might suppose that possessing a concept means having a word in one's language of thought that is dedicated to forming thoughts whose propositional contents contain that concept. For example, I possess the concept *mammal* in this sense because I can think, in English, "Some mammals lay eggs" and the word "mammal" expresses the concept *mammal*. At another extreme, one could hold that possessing a concept simply means having a mental representation that has a propositional content containing that concept, though this content need not be in any way reflected in the structure of the representation itself (the vehicle). A view in-between these two extremes can be defined if we suppose that perceptual representations, the vehicles in the head, though not analogous to sentences, nonetheless have a structure that can be described as conceptual structure. If someone thinks that concepts in some sense "shape" perceptual representations or that perceptions have a phenomenal character that determines their propositional contents, then one is supposing that perceptual representations have a structure, as vehicles, in which their propositional content is reflected. So a creature might in one sense *possess* a concept simply by having a perceptual representation that is in this sense structured by the concept.

There are at least two different things it could mean to say that a concept *characterizes* a content. To say that a concept characterizes a content could mean that the concept is literally a component of the content. But it could also just mean that in *describing* the content we would use words that express that concept. So even if one held that the contents of perceptions were Peacockean oriented scenarios, if one of those scenarios could be described as containing a cube, then the concept *cube* would in this sense characterize the content.

Again, the slogan that a representation has nonconceptual content if the agent need not possess the concepts characterizing the content will yield different conceptions of nonconceptual content depending on what is meant by *possessing* and *characterizing*. Peacocke's theory of nonconceptual content will be such a conception, because the concepts that we would use in describing a given way of filling space need not be in *any sense* possessed by an agent whose perceptual representation represents that way of filling space.[4] But such a conception could also be proposed by someone who held that the contents of perceptual representations were full-fledged propositions, provided that he or she allowed that a perceptual representation may have a propositional content though the bearer of that representation does not, in one or another sense, possess the concepts that compose the propositional content.[5] Such a conception would *not* be on offer, however, from someone who held both that perceptual representations have propositional content and that the concepts that make up the content are somehow reflected in the structure of the perceptual vehicle in a way that qualifies the perceiver as possessing the concepts.[6] Still, such a conception would be what is proposed by someone who held that perceptual representations have propositional contents *and* who held that when a perceptual representation has a proposition as its content the representational vehicle itself is shaped by or infused with the concepts that make up that content and is to that extent conceptually structured, *provided* that he or she then denied that the agent need *possess* the concept in the sense of being able to form nonperceptual judgments containing a word-like component dedicated to forming thoughts the propositional contents of which contained that concept.[7]

In any case, the theory I intend to defend will be that the contents of perceptual representations are not propositions at all. Naturally, it will be possible to *describe* in words the contents of perceptions even of the kind I will describe. But the content of a perception will in no sense be composed of concepts (not even in the guise of properties and kinds).

3. Perceptual Justification

In the past twenty years, it has been commonplace for philosophers to claim that perceptions justify beliefs. By this they do not mean merely that a belief may count as justified due the character of the perceptions that cause it. They mean, rather, that a perception is something like a premise from which, when it is joined with other premises, a conclusion may be drawn, or the truth of which would raise the probability of, or provide inductive support for some proposition that is a candidate for belief. This is the one motivation for attributing propositional content to perceptions that my alternative theory will not accommodate, and so I need to explain why I do not accept it.

If it were true that perceptions justify beliefs, then that would indeed be persuasive grounds for holding that perceptions have propositional content. The reason is that we have no models for the kind of justification at issue other than a passage from one kind of proposition-bearing state to another. Heck denies that perceptions need to have propositional contents in order to provide justifications, but he manages to deny it only by introducing a relation that he calls "conceptualization" that is supposed to hold between a belief and a perception that justifies it but which he tells us nothing about (2000, p. 511n). (See also Speaks 2005, p. 375.) Reliabilist theories of justification (e.g., Goldman 1979) have taught us to conceive of beliefs as being justified in the sense of being the product of a reliable process; but of course that is just not the kind of justification that people are thinking of when they infer that perceptions have propositional content, for the latter is supposed to be the kind of justification that a single mental state can lend to another by virtue of a relation between their representational contents.

In any case, among authors writing in the past twenty years, most, and perhaps all of those who hold that perceptions have propositional content are motivated in part by the assumption that perceptions justify beliefs. McDowell claims that unless we ascribe conceptual content to perceptions, we will have to extend the "space of reasons" beyond the "space of concepts", which, he claims, requires a confusion of "justifications" with "exculpations" (1996, p. 10; see also pp. 52–3, 165). In a paper in which Brewer argues that "sense experiences have conceptual content", he says he just takes for granted that "sense experiential states provide reasons for empirical beliefs" (2005, p. 217). Huemer writes that if experiences did not have propositional content we could not understand how an experience could be the "basis" for a belief, since "there would be no logical relations between them" (2001, p. 74).

Even authors who do not argue, but simply take for granted that perceptions have propositional content reveal in various ways that they are motivated by the assumption that perceptions justify beliefs. Thus, Pryor (2000, pp. 538–9) argues that there must be a category of *perceptually basic propositions* on the grounds that experiences can provide an immediate justification for some of our beliefs. Likewise, Glüer (2009) argues that the contents of perception are propositions about how things *look* by considering what that content must be if perceptions are to play their justificatory role. Siegel (2006b, p. 487–88; 2010, p. 10) claims that significance of her liberal account of the properties that can be represented in perception lies in the fact that it extends the range of justifications that we can suppose perceptions provide for beliefs.

3.1 The Argument from "Looks" Talk

Many contemporary authors treat the assumption that perceptions justify beliefs as a philosophical commonplace needing no defense. On the contrary, it is a recent innovation in the history of philosophy that picked up steam around the time of the publication of McDowell's *Mind and World* (1996, first published in 1994). The more usual view earlier in the 20th century had been that the entry-level justifiers were beliefs somehow *based on* but not *identical* to perceptions. One might form beliefs about one's sense data (Russell 1912) or one might "apprehend the given" (Lewis 1946, p. 183), or one might form beliefs about how one is *appeared to* (Chisholm 1977), but the perception *per se* was not conceived as an entry-level justifier.

Everyone will agree that "justification by experience comes to an end" (Wittgenstein 1953, §485). So there will be entry-level justifiers not in turn justified by anything else. That does not mean that the entry-level justifiers will not be justified at all; they might be *justified* even if they are not justified *by* their relation to another mental state that serves as justifier. (They might be justified as the products of a reliable process or because there is no reasonable basis to doubt them.) Since perceptions will not be justified by any other mental state even if empirical beliefs are justified by perceptions, there can be nothing absurd in countenancing justified mental states with empirical content that are not justified by any other mental state. So we cannot argue that empirical beliefs will not be justified at all if they are not justified by perceptions. Certainly perceptions must have some role in the formation of beliefs, and an account of the conditions under which an entry-level belief is justified will assign some role to perception. But it does not follow that the role of perceptions is to provide justifications.

Setting aside such fallacies, I find only one argument in the contemporary literature to back up the presumption that the epistemic role of perceptions is specifically to justify beliefs, namely, an inference from the following premises:

(1) Some claims about how things *look* (or, more generally, *appear*) report the contents of perception.
(2) Claims about how things look that report the contents of perception may defeasibly justify claims about how things *are*, which in turn express the contents of beliefs.

McDowell, Glüer, Huemer, and Pollock and Oved all offer such a rationale, and I find no other.[8] It is obvious that not *every* claim about how things look reports just the content of a perceptual representation. I might say, "That house looks like it was designed by Dr. Seuss", even though my perception does not represent Dr. Seuss. So premise (1) says only that *some* claims about how thinks look report the contents of perceptions. Premise (1) presupposes that in such cases there is content to report. I will question whether that content is propositional content, but I do not want to question it just yet, because the present question is whether there is a reason to suppose that perceptions have propositional content. What I want to question first is premise (2).

It is not very easy to keep the focus away from premise (1), because in many cases in which a statement about how something looks seems to support a statement about how things are, it is easy to read the *looks* statement as something other than a report on the contents of a perception. If I say that a certain object on my doorstep *looks* like a package, then I might take that as a reason to say that the books I ordered have arrived (an example from Ginsborg 2011, pp. 135–136). But my claim that the object *looks* like a package might be just a *hedged* way of expressing my *belief* that the object *is* a package (as well as the fact that the source of my belief is vision), in which case, it does not report the contents of a perception. If I say that a certain track in the mud *looks like* an ocelot track, then that might be taken to be a reason to say that the track *is* an ocelot track. But my claim that the track looks like an ocelot track might be just an expression of my belief that the track is similar in perceptible ways to an actual ocelot track and not itself a report on the contents of a perception.

To keep the focus on cases where the best case can be made that a *looks* statement reports the content of a perception, we should confine our attention to cases in which the justify*ing* claim says that an object *looks as though* it had a certain perceptible property and the claim to be justi*fied* says that the object *in fact* has that very same property. Thus, our question about premise (2) may be reduced to this: Where F might be taken to be a perceptible property, can a claim to the effect that x *looks as though it were F* (or x *looks F*) provide defeasible justification for a conclusion to the effect that x *is F*? For instance, can the claim that a tie *looks* green to me justify my claim that it *is* green?

But we also need to separate out extraneous information carried by the term "looks". In deciding whether to accept another's testimony, we may rightly be influenced by what we take the other person's source of information to be. If someone tells me that the river has broken through the levee and I know that she has just come back from the levee where she would have been in a position to *see* the river, the levee, and the water on the wrong side, I may believe her; whereas, if she had been simply relaying testimony that she had received from some stranger, I might not believe her. We may accept testimony that we consider to be the product of vision that we would not accept if we considered it to be the product of other testimony. Consequently, if someone tells me that it *looks* as though the river has broken through the levee (perhaps she is viewing it from a helicopter and speaking to me by radio), that may give me reason to believe that the river has broken through the levee, because I learn from what she says that she is acquiring her beliefs by means of vision.

So what we want to know is whether S's claim that x *looks F* can provide a justification for S's claim that x *is F* apart from the information about sensory modality contained in the claim that x *looks F*. If we abstract the information about sensory modality from the claim that x looks F to S, what is left is the claim that x *seems to S to be F* (considered as a claim about S's state of mind). So our question comes to this: Can a person's claim that something *seems* to him or her to be F ever justify, however defeasibly, his or her claim that x *is F*? One way to approach this question would be to consider what kind of state consists in its seeming to one that something is so. But what we are asking about is the soundness of one rationale for a particular answer to that question (viz., it is a state bearing propositional content). So that will not be my approach.

Off hand, an inference from a claim about how things seem to a conclusion about how they are might seem to be an innocent inference from effect to probable cause — an inference to the best explanation. The effect is a perception — its seeming to me that x is F, and the probable cause is the fact that x really is F (together with the fact that I am in position to be perceptually affected by that fact). But if the inference is an inference to the best explanation, then it is a confusion to say that it is the perception that justifies the belief. What justifies my conclusion that x is F is not its seeming to me that x is F but my *belief* that it seems to me that x is F and my *belief* that the probable cause of its seeming to me that x is F is x's being F.

Likewise, it would be a confusion to conclude that perceptions justify beliefs on the grounds that an agent S's subjective probability function may assign a higher value to the conditional probability of p given that *it seems* to S that p than it assigns to the unconditional probability that p. The rule of conditionalization says that if one starts out assigning a probability n to p *given q* and one then *learns* or somehow comes to *accept* that q, then one ought to revise one's probabilities so that the probability n is assigned to p. If the justification of belief through perception is supposed to be an application of this rule, then what is q? "It seems to S that x is F" is supposed to be our way of reporting on S's perception having the content *that x is F*. The words "It seems to S that" do not report any part of the content but only indicate that the words that follow report the content of a perception. So if we want to say that it is the *perception* that justifies S's belief, and not S's *belief* that S is having such a perception that justifies S belief, then we will have to say that q is the same proposition as p, namely, the proposition that x *is* F. In that case, the probability of p *given q* will be 1. But that proves too much. We certainly do not want to say that its seeming to S that p *proves* that p.

One way in which a premise that p can lend justification to a conclusion that q is by ruling out possible doubts about the proposition that q. My belief that my car keys are not on the kitchen counter may lend justification to my belief that they are in the car by ruling out a plausible alternative to their being in the car. Its seeming to me that p could not in that way lend support to my belief that p. If I am looking at a tie and wonder whether it really is green, perhaps because I am concerned that the lighting might be unusual, then reminding myself that the tie *seems* to be green does not rule out the possibility that it is non-green and does nothing else to resolve my doubt.

Once we have pared the question down to its pertinent core and set aside confusions and misbegotten defenses, there seems to be nothing to be said for premise (2). A reason to conclude that x is F would be a reason to pass from its merely seeming to one that x is F to believing that x is F, and its merely seeming to one that x is F, the starting state, cannot be a reason to make that move.

3.2 The Accessibility Assumption

On the basis of the assumption that perceptions justify beliefs and that this is why they must have propositional contents, I want to justify an assumption that I will use in the next subsection in challenging the thesis that perceptions have belief-justifying propositional content. Thus, from the assumption that perceptions justify beliefs by virtue of their propositional contents I intend, ironically enough, to draw a reason to doubt that perceptions have belief-justifying propositional content.

First, I want to make an assumption that has nothing especially to do with perception. This is that wherever there is propositional content, there is the possibility of expressing that propositional content in words — the words of a humanly possible language. Let us call this the *expressibility* assumption. This assumption does not mean that our language must already contain the vocabulary that we would need to have in order to express the content, only that through some kind of exercise in language-building we could introduce the necessary vocabulary. We all have the concept of the taste of a lemon. But as things stand, we cannot express that concept in words without making an irrelevant reference to lemons — by saying "the taste of a lemon". But I suppose that through an exercise in language-building we could introduce into our language a word that expresses the concept of the taste of a lemon without making an irrelevant reference to lemons.

The expressibility assumption, as I have explained it, says nothing about how the expression of propositional content is come by. But now I want to define (but not pin on anyone) a second assumption, namely, that if a person has a perceptual experience with a certain propositional content and has a language suitable for expressing that content in words, then the person should be able to express the propositional content of his or her perception in words and should be able to express it without undertaking any empirical investigation into the nature of his or her perceptions. Let us call this second assumption the *strong accessibility* assumption. In calling it that, however, I do not wish to presume any model of the mental processes of word choice. We may suppose that word choice is a nonreflective, nondeliberative, automatic process, or we may suppose that choosing the words to express a propositional content is a matter of reflecting on one's thought and in some sense comparing words to content. The strong accessibility assumption does not say that a perceiver ought to be able to find the words to express the propositional content of his or her perception without investing any kind of deliberation into the matter at all. It does not entail that philosophers reflecting on the nature of perception will not come up with different theories about the kinds of propositional contents perceptions may possess. However, it does entail that a person should not have to do empirical research in order to report the propositional content of his or her own perceptual representations.[9]

Having defined the strong accessibility assumption, but not attributed it to anyone, I now want to contrast it with the *weak accessibility assumption*, which I will argue should be accepted by anyone who infers that perceptions have propositional content on the grounds that perceptions justify beliefs. This says that if a person has a perceptual experience with a certain propositional content and has a language suitable for expressing that content in words, then, without empirical research, the person should be able to express in words *that aspect* of the propositional content of his or her perception that may serve to justify other beliefs. While the assumption that perceptions justify beliefs by virtue of their propositional content may, as I will argue, presuppose the accessibility of some aspects of the propositional content of a perception, one could have other reasons to attribute propositional contents to perceptions and on the basis of those maintain that other aspects of the propositional content of a perception are inaccessible. So the reason to distinguish between the strong and the weak accessibility assumption is that theorists who have multiple grounds for attributing propositional content to perceptions may be committed at most to the weak accessibility assumption.

Anyone who argues that perceptual representations justify beliefs by virtue of their propositional content should agree that those aspects of the propositional content of perception that justify beliefs ought to be accessible in the sense of the weak accessibility assumption. One could try to defend the weak accessibility assumption using the premise that, in general, a justification is the kind of thing a person can "give" in a sense that requires that one be able to *say* it. But I do not think we need to rely on general claims about the nature of justification. Rather, we have only to consider how we would react to someone who tried to attribute a perceptual justification, either to him- or herself or to another, while denying that the attributee could access the belief-justifying aspects of his or her perception.

Suppose that *A* says that *B*'s belief is actually justified, in part or in whole, on the basis of the propositional content of some of *B*'s perceptions. But, while not doubting that *B* has the vocabulary that would be necessary in order to express the content of those perceptions, *A* denies that *B* can in fact express the justifying aspects of the contents of the justifying perceptions. So by *A*'s account of the matter, *B* is so oblivious to the justifying aspects of the content of his own perceptions that he would not be able to appeal to his perceptions in answering other people's doubts about his belief or in answering doubts that he himself might consciously put to himself. We would have to say that, by *A*'s account of the situation, *B* does not know what the justification for his belief is. But in that case, we should not accept that *B*'s belief is actually justified by his perceptions. At most we could say that it was susceptible to such justification, pending his recognition of the justifying aspect of the content of his perceptions. *B*'s perceptions might be links in a subconscious process that reliably produced true beliefs. The belief in question might be *justified*, in the manner of a belief produced through such a process, but the perceptions would not qualify as its *justification*. So we cannot maintain that perceptions justify beliefs on the basis their propositional contents while denying the weak accessibility assumption.

If there is a relation of justification between two propositionally contentful states that does not require accessibility to the justifying aspects of the justifying state, then that relation is utterly unfamiliar in nonphilosophical contexts. So if any proponents of the thesis that perceptions justify beliefs by virtue of their propositional contents wish to deny the weak accessibility assumption, then they have some explaining to do that, as far as I know, they have not in fact done. So in questioning the assumption that perceptions justify beliefs, it will be fair to take the weak accessibility assumption for granted.

3.3 The Dilemma

Which concepts could possibly make up the belief-justifying propositional content of a perception? I will now raise some doubts about some broad categories of answers.[10] Most of the published criticism of the thesis that perceptions have propositional contents (starting with Heck 2000, Peacocke 2001, Kelly 2001) has employed a strategy of arguing that it is incompatible with the phenomenal richness of experience. In this context, the claim to beat has been that we can think of the propositional contents of perceptual representations as made up of "demonstrative concepts" (McDowell 1996, p. 56, pp. 170–171). My own strategy will neither support nor depend on this strategy.

In the previous subsection, I identified a couple of assumptions on which my challenge will rest, namely, the expressibility assumption and the weak accessibility assumption. In addition, I will assume that the properties represented by the concepts that make up the propositional contents of our perceptions would typically be concepts of properties of physical objects (or would *be* such properties if we are thinking of propositions as literally containing properties). That does not quite mean that they are physical properties in any especially narrow sense. But if, for instance, our perceptions represent colors, then the colors they represent are properties of physical objects, not properties of our own sensory experiences.[11] I do not see that there is any serious doubt about this in the contemporary literature. The assumption does not entail that we can never perceive the properties of our own experiences, but I will take no stand on the question whether we can do that.

Further, I will assume that the concepts of properties of physical objects that make up the propositional content of our perceptions are not typically complex concepts that *also* make reference to the states of the perceiver. The concept *thing that causes an experience such as the one I am now having*, for instance, would not be typical of the sorts of concepts that make up the propositional contents of our perceptions. In defense of this assumption one could argue that the perceptual representations of adult humans will not typically be very different in kind from those of young children and nonhuman animals and then argue that young children and nonhuman animals are not easily brought to think about their own experiences as such.[12]

Finally, I will assume that it makes sense to treat propositions as composed of concepts. As I observed in section 2, that might entail that concepts are properties, kinds, and individuals, which strikes us as odd terminology. Moreover, this seems to unfairly dismiss out of hand the idea that propositions may be identified with unstructured sets of possible worlds. But this latter charge can be evaded. By the expressibility assumption, the purported propositional content of a perception can be expressed in words. So a proposition that is the content of a perception will be the product of functionally composing other intensions corresponding to the words such as make up a sentence that expresses it. (I am assuming that context-relativity is no bar to a compositional semantics for thought.) The conceptual constituents of the proposition may be thought of as these other intensions. A proposition may be decomposable in this sense in more than one way, just as different sentences may express it, but my argument will question whether for the purported propositional contents of perceptions there is even one good way.

The challenge I will pose will turn on a distinction between *general* concepts and *maximally determinate* concepts. By *general* concepts I mean concepts of kinds or properties that subsume a number of various species, as the concept *chair* subsumes the species *Windsor chair* and the concept *blue* subsumes the species *cerulean blue*. By "maximally determinate" concept I mean concepts of kinds or properties that cannot be divided any further into species. By "species" I do not mean just any way of being a member of the kind or having the property. For example, if $blue_{57}$ is a particular shade of blue, *being a $blue_{57}$ chair* and *being $blue_{57}$ in France* are still not species of $blue_{57}$. But I will not now pause to try to define the distinction.

In outline, the dilemma I will pose is this: Either the concepts that are constituents in the belief-justifying propositional contents of perception include some general concepts or, instead, they are all maximally determinate concepts. The problem with supposing that the belief-justifying contents of perceptual representations include general concepts is that there does not seem to be any good way of fixing on any particular level of generality as uniquely appropriate. The problem with supposing that the concepts that make up the contents of perceptual representations are maximally determinate is just that our perceptual representations never do pick out anything so determinate.[13]

So suppose that the concepts included in the contents of perception include some general concepts. How general are they? Suppose I am looking at a wooden Windsor chair with arms. Even supposing that my perception is veridical, there are many different general concepts, having various overlapping extensions, that we might take to be constituents of the content. Candidates include: *chair, Windsor chair, wooden armchair, four-legged seat for one*, and so on. What would make it the case that one of these rather than the other was the predicate concept in the belief-justifying propositional content of my perception? Or, to take a simpler example, suppose I am looking at a box, 6 inches long, 3 inches tall and 3 inches wide. What does my perception tell me about its shape? Here are some options: That is it *box-shaped*, that it is *six-sided*, that it *has six sides that meet at 90° angles*, that it is *box-shaped and twice as long as high or wide*. The concepts that make up the belief-justifying propositional content of my perceptions do not have to be *precise* concepts; they could be vague. But there have to be some definite concepts that compose the belief-justifying propositional content of my perceptions.

I do not see any basis for answering such questions. By the weak accessibility assumption, I should not have to do any empirical work to find out which concepts belong to the belief-justifying propositional content of my perception. Provided that my language contains a suitable vocabulary, I should be able to tell you what the propositional content of my perception is, just as, if I *believe* that the object is a Windsor chair, I should be able, with due deliberation, to report that that's what I believe. My language may not contain a simple expression that exactly expresses the content of my perception, but by the expressibility assumption, my current lack of a suitable expression is ultimately no bar to my expressing the content of my perception in words. But on the contrary, I cannot in this way select the correct verbal expression for the content of my perception. I infer that the question, "Which general concepts are components in the belief-justifying content of my perception?", is mistaken in its presupposition that perceptions have general concepts as components of their belief-justifying propositional content.

Suppose, then, that the concepts that make up the belief-justifying propositional content of a perceptual representation are exclusively maximally determinate concepts. In that case, the question arises, what sorts of maximally determinate concepts might they be? Suppose the belief-justifying aspect of my perception of the chair includes a maximally determinate shape concept. Suppose I have a word in my language that expresses this concept: "shape$_{83}$". What exactly is shape$_{83}$? Is it the three-dimensional shape of the chair? It cannot be that, since there are features of the three-dimensional shape of the chair that I cannot see. For instance, I cannot see one of the legs, which is occluded by the seat. Visual experiences exactly like the one I am having now might equally represent any of a number of different particular objects having many different voluminous shapes. So, contrary to the assumption, there does not seem to be any maximally determinate voluminous shape that the belief-justifying aspect of my perception represents the object before me as having.

Perhaps, then, we should say that, with respect to shape, visual perception represents only the facing surface of an object. But there also does not seem to be any maximally determinate *facing surface shape* that my perception represents the object before me as having. Imagine two scenarios, one consisting of a rectangular board painted blue and another consisting of two rectangular boards painted blue, one a little larger and placed a little farther from me than the other. The two scenarios could be arranged so that from a certain angle they looked exactly alike to me. So there is no unique facing surface shape that my perception can be said to represent as before me.

It is the same with respect to color. Suppose that the belief-justifying propositional content of my perception of some point on the surface of the chair includes a maximally determinate color concept, a concept that applies to only a maximally determinate shade of brown. Suppose that I have a word that expresses my concept of this shade: "brown$_{909}$". Which shade exactly is brown$_{909}$? The visual experience that represents a colored surface will be affected by the lighting conditions and the colors of surrounding surfaces. Given compensatory background colors, two different shades of brown may be visually indistinguishable. So, contrary to the assumption, there is not any particular shade of brown that we can say my visual experience uniquely represents the object as having. That different colors might, under different conditions, look alike is an inevitable consequence of our assumption that the colors we represent are properties of physical surfaces and not properties of our sensory experiences. Since the cases of shape and color are representative, we may conclude that the concepts that make up the belief-justifying contents of perception do not represent things as having maximally determinate properties.

We should not assume that the propositional content of a perceptual representation would have to be *true*. It is certainly not the case that every quality that might *cause* a perceptual experience is the quality that an object is *represented* as having. We have to allow that the *cause* of a perceptual representation might sometimes be *mis*represented by that representation. Various spatial configurations might cause a perceptual representation though there is exactly one of these configurations that the resulting representation attributes to the scene perceived. Various colors might cause a perceptual representation though there is only one that the propositional content of the resulting representation represents the subject of the proposition as having.

Still, there will have to be some reason to pick out one of the spatial configurations, one of the colors, as *the* spatial configuration, *the* color, that the perceived object is represented as having. My problem is that I cannot see what basis there might be for fixing on exactly one completely determinate spatial configuration or one completely determinate color. Perhaps we could require that the determinate configuration and determinate color that the object is represented as having lie within the range of those that might cause the representation under a condition that qualifies as *normal*, in either a statistical or a teleological sense. On the contrary, any such proposal will put the belief-justifying propositional content of perception beyond access to the perceiving subject. In order for any such account of the belief-justifying content of perception to satisfy the weak accessibility assumption, we would have to suppose that perceivers can just "tell", without empirical research, which specific properties were the normal causes of perceptions such as those they are having, and that they cannot do.

Every concept is either general or maximally determinate. But neither sort can be constituents in the belief-justifying propositional contents of perceptions. So there would seem to be an error in the supposition that perceptions have belief-justifying propositional contents. At the very least, the dilemma I have posed puts the onus on the proponent to show that perceptions have belief-justifying propositional content. Until that obligation is plainly met, we have an incentive to develop other conceptions of perceptual representation, such as the one that I will develop presently.

4. Accuracy

Some philosophers observe that perceptions may be correct or incorrect, or accurate or inaccurate, and pass quickly from that assumption to the conclusion that perceptions have the sort of content that allows them to be either true or false.[14] One alternative to that conception, as Crane (2009) has observed, would be to think of the accuracy of perceptions as analogous to the accuracy of pictures. Crane himself takes this as a reason to endorse Peacocke's theory of scenario content. My problem with that theory is that, as I noted above, it is not obvious how to assign scenario content to perceptions. In any case, my own strategy, while it too might be viewed as an articulation of Crane's proposal, will be a different one.[15]

4.1 Perceptual Similarity Space

Every perceptible object, every perceptible arrangement of objects, can be modeled as a vector in a many-dimensional objective quality space. The dimensions of objective quality space, as I define it, are confined, for simplicity, to dimensions of perceptible variation. So since we can perceive colors, there will be a number of dimensions representing variation in color (hue, saturation, and brightness). There will be dimensions that measure variations in shape. As I said at the start, there will be dimensions that do not so readily come to mind, such as jerkiness of motion. In order to differentiate various arrangements of objects, there may be dimensions that differentiate various configurations of parts; for instance, there might be a dimension that measures the degree to which an arrangement of three objects is congruent to a certain triangle. Of course, not all dimensions of perceptual similarity space will be Euclidean. (The set of Euclidean dimensions forms a Euclidean subspace in which distance is measured by means of the Pythagorean Theorem. The set of dimensions measuring color, for instance, will not form a Euclidean subspace.)

While objective quality space measures the qualities that objects and scenarios actually have, a perceptual similarity space measures the qualities that objects and scenarios are perceived as having. For each dimension of objective quality space there will be a dimension of perceptual similarity space to which it corresponds (and, as I have defined it, the dimensions of objective quality space are chosen on this basis). When an object or scenario is perceived, its location in objective quality space is represented by a *mark* in perceptual similarity space. This mark in perceptual similarity space is likewise a vector, which measures the object's or scenario's location in objective quality space by including a value for each of a number of dimensions of perceptual similarity space. Perceptual representations, I propose, may be modeled as such marks in perceptual similarity space. Naturally, in saying that the mind "contains" such a perceptual similarity space I am merely proposing a model for some kind of neurophysiological structure, although I am not in a position to describe it in neurophysiological terms.

The marks in perceptual similarity space will play a role in guiding behavior. If I have to choose between two hors d'oeuvres, the one I choose might depend on the location of the marks that represent them in similarity space. If the mark representing hors d'oeuvres X is closer than the mark representing hors d'oeuvres Y to the mark representing some hors d'oeuvres that I previously ate and enjoyed, then the arrangement of these marks in perceptual similarity space may lead me to choose hors d'oeuvres X. Or suppose that I am trying to anticipate what a turtle will do if I poke it with my finger. I can imagine various things it might do. It might run away; it might bark at me like a dog; it might withdraw its head and limbs into its shell. Each of these episodes of visual imagery corresponds to a point in perceptual similarity space. (So not only perceptions may be modeled as marks in perceptual similarity space; also acts of perceptual imagination may be.) What I expect to happen may depend on the location of these points relative to marks representing my past experiences upon poking a turtle with my finger. Of the points representing the various things I imagine might happen, the one that is closest to the mark representing my past experience upon poking a turtle with my finger may be the point representing the turtle's withdrawing its head and limbs into its shell. In that case, that may be what I will expect to happen.

Many of the dimensions of perceptual similarity space will be part of the innate, nonlearned, cognitive equipment that the mind/brain brings to the task of understanding the world. But the mind's perceptual similarity space can be enhanced through learning as well. Once we have become familiar with a certain thing, we may add to our perceptual similarity space a dimension measuring similarity to that very thing. For example, an agent may become acquainted with a particular dog and observe its many different postures — sitting, standing, lying, running. The agent may recognize them all as postures of the same dog, because, if for no other reason, the agent may *track* that one dog as it passes through those various postures. Distance along such a dimension may defined in terms of distance from the various representations in the collection that make up one's representation of that dog. Similarly, one might add a dimension representing similarity to an arrangement of pieces of furniture in a certain dining room.[16] When such dimensions are added to an agent's perceptual similarity space, corresponding dimensions are added to that agent's objective quality space. (At this point I am introducing a relativization of objective quality spaces to agents.) The learning processes may affect not only the structure of the perceptual similarity space itself but also the ways in which it guides behavior. One person may, as a consequence of learning, be better at finding her way around in urban environments, and another person may, likewise as a consequence of learning, be better at finding his way around in thickly forested jungles.

The structure of perceptual similarity space is not open to introspection, but it can be investigated experimentally. If x is closer to y than to z in an agent's perceptual similarity space, let us say that the agent "judges" that x is more like y than like z. (I call these relations "judgments" for lack of a better word; they are not literally judgments with a conceptual content.) First, then, we need a number of behavioral indicators of an agent's similarity judgments. One of these might simply be that the subject will *say* (and literally judge), when asked, that x is more like y than like z. (But in drawing inferences from such assertions we will have to beware of the biases due to figure-ground effects. See Gleitman, et al., 1996.) Having assembled a large number of such similarity judgments on the basis of the agent's behavior, we can attempt, by means of multidimensional scaling, to construct a perceptual similarity space that represents them all. We will succeed if we construct a space in which the mark representing x is closer to the mark representing y than to the mark representing z if and only if the judgment that x is more like y than like z occurs on the list. We will know in advance that if we allow sufficiently many dimensions then we can succeed. However, we may find, as we continue to collect triples, that in order to accommodate new ones in our perceptual similarity space, we always have to add dimensions. In that case, we would have to conclude that our hypothesis, that the mind contains a perceptual similarity space, was not robust, and the present theory of perception would have to be abandoned.

The next step is to explain in these terms what a mark in perceptual similarity space represents and in what way it may be accurate or inaccurate. I will approach this in two stages. First I will define a kind of inaccuracy that I will call *mere misperception*. This will employ a mapping of points in perceptual similarity space into *points* in objective quality space, but will not employ a mapping of the *dimensions* of perceptual similarity space into the dimensions of objective quality space. Persistent illusions, such as the Müller-Lyer arrows, will not qualify as inaccurate in this sense. But then I will explain how the dimensions of perceptual similarity space may be mapped into dimensions of objective quality space. In terms of that mapping, we will be able to define the sense in which persistent illusions are indeed inaccurate.

4.2 Mere Misperception

For any given mark in perceptual similarity space, there are two points of interest in objective quality space. The first point will be identified by defining a causal relation between objects or scenarios and marks in perceptual similarity

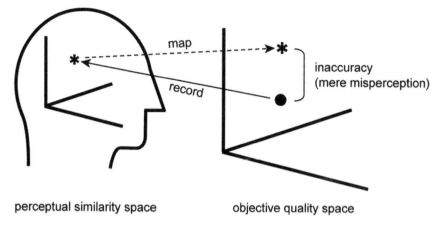

Figure 1

space, such that if the object or scenario is, in the defined sense, the *cause* of the mark's being recorded then the mark can be said to *record* the object or scenario, or record its location in objective quality space. (Here I am taking for granted that we have a solution to the so-called distality problem.) The first of the points of interest, then, will be the location in objective quality space that the object or scenario that a given mark *records* is actually at. For any given mark in perceptual similarity space, the second point of interest in objective quality space will be the point in objective quality space that that mark, in a sense to be defined, *maps into*. As I will explain presently, a mark in perceptual similarity space maps into the point in objective quality space that the object or scenario recorded *would have been at if the mark in perceptual similarity space had been recorded in the functionally normal way*.

In terms of these two points in objective quality space, we can define accuracy, to a first approximation, as follows:

> A mark in perceptual similarity space that records an object or scenario is *accurate* just to the extent that the point in objective quality space that the mark in perceptual similarity space is mapped into is *near* to the point in objective quality space that the object or scenario recorded is actually at.

So a mark in perceptual similarity space is perfectly accurate if the point in objective quality space that it maps into is the point in objective quality space that the recorded object or scenario is actually at. See figure 1.

Recall that the arrangement of marks in perceptual similarity space can play an important role in the production of behavior. Toward defining the requisite mapping between marks in perceptual similarity space and points in objective quality space, we may suppose that there is a certain *normal function* that perceptual similarity space, together with the marks recorded in it, plays in the production of behavior.[17] This will be the function that accounts for the promulgation of such a perceptual similarity space throughout the species through a process of natural selection. More precisely, to allow that dimensions of the perceptual similarity space may be the product of learning, we should say that it is the function from learning histories to perceptual similarities spaces that possesses a biologically normal function. Thus, I am assuming that there is a way of understanding the natural design of an organism that will allow us to distinguish between cases in which a perceptual similarity space, together with the marks recorded in it, guides behaviors in the ways that natural selection has selected for — the normal way — and cases in which it guides behavior in ways that natural selection has not selected for — an abnormal way.

In terms of the functionally normal way in which a perceptual similarity space, together with the marks recorded in it, guides behavior, we may define the functionally normal way in which marks are recorded in perceptual similarity space, thus: It is the way of recording marks in perceptual similarity space that allows the perceptual similarity space, together with the marks in it, to guide behavior in the functionally normal way. Psychological and neurophysiological studies of the processes by which sensory stimuli are transformed into perceptual representations will be studies of this functionally normal way of recording marks in perceptual similarity space.

We may now define the requisite mapping between marks in perceptual similarity space and points in objective quality space in terms of the functionally normal way of recording marks in perceptual similarity space, thus: A mark in perceptual similarity space will be *mapped into* a point in objective quality space if and only if that is the point in objective quality space at which the object or scenario that caused the mark in perceptual similarity space *would have been* located if the mark had been recorded in the functionally normal way. As we have seen, accuracy can be defined in terms of this mapping.

Inaccuracy, in the present sense, characterizes what we might call *mere misperception*. It is the kind of misperception that results from a defect in the sense organs or unfavorable circumstances. A defect may be congenital, or due to an injury, or due to a temporary condition such as drunkenness. Unfavorable circumstances might include bad lighting or inattention. Inaccuracy in this sense is merely a failure to function in accordance with a norm that we conceive biology to have set.

These definitions have the consequence that whether a perception is accurate is a matter of the natural history of the perceiver's biological species. According to this account, a person with red-green colorblindness never perceives the colors of red and green things accurately. But if a physiologically identical creature were a member of a species in which red-green color blindness were a normal feature of the visual system that natural selection had selected for that species, then his color perception might qualify as perfectly accurate. And if a creature physiologically identical to a member of our species were to rise out of a swamp as the product of some cosmic accident, then there would be no standard of accuracy for that creature at all. I think this will be an acceptable result, provided we do not try to make this concept of accuracy do too much work in epistemology (see section 5 below).

There is an ambiguity in these definitions having to do with what is functionally normal. Suppose I look at a blue sock under abnormal lighting. The result is that I record the sock with a mark in perceptual similarity space that is closer to marks representing black things than it is to marks representing blue things. As we might say, the sock looks black. Shall we say that my representation is inaccurate on the grounds that the mark in my perceptual similarity space would normally result from a sock with a different color? Or shall we say that it is accurate because my perceptual apparatus is operating just as it was designed to operate, albeit under circumstances that it was not designed for? My answer is that there is no reason to choose: we can draw either conclusion, so long as it is clear how we are deciding whether something is an example of normal function.

If accuracy can be defined as I have proposed, does this mean that perceptual representations have propositional content after all? Could we say that each perception *says*, of the object of perception, that it occupies such-and-such location in objective quality space? Or could we say that the propositional content is the set of possible worlds in which the object of perception does occupy a certain location in objective quality space? One could speak of a mark as "saying" that an object occupies such-and-such location, just as one could interpret a thermometer as "saying" that the surrounding atmosphere is 75° Fahrenheit. But I assume that proponents of the view that perceptions have propositional content have not meant only that perceptions have propositional content in the same way that a thermometer does. The assumption has been that perceptions represent particulars and represent general kinds and represent the particulars as belonging to some of the kinds. What we do not get on the present account of perceptual representation is representations of general kinds.

4.3 Persistent Illusions

According to the account of accuracy developed so far, many persistent illusions will count as accurate. The reason is that the marks representing the objects that instill persistent illusions are presumably recorded in the functionally normal way. The inaccuracy in such persistent illusions, as I will now explain, is due to the fact that their records are located in regions of perceptual similarity space where variation is not a *true measure* of variation in objective qualities. The Müller-Lyer arrows contain horizontal lines that we reliably perceive as having different lengths even though, in reality, they have the same length. So marks representing the two arrows are located in a region of perceptual similarity space where distance on the perceptual length dimension is not a true measure of distance on the objective length dimension. In developing this account, I will take for granted that we are given a correspondence between dimensions of perceptual similarity space and dimensions of objective quality space. In the next subsection, I will explain how that correspondence may be defined.

Let us designate *map* the mapping relation defined in the previous subsection from points in perceptual similarity space into points in objective quality space. Let *perc* be a measure of distance between points x and x' along a dimension D in perceptual similarity space. Let *obj* be a measure of distance between points y and y' along the dimension of objective quality space that corresponds to D. Variation along dimension D of perceptual similarity space is, within a given region of perceptual similarity space, a *true measure* of variation along the corresponding dimension of objective quality space if and only if there is a *uniform transformation, Tran*, of *perc* into *obj* such that for all points x and x' within the given region, $Tran(perc(x, x')) = obj(map(x), map(x'))$. What kind of function will count as a uniform transformation will depend what kind of dimension of perceptual similarity space is in question. If the dimension is Euclidean, then a uniform transformation will be a positive linear transformation. But, as noted above, not all of the dimensions of perceptual similarity space will be Euclidean.

In terms of the relation of true measure between dimensions of perceptual similarity space and their corresponding dimensions of objective quality space (in a region), we can introduce a new, improved definition of accuracy. Let us say that a mark in perceptual similarity space is a *candidate for accuracy relative to a set of dimensions of perceptual similarity space* if and only if the mark lies in a region of perceptual similarity space in which, for each dimension in the set, that dimension is, within the given region, a true measure of variation along the dimension in objective quality space that corresponds to it. Then we can say that *if* a mark in perceptual similarity space that records an object or scenario is a candidate for accuracy relative to a set of dimensions of perceptual similarity space, then it is *accurate relative to that set of dimensions of perceptual similarity space* just to the extent that the point in objective quality space that the mark in perceptual similarity space is mapped into is *near* to the point in objective quality space that the object or scenario recorded is actually at.

The reason why the marks representing the Müller-Lyer arrows do not qualify as accurate is that they are not even candidates for accuracy relative to any set of dimensions that includes the perceptual length dimension. They are not candidates because, in the region of perceptual similarity space containing those marks, variation in the perceptual length dimension is not a true measure of variation in objective length. The lines attached to the endpoints of the arrows, which are responsible for the illusion, place the marks representing the arrows in a region of perceptual similarity space where marks may occupy different locations on the perceptual length dimension but correspond to points in objective quality space that occupy the same position on the objective length dimension. Other marks may represent objects of the same length as those arrows but be in other regions of perceptual similarity space where variation on the perceptual length dimension is a true measure of variation on the objective length dimension.

4.4 Correspondence between Dimensions

In introducing the concepts of objective quality space and perceptual similarity space in subsection 4.1, I began by describing objective quality space, but in doing so, I took for granted that each dimension of objective quality space corresponds to a dimension of perceptual similarity space. Then I explained how we could define a mapping of points in perceptual similarity space into points in objective quality space. However, that explanation of the mapping made no use of the correspondence between dimensions. Moreover, the mapping from points to points does not immediately generate a mapping of the dimensions of perceptual similarity space into dimensions of objective quality space. But then in refining the definition of accuracy to accommodate the inaccuracy of persistent illusions, I took for granted that we could draw the correspondence between dimensions. So now I need to explain how that correspondence may be drawn.

It is evident that for any arrangement of points in a hyperspace, indefinitely many sets of lines through that space could be treated as the dimensions in terms of which we identify locations. Defining the correspondence between dimensions of perceptual similarity space and the dimensions of objective quality space is a problem precisely because, as the Müller-Lyer arrows illustrate, we cannot assume that distance on a dimension of perceptual similarity space is in all regions a true measure of variation on the corresponding dimension of objective quality space. So in searching for the dimension of objective quality space that corresponds to a given dimension of perceptual similarity space, we cannot simply go looking for *the* dimension such that variation on *that* dimension is truly measured by variation on the dimension of perceptual similarity space in question.

Toward defining the correspondence between dimensions, let us start with the case of length. Obviously, we can measure length in various ways (rulers, laser beams, etc.). Sometimes, provided the lengths are not too short or too long, we can judge whether one thing is longer than another just by looking. More precisely, the relative locations of marks in perceptual similarity space may guide our judgments of comparative length. Sometimes, as the Müller-Lyer arrows show, the length judgments that we form on this basis will be mistaken. Nonetheless, we might identify the length dimension of perceptual similarity space as follows: It is the dimension of perceptual similarity space such that *when we have nothing else to go by*, we will judge that x is shorter than y if and only if the mark representing x has a lower value on that dimension than the mark representing y.

Generalizing from the case of length, we may say that a dimension D of perceptual similarity space is the dimension to which a given dimension of objective quality space corresponds if and only if D is the unique dimension of perceptual similarity space that controls our judgments regarding the location of objects on that dimension of objective quality space when we have nothing else to go by. (Section 5 below will take steps toward explaining the sense in which a dimension of perceptual similarity space may "control" a judgment.)

On this account of persistent illusions, judgment has analytical priority over perceptual representation. We can distinguish the persistent illusions among the marks produced in the functionally normal way only insofar as we can correlate the dimensions of the perceiver's perceptual similarity space with dimensions of objective quality space and so only insofar as we can recognize the content of the perceiver's judgments. So if a creature is not literally capable of making judgments, then we cannot regard it as subject to persistent illusions. Even if we hold that nonhuman animals do not literally form judgments (as we should, I think, although this is not an issue I can take up here), that is a not implausible result. It is hard to think of any experimental manipulations that would show that, for example, a beaver was subject to the Müller-Lyer illusion. We might find that under certain circumstances, a beaver was reliably disposed to behave toward two logs of equal length as if it perceived one of them to be longer than the other. But we could do that only if we thought we knew how its perceptions varied with its responses. Instead of interpreting the beaver's behavior as demonstrating misperception of length, we could as well interpret it as guided by correct perception of some other property that really does differentiate the two logs (as the Müller-Lyer arrows really are differentiated by the orientations of the lines extending from their ends).

The incorrectness in our perception of the Müller-Lyer arrows does *not* consist in its tempting us to judge that the arrows have different lengths. Rather, it consists in the fact that the marks representing those arrows in perceptual similarity space have different values on the perceptual length dimension of perceptual similarity space. Nonetheless, when we *recognize* that our perceptions are incorrect, we typically do so by comparing two propositions. On the one hand, there is what we *would* judge the comparative lengths of the arrows to be, if we had nothing else to go by. On the other hand, there is what we *do* judge the lengths of the arrows to be as the result of measuring them in some way. We may recognize the error in our perception by noticing the disparity between these two propositions.

5. How Perceptions Guide Belief

Though perceptions do not justify beliefs, they do have a place in epistemology. Perceptions can *guide* belief and can do so in such a way that credit and blame for errors in belief can be attributed to perception.

Towards explaining how perceptions can guide belief, let us suppose that the mind can *associate labels* with marks in perceptual similarity space. A label could be thought of as a mark in perceptual similarity space representing a token of a *word*, by which I mean a type of utterance in a spoken language, such as English or Chinese. Alternatively, a label could be thought of as *itself* a token of a word in a language of thought. I will take the first option and treat a label as a perceptual representation of a token of a word. Even so, for simplicity I will refer to labels using the words whose tokens they represent. Thus, I may speak of the word "Katze" as a label, even though, strictly speaking, the label is a mark in perceptual similarity space representing a token of the word and not the word itself. An *association* between a label and another mark in perceptual similarity space will be a relation that plays a certain role, to be explained presently, in the production of speech. Associations in the present sense are not the object of learning; this theory posits no learning of associations that lead the mind to pass from an idea of one kind to an idea of another, "associated" kind.

Consider the following simple situation. A child has heard the word "Katze" in a number of situations involving a cat, so that the label "Katze" becomes associated with the marks representing those situations, and has heard the word "Hund" in a number of situations involving a dog, so that the label "Hund" becomes associated with the marks representing those situations. Moreover, the marks representing scenarios associated with "Katze" form a *cluster*, and those representing scenarios associated with "Hund" form a cluster. Here I will not try to define the concept of clustering, but the idea will be that the marks in a cluster will exhibit a kind of togetherness in perceptual similarity space. How best to define a cluster is an empirical question, and indeed empirical work led by Malt (Malt, et al. 1999) demonstrates quite persuasively that we should not expect clusters to occupy *convex* regions of perceptual similarity space. So it is not the case that for any mark x between two marks in a cluster, mark x needs to belong to the cluster as well.[18]

Suppose that the child encounters a novel situation and for some reason is disposed to label it herself. That is to say, the child is disposed to utter a word the utterance of which the child will represent by means of a label in perceptual similarity space. Suppose, moreover, that the child's choice of labels is for some reason limited to "Katze" and "Hund". In such a situation, the child's choice may be determined by the relation in perceptual similarity space between the mark representing the novel situation and the marks in the "Katze" cluster and the marks in the "Hund" cluster. Perhaps if the mark representing the novel situation is nearer to its nearest neighbors in the "Katze" cluster than it is to its nearest neighbors in the "Hund" cluster, the child will choose to utter "Katze"; and otherwise, if it is nearer to its nearest neighbors in the "Hund" cluster, then the child will utter "Hund". To the extent that the marks in perceptual similarity space accurately represent points in objective quality space, we may also say that the child's choice of label is driven by objective similarity relations between the novel situation and the objects and scenarios represented by the marks with which "Katze" and "Hund" are associated.

What this simple example shows is that we might in principle be able to explain how the location of marks in perceptual similarity space drives a developmentally early kind of speech behavior. Inasmuch as this speech behavior may be conceived as a developmentally early kind of judgment, or belief formation, it shows that in principle there might be ways in which the location of marks in perceptual similarity space might guide belief. Certainly there will be more to belief formation than labeling in this way on the basis of perceptual similarities. For instance, we might not wish to dignify a mental state as "belief" until it was sensitive to revision from nonperceptual sources, such as general theories. Nonetheless, we can see in this example that even on the present account of perceptual representation, the character of our perceptions can play a role in belief formation in at least one regular way.

Assuming that perceptions can guide beliefs in the manner indicated, we can acknowledge also that perceptions have a place in epistemology. Our errors in forming beliefs can sometimes be blamed on inaccuracies in perception, and our successes can sometimes be credited to accuracy in perception. Since accuracy is to be expected, and we normally explain events by citing those elements of their causation that are unexpected, we can expect that we will more often hear a judgment blamed on an inaccurate perception than we will hear a judgment credited to an accurate perception. Thus if a basketball player misses a shot, we may blame it on his misperceiving the distance between himself and the basket. (In that case, we ought to have to have some reason to think that the fault does not lie in his ability to convert his perception into a correctly calibrated push of the ball.) But by the same token, if he makes the shot, we can credit it to his accurately perceiving the distance.

However, the accuracy of our perceptions will not typically be a question we engage when we debate an issue. When we engage in a discussion with another person, or undertake empirical investigations, we may find that some of our prior judgments were mistaken. Sometimes our revisions may involve a reconsideration of the reasoning by which we arrived at the prior judgments we now deem mistaken. Sometimes we may simply find that the force of our present evidence and reasoning is sufficient to show that our prior judgment *must* have been mistaken, however it was arrived at. We do not in the same way reason about the correctness of our perceptions. We may conclude that the most reasonable explanation of an error in judgment is that we started with incorrect perceptions. But what we do not do is compare the content of our perceptions to the content of our present judgments and decide in favor of one or the other; the two kinds of contents are simply not comparable in that way.

6. Seeing-as

Another commonplace in the recent philosophical literature on perception is the supposition that perceptual representations have a *phenomenal character* and that the propositional content of a perception can be read off its phenomenal character. A favorite device for making salient the content-determining phenomenal character of a perceptual experience is to ask the reader to imagine a change in perceptual aspect. Thus, the duck-rabbit can be "seen as" either a duck or a rabbit. When we are seeing it as a duck, it is supposedly clear that our perceptual representation says, in effect, "That's a duck". When we are seeing it as a rabbit, then our perceptual representation says, "That's a rabbit". Or we are asked to imagine passing from a state of being unable to recognize a kind of thing perceptually to being able to recognize it. For example, we are to imagine being unable to recognize pine trees and then being able to recognize them (Siegel 2006b, 2010). What we are supposed to learn from such examples of aspect change is that at all times our perceptions have a phenomenal character that determines a propositional content.[19]

My answer to this sort of argument is that, while perceptions may have a phenomenological character, and while proposition-bearing representations may be involved in processing representations, there is no compelling reason to assume that it is the propositional content of perceptual experience that accounts for the phenomenological character of the perception. The alternative will be to suppose that phenomenological character is a matter of the perception's location in perceptual similarity space and that the associated propositional content is borne by a further act of the mind that the perceptual experience somehow elicits. This further act of the mind may not be *belief*. When we perceive the duck-rabbit drawing as a duck, we do not *believe* that there is a duck before us. When we perceive the lines in the Müller-Lyer arrows as unequal in length we need not *believe* that they are. Still, the propositional content may be conceived as carried by something other than the perceptual experience itself; we could call it *the subsumption of the object of perception under a concept*, or, for short, a *conceptualization*.[20]

Here, then, is how I would account for the phenomenon of seeing-as. It has two levels. The first level is the location of a mark in perceptual similarity space. One thing *looks* different from another (or, more generally, *appears* different from another) if the two of them are represented by marks at different locations in perceptual similarity space. This much of the process of seeing-as can take place even in creatures that lack concepts altogether. The second level is the level of conceptualization. Here a concept is applied to the object of perceptual representation in response to the representation. What is special about this conceptualization, which differentiates it from the conceptualization that occurs in other sorts of thoughts, such as those that result from inference, is that it is driven by the location of a mark in perceptual similarity space, in something like the manner described in the previous section. So if I perceive a dog *as* a dog, then I first place a mark representing the dog in perceptual similarity space. Then, as a consequence of the location of that mark in perceptual similarity space relative to other labeled marks in perceptual similarity space, I conceptualize it as a dog. Supposing that conceptualization may be accounted for along the lines indicated above, conceptualization may amount to labeling the dog (the object represented by the mark) with a word that means *dog*. As a speaker of English, my labeling the dog as a dog may take the form of my tokening in thought the English word "dog". Conceptualization in this sense may qualify as belief provided nothing about the circumstances elicits doubts in the agent that would prevent our treating it as such.

Cases of aspect change fall into at least two categories. In the case of ambiguous figures, which we see first as this and then as that, these may involve a certain amount of filling in. The lines of the drawing are schematic; so when we try to locate them as marks in perceptual similarity space we can imagistically "fill in" some of the missing values in various ways. (That is not to say that we mentally paint a duck or a rabbit into the outlines of the duck-rabbit. No such conscious visualization need be involved.) Alternatively, what happens in these cases may be that we attend to different features of the drawing when we see it as the one thing than we do when we see it as the other. In my terms, the consequence of either of these processes may be that we mark the drawing in different locations in perceptual similarity space — in one case closer to marks representing ducks and in the other closer to marks representing rabbits.[21]

The other category of aspect change are cases due to growth in expertise. After we know what the instruments in the orchestra sound like played solo, the whole symphony sounds somehow more articulate. Once we learn to read the Korean alphabet and acquire some Korean vocabulary, we can perceive Korean words in the Korean script, not just blocks of strange marks. In these cases, there is probably growth at both the level of perception and at the level of conceptualization. At the level of perception, we are able to mark the object of perception more precisely, perhaps due to the availability of a greater number of landmarks in perceptual similarity space. Before, the mark representing the sound of an oboe may occupy a range of values largely overlapping the range of values occupied by the mark representing the sound of a clarinet; afterward, their marks may be discrete. Moreover, with expertise our perceptual similarity spaces may acquire additional dimensions on which we can evaluate an object of perception (subsection 4.1 above). Thus, we might acquire a dimension representing similarity to the sound of an oboe. At the level of conceptualization, we acquire new labels, such as "the sound of an oboe" and "the Korean word for *person*".

7. Summary

The view that perceptions must have propositional content because perceptions justify beliefs may be questioned on the grounds that there does not seem to be any good way to identify the concepts that compose the purported belief-justifying propositional contents of perceptions. The other major rationales for attributing propositional contents to perceptions can be accommodated by means of an alternative theory of perceptual representation that does not attribute propositional contents to them. Perceptual representations can be modeled as marks in perceptual similarity space, and accuracy can be defined in terms of a mapping of marks in perceptual similarity into marks in objective quality space. The phenomenon of seeing-as can be divided into representing an object in perceptual similarity space and conceptually responding to the object on the basis of the location of that representation. Although perceptions do not justify beliefs, perceptions can guide beliefs in a epistemically relevant way.[22]

Notes

1. There is perhaps a fourth motivation in the fact that we use verbs of perception, such as "see", followed by "that"-clauses (Searle 1983, pp. 40–41). This motive is not very explicit in recent publications (an exception being Byrne 2005, p. 246), but its influence is perhaps evident in a persistent tendency of recent authors to use "that"-clauses in characterizing perceptions. I take it to be evidently unreasonable to assume that "that"-clauses in such sentences report the content of a perception. Suppose I report, "I saw that the vandals had left a skateboard in the foyer". Surely, the vandals are not represented in the act of perceiving a skateboard to which I am alluding.
2. One could cite Frege (1892/1994) here so long as one added a few qualifications about terminology. Concepts in my sense would be the Fregean senses of sub-sentential expressions. What he called *Begriffe* (the German word for *concepts*) were what we would call extensions.
3. Thus Crane writes: "For any state with content, S, S has a nonconceptual content, P, if and only if a subject X's being in S does not entail that X possesses the concepts that canonically characterize P" (1992, p. 143).
4. Peacocke does sometimes characterize nonconceptual content in terms of possession and "describing" in this way (e.g., 1992a, pp. 111–12). In view of his allusions to Peacocke, I think it is probably best to also interpret Bermúdez as thinking of nonconceptual content in this way when he writes that "it is theoretically legitimate to refer to mental states ["perceptual experiences" in his terminology] which represent the world but which do not require the bearer of those mental states to possess the concepts required to specify the way in which they represent the world" (Bermúdez 1995, p. 335).
5. In his 1992 paper, Crane's claim was that, while a perceptual state and a belief may have the same propositional content, when that content occurs as the content of a perception, it is not composed of concepts; because a perception could have such a content, though the perceiver lacked the concepts that are components of the corresponding belief content (p. 140, p. 155). That beliefs and perceptions both have propositional contents would also seem to be the position of anyone who, in the lingo of Jeff Speaks (2005), denies that perceptions have "absolute" nonconceptual content but affirms that they have "relative" nonconceptual content" (Speaks denies both). Crane now repudiates his earlier view (Crane 2009, p. 466).
6. Thus we would not describe McDowell as attributing nonconceptual content to perceptual representations. See his use of the metaphor of "shaping" in McDowell 1998, p. 460.
7. This is what I think Chalmers must be thinking when he writes that the contents of perception may be nonconceptual (2006, p. 122). He cannot mean to deny that perceptions have propositional contents; on the contrary, he ascribes to perceptions three different kinds of propositional content, Russellian (physical), Fregean and Edenic. Moreover, he accepts that perceptual representations are

conceptually structured (although that is not his term), inasmuch as he holds that the Edenic content of a perception is determined by the "phenomenal character" of the perception.

8. Both McDowell (1996, pp. 165–66) and Glüer (2009, p. 316) explicitly appeal to overt, spoken justifications. Huemer (2007) and Pollock and Oved (2005, p. 311) do not do that, but they do assert general principles to the effect that its seeming to one that p (or appearing to one as though p) provides defeasible justification for the belief that p.

9. Externalism about mental content is no evident bar to accessibility, properly defined. Even if the content of one of someone's beliefs can be equally described as the belief that water is wet and as the belief that H_2O is wet, and even if that person knows nothing about chemistry, her belief may be expressible by her with the words "Water is wet".

10. This argument, in a different form and aimed at a different target, appears also in my 2011 monograph.

11. To accommodate Chalmers's (2006) idea that the properties represented in perception are Edenic properties that nothing actually has, we could weaken this assumption to the following: The properties represented by the concepts that make up the propositional contents of perceptions are typically properties of a sort that only external objects *would* have if anything had them.

12. Siegel (2006a; 2010, chapter 7) argues that our ordinary perceptions represent relations to the perceptual experience itself. Searle (1983, chapter 2) has claimed that as well. I will not address their arguments.

13. Brewer (2006; 2011, section 4.3) hints at a critique of this sort. Brewer (who had earlier argued on the other side of this issue, e.g. in Brewer 2005) observes that any application of a general concept involves a classification and asks, in effect, how a perceptual representation can provide for the classification of its object.

14. In her 2006a (p. 485), Siegel describes the contents of perceptions as having "accuracy conditions", which she treats as truth conditions. She observes that some philosophers deny that perceptions have content in even this "minimal sense" and characterizes these philosophers as holding that perceptions are merely "raw feels". In her 2010, Siegel presumes at one point (p. 46) that if perceptions do not "present clusters of properties as being instantiated" then they can only represent bare particulars that *do not have* properties. Later, she takes the alternatives to be either raw feels or "pure objects" (2010, p. 65). In these ways, Siegel indicates that she conceives of no possibility of defining accuracy other than as the true ascription of properties.

15. The definitions in this subsection appear also in my 2011 monograph, where, however, they serve a different purpose.

16. My idea that perceptual similarity spaces may be augmented in this way was inspired by Shimon Edelman's "chorus model" of object recognition (Edelman 1995). Note, though, that I am not using the chorus model as a model of object *classification*.

17. Here I am taking my notion of biological normality from that developed by Ruth Millikan (see the papers in her 1993). In particular, I am defining the content of representations in terms of the biologically normal function of the representations' consumers. For my critique of Millikan's plan of building a general theory of intentionality on that ground, see my 1995. My own theory

is not subject to the circularity charge that I level in that review, because I do not define the normal function of perceptual similarity space in terms of the mapping relation.

18. I do not say, and elsewhere I have categorically denied (Gauker 2011, chapter 3), that concepts can be identified with such clusters.
19. This strategy is prominent in Searle 1983, p. 51, and Siegel 2006a, 2006b, 2010. Huemer (2001, p. 75) uses the duck-rabbit to argue that perceptions sometimes have *conceptual* content, which he distinguishes from *propositional* content. Chalmers (2006) does not appeal to aspect shifting, but, as noted in note 7 above, he does in other ways make an issue of how to derive the propositional content of a perceptual experience from its phenomenal character.
20. The term "conceptualization" sometimes refers to the application of theory-like structures to an object. As noted above, Heck (2000) uses it for the relation that underwrites the purported justification of beliefs by perceptions. My use is neither of these.
21. Price (2009) suggests both that such filling in and such variations in attention may account for aspect switching.
22. Versions of this material have been presented at various universities and conferences since 2008. I recall especially useful comments from Kathrin Glüer, Paul Griffiths, Magdalena Balcerak Jackson, Franklin Scott, and Tad Zawidzski.

References

Bermúdez, José. 1995. "Nonconceptual Content: From Perceptual Experience to Subpersonal Computational States." *Mind and Language* 10: 333–69.
Brewer, Bill. 2005. "Perceptual Experience has Conceptual Content." In *Contemporary Debates in Epistemology*, edited by Matthias Steup and Ernest Sosa, 217–30. New York: Routledge.
Brewer, Bill. 2006. "Perception and Content." *European Journal of Philosophy* 14: 165–81.
Brewer, Bill. 2011. *Perception and it Objects*. Oxford: Oxford University Press.
Byrne, Alex. 2005. "Perception and Conceptual Content." In *Contemporary Debates in Epistemology*, edited by Matthias Steup and Ernest Sosa, 231–50. Malden, MA: Blackwell.
Chalmers, David. 2006. "Perception and the Fall from Eden." In *Perceptual Experience*, edited by Tamar Szabó Gendler and John Hawthorne, 49–125. Oxford: Oxford University Press.
Chisholm, Roderick. 1977. *Theory of Knowledge*. 2nd edition. Englewood Cliffs, N. J.: Prentice-Hall.
Crane, Tim. 1992. "The Nonconceptual Content of Experience." In *The Contents of Experience*, edited by Tim Crane, 136–57. Cambridge: Cambridge University Press.
Crane, Tim. 2009. "Is Perception a Propositional Attitude?" *The Philosophical Quarterly* 59: 452–469.
Edelman, Shimon. 1995. "Representation, Similarity and the Chorus of Prototypes." *Minds and Machines* 5: 45–68.
Frege, Gottlob. 1994 [1892]. "Über Sinn und Bedeutung." In *Funktion, Begriff, Bedeutung*, edited by Günther Patzig, 40–66. Göttingen: Vandenhoeck and Ruprecht.
Gauker, Christopher. 1995. Review of Ruth Garrett Millikan, *White Queen Psychology and Other Essays for Alice*, *Philosophical Psychology* 8: 305–309.

Gauker, Christopher. 2011. *Words and Images: An Essay on the Origin of Ideas*. Oxford: Oxford University Press.

Ginsborg, Hannah. 2011. "Perception, Generality and Reasons." In *Reasons for Belief*, edited by Andrew Reisner and Asbjørn Steglich-Petersen, 131–57. Cambridge: Cambridge University Press.

Gleitman, Lila R., Henry Gleitman, Carol Miller, and Ruth Ostrin. 1996. "Similar and Similar Concepts." *Cognition* 58: 321–76.

Glüer, Kathrin. 2009. "In Defence of a Doxastic Account of Experience." *Mind and Language* 24: 297–327.

Goldman, Alvin. 1979. "Reliabilism: What is Justified Belief?" In *Justification and Knowledge*, edited by George S. Pappas, 1–23. Boston: D. Reidel.

Heck, Richard. 2000. "Nonconceptual Content and the 'Space of Reasons'." *Philosophical Review* 109: 483–523.

Huemer, Michael. 2001. *Skepticism and the Veil of Perception*. Lanham, MD: Rowman and Littlefield.

Huemer, Michael. 2007. "Compassionate Phenomenal Conservatism." *Philosophy and Phenomenological Research* 74: 30–55.

Kelly, Sean Dorrance, 2001. "Demonstrative Concepts and Experience." *Philosophical Review* 110: 397–420.

Lewis, C. I., 1946. *An Analysis of Knowledge and Valuation*. La Salle, IL: Open Court.

Malt, Barbara C., Steven A. Sloman, Silvia Gennari, Meiyi Shi, and Yuan Wang. 1999. "Knowing versus Naming, Similarity and the Linguistic Categorization of Artifacts." *Journal of Memory and Language* 40: 230–62.

Millar, Alan. 1996. "The Idea of Experience." *Proceedings of the Aristotelian Society* 96: 75–90.

Millikan, Ruth. 1993. *White Queen Psychology and Other Essays for Alice*. Cambridge, MA: MIT Press.

McDowell, John. 1996. *Mind and World*. Cambridge, MA: Harvard University Press.

McDowell, John. 1998. "Lecture II: The Logical Form of an Intuition." *Journal of Philosophy* 95: 451–70.

Peacocke, Christopher. 1992a. "Scenarios, Concepts and Perception." In *The Contents of Experience*, edited by Tim Crane, 105–35. Cambridge, MA: Cambridge University Press.

Peacocke, Christopher. 1992b. *A Study of Concepts*. Cambridge, MA: MIT Press.

Peacocke, Christopher. 2001. "Does Perception Have a Nonconceptual Content?" *Journal of Philosophy* 98: 239–64.

Pollock, John and Iris Oved. 2005. "Vision, Knowledge and the Mystery Link." *Philosophical Perspectives* 19: 309–351.

Price, Richard. 2009. "Aspect-switching and Visual Phenomenal Character." *Philosophical Quarterly* 59: 508–18.

Pryor, James. 2000. "The Skeptic and the Dogmatist." *Noûs* 34: 517–49.

Russell, Bertrand. 1912. *The Problems of Philosophy*. Oxford: Oxford University Press.

Searle, John. 1983. *Intentionality*. Cambridge: Cambridge University Press.

Siegel, Susanna. 2006a. "Subject and Object in the Contents of Visual Experience." *Philosophical Review* 115: 355–88.

Siegel, Susanna. 2006b. "Which Properties are Represented in Perception." In *Perceptual Experience*, edited by Tamar Szabó Gendler and John Hawthorne, 481–503. Oxford: Oxford University Press.

Siegel, Susanna. 2010. *The Contents of Visual Experience*. Oxford: Oxford University Press.

Speaks, Jeff. 2005. "Is there a Problem about Nonconceptual Content?" *Philosophical Review* 114: 359–98.

Wittgenstein, Ludwig. 1953. *Philosophical Investigations*. Translated by G. E. M. Anscombe. New York: Macmillan.

Philosophical Perspectives, 26, Philosophy of Mind, 2012

UNDERSTANDING THE INTERNALISM-EXTERNALISM DEBATE: WHAT IS THE BOUNDARY OF THE THINKER?

Brie Gertler
The University of Virginia

Since the work of Burge, Davidson, Kripke, and Putnam in the 1970's, philosophers of language and mind have engaged in extensive debate over the following question: Do mental content properties — such as *thinking that water quenches thirst* — supervene on properties intrinsic to the thinker? To answer affirmatively is to endorse internalism (or "individualism"); a negative answer is an expression of externalism.

There is no consensus about the correct answer to this question; a 2009 survey indicates that a bare majority of philosophers now characterize themselves as externalists.[1] The recent literature on this topic largely focuses on the implications of externalism and internalism. There is no consensus here either. Philosophers are sharply divided as to whether externalism is compatible with privileged access to one's own thoughts; whether externalism implies that we can achieve knowledge of the external world from the armchair; whether internalism is compatible with physicalism about the mental; and whether internalism implies that thoughts are incommunicable.

Disagreements are philosophers' stock in trade. But the disputes just mentioned have proven exceptionally intractable. The culprit, I think, is an ambiguity in the terms "externalism" and "internalism", which they inherit from an ambiguity in the notion of "intrinsic to the thinker" operative in these disputes. As employed in the debate over mental content, "externalism" and "internalism" are associated with a shifting set of claims encompassing a heterogeneous array of topics; these include the organism's contribution to thought contents, links between the individual and her community, the epistemic availability of thoughts, and relations between phenomenal character and intentional content.

I will argue that this ambiguity is ineliminable. Any way of explicating "intrinsic to the thinker" will clash with the usual taxonomy of leading externalist and internalist views, or construe these positions as involving claims that are standardly regarded as orthogonal to them — and, in some cases, explicitly rejected by their most prominent exponents.[2] The moral is stark. The sense that there is a substantive, defining commitment of externalism or internalism — even one that is vague or underspecified — is illusory. There is no univocal thesis of externalism or internalism.

The ambiguity of "externalism" and "internalism" helps to explain why contributors to this literature often seem to be arguing at cross-purposes, disagreeing about the truth and implications of externalism and internalism, and about the nature of the evidence that could resolve these disputes. Now this ambiguity would not be too worrisome if its effects were confined to disputes about mental content. But because the claims associated with externalism and internalism cover a diverse range of topics, philosophers routinely invoke externalism or internalism (or purported implications thereof) in evaluating a range of other questions — in the philosophy of language, epistemology, and the philosophy of mind. These include: Does the meaning of an utterance correspond to elements understood by the speaker? Do thinkers generally enjoy privileged access to their own mental states? Can we know contingent facts about the external world through introspection and *a priori* reasoning? Does phenomenal character supervene on intentional content, or vice versa? Can content be naturalized? The ambiguity endemic to discussions of externalism and internalism thus threatens progress on a broad spectrum of philosophical questions.

I begin by arguing, in Section 1, that an adequate explication of "externalism" or "internalism" must employ a criterion of "intrinsic to the thinker". The next three sections evaluate candidate criteria. Section 2 discusses the most familiar type of criteria, which explicate this notion in physical or spatial terms. Section 3 examines a recently proposed epistemic criterion. Section 4 considers the idea that what is intrinsic to thinkers are thoughts themselves — the bearers of content — which may not exhaust the factors determining content. Each of these candidates fails. Each commits externalists or internalists to positions that are strictly optional, according to the ordinary understanding of these views; conflicts with established classifications of particular views as externalist or internalist; or lacks the informativeness needed to illuminate this debate. Section 5 argues that other possible criteria of "intrinsic to the thinker" will likely share these inadequacies.

The debate about mental content, as it is currently framed, cannot be salvaged. I conclude by briefly suggesting more profitable uses for the philosophical energies conserved by abandoning this debate.

1. "Intrinsic to the thinker"

Internalism and externalism are standardly expressed as follows.

(I) Thought contents always supervene on properties intrinsic to the thinker.
(E) Thought contents do not always supervene on properties intrinsic to the thinker.[3]

My plan is to demonstrate that there is no univocal thesis of externalism or internalism, by showing that (I) and (E) are irremediably ambiguous: no way of explicating "intrinsic to the thinker" will cash out these statements in a way that makes sense of the existing debate.

Someone could object to my project by noting that the term "intrinsic to the thinker" is not present in every formulation of externalism and internalism. But while this term is not crucial, the distinction it marks — between properties intrinsic to the thinker and properties extrinsic to her — will be invoked in any plausible formulation of these positions. To see this, consider Kirk Ludwig's particularly clear formulation of externalism, which does not use the term "intrinsic to the thinker".

> The externalist thesis is, in short, that content properties are in part relational properties. A property *P* is a relational property just in case, necessarily, for any object *O*, if *O* has *P*, then there is an *X* such that *X* is (i) not an abstract object and (ii) *X* is not identical to *O* or to any part of *O*. (Ludwig 1993, 251)

On this interpretation, the content property *thinking that water quenches thirst* satisfies the externalist thesis *iff* my having a thought with that content entails the existence of some concrete entity (or other) distinct from myself. But arguably, X is a distinct concrete entity just in case *being such that X exists* is not intrinsic to me. So the notion of properties intrinsic to the thinker is implicit in this formulation of externalism. And this is how it should be, since — as the labels "externalism" and "internalism" indicate — these positions' defining theses make crucial use of the notion of features instantiated within (or outside) the thinking subject.

A more promising objection to my project denies that understanding "intrinsic to the thinker" requires identifying a *criterion*. This objection might take the following form.

> The search for a criterion here is misguided. Surely factors standardly regarded as internal, such as brain states, occur within the thinker. And those that serve as examples of external factors, such as the presence of H_2O in the environment and the use of "arthritis" by community experts, are external to the thinker. We should treat *being in brain state B* as a paradigm case of an intrinsic property; and we should treat *inhabiting an environment in which the watery stuff is H_2O* and *belonging to a community where experts use "arthritis" to refer to a joint disease* as paradigm cases of non-intrinsic properties. While the status of other properties may be less clear, these examples illuminate what "intrinsic to the thinker" means. We understand this term well enough, even if we are unable to specify a precise *criterion*.

Here is my response. Although the properties mentioned appear to be clear examples of intrinsic and non-intrinsic properties, it is conceivable that the best way to understand "intrinsic" and "non-intrinsic" will reclassify one or more of them. All else being equal, a way of drawing this distinction should count *being in brain state B* as an intrinsic property; and it should count *inhabiting an environment in which the watery stuff is H_2O* and *belonging to a community where experts use "arthritis" to refer to a joint disease* as non-intrinsic. But we cannot assume that an understanding of "intrinsic to the thinker" that remains loyal to widespread perceptions of the basic commitments of externalism and internalism will neatly match our intuitions about which properties fit this description. In other words, all else may *not* be equal. So even these seemingly clear instances of intrinsic and non-intrinsic properties are open to reclassification.

This last point is controversial. To see why these instances of (apparently) intrinsic and non-intrinsic properties should not be treated as sacrosanct, recall that a seminal externalist argument (Putnam 1975) uses *inhabiting an environment in which the watery stuff is H_2O* as an example of an external property. Many commentators have noted that this property could be regarded as intrinsic to the thinker, since humans are partly composed of H_2O. This complication is usually brushed off with the observation that H_2O is an unfortunate example. But it carries a valuable lesson: particular examples of properties claimed to be intrinsic (or non-intrinsic) may sit uneasily with the *intentions* guiding the use of these terms. And sometimes, as in the H_2O case, the intention is more important than the particular example. As we will see below, one philosopher has proposed that loyalty to the relevant referential intentions will count *being in brain state B* as a non-intrinsic property (Farkas 2003). Regardless of that proposal's ultimate merits, it seems reasonable not to foreclose, from the outset, the possibility that seemingly paradigmatic cases of intrinsic or non-intrinsic properties could conceivably be reclassified.

Here is another way to put this point. The standard examples of intrinsic and non-intrinsic properties are not genuine paradigms, in the strict sense of "paradigm" that is at work in paradigm case arguments. (In that strict sense of "paradigm", a paradigm case of an *F* cannot fail to be an *F*.) Rather, as the H_2O example illustrates, these examples are chosen because it is assumed that they qualify as intrinsic (or non-intrinsic) according to some principled, albeit unarticulated, conception of the boundary of the thinker: a boundary dividing factors within the thinker from those outside her. Making this implicit conception *explicit* requires identifying the criterion of "intrinsic to the thinker" that operates behind the scenes in the externalism-internalism debate.[4]

In attempting to unpack the notion of "intrinsic to the thinker" operative in this debate, we must balance a variety of factors. We must accord some weight to intuitions about how to categorize specific properties. But such intuitions may not carry the day, for they may conflict with standard classifications of particular views as internalist or externalist, or with widely shared assumptions about the commitments of internalism and externalism.

2. The Spatial Approach

Externalists often express their view by denying that thought content supervenes on properties instantiated within the subject's skin, brain, or head. The idea here is that the skin, brain, or head constitutes the outer spatial limits of the individual, conceived as an organism, or of that part of the individual directly involved in thought. It is easy to see why contributors to this debate have not felt it necessary to choose between these various biological boundaries. The central externalist claim is that some thought contents metaphysically depend on features of the physical environment or social practices, and these are presumed to fall squarely outside the human organism. (For convenience, I will use "the skin" to represent biological boundaries more generally.)

Expressions of externalism commonly assume that the supervenience base spatially located within the skin is constituted by physical properties. For instance, the normal test case for externalist claims are imaginary twins, characterized as "molecule-for-molecule duplicates". So the most familiar formulation of externalism relies on a spatiophysical construal of "intrinsic to the thinker": it interprets externalism as the thesis that thought contents can differ between individuals who are precisely alike as regards the physical properties instantiated within the space delineated by their skins. This suggests the following criterion. (Throughout the paper, "S" refers to a thinker and "F" refers to a property S instantiates.)

> **(Spatiophysical Criterion)** F is intrinsic to S iff F is a physical property instantiated within the spatial boundary constituted by S's skin.

While the Spatiophysical Criterion fits classic ways of stating the externalist thesis, it is plainly inadequate. This criterion interprets externalism as the claim that thought contents do not supervene on physical factors within the spatial boundary of the organism; it thereby links externalism to a seemingly unrelated question about mental ontology. Perhaps the clearest indication of this flaw is that this criterion classifies Descartes — standardly regarded as the archetypal internalist — as an *externalist*. For Descartes denies that mental contents metaphysically supervene on any physical properties. (Burge (2003a) notes that this flaw was present in his earlier (1986b) characterization of internalism.)[5]

Sensitivity to this issue about mental ontology has led some philosophers to take special care in formulating externalism (and internalism). Here is a good example of a carefully formulated externalist claim.

> [I]t is possible for thinkers that are alike in all intrinsic physical respects to differ in the contents of their thoughts by virtue of differences in their environments. (McLaughlin and Tye 1998, 349)

By specifying that it is environmental differences that are responsible for the difference in thought contents, this formulation adds a condition for externalism not present in the previous formulation. It is not clear whether McLaughlin and Tye intend this as a necessary condition for externalism, a sufficient condition, or both. But it will serve our purpose of expressing the externalist thesis only if it is both necessary and sufficient; so we must consider whether it satisfies that role.

Assume, for the moment, that the environmental differences in question are *physical* differences. (We revisit this assumption below.) This formulation then suggests the following criterion.

> **(Modified Spatiophysical Criterion)** F is intrinsic to S <u>iff</u> either (i) F is a physical property instantiated within the spatial boundary constituted by S's skin, or (ii) S's instantiating F does not metaphysically depend on any physical features of the environment.

Using this criterion, externalism is the claim that a difference in the physical environment can suffice for a difference in thought contents between two persons who are intra-skin physical duplicates.

The Modified Spatiophysical Criterion improves on the original Spatiophysical Criterion in that it classifies Descartes as an internalist. A Cartesian soul's thinking a particular thought (instantiating a particular content property) is independent of the physical features of the environment, and hence is intrinsic to the thinker, according to this criterion. And this criterion fits nicely with some of the principal examples used to support externalism. In these examples, the thought contents of physical duplicates differ purely in virtue of physical differences between their environments: e.g., differences in the microstructure of the local watery stuff (H_2O vs. XYZ).

But the Modified Spatiophysical Criterion contains the same flaw as the original Spatiophysical Criterion, though in a less obvious form. By construing externalism as the claim that thought contents depend on specifically *physical* features of the environment, the Modified Spatiophysical Criterion links externalism to a seemingly unrelated ontological issue. To see this, consider a view constituted by two claims.

(1) Possessing the concept <u>arthritis</u> is an irreducibly mental (i.e., nonphysical) property.
(2) A thinker's ability to entertain <u>arthritis</u> thoughts metaphysically depends on the possession of the concept <u>arthritis</u> by experts in her community (and on no other environmental factor).

On this view, the fact that community experts possess the concept <u>arthritis</u> is a nonphysical feature of the environment. *Thinking that arthritis is painful* thus satisfies condition (ii) of the Modified Spatiophysical Criterion, and is therefore *intrinsic* to the thinker, according to that criterion. So the Modified Spatiophysical Criterion will count the conjunction of (1) and (2) as an internalist view. However, this view seems patently externalist. In fact, Burge may hold something like this view.[6] (I will refer to the conjunction of (1) and (2) as Externalist Dualism, though of course it is only one brand of externalist dualism.)

So the Modified Spatiophysical Criterion is inadequate. It correctly classifies some externalist positions, viz., those that claim that two physical duplicates' thoughts can differ purely in virtue of differences in their physical environments. But it misclassifies another plainly externalist view, because it counts, as intrinsic to the thinker, an apparently non-intrinsic property (being in a community in which experts possess the concept arthritis).[7]

Both of the criteria we have considered cash out "intrinsic to the thinker" in partly physical terms. This leads to problems with each: the initial Spatiophysical Criterion misclassified Cartesianism, and the Modified Spatiophysical Criterion misclassified Externalist Dualism. The lesson is clear. Definitionally linking intrinsic (or non-intrinsic) properties with the physical entangles externalism and internalism with ontological issues that are orthogonal to them.

On reflection, this result is unsurprising. For internalism and externalism are, in spirit, ontologically neutral. This neutrality is reflected in the fact that each of the following positions has been defended by influential philosophers: internalist dualism (Descartes, David Chalmers); internalist materialism (Jerry Fodor[8], Frank Jackson[9], Gabriel Segal); externalist dualism (Tyler Burge and perhaps Donald Davidson[10]); externalist materialism (Fred Dretske, Hilary Putnam, Michael Tye, and numerous others).

An obvious strategy for avoiding these ontological complications is to abandon the assumption, present in condition (ii) of the Modified Spatiophysical Criterion, that environmental features are physical features. This tactic is suggested by the formulation of internalism (or "individualism") on which Burge seems to have settled.

> According to individualism about the mind, the mental natures of all a person's or animal's mental states (and events) are such that there is no necessary or deep individuative relation between the individual's being in states of those kinds and the nature of the individual's physical *or social* environments. (Burge 1986b, 3–4, my emphasis; compare Burge 2006, 152.)

Externalism is then the claim that this "necessary or deep individuative relation" sometimes does obtain.

This formulation correctly classifies Descartes, since Descartes would deny that thoughts are individuated by relation to the physical or social environment. And it also seems to yield the desired classification of Externalist Dualism, since community experts' possession of the concept arthritis is a feature of the social environment.

Crucially, this latter consequence depends on the assumption that the social environment qualifies as *external* to the thinker even if it is not a matter of *physical* features of the world beyond her skin. This assumption invites the question: in what sense is the social environment *external* to the thinker? One answer, which retains the desired ontological neutrality,[11] is that the social environment is external to the thinker in a *spatial* sense. The corresponding demarcation of the thinker's intrinsic properties is as follows.

(**Spatial Criterion**) F is intrinsic to S iff either (i) F is instantiated within the spatial boundary defined by S's skin, or (ii) S's instantiating F does not metaphysically depend on any features of the environment outside the spatial boundary defined by S's skin.

The Spatial Criterion avoids the ontological entanglements on which the previous criteria foundered. And it generates the appropriate classifications of Cartesianism (as internalist) and Externalist Dualism (as externalist).

However, the Spatial Criterion is disloyal to the spirit of the externalism-internalism debate. This point is aptly demonstrated with an ingenious case devised by Katalin Farkas (2003). Farkas imagines twins who are precisely similar except for one particular. One twin, on Earth, suffers from meningitis. The other, on Twin Earth, suffers from a disease that is superficially similar to meningitis, and is called "meningitis" on Twin Earth, but involves a bacterium different from the meningitis bacterium (meningococcus). Farkas designs this case to closely parallel Putnam's argument for externalism regarding *water*. A further similarity is that Farkas' case takes place in 1750, before the bacterium associated with meningitis was identified.

Putnam's example challenges internalism by prompting the intuition that two physical duplicates who differ only in the makeup of the watery stuff in their environment (H_2O vs. XYZ) entertain different contents when they think (what they would express by saying) "water quenches thirst". Given that Farkas' meningitis case parallels Putnam's example, one would expect internalism to be challenged by the intuition that Farkas' twins entertain different contents when they think (what they would express by saying) "meningitis is dangerous". But the Spatial Criterion does not deliver that result. According to the Spatial Criterion, the presence of the bacterium is *intrinsic* to each twin, since the bacterium is present within the spatial boundary defined by the skin. (Meningitis is a brain disease, so its presence falls within more restrictive spatial boundaries as well.) The claim that the difference between those bacteria can suffice for a difference in thought contents thus presents no challenge to internalism — it is perfectly compatible with internalism. The upshot is that the Spatial Criterion does not capture the spirit of the externalism-internalism dispute. Using that criterion, an argument relevantly similar to a classic argument against internalism does not threaten internalism.

The meningitis case fails to challenge internalism because meningitis occurs within the spatial boundary of the thinker. Its presence thereby satisfies the first clause of the Spatial Criterion. We might try to resolve this problem by eliminating that clause, and understanding "intrinsic to the thinker" solely by reference to the second, environmental clause.

> **(Modified Spatial Criterion)** F is intrinsic to S iff S's having F does not metaphysically depend on any features of the environment outside the spatial boundary defined by S's skin.

This criterion may be more loyal to Burge's intentions, since his formulation of externalism quoted above focuses exclusively on the contribution of the environment and says nothing about what occurs within the subject's skin.

The Modified Spatial Criterion is initially promising. But it is threatened by a variant of the meningitis example. (This variant is my own twist on Farkas' thought experiment.) Compatibly with the meningitis example as previously described, the twins' environments may be perfectly similar: this would be the case if each of the respective bacteria first appeared in the twins, and neither was yet present in their environments (outside their skins). Suppose this is the case. While this additional supposition weakens the parallel with Putnam's original case somewhat, it does not affect the basis for the intuition that drives the challenge to internalism. In the original case, the intuition was this: subjects can think *water* thoughts without being in a position to distinguish water (H_2O) from stuff that is only superficially similar (XYZ). In the meningitis case, the intuition is this: subjects can think *meningitis* thoughts without being in a position to distinguish meningitis from a disease that is only superficially similar (twin meningitis). In both cases, the difference in thought contents derives exclusively from the difference in natural kinds. The fact that the relevant natural kind is instantiated within the spatial boundary of the skin, rather than outside that boundary, has no bearing on the thrust of the thought experiment.

The insignificance of spatial location nicely explains why early discussions ignored the fact that the "twins" in the water example are not genuinely "molecule-for-molecule duplicates". These discussions treated the presence of H_2O as an external factor, despite the fact that water is present within the *spatial* boundary of the individual organism.

The Modified Spatial Criterion construes externalism and internalism as views about where content-individuating factors can be spatially located. Using that criterion, the claim that the twins in the meningitis case would differ presents no challenge to internalism. As Farkas convincingly argues, the meningitis case parallels the H_2O case in all crucial respects: if internalism is challenged by the intuition that the twins' thought contents differ in the latter case, it should be equally challenged by the corresponding intuition in the former case. If there is a single, clear notion of "intrinsic to the thinker" at work in this classic externalist argument, it is not a spatial notion.

To respect the ontological neutrality of externalism and internalism, an adequate formulation of these positions cannot employ a criterion that defines "intrinsic to the thinker" in physical terms. Retreating to a less committal, purely spatial criterion has some advantages. But this strategy ultimately fails, as a spatial criterion plainly conflicts with the spirit of the externalism-internalism debate.

3. The Epistemic Approach

Farkas' meningitis scenario reveals that what divides externalism from internalism is not a claim about the spatial location of content-individuating factors. She suggests that what leads us to take the meningitis case to be similar to Putnam's water example, as regards the potential challenge to internalism, is an epistemic feature: the subjects in both cases are blind to the differences between their thoughts and their twins'. On her view, the point at issue between externalism and internalism concerns the epistemic status of thought contents — specifically, whether differences in thought contents are subjectively distinguishable.

In a nutshell, Farkas' argument is as follows. The question of what is intrinsic to the thinker is primarily intended to concern the mind; in these discussions, the brain is at best a stand-in for the mind. And "[w]hat it is to have a mind is inseparable from what it is for example to have experiences, and this latter is a thoroughly epistemic notion." (Farkas 2003, 205) Moreover, most philosophers believe that externalism faces, and internalism avoids, at least a *prima facie* problem of compatibility with the phenomenon of privileged access. Farkas concludes that externalism and internalism are, at bottom, views about thinkers' epistemic relations to their thoughts. Specifically, internalism is the thesis that

> facts individuate mental contents only insofar as they *make a difference* to the way things appear to us. This means that any difference in the content of thoughts should be distinguishable from the subject's point of view and hence remains within the reach of privileged access. (ibid., 203)

The following criterion captures Farkas' proposal.

> (**Epistemic Criterion**) F is intrinsic to S iff S's instantiation of F makes a difference to how things appear to S, in a way that enables S to have privileged access to the fact that she instantiates F.

This proposal has significant benefits. As Farkas observes, it makes sense of the widespread impression that externalism faces a special burden in explaining privileged access. It correctly classifies Descartes as an internalist. It also correctly classifies Externalist Dualism as externalist (assuming that whether an expert in my community has the concept *arthritis* makes no difference to "how things appear" to me). Finally, this proposal captures the spirit of Putnam's argument and, relatedly, yields the appropriate construal of the meningitis case. The externalist reading of these cases is that one can think a determinately *water* (or *meningitis*) thought without being in a position to distinguish this thought from a *twin water* (or *twin meningitis*) thought.[12]

While Farkas acknowledges that the epistemic approach is unorthodox, she contends that it reflects the "motives [that] lie behind the externalist thesis" more accurately than spatial criteria (ibid., 193). It's not entirely clear to me whether Farkas' proposal is intended purely as an explication of the current debate. But our purpose is explicatory: we must examine whether the Epistemic Criterion reflects the current debate.[13]

The Epistemic Criterion has some problematic consequences. First, it ensures that externalism is incompatible with privileged first-person access, as a definitional matter. The Epistemic Criterion glosses externalism as the claim that content properties don't supervene on (and hence, aren't identical to) properties to which the thinker enjoys privileged access. Farkas embraces this consequence, saying that "one way to sum up my proposal is to say that externalism is a thesis about the nature of our access to our thoughts" (ibid., 204). While most externalists concede that their view initially appears incompatible with privileged access, most also maintain that these are ultimately compatible. Regardless of whether compatibilism is true, the controversy surrounding this issue casts doubt on the idea that incompatibility with privileged access is a simple analytic consequence of externalism.

A second worry about the Epistemic Criterion is that, by defining properties "intrinsic to the thinker" as those which (in Farkas' words) *"make a difference* to the way things appear"*, it renders externalism about the phenomenal incoherent. For surely phenomenal differences *"make a difference* to the way things appear". This result is especially troublesome because most advocates of phenomenal externalism take phenomenal character to be a species of intentional content (Dretske 1996, Lycan 2001, Tye 2000). So the sense of "externalism" operative in phenomenal externalism is precisely the sense operative in content externalism.

Finally, the Epistemic Criterion has difficulty making sense of the pivotal externalist claim that some intensional thought contents are wide. In Burge's terms, we must sometimes individuate thoughts widely in order to capture the thinker's "epistemic perspective": "how things seem to him, or in an informal sense, how they are represented to him" (Burge 1979, 25). This claim arguably constitutes the core externalist challenge to internalism. Internalists can grant that extensional content (e.g., what a *water* thought refers to, in a given context) is wide. So the key externalist claim is that some *intensional* contents — contents that reflect "how things seem to [the thinker], or ... how they are represented to him" — fail to supervene on his intrinsic properties.

A dilemma emerges when we try to make sense of this externalist claim using the Epistemic Criterion. This dilemma centers on the question whether a difference in a thinker's intensional contents (that is, in her epistemic perspective) must be subjectively distinguishable by her. Suppose the answer is "yes". On this supposition, the Epistemic Criterion classifies any factor on which the epistemic perspective depends as intrinsic to the thinker: hence, any way of individuating thoughts that captures the epistemic perspective will be a version of *internalism*. So on this first horn of the dilemma, a key externalist claim — that some intensional contents are wide — is incoherent.

The other horn of the dilemma is generated by denying that differences in intensional contents must be subjectively distinguishable. This horn allows for a coherent reading of the externalist claim just mentioned. But it implies that it is not (merely) a difference in intensional content that "enables S to have privileged access to the fact that she instantiates F". Some factor other than intensional content must explain privileged access. The only plausible alternative seems to be a thought's phenomenal character: *what it's like* to think that thought. Intrinsic properties — properties that make a difference to how things appear, in a way that allows for privileged access to the corresponding thoughts — would then be phenomenal properties. (Williamson (2000, 49) suggests identifying the internal with the phenomenal, as a way of sidestepping issues about physicalism.) Now if a difference in phenomenal character is what renders two thoughts subjectively distinguishable, then, given the Epistemic Criterion, the question dividing internalists and externalists is whether thought contents supervene on phenomenal character. But that question belongs to a different debate, one that is orthogonal to the debate over externalism. (Burge explicitly denies that the target of his arguments against internalism is the claim that content supervenes on phenomenal character.)

So the second horn of the dilemma is this: if differences in intensional content need not be subjectively distinguishable, then the only feature that could ground subjective distinguishability seems to be phenomenal character. On this horn, the Epistemic Criterion construes externalism as the view that thought contents fail to supervene on phenomenal character.[14] (Farkas accepts this implication in her 2008 book.)

The Epistemic Criterion is superior, in significant respects, to the previous criteria. It avoids entanglements with extraneous ontological issues, and makes sense of some classic externalist arguments (such as Putnam's "water" argument). Moreover, an epistemic approach to delineating the thinker seems more salient to philosophical concerns than physical or spatial approaches. But the Epistemic Criterion seriously distorts the current debate. It makes the denial of privileged access a simple analytic consequence of externalism. It renders phenomenal externalism incoherent. And it either renders a key externalist claim incoherent or mistakenly construes this debate as centering on the question whether intentional content supervenes on phenomenal character. The Epistemic Criterion does not satisfy our search for a univocal criterion implicit in the externalism-internalism debate.

4. The Neutral Approach

None of the criteria for "intrinsic to the thinker" we have considered provides an accurate construal of the mental content debate. These criteria cash out externalism and/or internalism as involving commitments that seem wholly unrelated to them — and which, in some cases, their leading proponents explicitly disavow. This pattern suggests that, to do justice to the current debate, an interpretation of "intrinsic to the thinker" must be relatively neutral, at least about ontological and epistemic matters.

In a valuable discussion, Richard Fumerton describes obstacles to establishing a precise definition of externalism and internalism. He responds to these obstacles by retreating to a highly neutral — even austere — understanding of what is intrinsic (or "internal") to the thinker.

> I suspect that in the end we will simply need to understand internal states as including both nonrelational properties of the self and the self's standing in certain sorts of nonnatural relations (such as acquaintance) with certain entities. Though inelegant, that's the only way I can see how to define internalism so that paradigm internalists stay in the right camp. (Fumerton 2003, 262)

The "certain entities" Fumerton mentions are universals. In effect, his proposal is similar to Ludwig's proposal (quoted in Section 1 above), with a verbal difference about whether standing in relation to a (presumably abstract) universal is a "relational property".

Reserving "relational property" for relations to concreta, the following roughly captures the Ludwig/Fumerton approach.

> **(Thinker Criterion)** F is intrinsic to S <u>iff</u> S's instantiating F does not entail the existence of any concrete entity wholly distinct from S.

The Thinker Criterion achieves the ontological neutrality required to correctly classify both Descartes' view and Externalist Dualism. Descartes qualifies as an internalist, since he would presumably deny that one's having a particular thought depends on (or entails) the existence of any other concrete thing. Externalist Dualism qualifies as externalist so long as community experts are concrete entities distinct from the thinker.

Another strength of the Thinker Criterion is that it captures at least part of the spirit of the externalism-internalism debate. For it characterizes externalism as the claim that, for some thought contents, having a thought with these contents requires that the thinker is appropriately related to certain contingently existing things distinct from her. And the classic externalist arguments center on the thinker's relation to contingently existing things distinct from her (H_2O, experts who use "arthritis" in a certain way, etc.).

One consequence of the Thinker Criterion may at first be surprising. This criterion classifies the "extended mind" view (Clark and Chalmers 1998) — also known as "vehicle externalism" — as neutral between externalism and internalism. According to this view, factors "external" to a thinker, such as a notebook, sometimes perform genuinely cognitive functions for the thinker, and hence partly constitute his beliefs and other attitudes.[15] Such factors thereby qualify as *part of* his mind and, hence, part of the thinker himself. The mind and the thinker are *extended* to include factors like notebooks.

> [The subject] himself is best regarded as an extended system, a coupling of biological organism and external resources. (Clark and Chalmers 1998, 18)

The claim that a notebook could partly constitute the thinker illustrates a point anticipated in Section 1: that even seemingly paradigmatic external factors may be glossed as intrinsic to the thinker.

Now if I am an extended system that includes my notebook, then my notebook is not wholly distinct from me. So the fact that my believing that p depends on my notebook does not entail externalism, according to the Thinker Criterion. Whether externalism is true depends on a question on which vehicle externalism is neutral, namely, whether my content properties entail the existence of any contingent entity that (unlike my notebook) is not within my extended mind or self. By contrast, the spatial criteria outlined in Section 2 classify vehicle externalism as externalist, since vehicle externalism denies that content properties supervene on properties instantiated within the skin.[16] (How the Epistemic Criterion classifies vehicle externalism is a complicated question.[17])

That the Thinker Criterion construes vehicle externalism as compatible with (content) internalism is not a strike against it. After all, vehicle externalism differs markedly from the paradigmatic content externalist positions of Burge, Davidson, and Putnam. These positions do not imply the vehicle externalist thesis that external factors can *partly constitute* mental states. Stephen Yablo (1997) highlights this contrast when he notes that Putnam's famous slogan "meanings ain't in the head" mischaracterizes Putnam's own conclusion. That slogan implies that external factors *partly constitute* meanings (and, by extension, beliefs). But classic externalist views say only that external factors sometimes *individuate* contents, making it the case that a belief is the belief that p rather than the belief that q. Moreover, Chalmers embraces both vehicle externalism and content internalism. Far from a strike against it, then, the result that vehicle externalism is neutral on the question of content externalism is plausibly a strength of the Thinker Criterion. (The label "vehicle externalism" reflects the influence of spatial construals of "intrinsic to the thinker".)

The Thinker Criterion does, however, face a serious problem. It fails to provide *informative* truth conditions for externalism or internalism. Consider the kind of truth conditions provided by the Spatiophysical Criterion. According to that criterion, externalism is true (and internalism is false) *iff* two thinkers who are precisely similar, as regards physical properties instantiated within the skin, may differ as to whether they think that *p*. This criterion has the potential to shed light on the debate about mental content, for it generates truth conditions for externalism and internalism that are informative, albeit ultimately flawed. By contrast, the Thinker Criterion says that externalism is true (and internalism is false) *iff* two thinkers can differ, as to whether they think that *p*, purely by virtue of differences in concreta existing outside them. But this is uninformative. To say that an entity exists *outside* — is wholly distinct from — the thinker is just to say that *being such that that entity exists* is not among the thinker's intrinsic properties.

In effect, the Thinker Criterion reintroduces our original question: how should we understand "intrinsic to the thinker" in (I) and (E)?

(I) Thought contents always supervene on properties intrinsic to the thinker.

(E) Thought contents do not always supervene on properties intrinsic to the thinker.

The Thinker Criterion does not illuminate these statements. The truth conditions for externalism and internalism generated by the Thinker Criterion are precisely those already inherent in the statements we are trying to explicate. Externalism is true (and internalism is false) *iff* two thinkers who are precisely similar, as regards intrinsic properties, may differ as to whether they think that *p*.

The Thinker Criterion's neutrality enables it to avoid saddling externalism or internalism with extraneous commitments. But this criterion is too neutral to be informative.

Clearly, what is needed is a criterion of "intrinsic to the thinker" that is informative (and thereby improves on the Thinker Criterion) yet also neutral in relevant respects (and thereby avoids entanglements with orthogonal issues). The contrast between vehicle and content externalism suggests a new tack. Construe externalism as the claim that some content-determining factors are external to content vehicles — e.g., to the thoughts possessing that content. In other words, thought contents don't always supervene on properties intrinsic to thoughts themselves. This yields the following construal of the externalism-internalism debate.

(Vehicle Construal) The defining thesis of internalism is that thought content always supervenes on properties intrinsic to the thought. The defining thesis of externalism is the denial of this claim.

This construal nicely matches the kind of relationship between thoughts and contents envisioned by (at least some) traditional externalists. Davidson (1987) illustrates this relationship with a sunburn analogy. A sunburn is located on the skin, but what makes it a sunburn is an external factor: that it was caused by sun exposure. Since a cause other than sun exposure could lead to precisely similar damage, two intrinsically similar bits of skin (on intrinsically similar organisms) could differ in that only one is sunburned. So the property *being sunburned* does not supervene on properties intrinsic to the skin (or organism). Analogously, according to content externalists some factors that contribute to fixing a thought's content may be external to the thought itself: such factors include the use of "arthritis" by experts in the community and (in the meningitis case) the presence of a certain bacterium in the brain. So the thought I'd express by saying "meningitis is dangerous" may have the same intrinsic properties as the thought my twin would express with those words, even if my thought is a *meningitis* thought whereas hers is a *twin meningitis* thought.

Unlike the proposals we've considered thus far, this construal of the debate is not based in a criterion for "intrinsic to the thinker". Nor does it provide such a criterion, since "intrinsic to the thinker" is not equivalent to "intrinsic to the thought" or even to "among the intrinsic properties of the thinker's thoughts". Being among the intrinsic properties of S's thoughts is plausibly *sufficient* for being intrinsic to S. But it is much less clear that this condition is *necessary* for being intrinsic to S. To restrict intrinsic properties of thinkers to intrinsic properties of their thoughts is to endorse the bundle theory of the self, or something very close to it. Because the bundle theory is highly controversial, it's unlikely that that theory (or anything close to it) is a foundational assumption of the debate about mental content.

This means that the question the Vehicle Construal takes to define this debate—whether thought contents supervene on properties intrinsic to thoughts—is not a plausible interpretation of the question ordinarily taken to define this debate, namely, whether thought contents supervene on properties intrinsic to the thinker. So an immediate worry about the Vehicle Construal is that it seems to conflict with the ordinary understanding of the point at issue between externalism and internalism. Whereas previous proposals were explications of this ordinary understanding, the Vehicle Construal is a competitor to it.

Let's put this worry aside for the moment, and consider how the Vehicle Construal fares in other respects. This construal appears to correctly classify Externalist Dualism. It may also correctly classify Descartes' view, though this is somewhat less clear.[18] It avoids the problem posed by the meningitis case, since even if meningitis occurs within the thinker, in some sense, *occurring in a brain in which meningitis is present* is plausibly a non-intrinsic property of a meningitis thought. And this construal shares, with the Thinker Criterion, the virtue of classifying vehicle externalism as neutral between internalism and externalism. The defining claim of vehicle externalism is that some content vehicles are partly constituted by factors outside the organism's biological boundary: vehicle externalism is silent on the question whether properties intrinsic to content vehicles exhaustively determine content properties.

But the Vehicle Construal faces a problem, stemming from its reliance on the distinction between the factors determining thought contents and thoughts themselves. This distinction is an instance of the more general distinction between *total* realizations and *core* realizations. A property's total realization is the set of conditions that jointly suffice for its being instantiated.[19] Its core realization is that part of the total realization corresponding to the thing that has the property. For example, the total realization of *being sunburned* is something like *having damage caused by sun exposure*. The core realization is just the skin, as it is the skin that has the property *being sunburned*. A thought's total realization is the set of conditions that jointly suffice for the instantiation of its content properties. E.g., if externalism is true the total realization of a particular thought that *water quenches thirst* may include the presence of H_2O in the environment. This thought's core realization is just the thought itself, which has this content.

According to the Vehicle Construal, the externalist thesis is that content properties sometimes fail to supervene on the properties intrinsic to thoughts. To cash out this thesis, we need some way of distinguishing properties intrinsic to a thought's core realization, on the one hand, from those that only belong to its total realization. In other words, we need some criterion for "intrinsic to a thought". The effect of replacing "intrinsic to the thinker" with "intrinsic to the thought", in our formulation of the point at issue in this debate, is to replace the need for a criterion for the former with a need for a criterion for the latter. Instead of asking how *thinkers* are delineated, in this context, we now need to ask how *thoughts*—core realizations of content properties—are delineated.

In some cases, like the case of sunburn, the distinction between core and total realizations is easily drawn. Properties intrinsic to the core realization of *sunburn* are distinguished from other parts of its total realization along biological and temporal lines. The properties intrinsic to the core realization (the damaged skin) are limited to those within a biologically salient region— in this case, the skin itself. And they concern the present time, whereas *having been caused by sun exposure* concerns the past. By contrast, properties intrinsic to a thought's core realization cannot be distinguished from other parts of its total realization in biological or temporal terms. Delineating a thought's core realization in biological terms would entangle the debate about mental content with questions of physicalism. A temporal delineation would construe plainly externalist claims, to the effect that thought contents are partly fixed by the natural kinds present in the environment *at the time of the thought*, as perfectly compatible with internalism.

It should be clear why spatial or epistemic approaches to understanding "intrinsic to the thought" will also be inadequate. These approaches will fail for precisely the reasons they failed regarding "intrinsic to the thinker": they will conflict with the ordinary taxonomy of views, or commit externalists or internalists to positions on which they are neutral (or, in some cases, which they explicitly reject). For example, identifying properties intrinsic to a thought with properties to which a thinker is epistemically sensitive, in a way that explains privileged access, would make the denial of privileged access a simple analytic consequence of externalism.

We should look for a new approach, one that diverges from the approaches to understanding "intrinsic to the thinker" we've previously considered. One obvious strategy for delineating something's core realization is to construe properties intrinsic to a core realization as those that underwrite the causal features of the thing. The total realization of a penny includes *being produced at a U.S. Mint*. But this part of the total realization seems irrelevant to the penny's causal features. A perfect duplicate of a penny that differed only in *not* being produced at a U.S. Mint would possess the same causal features: when run over by a train, both would flatten in precisely the same way; proffering a handful of such duplicates, as payment in a store, is as likely to exasperate a cashier as proffering a handful of pennies. So we might say that properties intrinsic to a thought are those directly responsible for the thought's causal features; causally irrelevant properties may belong to its total realization, but are not part of the thought itself.

But this strategy will not work. One problem is that the issue of causal relevance is not as straightforward as my example suggests. Some arguably causal explanations invoke properties not usually regarded as belonging to a core realization. That I gave the clerk a genuine penny seems to causally explain why I now have less money (legal tender) than I did a moment ago, whereas my handing over a counterfeit penny would not.

A more serious difficulty with this strategy is that it ensures that wide content is causally irrelevant. On the Vehicle Construal, narrow content is content that supervenes on the intrinsic properties of a thought's core realization. Wide content is content that metaphysically depends on factors beyond those intrinsic properties. (Because of this dependence, these latter factors belong to the thought's total realization.) So if properties intrinsic to core realizations are exclusively responsible for a thought's causal features, then we need not advert to wide content to explain a thought's effects on cognition or behavior. But the idea that wide content is irrelevant to such explanations is a standard *objection* to externalism, and is rejected by most externalists. So no plausible construal of externalism will interpret that view as straightforwardly entailing the causal inefficacy of wide content.

We might cast about for other ways to delineate thoughts, distinguishing properties intrinsic to a thought's core realization from properties merely belonging to its total realization. But this exercise is not likely to illuminate externalism and internalism. Any substantive principle used to distinguish core realizations is in danger of being insufficiently neutral. This was the flaw in the proposal just considered: that proposal used a substantive claim about what sorts of factors are relevant to causal explanations, and thereby committed externalists to a position that most of them reject.[20]

There is a more general reason to doubt that any way of delineating a thought will (when combined with the Vehicle Construal) yield an adequate explication of externalism and internalism. This is the worry expressed earlier: the Vehicle Construal does not provide for a suitable criterion of "intrinsic to the thinker", and therefore conflicts with the ordinary understanding of the externalism-internalism debate. Given the pervasiveness of the ordinary understanding, abandoning it in favor of the Vehicle Construal seems unwarranted.

There does seem to be something right about the Vehicle Construal. Internalists *may* generally accept, and externalists *may* generally deny, that a thought's content always supervenes on properties intrinsic to the thought. But I submit that, to the extent that the Vehicle Construal identifies a question that divides these two camps, this is because the distinction it relies on—between the factors determining content (a thought's total realization) and the thought itself (its core realization)—derives from a prior, more fundamental distinction between those properties of a thinker that are intrinsic to her and those that are not. If internalists disagree with externalists about whether a thought's content always supervenes on properties intrinsic to the thought, this is because "intrinsic to the thought" is understood by reference to what is *intrinsic to thinkers.*

Since this debate is not premised on the assumption that thoughts are the only features intrinsic to thinkers, the vehicle/content (or core realization/total realization) distinction will not explicate the notion of "intrinsic to the thinker". The Vehicle Construal accurately reflects an aspect of the current debate (if it does) only insofar as it relies on the assumption that properties intrinsic to a thought are intrinsic to thinkers—where the notion of "intrinsic to the thinker" remains unarticulated. So it cannot explicate that notion, or the externalism-internalism debate.

Let us review. The Thinker Criterion avoids the problematic commitments of previous criteria by defining externalism relative to a neutral conception of the thinker. While this criterion may be accurate, its neutrality prevents it from *explicating* the internalism-externalism debate. The Vehicle Construal aims to improve on the Thinker Criterion by providing informative truth conditions for externalism and internalism, while preserving the Thinker Criterion's ontological and epistemic neutrality. To achieve this latter goal, it exploits the neutral distinction between thoughts, as vehicles of content, and the factors that suffice for determining thought content. But absent a criterion of "intrinsic to the thought", the Vehicle Construal is no more informative than the Thinker Criterion. And any such substantive criterion—e.g., identifying properties intrinsic to a thought as those that ground its causal features—will threaten the Vehicle Construal's accuracy. This construal expresses a point on which externalists and internalists disagree (if it does) only by implicitly restricting properties "intrinsic to the thought" to properties intrinsic to the thinker. So it sheds no light on the externalism-internalism debate, or on the sense of "intrinsic to the thinker" operative therein.

5. Prospects for defining internalism and externalism

We have examined three approaches to defining internalism and externalism. The first approach accepts familiar construals of "intrinsic to the thinker" at face value. It glosses externalism as the claim that thoughts don't metaphysically supervene on (perhaps physical) properties instantiated within a certain spatial region, or that they metaphysically depend on (perhaps physical) properties instantiated outside that region. The second approach interprets externalism as the claim that distinct thoughts can be subjectively indistinguishable, perhaps because they are sometimes phenomenally similar. The third approach construes externalism as the claim that some content-determining factors are relational features of thinkers or of thoughts. None of these approaches succeeds in explicating the current debate. The first two approaches are overly committal about the nature or limits of the thinker. This lack of neutrality leads both of these approaches to conflict with the usual classification of familiar views, or to interpret internalism or externalism as committed to claims—about mental ontology, the subject's access to her own thoughts, or the relation between the intentional and the phenomenal—generally regarded as orthogonal to those positions. The third approach generally avoids these pitfalls. But its more promising versions implicitly rely on the distinction between intrinsic and non-intrinsic properties of the thinker. So this approach does not illuminate that distinction.

Should we persist in the search for a suitable criterion of "intrinsic to the thinker", one that is loyal to how philosophers ordinarily construe externalism and internalism? Participants in this debate do seem to have *some* common understanding of what is at issue; and there is relatively wide consensus about which sorts of positions are externalist and which are internalist. So perhaps there is some shared, implicit notion of intrinsic properties remaining to be discovered. In other words, perhaps our situation is similar to that which J.S. Mill described as the situation in ethics. Mill claimed that there was widespread agreement about which particular actions are right, and which are not right, but little consensus about the criterion of rightness. On his diagnosis, this curious situation was due to "the tacit influence of a standard [of rightness] not recognised"—namely, the Principle of Utility (Mill 1863, 3).

But there are strong reasons to doubt that there is a single, unrecognized criterion of "intrinsic to the thinker" operative in the current debate about content. First, the usual explicit gloss of this concept, in spatial (or spatiophysical) terms, has become deeply ingrained. Traces of this approach are ubiquitous in discussions of internalism and externalism: they are present in Putnam's famous slogan that meanings "ain't in the head", in the standard description of twins as "molecule-for-molecule duplicates", and in characterizations of intrinsic properties as those instantiated "within the skin". These familiar phrases have shaped our intuitions about what kinds of properties are intrinsic to thinkers, and about which views count as externalist and which as internalist. As noted above, the spatial approach is likely responsible for the fact that the extended mind view, which appears neutral about content externalism, nonetheless carries the label "vehicle *externalism*". As we saw above, the spatial approach is clearly inadequate: many of the intuitions rooted in this approach clash with the spirit of externalism and internalism, as ordinarily understood. Still, its influence on our intuitions dims the prospects for alternative approaches, as such alternatives will inevitably conflict with those intuitions.

The initial promise of each of the spatial criteria, and of the various ways of unpacking the Epistemic Criterion, supplies a second reason to doubt that there is a uniform tacit standard of "intrinsic to the thinker" at work here. Each of these proposals fits some dimension of the internalism-externalism debate, as ordinarily understood. For each of the following issues is implicated in *some* aspect of this debate: the relation between an organism's thoughts and the natural kinds in its physical environment; the division of linguistic and conceptual labor within a social community; the linguistic communicability of thoughts; privileged access to one's own mental states; and the relation between the phenomenal and the intentional. Because each of these issues is closely associated with some aspect of the externalism-internalism debate, and *no single criterion will capture all of them*, we have reason to doubt that there is a criterion of the internal that will do justice to the usual terms of this debate.

I propose, then, that we abandon the search for a criterion of "intrinsic to the thinker" that will capture the terms of the externalism-internalism debate, and discontinue the debate as it is now framed. To make progress on the diverse range of issues linked with this debate, we might focus our attention on more well-defined questions, of the sort that emerged from this discussion. We might ask whether thought contents supervene on physical properties that fall within the spatial boundary constituted by the skin; whether a difference in concepts possessed by experts (distinct from the thinker) can suffice for a difference in thought contents; whether distinct thought contents are subjectively distinguishable by the thinker; etc.

Alternatively, we might try to rehabilitate the question at the heart of the current debate, namely, "Do thought contents always supervene on properties intrinsic to the thinker?" This rehabilitative process involves two stages. The first, negative stage consists in surrendering our implicit associations with this question, including our present opinions about the implications of particular answers to it. The second, positive stage begins with an exercise in metaphysics: establishing a precise, principled conception of the boundary of the thinker, which can be used to unpack "intrinsic to the thinker". Only once such a conception is in hand can we address the question of supervenience.

One moral of this discussion is that any way of delineating the thinker will significantly reframe the debate over whether thought contents supervene on properties intrinsic to the thinker.[21] But if my arguments here succeed, they show that a fresh approach is overdue.[22]

Notes

1. Of the 931 "target faculty" responses to the Phil Papers 2009 survey, 51.1% chose the response "accept or lean toward externalism". Interestingly, only

19.9% chose "accept or lean toward internalism"; 28.8% chose "other". *Source*: http://philpapers.org/surveys/results.pl

2. I am not the first to notice these difficulties. Katalin Farkas (2003) and Richard Fumerton (2003) provide especially insightful discussions of them; I am indebted to both of these authors for helping me to appreciate the force of this problem. But while I regard these difficulties as fatal, Farkas and Fumerton each advance a proposal aimed to resolve them. I discuss their proposals in Sections 3 and 4, respectively.

3. By "thought contents" I mean content *properties*, such as the property *thinking that p*. I will usually talk of such properties as properties of thinkers, but in Section 4 I will discuss content properties—such as *having the content p*—as properties of thoughts themselves. (I assume that thoughts just are instantiations of contents; "having the content *p*" serves as shorthand for *being an instantiation of p*.) Some standard formulations of internalism and externalism use "internal" rather than "intrinsic"; nothing will turn on my choice of terminology.

4. Note that a viable criterion may allow for vagueness. The idea that there is a gray area, in which some properties are neither clearly intrinsic nor clearly extrinsic, is consistent with the availability of a general, principled criterion that distinguishes intrinsic from extrinsic features. By analogy: there is a general, principled criterion, along the lines of "having relatively few hairs on the head", that distinguishes those who are bald from those who are not bald. While this criterion is not specific enough to deliver a verdict in every case, it does explain why "bald" accurately describes Howie Mandel but not Oprah Winfrey. My search for an explication of "intrinsic to the thinker" would be satisfied by a similarly principled criterion, one that explains why "intrinsic to the thinker" accurately describes some properties but not others. A criterion could be adequate for this purpose even if it is less than maximally specific and hence fails to deliver a verdict in some cases. Indeed, a successful criterion may explain *why* certain cases are borderline.

5. Burge says that his earlier formulation (in Burge 1986a) "misleadingly suggests that failure of local supervenience of intentional states on the individual's physical states is to be identified with anti-individualism." (Burge 2003a, 302)

6. Burge seems committed to (2), or something very close to it. And he is at least attracted to the dualism expressed in (1): see especially Burge 2003a and 2003b.

7. The Modified Spatiophysical Criterion also faces the usual difficulty with the "water" example: it classifies *inhabiting an environment in which the watery stuff is H_2O* as intrinsic to the thinker, since that property satisfies condition (i) of the criterion.

8. This was Fodor's view in Fodor (1980).

9. See Jackson (2003). This marks a change from Jackson's earlier dualism.

10. I have in mind here the familiar idea that the predicate dualism advocated by Davidson (1970/1980) is really a kind of property dualism.

11. This answer retains the desired ontological neutrality only on the assumption that being spatially located does not entail being physical. If this assumption is false, the objections to the Spatiophysical and Modified Spatiophysical criteria may also defeat the Spatial Criterion.

12. The Epistemic Criterion also fits with the plausible idea that, as Farkas puts it, "what it is to have a mind" is tied to the epistemic.

13. If Farkas' proposal is not purely exegetical—e.g., if she is instead proposing a subtle reorientation of the debate—our evaluation of the Epistemic Criterion will not constitute an objection to it.

14. While the incoherence of phenomenal externalism followed from the idea that *all* phenomenal differences '*make a difference* to the way things appear', the second horn follows from the idea that *only* phenomenal differences make a subjective difference.

15. This follows from their so-called Parity Principle: "If, as we confront some task, a part of the world functions as a process which, were it to go on in the head, we would have no hesitation in accepting as part of the cognitive process, then that part of the world is (for that time) part of the cognitive process." (Clark and Chalmers 1998, 8)

16. Some versions of vehicle externalism, including the version advanced in Clark and Chalmers (1998), claim only that *dispositional* states—such as standing beliefs—are sometimes "extended". But most versions of content externalism concern *occurrent* states. I will ignore this complication.

17. Whether vehicle externalism qualifies as externalism, using the Epistemic Criterion, hinges on whether thinkers enjoy privileged access to "extended" mental states. Clark and Chalmers argue that it would be question-begging to deny that consulting a notebook to ascertain what one believes, say, is an introspective process. Be that as it may, vehicle externalism is most plausible as regards dispositional (non-occurrent) attitudes. Insofar as there is good reason to think that we enjoy privileged access only to occurrent thoughts and attitudes (as I argue in Gertler 2011, ch. 3), vehicle externalism counts as an externalist view, according to the Epistemic Criterion.

18. According to the Vehicle Construal, the internalist is committed to denying that content properties consist in relations to factors outside the thought but intrinsic to the thinker. While Descartes' view seems amenable to this position, it's not clear to me that it is committed to it.

19. A total realization may suffice for the property's being instantiated only on the assumption that certain background conditions are in place (Wilson 2004). I ignore this complication.

20. This point brings out an obstacle faced by content externalism, one which is not faced by internalism or by vehicle externalism. Both internalism and vehicle externalism can draw the boundary of the thinker, and her thoughts, at the boundary of total realizations. So neither of these views depends on some *other* way of delineating thinkers. By contrast, the standard version of content externalism construes thought contents as relational features of the thinker. So it must delineate thinkers in some other way. (In Gertler 2007, I argue that this obstacle is insurmountable, as there is no way of delineating the thinker that meets externalist requirements while preserving our basic conception of thinkers.)

21. I expect that the resulting conception of the thinker and her boundaries will be some sort of epistemic conception. In other words, I agree with Farkas that "what it is to have a mind ... is a thoroughly epistemic notion", understanding "epistemic" as encompassing the phenomenal (as she does). The arguments of Section 3 show that that result will constitute a significant departure from the current debate.

22. I presented an ancestor of this paper at the Australian National University, in January 2010, and received helpful feedback. For discussion or comments on earlier versions of this paper, I thank Anita Avramides, David Chalmers, Katalin Farkas, John Maier, Susanna Schellenberg, Lisa Shabel, Alan Sidelle, Daniel Stoljar, and especially Trenton Merricks.

References

Burge, T. (1979) "Individualism and the Mental". *Midwest Studies in Philosophy 4*, P. French, ed. (University of Minnesota Press), pp. 73–122. Reprinted in P. Ludlow and N. (1998).

Burge, T. (1986a) "Cartesian Error and the Objectivity of Perception". In *Subject, Thought, and Context*, edited by P. Pettit and J. McDowell. Oxford: Oxford University Press, 117–36.

Burge, T. (1986b) "Intellectual Norms and Foundations of Mind", *Journal of Philosophy* 83: 697–720.

Burge, T. (2003a) "Descartes, Bare Concepts, and Anti-Individualism: Reply to Normore". In Hahn, M. and B. Ramberg (2003) *Reflections and Replies: Essays on the Philosophy of Tyler Burge* (MIT Press), pp. 291–334.

Burge, T. (2003b) "Epiphenomenalism: Reply to Dretske". Hahn, M. and B. Ramberg (2003) *Reflections and Replies: Essays on the Philosophy of Tyler Burge* (MIT Press), pp. 397–403.

Burge, T. (2006) "Postscript to 'Individualism and the Mental'". In Burge, *The Foundations of Mind* (Oxford University Press, 2007), 151–81.

Chalmers, D. (2002) "The Components of Content". In Chalmers, ed., *Philosophy of Mind: Classical and Contemporary Readings* (Oxford University Press, 2002), pp. 608–633.

Clark, A. and Chalmers, D. (1998) "The Extended Mind". *Analysis* 58: 7–19.

Davidson, D. (1970/1980) "Mental Events", in his *Essays on Action and Events*, Oxford University Press, pp. 207–224.

Davidson, D. (1987) "Knowing One's Own Mind". *Proceedings and Addresses of the American Philosophical Association* 60: 441–458.

Dretske, F. (1996) "Phenomenal Externalism". In E. Villanueva, ed. *Philosophical Issues* 7: Perception (Ridgeview Publishing).

Farkas, K. (2003) "What is Externalism?" *Philosophical Studies* 112: 187–208.

Farkas, K. (2008) *The Subject's Point of View* (Oxford University Press).

Fodor, J. (1980) "Methodological solipsism considered as a research strategy in cognitive psychology". *Behavioral and Brain Sciences* 3: 63–110.

Fumerton, R. (2003) "Introspection and Internalism", in S. Nuccetelli, ed., *New Essays on Semantic Externalism and Self-Knowledge* (MIT: Bradford Books).

Gertler, B. (2007) "Content Externalism and the Epistemic Conception of the Self". *Philosophical Issues* 17: 37–56.

Gertler, B. (2011) *Self-Knowledge* (Routledge).

Jackson, F. (2003) "Narrow Content and Representationalism – or Twin Earth Revisited." Patrick Romanell Lecture, *Proceedings of the American Philosophical Association*, 77: 55–71.

Ludlow, P. and N. Martin, eds., (1998) *Externalism and Self-Knowledge*, Stanford, CA: CSLI Publications, 21–83.

Ludwig, K. (1993) "Externalism, Naturalism, and Method". *Philosophical Issues 4: Naturalism and Normativity*. (Ridgeview Publishing), pp. 250–64.

Lycan, W.G. (2001) "The Case for Phenomenal Externalism". In J.E. Tomberlin, ed., *Philosophical Perspectives, Vol. 15: Metaphysics* (Ridgeview Publishing).

McLaughlin, B. and M. Tye (1998) "Is Content-Externalism Compatible with Privileged Access?" *Philosophical Review* 107: 349–380

Mill, J.S. (1863/2002) *Utilitarianism*. G. Sher, ed. (Hackett Publishing).

Putnam, H. (1975) "The Meaning of 'Meaning'". In K. Gunderson, ed., *Language, Mind, and Knowledge* (Minneapolis: University of Minnesota) pp. 131–193.

Segal, G. (2000) *A Slim Book about Narrow Content* (MIT Press).

Tye, M. (2000) *Consciousness, Color, and Content* (MIT Press).

Williamson, T. (2000) *Knowledge and Its Limits* (Oxford University Press).

Wilson, R.A. (2004) *Boundaries of the Mind: the individual in the fragile sciences* (Cambridge University Press).

Yablo, S. (1997) "Wide Causation". *Philosophical Perspectives* 11: 251–281.

Philosophical Perspectives, 26, Philosophy of Mind, 2012

WHY AND HOW NOT TO BE A SORTALIST ABOUT THOUGHT[*]

Rachel Goodman
The University of Chicago

In this paper, I aim to intervene in the debate about *sortalism* (the view that individuating a particular object necessarily involves classifying it according to its kind) but to do so in a way that brings out several points and distinctions that, in my view, are too often passed over. In the title to the paper, I suggest that we should reject, not sortalism *per se*, but sortalism *about thought*, and that my task will be showing not just *why* this view should be rejected, but also *how* it can be rejected. This gives some clue as to the points and distinctions I want to make.

In rejecting sortalism *about thought*, I reject one particular claim made by the sortalist. This is the claim that it is a condition on the possibility of singling out a particular object in thought that one categorise it in some particular way, by bringing it under a sortal concept (a kind concept).[1] Many discussions of sortalism involve a conflation of this claim, which I will call *thought sortalism*, with an analogous metaphysical view about the role of facts about kinds in determining identity facts, which I will call *metaphysical sortalism*.[2] That these two views are distinct should not be controversial (although the seemingly obvious distinction is often ignored or obscured), so my aim is not just to clearly distinguish the two in the process of denying thought sortalism, but also to make some important and often neglected points about their relationship.

Most sortalists (and anti-sortalists for that matter) view metaphysical sortalism and thought sortalism as two sides of a single coin, to be accepted or rejected together. But, once we clearly distinguish the two views, we see that a common way of arguing for sortalism runs metaphysical and epistemological issues together. If we set aside the specifically metaphysical considerations that often figure heavily in discussions of sortalism, what remains of the sortalist's case are two arguments specifically about the structure of thought. One of my aims is to be clear about what these arguments are, in a way that the literature is not.

My next aim is to show not just *why* we should reject sortalism, but also *how* we can reject it. By clarifying the sortalist's arguments about the structure of thought, I try to show that, although these arguments do not actually support the sortalist's conclusions, they do contain important insights we should not ignore. Although there are fairly straightforward arguments against the sortalist's conclusion about thought, the arguments for her mistaken view (once they have been properly disambiguated) contain insights that shed light of the character of the very ability that she denies we have: the ability to think about particular objects *without* thinking of them as objects of particular kinds.

Philosophers of mind (or any philosophers who are interested in our capacity to have contentful thoughts about particular objects in the world) therefore have something important to learn from the debate about sortalism. This is the lesson that, although it *must* be the case that we are able to individuate particular objects for thought without classifying them as objects of particular kinds, there are difficult questions to be answered about *how* it is that we are able to do this. The sortalist gives us a way of formulating and pressing these questions. In recognising this (without accepting the sortalist's conclusions), we come to better understand our ability to think about particular objects without classifying them as members of particular kinds. The sortalist therefore teaches us something important about how we are able to achieve *conceptualisation without classification*.

*

Before outlining the sortalist's position and argument in detail, let me briefly say something general about the broadest aim of this paper. This is the aim of shedding light, through an examination of sortalism, on a puzzle about thought that is not recognized as such either by defenders or rejecters of sortalism: On the one hand, it must be possible to have sortal-free thoughts, otherwise, we would have no account available of the way that unfamiliar objects come into the subject-matter of thought; on the other, there are obstacles that make it seem as if this couldn't be possible.

At a broad level, the question is, how do particular objects[3] come to be the subject matter of thought? But, why is this a pressing question? Consider a case in which you stumble upon an *unfamiliar* object and have a thought,[4] which we would naturally express with an utterance of:

'I think this is an F'

We undoubtedly have thoughts like this all the time, but there is a puzzle about the thought's meaningfulness. That a thought like this is meaningful presupposes that one has succeeded in referring to something, or that the 'this' has a referent. So, to have a thought like this, one must individuate[5] the object it is about. But, there are considerations that make us think that an individuation we might express simply with the demonstrative 'this' must in fact have a hidden complex form. These considerations are sometimes voiced in terms of the inadequacy of mere pointing. If I point over there, what do I thereby pick out? A statue, or a lump of clay, or the statue's facing surface? The scope of the indeterminacy of my act of pointing seemingly depends on what range of kinds of thing we think there are over there.

Now, if, among other things, there is an *F* over there, and I believe there is an *F* over there, and wish to pick out that *F*, then I can make up for the inadequacy of merely pointing by specifying 'that *F*'.[6] On the other hand, it can't be that one always needs to rely on one's knowledge or true belief that there is an *F* over there in order to individuate an *F*. For a start, if it is to be a possibility that a thought like the one above is false—if thoughts to the effect that '*this* is an *F*' are to be something other than tautologies—then the object in question must be individuated independently of the thinker's believing or knowing it is an *F*.[7] Furthermore, what if I see the *F*, but don't know or believe it is an *F*. Finally, in order to be able to wonder or learn that this is an F you can't depend on already knowing or believing it is an F to pick it out. There is, of course, the possibility of picking out an F, (when you don't know or believe it is an *F*) on the basis of other knowledge or true belief about it—for example, your knowledge or true belief that it is a *G*—but this can't always be the way individuation goes. This would presuppose that we always have existing knowledge or true belief about particular objects at our disposal when we individuate those objects. But, this brings us back to the question of unfamiliar objects: How do *those* come into the subject matter of thought?

In the paper, I will argue that a solution to this problem emerges when we 1) disambiguate two points from the sortalist's larger case, 2) acknowledge these points as insights, and 3) let go of a fallacy that makes it seem as if these insights necessitate sortalism. The sortalist's insights are, first, that there is a structural requirement on any act of (even attempted) individuation–that the act is structured by the application of principles for individuating objects—and, second, that there must be some mechanism by which an act of individuation solves for an indeterminacy between objects and their parts. Disambiguating these insights from the sortalist's case is the work of §I & §III of the paper. In §II, I show why, despite these insights, sortalism cannot be true. In §IV, I argue that the key to reconciling these seemingly competing facts is giving up what I call *the descriptivist fallacy*: the fallacy that the only means by which an act of individuation can be structured by principles for individuating objects is through the use of a *concept*. I argue instead that the application of such principles can take place in perception, and therefore without the use of a sortal concept. Empirical work on perception, attention and infant cognition illustrates how this is so.[8]

I. The Sortal Dependency of Thought

The sortalist position is that 'individuation is sortal-dependent'.[9] What is meant by this is *both* that picking out an object for thought requires employing a sortal concept (a kind concept) and that what it *is* for an object to be the object it is, depends on the sortal under which it falls.[10] He views these claims as two sides of a single coin.

I.I *What is a sortal concept?*

A better understanding of what a *sortal concept* is helps us to better understand the sortalist's position.

According to the sortalist, a sortal concept is a kind concept, but there is a particular sense of 'kind' intended here.[11] There is a sense in which any old property is a kind (on this sense of 'kind', *blue thing* is a kind, just as *rabbit* is a kind) but a sortal concept is a concept of a special type of property:[12] a property that determines principles of identity and persistence for particular objects that possess it.

There are grammatical features that take us part way to distinguishing the category of properties that determine principles of identity and persistence for the particular objects that fall under them. For example, the predicates that pick out these properties can feature meaningfully in a *'how many?'* question about spatiotemporal objects. So, only nouns, not adjectives, and, within that category, count nouns not mass nouns, express sortal properties.[13] For example, *'how many talls/longs?'* and *'how many golds?'* do not usually yield sensible answers,[14] whereas *'how many cats?'* and *'how many cars?'* do. However, this grammatical distinction only gives us a preliminary grip on the category of sortal property. Noun phrases like 'brown thing' have the same grammatical role as 'cat' and 'car' but many such phrases underdetermine answers to the *'how many?'* question. Absent further instruction, for example, one might count brown chairs *and* brown surfaces *and* brown patches when asked to count brown things. Brown things extensively overlap one another and, in any given case, there might therefore be indefinitely many of them.[15]

'Puppy', 'duckling', 'ANZAC'[16] and 'passenger', all yield sensible answers to the *'how many?'* question, and thus determine principles of *identity* for particulars at a time, but they do not determine principles of *persistence* for the objects that fall under them. An individual can cease to be a puppy or a duckling without ceasing to exist.[17] An individual can become an ANZAC, but this does not mark the birth or creation of that individual. A person can become a passenger when he boards a plane, stop being one when he disembarks and become one again on his next journey, without these changes entailing any object being destroyed or created.[18] The fact that individuals persist through the change from, e.g., puppy-hood to non-puppy-hood, means that the property of being a puppy doesn't determine persistence conditions for the individuals that possess it. In contrast, 'human being' (arguably) does determine persistence conditions for the objects that fall under it, since (again, arguably) they cannot cease to be human beings without going out of existence.

In line with this contrast, there is a distinction between *phase sortals*, which do not necessarily apply to individuals over the course of their entire existence, and *substance sortals,* which, if they apply at all, necessarily do so over the course of an entire existence.[19] A substance sortal is therefore a concept of a property that, if possessed by an individual, is necessarily possessed—that is, it is a property that is a condition on the existence of individuals possessing it.[20] On the sortalist view, only substance sortals determine both principles of identity *and* principles of persistence.[21]

The sortalist claims (with a caveat I explain here) that all thoughts about particular objects employ concepts that determine identity and persistence conditions for those objects—that is, they all employ correct substance sortal concepts. The caveat is that, for example, a phase sortal, although it does not directly determine principles of identity and persistence for an individual, can be used to individuate that individual iff it *implies*[22] a substance sortal that correctly applies to it. Likewise, an *incorrect* substance sortal can be used to individuate an individual iff it implies a substance sortal that correctly applies to that individual. The notion of *implication* I have in mind here is the reverse of subsumption. Some sortals subsume others, in the sense that all objects falling under the latter sortal, also fall under the former, but not *vice versa*. This is so for some pairs of substance sortals: All dogs are animals, but not all animals are dogs. All men are human, but not all humans are men. *Animal* and *human* subsume *dog* and *man,* respectively. It is also true for phase sortals and the substance sortals they are phases of: The substance sortal *dog* subsumes the phase sortal *puppy*.[23] Since implication is the reverse of subsumption, sortal concepts (and predicates) *imply* all the sortal concepts (and predicates) that subsume them. If a sortal, F, is true of x, then all the sortals that subsume F will also be true of x. If an object falls under the phase sortal *duckling,* it is therefore implied that it falls under the substance sortal *duck*, and under the substance sortal *bird*, since *bird* subsumes *duck* and *duck* subsumes *duckling.*

This means that, with respect to their individuative resources, uses of concepts expressed by count nouns can be divided into three classes: Uses of concepts that directly determine principles of identity and persistence for the objects falling under them, uses of concepts that imply a concept that directly determines principles of identity and persistence for the objects falling under them, and uses of concepts that do not directly or indirectly determine such principles.[24] Given this, it is arguably the case that, by falling in the second class, uses of phase sortals like *puppy* or *duckling* could be appropriate sortal concepts with which to individuate not just puppies or ducklings, but also adult dogs and ducks. It is also arguable that, although the sortal *duck* does not correctly categorise a dog, it can nonetheless be used to individuate a dog because *duck* implies the sortal *animal*, which *is* correctly applied to a dog. This caveat will be relevant later in the paper.

I.II *An argument for sortalism*

As I've said, one of the sortalist's claims is that all thoughts about particular objects employ sortal concepts in order to individuate those objects. This is a claim about thought. But the most frequently discussed argument for this claim is in fact based on a claim about identity *itself*—that is, the argument for the claim about thought is usually premised on a *metaphysical* claim. In this section, I outline this argument in order to show, in the following section, that, if we set aside the sortalist's metaphysical commitments, what remains are two independent arguments specifically concerning the structure of thought.

The sortalist is committed to the following metaphysical claim: The relation of *identity* is really the relation of *identity under a sortal* (the relation of being '...*the same F as...*'). This claim is used as a premise in her argument for the sortal dependency of individuation. In order to clearly distinguish this metaphysical view, I'll call it *metaphysical sortalism* (MS):

> **(MS)** The identity relation is a three-place relation of *identity under a sortal*, identity (& difference) facts are fully specified by facts about this three-place relation, and claims involving the two-place identity relation are derivative on these facts

If there is a question as to whether *a* is the same object as *b*, this always *amounts to* the question of whether *a* is, e.g., the same *person,* or *animal*, or *puppy*, or *statue*, as *b*. This is, as I have already said, not a claim about thought, but one about identity itself.[25]

Given that sortal properties have been *defined* as properties that determine (either directly or indirectly) principles of identity and persistence for the objects that fall under them, this claim hardly looks surprising. But, the sortalist does not intend to be making a trivial claim. For her metaphysical claim to be more than trivial entails that the identity and persistence conditions determined by different sortal predicates sometimes *vary* or *differ*.[26] It would be vacuous to say that the facts about the identity of particular objects are determined by the sortal predicates that correctly apply to them unless there is a real and substantive *role* for sortal facts to play in constituting identity facts. The real substance of the sortalist's metaphysics of identity is therefore that the identity facts about particular objects are constituted by sortals that determine *varying* identity and persistence conditions for different kinds of spatiotemporal objects (she holds that kind membership and identity are inseparable and mutually dependent).[27] For example, an animal arguably ceases to exist when it dies, whereas non-living things do not have their persistence conditions determined in this way. What it would be to *reject* MS would be to hold that the identity conditions of spatiotemporal objects are determined simply by their *being* spatiotemporal objects *tout court*, independently of these objects belonging to certain kinds.[28]

MS therefore justifies what I will call *the argument that multiplies entities*, which, in turn, is used to argue for the sortalist's view about thought. This argument takes as its premises Leibniz's Law—that is, the Indiscernibility of Identicals: $(x)(y)((x = y) \rightarrow (\Phi x \equiv \Phi y))$—and the commitment just outlined to the idea that substance sortals (in some cases) vary in the principles of identity and persistence that they determine for the objects to which they correctly apply.

A very familiar example illustrates the argument. Let's say that, in an otherwise empty corner of my garden, there is a statue of Socrates. In the very same location as the statue, there is of course the piece of bronze from which it was cast. Are the statue and the piece of bronze the same object? Are they identical? Melting would destroy the statue, but the piece of bronze would survive this disfigurement (statues and pieces of bronze are different kinds of things and have different *persistence conditions*). Thus, Leibniz's Law dictates that the statue and the piece of bronze are distinct objects. Although it may be natural to point at the corner of my garden and claim there is but one object in it, according to the argument for multiplying entities, there are so far at least two. Once we take into consideration the identity and persistence conditions for statue surfaces, statue parts, aggregates of matter, etc., there will be indefinitely many distinct objects.[29]

MS and the argument for multiplying entities are then taken to entail the claim about thought that we are interested in. From here on, we will call this claim about thought, *thought sortalism* (TS):

> **(TS)** All thoughts that individuate particular objects employ sortal concepts.

The reasoning towards this claim is not always entirely clear,[30] but it goes something like this. If we can say of an agent that she is thinking of a particular object, x, then we are crediting her with an act that individuates x. This is an act that involves counting x (or conceiving of x) as a single thing to be distinguished from other things, and therefore involves an implicit judgment about identity.

Furthermore, the consequence of a metaphysics of varying identity and persistence conditions for different *kinds* of objects—that is, of MS—is that an act of individuation will not be successful unless it appeals to the notion of identity under a sortal and in fact specifies an individuating sortal. Recall the argument for multiplying entities and the statue occupying the corner of my garden. If it is true that there are in fact indefinitely many objects occupying this corner of my garden (a statue, a piece of bronze, a statue half, etc.) then singling out only *one* of them as the referent of thought demands a specification of *which* one. Pointing or demonstrating, or referring to 'the object over there' will not do the job, because, if there are many objects to choose from, it could always be asked, '*which* object over there?' The proponent of TS claims that distinguishing between the possibilities requires either a correct substance sortal concept, or a sortal concept that implies a correct substance sortal.[31]

I.III *The Statue/lump problem*

It is clear that the sortalist's argument for TS is presented as a worry about indeterminacy and, therefore, failure of reference. The broad shape of the sortalist's claim about indeterminacy is something like the following.

Without the employment of a sortal concept, an act of thought would fail to individuate a single object—and therefore fail of reference—because it would remain indeterminate between indefinitely many objects that co-occupy the location towards which, say, an attempted demonstrative identification is aimed.

However, there are in fact two distinct indeterminacy challenges, which discussions of sortalism often fail to distinguish. One of these challenges presupposes the sortalist's controversial metaphysical position. The other is an indeterminacy challenge that must be faced regardless of whether one accepts or rejects MS.

Both indeterminacy challenges have the same structure. They begin with the premise that, if a thought is to succeed in individuating a particular object, there must be something that *makes* it the case it is about one object rather than another. One's act of pointing, directed towards some source of information, is insufficient to secure reference. The sortalist asks, 'which of the indefinitely many objects at that location is the thought about?' She challenges us to account for a determinate answer without positing the use of a sortal concept.

I'll call the most familiar form of this challenge the *statue/lump problem*, because it is often illustrated with the example, which was discussed in §I.II, of a statue and the lump of, say, bronze or clay, which constitutes it. Take some location at a time, say, the corner of my garden with the statue in it, this afternoon. Despite the natural tendency to think there is only one object in this location, the sortalist argues there are indefinitely many objects that share the exact location in question:[32] a statue, a lump of clay, an aggregate of matter, etc. As a consequence, no purely spatial identification, no matter how exact, can distinguish one from the rest.[33] This indeterminacy challenge relies on a metaphysics of *varying* principles of identity and persistence for physical objects of different kinds—it relies on the truth of MS. It is only if we presuppose this metaphysics that the argument for multiplying entities generates the claim that a multitude of different kinds of objects share an exact location in space.

This argument therefore depends on a substantive and disputed claim: that distinct physical objects can share space at a time when one is not a part of the other. It therefore depends on rejecting the attractive conception of physical objects according to which they *exclude* one another in space. It is a compelling fact about ordinary medium-sized physical objects, and arguably part of our ordinary conception of them, that you can *bump into them*. If you wish to occupy the space currently occupied by an ordinary medium-sized physical object, you will need to *move* it. This point motivates some philosophers to reject the sortalist's metaphysics.[34] Aside from the worry that MS presupposes a distorted conception of the nature of physical objects, her view also poses problems for the idea that a single physical object could change from a statue into a mere lump of clay,[35] and for the idea that a single object could be *both* a statue and a lump of clay.[36] Wiggins famously introduces the notion of an 'is' of constitution to account for the sense in which the statue 'is' the lump of clay, and there is much to be said about the plausibility of this move and about the viability of the sortalist's metaphysics, but this debate is a debate in metaphysics. Thus, the statue/lump indeterminacy problem cannot be resolved independently of giving a substantive account of the metaphysics of physical objects and the nature of identity.

I.IV *Part/whole indeterminacy*

Arguments against sortalism often focus on questioning MS—that is, on disputing the claim that a statue and the lump of clay that constitutes it are distinct objects. But there is a second indeterminacy challenge we can pull out of the sortalist's argument, which does not rely on metaphysical sortalism. This challenge, firstly, *cannot* be rejected on the basis of rejecting the sortalist's metaphysics and, secondly, *can* be addressed on the basis of considerations about thought.

This second indeterminacy challenge is not based on the claim that distinct physical objects can share an exact location at a time, but on the more commonplace idea that whole objects share partial locations with their parts. This fact generates what I will call *the part/whole indeterminacy challenge*.

The part/whole indeterminacy problem can be illustrated by thinking about the account of perception-based demonstrative thought that is offered by Gareth Evans, in Chapter 6 of *Varieties of Reference*. Evans offers an account of perceptual demonstrative thought according to which these thoughts do not require a sortal concept to succeed.[37] He argues that successful demonstrative identification requires, firstly, that the thinker have a perceptual informational connection with the object of her thought that governs her conception of it and,[38] secondly, that she have knowledge of the object's *location* on the basis of this connection.[39]

It is this second condition that, according to Evans, accounts for the determinacy of demonstrative identification. For this to be so Evans must presume that physical objects exclude one another in space. If they did not, tracking the spatial location of an object would not serve to individuate it.[40] But, granting that this is the case, there is a further indeterminacy problem, which an account like Evans's must address. Let's agree for argument's sake that knowledge of the exact location of a physical object would serve to individuate that object from all other physical objects, because whole physical objects exclude one another in space. Even given this, it is hard to accept that ordinary perceivers ever *have* knowledge of the *exact* locations of objects on the basis of perception. Perception simply does not seem to supply us with knowledge of the exact boundaries of the objects we perceive. Take the case of me perceiving the statue in my garden. I have some sense of where it is located with respect to my body, but exactly how precise is this sense? How far away is the statue? How deep is the statue? How far does it extend in space on its unseen side? Are there any holes in it? This problem generalizes in an alarming way. I see a hydrangea bush in front of me clearly, but how deep are its roots? Is the apple on the counter a whole piece of fruit? It is possible that a slice been cut from the opposite side. If it is whole, is the unseen surface flat or lumpy? If it has been cut, where does the piece I perceive end?[41]

A more general version of this point has been important in the philosophy of perception. There is a worry that there is a tension (or gap) between the information we *strictly* speaking receive on the basis of perception, and that to which we take ourselves to have perceptual access on that basis.[42] Although parts of material objects are always out of view in perception, we often take ourselves to perceive a statue or an apple, not merely the facing surface of a statue or an apple-part.

Unaddressed, this problem puts pressure on the possibility of non-descriptive perception-based thoughts. If perception itself does not disambiguate between parts, surfaces, wholes, etc., then all successful perception-based thoughts have the hidden form of descriptions.[43] My thought about the statue in my garden either fails (because it is indeterminate whether it refers to the statue, or some visible statue part), is really only about a statue-surface, or in fact has a content (something) like,

1) *The statue whose surface I now perceive is F*,

which is descriptive in form.

The second indeterminacy challenge that can be abstracted from the sortalist's argument is therefore that there must be some means by which the object of a thought is distinguished from its parts. The sortalist's claim is that this disambiguation cannot be achieved without the use of a sortal concept.

I.V *The argument from structure*

The challenge I just discussed faces the theorist of thought even if she rejects the sortalist's metaphysics. But there is also an even more basic consideration that is raised by the sortalist, which is not merely an indeterminacy problem, but rather a fundamental and compelling point about the logical or cognitive structure of thought—a point about what it takes for a thought to so much as be an *attempt* at individuation.

At the heart of the sortalist's argument is an idea that is similar to one made by Frege in the *Foundations of Arithmetic*: To judge that $a = b$ (or to conceive of a as identical to b) is to judge that a and b ought to be counted as one. But there is no way of counting a, b or anything else as the same or different without applying principles for the count. Individuating an object for thought involves distinguishing it from other things, and doing so involves conceiving of it as distinct from other things. This in turn involves a kind of identity judgment (a negated identity judgment). And, making such a judgment must involve the application of principles of sameness or difference for the object in question. In order to *be*, in this implicit sense, a judgment of identity, a mental state must be structured by such principles. We'll call this, *the argument from structure*. The central thought behind the argument from structure is that there is an obligatory question we must ask about putative thoughts about particular objects: *What structure must a thought have in order to so much as be in the business of individuating?* According to the structure argument, the application of principles for carving things up is a structural requirement on an attempt at securing reference.

The sortalist takes the argument from structure to entail that thoughts about particular objects must be structured by a concept that determines the principles of identity and persistence for the object it applies to—that is, a sortal concept.[44] But, the argument from structure can be seen, more broadly, as laying down a condition that, in order to so much as be in the business of individuation, a thought about a particular object must be structured by some application of principles of identity.

II. *Why* to Reject Sortalism about Thought

We have abstracted from the sortalist's case two arguments that do not rely on metaphysical sortalism as a premise. These arguments suggest that there are two constraints on any account of thoughts about particular objects. Firstly, there must be something that accounts for the determinacy of such thoughts— in particular, successful reference to a particular object presupposes that there is some way that the thinker disambiguates a perceived object from its parts. Secondly, since a thought about a particular object presupposes individuation of that object, it must be structured by some application of principles of identity.

The sortalist claims that the use of a sortal concept as part of a thought would satisfy these constraints. It may be true that sortal concepts *can* play this role, but the sortalist does not appreciate the puzzle about thought with which this paper began. The puzzle is that, although sortal concepts are the right kind of thing to account for the determinacy and the individuative structure of thoughts about particular objects, and although there are reasons to think that there must be *something* that plays these roles, TS *cannot* be true. In §II.I, I argue that sortalism cannot be true because it forecloses the possibility of cases that do and must exist. In §II.II, I further illustrate the nature of these cases by expanding on their special conceptual features.

II.I *Counterexamples to TS*

Three kinds of case, all involving perception-based thought, illustrate why the sortalist's claim, that all individuation of particular objects involves the use of sortal concepts, must be false.

Firstly, TS forecloses the possibility of wondering, of a perceived object,

2) What *is* that?

But, we undoubtedly do this all the time. Imagine me in my garden, perceiving the statue in the corner, and thinking about it. Imagine, further, that I'm agnostic as to what *kind* of thing I'm seeing (the statue is obscured by foliage in such a way that I can make out its boundaries, and some of its properties, but not what kind of thing it is.) In fact, the nature of my thought is that I am wondering what kind of thing the object in front of me *is*: 'what on earth *is* that thing?', 'Is it a statue, a human being, or something else entirely?'.

TS rules out the very possibility of such a case. Without the employment of a sortal concept, TS holds, there simply *is* no particular object about which I am thinking—no object has been individuated. This would mean that it would not even be possible to sensibly formulate in one's mind the question, 'what *is* this thing?', because the lack of an answer to this question would preclude the question from having *content*. But, we meaningfully formulate this question all the time.

Over and above the fact that we *do* have thoughts in which we wonder, of an object, what kind of thing it is, there is also force to the argument that we *need* to sometimes do this. If we didn't, there would be no such thing as examining a thing in order to *learn* what kind of thing it is.[45] This would be a strange outcome, since one of the primary ways we have of making up our minds about what objects are like, and what kinds of things they are, is *looking at them* (or touching them, listening to them, etc.). If we could not think about things antecedently of knowing what kinds of things they were, we could not *answer* a question 'what kind of thing is *this*?' by looking. Furthermore, it is compelling to think that one way of acquiring concepts of kinds is through the process of recognising similarities and differences in the particular objects that fall under them.[46] In ruling this out, the sortalist rules out some of the primary and necessary functions of perception: learning and concept acquisition.

It is also a condition on any reasonable account of thoughts about particulars that it accommodates the possibility of thinking about a particular perceived object despite being *mistaken* about what kind of thing it is. If I see the statue in the garden, and form the belief

3) That is a man (who is sitting very still)

I will have entertained a thought that is *false* but nonetheless *contentful*: I think falsely, of the statue before me, that it is a man. The sortalist precludes the possibility of *many* such cases.[47] In claiming that a sortal concept is required to *determine* the referent of any thought that succeeds in referring to a particular object, the sortalist precludes the possibility of this kind of *failure within the scope of success*. On her view, since sortal concepts necessarily play the role of *determining content*, the kind of mistake involved in (3) must either be understood as an attempted act of individuation that fails of reference because it *lacks* the employment of an appropriate sortal, or as an attempted act of individuation that fails of reference because it employs a *mistaken* sortal concept.

If the case is theorised as one in which there is no sortal concept employed, then the sortalist is committed to the thought being indeterminate. If the case is conceived in the latter way, as employing a false sortal concept, then the thought will fail of reference. If the concept *man* is functioning as a sortal concept in the content of the thought (and plays a role in individuating the object of thought rather than merely playing the role of a predicational concept), then the content of that thought can be represented as having the following complex demonstrative form:

4) *That man* is a man

But, as an act of thought directed towards the statue in the garden, (4) is not false, but rather fails to pick out an object: There *is* no *man* in my garden. The thought fails of reference by virtue of my false belief about what kind of thing I am thinking about. In claiming that a sortal concept must always be employed in order to individuate a particular object, the sortalist rules out a case in which an object is individuated *independently* of the agent's belief that the object in question is, say, a *man*. She rules out the possible of my having a false belief *about that very object* to the effect that it is this or that kind of thing.

A third kind of case, which depends on the same possibility of failure within the scope of successful mental reference, involves disagreement. Walking through the garden together, you and I both see a small object in the grass. I think that it is a rabbit, paralysed by fear of our presence. You think it is a white ball of wool. We stand at a distance, and argue about this. The possibility of this argument rests on the fact that we disagree about whether a particular object is a rabbit or a skein of wool—it rests on us thinking about the same object. We have conflicting beliefs and no more than one of us could be correct. This could not be the case if not for the possibility of mistakes about kind within the scope of referential success. Thus, it could not be the case on the sortalist's view.

*

Whilst nobody would deny the possibility of these kinds of cases, the sortalist might respond by arguing that her view can accommodate them. For example, it might be suggested that a *mistaken* sortal concept can act to secure determinacy (and therefore reference) for a perception-based thought by *implying* a *correct* sortal concept. Secondly, but less compellingly, the sortalist might argue that TS claimed only that *some* sortal concept is employed as part of every successful individuation, not that a *correct* sortal concept is always employed. One could satisfy this condition, she might suggest, by employing a sortal concept that is not in fact true of the object one is thinking about.

These attempts to redeem TS fail, but they allow us to become clearer about exactly what the thought sortalist does commit herself to.

The suggestion that a mistaken sortal concept can (in some cases) secure reference should be conceded. But this concession does not protect TS from counterexamples. The notion of *implication* (introduced in §I.I) helps to precisify the suggestion, and the appropriate response to it. Recall that a sortal concept *implies* the sortal concepts that subsume it. In some cases, a mistaken sortal concept can *imply* a correct sortal concept. Thus, a mistaken sortal could serve to secure successful reference as long as it is subsumed by, and therefore implies, a correct sortal. Take a case in which I perceive a dog running through my garden and, mistaking it for a cat, think,

5) *That cat* is the largest cat I have seen

A thought like this would fail of reference because there is simply no cat present for me to think about, but, if a thinker is committed to (5) and is an adult concept-user with some grasp of the relationships between many of the concepts she possesses, she will also be committed to (6):

6) *That animal* is the largest cat I have seen

Unlike (5), (6) *is* (false but) contentful. It succeeds in picking out the dog in front of me.

But, this response does not explain away the counterexample I outlined with (3) above. Not *all* cases of thoughts involving mistaken sortal concepts leave open the possibility of successful reference in virtue of the relation of sortal implication. In some cases, the concepts used do not imply a correct sortal concept. In fact, the case I outlined earlier was one in which an artifact is mistaken for a living thing. There is therefore no implied higher sortal concept that could account for the success of the thought.[48] Thus, even allowing for the possibility of implied sortal dependent identifications, TS still rules out important cases of failure within the scope of success.

The second suggestion is less interesting (but I have heard it suggested often, so I will address it). It is sometimes claimed that the sortalist could retreat to the position that *some sortal concept or other* is required to be employed in an act of individuation.[49] The suggestion here is not that any sortal concept can play the required role by implying a correct sortal (this would amount to the suggestion discussed above), but rather that there need not be a *correct* sortal implicated in successful individuation, as long as some sortal concept or other is employed.

In making this suggestion, the sortalist is unfaithful to her own view. She has claimed that the employment of a sortal concept plays a special (and necessary) role in any thought about a particular object: it does essential work in individuating the object the thought is about. The *absence* of a sortal concept is meant to result in the indeterminacy of an act of perceptual individuation. This results in a failure to think a fully formed *content*. Furthermore, it is claimed that a thought involving, e.g., the concept *statue,* and one involving the concept *lump of bronze,* will have *different* contents—they will refer to different entities. Thus, the use of one sortal concept rather than another *makes a difference* to the content of the resulting thought. The sortal concept is supposedly doing the work of making the attempted act of individuation refer to some particular object (say, the statue) rather than some other (the lump), or none at all. But, this means the sortalist faces a dilemma. Either sortal concepts do indispensable *work* in generating the contents of thoughts, or they do not. If they do, then it doesn't make sense to claim that particular sortal concepts can be substituted without effect. If they don't, then this seems to impugn the sortalist's original claim; it seems tantamount to abandoning TS. If the use of any sortal concept at all can secure successful individuation, then how could the use of any particular one (ie., *statue* rather than *lump* or a *statue part*) solve a problem of indeterminacy, or secure referential success?

II.II *Conceptualisation without classification*

The cases discussed in §II.I stand as counterexamples to thought sortalism—they are cases in which a thinker successfully individuates a particular object in thought, without relying on a sortal concept to do so. We see the importance of these cases by recognising that they represent a special kind of possibility that the sortalist rules out with her view: the possibility of thoughts that involve conceptualisation of particular objects without classification of those objects. Aside from the mere fact, which was illustrated in the previous section, that these cases actually exist, it is also worth noting that they have distinctive conceptual features that do not show up on a picture of thought that embraces TS.

Imagine, that there is a single duck circling the pond in front of my cottage (let's call him Donald). Contrast two different kinds of thought I could have about Donald. The first is a descriptive thought:

7) The only duck who is now circling the pond in front of my cottage is yellow

What strikes us immediately about (7) is that thinking it obviously requires me to have and employ the sortal concept *duck* (as well as several other property concepts). This is because the concept is part of the content of the thought. And, possession and employment of the concepts composing the content of a thought is a condition on entertaining that thought. There are many different descriptive thoughts that might (under the right circumstances) relate a thinker intentionally to Donald, but they all require the possession and employment of property concepts (some of them sortal concepts) under which Donald in fact falls. They all achieve reference to Donald *through* classification of him as an object with x, y or z properties.

In contrast, there is a kind of thought I could have about Donald, which doesn't individuate him by classifying him as an object with certain properties or an object of a particular kind. If I look out at the pond in front of my cottage, I might *see* Donald and think,

8) *that* is yellow

(8) is an example of what philosophers call a perceptual demonstrative thought.

So, here is my suggestion. We could say that there is a relation—call it, the 'thinking-about-Donald' relation—that comes in two distinct forms. One form we'll call the *satisfactional*[50] thinking-about-Donald relation. It involves individuating Donald by his properties (Donald is the object on which the truth or falsity of a thought involving this relation turns because he *satisfies* the conditions laid out by the thought). The other we'll call the *non-satisfactional* thinking-about-Donald relation. It involves individuating Donald in some other way—some way that does not depend on his satisfying any descriptive conditions.

This difference is reflected in the contents of thoughts of the two kinds. The content of (8) does not contain the concept *duck* or any properties that serve to individuate Donald.[51] It is about Donald *independently* of anyone thinking or knowing that he is a duck. In contrast, the fact that Donald is a duck is essential to the fact that (7), the satisfactional thought, is about him. (7) picks out *whichever* thing happens to satisfy the description that features in its content. Since Donald happens to be the only duck circling the pond, (7) is about him.[52] If Donald were not a duck, it wouldn't be. (8) doesn't rely on Donald's *duckness* to individuate him. If Donald were a swan, or someone mistook him for a swan, this wouldn't preclude (8) from being about him.

It is essential to the nature of a *satisfactional thought* that it relates a thinker to an object through classification. In contrast, what is characteristic of (8), and the cases that are counterexamples to TS, is precisely that they relate thinkers to particular objects in a way that doesn't rely on classification—they involve *conceptualisation without classification*. This suggests that embracing TS involves foreclosing the possibility of genuinely non-satisfactional thoughts about particular objects.

Beyond the fact that this would, as we discussed in §II.I, rule out the possibility of cases whose occurrence we are familiar with, there are more general theoretical reasons why this would be problematic. The possibility of thoughts that involve conceptualisation without classification has an important role to play in our larger theory of thought and mental content. The distinctive epistemic and conceptual features of these thoughts—that is, the fact that they allow for mistakes, or agnosticism, about properties within the scope of successful reference—means that they can play an distinctive role in learning and concept acquisition. They might also have a special role to play in our understanding of how a system of thought in general could come to be contentful or to be about the world.[53]

III. The Sortalist's Insights

It seems to me that this leaves us with a problem to solve. We have good reason to reject the sortalist's conclusions about thought. It seems that we *can* individuate objects for thought without using kind concepts to do so. There are thoughts with contents of the form,

9) *this* is an *F*

and the content of such thoughts is not, as would appear to be the case on the sortalist's view, really elliptical for something of the partially satisfactional form of,

10) *this H* is an *F*

However, the sortalist's argument gives us reason to regard this as at least *puzzling*. A way of thinking about this puzzle is that we know there are thoughts that involve conceptualising objects without classifying them but, given the considerations brought to our attention by the sortalist, we need an explanation of *how* this could be so.

It is common that arguments against sortalism focus on the statue/lump problem, and attempt to argue against thought sortalism by arguing that physical objects exclude one another in space,[54] or that *physical object* in fact functions as a substance sortal,[55] and the sortalist is therefore wrong to posit an indeterminacy problem. However, there are two reasons why approaching the topic differently will be useful. Firstly, even if we set aside the problem of statue/lump indeterminacy, a proponent of the possibility of sortal-free thoughts must still show how the problem of part/whole indeterminacy can be solved without adopting sortalism. Secondly, it seems to me that, unlike the statue/lump problem, the part/whole indeterminacy challenge, and the argument from structure, raise questions that are specifically about thought (not the metaphysics of identity), which can be addressed through a discussion of the structure of thought. They force us to think carefully about how thought can succeed in individuating particular objects *without taking a satisfactional form.*[56]

So, in showing how we can address the part/whole argument and the argument from structure without adopting TS, we will establish some conclusions about how non-satisfactional or sortal-free thoughts *work* and, therefore, some important conclusions about our ability to think thoughts about particular objects.

IV. *How* to Reject Sortalism about Thought

Luckily, we can reject TS whilst also resolving the part/whole indeterminacy problem and addressing the argument from structure. In doing so, we will recognise two insights about thoughts about particular objects: 1) thoughts about particulars must be structured according to the application of principles of individuation and 2) thoughts about particulars must have some mechanism by which they distinguish between objects and their parts. My proposal for how we can accommodate these insights furthermore shows us where the sortalist goes wrong in her account of thought.

IV.I *Rejecting the descriptivist fallacy*

Let us begin with the argument from structure. This argument centers on the basic logical or cognitive point that there is no way to individuate a single object without structuring an act of individuation according to the application of principles of individuation. But, the sortalist concludes on this basis that the application of a sortal concept must structure any act of individuation. In order to generate TS as a conclusion, the sortalist makes an assumption: that the principles of individuation that structure an act of individuation must be contributed in the form of a *concept* (in particular, on her view, a sortal concept), which is employed in the thought—one that will therefore enter into the thought's *content*. And this claim has simply not been established. I am going to call the assumption that only the use of a property concept could provide the individuative structure required of an act of individuation, *the descriptivist fallacy*, because it entails that, in order to satisfy the demands set in place by the argument from structure, a thought must have a satisfactional, or descriptive, component.

By giving up the descriptivist fallacy, we can do justice to the argument from structure without adopting TS. If we recognise that employment of a *sortal concept* as part of the content of a thought is not the *only way* a thinker can bring to bear principles of individuation that structure her concept of an object, we will see that the sortalist's insight about the structure of thought can be vindicated without adopting thought sortalism. In particular, we can do this by seeing that our perceptual abilities themselves involve the application of principles of individuation that meet the demands of the argument from structure.

In §IV.II, I flesh out my suggestion that, by giving up the descriptivist fallacy, we can address the argument from structure without adopting TS. In §IV.III, I show how the account of perceptual abilities involved in rejecting the descriptivist fallacy also resolves the problem of part/whole indeterminacy. I then return, in §IV.IV, to say more about my claim about perception.

IV.II *Principles of individuation in perception*

My suggestion is that the sortalist is wrong to think that picking out a particular object for thought requires employing a property concept (in particular, a sortal concept) as part of one's act of individuation. Rather, we should recognize that, the application of principles of individuation comes 'built in' to our perceptual abilities.

A growing body of cognitive scientific results helps us to understand this suggestion. These results demonstrate that very young infants have a perceptual sensitivity to spatial information and are able to *bring this information to bear* in a systematic and reliable way in forming 'expectations'[57] about the identity and number of physical objects. These results are sometimes said to prove that infants operate with a concept *physical object*, which they use to make judgments about identity and number. But they seem to me to underdetermine this. They more clearly show that infants have a *perceptual ability* to attend to and successfully track objects on the basis of spatiotemporal information *before* they have developed a full-fledged system of concepts (among which are sortal concepts like *cup*, *dog*, etc., and concepts like *physical object*).

Xu (1997), for example, argues that infants are able to use spatiotemporal information to form expectations about identity well before they develop kind concepts or can harness kind information for the same purpose. The case she makes is of interest to me because it gives us a sense of what it would mean to have available an *implicit* understanding of principles of identity (in this case spatial principles), which could be brought to bear in providing the required individuative structure to thoughts about particular objects.

Xu makes a division between spatiotemporal information criteria and kind/property information criteria of individuation for physical objects.[58] Spatiotemporal criteria she mentions are that 1) two objects cannot be at the same place at the same time, 2) one object cannot be at two places at the same time and, 3) objects travel on spatiotemporally continuous paths (so that no object can move from point A to point B without traversing a continuous path in space in between).[59] Kind/property criteria she mentions are the following: 1) if one sees a member of a certain kind (eg. a cup) at a time t_1, and then a member of a different kind (eg. a dog) at a later time t_2, one has evidence that one has seen two numerically distinct entities and, 2) if one sees a member of a certain kind with some visible property (eg. a red block) at a time t_1, and then a member of the same kind with a different property (eg. a blue block) at a later time t_2, one has evidence that one has seen two numerically distinct entities.[60] She argues that infants as young as four or five months old make use of all three spatiotemporal criteria but fail to operate with kind criteria until much later.[61]

That infants of five months form expectations based on the criterion that objects exclude one another in space is demonstrated by Baillargeon et al. (1985), through experiments in which infants were shown displays involving a screen, which is rotated by 180° forward and then backward, in 'a drawbridge fashion'. After habituation to the display, a box was introduced to it, and then placed behind the screen. The infants were then shown two outcomes. The first, which is the expected outcome if you are operating with the principle that two objects cannot be at the same place at a time, was one in which the screen stopped short of its 180° rotation (because it is blocked by the box behind it). The second, the unexpected outcome, was one in which the screen rotated the full 180°. Infants looked longer at the unexpected outcome, suggesting that they form expectations about identity based on the generalization that objects exclude one another in space.

Baillargeon & Graber (1987) show that five month-olds have their expectations guided by the principle that objects cannot get from point A to point B without traversing a continuous path through the space in between. The subjects were shown rabbits that moved from one side of a stage, behind a screen that obscured them from view, and then appeared on the other side to complete their motion across the stage. They then watched a similar event that used a screen from which a 'cut-out' was taken from the middle section of the top-half of the screen and the rabbit was tall enough that motion from one side of the screen to the other would involve it appearing as it crossed behind the cutout in the screen. Again, two outcomes were shown. In the first, the rabbit moved across the stage, disappeared behind the screen, appeared behind the cutout as it moved behind the screen, and then appeared again on the other side of the screen. In the second, it disappeared behind the screen and did not appear again until it emerged from behind the other side. The second outcome produced longer looking times, indicating the infants expected that the rabbit would need to cross behind the screen to appear on the other side.

Spelke et al. (1995) demonstrate that infants as young as four months old take spatiotemporal discontinuity as evidence for the existence of numerically distinct objects, thus showing that they employ criterion (3) to form expectations about identity. These experiments involve a display of two screens with a gap between them, which are lowered onto a stage. A first test conducted is one in which a rod then appears from behind the left screen, moves to the far left end of the stage and then returns behind the left screen. An identical rod then appears from behind the right screen, moves to the far right of the stage, and then returns to its original place behind the right screen. There is a pause between the two events, (of the right length of time for a rod to travel between the two screens) but no rod appears between the screens during this pause. Infants are then shown two different outcomes as the screens are removed. In one outcome, the screens are removed to reveal only one rod while, in the other, the screens are removed to reveal two identical rods. Infants exhibited longer looking times for the outcome that revealed only one rod. In a second test, in which, during the pause between the two events, a rod *was* shown to move between the two screens (emerging from behind the left screen into the gap between the screens and then disappearing behind the right screen) the infants looked for equal amounts of time at the one-rod and two-rod outcomes. This suggests they formed an expectation that there were two numerically distinct rods in the first test, but that they were not surprised by either outcome in the second. Thus, it seems as if spatiotemporal continuity, or the lack thereof, guided their expectations about identity.[62]

Furthermore, Xu points out that the psychological literature shows that these expectations based on spatiotemporal information do not already draw on the employment of kind generalizations. Thus, she illustrates that we can isolate the use of particular information criteria (spatiotemporal information criteria, in this case) from other information criteria that might be employed in forming the same expectations. Xu & Carey (1996) attempt to establish that young infants do not bring to bear kind criteria with a one-screen variation of the Spelke et al. (1995) experiments. They are interested in whether infants use kind differences (like the difference between a ball and a bottle) to form expectations about identity and number. As such, they perform the same set of experiments on a group of ten-month-old, and a group of twelve-month-old infants. The experiments make use of the same kind of screen used in the Spelke split-screen (or double-screen) study, but only one screen is used. The single screen is lowered onto a stage. A *ball* then emerges from behind the left side of the screen, travels to the left end of the stage, and then travels back behind the screen. After a pause of appropriate length, a *bottle* emerges from behind the right side of the screen, travels to the right end of the stage, and then travels back behind the screen. Two outcomes are then presented to the infant when the screen is lifted: The first (expected outcome) is one in which there are two objects (a ball and a bottle) behind the screen, and the second (unexpected outcome) is one in which only one object is present. Ten-month-old infants failed to look longer at the unexpected outcome, but twelve-month-olds exhibited longer looking times in the one-object outcome test. In a control version of the experiment, the same procedure was followed, with the exception that infants were first shown the two objects simultaneously, thus providing them with spatiotemporal evidence that there were *two* objects involved. In the control version, both ten and twelve-month-olds looked longer at the one-object outcome.[63]

Xu concludes from these studies that infants use a *concept* of *physical object as* a sortal concept before they are able to use concepts like *cup, ball,* and *bottle* for the same purposes. But, there is reason to hesitate about this particular conclusion. Although the looking-time experiments demonstrate that infants are *surprised* by outcomes concerning identity and number that would be inconsistent with the spatiotemporal perceptual information available to them—and thus, demonstrate that they form expectations on the basis of this information in a reliable way—they do not go as far as to provide a theoretical defense of the claim that these expectations based on perceptual sensitivity amount to a fully fledged concept, *physical object*. This gives us reason to demur from the claim that these studies show that infants can think full-fledged thoughts whose conceptual content has the complex demonstrative form of (11):

11) *this physical object is F*

But it does seem to show that their perceptual systems at four or five months of age are already processing information in a way that adds up to a sensitivity to the identity and persistence conditions for those objects. This basic perceptual ability helps us to understand perception-based thoughts about particular objects, because it allows us to see that perception itself involves bringing to bear principles of individuation, which contribute necessary structure to an act of individuation.

The experiments therefore suggest an alternative to the descriptivist fallacy—one that nonetheless respects the sortalist's insight that individuation must involve at least implicit application of principles of individuation. When one perceptually attends to an object, one can exhibit a sensitivity to the identity conditions of spatiotemporal objects, which comes *built into* one's perceptual abilities. This sensitivity can be brought to bear in perceptual attention so as to make individuation of particular objects possible. In particular cases, this can happen in the absence of justification for applying a sortal concept, or the ability to apply a sortal concept, which would classify the object in question at the level of thought. In such cases, the thinker has implicitly (not explicitly) brought to bear criteria of identity for the objects she is thinking about—this is necessary for individuation—, but she has done this *through* perception. Concepts like *duck*, *cup* and *statue* are not required, but neither is *physical object*. What I am asserting, therefore, is that, *pace* the sortalist, there are different *forms* that the application of principles for carving up the world can take. A perceptual sensitivity to criteria of identity, which can give an act of individuation the structure it requires, can occur without the employment of a concept that determines principles of persistence and identity for those objects (a sortal concept).

Before returning to say more about what it means for individuation to be structured by application of principles of identity *in* perception, I want to illustrate how essentially the same suggestion also gives us the resources to deal with the part/whole indeterminacy challenge.

IV.III *Part/whole indeterminacy*

Above, I outlined an empirical argument that human beings are able to individuate medium sized physical objects by tracking their spatiotemporal properties and bringing to bear knowledge of, or true belief about, principles concerning how such objects *do* and *can* behave. My suggestion was that, rather than establishing that human beings operate with a *sortal concept* of *physical object* that allows them to individuate spatiotemporal objects by employing this concept as part of the content of thoughts, the way that infants are able to bring to bear spatiotemporal information in forming expectations about identity and number rather suggests an alternative to the *descriptivist fallacy*—that is, the fallacy that the *only way* that principles of individuation can be brought to bear to provide the requisite structure to an act of individuation is through the possession and employment of a property concept that enters into the content of a thought. I advocated instead for a view on which implicit knowledge of such principles is exercised *through* one's perceptual abilities—it is part of the ability to perceptually attend to an object.

We now face the question of how an act of perceptual individuation could disambiguate between whole objects and object-parts, object-surfaces, etc. The sortalist response to the part/whole problem is that a sortal concept (like *statue*) is required to disambiguate between parts and wholes, but the notion of a *whole object* would in fact serve just as well to disambiguate between the whole statue and its statue-parts (remember, we have set aside the disambiguation of statues and lumps in this paper, since it presupposes a particular metaphysics). Thus, employing a *concept* of a *whole object* would serve to disambiguate an object from, say, some visible part or surface of that object. However, if we reject the descriptivist fallacy, we should also be open to the idea that our perceptual abilities themselves involve implicit sensitivity to the principles of identity and persistence for whole objects and that this means that perception itself makes such objects available for thought. And, in fact, this suggestion is born out by empirical investigation of our perceptual abilities.

To see what I have in mind, we can look to a point made by Imogen Dickie, in a recent paper about the possibility of perceptual-demonstrative thought about ordinary empirical objects.[64] In the context of a larger argument that is not my specific concern here, Dickie points out that recent literature on visual attention shows a connection between the conditions for successfully sustaining attention on a visual object,[65] and the characteristics constitutive of ordinary objects.[66] As perceivers, Dickie points out, we are particularly good at attending to what she calls 'ordinary objects'.[67] For my purposes, the significant point is that human beings have perceptual systems that are *seekers of whole spatiotemporal objects* (not mere stuffs, or mere parts of larger wholes). When visual objects behave as whole spatiotemporal objects tend to, perceptual attention is successfully sustained. When they do not, attention often fails. This suggests the following response to the part/whole-problem. Human thinkers have perceptual systems that are fit to track whole spatiotemporal objects. Whole spatiotemporal objects are natural units of perceptual attention. Thus, thoughts based on perceptual attention net whole objects and, thus, these thoughts disambiguate between wholes and parts (about which we also receive information in perception), selecting whole objects by default.

This claim in fact lines up with the claim made in the previous section of the paper, that the application of principles of individuation is at work in our perceptual abilities. In this section, however, we are pausing to acknowledge that this accounts not only for the fact that acts of individuation must be structured by *some* such application of principles, but also that the principles applied make it the case that perception-based thoughts, by default, net whole objects (and are therefore not indeterminate between objects and their parts).

Two questions should be answered about this position. First, and most importantly, how is it that empirical investigation of perception could establish that human perceivers disambiguate between parts and wholes? Second, if perceptual attention is fit to track whole objects, does this mean that we *can't* have perceptual thoughts about parts of objects or surfaces of objects, or that we don't use the concept *whole object* in our thoughts about whole objects?

I'll start with the first question. What is at issue with the part/whole problem is whether there is anything in an act of perceptual individuation (unaided by a conceptual sortal classification) that disambiguates between whole objects and their parts. If the empirical facts about human perception are that the default objects of human perceptual attention are *whole objects*—if it is a fact that human perception tracks whole objects, not parts, or points, or surfaces, or aggregates of parts—then, in virtue of the *nature* of our perceptual abilities, an act of demonstrative or perceptual individuation (that does not involve employment of a sortal concept) indeed has the resources to disambiguate between an object and its parts, and this determines that the referents of perception-based identifications are whole objects.

And, as it happens, there is good evidence that this is the case. For example, there is evidence that the kinds of abilities Xu argues that infants have with respect to bounded, coherent whole objects that move as units through space, are not equally applicable to non-coherent, unbounded quantities of stuff (like piles of sand and puddles, etc.), even by much older infants.[68] And, this kind of evidence that human beings have a particular ability to automatically track and individuate whole objects is not limited to studies on infant cognition.[69] Studies of adult perceivers show that perceptual tracking abilities apply most naturally to whole objects, and that we are considerably less able to perform the same kind of tracking of object parts.[70] That the default units of perception are whole objects is further illustrated by the fact that the tracking of whole objects persists through occlusion,[71] and by the fact that changes and developments in the visual scene are processed much more easily and successfully when they are indexed to a single object, rather than spread across distinct objects.[72]

In short, human perceptual systems are in fact particularly *good* at tracking whole objects. The result of this is that our individuations *based* simply on perception net whole objects, not merely object parts or object surfaces. Even though it is *true* that the spatiotemporal information we have access to in perception is inexact, and that this creates a potential indeterminacy between objects and their surfaces and parts, the fact that our perceptual systems are sensitive to the behaviour of whole objects means that our tracking abilities train themselves on those whole objects despite limits on spatiotemporal information. This resolves the indeterminacy between wholes and parts that would exist if perceptual thoughts relied on the accuracy of spatiotemporal information alone. Someone like Evans is therefore right to deny that a sortal concept is required for successful demonstrative identification, but wrong to think the only resources that we have at our disposal for individuation without sortal classification is the spatiotemporal information we receive from objects. The sortalist, on the other hand, is wrong to think that the only thing that could solve the indeterminacy between parts and wholes is the use of a sortal concept.

But where does this leave the possibility of perception-based thoughts about *parts* of objects? If perceptual individuation, by default, determinately nets whole objects, does this mean that there are no perception-based individuations of object-parts or object-surfaces? It does not mean this at all. It is certainly possible to individuate, say, the arm of a statue, or a particular side of an apple, on the basis of perception, but the fact that our perceptual systems are particularly suited to tracking whole objects means that this is in fact a more sophisticated form of individuation, one that requires extra resources, and is more difficult. What this means is that the default in perception is to track whole objects, but that this can in particular cases be overridden. Whether this would require the use of a concept of *part* or *surface*, which operates like a sortal, or whether this individuation of parts is something that can take place through perception and without the need for sortal classification is beyond what I have space to discuss in this paper. The important point, however, is that my resolution to the part/whole indeterminacy challenge does not *foreclose* the possibility of thoughts about parts. Basically the same answer should be given to the question of whether this response to the part/whole problem amounts to rejecting that we use the concept *whole* object in our thoughts about whole objects. Although it is *available* to adult concept-users to employ a *concept* of *whole object* in their thoughts,[73] it is *also* possible to structure one's individuations in a different *way*, on the basis of one's perceptual abilities themselves.

IV.IV *What does 'in perception' mean?*

I have claimed that the sortalist is right to the extent that we must 1) account for the determinacy of thoughts about particular objects and 2) acknowledge and account for the fact that all acts of individuation must be structured by implicit application of principles of individuation. But, I have argued she is wrong to think this entails thought sortalism. In particular, she is wrong to draw this conclusion, because the use of a sortal concept is not the *only* way that an act of individuation can appeal to principles of individuation that can structure and disambiguate it. Rather, perception itself involves the application of principles of individuation that structure perception-based thoughts in the appropriate way and solve the indeterminacy between parts and wholes. But, what exactly does it mean to say that such principles are applied *in perception?* What is the difference between this work taking place in perception, and it taking place through the use of a sortal concept (which therefore features in the content of the thought in question)?

We can think of the difference in terms of whether it makes sense to think of the agent doing this kind of work at the level of concepts and thought (such that we would conceive of the content of her thought as containing a property concept in the role of a sortal concept),[74] or whether it makes better sense to think that this work is done at the level of the information processing and abilities that are employed to produce perceptual states. To see that there is a difference, think about the fact that the perceptual system itself does work in processing the information it takes as input, and generating *contentful states* as outputs.[75] An example of this work is that of parsing spatial information into representations of objects. The point to talking about the perceptual system as *itself* producing object representations that are formed according to the application of principles of individuation is that what the perceptual system receives in the form of information falls far short of what it generates as output (that is, awareness of persistent, moving, changing *objects*).[76] Another example is the fact that perceptual mechanisms are governed by generalizations about how spatiotemporal objects do and can behave (the kinds of generalizations that we see at work in the infants' formation of expectations about number and identity). Yet another is that human beings have specifically *perceptual* abilities to keep track of whole objects (which can be distinguished from an ability to keep track of objects in thought). It therefore makes sense to draw a distinction between the application of principles of individuation taking place through the use of a general concept in thought, and the application of such principles taking place in perception, such that this makes available *to* thought an object that the thinker can then form a concept of. What I have been trying to suggest is that the sortalist is right to think that, without the structure provided by the application of principles according to which individuation takes place, and without some mechanism that disambiguates between whole objects and object parts, there would *be* no individuation of objects, but wrong to think that these principles that allow for individuation could only be applied through the use of a sortal concept in the content of a thought.

That she is wrong to think this is evidenced, first, by our counterexample cases, second, by recognizing that the descriptivist fallacy is not obligatory and, third, by the way that empirical evidence can illustrate an alternative to that fallacy. The counterexamples show that, if the only way that the demands of the argument from structure and the part/whole indeterminacy challenge could be met were through the use of a sortal concept, then, it would not be possible, for example, to formulate a thought in which one wondered what kind of thing a particular thing was. This would make it unclear how *unfamiliar* objects could come to be the subject-matter of thought. The empirical results show not only that infants with underdeveloped conceptual systems nonetheless are able to bring to bear spatiotemporal generalizations about how ordinary objects behave in order to form expectations about identity and number, but also that adult perception is particularly adept at tracking whole objects and parsing visual information in terms of representations of whole objects.

V. Consequences

Let me clear about the implications of the claims I have made here.

I have denied the claim that all thoughts about particular objects must employ sortal concepts in order to individuate those objects. You might wonder, however, if I deny that we sometimes *do* think of statues *as* statues. Don't we often use the sortal concept *statue* to individuate particular statues? Isn't this what gives this concept a role to play in thought beyond that of a predicational concept? Part of what motivates the sortalist, for example, must be the idea that sortal concepts are important because they *facilitate* the individuation of particular objects.

It is important to recognise that the view I advocate here does not rule this out. Just as it is possible to think,

12) *That* is beautiful

of the statue, without classifying it as a statue, it is *also* possible to think

13) That *statue* is beautiful

When I think (13), I employ a sortal concept to play the role of facilitating my individuation of the statue in front of me. Although I don't always *need* to do this, I sometimes do it. It may even be the case that I sometimes *need* to do this, in order to succeed at individuating a statue. There may be many cases in which it would not be possible for me to, say, individuate the rabbit bouncing through the grass in front of me, if it were not for my concept *rabbit*. This concept supplies me with a particular understanding of how *rabbits* behave (how they move, e.g.) that is employed to track a particular rabbit in a context where I might otherwise fail to do so. My only claim in this paper has been that this is not *always* the case. Sometimes, we individuate rabbits without it mattering that they are rabbits.

My view is that, although (12) and (13) are about *the very same object*, their content is different. Part of the point of rejecting thought sortalism is preserving this difference. (12) is a thought that involves individuating an object without relying on classification. It therefore allows for agnosticism about kind, or mistakes about kind—all within the scope of successful reference. (13) is a perfectly good way of thinking about the statue in my garden, but it relies on classification in a way that (12) does not. Without allowing for the possibility that (12) can succeed without involvement from the sortal *statue*, it is hard to see what the *point* would be in distinguishing between the contents of (12) and (13). And, by saying that the real form of (12) is always (13), we would be denying ourselves of a notion—that of conceptualisation without classification—that has a role to play in our broader understanding of thought, knowledge and content.

I want it to be clear, also, that I have *not* claimed that we could simply *do without* sortal concepts, or that there is no distinction to be made (of a grammatical, philosophical or conceptual nature) between sortal concepts and ordinary predicative concepts.[77] That adult thinkers could do without sortal concepts is sometimes taken to be what one would have in mind in denying the truth of sortalism. In this spirit, Wiggins claims that what is at stake between sortalists and those who reject sortalism is the question, 'Could adults—could we—really operate with the concept *object*...as our one and only sortal concept?'[78] For me, this is not what is at stake *at all*. Wiggins, for example, holds a view according to which picking out a thing for thought—individuating it—is 'part and parcel' with treating it *as* a thing of a particular kind.[79] Here, I have been arguing for a possibility, which is foreclosed by this view: picking a thing out without the help of classification. So, what is at stake for me is not whether we need sortal concepts at all—it is whether *all* our thoughts about particular objects employ such concepts. These are different questions.

I also have not advocated the notion of a 'bare this' or 'bare particular'. There are two things it could mean to defend this idea, and I am committed to neither. Firstly, I have not claimed that there are objects that are not objects of particular kinds. The view I have argued for is consistent with the claim that *all* objects are objects of particular kinds.[80] A second sense in which one might advocate the idea of a 'bare this' is in the epistemic or cognitive sense. However, even though I have been concerned to preserve the possibility of genuinely *sortal-free* content (content with the simple form, '*this* is *F*'), part of my *point* has in fact been that this does not involve advocating a 'bare this'. I have rather argued that thoughts about particular objects always employ implicit application of principles of identity and difference for whatever one is thinking of. Other deniers of sortalism, for example Michael Ayers, have taken issue with this very point. Ayers expresses suspicion about the idea that judgments about particular objects appeal to employment of principles of individuation. He claims that 'we do not need 'criteria of identity' in addition to what the world and our perceptual and agent faculties give us, when it is a matter of picking out (and, maybe, picking up) *literally* discrete, concrete, durable objects.'[81] In contrast, I have claimed that the individuation of particular objects *does* make use of the application of principles of identity, but I have claimed that our 'perceptual and agent faculties' (as Ayers puts it) *involve* the implicit employment of these very principles.

Notes

* Thanks to Matt Boyle, Jason Bridges, Jim Conant, Michael Kremer, Christopher Peacocke and Josef Stern for discussion of this material, or comments on previous drafts. And, special thanks go to Aidan Gray and John Hawthorne.

1. As we'll see, this view in fact entails, with a caveat I will specify, that it is necessary to classify the object *correctly*, according to its kind—that is, according to a sortal concept that is true of it.

2. This is the claim that identity facts are dependent on facts about kind or, in terms that do not use the language of 'dependence' (which clearly cries out for precisification or explanation), that the identity relation is, at the most basic and explicit level, a three-place relation of *identity under a sortal*, and that the two-place identity relation is derivative on this three-place relation.

3. In this paper, I address the question of how particular spatiotemporal objects come into the subject matter of thought. I do not address the question of how, for example, other categories of objects (in the looser sense of 'object') come into the subject matter of thought (for example, events, sounds, properties, etc.). I will therefore use the term 'object' to mean spatiotemporal object, unless I specify otherwise.

4. When I talk about thoughts in this paper, I will be talking about mental states, not about abstract objects (e.g., Fregean thoughts). When I want to talk about the abstract objects we use to map mental states in terms of their intentional and truth-conditional properties, I will use the terms 'content' or, 'contents of thoughts'.

5. From here on in, 'individuate' and 'individuation' will be used as epistemic terms; as a way of talking about something an agent *does*. In thinking a thought that is true or false depending on a particular object, the agent must *individuate* that object. Thus, when I say in this paper that, e.g., '*a* is individuated by its location/kind/(or whatever)', I mean that this is the means by which some *thinker* picks out *a*. I do *not* mean that *a's* location/kind/whatever is that which *constitutes* *a's* identity. Since the difference between these two things is an issue addressed in the paper, it is especially important to be clear about the use of this term. The reader will have noticed that, in my very first gloss on sortalism (in the first sentence of the paper), I purposefully left the term 'individuating' ambiguous, as sortalists like Wiggins tend to. From now on, though, unless I am quoting the sortalist's ambiguous usage (in which case I will flag this fact), the term is not ambiguous.

6. As I say in n.1, I will later show that a coherent version of sortalism involves the claim that the thinker must correctly classify the object according to its kind. (There is a caveat to this that will be outlined in §I.I, and further discussed in §II.I). This means the view requires that the thinker has true beliefs about the kind of the object she individuates. There is a further possible claim one could make: that she must have *knowledge* of what kind of thing she is thinking about. For my purposes, I will count both views as varieties of sortalism.

7. Kripke gives arguments of roughly this form in *Naming and Necessity*. Unlike him, however, I will be talking specifically about *thought*, not *language*, in this paper.

8. Having said this, as we'll see, the argument does not stand or fall with its appeal to this work.

9. Wiggins (2001): 55–56.

10. That the sortal dependency of individuation is meant to imply both claims is clear. Wiggins, who is perhaps the most famous defender of sortalism, makes this clear from various remarks. For example, although he states that 'individuation' is something a thinker does (Wiggins, 2001: 6), thereby implying an epistemic reading of his position, he also states the thesis of the sortal dependency of individuation in terms of facts about identity, not in terms of facts about what thinkers do (e.g., Wiggins 2001: 56). Furthermore, he takes a 'theory of individuation' to address questions about the concept of identity, what it is to be a substance or enduring object, *and* what it takes to single objects out (Wiggins 2001: 1). His comments about meaning as use also imply that an examination of the concept of identity at once tells us about identity itself and about our practices of individuation—or that the two issues cannot be separated (Wiggins, 2001: 1–4).

11. We can distinguish between a *category concept*, which picks out a *category* of object (in the looser sense of 'object') like *sound, event, spatiotemporal object*, and a *sortal concept*, which (for our purposes, since we are concerned here with spatiotemporal objects) picks out a *kind* of spatiotemporal object, like

cat, cup, house. Since the discussion in this paper is restricted to sortalism about spatiotemporal objects, I can set aside the plausible suggestion that other categories of object fall under sortal concepts that distinguish particular kinds for the category of thing in question. See Marcus (2006), for example, for a discussion of the implications of sortalism about events for a metaphysics of mind.

12. I will speak in this paper both about *sortal concepts* and about *sortal predicates*. I use 'concept' to refer to a mental ability that is exercised in thought. A *sortal concept* is a concept of a sortal property. A sortal *predicate* is a predicate that refers to a sortal property. In what follows, I explain what a sortal property is.

13. I set aside the complication that some mass nouns also have uses in which they feature as count nouns, (as with 'how many coffees did you have today?'). However, it does seem that such usages are often elliptical (e.g., 'coffee' above is elliptical for 'cup of coffee').

14. There are certainly contexts in which these questions might yield answers. The claim here is only that they don't, absent some further information. In any case, this grammatical distinction is only meant to yield a preliminary way of distinguishing sortal properties from other properties.

15. 'Brown' is a *dispersive* term: a term that applies to individual objects that extensively overlap one another. It can combine with other terms to form complex count noun phrases but, when combined with other dispersive terms, like 'thing', it yields complex terms that are themselves dispersive. (see, Hirsch 1982: 48–49).

16. An ANZAC is a member of the Australian & New Zealand Army Corp. This is an example used by Geach (1980).

17. Wiggins 1980: 27. When a dog grows out of being a puppy, there is no passing away of anything, not even a puppy.

18. The airline might count this person as two passengers in its annual report, but this is exactly the point: The counting of two passengers (in the sense entailed by the airline's use of the term) does not entail the existence of two individuals (although counting two passengers on a single flight does).

19. Wiggins 1980: 24–27.

20. Wiggins 1980: 64.

21. As I mentioned in n. 2, there a question about how 'determination' is meant to actually work here.

22. This terminology is my own, but the point I use it to make is in line with a charitable interpretation of e.g., Wiggins's sortalism. The reason I make the point is that it will mean that I can direct my argument against the most compelling form of sortalism.

23. So, I am conceiving of subsumption in a general way here, which includes both phase subsumption and the hierarchy, for example, of genus to species.

24. I talk of uses of concepts here, rather than merely of concepts, because, depending on the context in which it is applied, the same substance sortal might either directly or indirectly determine the principles of identity and persistence for an object. In the case that *dog* is applied to a dog, there is direct determination. In the case that *dog* is applied to a cat, the determination is indirect (via implication of the sortal concept *animal*).

25. As I said earlier, this paper deals with the question as it applies to spatiotemporal objects. As I mentioned in n. 5, there is analogous position about other categories of objects (such as sounds, events, etc.). It is possible that e.g., Marcus (who I

mention in n. 11) is right that metaphysical sortalism about events is true but metaphysical sortalism about physical objects might still be false.

26. The sortalist can of course still hold (as Wiggins indeed does, for example) that there are some distinct sortal predicates that determine consistent identity conditions and persistent conditions.

27. This also means that she denies that *spatiotemporal object* is itself a sortal predicate. If different kinds of spatiotemporal objects have different principles of identity and persistence, then *spatiotemporal object* underdetermines these conditions.

28. MS should not be confused with the doctrine of the *relativity of identity*. A commitment to MS involves the claim that identity is *sortally dependent*, but *not* the claim that it is *relative*. This would be the claim, defended by Geach, that it is possible for *a* to be the same *F* as *b*, for *a* to be a *G*, but for it to be false that *a* is the same *G* as *b*. For example, imagine the following case (discussed in Ayers 1974: 118). A glass bottle, *a*, is melted down. The same mass of glass is then blown into a jampot, *b*. The proponent of relative identity might claim that *a* is the same piece of glass as *b* but not the same bottle as *b* (for this to imply relative identity *a* must indeed be a bottle). Wiggins argues that this is an infringement of Leibniz's Law, and he therefore denies the relativity of identity. On his view, if *a* is identical to *b*, then, if a is a *G*, the truth of the indiscernibility of identicals leaves no space for *a* not to be the same *G* as *b*. The indiscernibility of identicals entails that the piece of glass and the bottle are distinct entities. This rules out the relative identity claim. In order to account for the *sense* in which it is true that 'the piece of glass *is* the bottle', Wiggins famously introduces an 'is' of constitution: i.e., the piece of glass constitutes the bottle but is not identical to it. The details of this dispute and Wiggins resolution are not important for us here. What is relevant is that MS and the doctrine of relative identity are distinct claims. For our purposes, a metaphysical sortalist is someone who claims that identity is *sortal dependent* but *absolute*.

29. For Wiggins's endorsement of this view, see Wiggins 1980: 140 & 140, n. 13.

30. Wiggins, for e.g., is particularly cagey both in his statements of TS and about the steps that take us from MS to TS (he often talks as if the two claims are simply two sides of a single coin). But he is committed to TS. In particular, he frequently makes claims like the following: 'picking a thing out and tracing it through space and time is part and parcel with treating it as a thing with some specific way of behaving...'. (Wiggins 1977). And, in Wiggins 1980 (116–117) he claims that, for every object, there is some sortal concept that applies to that object which must be *treated* as invariant in even conditional or counterfactual 'envisagings' of that thing.

31. For this reasoning, see Wiggins 1980: 140.

32. For two objects to share an exact location, let us say, is for them to share exact boundaries in space, for it to be such that no part of either occupies any space that is not occupied by some part of the other. In claiming that indefinitely many objects share an exact location in this case, the sortalist can also allow that there are indefinitely many objects that share a partial location. I single out the case of shared exact location here, as a way to illustrate and distinguish a particular kind of indeterminacy that is grounded in a particular metaphysics.

33. It is worth noting that, if one is moved by this argument, it is not clear that supplying a correct sortal concept always solves the indeterminacy problem, since we might be able to generate cases in which two objects *of the same kind* share an exact location. For example, Kit Fine gives the example of Bruce and Bertha's letters, which are distinct entities of the same kind that share an exact location. (See his 2000: 357–36). We should therefore at least be aware of the possibility that, with the indeterminacy argument from shared exact location, the sortalist may generate a problem he does not actually have the resources to resolve.

34. See, e.g., Ayers 2005: 534–570.

35. Her view entails that we conceive of such changes in terms of the statue being destroyed or going out of existence and therefore rules out the idea that the object which is at time t a statue persists through the change out of statue-hood at time t^2.

36. Since her view entails that the statue and the lump are distinct objects.

37. Evans 1982: 178.

38. What it means for the informational connection to govern one's conception of an object is that one will be disposed to form beliefs about the object depending on the information he receives from it (Evans 1982: 121–122).

39. Evans 1982: 170.

40. While I stand by this reading of Evans's account of demonstrative identification, it should be noted that the account outlined in Ch.6 is in tension with remarks Evans makes elsewhere in his (1982), which contradict the account of Ch. 6 by suggesting that physical objects of different kinds can share space at a time (when it is not the case that one is a part of the other). For example, in discussing the *fundamental ground of difference* for physical objects, Evans writes, 'although two *G*'s may not be able to share a position at a time, a *G* may be able to share a position with a thing of a different kind: for instance a statue and a piece of clay.' (107) Essentially, what Evans does here is to endorse the argument for multiplying entities (§I.II of my paper). Remarks like this in fact lead Evans to make a series of remarks in which he attempts to reject TS in a way that accommodates MS and the argument for multiplying entities. Having spent much time trying to make sense of these remarks, I am inclined to think they do not culminate in a stable position. However, Evans's account of demonstrative identification from Ch. 6 can be extracted and taken on its own terms. Even in abstraction from the rest of his (1982) it is still the most insightful and systematic account of perceptual demonstrative thought to have surfaced in the literature. In my remarks here, I attempt to outline the part/whole indeterminacy challenge by focusing on the problems for this account. I set aside Evans's complicated relationship to sortalism in the book as a whole.

41. To be clear, the problem is *not* that agents' knowledge of the locations of perceived objects is not *objectively specified*. We can grant that egocentric or *indexical* knowledge of locations is sufficient but the problem that this knowledge is *limited* remains. Evans, e.g., argues that egocentric knowledge of the locations of objects suffices for demonstrative identification, so long as the agent has a general ability to map egocentric space onto objective space, in something like the way one would use a map to find one's way around by locating oneself on the

map. (Evans 1982: 162–163) But, this does not solve the problem we are now addressing.

42. Matt Boyle's excellent paper 'Sortalism and Perceptual Content' (unpublished) addresses this issue in a very helpful way. What he calls the 'Problem of Perceptual Presence' (a term of Alva Noe's) is at least close to what I have in mind. Boyle also points out that this is essentially the same problem Hume brings out in his criticism of the idea of substance. The problem, of course, surfaces again and again in discussions of perceptual content.

43. This is a view endorsed by Moore and Russell. For discussion, see Evans 1982: 144–145 & 177.

44. It is worth noting that the argument from structure does not itself seem to imply that, to fulfill the relevant structural requirement, the principles applied in an act of individuation must be principles that determine identity and persistence conditions. It may be that, to get from the argument from structure to TS, an indeterminacy argument is required.

45. For discussion of a similar point see Ayers 1974: 113–148, 115.

46. I don't claim that this is the only way we could or do acquire kind concepts. But I'm quite sure that *some* kind concepts are acquired in this way.

47. As we'll see in a moment, he does not preclude the possibility of *all* such cases. Some attempts at sortal-dependent individuation that involve mistaken sortals do nonetheless net a particular object in virtue of *implying* a correct higher sortal. But, even with this possibility in place, the sortalist rules out certain cases of mistakes that we should accommodate (for example, the mistake made in (3) above).

48. Without giving up her claim that physical objects have *different* identity and persistence conditions, the sortalist cannot claim that *physical object* is a higher sortal that can do the required work.

49. We should understand this as the claim that any concept that implies a substance sortal would be sufficient.

50. This terminology is due to Kent Bach, who makes a distinction between *satisfactional* and *relational* thoughts (Bach 1987). I mean the same thing by satisfactional as he does. I depart from Bach in contrasting satisfactional thoughts with *non-satisfactional* thoughts (rather than *relational* thoughts). My reasons for this have to do with trying not to beg the question against proponents of acquaintance-less singular thought, as well as with certain criticisms of purely causal accounts of acquaintance, but I need not go into these here.

51. Of course, it contains the concept *yellow*, but this concept is applied to Donald as a predicate. This presupposes that Donald has been individuated apart from his being yellow.

52. This way of talking is out of step with the notion, which appears sometimes in discussions of singular thought (and elsewhere) according to which *only* singular thoughts are really *about* objects. Descriptive thoughts are said to be rather about *properties*. This idea is inherited from Russell, who claimed that one could only think about the entities to which one was acquainted. The sense in which a descriptive thought was 'about' an object was therefore an attenuated sense. In contrast, I claim that descriptive thoughts are about the objects that satisfy their descriptive conditions, but that there are two *ways* a thought can be *about* an object. This divergence from the Russell-inspired terminology is harmless (it

does not do away with any philosophical distinctions). (For what it is worth, Russell would not have claimed, e.g., in 'On Denoting', that descriptions extend the reach of thought, if there were not some sense in which 'the shortest spy is Russian' were about the shortest spy, if there were one.)

53. It has often been suggested that singular thought 'supplies the content for thought in general'. For example, all of the following authors allude to this idea in one way or another: Evans 1982; Strawson 1959; Bach 2010; and Dickie 2010. The idea that this class of thoughts has special epistemic and conceptual features would make this claim more compelling.

54. For example, Ayers 1974.

55. For example, Xu 1997.

56. A longer, unpublished version of this paper also addresses the question of the relationship between thought sortalism and the statue/lump problem in greater detail.

57. The use of scare quotes here is meant to mark a sense in which one could have or form an 'expectation' without us saying that she has a *belief* (that is a contentful, conceptual mental state). Setting aside the question of whether they have beliefs, dogs have 'expectations'. Having marked this sense, I will not continue to use scare quotes in what follows.

58. Xu 1997: 370.

59. Xu 1997: 370.

60. Although Xu does not discuss the issue here, it seems that successful use of property criteria like (2) would require general knowledge about particular kinds. For example, blocks don't grow or change colour without being painted (or undergoing some other relevant physical process), but living things often grow, and some living things change colour frequently. So, seeing two instances of the same kind, which differ in colour, would provide evidence of numerical distinctness in the case of blocks (although the evidence would be defeasible) but not in the case of, say, some kinds of tree frog.

61. The studies discussed here make use of the 'Spelkean' methodology in which 'looking time' is taken to provide evidence as to the nature of the expectations formed by pre-verbal infants. (Spelke 1985)

62. Interestingly, there are also experiments showing that infants as old as eight months old fail to form such successful expectations when the tests make use of unbound, non-coherent quantities of stuff, like piles of sand. This suggests that they have and exploit general knowledge about how coherent objects behave, but not about how amorphous quantities behave. (Huntley-Fenner, & Carey 1995, also Cited in Xu 1997.)

63. A further control experiment was run in order to establish that these infants even *noticed* the difference between a cup and a ball, and concluded that they did. The point of this control is to show that the infants are sensitive to qualitative differences that could be used to distinguish kinds (they see that a cup looks different to a ball), they just don't *use* this information to form expectations about number and identity.

64. Dickie 210.

65. Where visual objects are conceived as configurations of features that attention is drawn to.

66. Dickie, 210: 232.

67. Apart from her appeal to an empirical story about attention as a grounding for an account of perceptual demonstrative thought, the other central component of Dickie's view is what she calls the MCP (Modal Containment Principle), which is essentially a category constraint on object-files. This principle is, on her view, a (necessary but not sufficient) condition on successful reference to particular objects. At least for purposes of the paper in question, Dickie's MCP is a *category* constraint, not a *sortal* constraint (see n. 11 above), so I need not reject it to make the current argument against sortalism. However, I am also not committed to endorsing this component of her view.

68. Huntley-Fenner & Carey 1995, cited in Xu 1997.

69. In giving her account, Dickie focuses on studies on adult perceivers. In particular, she focuses on the automatic spread of attention, amodal completion and multiple object tracking.

70. In a variation of the now well known multiple object tracking studies, Scholl, Pylyshyn and Feldman (2002) use a technique called *target merging* where subjects are presented with objects consisting of merged parts. The subjects' abilities to track a single *part* of the whole is tested and it is established that perceivers have a diminished ability to track parts in comparison with their ability to track whole objects.

71. Other variations of the multiple object tracking task performed by Scholl & Pylyshyn (1999) have been used to show that the ability to track multiple objects persists through occlusions. The perceptual system parses objects as wholes, even when they are occluded. These results are also reviewed in Scholl 2002: 25.

72. See, Scholl 2002: 8.

73. I am setting aside the question of whether very young children have and employ such a concept.

74. To play the *role* of a sortal concept, the concept plays the role in the thought of helping to pick out the object of predication, rather than that of predicating some property of an object picked out by some other means.

75. Or, if you prefer, meaningful states, as outputs.

76. In *Origins of Objectivity* (2010), Burge gives several examples of the non-trivial work the perceptual system does in generating objective representations. He also argues that this justifies talk of perceptual *content* that is not reducible to mere sensitivity but is also distinct from the content of thoughts.

77. What I say above about the existence of cases in which a sortal concept *is* what makes the difference between referential success and failure should already imply this.

78. Wiggins 1997: 413.

79. Wiggins, 1997: 413–414. It should be noted that Wiggins explicitly claims that treating a thing as a physical object is not enough.

80. Even if I committed to denying the sortalist's *metaphysics* of distinct principles of persistence for different kinds of objects (a position which I am in fact tempted to deny but which I do not commit to or defend here) this would not commit me to the existence of bare particulars. It would be possible, e.g., to claim that the statue in my garden could *persist* through change from, say, statue-hood into mere lump-hood, without anything being destroyed–that is, it would be possible to conceive of *statue* as a *phase* of the object in my garden. This would not entail denying that it is essential to all objects that they fall under kinds.

81. Ayers 1997: 393.

References

Ayers, Michael. 1974. 'Individuals Without Sortals.' *Canadian Journal of Philosophy* 4: 113–148.

———. 1997. 'Is *Physical Object* a Sortal Concept? A Reply to Xu.' *Mind and Language* 12: 393–405.

Ayers, Michael. 2005. 'Ordinary Objects, Ordinary Language, and Identity.' *The Monist* 88, 4: 534–570.

Bach, Kent. 1987. *Thought and Reference*. Oxford: Oxford University Press.

———. 2010. 'Getting a Thing into a Thought.' In *New Essays on Singular Thought*, edited by Robin Jeshion. Oxford: Oxford University Press.

Baillargeon, R., Spelke, E.S. & Wasserman, S. 1985. 'Object Permanence in 5-month-old Infants.' *Cognition* 20: 191–208.

Baillargeon, R. & Graber, M. 1987. 'Where's the Rabbit?: 5.5-month-old Infants' Representation of the Height of a Hidden Object.' *Cognitive Development* 2: 375–392.

Boyle, Matthew. Unpublished. 'Sortalism and Perceptual Content.'

Burge, Tyler. 2010. *Origins of Objectivity*. New York; Oxford University Press.

Dickie, Imogen. 2010. 'We Are Acquainted with Ordinary Things.' In *New Essays on Singular Thought*, edited by Robin Jeshion. Oxford: Oxford University Press.

Evans, Gareth. 1982. *The Varieties of Reference*. Oxford: Oxford University Press.

Fine, Kit. 2000. 'A Counterexample to Locke's Thesis.' *Monist* 83, 3: 357–36.

Frege, Gottlob. 1980. *The Foundations of Arithmetic*. Evanston; Northwestern University Press.

Geach, Peter Thomas. 1980. *Reference and Generality: An Examination of Some Medieval and Modern Theories*. Ithaca & London: Cornell University Press.

Hirsch, Eli. 1982. *The Concept of Identity*. New York: Oxford University Press.

Huntley-Fenner, G.N. & Carey, S. 1995. 'Individuation of Objects and Non-solid Substances: A Pattern of Success (Objects) and Failure (Non-solid Substances)', *Society for Research in Child Development*, Indianapolis, IN.

Kripke, Saul. 1972. *Naming and Necessity*. Cambridge, MA: Harvard University Press.

Marcus, Eric. 2006. 'Events, Sortals, and the Mind-Body Problem,' *Synthese* 150: 99–129.

Scholl, Brian J. & Pylyshyn, Zenon W. 1999. 'Tracking Multiple Items Through Occlusion: Clues to Visual Objecthood.' *Cognitive Psychology* 38: 259–290.

Scholl, Brian, J., Pylyshyn, Zenon W. & Feldman, Jacob. 2002. 'What is a Visual Object? Evidence from Target Merging in Multi-Element Tracking,' in *Objects and Attention*, edited by Brian J. Scholl, 159–179. MIT Press.

Scholl, Brian. Ed. 2002. *Objects and Attention*. Cambridge: MIT Press.

Spelke, Elizabeth. 1985. 'Preferential Looking Methods as Tools for the Study of Cognition in Infancy,' in *Measurement of Audition and Vision in the First Year of Postnatal Life*, edited by Gottlieb & Krasnegor. Norwood, NJ: Ablex.

Spelke, Elizabeth., Kestenbaum, R., Simons, D. & Wein, D. 1995. 'Spatiotemporal Continuity, Smoothness of Motion and Object Identity in Infancy.' *British Journal of Developmental Psychology* 13: 113–142.

Strawson, Peter. 1959. *Individuals*. London: Routledge.

Wiggins, David. 1997. 'Sortal Concepts: A Reply to Xu.' *Mind and Language* 12: 413–421.

———. 1980. *Sameness and Substance*. Cambridge: Harvard University Press.

———. 2001. *Sameness and Substance Renewed*. Cambridge: Cambridge University Press.

Xu, Fei. & Carey, Susan. 1996. 'Infants' Metaphysics: The Case of Numerical Identity.' *Cognitive Psychology* 30: 111–153.

Xu, Fei. 1997. 'From Lot's Wife to a Pillar of Salt: Evidence that *Physical Object* is a Sortal Concept.' *Mind & Language* 12: 365–392.

Philosophical Perspectives, 26, Philosophy of Mind, 2012

CONCEPTS, ANALYSIS, GENERICS AND THE CANBERRA PLAN[1]

Mark Johnston
Princeton University

Sarah-Jane Leslie[2]
Princeton University

My objection to meanings in the theory of meaning is not that they are abstract or that their identity conditions are obscure, but that they have no demonstrated use.[3]

—Donald Davidson "Truth and Meaning"

From time to time it is said that defenders of conceptual analysis would do well to peruse the best empirically supported psychological theories of concepts, and then tailor their notions of conceptual analysis to those theories of what concepts are.[4] As against this, there is an observation — traceable at least as far back to Gottlob Frege's attack on psychologism in "The Thought" — that might well discourage philosophers from spending a week or two with the empirical psychological literature. The psychological literature is fundamentally concerned with mental representations, with the mental processes of using these in classification, characterization and inference, and with the sub-personal bases of these processes. The problem is that for many philosophers, concepts could not be mental items. (Jerry Fodor is a notable exception, we discuss him below.)

We would like to set out this difference of focus in some detail and then propose a sort of translation manual, or at least a crucial translational hint, one which helps in moving between philosophical and psychological treatments of concepts. Then we will consider just how, given the translation, the relevant psychology, particularly including recent work on the generic character of many of our 'platitudes' or early developing central beliefs (Gelman, 2010; Hollander, Gelman, & Star, 2002; Leslie, 2007, 2008, in press a; Leslie & Gelman, 2012; Leslie, Khemlani, & Glucksberg, 2011; Mannheim, Gelman, Escalante, Huayhua, & Puma, 2011; Tardif, Gelman, Fu, & Zhu, 2011), bears upon philosophical theories of concepts, and especially on the new style of conceptual analysis that now goes under the heading of "the Canberra plan".

A Philosophical Theory of Concepts

What follows in this section is a short account of the general form of a substantial philosophical theory of concepts. We do not endorse it. We simply take it to be a widely held view, at least in its significant sub-parts; we also take it to be a view that animates the common practice of conceptual analysis within philosophy, along with the so-called conceptual theory of the a priori — the idea that the source of the a priori lies in the application conditions of concepts.

On the substantial theory, *concepts are abstract objects individuated by their conditions of application to entities, and it is possession or grasp of these concepts which guides the use of terms.* Thinkers who grasp or possess a given concept C will often come to associate it with a term or representation "T" and then use "T" to classify or characterize entities in accord with the specific conditions of application of the concept C. For such thinkers "T" will then express the concept C. Other thinkers, who do not even implicitly know the application conditions associated with C might nonetheless defer to those who use "T" to express C, and intend to do likewise even though they themselves do not use "T" to classify or characterize entities in accord with the specific conditions of application of C. They can thus make conceptual mistakes, such as supposing that arthritis is a more general infirmity than inflammation of the joints. They can then be said to have an imperfect or incomplete grasp of the concept expressed by "arthritis".

Thus far, concepts are abstract objects encoding conditions of application of words, phrases and the like; in effect, they are rules of reference determination across possible situations, rules that we grasp and employ as guides in our use of terms. They are what give spoken and written words 'life'; that is, it is by being associated with this or that concept that a word or phrase comes to have conditions of application. They would also explain how it is that words and phrases — like "si" — that appear in distinct languages can have double lives. The speakers of the distinct languages associate different concepts with the same words. Likewise, within a language, the association of different concepts with the same words and phrases is what accounts for ambiguous words and phrases such as "bank" and "the bank he built up".

The postulation of concepts, and the hypothesis that it is the grasp of these concepts — if not by us then by the experts and lexicographers to whom we defer — that properly guides our use of words, makes for *concept publicity*; that is, the possibility of two speakers with very different beliefs about a subject matter sharing the same concept of that subject matter. Someone who knows that arthritis is a disease of the joints can genuinely disagree with someone who believes it can spread to the bones. The second is in error about the application conditions of a concept that both speakers share. As a result he can be meaningfully corrected by the experts; for example they are not changing the subject on him when they tell him that one cannot have arthritis in the thigh.

Since words can combine compositionally to produce phrases of any arbitrary length, the life-givers that are concepts *had also better combine compositionally* to give life to phrases of arbitrary length (see, e.g., Fodor, 1998, Fodor & Lepore, 2002). So the concept female lion had better be some computable construction out of the concept female and the concept lion. Very likely, it had better amount to an intersection of these concepts; that is, a concept whose conditions of application are given by the conjunction of the application conditions of the constituent concepts.

A natural extension of this whole way of thinking involves associating a certain sort of concept with a whole sentence. The concept associated with a whole sentence is a computable construction out of the concepts associated with the sentence's constituent words and phrases. The special name for such a concept is "a thought", where a thought is not a sentential or representational vehicle but rather what is expressed by such vehicles. On this view, it is precisely because sub-sentential concepts have application conditions that sentences express thoughts, and so can be true or false. The special name for the application conditions of these structured concepts, the ones that are expressed by whole sentences, is "truth conditions".

On the substantial theory, if there are concepts, and if our use of terms is explained by our grasp of the associated concepts, then *there will be certain immediate inferences that will look like good candidates to be underwritten simply by our grasp of the relevant concepts,* since those inferences seem utterly reliable and do not seem to depend on any intermediate empirical premise. So it is with the inference from

Bonnie is a mare

to

Bonnie is a horse.

Furthermore, there is a route to recognizing the truth of the corresponding conditionals of such inferences by appealing simply to our grasp of the relevant concepts. So it is said that it is a priori that

If x is a mare then x is a horse

where this means that there is a route to recognizing its truth that does not depend for its justifying force on any empirical information about how the world works.

This also explains why the conditional could not be false. The conditional gives no hostages to fortune; it involves no bet on any contingent way the world is. Accordingly, the conditional has the defining feature of a so-called conceptual truth: it is not only a priori but necessary.

Finally, if our use of terms is explained by our grasp of the associated concepts, and if concepts have necessary and sufficient conditions of application, then we might well hope to make our implicit knowledge of the application conditions of our terms *explicit*, by reflecting on what seems to be guiding us when we apply them in the vast range of imaginary cases that we can conjure up in the philosophical armchair. We can then form various hypotheses about just which sets of application conditions lie behind which terms, and we can test these hypotheses further by means of the method of consulting real and imaginary cases. The aim is, for each significant philosophical concept that is not simple — that is, for each concept that is compounded out of other concepts — to arrive at an a priori and necessary biconditional of the form

x is T if and only if x is . . .

where "T" is a term expressing the concept in question.

Not just any such biconditional will do. It has to be non-trivial. And it has to be rich enough to enable the derivation of all the a priori and necessary truths that arise from the concept associated with "T". *Finding a rich enough a priori and necessary biconditional is not easy; but if we succeeded we would have an 'analysis' of the relevant concept.* Generalizing, if we were to provide such analyses for all of the concepts of philosophical importance — *person, cause, essence, knowledge, mental state, matter, good* and so on and so forth — we would have articulated the bases for all of our distinctively philosophical a priori knowledge.

Something like this substantial picture has a good claim to be at the motivating core of what was once called 'analytical philosophy' (from Gottlob Frege, Kurt Gödel, A.J. Ayer, H.P. Grice and Roderick Chisholm through to George Bealer and Frank Jackson). Arguably, with the simple addition that the abstract objects that encode the application conditions of terms are *the rules we grasp* and which then determine our sense of the rightness of our applications of the term in particular cases, the picture is the real target of the skepticism about meaning that Saul Kripke (1982) saw in certain passages in Wittgenstein. Whether or not one accepts the picture, it goes some way toward illuminating just why a philosophical theory of concepts might take little notice of mental entities or mental processes.

Of course, the picture raises many questions: What are the specific application conditions of this or that particular concept? What it is to grasp a concept? What is it for a concept to be associated with a word or phrase? Are concepts really 'life-givers' or is talk of them simply a way of encoding, as it were after the fact, the details concerning the extension of this or that word- or phrase-in-use? Are concepts then idle wheels? Is a priori knowledge really knowledge deriving from knowledge of the application conditions of our concepts? If so, is there any that goes beyond knowledge of merely stipulative definitions? Is the method of imagining a case and calling on our intuitions about whether a given concept applies in such a case a good way of making explicit our implicit grasp of the application conditions of the concept? Are some concepts, for example the familiar concept *plus,* more natural than others, in the sense of being privileged attractors of the terms that we use, attractors which we can only avoid by explicitly intending to use our terms in certain specific ways? Is this why our term "+" expresses the concept *plus* rather than the concept of some finite function that is like plus for a huge finite stretch but gives no answer just where our capacity to add actually gives out?

It may well turn out that these questions have disappointing answers. (For some of best arguments that this is so, see Willard van Orman Quine (1951), Hilary Putnam (1962, 1975), Gilbert Harman (1974, 1975), Jerry Fodor (1998), Timothy Williamson (2003) and Michael Devitt (2005).) Concepts may not be guides in any psychologically real sense. There may be no non-trivial biconditionals that neatly capture the application conditions of our concepts. There may be no a priori knowledge, period, or, at least, almost none beyond that delivered by logic and mathematics. Furthermore, the now popular idea of certain concepts, or the properties they demarcate, being privileged attractors may just be hopeful mysticism. At the end of the day, the frame provided by philosophical talk of concepts, analysis, and the distinctively philosophical a priori may have nothing very interesting left in it. (Obviously that pessimistic view also has its distinguished opponents; among them David Lewis (1970, 1994, 1997), Christopher Peacocke (1992) George Bealer (1987), Frank Jackson (1994, 1998), David Chalmers (Chalmers & Jackson, 2001) and Paul Boghossian (2003).)

What has so far been missing from the debate over these central philosophical issues is any systematic account of just how the psychological literature might bear upon them. By way of beginning to fill that gap, we will revisit these issues at the end of the paper, once the interrelations between philosophical and psychological theories of concepts have been set out in appropriate detail. Our ultimate view is that the psychology does resolve the philosophical standoff in a fairly convincing way.

In any case, it should be clear that on what we have been calling the substantial theory, concepts are abstracta that encode conditions of application; they are not mental processes or mental representations. One obvious route to the conclusion that concepts are not mental is to note that on the substantial view of concepts, the content of what is thought is a kind of concept, and only someone in the grip of the vehicle/content confusion would think that what is thought is a mental representation. Mental representations might be vehicles that *express* thoughts, but a mental representation is not the *content* of what is thought. Representations have characteristic effects, but no one is in danger of coming under the causal influence of a thought content, as opposed to a representation of it, or a proponent of it. So the concepts that are the variety of things that are thought are none of them mental representations, and neither are their constituent concepts. Furthermore, as Christopher Peacocke (1992) emphasizes, once the substantial theory of concepts is up and running, it seems obviously coherent to suppose that many or most concepts are beyond our grasp, so that we will never bear any interesting mental relation to them.

However, psychologists who theorize about concepts are directly concerned with putatively mental entities, namely mental representations (including mental images and the like) that play a central role in our activities of classifying and characterizing and making immediate inferences about objects. A psychological account of our concepts in this sense is an account of just how it is that we, or our cognitive systems, systematically exploit certain sorts of general information to use the relevant mental representations to classify and categorize objects, and make inferences about them.

In fact, when psychologists do focus on mental representations they show little or no interest in the rules which determine their possible world extensions. What then is the relation of the psychological literature to the philosopher's interest in concepts? Is it simply a confusion of tongues to suppose that psychologists and philosophers are concerned with the same subject matter?

We believe that once the import of the psychology is made clear, a different philosophical view of concepts, one which attributes less knowledge to concept-users as such, becomes much more plausible. On this 'concepts as terms-in-use' view, a concept is a term, and a term is just an interpreted string in a language; a string which has, thanks to its conventional use, an extension, i.e. a range of items to which the term applies. Accordingly, it is only use, perhaps only conventionally governed use, which gives terms the 'life' that arbitrary strings lack. There need be no more to specifying a term than characterizing its syntactic form and giving a rule that determines its extension. There need be nothing *behind* terms — at least nothing like concepts understood as meanings or senses or extension-determining rules — that speakers *grasp* and which then guides their use of the relevant terms. Mutual correction while participating in a convention for using a term selects for a variety of effective heuristics or criteria that then guide individuals in their use of that term. To 'know how to use a term' is just to have some such effective criterion, and this will often fall far short of even a tacit understanding of the conditions of application of the term. Hence, on the concepts as terms-in-use view, there is no reason to suppose that speakers can render explicit the conditions of application of their terms simply by reflecting on how they would use them in a variety of circumstances. For such actual and counterfactual usages reflect only the speakers' empirical criteria, which may fall short of any grasp of application conditions. Thus 'armchair' philosophical analysis, as traditionally conceived, can at best produce fragmentary and inconclusive results. It can be no more than the articulation of the criteria we presently use in deciding whether to apply a term.

Problems with Psychological Theories of Concepts?

By starting with the philosopher's substantial notion of a concept, and adopting a translation of the following sort

> "Concept" in the psychological literature means pretty much what philosophers who have accepted significant parts of the substantive theory have meant by it

one can quickly make mincemeat out of the psychological literature. Jerry Fodor has already done much of this work for us in his *Concepts* (1998), where he points out that so construed, most, if not all, psychological theories of concepts fail the straightforward requirements of compositionality and publicity. To put it in the broadest possible terms, psychologists seem most interested in discovering our criteria or ways of telling when a given individual has a property or falls within a specified kind, and our criteria or ways of telling which inferences about members of a kind are the ones to make. But it will not be in general true that our ways of telling that something falls under a complex concept *F&G* is a joint application of our ways of telling whether something falls under the concept *F* and our ways of telling whether something falls under the concept *G*. Moreover, there is massive individual variation in our ways of telling whether something falls under the concept *F*; we may only be able to look it up in a book, you may have written the book and conducted the complex experiments needed to determine that it is F, and yet — so the substantial theory has it — all of us can share the same concept *F*.

Someone more enamored than Fodor of the conceptual theory of the a priori – say the Christopher Peacocke of A *Study of Concepts* (1992) and more recently "The A Priori" (2004) – might continue in the same general vein, by noting that, if we simply focus on our ways of telling which inferences about members of a kind are the ones to make, we will fail to distinguish between those inferences underwritten by our grasp or possession of the concept of the kind in question, and those inferences that appeal to collateral knowledge about members of the kind. Yet psychologists studying concepts happen to show no interest in this distinction. Instead, they focus on what generalizations and inferences are cognitively fundamental, in the sense of being (i) early developing and (ii) central to our a posteriori conceptions of the kinds in question.

We believe that the perception that these are — in any sense — defects in the psychological literature derives from the naive translation principle, and not from the psychological theories themselves. We will briefly review the relevant literature, emphasizing as we go just how recent discoveries concerning generics bear on that literature, then propose a different translation scheme, and finally examine the ways in which the psychological theories might put pressure on philosophical theories of concepts.

Some Psychological Theories of Concepts

The focus and the questions that drive psychological theorizing differ significantly from those which organize philosophical discussions of concepts. This is partly obscured by the fact that almost all reviews of the psychological literature on concepts begin with the so-called 'classical view', which is easy to misconstrue as simply a version of the substantial philosophical theory of concepts. On the classical view, when applying most lexical concepts (a lexical concept is a concept that is expressed by a single word) subjects actually exploit represented necessary and sufficient conditions for falling under the concept. The standard illustration of the classical view is the concept *bachelor*, which, it is claimed, is composed of the concepts *unmarried* and *man*, such that anything is a bachelor just in case it is an unmarried man. Of course, not all concepts can be decomposable in this way; there must be some or other stock of primitive concepts, out of which all other concepts are ultimately composed. Nevertheless, concept learning, on this view, involves combining such primitive concepts to form complex ones, and classifying an item under a decomposable concept really is supposed to be a matter of checking whether the item satisfies the necessary and sufficient conditions specified by the decomposition. Thus, someone who possesses the concept *bachelor* will classify items as bachelors *based on* their gender and marital status, in such a way that she will classify something as a bachelor *just in case* it is a man and unmarried. Mutatis mutandis for concepts such as *lion, dog,* and *table.*

Notice that, despite the initial appearances, the classical view of the concept bachelor is not just the (false but) banal remark that someone is a bachelor if and only if he is an unmarried man; it is instead the rather heady empirical thesis that we actually use the concepts *unmarried* and *man* in deciding whether to count something as a bachelor. It is distinctively a thesis about the criteria we actually use, not, or not just, a thesis about the application conditions of our concepts.

Since the 1970s, the classical view, understood as a thesis about the criteria we actually use, has been quite roundly rejected. Much of the reason for its rejection has to do with the discovery by Eleanor Rosch and her colleagues of so-called *typicality effects* (e.g., Rosch, 1973, 1978; Rosch & Mervis, 1975). For many categories, some members of a category are perceived as being more typical examples of the category than others, and it turns out that how typical a category member is actually predicts a very wide range of experimental results. For example, people are quicker to categorize typical members, and are more confident and consistent in their categorization of typical members. When learning a novel concept, people learn to categorize the typical members first, and they learn the concept faster when presented with typical members in the learning phase. There are also myriad effects of typicality on language learning and use, on reasoning, and so on so forth. (For some very helpful reviews, see Laurence & Margolis, 1999; Murphy, 2002; Smith and Medin, 1981).

Positing that people represent and exploit necessary and sufficient conditions does not explain typicality effects. Knowing that something is a bachelor just in case it is unmarried and a man does not give any information about what makes for the typical versus the atypical bachelors; for they are all alike in respect of being unmarried men. The pope is an unmarried man, but quite an untypical bachelor. Something else has to be posited to explain typicality effects; but once we have posited this something else there may be no empirical reason to also posit the representation of necessary and sufficient conditions. That is, suppose we posit some sort of mental representation that explains the powerful effect of typicality on people's categorization practice, and suppose we satisfy ourselves that this posited representation explains the experimental findings concerning people's dispositions to categorize items and generalize and reason about them. Then we will have accounted for all the data without positing operations on subjects' representation of necessary and sufficient conditions. From the perspective of explaining and predicting the target empirical results, knowledge of necessary and sufficient conditions then looks like an idle wheel — there are no results whose explanation demand positing the representation of necessary and sufficient conditions. The classical view has fallen into disrepute because many investigators believe that something like this has turned out to be true.

There may be some confusion concerning the rejection of the classical view: the evidence does not, it is sometimes said, *prove* that for most of our lexical concepts subjects do not represent and exploit necessary and sufficient conditions. That is correct; the findings of Rosch and her colleagues do not *prove* that there cannot be necessary and sufficient conditions lurking somewhere in our mental representations. However this form of resistance misses the real thrust of the psychological data; the issue is not that certain empirical results prove the absence of represented necessary and sufficient conditions, but rather that there is simply *no evidence for* their representation in the case of most lexical concepts.[5] Consider, for example, an experiment conducted by Jerry Fodor and his collaborators, in which they asked whether one could find any differences in processing time that would indicate that one concept is composed in part of another. If, e.g., the concept *murder* is composed in part by the concept *kill* (as has been claimed), then it should take longer to process *murder* than *kill*, since processing the former involves processing the latter as a proper part. However, this prediction of the classical view is not borne out (Fodor, Garrett, Walker, & Parkes, 1980). Again, no evidence in favor of the classical view emerged from that experiment. It is for this sort of reason that psychologists have moved beyond the classical view of concepts.

Driven by the need to explain typicality effects, many psychologists have embraced the prototype theory of concepts, where prototypes are statistical functions over properties, which assign weights to features based on how likely a category member is to have that feature, or conversely, based on how likely something with that feature is to be a category member. There are a number of different proposals that fall under the heading of the prototype theory (see Murphy, 2002, for an extensive review), but they generally appeal to features that are in some way statistically related to category membership. For example, the prototype for *dog* might include features such as *barks*, *has four legs*, *has a tail*, *wears a collar* and so on. These features are not candidates to figure in universal necessary and sufficient conditions since not all dogs have these features; an unfortunate creature can still be a dog even if it has three legs, no tail, no collar and no voice. However, the basic idea behind prototype theory as applied to dogs is that if one is confronted with an animal and wishes to determine whether or not it is a dog, one will use this animal's features, or lack thereof, in a complex sub-personal calculation based on the weights of the various features in the prototype of *dog*. (The details of this calculation differ a great deal depending on the particular version of the theory.)

The weight that a feature receives in the prototype is generally taken to be determined by two sorts of statistical facts, namely the *prevalence* of the property among *dogs* (so *barks, has a tail*, etc would receive high weights since most dogs have these features), and/or the *cue validity* of the property; that is, how likely it is that something with that feature is a dog. Thus even though, perhaps, most dogs don't wear collars, the probability of something being a dog if it wears a collar is high, so *wears a collar* might receive a significant weight in the prototype. The more highly weighted features an individual has, the more typical an exemplar of the kind it will be; prototype theory thus places typicality effects first-and-foremost among the data it aims to explain.

Of course, one could try to express the prototype view in terms of some set of necessary and sufficient conditions; for example

> x is a bachelor if and only if his lifestyle and behavior resembles an appropriate paradigm, e.g. the one presented by Sean Connery in the early James Bond movies.

Clearly, when expressed this way, the prototype theory for *bachelor* fails miserably. This is just one sign that prototype theory is just not intended as an account of the application conditions — as, in effect, an analysis — of the term "bachelor". Another sign is that, as this very dated example suggests, the paradigms can change over time without thereby producing any change in the application conditions of the term.

Prototype theory has many adherents, and many well-motivated critics. While we may often rely on statistically weighted features in categorization, particularly in rapid, perceptually-based categorization, it seems that this cannot be the whole story. Imagine, for example, that you are presented with a raccoon. A perverse scientist then comes along and alters the creature, dying its fur so that it takes on the markings that are typical of a skunk, and even goes so far as to implant a sac of smelly liquid that the creature can use to spray smells when it is under stress. How would you categorize this creature? It now has all the typical features of a skunk, yet overwhelmingly, from elementary school on up, people say this is still a raccoon (Keil, 1989). This finding is hard for standard prototype theories to accommodate. Furthermore, it seems increasingly clear that typicality ratings are not solely driven by statistical facts; crucially, the causal status of features also matters. Imagine that two features are equally prevalent among members of a kind, but that one is understood as generally being the cause of the other. Suppose then that an instance of the kind has one feature but not the other. Since the statistical facts are the same in both cases, prototype theory would seem to predict that typicality ratings of the individual would not be affected by *which* feature is lacking. However, individuals exhibiting the effect but not the cause are rated as less typical than those exhibiting the cause but not the effect (Ahn, Kim, Lassaline, & Dennis, 2000).

These results and many others suggest that our ways of categorizing things, and reasoning about things in categories, involve a richly structured knowledge base that is responsive to causal-explanatory factors as well as statistical factors (e.g., Carey, 1985, 2009; Gelman, 2003; Gopnik & Meltzoff, 1997; Keil, 1989). As we will use the term here, this is the outlook typical of the so-called theory-theory of concepts.[6] Since theory-theory, so construed, posits that our concepts or criteria for categorization and generalization are sensitive to theory and causal-explanatory structure, there is not too much to be said beyond that about the *general* features of our concepts. Rather, it may be useful to go on to consider concepts within each broad domain, e.g., natural kind concepts, artifact concepts, social concepts, mental state concepts, mathematical concepts and so on so forth. For example, a view known as *psychological essentialism* seems to provide a great deal of insight into how our natural kind concepts are structured from a very young age (e.g., Gelman, 2003; Leslie, in press b). However, this view is very likely not applicable to artifact concepts or mental state concepts, and certainly not to mathematical concepts. That sort of domain sensitivity should not be seen as a failing of theory-theory, but as an appropriate response to the complex and myriad ways we have of categorizing things, and of generalizing on the basis of those categories.

Probably the view that fits best with the mass of empirical material on concepts is a hybrid of theory-theory and some elements drawn from prototype theory. There are terms like "red" or "dog" which we can apply rapidly and without reliance on theory, at least in some circumstances. It is natural to think that this goes by way of sub-personal processing of sensory and perceptual information with subsequent comparison with paradigmatic or prototypical sensory and perceptual profiles. The characterization of such prototypical profiles — in particular whether and to what extent they use prevalence and cue validity — is a complex piece of empirical psychological theorizing, yet to be completed. Obviously, subjects who use such prototypical profiles are not thereby using the yet-to-be-completed psychological theory. When it comes to the immediate sensory or perceptual application of terms like "red" or 'dog", subjects exploit a range of prototypical sensory and perceptual profiles, but they do not exploit a theory of those prototypical profiles.

In what follows, we will take this qualification to theory-theory as read, and emphasize instead the explicitly theoretical elements in our criteria for applying terms.

Concepts and Generalizations

One feature that the foregoing psychological theories of concepts have in common is that they all make some reference to properties that are possessed by member*s* — plural — of the target category; they all involve focus on forms of *generalization* concerning the category and its properties. According to the classical theory, the relevant generalizations are (modalized) universal generalizations; the prototype view treats them as probabilistic generalizations; and on the theory-theory, they are complex and theory-laden general beliefs. These observations suggest a possible alternative route to studying the nature of our classificatory and inferential heuristics: we should look to the empirical investigation of our earliest and most fundamental generalizations.

Suppose, for example, that it was possible to identify and describe our most basic way of forming general judgments about kinds or categories — of moving from information concerning individual members of a category to judgments concerning the category in general. It would be quite surprising if this fundamental manner of generalization was not centrally connected with the heuristics for categorization and inference concerning kinds or categories. Thus a natural and conservative empirical hypothesis would be that our conceptual heuristics in large part consist of such fundamental types of generalizations.

Recent interdisciplinary research suggests an intriguing possibility along these lines; namely that our basic way of generalizing information issues in *generic generalizations*, which are articulated in language via generic sentences such as "tigers have stripes", "lions have manes", and "mosquitoes carry malaria" (e.g., Gelman, 2010; Hollander et al., 2002; Leslie, 2007, 2008, in press a; Leslie & Gelman, 2012; Leslie et al., 2011; Mannheim et al., 2011; Tardif et al., 2011). Such generic sentences exhibit a puzzling truth-conditional profile, as a few familiar examples quickly illustrate. Consider, for example, "lions have manes" — this strikes most people as obviously true, yet only mature male lions have manes. Thus, there are perfectly normal lions (i.e. female ones) who lack manes, and yet the generic seems true. Further, there are *more* male lions than there are maned lions (since some males are immature or lack manes for genetic or environmental reasons), yet the generic "lions are male" is widely rejected. Perhaps more puzzling are generics such as "mosquitoes carry malaria", which are accepted despite the fact that only about one percent of mosquitoes carry the virus. Yet, generics such as "books are paperbacks" are robustly rejected, even though over eighty percent of books are paperbacks (for more discussion of generics, see Carlson & Pelletier, 1995; Cohen, 1996; Leslie, 2007, 2008; for empirical investigation of people's judgments of these sorts of generics and others, see Prasada, Khemlani, Leslie, & Glucksberg, in press).

Most importantly for our purposes here, generic generalizations are obviously not equivalent to universal generalizations, as is illustrated by the truth of "lions have manes" and "mosquitoes carry malaria". Even generics such as "tigers are striped" and "dogs have four legs" tolerate exceptions in a way that their universal counterparts do not. "All tigers are striped" is falsified by a single stripe-free albino tiger, and similarly for "all dogs have four legs"; the generics are more robust, however, and remain true in the face of exceptions. Thus, if generic generalizations constitute our most fundamental way of making general judgments about categories, this would seem to raise a further empirical challenge for the classical view. A proponent of the classical view would have to argue that the general information employed in our classificatory heuristics does not originate from our most basic way of forming general judgments. The information that we use to identify members of a category would not come by way of our basic means of forming general judgments about the category. This is not incoherent, but given the overwhelming absence of empirical evidence in favor of the classical view, it amounts to positing another unmotivated defensive epicycle.

But why should we think that generic generalizations are more cognitively fundamental than universal ones? Some of the data in favor of this hypothesis comes from the study of language acquisition. As noted, generics have a very complex truth conditional profile; providing an account of when generic sentences are true or false is a quite demanding task (see e.g., Carlson & Pelletier, 1995; Cohen, 1996; Leslie, 2008). In contrast, it is very easy to provide an account of when universally quantified statements are true ("all Ks are F" is true iff the set of Ks is a subset of the set of Fs). In light of this, one might expect that universals would be easier for young children to acquire and process than generics; however, this is precisely the opposite of what we find. Generics are produced and understood by preschool-aged children, and the data collected to date suggest that these young children have a remarkably adult-like understanding of generics. For example, preschoolers who know that only 'boy' lions have manes will accept "lions have manes" but reject "lions are boys" — despite implicitly understanding that there are at least as many 'boy' lions as there are maned lions (Brandone, Cimpian, Leslie, & Gelman, 2012; see also Gelman & Raman, 2003; Gelman, Star, and Flukes, 2002; Graham, Nayer, & Gelman, 2011; for a summary of available evidence on generic acquisition, see Leslie, in press a).

Preschoolers are generally competent with the quantifier "all" *when it is applied to a specific set of individuals* (e.g., Barner, Chow, & Yang, 2009). For example, if preschoolers are shown six crayons and asked "are all *of these* crayons in the box?" they are usually able to answer the question correctly. Most of the work on quantifier acquisition has focused on such situations; however it should be clear that these sorts of limited, non-projectable pseudo-generalizations are not the sort that are involved in conceptual heuristics. The question, then, is how young children fare with open-ended, category-wide universals — not "all of these crayons", but "all crayons". Several studies indicate that they have considerable difficulty processing universal quantifiers in such kind-wide generalizations. Most intriguing, though, is that when preschoolers are confronted with such kind-wide universals, they do not simply provide random, incorrect answers, instead *they treat the universals as though they were generics*. That is, preschool children not only consistently evaluate generics just as adults do, they also evaluate kind-wide universals as generics (Hollander et al., 2002; Leslie & Gelman, 2012; Tardif et al., 2011; for a detailed review, see Leslie, in press a). In addition to English-speaking children, such findings have also been documented among Mandarin Chinese- and Quechua-speaking children; similar results have also been found with other quantifiers (Brandone, Gelman, & Hedglen, submitted; Hollander et al., 2002; Mannheim et al., 2011; Tardif et al., 2011).

Importantly, these findings are just what one would expect on the hypothesis (Leslie 2007, 2008, in press a) that generics, unlike universals (or "some"- or "most"-quantified statements), articulate cognitively fundamental generalizations. If the cognitive system has a basic, default way of forming general, open-ended judgments then it may sometimes fall back on this means of generalizing when asked to process a more taxing and sophisticated generalization. This tendency would be most pronounced in young children, who would be expected to struggle with the more taxing generalizations. Not only do young children apparently not struggle with generic generalizations, they substitute their understanding of the generic when asked to consider category-wide quantified generalizations.

If generics truly do article cognitively fundamental, default generalizations then one would expect that these effects might not be limited to young children. Adults might also be susceptible to the error of treating quantified statements as generics. Indeed, under a variety of circumstances, adults do show a robust tendency to accept universally quantified statements such as "all ducks lay eggs", despite knowing that male ducks do not lay eggs (where the tendency to accept the universal was *not* due to participants interpreting the universal as quantifying over only females, or over sub-kinds of ducks; Leslie et al., 2011; see also Meyer, Gelman, & Stilwell, 2010). This finding would be explicable if adults were not always evaluating the universal claim, but were instead, like preschoolers, sometimes substituting their evaluation of the corresponding generic. Further confirming evidence can also be found in the study of adult reasoning errors. For example, Steven Sloman (1993, 1998) investigated adults' evaluations of arguments that involve the quantifier "all", and found that their evaluations did not conform to the logic of universal quantification. His participants judged that arguments such as (A) are strictly stronger than arguments such as (B), despite judging that reptiles are indeed animals:

(A) All animals use norepinephrine as a neurotransmitter; therefore all mammals use norepinephrine as a neurotransmitter
(B) All animals use norepinephrine as a neurotransmitter; therefore all reptiles use norepinephrine as a neurotransmitter

This pattern of judgment is simply mistaken given the logic of the universal quantifier; however, if we replace the universals in the arguments with generics, then the judgments of the participants would be very reasonable. Since generics tolerate exceptions, the claim "animals use norepinephrine as a neurotransmitter" can be true even if some animals are exceptions to the claim. If one judges then that reptiles are more likely than mammals to be exceptions to the generic, then argument (A) is indeed stronger than argument (B). Hence these results are as one would expect if adults have a tendency to evaluate universals as generics.

Note that adults also judge that universals such as "all ravens are black" are more likely to be true than universals such as "all young jungle ravens are black", despite understanding that the latter are a subset of the former (Jönsson & Hampton, 2006). Again, this is incoherent if one is really dealing with universally quantified statements; however, if one were instead evaluating these universals as generics, this would be a reasonable judgment, since for all one knows young jungle ravens may be exceptions to the generic "ravens are black". These results are thus naturally read as lending support to the hypothesis that adults are treating these universals as generics. As a further piece of converging evidence from another experimental paradigm, it has been found that both preschoolers and adults *recall* previously presented quantified statements as generics (Leslie & Gelman, 2012).

The hypothesis that generics, unlike quantified statements, articulate cognitively fundamental, default generalizations thus has a fair amount of empirical support at this time. As a final observation in favor of the hypothesis, we might note that quantified statements require a phonologically articulated element, namely the quantifier itself. That is, we say "*all* tigers are striped" or "*most* tigers are striped"; however, in the case of the generic, there is no corresponding articulated element (e.g., "*gen* tigers are striped"). This is not an isolated fact about English, but rather it would appear that few, if any, natural languages have a dedicated, articulated generic operator (Carlson & Pelletier, 1995; Dahl, 1985).

The generics-as-default-generalizations hypothesis offers an explanation for this otherwise puzzling fact: if one wishes to interact efficiently with a system, and the system has a basic, default way of proceeding or performing a task, then one need only issue an explicit instruction to the system if one wishes it to *deviate* from this default way of proceeding. To convey the idea in more intuitive terms, if one is dealing with a child who, say, by default does not pick up her toys, one only needs to say something if one wishes the child to *deviate* from her default and actually pick up her toys. If one does not wish the child to pick up her toys on a given occasion, it would be a waste of breath to say "don't pick up your toys!" since this is what will happen even if one remains silent. Thus, quantifiers may be articulated in language because one needs to *tell* the cognitive system, as it were, to deviate from its default, generic mode of generalizing, and instead generalize in the universal manner or the existential manner, and so on and so forth (for more details, see Leslie, 2008, in press a). Generics, by virtue of expressing the default mode of generalization, require no such phonological marking.

The Nature of Generic Generalizations

Suppose that, in the light of the foregoing, we were to go further and adopt the *generic encoding hypothesis*; namely that the heuristics which most fundamentally guide our use of terms are properly formulated in generic terms.[7] How would this impact the extant psychological theories of concepts? That depends on just how we as theorists should understand generic generalizations. There would be minimum impact on the classical view if generics were to be understood either as *ceteris paribus* generalizations as in "other things being equal, all ravens are black" or as universals over what is normal as in "all normal ravens are black". Likewise, the prototype theory would find support if generics could be explained either in terms of the conditional probability of the kind in question having the feature in question or in terms of the cue validity of the feature; that is, its predictive value as an indicator of the kind.

Universally quantified generalizations are easily analyzed, since "all Ks are F" is true just in case the Ks form a subset of the Fs. Yet, as we have seen, generic generalizations of the form "Ks are F" are not universals, since they tolerate exceptions. Can such generics be analyzed as equivalent to claims that are quantified with "most", "usually", or "generally"? This might seem promising for generics such as "tigers are striped" or "ravens are black". There are, however, generics that can be true even though most members of the kind *lack* the property: consider "mosquitoes carry West Nile virus", "lions have manes", "sharks attack swimmers". Paraphrasing these true generics with "most", "usually" or "generally" results in false claims, suggesting that this is not the correct analysis. Conversely, a range of false generics become true when paraphrased with "most", "usually" or "generally": "most school teachers are female", "usually, books are paperbacks" and "generally, humans are right-handed" are all correct claims, yet the corresponding generics ("school teachers are female", "books are paperbacks", "humans are right-handed") would seem to be false. Clearly this latter point also rules out the idea that generics are equivalent to any logically weaker claims, such as statements quantified with "some".

In the semantics literature, it is often proposed that generics are in some sense or other equivalent to claims about what is normal for members of the kind. There are subtle variants on these accounts (see, e.g., Pelletier & Asher, 1997), but they share the core notion that generics tell us something about the properties of all of the normal members of the kind. Again, this seems promising for generics such as "tigers are striped", since albino tigers may be counted as in some way abnormal. More challenging are generics such as "lions have manes" and "ducks lay eggs", since there is nothing abnormal about maneless female lions, or eggless male ducks. The standard response to such examples is to suggest that these generics involve covert restriction to the relevant sex (or other natural sub-kind) — that is, "lions have manes" is just elliptical for the claims "male lions have manes", which is arguably amenable to an 'all normal' analysis.

However, if it sufficed for the truth of a generic that all the normal members of one sex have a property, we would expect that a range of clearly false generics would instead be true. For example, it is surely true that all normal male lions are male; why then does the generic "lions are male" strike us as clearly false? Further, it is normal for male ducks to *not* lay eggs, yet "ducks don't lay eggs" would seem to be false (for further discussion of the point, see Leslie, 2008). Recent empirical evidence also raises some additional difficulties for any approach that appeals to implicit restrictions. Andrei Cimpian and his colleagues investigated whether people think that a kind in which a property is had only by one sex (that is, where an effective domain restriction to a single sex is possible) is a better satisfier of a generic such as "Xs have manes" than a kind in which half the members, regardless of sex, have the property (that is, where no such effective restriction to single sex is possible). If generics of the form "Xs have manes" are only accepted because people are implicitly restricting the domain to a sub-kind whose members normally possess the property, then they should think that a kind in which the property is had by one sex is a better satisfier of the generic – that is, a better satisfier than a kind in which half the males and half the females have the property. However, no such preference was found (Cimpian, Gelman and Brandone 2010; see also Khemlani, Leslie, & Glucksberg, 2009, for distinct empirical considerations against the notion of implicit domain restriction).

If generics such as "lions have manes" do not implicitly mean "male lions have manes", then they would seem to count against the analysis of such generics in terms of what is normal for members of the kind. There is after all nothing abnormal about the maneless female lions. Further challenges are also posed by generics such as "mosquitoes carry West Nile virus" and "sharks attack swimmers". Very few members of the kinds in question have the relevant properties, and it is hard to maintain that this tiny minority represents what is normal, while, e.g., the virus-free mosquitoes are somehow abnormal. Examples such as these suggest that generics need not always involve properties that are normal for the kind, or even for any of its sub-kinds. Nor does it seem plausible to suppose that these generics are, respectively, equivalent to "other things being equal, all mosquitoes carry the West Nile virus" and "other things being equal, all sharks attack swimmers". There is another possible approach to the analysis of generics, one which might be favored by prototype theorists trying to accommodate the generic encoding hypothesis. Perhaps some generics such as "tigers have stripes" are accepted because the property is highly prevalent among members of the kind (i.e., because *most* tigers have stripes), while other generics such as "mosquitoes carry West Nile virus" are accepted because if something carries West Nile virus, it is very likely to be a mosquito — that is, because the *cue validity* associated with the generic is high. If such an account of generics were successful, then this would constitute evidence in favor of the prototype theory of our classificatory heuristics. Since prototype theory standardly involves features that are either highly prevalent or highly diagnostic (or some combination of the two) it would then fit well with the generic encoding hypothesis, and it could naturally assimilate the considerable evidence in favor of that hypothesis.

Problems arise for such an account along several dimensions. First and most importantly, even the *combination* of high prevalence and high cue validity does not suffice for the truth of a generic. Consider examples such as "books are paperbacks" or "tigers are Bengal tigers", (As it happens, there are six remaining subspecies of tigers in the world, with Bengal tigers being more numerous than all the other subspecies combined). In both cases, the majority of the members of the kind have the property in question, and furthermore the property is highly diagnostic of being a member of the kind; still these generics seem to be false. Second, recent empirical work suggests that peoples' judgments of low-prevalence generics (such as "mosquitoes carry malaria") are not especially sensitive to their estimates of cue validity. If low-prevalence generics were accepted only because the associated cue validity was high, then one would expect that people's judgments of these generics would scale to some extent with their estimates of cue validity. However, this was found not to be the case (Prasada et al., in press).

If the notions of normalcy, prevalence and cue validity do not allow us to give an account of generics, where does that leave us? As noted above, it would be reasonable to suppose that the best account of our classificatory heuristics should mesh with our best account of generics, since the former involves features that are generalized to kinds and categories, while the latter are language's way of letting us articulate our most cognitively basic generalizations. That is the basis of our advocacy of the generic encoding hypothesis. We have also just seen that generics are simply not equivalent to universals (which means the generic encoding hypothesis does not mesh with the classical view), nor do they seem especially amenable to treatment in terms of probabilistic notions such as prevalence and cue validity (which means that the generic encoding hypothesis does not mesh with the prototype theory). Perhaps, then, in accord with the theory-theory, we need to take into account theoretically rich, content-based factors in giving an account of generics.

Consider, for example, the low-prevalence generics that have been discussed throughout this section: "mosquitoes carry West Nile virus", "sharks attack swimmers", "ticks carry Lyme disease". We might add to the list as follows: "pit bulls maul children", "tigers eat people", "lead toys poison children", and so on so forth. Once we are on the lookout for *content-based* factors — as opposed to merely formal statistical relations like prevalence or cue validity — we can make something of the fact that these generics all share a common feature: the predicates in question all express properties that make their possessors dangerous or threatening; they involve the sort of property about which we would wish to be forewarned. Indeed, it is natural to suppose that it would be beneficial for us if our most basic way of generalizing was sensitive to such a higher-order feature of the properties predicated of the relevant kinds. Perhaps, then, generics are accepted even at low prevalence levels if the property in question has this type of higher-order feature (see Leslie, 2007, 2008, in press c for detailed discussion; for empirical support see Cimpian, Brandone, & Gelman, 2010).

If generic generalizations are indeed sensitive to the nature of the property being generalized, might that account for other 'troublesome' generics? Suppose that, as part of our theoretical knowledge — as this is understood by the theory-theory — concerning animal kinds, we register that animals kinds tend to be very similar to each other at a certain level of abstraction: by and large, animal kinds have characteristic noises, characteristic modes of locomotion, characteristic diets, characteristic salient physical features, characteristic methods of reproduction/gestation, and of nurturing the resultant young. Outside the domain of animal kinds, artifact kinds have characteristic functions, kinds of professionals have characteristic social roles, and so on.

Suppose that this general structural knowledge is exploited by our cognitive system, so that for each of the relevant characteristic dimensions for each type or kind with which we are presented, we first seek to fill in the relevant values. We might call these values the *characteristic properties* of the kind. Examples of characteristic properties of kinds would include salient, distinctive physical features (e.g., "lions have manes"), methods of reproduction and nurturing the young for animal kinds (e.g., "ducks lay eggs", "pigs suckle their young"), and for artifact kinds, functions (e.g., "Orange-Crusher-2000s crush oranges" — which could be a true generic even if every Orange-Crusher-2000 is destroyed before it is used).

There is thus a sense in which these generics are 'answering an implicit question' about, e.g., how ducks reproduce, or what the function of Orange-Crusher-2000s is. They do not reflect merely statistical claims about how prevalent the property is among members of the kind. Indeed, if a generic attributes a characteristic property to the kind, then the generic may be accepted even if few members of the kind have the property in question (see Leslie, 2008 for more details).

Given that generics are indeed sensitive to rich, content-based factors, it may be possible to explain why some generics are accepted even though the property is not prevalent among members of the kind. What, though, of generics such as "books are paperbacks", "school teachers are female", or "Canadians are right-handed"? People tend to reject such generics, despite judging that the property in question is highly prevalent (Prasada et al., in press). One proposal is that generics may be sensitive to the nature of the *exceptions* to the generic claim (Leslie, 2007, 2008). That is, amongst the members of the kind that fail to have the predicated property, it may matter *how* they fail to have the property; in particular whether they simply lack the property, or whether they have an equally salient, concrete, positive property *instead*. "Ticks carry Lyme disease" is accepted even when the prevalence estimate is low, but the non-infected ticks are known to simply *not carry Lyme disease;* they do not have a specific alternative property instead. However, the books that are not paperbacks are instead hardcover. Similarly, people who are not right-handed are instead *left-handed*; elementary school teachers who are not female are *male*. Intuitively, one might feel as though one would be 'overlooking' these hardcover books, these left-handed individuals, and these male school teachers if one accepted the generics in question. Thus, a promising proposal is that generics may be also sensitive to the nature of the exceptions to the generalization.

Of course, the study of generics does not provide decisive evidence regarding the nature of our heuristics and criteria. However, if the best account of generic generalizations meshes with theory-theory but not other accounts, this could be naturally construed as providing support for the theory-theory approach to categorization and inference. In our terms, the theory-theory fits best with the generic encoding hypothesis; the empirical claim that the heuristics or, more generally, the criteria we use in applying terms frequently take a generic rather than a universal form. Therefore, in what follows, we will assume that the theory-theory offers the best account of our heuristics of categorization, and that the generalizations involved are articulated in language via generic sentences, whose interpretations are governed by rich, content-based factors.

This tentative vindication of the theory-theory, because of its capacity to incorporate the generic encoding hypothesis, may initially seem to raise the stocks of the Canberra plan. To the casual eye the Canberra plan, focusing as it does on the theory, or alternatively the set of platitudes, that guides us in the use of a term may seem to best comport with the theory-theory of concepts. As we shall see, this first impression is badly wrong; the theory-theory is plausible only as an account of the heuristics or criteria we employ in using a term, while the Canberra plan is intended as a general account of how we should specify the application conditions of a term. Moreover, as we will see, the generic character of many of our platitudes raises quite systematic problems for the Canberra plan, at least when it is applied to arenas where the relevant generic platitudes are not backed up by the corresponding universal truths (as they typically *are* in logic and mathematics).

Some Suggestions about "Translation"

As even this brief review of the psychological literature makes clear, when relating philosophical and psychological theories of concepts, we need a better translation scheme than the following

"Concept" in the psychological literature means pretty much what philosophers who have accepted significant parts of the substantial theory have meant by it.

Otherwise, philosophers might all too easily follow Jerry Fodor's lead in despairing of psychological theories of concepts, while psychologists will be immediately led to think that the philosophical discussion is derisory.

The naïve translation principle implies that psychologists should be interested in the application conditions of concepts, but of course they are not. They show no interest in studying those who would be best placed to know the application conditions of concepts, namely clear-headed taxonomists and experts in philosophical analysis. Indeed, given the naïve translation manual, it would have be said that psychologists exhibit what can only be seen as a curious and indefensible fixation; they study the cognitive performance of untutored adults and even of young children! So they might discover, for example, that children and untutored adults withhold the term "fruit" from tomatoes, olives and peppers. But that just entails that such people are not full masters of the concept *fruit*, which does indeed apply to these ovaries of flowering plants. That is, these subjects simply do not know the application conditions of the term "fruit". Why then is *their* performance at all relevant in the study of concepts? Is this not an *appalling* waste of time and money?

That line of questioning, which is on its face rather silly, would be quite sensible if the naïve translation were adequate. So it is not adequate. We should do better.

Often psychologists simply mean by "concept of Ks" what ordinary speakers mean, namely a contextually relevant part of someone's conception or total theory of Ks. In *Doing Without Concepts* (2009), Edouard Machery has recently argued that in so far psychologists mean just that, and in so far as they appeal to *different* parts of a subject's conception of Ks when they explain her perception of Ks, memory of Ks, classification of Ks and inferences concerning Ks there is then nothing uniform to go under the heading of "a psychological theory of concepts".

However, there seems to us to be more relevant uniformity in the psychological literature on concepts. Mostly psychologists mean by "concept of Ks" psychologically real clusters of heuristics, or more generally criteria, which guide us in classification, characterization and inference concerning Ks. The crucial interpretive point is that most psychologists working on concepts are not concerned with what an analysis would deliver, namely application conditions of concepts, but with heuristic criteria for classification, characterization and inference. If this is right then we should also avoid the opposite error that could be driven by the naïve translation principle, namely the idea that we could use the experimental methods of psychology, or the methods of opinion surveys, to directly study not just the criteria or heuristics we use, but the application conditions of our concepts, thereby letting the empirical work do our analyses for us, as it were.

Three Main Theses

This overview of the relation between philosophical and psychological theories of concepts naturally suggests the following thesis:

> Philosophers who believe in concepts/conceptual knowledge/the distinctively philosophical a priori should treat the psychological theories outlined above, along with other psychological theories in the same line of country, as in significant part accounts of the *heuristics or more generally the criteria* we actually use to apply terms to things.

This, in its turn, suggests a second thesis, concerning the crucial relevance of the psychology to philosophical theories of concepts:

> Philosophers should then ask whether and to what extent their theories of concepts, when combined with the best psychological accounts of the heuristics we actually use to apply terms, will entail massive underdetermination in respect of just which concepts we are using those terms to express.

Thirdly,

> To the extent that there is such massive underdetermination of concepts and their associated application conditions by the criteria we use in applying terms, philosophers should lose confidence in the usefulness of conceptual analysis, understood as the making explicit of the conditions of application of concepts by means of the method of cases. To that same extent, we should be pessimistic about the range of the distinctively philosophical a priori.

Dogs, Wolves and German Shepherds

In order to illustrate the last two theses, suppose that in actual fact our heuristics for applying the term "dog" are exhausted by the following down-and-dirty criteria:

Is it an animal?

Does it have one of the characteristic looks, smells, coat textures, etc, of one of the familiar kinds of dogs?

Is it the offspring of an animal with one of the characteristic looks, smells, coat textures, etc, of those one of those familiar kinds of dogs?

As things actually go in suburban environments these three criteria may be good heuristics for collecting together observed instances of the kind dog, the kind we now know to be the species *Canis lupus familiaris*. However, this is due to the contingent fact that the canines around us are almost all of them from that species. In fact *Canis lupus familiaris*, as the name suggests, is a subspecies of the kind grey wolf, *Canis lupus*, which includes wolves that are not dogs, but which happen to look very like German Shepherds. Wolves typically don't roam in suburban neighborhoods. So, what we in fact track by means of these heuristics are dogs, but in another environment the same heuristics might lead us to track a larger group, namely the grey wolves.

What concept in the philosophical sense should we then assign to our word "dog": the concept that comports with membership in *Canis lupus familiaris* or the concept that comports with membership in *Canis lupus*? Notice that some background intention to use "dog" to refer to *the same sort of animal* as the ones around us won't really help here. First, we may not in fact have that intention, and yet presumably we would still have a concept associated with "dog". Second, the intention itself does not eliminate *Canis lupus* from contention, for there is no good reason to suppose that all the grey wolves considered together are not *the same sort of animal*. In general there are too many *sorts of animals* for underdetermination to be reduced in this way.

Moreover, even on the assumption that these heuristics enable us in our environment to use "dog" to pick out members of *Canis lupus familiaris*, the heuristics themselves will be poor candidates to figure in the analysis of the concept *dog*. For it is not a priori and necessary that

> If x is an animal which has one of the characteristic doggish looks, smells, coat textures, etc., and is the offspring of that ilk then x is a dog.

Other animals can be made to look like dogs. A coiffed squirrel can be made to look like a chihuahua, and so can the squirrel's immediate forebears. The lesson is that the heuristics are simply *indicators* of when something around here is a dog. It is a bad verificationist error to mistake such heuristics for the application conditions of the relevant concept.

A similar argument goes through on the assumption that these heuristics in fact enable us, at least in our typical environment, to pick out the kind *Canis lupus*. Animals that are not grey wolves can be made to look, smell and feel like grey wolves. So can their immediate forebears. Satisfying the criteria for applying a concept — or better, for applying a mental representation or a term — is not satisfying the application conditions (in the philosopher's sense) for the concept associated with the representation or term.

Indeed, once the criteria/conditions distinction is made, why should we think that application conditions rather than our criteria are what is articulated by our judgments about cases? Once that distinction is made clear, the method of appealing to our judgments as to whether we should apply or withhold a term in a variety of imaginary cases is obviously a way of manifesting our criteria or ways of telling whether the term applies. It is not obviously a way of manifesting our 'implicit grasp' of the application conditions of terms. Indeed, the empirical explanation of our use of terms, by way of one or another psychological theory of concepts, seems to *drive out* the supposed explanation by way of implicit grasp of application conditions. But the supposed explanation was doing the crucial work of justifying the method of cases as the royal road to the analysis of our concepts.

A Temptation to be Resisted

Some may still be tempted by the thought that *if* our heuristics for applying the term "dog" are in fact just exhausted by the down-and-dirty criteria

Is it an animal?

Does it have one of the characteristic familiar doggish looks, smells, coat textures, etc.?

Is it the offspring of an animal with one of those characteristic looks, smells, coat textures, etc?

then it just follows that the concept we express by "dog" is the concept of an animal which has one of the characteristic domestic doggish looks, smells, coat textures, etc., and which is the offspring of an animal with one such perceptual profile. Accordingly, they will say that given how we use the word "dog" it is a priori and necessary that

x is a dog iff it is an animal with one of the characteristic patterns of domestic doggish looks, smells, coat textures, etc., and it is the offspring of that ilk.

Here we no longer have underdetermination, understood in terms of there being multiple kinds — *Canis lupus familiairis, Canis lupus* — that are equally good candidates to fall under the concept *dog*. Instead we have lack of specificity in the concept expressed by "dog"; it turns out to be a concept under which the more general kind *Canis lupus* falls.

The problem then is to explain how it could have been rational on our part to accept the scientific discovery that

All dogs are members of the kind *Canis lupus familiaris.*

At the very least, accepting this will involve a conceptual change, by changing from the topic we had in mind when we use "dog" to a much more specific topic. That is odd, for it suggests that we could reasonably reject such scientific discoveries out of hand because they confuse a kind with one of its sub-kinds in precisely the same way as the following claim does:

All human beings are men.

Obviously, such a rejection of the scientific discovery that all dogs are members of the kind *Canis lupus familiaris* is wildly out of place, therefore the temptation that prompts it is not to be followed.

What then is wrong with the temptation to make the conditions of application of a concept exactly as unspecific as the heuristics which govern its use? Once again, it confuses useful heuristics or criteria for the employment of a term with a priori and necessary conditions for the term's correct application.

The usefulness of a heuristic is invariably situation-dependent. In the suburbs of New York, the heuristics are a fair guide to the presence of a member of *Canis lupus familiaris*. In the Arctic hinterlands, where there are lots of wolves, they are not. The conditions of application of the concept *dog* are not in this way situation-dependent.

Are There Any Concepts in the Sense of Things to be Analyzed?

Philosophical reflection on the psychological literature yields the following straightforward challenge:

Premise 1: The concept that subjects express in their use of a term "T" is not fixed by the heuristics that subjects employ in applying "T".

Premise 2: All that subjects could have introspective or armchair access to, even in the best case of articulating what they know about Ts by means of an large inventory of real and imagined possible cases in which "T" is applied and withheld are (i) the various deliverances of their heuristics in the real and imagined possible cases, and (ii) by way of inferences to the best explanation of such deliverances, the details of their own heuristics.

Conclusion: The method of trying to extract a conceptual analysis, a statement of the necessary and sufficient conditions of application of a concept, from armchair intuitions about cases typically will not work. For if there is a concept that subjects express in their use of a term "T", the relevant heuristics will typically underdetermine which concept that is.

This challenge has only been illustrated, not vindicated, by the toy example of our heuristics for "dog". For it is open to someone to maintain that when we really take *all* the heuristics or criteria that we employ in applying "T" into account then the conditions of application of the concept expressed by 'T' *are* determined or fixed (or fixed modulo the further facts about which concepts, properties or extensions are privileged attractors).

That response will be taken up in detail later in the paper, in the context of discussing the general program of philosophical analysis known as the Canberra plan. Obviously, the actual facts about the kind of heuristics or criteria we really are employing are highly relevant to the claim that the totality of the heuristics or criteria we use determines the conditions of application of the relevant term or concept. The overall challenge from psychology can only be met — if it can be met at all — by looking at what psychologists have discovered about these matters.

As we noted above, recent psychological results are now converging on the suggestion that many of the heuristics or criteria we use in applying terms involve beliefs that are best expressed in generic form. If this is so then we believe that it can be shown that it is very unlikely that the totality of our heuristics or criteria fix the application conditions of the relevant terms.

Isn't "Reference Fixing" Analysis Still Viable?

Once upon a time, there *was* a privileged way of telling whether something was Neptune; all we had to determine was whether it was the planet which caused perturbations in the orbit of Uranus. And, arguably, this way of telling was semantically tied to the name "Neptune" in the sense that this name was in fact introduced to denote whatever planet was causing the already observed perturbations in Uranus. According to the well-known tale, Alexis Bouvard observed odd perturbations in the orbit of Uranus and hypothesized that these were caused by the gravitational influence of an unknown planet, which was then dubbed "Neptune". Then, in 1846, Johann Galle discovered the planet in question. Some would then say that it is a priori that

(1) Neptune is the cause of perturbations in Uranus

and hence that it is a priori and necessary that

(2) Neptune is the actual cause of perturbations in Uranus

Finally, someone might say, we now have just what we wanted from an analysis. We have identified a privileged way of telling whether something is Neptune, a way of telling that is semantically tied to the term "Neptune", and one which can be used to guide us in determining the application conditions of the term across all possible situations. All we have to do is look to see whether the thing in the possible situation is identical with the actual cause of perturbations in Uranus.

The idea can be generalized if we indulge ourselves in various 'as-if' stories about the introduction of our terms. Suppose the term "water" was introduced to denote the same stuff as the potable liquid found in rivers, lakes and streams, and that falls from the sky when it rains. Then, according to the line of thought in question, it is a priori and necessary that

(3) Water is the stuff that is the actual potable liquid found in rivers, lakes and streams, and that falls from the sky when it rains.

Once again, we have something that can play the role of an analysis of the concept *water*, for if (3) is a priori and necessary then it specifies the application conditions of "water" across all possible situations.

Why then is there any problem about analysis? Analysis is just the articulation and rigidification of the reference fixers of our terms!

However, as our brief survey of the psychological facts suggests, ordinary users of terms do not themselves privilege such reference fixers among their ways of telling. Indeed, as in the case of "water", they often apply terms on the basis of prototypical perceptual profiles, profiles which may resist any discursive characterization that could appear on the right hand side of an analysis, even a reference fixing analysis. Do they then have different concepts from those who explicitly treat (2) and (3) as a priori?

The friend of reference-fixing analyses need not say this. He or she can say that, as Kripke and Putnam have shown, ordinary users of the terms "Neptune" and "water" respond to possible cases as if they did treat (2) and (3) as a priori and necessary. So although they have anticipated one important upshot of the psychological literature, namely that ordinary users of terms employ at most fallible heuristics or criteria in their use of those terms, Kripke and Putnam have nonetheless shown us the way to provide thoroughly modern conceptual analyses: namely, find the reference-fixer for the term in question and rigidify the reference-fixing condition. It is Frank Jackson, more than anyone else, who has done the most to advance this route to refurbishing the credentials of analysis.

The main difficulty for the thought that reference fixers can provide analyses is that, although in some cases reference fixing descriptions may have played a 'semantic' role precisely in serving, *at a particular time*, to fix the reference of a term, it is a notable fact that even in these very cases the relevant rigidified reference fixers need not in fact fix the *subsequent* application conditions of terms across all possible situations. That is, (2) and (3) and their various analogs are not a priori and necessary.

To see that (2) and its ilk are not a priori imagine that after Johann Galle's observation of Neptune, Alexis Bouvard subsequently noticed odd perturbations in the orbit of Neptune, though of a less dramatic sort than those he found in Uranus. Bouvard then hypothesizes that these too are the gravitational effects of still another planet, one that remains to be observed. The question arises as to how to name the planet that is doing this to Neptune, and it comes to be called "Pluto". Galle then subsequently observes Pluto. If history had gone that way, then if (2) is a priori and necessary, the same would hold of

(4) Pluto is the actual planet that is causing perturbations in Neptune.

However, (4) is certainly not a priori and necessary, even in the scenario imagined. For our little story about Galle's second success is compatible with what actually happened in the early 21st century, when shockingly, Pluto was demoted from the status of a planet, because it turned out to be more similar to large asteroids than to planets. If (4) were indeed a priori and necessary that could not have happened. Instead the only option would to have been to conclude that Pluto never existed. Likewise, we could discover that Neptune is a huge, well-disguised, alien spaceship, so (2) is not a priori and necessary. The crucial lesson is this: an established pattern of usage can override original reference fixers. So long as we are not dealing with what Putnam called 'one-criterion' terms, as, perhaps, in the artificial example of the name "Julius" introduced just to denote the inventor of the zipper, we can find examples where the term survives the falsity of its initial reference fixing description. Reference fixing descriptions for terms do not in general hold a priori of the items that the terms pick out.

This is even more obvious in the case of so-called natural kind terms such as "water". (For an extensive discussion of crucial, but often suppressed, complexities surrounding natural kind terms see Leslie (in press b).) We can discover that the water cycle is much more complicated than we supposed, so that the stuff that falls from the sky changes its chemical structure as it approaches the surface of the earth, with the consequence that there is no natural unity in the stuff that falls from the sky and the stuff in lakes and streams. This is not the discovery that water does not exist, as it would have to be if (3) is a priori. Again, an established pattern of usage can override almost any original reference fixer.

There is an appealing response that Frank Jackson and David Chalmers offer to these kinds of counter-examples (Chalmers & Jackson, 2001; Jackson, 1994, 1998). They say that, in order for us to have these very intuitions about the possible cases in question, we must be using some other criterion for being Pluto, or Neptune or water. Otherwise, how can we identify the possible situation before us as one in which we have Pluto, though (4) is false, or as one in which we have Neptune, though (2) is false, or as one in which we have water, though (3) is false?

That may seem like a compelling question, at least if we take seriously what Kripke (1980) called the 'vernoscope picture' of our relation to possible worlds. On this picture, a possible world is presented to us neutrally, leaving open whether it contains Pluto, or Neptune, water or whatever target phenomenon or feature. It is then up to us to bring to bear our a priori and necessary criteria for telling whether it contains Pluto, or Neptune or water or whatever other target we have in mind. An articulation of our ultimate a priori and necessary criteria for telling will then be the proper analysis of the term for the target. So, say Jackson and Chalmers, counterexamples to analyses are themselves indications that we implicitly possess a priori and necessary conditions for telling, i.e. that we know the true analysis.

However, the vernoscope picture, as Kripke (1980) emphasized, systematically misrepresents the nature of our thoughts about possibilities. We happen to know that certain things are possible, and this knowledge of possibilities already comes laden with subject matters, e.g. Pluto, or Neptune, or water. Possible worlds neutrally described are not our basic epistemic starting points in arriving at knowledge of possibilities; they are simply useful devices for defining validity in modal languages.

In particular, in urging the argument above, did we actually find ourselves in such a situation of surveying a possible world neutrally described so that we then had to bring to bear a priori and necessary criteria to determine whether that possible world contains Pluto, or Neptune, or water? No, for the purposes of the argument above, we simply found ourselves in this epistemic situation: the following individual claims are very plausible

Pluto could exist even if (4) were false.

Neptune could exist even if (2) were false.

Water could exist even if (3) were false.

Clearly we do not need to be relying upon even an implicit analysis of "Pluto", "Neptune" and "water" to be in that, fairly minimal, epistemic situation. That should be clear because the possession of an implicit analysis is a very strong condition; an implicit analysis would decide every case. For the purposes of the argument above, we needed only to decide three cases. Obviously, something much more fragmentary and thus much less committal than an implicitly possessed analysis could suffice for that. After all, our grounds for the three claims above were simply that established usage can simply override the reference fixers of old. In saying that we need simply be relying on some reasonable criteria for counting as Neptune, Pluto and water, criteria that do not themselves amount to an analysis, and which may not themselves figure in any plausible analysis of the application conditions of the terms "Neptune", "Pluto" and "water".

Laura Schroeter has offered a very useful way of understanding the general approach of Jackson and Chalmers when it comes to the analysis of our terms. She writes

> However exactly we choose to cash it out, it seems that Jackson's and Chalmers's account is ultimately grounded in the conceptual [or term-using] dispositions the subject would form after ideal reflection on hypothetical cases. The rigidified definite descriptions Chalmers and Jackson offer as an analysis of "water" are correct just in case they accurately summarize the ideal conceptual dispositions the subject would converge on, irrespective of which world she considers as actual (2004, p. 449).

The thought is that *something* is guiding our use of terms in thinking about merely possible situations. Imagine a huge list of the positive and negative verdicts about whether the term under consideration applies in a fully representative range of possible cases — verdicts we would give under ideal conditions; that is, conditions such as no distractions, plenty of computational ability, no straightforward irrationality. If we could codify the pattern found in such a list, we would have an analysis of the concept expressed by the term; equivalently, we would have an account of the application conditions of the term. If not, we will not have an analysis, but there is no more to know about the application conditions of the term in question than the list of verdicts. What else, Jackson and Chalmers might ask, could determine the application conditions of the term?

Having worked through the toy example of dogs, we hope that the reader can now recognize this kind of idea. Once again, it amounts to the conviction that what we rely upon in making judgments about cases, namely our criteria, themselves determine the application conditions of terms.

What else could determine the application of our terms? Recall the concepts as terms-in-use view. Mutual correction while participating in a convention for using a term selects for a variety of effective heuristics or criteria that then guide individuals in their use of that term. To 'know how to use a term' is just to have some such effective criterion, and this will often fall well short of even a tacit understanding of the conditions of application of the term. Accordingly, on the concepts as terms-in-use view, there is no reason to suppose that speakers can render explicit the conditions of application of their terms simply by reflecting on how they would use them in a variety of circumstances. For such actual and counterfactual usages reflect only the speakers' criteria, which may fall short of any significant grasp of application conditions. (Remember how Sean Connery was once more central to the criteria for counting as a bachelor than were the properties of being male and being unmarried.) Thus philosophical analysis, as traditionally conceived, can at best produce fragmentary and inconclusive results, *even under conditions of ideal reflection.*

One way to press this point home is to characterize just what knowledge is required to fix the application conditions of our terms, and how far that knowledge transcends anything that could be fixed even by full knowledge of the criteria we actually use in applying our terms. As the examples of Neptune, Pluto and water themselves show, scientific discoveries can entail surprising facts about the application conditions of our terms. Neptune may not be the cause of the very perturbations which were cited in the fixing of the reference of the term "Neptune"; "Pluto" need not refer to a planet, and "water" may not apply to rain.

In fact, as we shall now see, in order to have the knowledge required to fix the application conditions of our terms, we would either have to know (i) the true total theory of the world (encompassing all the potential sources of surprises about the application conditions of our terms) or (ii) conditionals which specify *for each epistemically possible total theory of the world* just what the application conditions of our terms would be relative to that total theory. Surely both (i) and (ii) massively transcend what can be extracted from our criteria, even under ideal conditions, at least as those conditions have so far been defined.

To see just why the Jackson and Chalmers view that our dispositions to classify possible cases are rich enough to determine the application conditions of our terms leads to one or another of these positions, consider the following example, which simply recalls the traditional Quinean worries about the inter-animation of application conditions and empirical theory. Suppose that a subject has never understood or even heard of special relativity, and suppose that its important claims do in fact figure in the total true theory of the world. When asked to clearheadedly consider a world in which there is no relevant two-place temporal relation between events that can count as a candidate to be simultaneity, our subject will wrongly conclude that there is no simultaneity in that world, because he has not had the benefit of the relevant scientific understanding of the widespread explanatory advantages associated with special relativity — the very ones that justify thinking of simultaneity as frame-dependent. The general lesson is this; if actual science as we know it can reveal surprising facts about the extensions of our terms, for example that "simultaneity" applies in a world in which there is no relevant two place temporal relation between events that can count as simultaneity, then absent the knowledge of the total true science of our world, we will be liable to make systematic errors about the extensions of our terms when presented with possible cases.

Of course, our subject can be presented with an explanation of special relativity, and then asked "What is the extension of our term "simultaneity" under those circumstances?" Then he may get it right. But suppose he is given a description of a possible case in a possible world, without knowing just how the ultimately correct scientific theory of our world reveals, as it likely will reveal, surprising facts about the extensions of our terms. Suppose, as is likely, that this forever unknown theory would be even more revisionary and surprising than special relativity. As the history of science's impact on our use of terms already reveals, if we are in ignorance of the true theory of the world, then we should treat our reactions to 'vernoscope' presentations of possible worlds — presentations in which it is left open whether the target things in question are in them — as hypotheses, not as data. They could well be overturned by subsequent scientific developments.

On the Jackson and Chalmers view that our dispositions to classify possible cases are rich enough to determine the application conditions of our terms, there are two ways of assimilating the familiar point about the unknown surprises that the true theory of the world might deliver. On the first, in order to be sure that our 'ideal' reactions to possible cases get the extensions of our terms right, we need to be in ideal conditions *that include knowledge of the surprising implications of the extensions of our terms due to the ultimately correct theory of our world.* Only then can we properly evaluate the extensions of our terms in the possible situations presented to us.

Let us suppose that for each term "T" there is such a thing as the list of those reactions we would have to the full range of possible cases, under the following conditions: we have no distractions, plenty of extra computational ability, no straightforward irrationality and *we know the surprising implications of the extensions of our terms due to the ultimately correct theory of our world.* What are we to make of that list?

First, it looks unlikely that for many terms there will be any useful finite codification of the infinite number of reactions on the relevant list. So, we may have here a final account of what would make an analysis true, without there ever being any analysis, i.e. any actual statement of an analysis, which is true. Second, given the nature of the idealization required, it would be utterly forced to say that for each term we even *tacitly know* its list, let alone the codification of the list if there is one. Third, and most importantly, we have arrived once more at a central theme of this paper; the real problem with concepts, and with the conceptual a priori and with analyses, is that they have no demonstrated use. Certainly, given the idealization in question, it is not our knowledge of them (explicit or tacit) which guides our use of terms in ordinary life, where we manifestly do not know *the surprising implications of the extensions of our terms due to the ultimately correct theory of our world.* It is rather our heuristics, our criteria, which guide our use of terms. Whereas the psychological approach to concepts as clusters of heuristics has an explanatory relation to a subject-matter, the philosophical treatment of concepts that goes by way of such highly idealized outputs does not.

The same conclusion emerges on the alternative way of assimilating the point about the surprises concerning the extensions of our terms that the true theory of our world might force. Imagine the following response to the worries just raised.

> We agree that the comprehensive scientific theories we accept can involve surprising consequences for the use of our terms. What is true for users of a term "T" is that under ideal conditions of the more restrictive sort, involving only no distractions, plenty of extra computational ability, and no straightforward irrationality, the users will be disposed to give a verdict for each epistemically possible true total theory of the actual world whether, under that theory, "T" applies in this or that possible case.

This massively multiplies the computational complexity required to generate the relevant list, and so intensifies the worry that there will be no codification of the list. But it also means that the items on the list will themselves be conditional in form; for example, when it comes to the concept of simultaneity, the relevant conditional will look like

> If special relativity holds up in the true total theory of our world then...

So now the obvious problem is this. Thus articulated, our conceptual knowledge leaves us in the following situation: we should make no judgment about any cases with respect to whether they fall in the extension of the term in question or not *until we know the total true theory of our world.* Hence, on this alternative way of going, our main point holds a fortiori; if this is the content of our conceptual knowledge, it not only has no demonstrated use, its lack of usefulness is itself demonstrable.

Jackson and Chalmers might insist that there is indeed one remaining use for talk of a priori or conceptual knowledge here, however idealizing it may be. For they each identify physicalist reductionism with a very distinctive thesis, namely with so-called 'type A' physicalism. This is the thesis that the deliverances of ideal reflection about all relevant cases will in principle support rich enough intermediate a priori premises to provide a derivation of the truths about all that there is, from the truths about what there fundamentally is at the physical level. Chalmers denies this thesis and Jackson now defends it, but they both understand physicalist reductionism in this same way. The fact that the deliverances of ideal reflection may not be codifiable is not crucial here, for that only means that *we cannot carry out the derivation.*

As against this highly theoretical use of the conceptually based a priori, we have only the following plausibility argument. Consider what ideal reflection, on this way of going, is. It is no more than having no distractions, plenty of extra computational ability, and being subject to no straightforward irrationality. Consider the input that ideal reflection takes in, namely the dispositions of use associated with the heuristics and criteria we employ in deciding how to use terms. Now consider the massive output needed to meet the standards of type A physicalism: for each term in our language which is not part of the logical or basic physical vocabulary we need a conditional which specifies, for each epistemically possible total theory of our world, just what the possible world application conditions of the term would be relative to that epistemically possible total theory.

Is it really credible that ideal reflection using the input yields *anything like* this output? Is this not a massive, and extremely adventurous, empirical psychological speculation?

In any case, it was an important line of inquiry to ask whether the externalist semantics of Kripke and Putnam reintroduced something like analysis by the back door. We take ourselves to have argued for a negative judgment on this more restricted point; reference fixing descriptions do not (except in very artificial cases, where there is one, simple and theory-free, criterion) hold a priori, and in arguing for that conclusion we ourselves need not be evidencing an implicit grasp of an analysis.

Total Theory as a Criterion

A theory of Ts, that is, a theory of the things to which the term "T" applies, can be readily re-interpreted as a heuristic for applying the term "T". Simply proceed as follows: first put a variable "X" for every occurrence of "T" in the statement of the theory. You then have a vast open sentence. You now look around the world for the things which satisfy the open sentence. Your heuristic is: apply "T" to *those* things and those things only.

Furthermore, if we abstract away from the actual psychological limitations which make it reasonable to use only smallish subparts of what one believes about

Ts when determining whether we have a T before us, then one's *total* theory of Ts at some given moment should be the theory from which one derives one's T-sensitive heuristic. For suppose you omit something you do in fact believe about Ts; then you are not abiding by the requirement of total evidence, the requirement that you bring all relevant beliefs to bear on the question of whether you have a T before you.

Of course, your total theory of Ts is likely to evolve over time, and so your ideal heuristic will also change over time. What changes here are not the application conditions of the term "T", but your ways of telling whether to apply it. Imagine a child who starts out with the following theory of dogs

> If x is an animal which has one of the characteristic doggish looks, smells, coat textures, etc., and is the offspring of that ilk, then x is a dog.

and then becomes a biology major, adding to her earlier theory of dogs the thesis that

> Dogs are members of the subspecies *Canis lupus familiaris*, distinct from the members of the wider species *Canis lupus* in the following ways: A, B, C.

Obviously, she now has *better* criteria for telling when something is a dog; she is less likely to confuse dogs and grey wolves. Has her concept *dog* changed as a result? Has she moved from a concept with the application conditions determined by the smaller childhood theory to a concept whose application conditions are determined by the larger adult theory? As we noted earlier, there is an everyday use of the term "concept", on which one's concept of Ks is just some contextually relevant part of one's total theory of Ks. In this sense, in certain contexts, it will be right to say that her concept has changed. However, this is manifestly not the philosophers' use of "concept", which ties concepts essentially to conditions of application. Once we have that use in mind, the thing to say is that she has just learnt more about the things the concept *dog* applies to; the extension of the term "dog" could have remained the same for her, even as she acquires more and more knowledge about the nature of the items in that extension.

Suppose instead that there were, earlier and later, two concepts in play; not in the trivial everyday sense of there being two conceptions in play, but in the philosophical sense of two extension-determiners in play. Then the biology major would have made a conceptual error in simply conjoining her later knowledge with her earlier knowledge and treating them as knowledge concerning the same kind of animal. To assume that our total theory determines the application conditions of its concepts, makes what we call "learning" typically count as conceptual confusion.

This is obviously not an objection to the total theory-theory of concepts, so long as we understand that as merely an empirical account of theory-based criteria we use in applying concepts. But if we instead treat the total theory-theory of concepts as an account of the application conditions of concepts, then the urgent objection will be "How is significant learning — specifically learning that narrows or broadens our conception of the range of entities a term is to be applied to — possible?" Moreover, if the total theory-theory account of application conditions were true, someone could not learn a theory in the obvious way; that is, by having it explained to them using words he or she already understands. For the total theory-theory account of application conditions implies that in order to know what the words that occur in the total theory mean, one must already know the total theory.

The total theory-theory account of the application conditions of our terms faces a second objection: it wrongly represents cases of genuine disagreement as cases in which the disputants are talking past each other. Suppose, as David Lewis (1970, 1994) argues, that our total folk theory of mental states represents them as inner sates that occupy certain characteristic causal roles, in particular with respect to other such inner states, sensory input and behavioral output. On the face of it, the folk theory is at odds with behaviorism, which represented being in a mental state merely as exhibiting certain patterned connections between sensory input and behavioral output. The folk theory is even more obviously at odds with epiphenomenalism, which denies that mental states are causes, and with the parallelism of Leibnitz, which keeps the mental and the physical realms causally isolated, but running in harmony with each other, so that they behave as if they were interacting.

But now suppose that we adopt the total theory-theory view of the application conditions of our terms, and accordingly consider the four theories just discussed — folk theory, behaviorism, epiphenomenalism, parallelism — as different total theories that thereby establish different application conditions for mental state terms such as "belief", "desire", "pain" and so on. Now the manifest disagreement about the nature of the mental among the defenders of such theories is lost. There are simply four different term defining theories, and their proponents are simply talking past each other.

The familiar response to both the objection from learning and the objection from disagreement involves a restriction of the theory of Ts to a sub-theory that involves just those criteria that are analytic as opposed to empirical. ("Analytic" in this context can be taken to mean both a priori and necessary.) The thought is that, quite generally, part of the theory ordinary speakers use in applying a term T will involve a priori and necessary criteria, where this entails, crucially, that these criteria are immune to empirical revision, and so should persist throughout any amount of learning. Likewise, disputants with differing total theories of a domain can still genuinely be in dispute over a common subject matter. For that subject matter can be defined by a common shared core of a priori and necessary criteria.

Even setting aside general philosophical skepticism about the analytic/synthetic distinction, the response seems inadequate. It faces a dilemma: are the analytic *criteria* for a term "T" themselves sufficient to fix the application conditions of T, or not? The supposition that they typically are appears to have been empirically embarrassed; that is, the accumulated evidence against what Rosch called the classical view is precisely evidence to the effect that speakers in using terms do not know, and so do not employ, analytic criteria — a priori necessary and sufficient conditions — that fix the application conditions of those terms.

So at best the analytic criteria, in so far as speakers possess them and associate them with terms, will somewhat constrain, but not fix, the application conditions of terms. A number of difficulties now arise on this horn of the dilemma. First, in the case of many of our terms, there is reason to doubt that we actually possess *any* analytic criteria. Consider the biology major who comes to hold the consolidated theory about dogs:

> If x is an animal which has one of the characteristic doggish looks, smells, coat textures, etc. and is the offspring of that ilk then x is a dog. Dogs are members of the subspecies *Canis lupus familiaris*, distinct from the members of the wider species *Canis lupus* in the following ways: A, B, C.

None of this is analytic, i.e. utterly insulated from being overturned by surprising empirical discoveries. As Hilary Putnam made clear long ago, we could discover that the things we call "dogs" are not members of the subspecies *Canis lupus familiaris*, and indeed are not animals, but instead are cleverly disguised bionic robots collecting information about our domestic habits. Moreover, recall the coiffed squirrels that look like Chihuahuas. What actually is analytic for speakers when it comes to the term "dog"?

Second, consider the cases where we might suppose that some criterion possessed by speakers is at least a pretty good candidate to be "analytic". What are we then to make of subsequent learning of empirical matters of fact that intuitively work to restrict the extension of the term? How is that really possible? Suppose for example that for some user of the term "arthritis" the criterion "arthritis is a disorder" is an analytic criterion, and so one that constrains, but does not fully specify, the application conditions of his term "arthritis". Suppose he now learns the synthetic medical fact that arthritis is inflammation of the joints. How exactly *can* he have learned this, given the present theory of the application conditions of terms? Prior to the supposed learning, he associated one analytic criterion with arthritis, namely its being a disorder. So, on the hypothesis that only one's analytic criteria constrain the application conditions of one's terms, he is using a term which is no more specific in its application conditions than the term "disorder" or the phrase "some disorder or other". On the hypothesis that only the analytic criteria one associates with a term can constrain its application conditions, the most he can learn is that some disorder or other is inflammation of the joints. But clearly he is in a position to learn more than this, namely that *arthritis* is inflammation of the joints.

Have we crucially under-estimated what is analytic for our subject? Maybe it is something like "arthritis is the disorder that my speech community refers to by the term "arthritis"". Now perhaps we can explain, consistent with the hypothesis that only one's analytic criteria constrain the application conditions of one's terms, how our subject can learn that specifically *arthritis*, and not just some disorder or other, is inflammation of the joints. One familiar worry for this line of response is that many speakers who use terms do not have views about how their speech community uses those terms. That is not very telling, since a defender of the view that we have analytic criteria, and that only they constrain the application conditions, could say that rational speakers would come to recognize the truth that *arthritis is the disorder that my speech community refers to by the term "arthritis"*, just by understanding that truth.

A more telling objection is this: upon reflection it is obviously a synthetic or empirical matter of fact that one's speech community refers to arthritis by "arthritis". For just how far one's speech community extends is an empirical matter, and, crucially, it is an empirical matter just how good or bad the members of one's speech community are at spelling and pronunciation. It is manifestly not a priori that many of them are not severely impaired when it comes to spelling and speech production. They may, many or most of them, systematically fail to produce the right graphemes and phonemes, and so not refer to arthritis by "arthritis".

These points aside, we should say that our target is not the idea that we have *some* analytic or a priori criteria for applying *some* concepts. Our point is that the empirical literature makes this look like a special kind of case. This is especially so if the generic encoding hypothesis is true. Our earliest forms of generalization are generic in nature, so the little theories we use as criteria for applying terms are from the beginning generic in form. Even as adults, our thought is rife with generics, and we can relatively easily be gotten to evaluate universal generalizations as generics (Leslie et al., 2011). Thus it is very likely that our general criteria for the use of the concepts are generic in form. Here is the crucial observation in this context: the only generics that are plausibly taken to be a priori are those for which the corresponding universal generalization is a priori. These are the sorts of cases we have in mind:

Yellows are brighter than browns.

Primes are divisible by themselves.

Irrational numbers are not expressible in the form m/n where m and n are rational.

Conjunctions entail their separate conjuncts.

These are the special cases; and our point is that even in these special cases it remains a question whether the application conditions of the constituent concepts can be *defined* by way of the backing universal generalizations. (For what it is worth, our best guess is "yes", for some simple mathematical and logical concepts, like *prime* and *conjunction*, and "no", for almost everything else.)

For all these reasons, we should reject any simple identification of the application conditions of the term "T" with the criteria — even the analytic criteria — derived from our best theory of Ts. The theory-theory of *criteria* is tenable; it is the favored psychological theory of concepts, and as we have seen, it meshes with the generic encoding hypothesis better than pure prototype theory; but the theory-theory of application conditions, at least in the simple form just considered, is not tenable.

The question remains as to whether there is some sophisticated tweaking of the theory-theory of application conditions that is tenable. Hence the relevance of the so-called Canberra plan, which we take to be just such a theory.

Lewis on Defining Terms

John Hawthorne and Huw Price coined the term "the Canberra plan" in 1996 to denote what was then a growing tendency among Australian philosophers, several of them then located in Canberra, to apply David Lewis's method of defining terms quite generally as a part of a revival of the program of philosophical analysis. Lewis' own analyses of the concepts of mind (1970), value (1989) and color (1997) are taken to be paradigms of the Canberra plan. Michael Tooley (1987) provided an analysis of causation which can be easily assimilated to the plan. Johnston's (1992) discussion of color is sometimes cited as an example of the plan, since it begins with central beliefs about color that we would find hard to give up, but unlike Lewis's (1997) somewhat similar discussion of color, the general apparatus of the plan is in fact absent. David Braddon-Mitchell and Robert Nola have recently edited an important collection of papers, *Conceptual Analysis & Philosophical Naturalism* (2009), a collection which is on the whole extremely sympathetic to the plan.

David Lewis is rightly viewed as the father of the Canberra plan, and his "Psychophysical and Theoretical Identifications" (1972) and "How to Define Theoretical Terms" (1970) are taken to be its founding documents, with an important addition arising from Lewis's emphasis in "New Work for a Theory of Universals" (1983) and "Putnam's Paradox" (1984) on natural properties as default referents. One way to see Lewis's proposal, and the Canberra plan more generally, is as a very sophisticated revision — one developed over fifteen years — of the general idea that the criteria derived from our theory of Ts are indeed the application conditions of the term "T".

Lewis makes three crucial revisions to the simple version of this idea, the version we have already found to be unworkable. The Canberra plan is the idea that, given these revisions and some associated qualifications, the criteria derived from our common theory of Ts are the application conditions of the term "T".

Precisely what revisions to the simple criteria/conditions identification are required, according to Lewis? First, instead of focusing on analytic criteria, which, even if they exist, are in fact very sparse on the ground and obviously insufficient to determine the application conditions of terms, Lewis resorts to what in various places he calls "platitudes". Thus in "Psychophysical and Theoretical Identifications" he writes

> Collect all the platitudes that you can think of regarding the causal relations of mental states, sensory stimuli, and motor responses . . . Add also all the platitudes to the effect that one mental state falls under another—"toothache is a kind of pain", and the like. Perhaps there are platitudes of other forms as well. Include only platitudes which aie common knowledge among us — everyone knows them, everyone knows that everyone else knows then, and so on. (1972, p. 256)

Notice that the items of common knowledge considered individually need not be a priori; they can be highly informative. As an example, Lewis (1997) has the platitudes concerning *red* include such things as that British postboxes are red.[8] It is clear also that Lewis allows that platitudes can be false, for he immediately adds

> Form the conjunction of these platitudes; or better, form a cluster of them—a disjunction of all conjunctions of most of them. (That way it will not matter if a few are wrong.) This is the postulate of our term-introducing theory (1972, p. 256).

The platitudes embedding a term "T" used by our speech community make up the knowledge or supposed knowledge common to the members of our speech community. They are the relevant things 'that are known' in the sense that we take ourselves to know them, and we take them to be widely known, at least implicitly, throughout our speech community. Since these platitudes are common (supposed) knowledge, a certain kind of informed and reflective thinker can access them from the armchair, i.e., without any *further* empirical investigation.[9] Though some have tried to place further constraints on the Canberra plan, most notably that the platitudes be genuinely a priori or immune from empirical revision, Lewis's own more liberal account is more realistic, given the actual psychological literature. For each of our terms, we have a rich set of relevant things we take 'to be known'; but outside of logic and mathematics there is little that looks a priori.

Second, as the last quotation makes clear, in "Psychophysical and Theoretical identifications" Lewis adopts a cluster theory of application conditions. Instead of requiring that all of the platitudes taken together determine the application conditions of our terms, he assigns that work to a disjunction of conjunctions, each of which contains collections of most of the platitudes. As he notes, this has the attractive consequence that the term "T" can have a reference even when many (though not most) of the platitudes involving it turn out to be false.

Third, in "New Work for a Theory of Universals" and "Putnam's Paradox" Lewis crucially departs from the idea that the reference of our terms is fixed solely by our total set of platitudes involving them. He recognizes that such an account, especially when it takes an appropriately clustered form, may well underdetermine the references of our terms in recognizable ways. Moreover, as Putnam (1980) pointed out, there will be intuitively wrong interpretations of "T" that are nonetheless compatible with making the "T"-involving platitudes true. Thus Lewis is led to endorse an external constraint on the reference of terms — one that turns on a notion that he finds indispensible for ontology, namely the notion of one property or class of individuals being more natural than another property or class of individuals. A property or class is perfectly natural when it is suited to figure in a fundamental ontology; when things share such a property they exhibit a respect of perfect similarity. The more natural a property or class, the more the sharing of a property, or membership in the class, makes for genuine similarity. For example, the property of being green makes for a genuine similarity among the things that have it, and so is more natural than the property of being grue, i.e. the property of being green and observed before the year 2000 or blue and observed after the year 2000, which does not make for a genuine similarity among the things that have it. Moreover, the class of electrons is more natural than the class of particles; the electrons collectively exhibit a higher degree of genuine similarity than does the wider class of particles.

Lewis's external constraint on reference fixing may now be put as follows; the more natural a property or class, the more it works as a default reference-attractor; that is, where there are two interpretations of "T" that do as well in making our "T"-involving platitudes true, or mostly true, we should prefer that interpretation which assigns "T" the more natural property or class. Notice that this way of putting it ranks the satisfaction of most of our "T"- involving platitudes lexically above the appeal to naturalness.

Alternatively, but still in the spirit of Lewis, one could adopt a principle which says that the preferred assignment of an extension to "T" is one that optimizes both the making true of platitudes and the degree of naturalness of the extension of "T". Depending on which way one goes, there will be a difference in what will count as the best analysis of a term or concept. For example, it is now a platitude, among philosophers at least, that justified true belief must somehow be 'de-Gettierized' in order to count as knowledge. If knowledge is a conjunctive property, then the identification of it with the tripartite conjunctive property — true and justified and believed — will hew to the naturalness constraint better than the identification of it with the four part conjunctive property true and justified and believed and de-Gettierized. Of course, the second identification will make one more platitude true, namely the very platitude that amounts to the standard philosophical intuition in Gettier cases. On the lexical ranking version of the naturalness constraint, this latter fact means that the second, and philosophically favored, interpretation wins the day. On the other hand, the optimizing form of the naturalness constraint would treat this as a trade-off situation, and might deliver the result that our term "knowledge" can equally well be associated with either the three-part or the four-part conjunction. (Hereafter, the difference between the lexical and the optimizing forms of the naturalness constraint will not make much difference.)

General Empirical Problems with the Plan

By the Canberra plan we here specifically mean the idea that Lewis has thus outlined a quite general method of analysis. (Variants on this straightforward characterization will be considered as we go.) Lewis himself seemed more cautious than the planners so defined; after all, his own counterfactual analysis of causation does not go by way of the 'Ramsey/Lewis' method. In part, this was because Lewis (1973, 2000) believed that there are two very different forms of causation, causation by 'biff', roughly, by the transference of energy, and causation by absence, which are not in fact *platitudinously* identified as two forms of causation. (As it turns out, some friends of the Canberra plan such as David Liebesman (2011) have chided Lewis on just this point.)

If we follow the planners in viewing Lewis's account as a quite general method of analysis, we then have an account which (modulo considerations of naturalness) tightly connects the application conditions of a term to a certain privileged criterion that users of the term implicitly possess, namely the criterion which is determined by the disjunction of conjunctions of most of the platitudes involving the term. For Lewis, and for the planners more generally, "implicitly possess" now has a definite empirical content. Many or most of the users of the term will recognize the relevant platitudes as such upon appropriate reflection.

One immediate empirical problem with any specific application of the plan is deciding whether there are in fact enough platitudes on offer in order to fix the application conditions of the term in question. Being platitudinous within a speech community is not like being a priori or being analytic. Those latter properties are — at least according to theories which give them any significant role — properties a member of the speech community can in principle recognize claims to have simply by considering the claims themselves. In contrast, being platitudinous within a speech community is a substantial psycho-social property; I am only in a position to treat some claim as a platitude in this sense, and so incorporate it into a Lewis-style analysis, if I both take myself to know it and take it to be widely known, even if only implicitly, throughout my speech community. This latter condition is on its face an empirical belief about the claim's general uptake in my speech community, and there are reasons to think we have a tendency to overestimate how many of our deep convictions are obvious to others. The first worry then is this: for any given term there do seem to be more platitudes connected with it than there are genuine a priori or analytic claims involving the term, so that a platitude analysis initially seems more promising as an account of what determines application conditions; however, it turns out to be an empirical question just which claims are platitudes, and there are reasons to believe we may often be mistaken about such questions. So we need to get out of the armchair and do some empirical social psychology in order to perform our "analysis" by platitudes. So the analysis is not in any real sense a priori. That point could be given an extra twist: since we need to get out of the armchair anyway, why not instead investigate the worldly phenomenon associated with the term? Is that not invariably of more philosophical interest than the investigation of the adventitious *social status* of claims?

Moreover, a claim's being platitudinous within a speech community can be a temporary property of that claim; many of the platitudes in which a term figures can suddenly be given up. Suppose investigators seem to discover that Neptune is not a planet but a massive space ship, a space ship that does not orbit the Sun, but simply occupies positions consistent with that, during just the periods when the space ship is visible from the Earth. The discovery gets widely put about. Should we then have any confidence that there are claims about Neptune which still are platitudinous in the relevant sense? (Recall that it need not be known by the members of my speech community that "Neptune" denotes Neptune; they need not be readers or writers to be speakers, and they may badly mispronounce the names of planets.) Does "Neptune" cease to have a reference in such conditions? It seems not. Reference seems a more persistent feature than the adventitious social status of claims.

A third problem arises from the residual truth in prototype theory, at least when it is restricted to what some philosophers have called "partly recognitional terms". These are terms like "red" or "dog", which we apply at least in part on the basis of paradigmatic or prototypical sensory and perceptual profiles, profiles whose linguistic characterization is a complex empirical psychological matter. We are not saying that an extensionally adequate linguistic characterization of the prototypical look of red or of the prototypical looks of dogs can never be given. The point is that even if we had such characterizations they would not be platitudinous in the defined sense. They would be complex bits of empirical psychological theorizing. The same is true of the very claim that the term "dog" is partly recognitional; philosophers can plausibly speculate that this is so, but it is not a platitude in the relevant sense. It is a bit of tentative, if plausible, psychological theorizing that goes beyond 'what is known' in our speech community. However, if the term "dog" is in fact partly recognitional then it is fairly likely that its extension is at least partly determined by our dispositions to treat certain looks as prototypical dog-looks. The upshot will then be that a crucial determiner of the extension of our term "dog" will not be incorporated into an analysis via platitudes. That method of analysis will thus be susceptible to being systematically thrown off for partly recognitional terms like "dog" or "red". (Notice that this point would hold a fortiori if we departed from Lewis, as Michael Smith does, and restricted the platitudes to those claims that are ostensibly a priori. As observed in footnote 8, Smith agrees.)

Some may say that this just shows that philosophers have no business analyzing partly recognitional terms. However, many terms of peculiarly philosophical interest may well turn out to be partly recognitional. Color terms are an obvious example. The attributive adjectives "good" and "bad" may be partly recognitional. You need to have visual recognitional capacities to identify a good tennis swing as such. You need to have visual recognitional capacities to identify any badlooking thing as such, including morally-badlooking things such as the torturing of a cat. And as Albert Michotte's (1963) work reflects, there are a range of recognizable perceptual prototypes for causation, at least of the biff variety. Even six-month-old infants are sensitive to this profile, as Alan Leslie and Stephanie Keeble (1987) demonstrated.

Generics and the Plan

The Canberra plan, inspired by Lewis's account of the definition of terms, proposes a general method for the analysis of concepts: identify the term or terms which express the target concept, collect the platitudes involving the term that expresses the target concept, and then find the most natural satisfier of at least most of those platitudes. (If there is no satisfier of most of the platitudes, the term will then be empty.) Although the planners confine their attention to philosophically interesting concepts, there is, in fact, no such in-principle limitation built into the plan. If the plan works, then it should work quite generally. If it fails quite generally, then absent special pleading for the concepts of philosophical interest, we should expect it to fail in the philosophical cases as well.

One kind of special pleading we regard as very unpersuasive, given the psychological evidence, is that in philosophy our platitudes are invariably universals and not generics. That would be remarkable if true. "Events have causes", "true justified belief is knowledge", "lying is wrong", "people choose those acts that seem to them, given their beliefs, to advance the satisfaction of their desires" — these generics are platitudes, but the various attempts to find universal truths backing each of them has not resulted in anything that is likewise platitudinous.

Only if the plan works quite generally for concepts in whatever subject area we choose can it be seriously put forward as a method of conceptual analysis. *Concept* and *conceptual analysis* are topic neutral or quasi-formal notions that apply across all subject matters. The moral is that if the plan fails for many subject matters then whatever the plan is achieving in the philosophical cases it is not the analysis of concepts.

The plan does fail quite generally when interpreted as a philosophical analysis of concepts in any interesting sense of "concepts". First, let's set aside an uninteresting sense. As noted earlier, a term of the form "concept of Ts" is often used to pick out contextually relevant part of someone's or some group's conception of Ts, as in "their concept of men is so old-school". A conception of Ts can be articulated or explicitly set out, but this is not analysis in any interesting sense, nor is it a distinctively philosophical enterprise, even when the term T is widely employed in philosophy. The articulation of conceptions is a matter for history, psychology and sociology; which is not to say that philosophers are to be prevented from pursuing such matters.

Suppose instead that we understand concepts as terms-in-use. If we want to know the extension of a concept understood as a term-in-use, we should consult the lexicographer, who has studied the relevant empirical questions about the extensions of our terms. Still, the plan might be put forward as a general account of what makes it the case that any given term in use has the (possible worlds) extension that it does, namely that the extension is determined by the most natural satisfier of the platitudes which involve the term. But now we face problems. Terms in use combine compositionally to give more complex terms in use. However, many of our platitudes are generic in form, and the structure of generics systematically interferes with compositionality. Furthermore, the requirement of naturalness and the structure of platitudinous generics can work together to assign manifestly incorrect extensions to terms.

The same points apply when we understand concepts by way of the substantial conception; that is, as items speakers grasp and which themselves determine (modulo considerations of naturalness) the extensions of our terms. Concepts, so understood, combine compositionally. Yet many of our platitudes are generic in form, and the structure of generics systematically interferes with compositionality. Moreover, the requirement of naturalness and the structure of platitudinous generics can work together to assign manifestly incorrect extensions to terms. Finally, when the plan relies on disjunctions of conjunctions of platitudes in order to insulate itself from the possibility of platitudes turning out to be false, it thereby breaks with another requirement on conceptual analysis, namely that good conceptual analyses should underwrite inferences like

Bonnie is a mare

to

Bonnie is a horse.

that is, the rare inferences where we *do* seem to possess (what looks like) an a priori justification for proceeding from the first belief to the second.

Generic Platitudes that Hold Only in the Minority of Cases

There can be generic platitudes that are true even though they hold of a minority of the very kind those generics concern. "Lying is wrong" holds true, and may even be platitudinous, in a world in which people are quite honest and mostly lie *righty*, say to crazed axe-men at the door. Whenever we have generic platitudes that hold of a minority of cases, there is the likelihood that a platitude analysis will produce failures of compositionality. This is most easily seen in the case of sex-typed generics, but the point is quite general.

The possible world extension of the concept *female lion* should be a specific compositional function of the possible world extension of the concept *female* and the possible world extension of the concept *lion*. In particular, the concept *female lion* is intersective; that is, its extension in a possible world is the intersection of the extension of the concept *female* in that world with the extension of the concept *lion* in that world. (Contrast attributively qualified concepts like *small lion*, which though compositional are not intersective in this sense.) The Canberra plan applied to these three concepts *female*, *lion* and *female lion* will generate the required result that the concept *female lion* is intersective only if the platitudes concerning *female lion* are a union of the platitudes concerning *lion* and the platitudes concerning *female*.

Since being a platitude is a substantial psycho-social property there is no general guarantee that this is so. If it is not so, then there will be a failure to find the right kind of compositionality for the concept *female lion*. And the point will generalize for every intersective concept for which the platitudes do not align in the proper way. This kind of problem, if and when it arises, has always been taken to be a disabling objection to a philosophical theory of concepts. Recall that Fodor (1998) used this kind of objection against psychological theories; although we think it was misplaced there, the objection is disabling if it applies to a proposed theory of the application conditions of our concepts. We want concepts to combine compositionally, since the (possible worlds) extensions of our terms combine compositionally and concepts are, minimally, extension-determiners.

The generic encoding hypothesis suggests one way in which the right alignment of platitudes might not be in place. From a very young age, we are interested in what psychologists call "basic-level" kinds, kinds such as *dogs, lions, tigers, tables,* and *chairs.* Basic-level kinds can be contrasted with superordinate kinds (e.g., *mammals, furniture*), and subordinate kinds (e.g., *Bengal tigers, formal dining tables*). The first count nouns we learn usually denote basic-level kinds, and even into adulthood, they are the first terms we supply to answer the question, "what is this?" (e.g., if shown a picture of Princeton University's mascot, and asked what it is, one would naturally reply "a tiger", rather than "a mammal" or "a Bengal tiger"). Our knowledge concerning such kinds — knowledge passed on to us in childhood in generic form — is likewise encoded in as generic generalizations.

When taken collectively for each such kind, this mostly generic knowledge forms perhaps the best candidate to be the platitudes applicable to the kind. After all, we not only 'know' such things but we 'know' that our parents and teachers 'know' them. It would be very implausible to suggest that we only have a concept of a basic-level kind like the kind lion when and if we arrive at exceptionless generalizations concerning it, and then come to know that these exceptionless generalizations are widely known in our speech community. For one thing, the exceptionless generalizations will not be widely known in our speech community.

So our platitudes for such basic-level kinds are, many of them, generic in form. Moreover, in the case of animal kinds, some of these generic platitudes involve properties that are only had by one sex. These include generics that describe methods of reproduction, such as "ducks lay eggs" and "horses give live birth", but also characteristic salient physical traits that happen to be had only by members of one sex, such as "lions have manes", "deer have antlers" or "peacocks have fabulous blue-green tails". As emphasized earlier, these generics are just not plausibly interpreted as contextually restricted universals respectively applying to female ducks and horses, or male lions, deer or peacocks. Nor, as noted above, are they encoded as sex-restricted generics such as "male lions have manes" (e.g., Cimpian, Gelman et al., 2010; Leslie, 2007, 2008, Khemlani et al., 2009). Rather, these are generics that are true despite there being a substantial number of exceptions to the generalization. These sex-typed generics are understood and accepted by preschool children; and plausibly are accepted as platitudes even at this age (Brandone et al., 2012). Surely, if anything is a platitude, *lions have manes* is a platitude.

We now have the following concrete situation. The platitudes for the concept *female lion* are not a union of the platitudes for the concept *female* and the platitudes for the concept *lion*. Even though it is a platitude that *lions have manes*, it is not a platitude that *female lions have manes*. Some of our fellow speakers of the language do not regard this as true because they know that female lions do not have manes; others do not regard it as true because they do not know whether it is the male lions or the female lions that have manes. The platitudes associated with an intersective concept such as *female lion* thus are not given by the union of the platitudes associated with *female* and the platitudes associated with *lion*. Note that if platitudes took universal rather than generic form, this particular issue would not arise, for if the only platitudes associated with *lion* were ones that were satisfied by *all lions*, and similarly for *female*, then the platitudes associated with *female lion* could consist of the union of these platitudes. However, it is simply not empirically plausible that our platitudes here take universal rather than generic form.

What if *only male lions have manes* was also a platitude? It is not clear how this could help. The point is simply that *lions have manes* is a platitude associated with *lions* but not with *female lions*, no matter what other platitudes may be also associated with the relevant concepts; therefore the platitudes associated with an intersective concept are not the union of the platitudes associated with both concepts. Further, it is much less plausible that *only male lions have manes* is a platitude, certainly it need not be. (In fact, a recent study found that some twenty percent of adult participants were ignorant of this fact, and a full third did not know that only male goats have horns and only female kangaroos have pouches

(Leslie et al. 2011).) We can't plausibly maintain that these adults who do not know that it is the male lions that have manes therefore do not have the concept lion, and hence do not have the concept female lion.[10]

What then can the friend of the Canberra plan say in order to defend the idea that it is a general method of conceptual analysis?[11]

Clustering to the Rescue?

There is one feature of the Canberra plan that might be thought to be helpful here. Lewis proposed that we 'cluster' our platitudes; that is, we should take the extension-determiner for a term not to be the totality of platitudes which govern it, since this would make the term empty if even one platitude was false, but rather to be a disjunction of conjunctions, each disjunct of which contains most of the platitudes, with each platitude appearing in at least one disjunct. So if there are three platitudes, "P1", "P2" and "P3", governing a term "T" we have in effect the claim that the possible worlds extension of "T" is fixed in the following way

A as it is in W satisfies "T" if and only if either

  (i) the open sentence formed from "P1 and P2" by substituting the variable "X" for "T" throughout is true of A as it is in W, *or*
  (ii) the open sentence formed from "P1 and P3" by substituting the variable "X" for "T" throughout is true of A as it is in W, *or*
  (iii) the open sentence formed from "P2 and P3" by substituting the variable "X" for "T" throughout is true of A as it is in W.

Thus Lewis says that all his account requires is that the platitudes be mostly true of the target extension, which on the famous Lewisian account of adverbs (1975) amounts to the claim that all that is required is that most of the platitudes be true of the target extension. (We confess that we cannot make out anything helpful here in the alternative suggestion, sometimes heard, to the effect that *each* platitude should be true of most of the items in the extension. This fails for the same reason that accounts that assimilate generics to "most"-statements fail. For example, the platitude that lions have manes is not 'mostly true' of lions; most lions lack manes, since only *typically developing adult male* lions have manes.)

The relevance of Lewis's clustering proposal is this: clustering allows us to effectively shed or neutralize platitudes that turn out to be problematic, and thus avoid having them constrain the extensions of the relevant terms. Platitudes can be problematic if they are false, and this is what motivated the clustering account in the first place; for not every false platitude makes for an empty concept. Perhaps platitudes can also be problematic if they interfere with the compositional derivation of intersective concepts from their components. Only one of the disjuncts —itself a conjunction — needs to hold for the disjunction to hold. So perhaps we can effectively neutralize the impact of the problematic platitude that lions have manes.

A moment's reflection will show that to resort to clustering here is to jump from the frying pan into the fire. First, we need not change our concept *female lion* by getting very interested in female lions, thereby coming to have more platitudinous knowledge of them than we do of lions in general. But when we do this, the disjunction of conjunctions of platitudes associated with female lions will change. Is this not a change in concept, according to the cluster view (just as it is a change in concept on the non-cluster view)? Certainly the extension determining cluster itself has changed.

Second, a single platitude or two may be all that is holding the possible world extensions of two distinct concepts apart, keeping them disjoint as it were. Such is the case, perhaps, with the concepts *Siberian tiger* and *Bengal tiger*, where the relevant true platitudes might be as follows

For Siberian Tigers

P4: Xs are predominantly located in or derive from the territory surrounding Siberia

P5 : Xs are striped

P6 : Xs are large cats

For Bengal Tigers

P7: Xs are predominantly located in or derive from the territory surrounding Bengal.

P8: Xs are striped

P9: Xs are large cats

The 'clustering' approach now produces chaos. Bengal tigers in any possible world will satisfy a disjunction of three distinct conjuncts each containing two of P4, P5, and P6, since they satisfy P5 and P6. Yet no Bengal tigers are Siberian tigers. Siberian tigers in any possible world will satisfy a disjunction of three distinct conjuncts each containing two of P7, P8 and P9, since they satisfy P8 and P9. Yet no Siberian tigers are Bengal tigers.

What if we add this last observation to the list of platitudes; what if we add *Siberian tigers are not Bengal tigers* to the lists? Even this will not help. It is, in effect, a numbers game; for suppose we also add one more platitude that Siberian and Bengal tigers 'agree' on, say "Xs are ferocious". Now there will be five platitudes associated with each concept, and so there will be a disjunct that contains only the three platitudes that both Siberian and Bengal tigers both satisfy. This disjunct will suffice to give the two concepts the same extension, despite it being a *platitude* that they do not share the same extension.

As an elaboration of this point, let us return for a moment to the case of female lions. Suppose we were able to deal with the earlier difficulty about compositionality by insisting (implausibly) that platitudes must be universals, not generics. The set of platitudes associated with *female lion* could then be the union of the platitudes associated with *female* and with *lion*. But consider the possibility that there are *more* platitudes associated with *lion* than with *female*. Then there will be a disjunct that contains *only* platitudes associated with *lion*, and none with *female*. Clearly, male lions will satisfy this disjunct, and so we have the result that male lions fall in the extension of *female lion*.[12]

It is important to notice that this problem does not lie specifically with the idea that a given disjunct should contain *most* of the platitudes. Even if we raise the requirement to, say, 90% of the platitudes, we need only consider a context in which there are nine times as many platitudes associated with *lion* than with *female*. (This could be the result of a case of extreme female sequestration, across the entire animal kingdom.)

A final difficulty with clustering may now be noted. Suppose we persuade ourselves that there is an a priori and necessary connection between two concepts; given clustering, how can we be sure that the a priori and necessary status of this connection will be preserved? Perhaps a plausible case is the concept *mare* and the concept *horse*, so that it is a priori and necessary that if x is a mare then x is a horse. Intuitively, if anything is due to concepts, this is due to the concept *mare* and the concept *horse*, and so the relevant platitude "if x is a mare then x is a horse" should be part of the roster of platitudes for both concepts. But depending on how many platitudes there are for mares, something, say a perfect inorganic simulacrum of a mare, can fall under *most* of the platitudes on the roster for the concept mare, even though it is not a horse. How then can it be a priori and necessary that if x is a mare then x is a horse?

It should be noted that that many of these objections would still apply even if we limited the platitudes to prima facie a priori claims, as Smith (1994) suggests. Clustering would thus appear to be an inherently problematic strategy. But then how do we avoid the unwanted result that a single false platitude makes the target term empty?

Striking Property Generics and the Requirement of Naturalness

Earlier, we indicated that we wanted to consider some variants of Lewis's view that might be considered further 'tweaks' to which a particular planner might be attracted. Consider the following variant on Lewis's stated theory, one which does not in general associate application conditions with concepts, but only gives a criterion for deciding when one competing account is to be preferred to another: where we have two or more competitors we should prefer, other things being equal, the account that vindicates *more* of the relevant platitudes. This criterion would generate a preference even in a case in which almost all of the relevant platitudes are false. In such cases, we believe Lewis would have said that there is no good account of the extension determiner of the concept. So it is a significant weakening of Lewis's actual view. Consider also the following significant strengthening of Lewis's view: the extension-determiner expressed by a term encompasses almost all of the platitudes associated with the term. Both the weakening and the strengthening of Lewis's view run into difficulties when we see that many of our platitudes are generic in form, and then come to understand the import of generic platitudes.

Recall that some generics, such as "sharks attack bathers," "manipulators are evil" and "mosquitoes carry West Nile virus", can be true even though very few members of the kind in question have the property.[13] Such cases arise if the property in question makes its bearers dangerous. One tempting first response is to suppose that, if a property has this feature, then a generic is true if just *some* members of the kind have the property in question. However this is too simple: consider "fish attack bathers" and "mammals maul children". Some great white, oceanic white-tipped, bull and tiger sharks attack bathers, and some pit-bulls maul children, yet the more general generics concerning fish and mammals do not seem right.

Leslie (2007, 2008, in press c) proposes that these sorts of generics are only true if the kind in question is a *good predictor* of the striking property, where a kind is a good predictor if its members are *typically disposed* to have the property in question, even if they do not manifest it. "Fish attack bathers" is false because trout and salmon and sea bass have no such disposition. However, we do not often have access to detailed information about unmanifested dispositions; so the question then arises, how do we in fact select a kind to be the locus of a 'dangerous-making property generic' in the absence of this sort of information? A plausible hypothesis is that, by default, we generalize the property to the basic-level kind. These kinds make up the psychologically privileged level of the subjective taxonomy, which includes kinds such as *sharks*, *tigers*, and *lions*. This pattern of generalization allows us, by default, to generalize these properties to kinds that can be easily and efficiently identified (see Leslie, 2008, in press c for more details). However, there is no guarantee that such kinds will not be overly inclusive; their members may not, in fact, be typically disposed to have the property in question. For example, consider "sharks attack bathers". It is plausible to suppose that this generic is, in fact, false, since arguably only great white, oceanic white-tip, bull and tiger sharks have this disposition. This is plausibly a case in which our default practice of generalizing to the basic-level kind leads us to over-generalize the property.

It would, however, seem to be a platitude that sharks attack bathers. It certainly satisfies the intuitive test, namely that it is natural to say, in an authoritative tone, "*it is widely known* that sharks attack bathers!" In fact, of course, this is one of those cases that Lewis deliberately allowed for, a case in which a platitude, something supposedly widely known, is false. It is only the great white sharks, the oceanic white-tip sharks, the tiger sharks and the bull sharks that ever attack bathers; for example, basking sharks, whale sharks and megamouth sharks feed only on plankton. But this is not widely known, and so not a platitude. Suppose then, for purposes of argument, that great white sharks possess all the properties platitudinously predicated of sharks. After all they are sharks, and clustering aside, that is how you get to count as a shark on the Lewis view. Thus the great white sharks satisfy more of the platitudes on the roster for the concept shark, since they *do* attack bathers. So we now have an unintuitive result, namely that the extension of "sharks" is great white sharks. (By now it should be clear that "unintuitive" in such contexts does not mean: at odds with the proper analysis of the concept *shark*. It just means hard to believe, even given the circumstances imagined.)

Alternatively, suppose that there is one platitude on the roster of the concept *shark* that great white sharks do not satisfy. Then we indeed might have a tie, where both sharks and great white sharks each satisfy all but one of the platitudes on the roster of the concept *shark*, a different one in each case. Then the third distinctive feature of Lewis's account of how to define terms will kick in; when we have such a tie we should take the extension of the term to be the more natural set of things that satisfies the platitudes.

As we noted earlier, for Lewis a property or class is perfectly natural when it is suited to figure in a fundamental ontology; when things share such a property or are in such a class they exhibit at least one respect of perfect similarity. When we depart from the perfectly natural, the controlling rule is that the more natural a property or class, the more the sharing of a property or membership in the class makes for genuine similarity. So the class of electrons is more natural than the class of particles; the electrons collectively exhibit a higher degree of genuine similarity than does the wider class of fundamental particles. Likewise, the great white sharks exhibit a higher degree of genuine similarity than the sharks.

Thus, if we apply Lewis's criterion of naturalness to break the tie between sharks and great white sharks in the case where each satisfy all but one of the platitudes on the roster of the concept *shark*, we then get the unwanted result that the extension of "sharks" is the great white sharks. That unwanted result is the upshot of an unavoidable fact about platitudes, namely that just what the available platitudes are at a time is a contingent psycho-social matter, and a typical feature of naturalness, namely that a so-called "basic-level" kind like *shark* is less natural than its sub-kinds such as *megamouth shark* and *great white shark*.

It may even be possible to generate this sort of unwanted result simply from the facts about naturalness alone. Suppose we have a kind, namely *Panthera tigris*, more typically known as the kind tiger, and suppose that this kind satisfies *all* the platitudes governing the term "tiger". Depending on how the facts of genetics stand there may be a more natural sub-kind or sub-class of the kind tiger, which also satisfies all the platitudes in question. Here is a way of looking for it; identify some mutant tigers of a very distinctive sort, and consider the kind or class that includes just the tigers that do not have that mutation. It will be very likely that this sub-kind or sub-class exhibits more genetic and phenotypic similarity among its members than does the kind tiger. To take a concrete example; consider the albinos, mutant tigers with a homozygous occurrence of a recessive gene that controls coat color, which has the effect of producing a stripe-free white coat. The albinos lie among the tigers, but thanks to the generic character of platitudes like "tigers have stripes" this does not prevent the kind tiger or the class of tigers from satisfying *all* the platitudes. But now consider the non-albino tigers, they may also satisfy all the platitudes, for the fact that some tigers are albinos is a relatively recherché fact, and so need not be a platitude. The non-albino tigers are not only more phenotypically similar among themselves than are the tigers; they are genetically more similar among themselves than the tigers. The non-albino tigers are, accordingly, the more natural class. Applying the Canberra plan, we get the unwanted result that our term "tiger" applies just to the non-albino tigers.[14]

We could go on in much more detail, but perhaps enough has been said to show that the Canberra plan, understood as a generalization or natural variant on Lewis on defining terms, is not really viable as a method of conceptual analysis.

There is another, much more deflationary way of construing the interesting work the advocates of the plan have done on color, mind and value; on this construal the work has been very useful, but it is not the implementation of a recognizable successor to conceptual analysis, let alone a newfangled method of conceptual analysis. It is just the humdrum, old-fashioned method of starting our inquiry with what we happen to take ourselves to know or firmly believe. That method is more or less compulsory anyway, and its credentials do not improve if it is further adorned with implausible aspirations to thereby provide an analysis, or explain the appearance of the a priori.

Conclusion

There are strong grounds for doubting that even when one takes into account all the heuristics and guiding theoretical commitments that we employ in applying a term "T" they will determine the conditions of application of the concept we express by "T". Indeed, there is good reason to doubt that when one takes all the heuristics that we employ in applying "T" into account, *and* all the facts about the relative naturalness of the extensions that could be captured by those, then all of this together will determine the conditions of application of the concept we express by "T". Just this emerged in the discussion of the Canberra plan.

Furthermore, once we assimilate the relevant psychology and philosophy, the following picture presents itself as plausible overview of the subject area that goes under the title of "concepts".

1. There are terms, both linguistic and mental. Terms *somehow* respectively get to be about individuals, classes, kinds, properties, etc. They *somehow* come to have these worldy items as their extensions. The unsolved mystery of reference or intentionality remains; we have shed no positive light upon it, but have only tried to rule out certain popular conceptions of how it works. Perhaps one crucial determiner of reference is the acceptance correction by others whom we regard as speaking our common tongue, so that we can then cull hopeless hypotheses about the reference of our common terms, and refine useful ones.

2. As a matter of psychological fact, subjects associate criteria with a term; these are heuristics, including perceptual prototypes, and guiding theoretical commitments, which put us in a good position to recognize many items in the extension of the term. These heuristics may be effective only in certain restricted situations, and the guiding theoretical commitments may be, even in large part, false.

3. Even when they are true, the guiding theoretical commitments are likely to be generic in form, allowing for many exceptions which are not counterexamples. (The generic encoding hypothesis.)

4. The psychologically real analog of Frege's notion of sense, namely the set of criteria a subject associates with a term, does not determine the reference of terms. It does not guarantee the compositionality of our concepts. It does not make for publicity, for different speakers using the same term with the same extension can employ different theories and different heuristics as guides.

5. The psychologically real analog of sense may serve to explain how it is that terms with the same possible word extensions can have different cognitive values for a given speaker. It can be informative to learn that vixens are female foxes because it unites the criteria we use for "vixen" with those we use for "female foxes".

6. The method of cases, the method of trying to articulate what we know in using a term by considering how we are inclined to apply it to real and merely possible cases, is at best a way of articulating our criteria. It is not a method for analyzing concepts, as is shown by the fact that our reaction to cases is typically explained by our criteria, and not by some supposed grasp of the application conditions of our concepts.

7. There is no empirically explanatory need to postulate concepts, understood as abstract entities (i) which encode the conditions of application of our terms and (ii) grasp of which guides in the use of our terms. Talk of grasping a concept is either an unhelpful metaphor or a description of a supernatural theory of language use, one rendered otiose by the actual empirical psychology of language use.

8. There is accordingly no good reason to think that there are concepts in any substantial philosophical sense. There are terms, public languages,

the extensions of terms, and criteria for applying terms. There is the something or other that gives terms their particular extensions, and hence their conditions of application. But this something or other is never a concept in the substantial philosophical sense. Concepts in the substantial sense have no demonstrated use.

Notes

1. Special thanks to Shamik Dasgupta, Frank Jackson, Joshua O'Rourke, Nathaniel Tabris, and Gideon Rosen for helpful comments on an earlier draft.
2. Preparation of this article was supported by NSF grant BCS-1226942, awarded to Leslie.
3. 1967, p 22.
4. See, for example, Ramsey (1992), Stich and Weinberg (2001), Laurence and Margolis (2003), Sytsma (2010), and Banicki (2012).
5. It is interesting here to consider the findings of Armstrong, Gleitman, and Gleitman (1983), who found some of the typicality effects even for concepts such as *odd number*. This shows, of course, that typicality effects are *compatible* with representing necessary and sufficient conditions. However, the crucial point is that in the case of concepts such as *odd number* we have independent reason for supposing that we represent necessary and sufficient conditions — namely that we (i.e., typical competent adult users of the term "odd number") can articulate what they are. There is no corresponding case to be made for the majority of concepts. Thus while the in-principle compatibility point concerning typicality effects and necessary and sufficient conditions is illustrated by Armstrong et al.'s findings, it does not address the fact that, for most concepts, we simply have no reason to suppose that typical, competent adults represent and exploit necessary and sufficient conditions.
6. Sometimes "theory-theory" is reserved for the specific view that our concepts, including young children's concepts, are *exactly like* scientific theories. We follow many in the field by using the term more inclusively.
7. It is, perhaps, rather telling that psychological experiments concerned with concepts almost invariably use the generic form to articulate conceptual knowledge.
8. Some friends of the Canberra plan, such as Michael Smith (1994), reject this liberal attitude to platitudes. For Smith, platitudes must be "prima facie a priori", i.e. such that if they are true then their truth is not an empirical matter. However this means that the plan will often fail, since, as we have seen, in general there are just not enough prima facie a priori truths around to determine the application conditions of our terms. Indeed, as in the case of space not in fact being Euclidean makes clear, empirical inquiry is itself highly relevant to the question of whether it is the case that if S is true then its truth is an a priori or instead an empirical matter. We often simply cannot imagine what would undermine our central beliefs. So, the category of what we can legitimately take to be prima facie a priori will shrink as we become more and more aware of the inter-animation of the putatively a priori and the empirical. In fact, Smith's own conclusion is that the plan does fail in both of the cases he is concerned with, namely the analysis

of "red" and in the analysis of "right". And he provides a plausible diagnosis of this failure; in such cases competence with the term consists in part in a disposition to use it to classify cases correctly on the basis of certain patterns of features. There is no reason to believe that there is any prima facie a priori encapsulation of the relevant patterns.

9. Although Lewis drops the term "platitudes" in "Reduction of Mind" (1994) he crucially still talks in terms of putative common knowledge. He writes "We have a very extensive shared understanding of how we work mentally. Think of it as a theory: FOLK PSYCHOLOGY. It is common knowledge among us; but it is tacit, as our grammatical knowledge is. We can tell which particular predictions and explanations conform to its principles, but we cannot expound those principles systematically" (p. 56). Our use of "platitudes" throughout is meant to conform simply to this idea that we can articulate the relevant putative common knowledge in which our terms are entangled, and then use it to define our terms. In fact, Lewis (1997) seems to persist with a platitude-based analysis of color terms.

10. We have argued that the platitudes associated with intersective concepts do not always include the union of the platitudes associated with the component concepts. A related point that Jerry Fodor (e.g., 1998) has often made is that the platitudes associated with the complex concept will also not usually be *exhausted* by this union of platitudes. That is, it could be a platitude that *black bulls are dangerous* without it is being a platitude that *black things are dangerous* or its being a platitude that *bulls are dangerous*.

11. One response to failures of compositionality due to the widespread application of one's favored technique of analysis is instead to identify a base of uncompounded terms, apply one's favored technique of analysis only to them and then simply let the syntactical methods of combination by which the language generates compound terms determine the extensions of compound terms. This, however, would be an unhappy way to patch up the failures of compositionality due to widespread application of the Canberra plan. First, it is likely that many terms in any plausible base will be partly recognitional terms like "red" and "dog" and "cause", for which the platitude-based analysis is ill-suited because of the reasons noted earlier. Second, many of the target terms of philosophical analysis are unlike "physical cause" and more like "free will" in being themselves complex though not simply intersective combinations (or any other simple combination) of their respective components (here "free" and "will").

12. Note that it will not help to insist, implausibly, that each concept have the same number of platitudes associated with it. For consider then the complex concept *adult female lion*. By assumption there is the same number of platitudes associated with all three concepts, so each concept contributes one third of the total number of platitudes. But then again there will be a disjunction that contains only platitudes associated with *adult* and *lion,* and none with *female.* Adult male lions will again satisfy this disjunction.

13. Far and away, most cases of manipulation involve parents and children; you get to count as a manipulator by manipulating a bit now and then, but the overwhelming majority of parents and children who manipulate a bit now and then are not evil. The same holds for lawyers, politicians and the police.

168 / Mark Johnston and Sarah-Jane Leslie

14. For an analog of this sort of point in the case of Lewis's analysis of the concept of personal identity, see Johnston (2010), pp. 79–80 "On the Unhelpfulness of Reference Magnetism".

References

Ahn, W., Kim, N. S., Lassaline, M. E., & Dennis, M. J. (2000). "Causal Status As A Determinant of Feature Centrality." *Cognitive Psychology*, 41, 361–416.

Armstrong, S.L., Gleitman, L.R., & Gleitman, H. (1983). "What Some Concepts Might Not Be." *Cognition*, 13, 263–308.

Banicki, K. (2012). "Connective Conceptual Analysis and Psychology." *Theory and Psychology*, 22 (3), 310–323.

Barner, D., Chow, K., & Yang, S. (2009). "Finding One's Meaning: A Test of the Relation Between Quantifiers and Integers in Language Development."*Cognitive Psychology*, 58, 195–219.

Bealer, G. (1987). "The Philosophical Limits of Scientific Essentialism." *Philosophical Perspectives*, 1, 289–365.

Boghossian, P. (2003). "Blind Reasoning." *Proceedings of the Aristotelian Society, Supplementary volume*, 77, 225–248.

Braddon-Mitchell, D., & Nola, R. (2009). *Conceptual Analysis and Philosophical Naturalism*. Cambridge, MA: MIT Press.

Brandone, A., Cimpian, A., Leslie, S. J., & Gelman, S. A. (2012). "Do Lions Have Manes? For Children, Generics are About Kinds, Not Quantities." *Child Development*, 83(2), 423–433.

Brandone, A., Gelman, S. A., & Hedglen, J. (submitted). "Young Children's Intuitions about the Truth Conditions and Implications of Novel Generics."

Carey, S. (1985). *Conceptual Change in Childhood*. Cambridge, MA: MIT Press.

Carey, S. (2009). *The Origin of Concepts*. New York: Oxford University Press.

Carlson, G.N., & Pelletier, F.J. (1995). *The Generic Book*. Chicago: Chicago University Press.

Chalmers, D. (1996). *The Conscious Mind*. New York: Oxford University Press.

Chalmers, D., & Jackson, F. (2001). "Conceptual Analysis and Reductive Explanation." *The Philosophical Review*, 110, 315–361.

Cimpian, A., Brandone, A. C., & Gelman, S. A. (2010). "Generic Statements Require Little Evidence for Acceptance But Have Powerful Implications." *Cognitive Science*, 34(8), 1452–1482.

Cimpian, A., Gelman, S. A., & Brandone, A. C. (2010). "Theory-Based Considerations Influence The Interpretation of Generic Sentences." *Language and Cognitive Processes*, 25(2), 261–276.

Cohen, A. (1996). *Think Generic: The Meaning and Use of Generic Sentences*. Ph.D. dissertation, Carnegie Mellon University.

Dahl, O. (1985). *Tense and Aspect Systems*. Oxford: Blackwell.

Davidson, D. (1967). "Truth and Meaning." *Synthese*, 17, 304–323.

Devitt, M. (2005). "There is No A Priori." In E. Sosa and M. Steup (eds.), *Contemporary Debates in Epistemology*, pp. 105–115. Cambridge, MA: Blackwell Publishers.

Fodor, J. A. (1998). *Concepts: Where Cognitive Science Went Wrong*. Oxford: Oxford University Press.

Fodor, J. A., Garrett, M. F., Walker, E., & Parkes, C. (1980). "Against definitions." *Cognition*, 8, 263–367.

Fodor, J. A., & Lepore, E. (2002). *The Compositionality Papers.* New York: Oxford University Press.

Frege, G. (1956). "The Thought: A Logical Inquiry." *Mind*, 65, 289–311

Geach, P.T. (1967). "Identity." *Review of Metaphysics*, 21, 3–12.

Gelman, S. A. (2003). *The Essential Child: Origins of Essentialism in Everyday Thought.* New York: Oxford University Press.

Gelman, S. A. (2010). "Generics as A Window onto Young Children's Concepts." In F. J. Pelletier (ed.), *Kinds, Things, and Stuff: The Cognitive Side of Generics and Mass Terms* (New Directions in Cognitive Science v. 12.), pp. 100–123. New York: Oxford University Press.

Gelman, S.A. & Raman, L. (2003). "Preschool Children use Linguistic form Class and Pragmatic Cues to Interpret Generics." *Child Development*, 74, 308–325.

Gelman, S. A., Star, J., & Flukes, J. (2002). "Children's Use of Generics in Inductive Inferences." *Journal of Cognition and Development*, 3, 179–199.

Gopnik, A., & Meltzoff, A.N. (1997). *Words, thoughts, and theories.* Cambridge, MA: MIT Press.

Graham, S. A., Nayer, S. L., & Gelman, S. A. (2011). "Two-Year-Olds use the Generic/Non-Generic Distinction to Guide Their Inferences About Novel Kinds." *Child Development*, 82, 493–507.

Harman, G. (1974). "Meaning and semantics." In M. K. Munitz and P. K. Unger (eds.), *Semantics and Philosophy*, pp. 1–16. New York: NYU Press.

Harman, G. (1975). "Language, Thought, and Communication." In K. Gunderson (ed.), *Language, Mind, and Knowledge: Minnesota Studies in the Philosophy of Science* VII, pp. 279–98. Minneapolis, MN: University of Minnesota Press.

Hawthorne, J., & Price, H. (1996). "How to Stand Up For Non-Cognitivists." *Australasian Journal of Philosophy*, 74 (2), 275–292.

Hollander, M. A., Gelman, S. A., & Star, J. (2002). "Children's Interpretation of Generic Noun Phrases." *Developmental Psychology*, 38, 883–894.

Jackson, F. (1994). "Armchair Metaphysics." In M. Michael and J. O'Leary-Hawthorne (eds.), *Meaning in Mind*, pp. 23–42. Boston: Kluwer Academic Publishers.

Jackson, F. (1998). *From Ethics to Metaphysics: A Defense of Conceptual Analysis.* Oxford: Clarendon Press.

Johnston, M. (1992). "How to Speak of the Colors." *Philosophical Studies*, 68(3), 221–263.

Johnston, M. (2010). *Surviving Death.* Princeton, NJ: Princeton University Press.

Jönsson, M. L. & Hampton, J. A. (2006). "The Inverse Conjunction Fallacy." Journal of Memory and Language, 55, 317–334.

Keil, F. (1989). *Concepts, Kinds, and Cognitive Development.* Cambridge, MA: MIT Press.

Khemlani, S., Leslie, S. J., & Glucksberg, S. (2009). "Generics, Prevalence, and Default Inferences." *Proceedings of the 31st Annual Cognitive Science Society.* Amsterdam: Cognitive Science Society.

Kripke, S. (1980). *Naming and Necessity.* Cambridge MA: Harvard University Press.

Kripke, S. (1982). *Wittgenstein on Rules and Private Language.* Cambridge, MA: Harvard University Press.

Laurence, S., & Margolis, E. (2003). "Concepts and Conceptual Analysis." *Philosophy and Phenomenological Research*, 67 (2), 253–282.

Leslie, A.M., & Keeble, S. (1987). "Do Six-Month-Old Infants Perceive Causality?" *Cognition*, 25, 265–288.

Leslie, S. J. (2007). "Generics and the Structure of the Mind." *Philosophical Perspectives*, 21, 375–403.

Leslie, S. J. (2008). "Generics: Cognition and Acquisition." *Philosophical Review*, 117(1), 1–47.

Leslie, S. J. (in press a). "Generics Articulate Default Generalizations." *Recherches Linguistiques de Vincennes.*

Leslie, S. J. (in press b). "Essence and Natural Kinds: When Science Meets Preschooler Intuition." In T. Gendler and J. Hawthorne (eds.), *Oxford Studies in Epistemology*, 4.

Leslie, S. J. (in press c). "The Original Sin of Cognition: Fear, Prejudice, and Generalization." *The Journal of Philosophy*.

Leslie, S. J., & Gelman, S. A. (2012). "Quantified Statements are Recalled as Generics: Evidence from Preschool Children and Adults." *Cognitive Psychology*, 64, 186–214.

Leslie, S. J., Khemlani, S., & Glucksberg, S. (2011). "All Ducks Lay Eggs: The Generic Overgeneralization Effect." *Journal of Memory and Language*, 65, 15–31.

Lewis, D. (1970). "How to Define Theoretical Terms." *Reprinted in his Philosophical Papers*, pp. 78–95, vol. 1, (1983), New York: Oxford University Press.

Lewis, D. (1972). "Psychophysical and Theoretical Identifications." *Australasian Journal of Philosophy*, 50, 249–259.

Lewis, D. (1973). "Causation." *Journal of Philosophy*, 70, 556–567.

Lewis, D. (1975). "Adverbs of Quantification." In E. L. Keenan (ed.), *Formal Semantics of Natural Language*, pp. 3–15. Cambridge: Cambridge University Press.

Lewis, D. (1983). "New Work for a Theory of Universals." *Australasian Journal of Philosophy*, 61, 343–377.

Lewis, D. (1984). "Putnam's Paradox." *Australasian Journal of Philosophy*, 62, 221–236.

Lewis, D. (1989). "Dispositional Theories of Value." *Proceedings of the Aristotelian Society*, Supplementary volume 63, 113–137.

Lewis, D. (1994). "Reduction of Mind." In S. Guttenplan (ed.) *A Companion to the Philosophy of Mind*, pp. 412–31. Oxford: Basil Blackwell.

Lewis, D. (1997). "Naming the Colours." *Australasian Journal of Philosophy*, 75(3), 325–342.

Lewis, D. (2000). "Causation as Influence", *Journal of Philosophy*, 97, 209–212.

Liebesman, D. (2011). "Causation and the Canberra Plan". *Pacific Philosophical Quarterly*, 92(2), 232–242.

Machery, E. (2009). *Doing Without Concepts*. New York: Oxford University Press.

Mannheim, B., Gelman, S. A., Escalante, C., Huayhua, M., & Puma, R. (2011). "A developmental analysis of generic nouns in Southern Peruvian Quechua." *Language Learning and Development*, 7(1), 1–23.

Margolis, E., & Laurence, S. (1999). *Concepts: Core Readings*. Cambridge, MA: MIT Press.

Meyer, M., Gelman, S. A., & Stilwell, S. M. (2011). "Generics are a Cognitive Default: Evidence from Sentence Processing." In *Proceedings of the 33rd Annual Conference of the Cognitive Science Society*. Boston, MA: Cognitive Science Society.

Michotte, A. (1963). *The Perception of Causality*. Andover: Methuen.

Murphy, G. (2002). *The Big Book of Concepts*. Cambridge, MA: MIT Press.

Peacocke, C. (1992). *A Study of Concepts*. Cambridge, MA: MIT Press.

Peacocke, C. (1993). "How Are A Priori Truths Possible?" *European Journal of Philosophy*, 1, 175–99.

Peacocke, C. (1997). "Metaphysical Necessity: Understanding, Truth and Epistemology." *Mind*, 106, 521–74.

Peacocke, C. (1998). "Implicit Conceptions, Understanding and Rationality." in E. Villanueva (ed.), *Philosophical Issues 9: Concepts*, pp. 121–48.

Peacocke, C. (2005). "The A Priori." In F. Jackson and M. Smith (eds.), *The Oxford Handbook of Contemporary Philosophy*, pp. 739–767. Oxford: Oxford University Press.

Pelletier, F. J. & Asher, N. (1997). "Generics and Defaults." In J. van Benthem and A. ter Meulen (eds.), *Handbook of Logic and Language*, pp. 1125–1179. Cambridge, MA: MIT Press.

Prasada, S., Khemlani, S., Leslie, S. J., & Glucksberg, S. (in press). "Conceptual Distinctions Amongst Generics." *Cognition*.

Putnam, H. (1962). "It Ain't Necessarily So." *The Journal of Philosophy*, 59, 658–671.

Putnam, H. (1973). "Explanation and Reference." Reprinted in his *Mind, Language and Reality: Philosophical Papers*, vol. 2, (1975), pp. 196–215. New York: Cambridge University Press.

Putnam, H. (1975). "The Meaning of 'Meaning'." Reprinted in his *Mind, Language and Reality: Philosophical Papers*, vol. 2, (1975), pp. 215–272. New York: Cambridge University Press.

Putnam, H. (1980). "Models and Reality," *Journal of Symbolic Logic*, 45(3), 464–482.

Quine, W.V.O. (1951). "Two Dogmas of Empiricism." Reprinted in his *From a Logical Point of View*, (1953), pp. 20–47. Cambridge MA: Harvard University Press.

Ramsey, W. (1992). "Prototypes and Conceptual Analysis." *Topoi*, 11, 59–70.

Rosch, E. (1973). "Natural Categories." *Cognitive Psychology*, 4, 328–350.

Rosch, E. (1978). "Principles of Categorization." In E. Rosch & B.B. Lloyd (eds.), *Cognition and Categorization*, pp. 27–48. Hillsdale: Lawrence Erlbaum Associates.

Rosch, E. & Mervis, C.B. (1975). "Family Resemblances: Studies in the Internal Structure of Categories." *Cognitive Psychology*, 7(4), 573–605.

Schroeter, L. (2004)."The Limits of Conceptual Analysis." *Pacific Philosophical Quarterly*, 85, 425–453.

Sloman, S. A. (1993). "Feature-based induction." *Cognitive Psychology*, 25, 231–280.

Sloman, S. A. (1998). "Categorical inference is not a tree: The myth of inheritance hierarchies." *Cognitive Psychology*, 35, 1–33.

Smith, E. E., & Medin, D. L. (1981). *Concepts and Categories*. Cambridge, MA: Harvard University Press.

Smith, M. (1994). *The Moral Problem*. Oxford: Wiley-Blackwell.

Stich, S.P., & Weinberg, J.M. (2001). "Jackson's Empirical Assumptions." *Philosophy and Phenomenological Research*, 62 (3), 637–643.

Sytsma, J. (2010). "The Proper Province of Philosophy." *Review of Philosophy and Psychology*, 1(3), 427–445.

Tardif, T., Gelman, S. A., Fu, X., & Zhu, L. (2011). "Acquisition of Generic Noun Phrases in Chinese: Learning about Lions without An "-S"." *Journal of Child Language*, 30, 1–32.

Tooley, M. (1987). *Causation: A Realist Approach*. New York: Oxford University Press.

Williamson, T. (2003). "Understanding and Inference." *Proceedings of the Aristotelian Society*, 77, 249–293.

Philosophical Perspectives, 26, Philosophy of Mind, 2012

WHAT SHOULD THE NAÏVE REALIST SAY ABOUT TOTAL HALLUCINATIONS?

Heather Logue
The University of Leeds

Naïve Realism is a theory of *veridical* experience — the sort of experience in which a subject perceives things, and they appear to the subject to have certain properties because the subject *perceives* those properties. For example, I'm currently having a veridical visual experience of the banana on my desk. I see the banana, and it looks to me to be yellow and crescent-shaped because I perceive the banana's yellowness and crescent-shapedness. What Naïve Realism says about veridical experience is that it *fundamentally consists in the subject perceiving things in her environment and some of their properties*. For example, it says that my veridical experience of the banana fundamentally consists in my perceiving it, and its yellowness and crescent-shapedness.

Whatever there is to be said in favor of Naïve Realism, many reject the view because it comes with a commitment to a rather counterintuitive account of *total hallucination* — the sort of experience in which the subject doesn't perceive anything in her environment at all (e.g., an experience had by a brain in a vat). Since total hallucinations *don't* involve the subject perceiving anything in her environment, they can't *fundamentally consist in* perceiving things in her environment. So the Naïve Realist has to give a totally different account of total hallucination.

The received view is that the Naïve Realist must say that total hallucination "... is nothing but a situation which could not be told apart from veridical perception" (Martin 2004: 72). All she can say is that a total hallucination is subjectively indiscriminable from a veridical experience of a certain kind; she cannot characterize it in terms of a more substantive psychological property. Many find this kind of account deeply unsatisfying. Surely we can and *should* say more than this in giving a philosophical theory of total hallucination.

I will argue that the Naïve Realist should say more than this — but also that what she can say is still rather counterintuitive. Nevertheless, I think that this reaction stems from a failure to appreciate the broader dialectical context;

whereas the same cannot be said of dissatisfaction with the standard Naïve Realist account of hallucination.

Before I can make the case for that claim, more must be said about exactly what Naïve Realism is and why it is thought to lead to an account of total hallucination in terms of subjective indiscriminability. In the first section, I will elaborate Naïve Realism and sketch the space of options the Naïve Realist has in accounting for hallucination. In the second section, I will elaborate the subjective indiscriminability account, explain why I think it is unacceptable, and why it is commonly supposed that the Naïve Realist is forced to it. In the third section, I will identify a loophole in the reasoning that takes us from Naïve Realism to a subjective indiscriminability account of hallucination, and then outline (but ultimately reject) an attempt to exploit that loophole. In the fourth section, I will argue that we can avoid a subjective indiscriminability account of total hallucination if we reject (the admittedly natural) assumption that there is something it is like to hallucinate. Finally, in the fifth section, I will reply to several objections to this counterintuitive account — in a nutshell, I will argue that *if* a certain motivation for Naïve Realism holds, the objections dissolve.

1. Naïve Realism and Disjunctivism

As I said above, Naïve Realism holds that veridical experience fundamentally consists in the subject perceiving things in her environment and some of their properties. This might not sound like a controversial or even informative theory; after all, no one but an idealist would deny that the subject of a veridical experience perceives things in her environment and some of their properties. The controversial component of the theory is the claim that veridical experience *fundamentally* consists in such a state of affairs.

What an experience fundamentally consists in are the features of it that pro-vide the ultimate *personal-level psychological* explanations of certain phenomenal, epistemological, and behavioral facts. For example, there's "something it's like" to have the perceptual experience I'm having right now, and in virtue of having it, I'm inclined to believe that there's a banana before me (given that, e.g., I don't believe that there are lots of faux bananas about) and to move my arm in a certain direction (given that, e.g., I want to eat a banana). Of course, there are further *subpersonal* psychological facts concerning the information processing that generates experience, and further *non-psychological* facts concerning the biological and chemical underpinnings of such processing. Such facts are of course explanatorily relevant, but it's not the job of a *philosopher* to identify them. They are *causally* relevant to the features of experience mentioned above, but the aim of a philosophical theory of perceptual experience is *metaphysical* explanation. For example, a given perceptual experience is apt to cause certain beliefs and behaviors, but what a philosopher of perception wants to know is *why* this is so — what it is about that experience that makes it apt to cause *those* beliefs and behaviors as opposed to others.

It will be helpful to compare Naïve Realism to its main rival, *Intentionalism*. There are quite a few varieties of Intentionalism, but the core of the view is the claim that all perceptual experiences fundamentally consist in the subject *representing* her environment as being a certain way. For example, according to an Intentionalist, my current veridical experience fundamentally consists in my visually representing that there's a yellow, crescent shaped thing before me. Of course, an Intentionalist doesn't deny that the subject of a veridical experience perceives things in her environment. She simply denies that veridical experience *fundamentally* consists in this fact — that this fact is the *most basic* personal-level psychological explanation of the phenomenal, epistemological, and behavioral explananda mentioned above.

Discussion of Naïve Realism is usually intertwined with discussion of *disjunctivism*, which is basically the claim that veridical experiences and at least total hallucinations are fundamentally different.[1] The discussions are intertwined because Naïve Realism leads naturally to disjunctivism — as I noted above, since total hallucinations *don't* involve the subject perceiving anything in her environment, they can't *fundamentally consist in* perceiving things in her environment. So the Naïve Realist is pushed towards holding that total hallucinations have a radically different metaphysical structure than veridical experiences.[2]

Of course, a Naïve Realist disjunctivist cannot simply state that total hallucinations are fundamentally different from veridical experiences — she must tell us what total hallucinations fundamentally consist in. There are two broad options: *positive* or *negative* disjunctivism. Positive disjunctivism is the view that hallucination fundamentally consists in a psychological property that can be specified *independently* of veridical experience, for example, the property of *perceptually representing* one's environment as being a certain way. This would be a version of positive disjunctivism: saying that the subject of a hallucination perceptually represents her environment as being a certain way involves neither explicit nor implicit reference to veridical experience.[3] Negative disjunctivism is the view that hallucination fundamentally consists in a psychological property that *cannot* be specified independently of veridical experience, for example, the property of being in a state that is *subjectively indiscriminable from a veridical experience of a certain kind*. Obviously, saying that the subject of a hallucination is in a state that is subjectively indiscriminable from a veridical experience of a certain kind involves explicit reference to a veridical experience of a certain kind. For example, this account holds that a hallucination as of a yellow, crescent-shaped banana fundamentally consists in being in a state that is subjectively indiscriminable from a veridical experience of a yellow, crescent-shaped banana. As far as I know, the only version of negative disjunctivism out there is the one just outlined in terms of subjective indiscriminability. In the next section, I will elaborate this view, highlight its problems, and explain why it is nevertheless the most popular account of hallucination among Naïve Realists.

2. Subjective Indiscriminability Negative Disjunctivism

In order to understand subjective indiscriminability negative disjunctivism (hereafter 'SIND' for short), we must clarify exactly what it means to say that a hallucination is *subjectively indiscriminable* from a veridical experience of a certain kind. For M.G.F. Martin, the originator of SIND, the relevant notion is a purely *epistemic* one: a hallucination is subjectively indiscriminable from a veridical experience of a certain kind just in case the subject is *not* in a position to *know by introspection alone* that the hallucination is *not* a veridical experience of that kind (2004: 48). ('Introspection' refers to the special mode of access one has to one's own mental states, whatever that is, exactly.)

There are two different ways of interpreting such claims, which differ with respect to what the relata are. The first is a *de re* claim about two particular experiences: there is a particular hallucination that the subject cannot tell apart from a particular veridical experience by introspection alone. The second interpretation is a claim about a particular hallucination and the *property* of being a veridical experience of a certain kind: there is a particular hallucination such that the subject cannot tell that it *doesn't have the property of being* a veridical experience of that kind (e.g., the property of being a veridical experience of a yellow, crescent-shaped thing). On the first interpretation, the relation is symmetric, but on the second it isn't — the latter concerns a relationship between entities in different ontological categories (an experience, and a *property* of experiences).

Now, one might want to deny that any given veridical experience is subjectively indiscriminable from a particular hallucination (e.g., for anti-skeptical reasons). Since the *de re* interpretation is *symmetric*, this requires denying that any given hallucination is subjectively indiscriminable from a particular veridical experience. But one could still accept that a hallucination is subjectively indiscriminable from a certain kind of veridical experience on the *non-symmetric* interpretation of this claim: in principle, it's possible that one *couldn't* be in a position to know that a given hallucination doesn't have the property of being a veridical experience of a yellow, crescent-shaped thing, even if one can be in a position to know that a given *veridical experience* doesn't have the property of being a *hallucination* as of a yellow, crescent-shaped thing. Since SIND can be elaborated in terms of the uncontroversial non-symmetric interpretation, let us set the symmetric interpretation aside for simplicity's sake.[4]

So, according to Martin's version of SIND, total hallucination fundamentally consists in being a state that is subjectively indiscriminable from a veridical experience of a certain kind, where this is a matter of the subject not being able to know by introspection alone that the state lacks the property of being a veridical experience of that kind. This view faces some difficult objections. For example, one that has loomed particularly large concerns cognitively unsophisticated creatures — creatures that don't have the capacity to form beliefs, and hence are *never* in a position to know anything at all (Siegel 2008: 210–4). Since Martin's version of SIND utilizes a purely epistemic notion of indiscriminability, *prima facie*, it cannot adequately account for the hallucinations of such creatures. For such a creature, any given hallucination is subjectively indiscriminable from *every* kind of veridical experience, and so we cannot even formulate a SIND account of its hallucinations (as there isn't a specific kind of veridical experience from which it is subjectively indiscriminable).[5]

In order to circumvent objections in this vicinity, William Fish proposes a version of SIND that utilizes a *broader* notion of indiscriminability. On his view, what it is for a hallucination to be subjectively indiscriminable from a veridical experience of a certain kind is for it to produce the same *cognitive effects* as the latter would in a rational subject, holding fixed all the subject's other mental states (2009: 94–5). The cognitive effects Fish has in mind include beliefs, but they also include *actions*. This is how he proposes to deal with the problem of cognitively unsophisticated hallucinators — holding other mental states fixed, for any given hallucination, there is a specific kind of veridical experience that would generate precisely the same behaviors (2009: 101–2). So, on this broader notion of subjective indiscriminability, there is a reasonably specific kind of veridical experience from which a cognitively unsophisticated creature's hallucination is subjectively indiscriminable.

Siegel offers objections to Fish's version of SIND (see her 2008: 214–7). But rather than explore the existing dialectic further, let us take a step back to consider what is arguably the most important problem with any version of SIND. In a nutshell, the problem is this: any version of SIND takes subjective indiscriminability *for granted*, rather than explaining it in terms of personal-level psychological facts.

Martin's version of SIND cannot explain *why* a hallucination is subjectively indiscriminable from a veridical experience of a certain kind in the relevant sense — that is, it cannot explain why a hallucinating subject isn't in a position to know by introspection alone that her experience doesn't have the property of being a veridical experience of a certain kind. According to this version of SIND, a hallucination *fundamentally* consists in being subjectively indiscriminable from a veridical experience of a certain kind. So it's *built in* to the view that there is no personal-level psychological explanation of the fact that a hallucination is subjectively indiscriminable from a veridical perception of a certain kind. I suspect that much of the resistance to Martin's version of SIND is rooted in the idea that it's part of the job of a philosophical theory of perceptual experience to provide such explanations. Now, Martin would simply reject this part of the job description. But arguably, it's a crucial component of explaining the epistemological role of perceptual experience. Perceptual experience is the source of perceptual knowledge about one's environment, but it is also an *object* of *introspective* knowledge. So, just as we need to explain what it is about a given perceptual experience that suits it to generate and justify specific beliefs about one's environment, we also need to explain what it is about a given hallucination that renders introspection unable to tell it apart from a veridical experience of a certain kind.[6]

Similarly, Fish's version of SIND cannot explain *why* a hallucination is subjectively indiscriminable from a veridical experience of a certain kind in the relevant sense — that is, it cannot explain why the former produces the same cognitive effects as the latter would (in a rational subject, holding fixed all the subject's other mental states). According to this version of SIND, a hallucination fundamentally consists in being a state that generates the same beliefs and behaviors as a veridical experience of a certain kind would (with the aforementioned qualifications). So it's *built in* to the view that there is no personal-level psychological explanation of the fact that a given hallucination generates the beliefs and behaviors that it does. This clearly runs afoul of part of the job description of a philosophical theory of perceptual experience outlined above — namely, the requirement of specifying the personal-level psychological features of a hallucination that render it apt to cause certain beliefs and behaviors. Now, Fish rejects this part of the job description: basically, he says that if his theory of hallucination is correct, then this explanatory burden isn't part of the job description after all (2009: 114). However, this attempt to evade the explanatory burden is dialectically ineffective. Fish's opponent *accepts* this conditional — she's simply using it in a *modus tollens* inference to the falsity of Fish's account. She will not reject the job description without good reason for doing so (one that's *independent* of the details of any particular theory).[7]

In short, the basic problem with SIND is that on any version of it, the relevant sort of subjective indiscriminability is just left *unexplained*.[8] Nevertheless, it is commonly supposed that the Naïve Realist simply has no other option in accounting for hallucination. This is because of Martin's influential "screening-off" argument against positive disjunctivism (2004: 52–68).[9] The first premise of the argument is this: if we say that hallucination fundamentally consists in (say) the subject perceptually representing her environment as being a certain way, then we have to say that veridical experience does too. Martin's argument for this claim is that a hallucination can have the same proximal neural cause as a veridical experience. So if that proximal neural cause gives rise to a representational state in the case of hallucination, then it gives rise the same kind of representational state in the case of a veridical experience — it would be *ad hoc* to deny that it does.[10] The second premise of the argument is this: if veridical experience also fundamentally consists in being in a representational state, then this state "screens off" the Naïve Realist account from doing any significant explanatory work. The idea is that whatever the experiences have in common (e.g., their phenomenal character, and their tendency to generate certain beliefs and behaviors) will be best explained by *further* features they have in common (e.g., their representational properties). Hence, there wouldn't be much left over for *Naïve Realism* to explain; we could adequately account for the phenomenal, epistemological, and behavioral features of veridical experience entirely in terms of perceptual representation. Hence, if hallucination fundamentally consists in perceptual representation, then Naïve Realism is explanatorily redundant. So if we want to hang on to Naïve Realism, we have to endorse a version of SIND.[11]

We have now arrived at the present state of the dialectic concerning how the Naïve Realist should account for hallucination. Whatever Naïve Realism has going for it as an account of *veridical* experience, the screening-off argument seems to show that the view brings a commitment to an account of hallucination that simply cannot explain one of the main things it's supposed to explain (viz., subjective indiscriminability). Fortunately, as I will explain in the next section, there is a loophole in the screening-off argument. Unfortunately, as I will also explain, it's not clear how the Naïve Realist can exploit it.

3. Positive Disjunctivism, First Pass

As I have argued elsewhere (Logue forthcoming-a: section 4.3) the loophole in the screening-off argument is this: even if the positive disjunctivist is forced to conclude that veridical experience involves perceptual representation, she is *not* forced to conclude that veridical experience *fundamentally consists* in perceptual representation. For example, there is logical space for the following sort of Naïve Realist positive disjunctivist package. Hallucination fundamentally consists in the subject representing her environment as being a certain way — that is, the most basic, personal-level psychological explanation of the phenomenal, epistemological and behavioral features of a hallucination is in terms of such a representational state. As for veridical experience, the Naïve Realist can accept that if a hallucination involves a certain kind of representational state, then so does any veridical experience that involves the same kinds of brain states; and she can accept that a veridical experience's phenomenal, epistemological, and behavioral features are explained in terms of the subject being in a certain representational state. However, the Naïve Realist can *deny* that a veridical experience *fundamentally* consists in the subject representing her environment as being a certain way. That is, she can insist that there is a *further* personal-level psychological fact in virtue of which the subject is in this representational state — a natural candidate would be *the subject perceiving things in her environment* (I'll call this the 'Naïve Realist state of affairs' for short). This is the Naïve Realism the positive disjunctivist aims to preserve: a view on which veridical experience fundamentally consists in the subject perceiving things in her environment.

This Naïve Realist positive disjunctivist package is short on detail. In particular, I haven't specified *what it is* about the representational state that is explained by the Naïve Realist state of affairs. (What its content is? The mere fact that the subject is in it?) And unfortunately, it's not clear how to make the proposal more precise. I suspect that this is because the view mischaracterizes the relationship between the representational state and the Naïve Realist state of affairs. It's not that the Naïve Realist state of affairs *explains* anything about the representational state. It's rather that the representational state is simply a *constituent* of the Naïve Realist state of affairs.

Note that the Naïve Realist state of affairs has *the subject* as a constituent (in addition to the objects of experience and the perceptual relation the subject bears to them). This raises the question: *which aspects* of the subject count as part of the veridical experience? Plausibly, not *all* of them do. Some of them are causal *consequences* of the experience (e.g., the belief that there's a yellow, crescent-shaped thing before her). Some of them operate in *conjunction* with the experience to produce such consequences (e.g., the desire to eat a banana operates in conjunction with the veridical experience to produce the action of reaching for the banana). And some of them are just plain *irrelevant* to the experience (e.g., the shirt she's wearing). But the Naïve Realist's account of veridical experience can and should include states of the subject that have a role to play in explaining the phenomenal, epistemological, and behavioral aspects of the experience — such as personal-level perceptual representational states (if such there be). Hence, given that veridical experience involves a perceptual representational state, it is best thought of as a constituent of the state of affairs that the Naïve Realist identifies with the experience.

So, in summary, it seems that the initial proposal started off on the wrong foot. The representational state involved in veridical experience isn't something entirely distinct from the Naïve Realist state of affairs to be explained in terms of it. Rather, it is simply a constituent of that state of affairs — one that can be appealed to in explaining various aspects of the veridical experience. And the Naïve Realist can say that the representational state involved in hallucination isn't embedded within a Naïve Realist state of affairs. The subject perceptually represents her environment as being a certain way without perceiving anything in it, and this representational state can be appealed to in explaining various aspects of the hallucination.

However, this change of heart has pushed us back into the crosshairs of the screening-off argument. The initial proposal avoided the screening-off argument by claiming that some aspect of the representational state was to be *explained in terms of* the Naïve Realist state of affairs — which would mean that the latter isn't explanatorily redundant after all. But now I've suggested that we *abandon* the idea that we can explain the representational state in terms of the Naïve Realist state of affairs, and instead hold that the former is a constituent of the latter — one which has some role to play in explaining the experiential phenomena at issue. By the reasoning of the screening-off argument, if a perceptual representational state suffices to explain the phenomenal, epistemological, and behavioral explananda in the case of hallucination, then it *also* suffices to account for those explananda when they occur in the case of veridical perception. So if we give up on the idea that the representational state is explained in terms of the Naïve Realist state of affairs, it appears that the screening-off argument goes through. There would be no reason to identify the veridical experience with the entire Naïve Realist state of affairs; we might as well just identify it with the constituent representational state (since it explains everything that needs explaining).

The only way out for the positive disjunctivist is to deny that the representational state explains *everything* that needs explaining. For positive disjunctivism to thwart the screening-off argument, there must be some feature of veridical experience that is explained by the Naïve Realist state of affairs *as a whole*, rather than just its component representational state. But it's not immediately clear how to defend such a claim. It is typically assumed that a hallucination has pretty much exactly the same phenomenal, epistemological, and behavioral features as a veridical perception of a certain kind (with a few minor exceptions to be noted later), and a perceptual representational state is sufficient to explain these common features. However, in the next section, I will present and defend a version of positive disjunctivism that *denies* that a hallucination has the same features as a veridical experience of a certain kind.

4. Eliminativist Positive Disjunctivism

What might veridical experience have that hallucination lacks? Of course, a hallucination and the kind of veridical experience from which it's subjectively indiscriminable differ in their causal histories — veridical experience is caused in a "non-deviant" manner, whereas hallucination is "deviantly" caused. Spelling out what this notion of deviant causation of an experience amounts to is a non-trivial task. But *whatever* it amounts to, the difference isn't one the positive disjunctivist can appeal to in order to avoid the screening-off argument. For we don't need an *explanation* of why veridical experiences and hallucinations differ in their causal histories; plausibly, this is true simply as a matter of *definition*. Part of what it is to be a hallucination is to be an experience caused in a deviant way. And what we're looking for is an aspect of veridical experience that could be best *explained* by the Naïve Realist state of affairs.

As I've been insisting, the job of a philosophical theory of perceptual experience is to explain its phenomenal, epistemological, and behavioral aspects. So let us consider these aspects to see whether there's anything that veridical experience has that hallucination lacks. The prospects for appealing to doxastic or behavioral aspects of veridical experience are grim, as a hallucination will have pretty much the same doxastic and behavioral features as the kind of veridical experience from which it's subjectively indiscriminable.[12] Just as the subject of a veridical experience of a yellow, crescent-shaped thing is inclined to believe that there is a yellow, crescent-shaped thing before her (other things being equal), so is the subject of a hallucination as of a yellow, crescent-shaped thing. And just as the subject of the veridical experience will reach in a certain direction if she wants to eat a banana, so will the subject of the hallucination.

Now, there are some doxastic and behavioral differences between the subjects — arguably, only the subject of a veridical experience is in a position to form beliefs with object-dependent content (e.g., that *this thing* is yellow and crescent-shaped), and her actions are much more likely to be successful (unless the hallucinator's experience happens to be accurate, she will fail to get her hands on a banana). Nevertheless, these differences can be easily explained in terms of the subjects' representational states. We can say that the subject of the veridical experience perceptually represents the relevant object-dependent proposition, and (arguably) we can account for the success of her action in terms of the truth of that proposition.[13]

What about the *phenomenal* aspects of the veridical experience? On the face of it, the prospects look even *more* grim here — surely what it's like for a subject to have a hallucination as of a yellow, crescent-shaped thing could be *exactly the same* as what it's like to veridically perceive such a thing. But what was once regarded as an obvious truth is now up for debate. In a recent book, William Fish has argued that hallucinations lack perceptual phenomenal character entirely (2009: Ch. 4). Fish is forced to this conclusion because he holds that perceptual phenomenal character is *relational* in nature — i.e., that it fundamentally consists in a relation to a mind-independent entity. In particular, he holds that that it fundamentally consists in the subject *perceiving* things in her environment and some of their properties.[14] *If* perceptual phenomenal character is relational in nature, then total hallucinations don't have it — since they don't involve the subject perceiving things in her environment.[15]

Now, the Naïve Realist need not claim that hallucinations lack phenomenal character *entirely* in order for there to be something for the Naïve Realist state of affairs to explain. For she could claim that hallucinations have *non-perceptual* phenomenal character (perhaps the typically fainter but similar sort of phenomenal character associated with perceptual imagination). This option has the advantage of making a hallucinator's introspective error less egregious (see the objections from introspection in section 5). The error is that she is inclined to believe that her state has perceptual phenomenal character even though it doesn't. But if hallucinations have imagination-like phenomenal character, rather than the subject being inclined to mistake a *non-phenomenal* state for a phenomenal one, she would be inclined to mistake *imagination-like* phenomenal character for perceptual phenomenal character. One might find the latter mistake more palatable than the former. However, this option faces another objection. It entails that *veridical* experiences have too many phenomenal characters — the phenomenal character associated with sensory imagination *in addition to* perceptual phenomenal character. This claim is in tension with the deliverances of introspection of veridical experience. As I'm not entirely sure how to respond to this objection, I will defend the claim that hallucinations lack phenomenal character entirely.

Of course, the obvious question at this juncture in the dialectic is: why on earth should we think that perceptual phenomenal character is *relational* in nature? This question is too big to address within this paper. I refer the reader to other works that address it: Fish argues (briefly yet tantalizingly) that a relational account of phenomenal character can give us traction with one aspect of the "hard problem" of consciousness (2009: 75–9). And I have argued that a relational account of phenomenal character is required to explain how veridical experience puts us in a position to know what the things we perceive are like independently of experience (Logue forthcoming-b). In light of the main aim of this paper, I will assume for the sake of argument that the Naïve Realist has a sound case for the claim that perceptual phenomenal character is relational in nature — for this is the only motivation for denying that total hallucinations have perceptual phenomenal character, and this denial affords a version of positive disjunctivism that avoids the screening off argument.

Let us now spell out this combination of positive disjunctivism with elimi-nativism about hallucinatory phenomenal character. The basic idea is that total hallucinations fundamentally consist in the subject perceptually representing her environment as being a certain way, but they lack phenomenal character. The first part of the proposal is a positive account of hallucination, and the second part is intended to thwart the screening-off argument. According to the first plank, the most basic personal-level psychological explanation of the epistemological and behavioral effects of a hallucination is in terms of the subject perceptually representing her environment as being a certain way. For example, the subject of a hallucination as of a yellow, crescent-shaped thing is inclined to believe that there is such a thing before her (other things being equal) in virtue of the fact that she *perceptually represents* that there is such a thing before her. And given that the subject believes that bananas are yellow and crescent-shaped and that she wants to eat a banana, she will be inclined to reach in a particular direction. She has this inclination partly in virtue of the fact that she *perceptually represents* that there is a yellow, crescent-shaped thing in that direction. According to the second plank of this positive disjunctivist proposal, hallucinations lack perceptual phenomenal character. That is, there is *nothing it is like* to hallucinate. Note that it doesn't follow that hallucinators are philosophical zombies. For they may be in *other* mental states that have phenomenal character, e.g., states of pain, imagination, or memory (Fish 2009: 98–9, fn. 19).[16]

Of course, as I noted above, the subject of a hallucination will be *inclined to believe* that she is in a state with perceptual phenomenal character. Eliminativist positive disjunctivism is committed to claiming that this belief is *false*. Hence, we need an account of why hallucinating subjects are inclined to form false beliefs of this sort. As a first pass, one might suggest that the subject of a hallucination is inclined to believe that her experience has perceptual phenomenal character because it is *subjectively indiscriminable* from a kind of state that *does* have it — namely, a veridical experience of a certain sort. A subject of a hallucination as of a yellow, crescent-shaped thing cannot know by introspection alone that her experience doesn't have the property of being a veridical experience of such a thing, and is thereby inclined to believe that her state has the same phenomenal character as such a veridical experience. But of course the story cannot end here. For we need to explain how a hallucination could be *subjectively indiscriminable* from a certain kind of veridical experience when they differ *so radically* — when there is something it's like to be in the former kind of state, but nothing it's like to be in the latter.

It will be helpful to consider the general forms an explanation of indiscriminability might take. If an X is indiscriminable from the Ys via a given mode of epistemic access, that's because the X *seems* exactly the same as a Y via that mode of epistemic access. And there are three broad kinds of explanations of why the X would seem exactly the same as a Y. The first is that the X *is* exactly the same as a Y. The second is that (a) the X differs from a Y in some but not all respects, but (b) the X is exactly the same as a Y *with respect to those features the relevant mode of access is sensitive to*. The third is that (a) the X differs from a Y in some or all respects, (b) the relevant mode of access *isn't* sensitive to any similarities there may be, and (c) the relevant mode of access is simply insensitive to differences *in any respect whatsoever*.

Obviously, when it comes to explaining the subjective indiscriminability of a hallucination from a certain kind of veridical experience, the first sort of explanation isn't available to an eliminativist positive disjunctivist (since there is a phenomenal *difference*). So the explanation must take either the second or the third form. Now, unless we have reason to believe that the mode of access at issue has the severe limitations postulated in the third form of explanation, arguably this form of explanation should be avoided if at all possible. That is, we shouldn't place all the "blame" for indiscriminability despite differences *on the mode of access*. Provided that the mode of access is supposed to be reasonably acute, we should favor an explanation of the epistemic appearance of total sameness that it generates in terms of its detecting some similarity (rather than an explanation solely in terms of a brute failure to detect any differences). And surely, introspection is *at least* reasonably acute with respect to perceptual experience.

So given that the second form of explanation is what we're after, let's make it less abstract by considering an example involving perception rather than introspection — J.L. Austin's lemon-like bar of soap (1962: 50). It is *visually* indiscriminable from lemons of a certain kind (i.e., those with a certain shape, color, and so forth) because it seems exactly the same as a lemon of that kind solely on the basis of vision. And it seems exactly the same as a lemon of that kind because, although it is different in many respects (e.g., chemical composition), it is exactly the same with respect to the properties vision is sensitive to (color, shape, and so forth). Similarly, we can explain the *subjective* indiscriminability of a hallucination from a certain kind of veridical experience as follows: a total hallucination is *subjectively* indiscriminable from a certain kind of veridical experience because it seems exactly the same as a veridical experience of that kind solely on the basis of introspection. And it seems exactly the same as a veridical experience of that kind because it *is* exactly the same with respect to the features introspection is sensitive to.

But which features do they have in common that introspection is sensitive to? At this point, the positive disjunctivist plank of the proposal comes in handy. The positive disjunctivist holds that there is a personal-level psychological commonality between a total hallucination and the kind of veridical experience it is subjectively indiscriminable from — on the view being developed here, this commonality is a perceptual representational state. And plausibly, introspection is sensitive to such states. Now, I'm not suggesting that a subject can tell by introspection that she is in a perceptual representational state. If we could, there would be no room for debate about whether experiences have representational content — a claim which some Naïve Realists dispute (see, e.g., Brewer 2006). Rather, I mean that the *content* of the representational state is introspectively accessible by the subject (e.g., that there is a yellow, crescent-shaped thing before one).

A worrying consequence of combining this explanation of subjective indiscriminability with eliminativism about phenomenal character is that the subject of a total hallucination is *not* introspectively sensitive to the presence or absence of *perceptual phenomenal character*. The proposed explanation holds that the hallucination is exactly the same as veridical experiences of a certain kind with respect to features that introspection is sensitive to. But eliminativism says that they are *not* the same with respect to phenomenal character — veridical experiences have phenomenal character, while the total hallucination doesn't. Hence, in order to reconcile the explanation with eliminativism, we must conclude that the subject of a total hallucination is not introspectively sensitive to whether or not her experience has perceptual phenomenal character; which is a counterintuitive result.

I will address this worry at great length in the next section. But first, let us compare eliminativist positive disjunctivism with the other views we've discussed so far. Unlike SIND and like Intentionalism, eliminativist positive disjunctivism offers a personal-level psychological explanation of subjective indiscriminability. But unlike Intentionalism, eliminativist disjunctivism does not appeal to sameness of phenomenal character in its explanation. Recall that SIND holds that hallucination *fundamentally* consists in being subjectively indiscriminable from a veridical experience of a certain kind, which means that there is no personal-level psychological explanation of the fact that a given hallucination is subjectively indiscriminable from a veridical experience of a certain kind. Intentionalism, on the other hand, explains subjective indiscriminability in terms of phenomenal sameness, which it in turn explains in terms of sameness in representational state. For example, it explains the fact that a hallucination as of a yellow, crescent-shaped thing is subjectively indiscriminable from a certain kind of veridical experience by appeal to the fact that the experiences have the same phenomenal character. And it explains this sameness in phenomenal character in terms of sameness in representational state (e.g., by holding that the phenomenal character of an experience fundamentally consists in perceptual representation, and holding that both states involve visually representing that there is a yellow, crescent-shaped thing before one). By contrast, we can think of eliminativist positive disjunctivism as offering an explanation in terms of personal-level psychology, but one that cuts out the Intentionalist's middle step: it explains subjective indiscriminability *directly* in terms of sameness of perceptual representational state.

Now that eliminativist positive disjunctivism has been elaborated, let us address some objections to it.

5. Objections and Replies

One could object to eliminativist positive disjunctivism by taking issue with either its "eliminativist" plank (i.e., the claim that hallucinations lack perceptual phenomenal character) or its "positive" plank (i.e., the claim that hallucinations fundamentally consist in perceptually representing one's environment as being a certain way). First, I will discuss an objection directed at the "positive" plank, and then I will discuss two objections directed at its "eliminativist" plank.

The objection targeted at the "positive" plank concerns the proposed explanation of a hallucinator's inclination to believe that she's in a state with perceptual phenomenal character. In a nutshell, the worry is that this explanation applies to a *veridically perceiving* subject as well.[17] Recall that eliminativist positive disjunctivism explains a hallucinating subject's inclination to believe that she's having an experience with perceptual phenomenal character by appealing to the fact that her experience is subjectively indiscriminable from a veridical experience of a certain kind (which *does* have perceptual phenomenal character), and in turn explains the subjective indiscriminability in terms of the fact that both experiences involve the same kind of *non-phenomenal* perceptual representational state. Applying the same kind of reasoning used in Martin's "screening off" argument, we reach the following conclusion: if being in a certain kind of non-phenomenal perceptual representational state is sufficient to explain why the subject of a hallucination is inclined to believe that she's having an experience with perceptual phenomenal character, then being in this kind of state is sufficient to explain why the subject of a *veridical experience* is inclined to believe this as well. The fact that a veridically perceiving subject is having an experience with phenomenal character *drops out* of our explanation of why she is inclined to believe that she's having such an experience, which is an odd result. Surely the fact that she is having an experience with perceptual phenomenal character should play a central role in the explanation of why she *believes* that she does.

However, being in a certain non-phenomenal perceptual representational state plausibly *isn't* sufficient to explain why the subject of a hallucination is inclined to believe that she's having an experience with perceptual phenomenal character. As I argued in section 3, in the case of veridical experience, the perceptual representational state is a constituent of that experience — it is but one part of a larger state of affairs that the Naïve Realist identifies with the experience (viz., the subject perceiving things in her environment and some of their properties). Now, being in such a state presumably *wouldn't* generate the inclination to believe that one is in a state with perceptual phenomenal character if it weren't *normally* a constituent of a state with perceptual phenomenal character — namely, a certain kind of veridical experience. In the absence of a normal association between perceptual representational states and states with perceptual phenomenal character, there would be no reason to suppose that the former would generate inclinations to believe anything whatsoever about the latter.[18] So a hallucinating subject's being in a non-phenomenal perceptual representational state *isn't* sufficient to explain why she is inclined to believe that she's having an experience with perceptual phenomenal character — another crucial part of the explanation is that the representational state is normally a constituent of a state that *does* have perceptual phenomenal character. The explanatory power of the representational state depends upon it normally being a part of a Naïve Realist state of affairs. Hence, the fact that the subject of a *veridical experience* is in a state with perceptual phenomenal character *does* figure in the explanation of her inclination to believe that she's in such a state. Her perceptual representational state generates that inclination because it's normally a constituent of a state with perceptual phenomenal character — in particular, a veridical experience of the sort she's currently having.

Let us now turn to objections to the controversial "eliminativist" plank of eliminativist positive disjunctivism. Probably the most obvious objection to eliminativism is based on the claim that *neural stimulation* is *sufficient* for the generation of an experience with phenomenal character. The idea is that since such neural stimulation is also sufficient for the generation of a *hallucination*, hallucinations must have phenomenal character. This objection has been discussed at great length by Fish (2009: Ch. 5). In my view, Fish does an excellent job of dismantling it; so my discussion will be relatively brief.

Fish points out that the *brute assertion* that neural stimulation is sufficient for phenomenal character simply begs the question against the Naïve Realist, who is claiming that phenomenal character fundamentally consists in bearing a certain *relation* to things in one's environment. So this assertion stands in need of an argument. One might seek from it the armchair (by employing thought experiments), or one might appeal to empirical considerations.

As for the first option, one might suggest that it is conceivable that neural stimulation is sufficient for perceptual phenomenal character — e.g., that we can conceive of a brain in a vat being in states with perceptual phenomenal character. From there, one could say that if it's conceivable, then it's possible; and if it's possible, then perceptual phenomenal character isn't relational after all. However, the first step in this conceivability argument is inadmissible in this dialectical context. Given that there is a sound argument for the claim that perceptual phenomenal character is relational (which I'm assuming for the sake of argument here), then it isn't *ideally* conceivable that neural stimulation is sufficient for perceptual phenomenal character. It was *prima facie* conceivable before we were convinced by the argument, but that sort of conceivability is not a reliable guide to possibility (Chalmers 2002). Hence, this conceivability argument gets off the ground only if the Naïve Realist cannot defend her argument for the claim that perceptual phenomenal character is relational — in which case the conceivability argument becomes *unnecessary* (since there would no longer be any *motivation* for claiming that hallucinations lack perceptual phenomenal character in the first place).[19]

The other strategy is to appeal to empirical considerations in support of the claim that neural stimulation is sufficient for perceptual phenomenal character. For example, one might suggest that since there is a strong correlation between certain kinds of neural goings-on and experiences with a certain kind of perceptual phenomenal character, it is plausible that bringing about such neural goings-on is sufficient for bringing about experiences with that kind of perceptual phenomenal character (Fish 2009: 134–6). However, as Fish points out, an equally plausible explanation of the correlation is that the neural goings-on are *necessary* but not *sufficient* for perceptual phenomenal character. In particular, it could be that the visual processing carried out by neurons is a necessary condition of getting into a state with *relational* perceptual phenomenal character — it is but one component in the process that reveals some qualitative aspects of a subject's environment to her, rather than *the* component that generates an experience with (non-relational) perceptual phenomenal character all on its own (Fish 2009: 137–8). What we would need in order to support the sufficiency claim is a uncontroversial case of neural stimulation *without perception* accompanied by perceptual phenomenal character, and Fish argues that there is no such case (2009: 123–34).

Let us now turn our attention to a family of objections to the eliminativist plank that Fish does not address. The basic worry is that eliminativist disjunctivism characterizes introspection of perceptual experience as being considerably less powerful than it really is. One way of developing this idea is to claim that the belief that one is in a state with perceptual phenomenal character is *infallible* — if a subject believes it, then it's true. But eliminativist disjunctivism entails that such beliefs *aren't* infallible, since it holds that such a belief would be false if it were formed by hallucinating subject.

Why might one think that such beliefs are infallible? One potential reason is the idea that beliefs about "feelings" in general are infallible.[20] A way of getting a grip on the notion of perceptual phenomenal character is by characterizing it as the distinctive kind of *feeling* associated with perceptual experiences (or at least some of them, if eliminativism about hallucinatory phenomenal character is correct). Now, when it comes to other feelings, such as bodily sensations like pains and tickles, it might seem absurd to suppose that one could be wrong about whether one has them. If one believes that one is in pain, then one *is* in pain. So why shouldn't we say the same about feelings in general, and perceptual phenomenal character in particular?

However, this line of thought is too quick. Note that I'm *not* denying the analogous claim about perceptual experience, namely: if one believes that one is having a perceptual experience, then one is having a perceptual experience. Infallibility about whether one is having a *perceptual experience* is in principle compatible with fallibility about whether one's experiences have *perceptual phenomenal character*. I'm denying only that we are infallible about whether our perceptual states have perceptual phenomenal character. So the analogous claim in the case of pain is really this: if one believes that one is in a state that has the sort of phenomenal character associated with pain states (let's call it 'painful phenomenal character'), then one is in such a state.[21]

Even so, one might find the strictly analogous infallibility claim just as plausible — that if one believes that one is in a state with painful phenomenal character, then one must be in such a state. However, matters are not quite so straightforward in this dialectical context. Arguably, if a certain kind of phenomenal character is *relational* in nature, then one is *not* infallible about whether one is in a state that has it. In particular, if a certain kind of phenomenal character consists in a certain kind of *awareness of* an entity of some sort, and the subject can be *mistaken* about whether she is aware of such an entity, then she can be mistaken about whether or not she is in a state with that kind of phenomenal character.

To make this rather abstract point more concrete, let us illustrate it with an example. There is at least logical space for a relational theory of painful phenomenal character, and on such a theory, it would be possible to falsely believe that one is in a state with painful phenomenal character. Suppose (for the sake of argument) that painful phenomenal character fundamentally consists in interoceptive awareness of bodily damage. Now, in principle, one can be mistaken about whether one is interoceptively aware of bodily damage. An unwitting amputee waking from surgery might believe that she is interoceptively aware of bodily damage in her left calf, but be wrong (because her whole left leg has just been amputated, and so she has no interoceptive access to it). This possibility, in conjunction with the toy theory of painful phenomenal character just sketched, entails that one can be mistaken about whether one is in a state with painful phenomenal character. If one wrongly believes that one is interoceptively aware of bodily damage, one is nevertheless inclined to believe that one is in a state with painful phenomenal character. But, given the theory, this belief will be *false*: according to the theory, there is no painful phenomenal character without interoceptive awareness of bodily damage. Now, I'm not suggesting that this theory of painful phenomenal character is correct. The moral is simply that there is a connection between infallibility about a mental phenomenon and whether or not it is relational: in particular, *if* a mental phenomenon is relational in nature, *and* if one can be mistaken about whether that relation obtains, then one is not infallible about that mental phenomenon.

This general point has implications for the dialectic concerning eliminativism and infallibility about perceptual phenomenal character. Recall that I am assuming for the sake of argument that perceptual phenomenal character is relational in nature. (That's the whole motivation for claiming that hallucinations lack perceptual phenomenal character in the first place, so there's really no point in taking this claim seriously unless we spot the Naïve Realist the motivation behind it.) So given that we are assuming that perceptual phenomenal character is relational, and the fact that one can be mistaken about whether one perceives things in one's environment, we must also assume in this context that one is *not* infallible about whether one is in a state with perceptual phenomenal character. Hence, the claim that we *are* infallible about this is not admissible in this dialectical context — at least, not as a brute assertion. If the objector can offer an *argument* for this infallibility claim, that argument (in conjunction with the reasoning above) would count as an argument against the claim that perceptual phenomenal character is relational. But, at least as far as I can tell, there is no such argument. Many regard the claim that one is infallible about whether one is in a state with perceptual phenomenal character as simply obvious and intuitive, but such considerations are relatively flimsy compared to a sound argument for the claim that perceptual phenomenal character is relational (which, again, I'm assuming that there is for the purposes of this paper). So, in short, the claim that we are infallible about perceptual phenomenal character is not admissible in this dialectical context as a brute assertion of an allegedly obvious intuition.

Nevertheless, even if we retreat from the infallibility claim, there still seems to be something wrong with the idea that introspection could be susceptible to such a *massive* error. Of course, introspection can get the finer details wrong, especially when we're being hasty or inattentive — for example, I might hastily judge that something looks scarlet to me when it actually looks vermillion. In special cases, introspection can even get it wrong when it comes to something as coarse-grained as *which mental states* one is in — for example, one might deceive oneself into thinking that one is happy even though one isn't. But eliminativism seems to imply that even an attentive, careful subject who isn't at all prone to self-deception is inclined to believe that her experience has perceptual phenomenal character even though it doesn't. It's hard to believe that introspection can systematically lead one astray with respect to the very coarse-grained question of whether one is in a state with perceptual phenomenal character. As I myself have previously argued:

> Introspection might be unreliable when it comes to certain fine-grained mental matters, and even about coarse-grained mental matters when it is employed in unfavorable contexts (e.g., in the presence of motives conducive to self-deception). But surely introspection isn't *so* bad as to systematically generate the belief that one has an experience with phenomenal character when in fact *the state lacks it entirely*. It is plausible that introspection is extremely reliable when it comes to the very coarse-grained question of whether one is in a state

with phenomenal character, at least when the context is favorable for its operation (e.g., one isn't suffering the delirium typical of dreams). (Logue 2010: 35)

And although the result that introspection is an unreliable guide to perceptual phenomenal character is bad enough in itself, it leads to an even worse conclusion: for one could use it to argue that eliminativist disjunctivism leads to *scepticism* about perceptual phenomenal character. Of course, we want to be able to say that a subject of a *veridical experience* can know that she is in a state with perceptual phenomenal character by introspection. Now, plausibly, for introspection to afford knowledge that one is in a state with perceptual phenomenal character, it is at least a necessary condition that introspection is a *reliable* guide to whether one is in such a state. But, as we've seen, eliminativism about hallucinatory phenomenal character entails that introspection is *not* a reliable guide to the instantiation of perceptual phenomenal character. So it appears that eliminativism leaves us in a sceptical predicament: given that it entails that introspection is an unreliable guide to the instantiation of perceptual phenomenal character, it also entails that we cannot know by introspection that it *is* instantiated.

I think the eliminativist disjunctivist should respond to these objections by arguing that any situation in which a subject is having a total hallucination is an *unfavorable* context for introspection of perceptual experience. If this is right, then we would be able to soften the blow of the result that introspection isn't a generally reliable guide to the instantiation of perceptual phenomenal character. For we would be able to maintain that it is at least reliable in *favorable* contexts, which in turn affords a response to the skeptical worry outlined above — the unreliability of introspection in *unfavorable* contexts does not impugn its ability to generate knowledge about experience in *favorable* contexts. Compare: the unreliability of *perceptual experience* in unfavorable contexts (e.g., in unusual lighting conditions, from great distances, and so forth) does not impugn its ability to generate knowledge about *things in one's environment* in favorable contexts.[22]

One might think that the suggestion that total hallucination constitutes an unfavorable context for introspection is rather *ad hoc*. Indeed, I used to think so: "Surely it is in principle possible for a hallucinating subject to be exceedingly attentive to her experience, to suffer no distractions from such a careful introspective endeavor, to have no motives conducive to self-deception regarding the phenomenal aspects of her mental situation, etc." (Logue 2010: 36). I think my past self was too hasty. In particular, I was assuming that we could identify all of the features of a situation that make it an unfavorable context for introspection of perceptual experience *independently* of which theory of introspection we adopt. Now, an ability to be exceedingly attentive to one's experience, and free of distractions and motives conducive to self-deception, are plausibly *necessary* conditions on a context's being favorable. But arguably, at least on some theories of introspection of perceptual experience, they are not *sufficient*. In what follows, I will outline a theory of introspection of perceptual experience on which total hallucination constitutes an unfavorable context for introspection of perceptual experience (including its phenomenal character). I will not argue that this theory of introspection is *correct* — such a task is too large to accomplish in this paper. Rather, my aim will be the less ambitious project of arguing that the objections just outlined are not decisive unless this theory can be ruled out.

The broad kind of theory of introspection I have in mind is one on which it involves attending to what one's mental state is *about*. This sort of theory has been mostly discussed in relation to introspection of *belief*. An inspiration for this sort of theory is Evans' famous suggestion that "...in making a self-ascription of belief, one's eyes are, so to speak, or occasionally literally, directed outward — upon the world. If someone asks me 'Do you think that there's going to be a third world war?' I must attend, in answering him, to precisely the same outward phenomena as I would attend to if I were answering the question 'Will there be a third world war?'" (1982: 225) The idea is basically that introspection of belief doesn't involve "looking within", whatever that might amount to. Rather, we acquire knowledge about our beliefs by attending to *extra-mental* facts pertaining to what our beliefs are about (e.g., facts that could precipitate or prevent a third world war). (Of course, on this model, '*intro*spection' is not an apt label for the mode of access one has to one's own beliefs. But I will continue to use it nonetheless.)[23]

Although Evans thought that there are important differences between introspection of belief and introspection of perceptual experience, he thought that they are broadly similar in that the latter also involves "looking without" (1982: 227–8). Plausibly, in making a self-ascription of *perceptual experience*, one's eyes are *literally* directed outward upon the world. To continue to adapt Evans' language to the analogous point concerning experience: if someone asks me 'Do you have a visual experience of something yellow?", I must attend, in answering her, to precisely the same outward phenomena as I would attend to if I were answering the question 'Is there something yellow before you?' The basic idea is that introspection of perceptual experience is mainly a matter of attending to the *objects* of one's experience. In the phrase 'objects of experience', I'm using 'objects' broadly to refer to *the entities one perceives* — including not just objects in a narrower sense of the term, but also regions of space, events, property instances, and so forth. So, for example, I know that I'm having a visual experience of a yellow, crescent-shaped thing by attending to my immediate environment: in particular, the thing I see, and its yellowness and crescent-shapedness. This proposal captures how we actually go about introspecting our perceptual experiences. If someone were to ask me about my current visual experience, or instruct me to introspect it, I would have no idea what to do other than attend to what my experience is *of*.

More recently, Alex Byrne (2012) has offered a theory in this spirit. Unlike the theory just sketched, his theory is restricted to *seeing*. That is, it's only a theory of knowledge that one is *visually* perceiving something, as opposed to perceiving something in any of the other sense modalities (although, at least *prima facie*, one could easily extend the theory to the other modalities). Moreover, as stated, Byrne's theory isn't a theory of how one knows about one's *visual experiences* (which don't always involve seeing things, as in the case of a visual total hallucination). Regardless of these differences, there are some initial obstacles that any theory of this sort must overcome, and Byrne elaborates his theory in order to deal with them. I won't get into these obstacles or the details of Byrne's view, as they aren't of immediate importance for our purposes. Here, I just want to argue that if we generalize *something* along the lines of Byrne's theory to introspection of perceptual experience in general, it turns out that total hallucination constitutes an *unfavorable* context for introspection of one's experience.

Of course, this kind of theory cannot be straightforwardly extended to introspection of total hallucination. It holds that one gets knowledge about one's experience by attending to the things in one's environment one perceives, but in the case a total hallucination, one doesn't perceive any such thing. Nevertheless, this kind of theory still seems to capture how the subject of a total hallucination would go about introspecting her experience: plausibly, the subject would have no idea of what to do other than to attend to her surroundings. A natural way of extending this sort of theory to accommodate introspection of total hallucination is as follows: introspection of non-hallucinatory perceptual experience involves attending to things in one's environment (the objects of the experience), whereas introspection of total hallucination involves *trying and failing* to attend to such things.[24]

This proposal allows us to capture how the subject of a total hallucination would actually go about introspecting her experience. And, with a natural addition, it gives us a principled story to tell about what makes total hallucination an *unfavorable* context for introspection of one's experience. Once we've accepted that introspection of perceptual experience involves *trying* to attend to things in one's environment, it is natural to suppose that *ideal* introspection involves *succeeding* in this attempt — whereas trying and *failing* amounts to a *defective* form of introspection. Now, if ideal introspection requires successfully attending to the objects of one's experience, then any introspective endeavor carried out by the subject of a total hallucination is *guaranteed* to be defective (since there are no objects of experience to attend to). Hence, if something along the lines of this theory is right, then total hallucination constitutes an unfavorable context for introspection of perceptual experience.

One might worry that this theory entails that the subject of a total hallucination cannot know *anything at all* about her experience via introspection. For if only *ideal* introspection of one's experience can afford knowledge about it, then the subject of a total hallucination cannot have any introspective knowledge about her experience. One option is to embrace the conclusion that the subject of a total hallucination doesn't know anything about her experience. Of course, the subject will have *beliefs* about her experience, but there is room to deny that these beliefs amount to *knowledge*. Another, less radical, option is to deny that ideal introspection is the only route to any knowledge about one's experience whatsoever.

All we need in order to counter the objection to eliminativism is that introspection in an unfavorable context deprives the subject of knowledge about *perceptual phenomenal character*. It could still be the case that defective introspection can put one in a position to know about *other* aspects of one's experience — e.g., that one's experience is as of a yellow, crescent-shaped thing (in other words, what its representational content is). Of course, we would need a principled reason for thinking that defective introspection deprives one of knowledge about perceptual phenomenal character, but doesn't deprive one of knowledge about other features of one's experience. I think that the account of hallucination I'm defending can provide such a reason. Roughly, the idea is that successful attention to the objects of experience is required for knowledge of *relational* features of the experience (e.g., its perceptual phenomenal character), but it is not required for knowledge of *non-relational* features of the experience (e.g., its representational content).[25] Developing the details of this story, however, would take us too far afield.

Let's take stock. I've argued that the objections from introspection can be avoided if total hallucination constitutes an unfavorable context for introspection of experience, and that this is the case if ideal introspection involves successfully attending to the objects of experience. At this point, one might wonder: why should we think that ideal introspection of experience involves attending to its objects? The response to the objections depends upon a controversial claim about how introspection of experience works, and if it's false, the whole house of cards collapses.

However, the situation might not be quite so precarious. What introspection of experience involves might depend on what experience *is*. That is, in principle, one could argue from a theory of the *metaphysical structure* of perceptual experience to a theory of *introspection* of perceptual experience. Recall that, according to Naïve Realism, veridical experiences are *relational* states of affairs that encompass things outside of one's head. If veridical experiences really do encompass things outside one's head, then one might reasonably expect that introspection is at least partially directed *outward* towards those very things (after all, they're part of the experience too). Of course, there are many gaps in this line of thought that need to be filled in. In this context, I simply want to suggest that the theory of introspection that the response depends upon *might* be considerably less controversial if Naive Realism is true. Alas, defending this suggestion will have to wait until another time.[26]

6. Conclusion

The standard Naïve Realist account of total hallucinations, subjective indiscriminability negative disjunctivism (SIND), is typically regarded as counterintuitive. I have argued that this reaction is likely rooted in the fact that SIND cannot discharge a key explanatory burden of a philosophical theory of perceptual experience, namely, the task of giving an account of *the personal-level psychological facts in virtue of which* a total hallucination is subjectively indiscriminable from a certain kind of veridical experience. I argued that the Naïve Realist can avoid SIND and explain subjective indiscriminability in terms of perceptual representational states. However, this comes at the cost of embracing what some might take to be an even more counterintuitive claim — the claim that total hallucinations lack perceptual phenomenal character.

Nevertheless, several of the objections underlying this understandable reaction to eliminativism about hallucinatory phenomenal character lose their force once we appreciate the bigger dialectical picture. We must ask: is there any *good reason* to think that total hallucinations lack perceptual phenomenal character? A natural answer for the Naïve Realist to give is that perceptual phenomenal character is *relational* in nature, fundamentally consisting in the subject perceiving things in her environment. This answer undermines several of the objections. Some of the objections beg the question because they are based on claims that presuppose that perceptual phenomenal character is *non-relational* (e.g., the claim that neural stimulation of a certain sort is sufficient for perceptual phenomenal character, and the claim that we are infallible about whether a state has perceptual phenomenal character). And, if perceptual phenomenal character is relational, there is a way to avoid the unwelcome result that introspection is generally unreliable regarding the instantiation of perceptual phenomenal character. If introspection of perceptual experience involves attending to its objects, then it can be argued that total hallucination is an *unfavorable* context for introspection of perceptual experience — which would mean that its unreliability in the case of total hallucination doesn't impugn its reliability in the case of veridical experience. Moreover, if perceptual phenomenal character is relational, that would provide at least some support for a theory of introspection of this sort.

So the structure of the dialectic is this: if perceptual phenomenal character is relational, then the Naïve Realist can dispense with some of the most troubling objections to eliminativist positive disjunctivism. As I said above, the question of whether the antecedent is true is beyond the scope of this paper. My point here is simply that the viability of these objections depends upon whether perceptual phenomenal character is relational. Hence, we cannot simply dismiss eliminativist positive disjunctivism on the basis of the former without engaging with the arguments for the latter.[27]

Notes

1. Obviously, this statement of disjunctivism is very rough. For one thing, it doesn't cover illusion — i.e., an experience in which the subject perceives something

in her environment, and it appears to have a certain property, but *not* because the subject perceives an instance of that property. Nor does it cover *partial hallucination* — i.e., an experience in which the subject perceives things in her environment, but *some* aspects of the way things perceptually appear to be aren't due to the fact that she perceives these things (but rather to, say, causally independent goings-on in her brain). Since the our focus is what the Naïve Realist should say about *total hallucinations*, we need not trouble ourselves with the related refinements of disjunctivism here. (Unless I say otherwise, in what follows when I use 'hallucination' I mean *total* hallucination.) That said, there are tricky issues regarding the implications of the account of total hallucination I will propose for what the Naïve Realist should say about illusions and partial hallucinations. Unfortunately, I must leave this issue until another time.

2. Although see Johnston 2004 for a non-disjunctivist theory of perceptual experience that is compatible with Naïve Realism. However, this theory comes with commitments that most Naïve Realists aren't willing to take on (see fn. 15 below), which is why most Naïve Realists are disjunctivists.

3. Throughout this paper, I will assume that the positive psychological property is a perceptual representational state, because I think that sort of state is the most plausible candidate for being what total hallucination fundamentally consists in. However, in principle, it could be a positive psychological property invoked by theories of perceptual experience *other* than Intentionalism (e.g., awareness of sense-data).

4. See Fish 2009: 86–8 for a more detailed discussion of these interpretations.

5. Martin replies to this objection in his 2004: 51 and his 2006: 381, and Siegel rebuts this reply in her 2008: 211–3.

6. In principle, we could explain this inability in our theory of *introspection* of perceptual experience, rather than in our theory of perceptual experience. The idea is that hallucination seems exactly like a veridical perception of a certain kind to introspection (even if they have no personal-level psychological commonalities whatsoever) *simply* because introspection is not sensitive to the differences. But as I will argue below in section 4, this kind of explanation is an option of last resort.

7. See Logue 2010: 32–4 for a more detailed discussion of this objection to Fish's account, his response, and why this response isn't dialectically effective.

8. It's not as though SIND has *no* explanation of subjective indiscriminability at its disposal. A proponent of SIND might appeal to *neural* commonalities in explaining it (Thau 2004: 249–50). But what we're after in giving a philosophical theory of perceptual experience is *personal-level psychological* explanation.

9. Martin presents this argument in painstaking detail, but for our purposes here it's sufficient to summarize the key moves in it.

10. One might object to this case for the first premise because of skepticism about there being a "'last' brain state that then causes [perceiving]" (Johnston 2004: 138–9). But as long as the sort of brain state that Martin has in mind is a *constituent* of both veridical and hallucinatory experience, and it either causes or constitutes a perceptual representational state, the first premise of the screening-off argument holds.

11. Note that an analogous argument applies to any other positive account of hallucination.

12. Of course, a crucial difference in the epistemological roles of veridical experience and hallucination is that the former affords *knowledge* of one's environment. I will not pursue this avenue here, however; as I've argued elsewhere (Logue 2011) that this facet of the epistemological role of veridical experience can be adequately accounted for in terms of perceptual representation.

13. There is room to criticize the proposed explanation of successful action. As Martin notes, some have argued that "the explanatory potential of . . . a relational explanans [e.g., perceiving an object] cannot necessarily be matched by a conjunction of a non-relational psychological fact [e.g., perceptually representing that there is something at a certain location relative to one] and some non-psychological relational facts in addition [e.g., the fact that there *is* an object at that subject-relative location]" (2004: 64). Nevertheless, Martin does not pursue this strategy for vindicating the explanatory power of the Naïve Realist state of affairs, on the grounds that it would leave it open that a Naïve Realist explanation of *phenomenal character* is redundant (2004: 64). Since I agree with Martin that such an explanation is *not* redundant (Logue forthcoming-b) I will not pursue this strategy either.

14. Note that this is only a proposal about *perceptual* phenomenal character — it could still be that the phenomenal character associated with *other* sorts of mental states (e.g., imagination) is non-relational.

15. Actually, the matter is not quite so straightforward. Mark Johnston holds that the phenomenal character of hallucination fundamentally consists in the subject perceiving "sensible profiles", which are complexes of properties — in particular, the ones that would be instantiated by things in one's environment if one's experience were veridical (2004: 134). Sensible profiles aren't mind-dependent sense-data; they are complexes of mind-independent, uninstantiated properties. Hence, there is at least logical space for a relational theory of hallucinatory phenomenal character. This theory entails that we can perceive *uninstantiated* (and presumably *abstract*) properties, a claim I think is false (although explaining why would take me too far afield). Suffice it to say that I don't think we should try to avoid the conclusion that total hallucinations lack phenomenal character by embracing Johnston's theory.

16. I should note that I am not inclined to extend this account to illusions or partial hallucinations. Both sorts of experience involve the subject perceiving things in her environment, so there is scope for claiming that they have relational perceptual phenomenal character. However, formulating the details of such an account will be tricky — for example, what's it's like to perceive something as being yellow when it *isn't* obviously cannot be accounted for in terms of perceiving an instance of yellowness. In the case of illusion, I am inclined to adopt something along the lines of the account offered in Brewer 2008. However, this issue is beyond the scope of this paper.

17. Thanks to David Chalmers for raising this objection.

18. I mean 'normal' in the normative sense. There is something *defective* about hallucination; given that a primary function of a perceptual system is to convey information about the subject's environment to her, the system fails

to perform this function in a case of hallucination. So even in a situation in which total hallucinations are the norm in the *statistical* sense (e.g., the Matrix), the perceptual representational states at issue would normally be constituents of veridical experiences (in the *normative* sense).

19. I should note that this reply to the conceivability argument isn't Fish's. He concedes that it is conceivable (in a possibility-entailing sense) that neural stimulation is sufficient for perceptual phenomenal character, but says that this shows only that non-relational perceptual phenomenal character is logically possible, not that it's *physically* possible (2009: 122). I don't think the Naïve Realist should be too quick to concede the ideal conceivability of the scenario at issue. For if the argument that perceptual phenomenal character is relational *isn't* based on contingent facts about the physical constitution of our perceptual apparatuses, then it may well be incompatible with even the logical possibility of non-relational perceptual phenomenal character.

20. Thanks to Anandi Hattiangadi for raising something along the lines of this objection.

21. One might suggest that there is no difference between painful phenomenal character and pain itself. Now, the word 'pain' is sometimes used to refer to painful phenomenal character. But it is also used to refer to a mental state that *has* that phenomenal character, along with other features (e.g., a certain functional role). This is the sense in which I am using the word here, because it is analogous to the sense of 'perceptual experience' in play in this context — the latter term is intended to refer to a mental state that might have perceptual phenomenal character, along with other features (e.g., a certain functional role). (The point of the 'might' is to allow for eliminativism about hallucinatory phenomenal character.)

22. Of course, there are *other* well-known arguments for the claim that perceptual experience cannot afford knowledge about one's surroundings (e.g., arguments from the inability to rule out skeptical scenarios). But the point here is that the *unreliability* of perceptual experience in certain restricted contexts is not a basis for such an argument.

23. This kind of theory is controversial. But for our purposes, it only matters whether an analogous theory concerning introspection of *perceptual experience* is true; we need not take a stand on the theory concerning introspection of belief.

24. Of course, the subject of a total hallucination wouldn't be in a position to *know* that she's failed to attend to things in her environment, given that her experience is subjectively indistinguishable from a veridical experience of a certain kind.

25. Given externalism about mental content, there is a weaker sense in which the content of experience is relational — being in a state with that content requires that (say) one's evolutionary ancestors bore the right sorts of relations to certain things. However, the content of an experience is non-relational in the stronger sense of the term being used in this context: one can perceptually represent that there is something yellow before one without *perceiving* anything yellow.

26. Another objection to eliminativism is based on the claim that one can learn what it's like to experience a property by hallucinating it (Johnston 2004: 130–1). If hallucinations lack perceptual phenomenal character, it's not obvious how

they could afford such phenomenal knowledge. I don't know what to say in response to this objection at present, other than to bite the bullet and deny that hallucinations are a source of such knowledge.

27. Various versions of this paper were presented at the Centre for Metaphysics and Mind at the University of Leeds, the Philosophical Society at the University of Oxford, and a conference on Phenomenality and Intentionality hosted by the University of Crete. Many thanks to the members of the audiences for their helpful comments and questions.

References

Austin, J. 1962. *Sense and Sensibilia*. Oxford: Oxford University Press.

Brewer, B. 2006. Perception and content. *European Journal of Philosophy* 14: 165–81.

———. 2008. How to account for illusion. *Disjunctivism: Perception, Action, Knowledge*. ed. A. Haddock and F. Macpherson. Oxford: Oxford University Press.

Byrne, A. 2012. Knowing what I see. *Introspection and Consciousness*. ed. D. Smithies and D. Stoljar. Oxford: Oxford University Press.

Chalmers, D. 2002. Does conceivability entail possibility? *Conceivability and Possibility*. ed. T. S. Gendler and J. Hawthorne. Oxford: Oxford University Press.

Evans, G. 1982. *The Varieties of Reference*. Oxford: Oxford University Press.

Fish, W. 2009. *Perception, Hallucination, and Illusion*. Oxford: Oxford University Press.

Johnston, M. 2004. The obscure object of hallucination. *Philosophical Studies*, 120: 113–83.

Logue, H. 2010. Getting acquainted with Naive Realism: critical notice of Perception, Hallucination, and Illusion. *Philosophical Books*, 51: 22–38.

———. 2011. The skeptic and the Naive Realist. *Philosophical Issues*, 21: 268–88.

———. forthcoming-a. Good news for the disjunctivist about (one of) the bad cases. *Philosophy and Phenomenological Research*.

———. forthcoming-b. Why Naive Realism? *Proceedings of the Aristotelian Society*.

Martin, M. G. F. 2004. The limits of self-awareness. *Philosophical Studies*, 120: 37–89.

———. 2006. On being alienated. *Perceptual Experience*, ed. T. Gendler and J. Hawthorne. Oxford: Oxford University Press.

Siegel, S. 2008. The epistemic conception of hallucination. *Disjunctivism: Perception, Action, Knowledge*, ed. A. Haddock and F. Macpherson. Oxford: Oxford University Press.

Thau, M. 2004. What is disjunctivism? *Philosophical Studies*, 120: 193–253.

Philosophical Perspectives, 26, Philosophy of Mind, 2012

DESIRE CONSIDERED AS A PROPOSITIONAL ATTITUDE

William G. Lycan
University of North Carolina and
Victoria University of Wellington

We speak of "belief-desire psychology." Beliefs and desires are roughly equal partners in producing action, most likely by resulting in intentions which produce the actions more directly, and all in terms of content: We desire that P, and, guided by our beliefs, we come to intend that P, and then we act so as to make it the case, or make it more likely, that P. So much is endorsed by nearly all philosophers of mind other than eliminativists.[1] (They do not all mean the verbs like "producing" and "resulting in" in any robustly causal sense.) Some would say the belief-desire view is plain common sense; I doubt that.

Mainstream philosophers of mind have implemented this picture in any of several ways. But they have just assumed that a single model of "the propositional attitudes" fits desire (and the other attitudes) as well as belief. That is not so. Or such is my thesis.

Again not counting eliminativism, we inherit two main paradigms regarding the propositional attitudes: Dennettian interpretivism/instrumentalism, and the Sellars-Fodor language-of-thought model.

I.

To begin with Dennett (1987): Behavior prediction from his "intentional stance" is a matter of extrapolating from what a creature *ought to* believe given its circumstances and perceptual capacities, and what it *ought to* desire in those circumstances given its needs. We then presume that it does believe and want those things, and predict that it will reason and behave rationally given those beliefs and desires. Metaphysically, Dennett maintains that for the creature to have beliefs and desires just is for this method to succeed in its case.

But Fred Schueler (1995) has made what I think is a compelling argument against the desire side of Dennett's epistemology.

Everyone who works in this area agrees that "desire" is ambiguous as between at least two readings.[2] Terminology differs, and the distinction is drawn in slightly different ways, but it is at least the following.

In one sense of the term, it is entirely commonplace that we do things we do not want to do. I often do things I have no desire *at all* to do; I do them against my will, but for what I consider good and overriding reasons; and I am quite sure the same is true of you. Schueler calls desires in this sense "desires proper."

But there is also a sense in which, if I did do X voluntarily, I must have ultimately wanted to do X; after all, I did choose to do X. Schueler calls desires in this sense "pro-attitudes." That is a more general, presumably the most general, conative category; of course it includes desires proper.

Now Dennett faces a dilemma. Suppose that by "desire" he means merely pro-attitudes. Then desires cannot be used to predict behavior at all, because you cannot learn what pro-attitude someone has in the choice of doing X vs. doing Y until the person has actually done X or Y.

But suppose Dennett means desires proper. Then you will get predictions, but often the wrong ones. For, as noted above, we often go against our desires proper. A different sort of conation overrides, and we do something we do not desire-proper to do.[3]

Though Schueler presents his dilemma as a critique of Dennett, notice that it applies against the entire belief-desire picture.[4] If "desire" means desire-proper, then as before desires are only one kind of pro-attitude; they do not predict action with any reliability and they only sometimes explain it. But if "desire" means just any pro-attitude, desires cannot in principle predict behavior and can only vacuously explain it.[5]

Moreover (I add), either way there is no case for Hume's view that beliefs alone cannot produce action, because one common pro-attitude that motivates is the belief that one ought (morally or otherwise) to do such-and-such. (Since it itself motivates,[6] that belief need not be accompanied by any further pro-attitude such as a desire-proper.)

II.

According to Fodor (1975, 1981, following Sellars (1956)), intentionality is mental representation, and propositional attitudes have their characteristic features because the internal physical states and events that realize them represent actual or possible states of affairs. The existent-or-nonexistent states of affairs that are their objects are just representational contents, akin to the meanings of sentences. So, to believe that P is to bear the Belief relation to an internal representation whose semantic content is that P. What makes the belief that P a *belief* rather than a desire that P or a hope or a regret or a fear is its functional profile; what makes it the belief *that P* is its representational content.

With beliefs, *content* is a fairly straightforward matter. Of course I do not mean that psychosemantics is easy; whatever Fodor himself may say, we have no good naturalistic account of what it is that makes my belief about Jerry a belief about him, or (worse) of what makes my belief about Emma Bovary a belief about her, or (still worse) what makes my belief about the lore of our fathers' being a pale grey lore a belief about that. What is simple is saying what a belief's content is: the content of the belief that P is that P, and the belief is true iff P. And of course the latter is exactly what is predicted by Fodor's internal-representation model.

Desire content is not so straightforward. (I should begin by warning you that I have no settled views in this area. My main point will be just that serious issues arise for the notion of desire content that have to be adjudicated and that have no analogues for belief.)

We do not speak of desires as being true or false, because it is not their job to describe or otherwise correctly represent the world. The desire analogue of truth is *satisfaction* or fulfillment. But as we shall see, it is not a perfect analogue.

There is an apparent parallel in the philosophy of language, which I mention only to get it out of the way: We do not speak of nondeclarative sentences, particularly interrogatives and imperatives, as being true or false, because it is not their job to describe or otherwise correctly represent the world. This is sometimes put forward as an objection to the truth-condition theory of linguistic meaning. But that difference, according to me, is superficial and of no theoretical importance. Interrogatives and imperatives do have bipolar semantic values which might just as well have been called truth-values even though they normally are not. An imperative is *obeyed* or not (depending on whether its propositional complement turns out to be true or false) and a question has the correct answer "yes" or "no" (depending on whether its corresponding declarative is true or false).[7] The custom of not calling nondeclaratives true and false is only that, a custom, and is expendable; without detriment to the language, we could have called imperatives "true" or "false" depending on their being obeyed, and questions "true" or "false" depending on their correct answers. End of issue.

Now, desire does have an exact semantic parallel of this sort to belief: We could call a desire that P "true" just in case P, without detriment to the language. Or we could just continue use the more traditional term "satisfied," as a functional synonym for "true." And indeed that is a perfectly clear notion; let us call it "*semantic* satisfaction" for desires.

The trouble is that semantic satisfaction does not coincide with what we more commonly mean when we speak of a desire's being satisfied or fulfilled. So it is not true that the desire that P is satisfied (in the ordinary sense) iff P. Nor, more to the point, is "semantic satisfaction" as important to us as is satisfaction in the ordinary sense. It is what we do ordinarily call satisfaction that counts, not semantic satisfaction.

(I) Dennis Stampe has argued (1986, pp. 153–54) that a desire is not satisfied until its content proposition actually *comes* true. I now desire to be invited back to Victoria University of Wellington, for a fifth term-long visit.[8] Suppose it is (in fact) true that in 2015 I will be invited back to Vic. Then my content proposition is true, but my desire is not yet satisfied. Someone might think that this is really only a psychological fact, in that *I* cannot be said to be satisfied on the point so long as I do not yet know that I will be invited. But Stampe's claim is stronger, in each of two ways: (i) It is still the desire itself that is not satisfied, not just me and my feelings, and (ii) even if I do come to know that I will be invited and so am happy, the desire itself will still not have been satisfied until I actually get the invitation; the *present-tense* truth of the content proposition is at least necessary for satisfaction. And I think Stampe is right on each count.

The second point makes a further prediction: that even if I firmly believe and take myself to know that I have received the invitation, my desire is not satisfied unless I am right. Suppose I have been told that I will be invited, and then a missive arrives on Vic letterhead, signed (apparently) by the Vice-Chancellor and offering me the visiting position. At that point *I*, psychologically, am happy and very satisfied. But the letter is forged; it is a cruel practical joke by a disgruntled former student (the one I... —never mind). In fact, the money for the position has fallen through, and the Head of Philosophy is about to e-mail me with the bad news. We cannot say that my *desire* has been satisfied. My desire has been frustrated, even though I do not know that.

(II) As Robert Gordon (1986) points out, some desires ("the appetites") can be satisfied only while they still exist. For example, if I desire to have lunch, but cause that desire to cease by taking a diet pill, the desire is not satisfied. Nor is it frustrated, even though I do not eat. Even if I do that and then (for whatever reason) do eat, the now extinct desire is not satisfied, despite the truth of the object proposition. Finally, if I eat but it fails to quench the desire, the desire is not satisfied.[9]

—For what all that is worth. Even if these conceptual claims are true, one may wonder why they are important. In particular, they do not obviously *refute* either Fodor's theory of the propositional attitudes or his or anyone's informational etc. psychosemantics.

Now (though this is not his main project), Stampe goes on to offer an alleged explanation of (I), in terms of a *differential* psychosemantics for the belief that P and the desire that P (p. 154). (All standard psychosemantics has assumed uniform treatment of attitude contents, attitude types differing only functionally. We should bear in mind that Stampe's alternative is an option, since then overlooked.) Stampe's psychosemantics adverts to the ideal *effect* of a desire that P, as contrasted with the ideal cause of the belief that P. Here is the explanation (pp.154–55):

> My belief that I will win the match is a state the ideal causes of which are such that I will win: its causes are, for instance, states of affairs that comprise *evidence* that that is what will happen. My desire that I win is a state of mind the ideal effect of which is that I win. Since the causes of a state are fixed at the time someone enters into it, a belief is satisfied or not—i.e., true or not—at that

time. If the satisfaction of a desire consists in the occurrence of events which are ideally the effects of that desire, then the desire that something be the case will not be satisfied until it comes to be the case, if it is to do so.

There is something to this. But I do not see how the explanation goes. First, the point about belief and its ideal causes is a fudge: Who says those causes "are such that I will win" (except vacuously, assuming the fact is I do win)? Second, the concluding conditional about desire seems to me a non sequitur. It may sound nearly tautologous, until one remembers that Stampe's "consists in" is the modality of psychosemantics: the desire that P is the desire *that P* in virtue of its ideal effect. "Its ideal effect" is a property it has *now*, that is currently constituting its content, just as a belief's ideal cause is a property it has now, ditto. And it is already true (or not) that I will win the match.[10]

Jesse Prinz (2008) offers a competing view:

[(I)] shows something about desire satisfaction. S desires that P is satisfied only if P is true in the present. But notice that this formulation makes reference to P being true. And P being true can be explained in the usual way (e.g., correspondence). It's part of the functional role of desire that satisfaction (being assuaged) has a temporal parameter. This is unsurprising. Desire also has a future directed temporal parameter (one can't desire what one believes is already the case). The functional role of desire involved keep track of when the desired thing becomes true (compare other attitudes like anticipation, regret, hope, recollection, etc.). But the theory of truth here is just the normal beliefy kind.

Which seems right to me, given that I am unconvinced by Stampe's alternative.

What (I) and (II) do show is that Fodor's model *does not illuminate* desire in the way that it illuminates belief. Contra Stampe, it may not require nonstandard psychosemantics for desire, but by itself it has nothing to say about desire satisfaction in the central and important sense.

This comes out a bit more clearly if we consider Sellarsian/Fodorian semantics for attitude ascriptions. On that view, "S believes that P" is to be parsed as roughly,

"($\exists$r)($\bullet$P$\bullet$(r) & BEL(S,r))"; r is a token of some kind (on Fodor's view, an internal, brain state of S), and the Sellarsian dot-quoted predication classifies r as being the same in kind as the filler, the complement sentence. (Think of answering the question, "What color is your new car?" by holding up a piece of colored paper and saying "This color.") Sameness of kind might be sameness of truth-condition (as Fodor would normally have it), or sameness of conceptual or inferential role (Sellars).[11] Either way, the attitude ascription's meaning is exhausted by the pairing of the subject via a particular attitude with a semantic property fairly narrowly specified. For belief, that seems fine. But for desire, it leaves out the distinctive features of satisfaction. (Though if we insist that those are part of the meaning of "desire," the Sellarsian/Fodorian may fairly say that they are packed into the lexical meaning of the "DES" operator.)

III.

(III)   There is an issue of grain. Suppose you desire to have lunch. Helpfully, I force-feed you twenty-five old and soggy Brussels sprouts, each covered in suppurating mold. "(Ghack, gag), not *that* lunch!" Or you desire to be famous. You publish something, but it contains a fallacy so incredibly stupid that the news of your gaffe spreads to the entire English-speaking world. "I didn't mean *that* way / famous for *that*." Again, mere semantic satisfaction is the least of what we care about.[12]

I have not seen this particular issue addressed in the literature, and I am not sure how to parse the phenomenon. But several options suggest themselves:

First, we might again appeal to the distinction between technical satisfaction of the desire itself and a psychological notion. Prinz (2008) does that:

It seems we often have desires that are underdeveloped in our own minds and only afterwards [realize] that there are ways of satisfying them that are unsatisfying. I put it this way because I think these examples mostly expose an ambiguity in "satisfaction." In some semantic sense, a desire is satisfied when the content expressed by its ascription comes true. So the mold[y Brussels sprout collation] satisfies my desire. But it doesn't satisfy me. One way to think about this is that satisfying *me* is a matter of my being in a state that feels satisfied overall. If something happens to me that I don't like, I will to that degree be unsatisfied. All things considered, eating mold leaves me feeling unsatisfied, even if I really wanted to eat. I am satisfied in one dimension—eating—but not overall. If I were starving, I might be satisfied overall. So it makes sense to say, I got something I wanted along with something I intensely didn't want. I think the main lesson of this is that desire satisfaction doesn't always make us happy.

I cannot refute the suggestion that the subject got something he wanted; maybe he did. But as before, the disambiguation move is too simple. The question is not how the subject feels, but whether his desire itself counts as having been satisfied. That depends on how far we respect the subject's protest, "Not *that* way!," or "*That* wasn't what I wanted." The protest does not have the force of law, and Prinz might be right, but let us review some further options, in increasing order of respect.

Second: In much the same spirit, we might see an ascriber as having implied that what the subject wants is a *decent, pleasant* lunch, the implication having been pragmatically conveyed in the context rather than part of the ascription's semantic meaning. (Of course, the present issue is about desire itself, and does not depend on any actual ascribing; it arises whether or not anyone including the subject attributes the desire in question. But someone may think that my own description of the case only implicates the "decent, pleasant" part.) Prinz himself might suggest that what we have here is merely a conversational implicature, though a strong one. On this view unlike the first, I did commit a solecism in feeding him the Brussels sprouts: I ignored a clear and obvious implication, and I did something that the subject obviously did not want me to do.[13]

That would be in keeping with Prinz's view that the original ascription was literally true, and it would be to downplay the protest as merely backing off an implicature that one did not intend or anyway should not have intended. On the present view as on the first, the subject did get what he wanted, though he did not get what he importantly implicated he wanted and he also got something he very much did not want. But if we do not feel that his desire itself was satisfied, that is as much an objection here as to Prinz's original view.

Third try, an error theory: One could insist that the simple desire-ascriptions are inaccurate, strictly false, because what the subject really wanted was much more qualified and otherwise complicated.

This (finally) respects the view that although *as a first approximation* the subject wanted to have lunch, his ingestion of the Brussels sprouts did not satisfy that desire, and he did not really have it; he did not get anything he (relevantly) wanted. But where does this error hypothesis end? Must a desire-ascription, in order to be strictly true, detail the nuances of what would and what would not satisfy the desire that the subject *really* has? Then, probably, no actual desire-ascription is ever true.

Fourth: Suppose we take seriously the bold idea that the desire-ascriptions are correct but so are the protests. Then, obviously, the ascriptions cannot be taken at face value, even though we insist on their truth in context. In response to thesis (II) (not (III)), Gordon offers an explanation that meets the present description (preserving the correctness both of the desire ascription and of the protests by offering a non-face-value analysis of the ascription). It is that the desire is not only to eat but also, by eating, to quench the appetite. (If the appetite does not exist at the time of eating, it is not quenched.)

How would this address the Grain problem (III)? When I force-feed you the Brussels sprouts, do I quench your desire for lunch? Yes and no. I very probably *end* it; you are not likely to be hungry again for some hours or days. But I do not merely end it, as with a diet pill, because I do give you lunch, and it is *in part* the fullness of your stomach that ends the desire. In that sense, at least, it is quenched, and so Gordon's proposed content is satisfied.

Also, as Gordon is well aware, not all desires are quenched once fulfilled. He gives the example of health, which I continue to desire no matter how healthy I already am. My desire for fame is not stilled even if I achieve fame through merit and not through monumental stupidity, so Gordon's explanation does not cover it.

Fifth, let us try a nonstandard semantics. On the usual Hintikka-style view, just as to believe that P is for P to be true in every one of your doxastic alternatives (intuitively, the worlds compatible with your beliefs), to desire that P is for P to be true in every one of your orectic alternatives, intuitively those worlds in which all your desires are semantically satisfied. That fits with the usual Fodorian practice of treating desire in a way exactly parallel to belief. But let us now import Lewisian considerations of world *similarity* or, less misleadingly,[14] closeness. We may say that to desire that P is for P to be true in all your *nearby* desire worlds. Thus, we distinguish between the actual contextual meaning of the desire ascription and what it would mean if taken unrestrictedly. You desire to eat lunch because in every nearby world compatible with your desires you do eat lunch; worlds at which you get force-fed are nowhere nearby. And you want to be famous, because in every nearby world semantically compatible with your desires you do become famous, and in none of those worlds do you become famous for stupidity or fallacious thinking.

Unfortunately, this threatens to be a distinction without a difference, because we may presume that you desire *not* to eat mold and *not* to be exposed as an idiot; so the Brussels-sprout lunch and the famous gaffe occur in none of your desire worlds anyway, even remote ones. The difference shows up only when there are cases in which you are neutral: for lunch X or basis for fame Y, you neither desire it nor desire not it. But you still desire only what holds in all the nearby desire worlds, not in all of them.

On this view, you do desire what you and we say you desire, but at the same time your protest is strictly accurate. (On the Error view, your actual desire is the one supposed here, and the protest is accurate, but the desire ascription does not match the actual desire and is false.)

To head off a possible misunderstanding: The similarity of my closeness semantics to a common semantics for conditionals ("A > C' is true iff C holds in every nearby A-world"[15]) may encourage the response: "So, you're saying that what someone really desires is conditional. On the common semantics, the content of the lunch desire is equivalent to, '*If* I eat lunch, it will be a decent, pleasant lunch.' But the subject's desire is not conditional at all, much less conditional upon eating lunch; he damn well wants to eat lunch. So the closeness semantics for desire-ascriptions makes a plainly false prediction." —But this misses the semantics' revisionary point: First, the desire-ascription whose semantics it is is, precisely, "S desires to eat lunch," and that target sentence is taken as true; it is not being denied. Second, the objector applied the common semantics for conditionals directly to the desire-ascription's complement clause, and that is exactly the Fodorian idea that the closeness theorist is now rejecting; at best, the objector would have to interpret the conditional-desire sentence "S desires that if S eats lunch, it will be a decent, pleasant lunch" as "'If S eats lunch, it will be a decent, pleasant lunch' holds in every *nearby* desire world [not in every single one however remote]."

Yet I do not think the closeness theory is intuitively illuminating, at least not without adversion to a recent idea of Kris McDaniel's and Ben Bradley's (2008) about conditional desires in particular.

So, sixth: According to McDaniel and Bradley, conditional desire is a relation, not between a subject and a proposition, but between the subject and two propositions: such a desire has both an "object" proposition and the relevant "condition." The assumption here is that there are very few genuinely unconditional desires—which seems right: how often does someone desire that P *no matter what*, including the murder of her/his child, nuclear holocaust, etc?[16]

The ternary relation is taken as primitive. The condition may be tacit and quite complex; it need not be fully represented, but is normally the value of a contextual parameter. The authors go on to write satisfaction and frustration clauses on this basis; when a desire's condition fails, the desire is neither satisfied nor frustrated, but "cancelled" (p. 274). (In light of (I) and (II), those conditions would have to be tweaked, but that does not matter for now.)

Though they were not addressing my Grain problem, McDaniel's and Bradley's model bears directly upon it. If nearly every desire ascription has a vague and messy "condition" parameter, then finally it is straightforward that our problematic desire-ascriptions are correct but so are the protests. You want lunch, on the condition that the proffered lunch is decent and pleasant. You want fame, on the condition that it be based on something admirable. Absent those conditions, your desire is not satisfied, even though it is semantically satisfied. Your assertion, "I want to have lunch," was true in the context, and so was your protest that you did not want to have the lunch I force-fed you. (Your desire was real, but it was conditional, and "cancelled" in this case.)

This is our best option to date.[17] But it is a kind of "no-theory theory," in Steve Schiffer's phrase. We are not told what relation the new ternary relation is. Nor, more specifically, does the account succeed in comparing to genuinely conditional speech acts, such as conditional bets and conditional requests (though McDaniel and Bradley venture such a comparison (p. 276)): When a bet is conditional and its condition fails, the bet is off, period, and so too for requests; it is precisely as if no bet or request had been made. But a conditional desire whose condition fails still exists and is psychologically significant; it is not as if there had been no such desire.[18]

So McDaniel and Bradley have shown that our Grain situation has a model; but they have done nothing to explain what is going on. They have essentially just asserted that conditional desires have the features in question. I think they are right, but we should seek a deeper analysis.

The closeness theory is compatible *in form* with McDaniel and Bradley's thesis that the desires in question are conditional desires; a conditional desire in their sense is not an unconditional desire directed upon a conditional proposition. (Neither, of course, is it a conditional truth whose consequent is an unconditional desire. In that respect it is like conditional obligation.[19]) And intuitively, what is desired is a lunch, or fame, that meets certain tacit conditions. That they are tacit is the reason the corresponding desire ascription is put categorically and is not overtly conditional.

Therefore, seventh: We adapt the closeness theory to McDaniel and Bradley. "Nearby" is not right, if it is meant in Lewis' sense of similarity. The subset we want of the semantic desire worlds is, rather, that in which all the tacit conditions are met. This no longer is any notion of similarity, so let us call the worlds in the subset the "compliant" worlds

Having thus given our contextual semantics, we can dispense with McDaniel and Bradley's hidden parameter. There is no longer the need to take desire as a relation between two propositions, and accordingly no need for either of them to be mentioned in logical form.

(This compliance theory inherits the distinction-without-a-difference problem, but as before, there *is* a difference even if it is not as large as we would like.)

I promised explanation. You may be disappointed, or even moved to derision. Appeals to possible worlds are not known for their explicatory accomplishments. ("What is it for a proposition P to be possible?"—"It's for P to be true in every possible world." "What is it for someone to believe that P?"—"It's for P to be true in all that person's doxastic alternatives."—"Oh, I see.") Of course, if David Lewis' infamous modal concretism is assumed as the background metaphysics, such explanations become *highly* substantive—a little too substantive for many. But even absent concretism, the appeal to worlds does illuminate to some degree. It puts desires, especially conditional desires, in a familiar formal context, and thereby affords comparisons with beliefs, obligations, conditionals themselves and so on. And as always it explains patterns of valid and invalid inference.

Rejecting the Fodorian idea aforementioned (that we get a semantics for conditional desire by applying a semantics for conditionals directly to the relevant desire sentence's complement) brings us back to one of the Stampe issues: Since the compliance theory does not simply read the propositional content of the complement clause out from under the desire operator, does it propose a *different psychosemantics* for desires? This proves to be a tricky question. Conservatively: For all that has been shown, the referents of the mental terms that figure in a Fodorian representation underlying a desire are determined in whatever is the usual psychosemantic way (indicator, asymmetric dependence, causal-historical, teleological or whatever). Assuming the subject's desire is an occurrent one, the same concepts EAT and LUNCH figure in it as are the corresponding constituents of his belief that he will eat lunch. But that does not settle the matter, since the belief is uncomplicatedly true if the fact is he will eat lunch, and according to the compliance theory, nothing parallel holds for desires. And a pointed question arises: If Fodor is right and what makes the desire-ascription true is a representation harbored within the subject's brain, what exactly is the content of that representation itself?

Despite the close relation between the Sellarsian semantics for attitude ascriptions and Fodor's ontology of the attitudes, the former is not always a reliable guide to the latter.[20] If we assume the Sellarsian form of semantics but go with Fodor in the matter of content individuation, we're told that "S desires that P" is true iff $(\exists r)(\bullet P\bullet(r)\ \&\ DES(S,r))$," r being a token that shares the truth-condition of the complement sentence that replaces "P," which would mean that the putative representation in the subject's brain would have to be "true" or semantically-satisfied iff he will in fact eat lunch. And so it is, trivially by definition of "semantic satisfaction." But as before, that does not settle the matter at issue. It is not a given that semantic satisfaction matters, with desires, and (I), (II) and (III) suggest that semantic satisfaction is at best a necessary condition for what does matter. An adequate psychosemantics will have to predict the desire's semantic-satisfaction condition, but it, or something, would also have to attach a *real* satisfaction condition to the brain state in question, and that is what the compliance theory proposes.

(But does the compliance theory help with (I) and (II)? Alas, no. It would predict (I) only if we were to assume that every compliant world is one in which the desire's reference time has already arrived, which is silly. It would predict (II) if we stipulate that at every compliant world, the subject's desire continues to exist; but the stipulation would be purely ad hoc.)

I await further three-cornered debate, with deflationist followers of Prinz and error theorists.[21]

IV.

(IV) Tal Brewer (2006) and Paul Thagard (2006) have argued that, far from having propositional contents that parallel those of beliefs, desires need not (and perhaps characteristically do not) have *propositional* contents at all. Desires can be simply for things.[22]

Of course it seems that when a desire ascription has only a singular term or an indefinite description marking its object position, something needs filling in. "I want X" and "I want an F" invite the question "What is it you want to do with/to...?"; a transitive verb is called for. Searle (1983, p. 30) offers a wonderfully specific syntactic argument on this point: Consider the sentence "I want your house next summer." The adverbial "next summer" does not modify "want"; but it has to modify a verb. So there is a second, ellipsized verb, though the hearer may have no idea what verb it is. ("Actually I want to drop it on the Wicked Witch of the East.")

Of course, Searle's argument shows only that a desire ascription *that contains such an adverbial* has a hidden verb. Nor does it offer any way of determining what verb it is. We may think that the verb is at least in the speaker's mind, but that may well not be so.[23] The speaker may have no specific intentions regarding the house, though there are plenty s/he does not have. We might try something general, such as "use," but it may not be true that the speaker wants to *use* the house for anything. Or we may offer a dummy term such as "have," but that only leads to ambiguity: "I will have your house next summer" does not express any single proposition.[24]

Brewer (2006) argues that desires for things are themselves often genuinely indeterminate in this way. Dorothy (p. 263—not Dorothy Gale) definitely wants a Harley-Davidson. But does she want to *own* one in the legal sense? Not necessarily. Does she want to ride one? Maybe or maybe not. The point is not epistemological, not merely that Dorothy may not know exactly what she wants; it is that her desire state is focused on a Harley-Davidson even though nothing in (or outside) her psychology determines any but a broadly and vaguely disjunctive relation she might bear to one.

Undeniably, we have some crisply propositional desires. Dennett (1987, p. 20) points out that there are desires you cannot have without knowing a public language (or at least having a representational system of comparable power): "I want a two-egg mushroom omelet, some French bread and butter, and half a bottle of lightly chilled white Burgundy." But Brewer argues that (typically) the desire or desire complex in question goes beyond that content; the words, though accurate so far as they go, flatten the thing actually wanted.

Thagard (2006) appeals to the case of nonhuman animals, which certainly desire things like *food* and *warmth* but, he contends, not propositional expansions of those. (a) The animals cannot represent themselves, as in "...that *I* eat food"; (b) they are not good at representing relations, as in "...that I *eat* food."

Such arguments can be resisted.[25] But here again, desire differs from belief in that there is a serious issue about the nature of its contents.

I shall leave that issue, and the others, at this point. But I hope I have said enough to convince you that the notion of desire content is fraught, and that desire is not, or not obviously, a propositional attitude in the same way as belief is. Wishing, resenting, regretting, and being embarrassed will require at least another paper.[26]

Notes

1. It was not always so. In their respective famous catalogues of mental states, neither Ryle (1949) nor Armstrong (1968) said anything about desires. Rather, talk of desire came out of action theory, most notably from Davidson (1963), and entered mainstream philosophy of mind only in the 1970s. Philosophy papers on propositional attitudes, attitude content and related matters occasionally acknowledge that there are propositional attitudes other than belief: desire, intention, remembering, guessing, speculating, wondering, hoping, wishing, resenting, regretting, being embarrassed, etc. Those same philosophy papers then discuss only belief. Desire, intention and memory very

occasionally receive attention from philosophers of mind and philosophers of psychology; the other attitudes almost never. It is an interesting question why belief holds this overwhelming social preëminence over the other attitudes.

2. The point goes back at least to Locke (1974).

3. Dennett has nowhere replied to this objection.Wall (2012) argues that desire parallels belief at least in admitting Moore's-Paradox-like cases, but he takes that finding to count against instrumentalism regarding desires.

4. Thanks to Annette Baier for a useful conversation about this. And Don Locke (1982, p.243) made a quick version of this argument.

5. Of course, one may come much closer to predicting behavior if one has some independent access to the subject's *other pro-attitudes*.

6. See Lycan (1986).

7. This of course ignores *wh*-questions, but *wh*-questions have true or false answers depending on the singular term that gets plugged into their matrices. For example, "Who left the gate open?" generates the answer-class {"Alice left the gate open," "Bill left the gate open,". . .}, and is correctly or incorrectly answered by a member of that class accordingly as that member is true or false. Similarly, "When does the game start?" generates {"The game starts at 2:00 p.m.," "The game starts at 2:30 p.m.,". . .}. And, intuitively, the meaning of a *wh*-question is parasitic on the meanings of its admissible answers.

8. Members of audiences to which I presented early versions of this paper in 2009 and 2010 can confirm that the text then spoke of a *fourth* visit in *2012*. Precognitive? Or perhaps someone took the hint.

9. Gordon takes these points to show that the "object" (p. 109) of the desire is not simply to eat. He suggests that the object is that one eat *and* by doing so quench the appetite. (On this, see sec. iii below.) I think Gordon does not sufficiently distinguish between hunger, a drive and/or sensation or feeling, and a desire qua propositional attitude (one may desire to eat even though one is not at all hungry, and vice versa), but the difference does not much matter to his four claims. Perhaps the fourth one depends: In one sense the desire would be satisfied, because what I wanted was to eat and I did eat; it is just that now I want to eat more. Maybe that sense is only that of semantic satisfaction; I am inclined to think not.

10. For a much fuller and richer presentation of Stampe's theory of desire, see his (1987).

11. Lycan (1985, 1994) and Boër and Lycan (1986) maintain that attitude ascriptions are contextually ambiguous as between roughly these two individuation schemes for dot-items; it is that difference of scheme that determines opaque vs. transparent readings.

12. This phenomenon is the main theme of the 1967 movie *Bedazzled*, starring Peter Cook and Dudley Moore.

13. It may be felt that the force-fed Brussels sprouts do not qualify as *lunch* at all. If so, delete the mold and the force-feeding; I merely invite you to lunch and then place twenty-five boiled soggy Brussels sprouts on a plate before you. Politeness compels you to eat them.

14. Lewis (1979) admits that his closeness relation does not always track intuitive similarity.

214 / William G. Lycan

15. Not Lewis' (1973) own semantics, of course, but a simpler one adopted by Nozick (1981) and Lycan (1984, 2001).
16. McDaniel and Bradley represent genuinely unconditional desires as desires that are conditional on necessary truths such as "that something is the case" (p. 278), thereby preserving their model of desire as a relation of a subject to two propositions.
17. In conversation, Cei Maslen has suggested what may be a further option: to understand desire ascriptions as containing tacit *ceteris paribus* clauses. To assess that plausible idea, we would have to go through each of the various analyses there are of c.p. clauses in turn (Reutlinger et al. (2011)). But intuitively, c.p. clauses are vague conditional antecedents, and so a c.p. view would be a species of conditional account.
18. McDaniel and Bradley (ibid.): "[I]n an important respect it is as if the desire never happened." I do not see that at all.
19. I am thinking of the approach to conditional obligation pursued by van Fraassen (1972), Lewis (1973, 1974) and especially Feldman (1986), on which conditional obligation is itself a relation between two propositions. However, for a critique of that approach, see Bonevac (1998).
20. As we were reminded long ago by Devitt (1984).
21. Stampe raises a further issue about closure (of belief and desire under entailment), and he tackles it by applying his variant psychosemantics.
22. Hanoch Ben-Yami (1997) defends the much more general thesis that mental states generally are not propositional attitudes—not even belief.
23. I think this point is of some syntactic interest, but I have not yet discussed it with any linguist.
24. Humberstone (1990) resists that contention, maintaining that the dummy "have" is merely nonspecific rather than ambiguous. But the point remains that either way, it is vacuous and does not reflect any determinate psychological property of the subject.
25. Vs. Thagard: (a) is true but does not show that the creature itself does not figure in the semantic satisfaction condition. (b) is true but does not show that the creature does not represent a relevant relation in any way at all.
26. I am grateful to audiences at East Tennessee State University, the University of Sydney, the University of Otago, Victoria University of Wellington, and the APA Pacific Division meeting in Vancouver, 2009. Thanks also to Fred Schueler, Bob Gordon and Tim Schroeder, my expert co-symposiasts on that last occasion. And to Paul Bloomfield and Dan Moseley for detailed comments on a subsequent draft.

References

Armstrong, D.M. 1968. *A Materialist Theory of the Mind*. London: Routledge and Kegan Paul.
Ben-Yami, H. 1997. "Against Characterizing Mental States as Propositional Attitudes." *Philosophical Quarterly* 47: 84–89.
Boër, S.E., and W.G. Lycan. 1986. *Knowing Who*. Cambridge, MA: Bradford Books / MIT Press.
Bonevac, D. 1998. "Against Conditional Obligation." *Noûs* 32: 37–53.

Brewer, T. 2006. "Three Dogmas of Desire." In *Values and Virtues: Aristotelianism in Contemporary Ethics*, edited by T.D.J. Chappell, 257–84. Oxford: Oxford University Press.

Davidson, D. 1963. "Actions, Reasons and Causes." *Journal of Philosophy* 60: 685–700.

Dennett, D.C. 1987. *The Intentional Stance.* Cambridge, MA: Bradford Books / MIT Press.

Devitt, M. 1984. "Thoughts and Their Ascription." *Midwest Studies in Philosophy* 9: 385–420.

Feldman, F. 1986. *Doing the Best We Can.* Dordrecht: D. Reidel.

Fodor, J.A. 1975. *The Language of Thought.* New York: Crowell.

Fodor, J.A. 1981. *RePresentations.* Cambridge, MA: Bradford Books / MIT Press.

Gordon, R. 1986. "The Circle of Desire." In Marks (1986).

Humberstone, I. 1990. "Wanting, Getting, Having." *Philosophical Papers* 99: 99–118.

Lewis, D.K. 1973. *Counterfactuals.* Cambridge, MA: Harvard University Press.

Lewis, D.K. 1974. "Semantic Analysis for Dyadic Deontic Logic." In *Logical Theory and Semantic Analysis: Essays Dedicated to Stig Kanger on His Fiftieth Birthday*, edited by S. Stedlund, 1–14. Dordrecht: D. Reidel.

Lewis, D.K. 1979. "Counterfactual Dependence and Time's Arrow." *Noûs* 13: 455–76.

Locke, D. 1974. "Reasons, Wants, and Causes." *American Philosophical Quarterly* 11: 169–79.

Locke, D. 1982. "Beliefs, Desires, and Reasons for Action." *American Philosophical Quarterly* 19: 241–49.

Lycan, W.G. 1984. "A Syntactically Motivated Theory of Conditionals." *Midwest Studies in Philosophy*, Vol. IX. Minneapolis: University of Minnesota Press.

Lycan, W.G. 1985. "The Paradox of Naming." In *Analytical Philosophy in Comparative Perspective*, edited by B.-K. Matilal and J.L. Shaw, 81–102. Dordrecht: D. Reidel.

Lycan, W.G. 1986. "Moral Facts and Moral Knowledge." *Southern Journal of Philosophy* 24, Supplement: 79–94. Reprinted as Ch. 11 of *Judgement and Justification* (Cambridge: Cambridge University Press, 1988).

Lycan, W.G. 1994. *Modality and Meaning.* Dordrecht: Kluwer Academic Publishing, Studies in Linguistics and Philosophy series.

Lycan, W.G. 2001. *Real Conditionals.* Oxford: Oxford University Press.

Marks, J., ed. 1986. *The Ways of Desire.* Chicago: Precedent.

McDaniel, K., and B. Bradley. 2008. "Desires." *Mind* 117: 267–302.

Nozick, R. 1981. *Philosophical Explanations.* Cambridge, MA: Harvard University Press.

Prinz, J. 2008. "No Satisfaction? The Mundane Truth about Desire." MS, University of North Carolina.

Reutlinger, Alexander, G. Schurz and A. Hüttemann. 2011. "Ceteris Paribus Laws." *Stanford Encyclopedia of Philosophy*, E.N. Zalta (ed.), URL = <http://plato.stanford.edu/archives/spr2011/entries/ceteris-paribus/>.

Ryle, G. 1949. *The Concept of Mind.* London: Hutchinson.

Schueler, F. 1995. *Desire.* Cambridge, MA: Bradford Books / MIT Press.

Searle, J.R. 1983. *Intentionality.* Cambridge: Cambridge University Press.

Sellars, W. 1956. "Empiricism and the Philosophy of Mind." In *Minnesota Studies in the Philosophy of Science*, vol. I, edited by H. Feigl & M. Scriven, 253–329. Minneapolis, MN: University of Minnesota Press.

Stampe, D. 1986. "Defining Desire." In Marks (1986).

Stampe, D. 1987. "The Authority of Desire." *Philosophical Review* 96: 335–81.

Thagard, P. 2006. "Desires Are Not Propositional Attitudes." *Dialogue* 45: 151–56.

Van Fraassen, B. 1972. "The Logic of Conditional Obligation." *Journal of Philosophical Logic* 1: 417–38.

Wall, D. 2012. "A Moorean Paradox of Desire." *Philosophical Explorations* 15: 63–84.

Philosophical Perspectives, 26, Philosophy of Mind, 2012

ARE THERE MENTAL INDEXICALS AND DEMONSTRATIVES?

Ruth Garrett Millikan
University of Connecticut

1. Plan of the Essay

The answer to our question turns, I think, on three prior issues.

First, since the notions of mental indexicals and demonstratives are derived from those of linguistic indexicals and demonstratives, we need to start with a description of the latter forms. David Kaplan (1989a,b) suggested that we represent their semantic meanings as functions from the contexts in which they are tokened to elements of propositional content. Manuel Garcia-Carpentero (2000) has proposed an account of indexicals according to which reflexive reference to the indexical token constitutes part of the sense of the indexical. John Perry has offered a not dissimilar account according to which indexicals and demonstratives have reflexive content that is not part of what is "said" but still helps us to "understand the reasoning that motivates the production of utterances, and the reasoning that is involved in their interpretation" (Perry 2006, p. 323). These authors seem to agree on the nature of the extensional relations between indexicals and demonstratives and their referents, that is, on how their contributions to truth conditions are determined, though they describe these extensional relations in different ways. I will start by suggesting still a fourth way of looking at the truth condtional semantics of indexicals and demonstratives, one that is extraordinarily simple. I do not think that this simple analysis is in any way mandatory. It is just one more way of describing the same mapping from language to world. But it is a way of describing this mapping that greatly simplifies and clarifies the question whether indexicals and demonstratives might have mental counterparts.

Second, we need to know what kind of relation between a linguistic indexical/demonstrative and a thought would count as showing that the thought is indexical/demonstrative too. Is a thought to be called "indexical" or "demonstrative" because it is of a peculiar kind that is expressed or transmitted whenever one uses or understands a linguistic indexical or demonstrative properly? Or is the thought to be called "indexical" or "demonstrative" because it is a representation whose truth conditional semantics is like that a linguistic indexical or demonstrative? I will argue against the view that different linguistic forms having the same referents correspond, as such, to different kinds of thoughts expressed. I will argue, that is, against, the view that referential terms possess any relative of Fregean sense — yes, even for the case of referential descriptions. In particular, there is no such thing as a peculiar "cognitive significance" of an indexical or of a demonstrative as such. If there are mental indexicals or demonstratives then, they must be thoughts that have are truth-conditional semantic analogs of linguistic indexicals.

Third, I will try to show that although indexical terms do not generally correspond to indexical thoughts, still there probably is an interesting analogy between the truth conditional semantics of a restricted set of linguistic indexicals and certain kinds of thoughts which might therefore be called "indexical." And although demonstrative terms do not necessarily correspond to demonstrative thoughts, there is also an interesting analogy between the way linguistic demonstratives work and the way thoughts sometimes work when they concern things one is currently perceiving, thus making it sensible to call them "demonstrative thoughts."

2. Linguistic Indexicals and Demonstratives

There are three ways the truth conditional semantic analyses I will give of linguistic indexicals and demonstratives do not come directly out of the box. First, I will discard the commonly made assumption that conventional language forms include only spoken or written parts, or more broadly, only parts that are produced, made, fashioned, by the speaker or writer herself. I will argue that part of what is typically labeled as the "context" in which a token of a linguistic form occurs can sometimes be illuminatingly considered as a proper part of the conventional sign itself. Sometimes it is part of the pattern that a language learner has learned to use in a conventional way in learning the basic conventions of a language.

Second, I will refuse the assumption, often made implicitly even when denied explicitly, that the relation of a linguistic sign that expresses a proposition to its extension is built up by combining its parts which have independent prior extensional meaning. I will bring to center focus that the sign-signified relation is always at root a relation between complete states of affairs, not reducible to a set of relations between parts of signs and parts of states of affairs.

Third, with these ideas clearly in mind it will emerge that there are such things as conventionally self-signifying signs, things that figure both in a state of affairs that is being conventionally used as a sign and in the state of affairs that is conventionally signified by it. Sometimes, that is, things are conventionally used to stand for themselves. Also, less dramatically, sometimes things are used to stand, conventionally, for other things that bear to them not the identity relation but some other identity-determining relation. (Compare the relation of an inch-long line on an architect's scale drawing to the length — say a foot — that it represents.) In these latter cases we can interpret what Kaplan called "character" more simply, as functions, not from context to content, but from natural properties of the very sign itself to its content.

I will use the word "signers" to cover speakers, writers, deaf language signers, those who manage to communicate in any other linguistic media such as hand-spelling, brail, semaphore, whatever.

We tend to think of conventional linguistic forms as composed entirely of parts that are fashioned by the signers themselves, parts such as vocal sounds, ink patterns, or in the case of sign languages, gestures. It is true that gestures have as aspects certain physical body parts, and these parts are not of course created by signers in the act of signing. But these parts are typically involved in the language not as such, but only as occurrently shaped, positioned and moving in certain ways, these ways being fashioned by the signers themselves. That its meaningful elements should be wholly created by the signer, however, is not intrinsic to the conventionality of a language. One could imagine, for example, having a box full small blocks with symbols on them and communicating or making up stories by setting these blocks in rows to make sentences. Using this kind of language would be rather limited and inconvenient, but the example makes clear that it is not the manufacturing by signers of individual word tokens that is intrinsic to conventional language, but the arranging of the parts into new sentences.

With the above in mind, consider certain words in ASL that apparently contain as parts tokens that fall within their own extensions. Words for body parts typically are such words. The words for tongue and for chin and for hair, for example, consist in certain ways of pointing to the signer's own tongue or chin or hair. Clearly in these cases the signer does not create those significant parts of the sign. Those parts of the sign are just handily found to be close by and incorporated as such into the pattern that is a full ASL sentence. One might suppose that within the context of such an ASL sentence, these body parts stand for their own types according to a conventional function from a token body part to its general kind. But although it certainly makes ASL easier to learn that body parts are typically named by making some kind of gesture towards them, and although it is clear that these signs originated as mere pointings, that general supposition would be wrong. There is no general rule in ASL that gesturing toward a body part constitutes a name for that part. Moreover, in each case the exact manner of gesturing toward the part so named is conventionalized in its own way. My immediate interest in these signs is rather as illustrations that things conveniently found lying around in the context of the rest of a language, rather than wholly created during the production of the language, may sometimes be fully incorporated into the language itself as elements helping to complete fully conventional linguistic patterns. The lesson is only that we need to be careful not too readily to make assumptions about where the line between language and context is to be drawn. Context need not include everything that was there before the signer came along. Some of the things that were there before the conventional sign was produced may have been co-opted to help in composing the sign.

Return now to the language that is signed by arranging small blocks with words written on them into sentences. One could imagine that besides just rearranging these blocks, it was conventional to accompany one's constructions with manual or auditory gestures whose function was to indicate whether one's constructions were to be taken as representing states of affairs being described, or instead being requested, or demanded, or wished for and so forth, and perhaps also whether the states of affairs were past, present or future. Just as it is not intrinsic to language that it create all its parts on the fly, it is not intrinsic to language that it use only one medium of expression, all significant parts occurring in the same modality. Conventional linguistic patterns that arrange together parts from several sensory modalities are surely possible.

Coupling the observation that a conventional language need not create all its utilized parts with the observation that it might utilize parts from more than one medium, there seems no principled reason to assume that the boundaries of a conventional spoken language lie exactly where the sound ends and the rest of the world begins. It is possible that pieces of the neighboring world are sometimes incorporated right into the linguistic conventions themselves.

Consider, for example, the convention of writing or pasting labels on things — a can with a label on it that says "spinach" or a bridge with a sign that says "unsafe for lorries." The conventional signs that result are not composed just of words. The word "spinach" obviously says nothing hanging by itself in the air. It is true that we sometimes say, for example, just "black clouds mean rain" or just "a fever probably means an infection." But speaking more carefully, it is not the black clouds that have a meaning. Rather, the fact that black clouds are forming over a certain place at a certain time means it will soon rain in that place at that time. Or the fact that someone, say Johnny, has a fever means that that person, Johnny, has an infection. Signs, in the first instance, always sign complete propositions. Coordinately, signs themselves (tokens), in the first instance, are complete states of affairs. Johnny's fever, taken by itself, fails to signify anything in the same way that "... has an infection" fails to signify anything. In each case, more parts of the sign need to be filled in before we have a complete sign. Similarly for "spinach" taken by itself. It is not a complete sign until the rest of a propositional sign is filled in. In the case of "spinach" as a label on a can, the rest of the sign is the filled can. One might think of the relation of the physical word "spinach" to the contents of the can — the relation being-on-a-container-with-X-contents — as the syntactic form of the sign.

Notice further that the "sign design" (Wilfrid Sellars), that is the shape, "spinach," taken just by itself, doesn't even compose the English word "spinach," unless it occurs as a reproduction of prior instances of that very word.[1] Formed accidentally in the clouds, exactly the same shape as the English word "spinach" would no more be that word than the sign design "rot" is the German word "rot" in my sentence, "that words are individuated as nothing more than sign designs is just rot." If scratched accidentally by an infant on a blank label, the physical sign design "spinach" is not a word any more than if it had been scratched on a rock by a glacier. Exactly conversely, if following our ordinary labeling conventions, a filled can is purposefully placed under a lable saying "spinach," the filled can *does* become, if not exactly a word, certainly a significant part of a meaningful conventional sign. In both cases, what makes the thing a symbol, a part of a conventional sign, involves that is has purposefully been used to help complete a pattern of a kind conventionally used for communication.

What completes the state of affairs constituting the sign that there is spinach in the can is the very can-of-something resting under the label. The can-with-contents stands for itself. When the relation between a sign and its signified is partly constituted by an identity of parts or aspects, a self-sign doing the major work of connecting the sign token with the signified state of affairs, it is very easy to overlook that particular feature of the sign-signed relation. Indeed, to be guided by a self-sign in the production of appropriate thought or behavior to understand the self-sign is the same as to be directly guided, in part, by that which is signified. The illusion then is that no interpretation of the self-sign part of the sign is needed; the distinction between this part of the sign and its signified disappears. The self-signed part of the sign is perceived directly, not merely understood by means of a sign. But being more careful, we can see that the distinction is there. The self-sign's relation to the rest of the completed sign is one thing, the self-sign's (qua self-signified's) relation to the rest of the completed signified is another.

Now consider a stop sign. The convention is that a stop sign is placed just before the place at which one is to stop. Where the stop sign is placed signifies where one is to stop. The complete sign consists not just in a sign saying "stop" but in its standing in a certain place. Subtracting the place, the bare sign does not signify anything. So it seems that not only can an object such as a can and its contents become incorporated into a sign and made to stand for itself, a place can be incorporated into a sign and made to stand for itself.

Consider a red stop light. Not only its place but also the time it occurs stands for itself. Using particular places and particular times to stand for themselves is such an obvious thing to do that it disappears. It is nearly invisible because of its very ease and simplicity. Similarly, the color on the outside of a marking pen conventionally stands for itself — for the same color — on the inside. Sensible, but conventional. And one inch can stand for itself — for one inch — on a scale drawing. And when I shake my fist at you I make a conventional sign that RGM, the one shaking the fist, is angry at you, the one being addressed with the fist. I stand for myself and you stand for yourself.

Sentences are often completed by inserting them into contexts so as to incorporate aspects of the context into the sign itself in a conventional way. Both time and place are often used in this way. When someone observes "It's raining," the place it is said stands for the place it is said to be raining.[2] The time it is said stands for the time it is said to be raining. The time at which a past tense sentence is tokened is also a sign of the time of the state or event that it represents, but in this case the sign is not a self sign. The convention is that the time of the affair represented is determined as a function of the time the past tense sentence is tokened. Similarly for tokens in future tense. Compare again an architect's drawing where one inch stands for a length twelve times as long. Many natural signs work the same way. Lightning here now serves as a natural sign of thunder here soon; the time of the affair signified is an identity-determining function of the time of the sign.

One more example before turning directly to the role of those signed elements that have traditionally been called "indexical" and "demonstrative." English directives are generally given in the imperative mood, a standard feature of which is the absence of an articulated subject term. Consider "Please go!" The satisfaction condition for a token of this type is the obtaining of a full state of affairs, namely, that the person addressed goes out or away shortly after the sentence is spoken. Clearly, both the time of speaking and the person addressed are being used here as part of the sign; the person addressed is a self sign. If there is no addressee, no satisfaction condition is determined. If you hear the directive but cannot tell to whom it is being addressed, you will not grasp its satisfaction condition. Whatever you have to observe in order to interpret the meaning of a sign you have learned may reasonably be considered to be a part of the sign. So, like the can with a label on it, the addressee may be considered to stand for himself or herself.[3] In ASL, there are no first and second person personal pronouns. Instead, the speaker or the hearer are pointed to at appropriate points in the temporal syntax. They stand for themselves.

Now instead of "Please go" one could of course say, "Would you please go," in which case "you" stands for the person who is to go. "You" has traditionally been called an "indexical," the question for truth-functional semantics being how the referent of "you" is determined. Unlike the case of proper names and of most other extensional words, the referent of "you" shifts from occasion to occasion. But unlike the way in which the sign design "John" shifts its referent from occasion to occasion depending on which John is meant, the way the referent of "you" shifts is systematic. Quite obviously, the referent is determined as whoever the speaker happens to be addressing. Thus anyone who would grasp it's satisfaction condition must know to whom it is addressed. As before, what this suggests is that the addressee is actually part of the sign. The addressee is part of the sign on the assumption (or stipulation) that whatever it is necessary to observe or know of in order to grasp the conventional truth conditions of a sign, granted that one knows all the relevant conventions, must be part of the sign. Without it the sign is incomplete.

The interesting result is that the "you" in "Would you please go" now appears merely to be *anaphoric*, requiring no special analysis under a special label "indexical." As anaphoric — call this "intermodal anaphora" — its contribution is merely to make explicit the place of the addressee *qua self-sign* within the syntactic form of the sentence, hence the place of the addressee *qua signified* within the state of affairs rpresented.[4] In ASL, the second person pronoun is formed by sharply jabbing the first finger of the right hand at the addressee *at the syntactically appropriate time* in the sign sequence. In a spoken language it is impossible to incorporate the actual referent intended into the spoken syntactic form of the sentence, so an anaphoric element is inserted into that position instead.

Consider the general form of the problem that is solved by using intermodal anaphora to designate things present to both speaker and hearer. If part of what you want to talk about — perhaps an object, perhaps a property and so forth — is itself present as you speak, it may be convenient to use it as a sign for itself rather than trying to find some different sign for it that your hearer will easily understand. You would like to *label* this something — as one might label a can — with a linguistic description that will provide some information to your hearer about it. But there is a practical difficulty. In a spoken language, the logical position of an object or property within a state of affairs to be represented is usually indicated by the syntactic position of the sign for this thing, the syntactic position being determined by inflection or by position within the sentence order. With rare exceptions ("Gargantua was so called because of his size"), neither of these ways can be used with an object or property that stands for itself. The object cannot itself be placed, say, in the subject or direct object position, or have its form inflected. The spoken part of your sentence needs to be attached at the right place somehow to the object that is to form the rest of your conventional sign. So you insert a dummy anaphoric "pro-word" into the needed syntactic position.

But, of course, there must also be a way for the hearer to know to what the anaphoric word refers. There must be a way of anchoring the part of the environment that you wish to use as a self sign to the spoken part of your sign. The spoken label has to be stuck, somehow, onto the bottle, not just left fluttering about. This anaphoric anchoring may be achieved in a number of different conventional ways, sometimes also in nonconventional ways, the latter being a matter for pragmatics. Here I want to emphasize first the conventional ways, because owing to the traditional focus that considers only the audible aspects of a (spoken) language to be parts of the linguistic signs themselves (indeed, often only the audible parts that are analyzable into rearrangements of conventional phonemes), it is underappreciated that there are various conventional ways of aligning spoken forms with outside things so as to fuse them into a single conventional representation.

These ways require the fashioning of a conventionally specified relation of some kind between the environmental element that stands for itself and its spoken pro-word. Taking "he," "she," "then" and "there" as our first examples, sometimes the pro-word word helps out by restricting the category of its referent, in the above cases to a male, to a female, to a time, to a place. Restrictions may also be imposed with a description, as in "that girl" or "this chair" or "the fountain over there with dolphins." In the case of "I," of "you," of "here" of "now" and of "yesterday," for example, the antecedents are not just restricted but fully determined by the relations they bear to the pro-word token. "I" refers back to the speaker of the token, "you" back to the addressee, "yesterday" back to the day before the tokening, and so forth. In the less determinate cases of third person pronouns and of "there," and "then," "this" and "that," often the anaphoric reference is intramodal rather than intermodal. Then the antecedent may be determined according to syntactic rules that work just as strictly as the rules for "I," "you" and "now." (In the case of English at least, these rules have been carefully studied.) But where these pro-words appear as so-called "demonstratives," that is, when they are intermodally anaphoric, issues involved in their analysis have generally been relegated to pragmatics, which is thought of as dealing with uses of language that lie beyond what is merely conventional.

Our reflections above that aspects of the environment may serve conventionally as parts of conventional linguistic signs suggest that we should postpone pragmatics and look first for conventional ways of anchoring demonstrative pro-words to their intermodal antecedents. Obvious candidates are various conventional ways of pointing, with body parts, with arrows, with spatial position relative to the signer or to the sign. I have noted that a label's position on the thing labeled can be viewed as a conventional syntactic form that fuses label and labeled into a single multimodal conventional representation. Similarly, when they are conventional or conventionalized, the relations that serve to tie demonstratives to their referents can be viewed as syntactic relations. These relations may not, however, be strongly digitalized, as what counts as the same word or sentence again is digitalized by strong digitalization of its component phonemes. What is allowed to count as a copy of an anchoring relation that has been used before may not be set in stone. A variety of different ways of pointing have become conventionalized, hence perhaps also fairly digitalized, in different cultures, pointing with this hand or that, with this finger or that, with the lips in various ways, with the eyes and head in certain ways. But these digitalized ways may also merge into less digitalized ways. Other conventionalized means of creating intermodally anaphoric signs have not, to my knowledge, been looked for, but perhaps a search would be fruitful.

When conventional ways of demonstrating merge into less conventional ways that rest more heavily on a hearer's capacity to discern what might coherently be meant, it has been traditional to assume that the referent of the demonstrative token is determined by whatever the speaker had in mind as the referent. Notice that the present analysis suggests a somewhat different formulation. The referent is determined by what the speaker had in mind *as composing the unspoken rest of his conventional linguistic sign.* Or, reading that transparently so as to retreat from the suggestion that the speaker has to think of his sign as a sign in order to use it, and retreating also from the Gricean mood in which all purposes are taken to be conceptualized intentions, we can put it thus. The referent is determined as that into which the spoken part of the sign was purposively put in relation, as the speaker copied a linguistic precedent, patterning this relation on relations that have previously served to specify external antecedents of such demonstratives for hearers. There is, that is, some kind of relation between his demonstrative word and its extramodal antecedent that was salient for him and that he used in reproducing, as he saw it, certain past salient relations between demonstratives and their extramodal relations. We can take the reproducing here to be sheer copying, unaccompanied by thoughts of likeness or thoughts of reproducing.[5] (Wiping away the Gricean intentions sometimes assumed to accompany all language use is not the project of this essay, although further themes relevant to such a project will surface in part III.[6])

3. How are linguistic forms related to forms of thought?

I'm not, as I said, proposing the above description of how indexicals and demonstratives determine their truth conditions as in any way mandatory. But the fact that this perspective is possible raises a question for the Fregean or neoFregean who would seek to find a particular and peculiar kind of thought that is expressed by indexicals or by demonstratives. Consider a Fregean to be someone who holds not only that different kinds of thoughts can correspond to or grasp the very same state of affairs, but that language works by transmitting, specifically, these different kinds of thoughts from speaker to hearer rather than by transmitting brute graspings of states of affairs. In addition to having referents, extensions and truth conditions, words and sentences bear certain "cognitive significances," meanings of a more fine grained type, many of which meanings may correspond to one and the same extensional meaning. Cognitive significance may be posited as the way that what is in or before the mind determines its reference, that is, as what Frege called a "mode of presentation" of the referent/extension. And/or it may be posited as what determines the kinds of inferences that can rationally be made using the thought, hence as helping to explain differences in inferences and action where simple grasp of extension would fail to do so.

A well known problem for Fregean positions has been the status of proper names. Direct reference theorists have argued that understanding a proper name does not involve a designated way of latching in thought onto its referent, or of making inferences concerning its referent. No special "cognitive significance" distinguishes one proper name from other proper names for the same individual. If we take seriously that the things referred to using indexicals and demonstratives stand for themselves, similar questions arise how *these* linguistic parts could possess, beyond their reference, some special kind of cognitive significance transmitted from speakers to hearers. We cannot assume, for example, that the way the signer grasps a self sign must be the same as the way the interpreter grasps it, for they will be observing the self sign from different perspectives, perhaps even using different sensory modalities. The view that there are special kinds of thoughts that should be called "indexical" or "demonstrative" for the reason that they are assigned specifically to the understanding of linguistic indexicals or demonstratives becomes problematic. However, rather than pressing this issue directly, trying to anticipate neoFregean replies, I am going to propose, or better, review,[7] a picture of the relation of language to thought that extends a direct reference analysis not just to self-signing linguistic constituents but to the majority of all extensional terms. On this analysis it will turn out that proper names, self-signing constituents and most other extensional terms are understood in exactly parallel ways, the thoughts that correspond to them across all competent users of a language having only reference or extension in common. They carry no public cognitive significance; no Fregean baggage.

Let me begin with the kinds of thoughts, the "ideas" in classical idiom, that lie behind one's uses of proper names for the people with whom one is most familiar. Begin, for example, with your idea of a parent or a sibling, a spouse or a best friend.[8] You will have accumulated piles of information about this person perhaps over many years. Consider by what means you have done this, the various ways you have used or might use to recognize when you were receiving more information about this same person.

You could do this by seeing them in the flesh, 20 meters up the street, perhaps at 1000 meters by his or her walk, certainly at 30 centimeters, from the front, from the back, from the left side or the right or most any other angle, half hidden behind another person or a chair or a table or a book, sitting, standing, lying down, yawning, stretching, running, eating, holding still or moving in any of various ways, in daylight or moonlight, under a street lamp, by candlelight, through a fog, in a photograph, on TV, through binoculars, by hearing their voice from any of many distances or as it passes through a variety of media such as lightweight walls, under water, over the phone, despite many kinds of masking sounds such as wind, or rain, or other people talking, and so forth.

Now generalize the ordinary notion of recognizing a person just a bit so that it encompasses your wider ability to keep track of when information is arriving at your various senses in other forms about this same person. You might recognize them, or signs of them that enabled you to gather information about them, by recognizing their signature or handwriting, their style of prose or humor or, perhaps, of musical interpretation or of some other activity, by the sound of the instrument they play coming from the next room or the hammering that accompanies their current home project, by recognizing their name when someone talks about them or when it is written, by hand or in any of hundreds of handwritings or fonts, and so forth.[9] You can also recognize that the information arriving is about them through many hundreds of descriptions: the person who was or did this or that, about whom this or that is true. Or you may recognize whom the information is about using various kinds of inference, induction or abduction. If these less immediate ways of recognizing a person seem to you to divide off rather sharply from recognizing them "in the flesh," recall that recognizing a person by their looks or voice is also gathering information about them *through signs*. The light that strikes your eyes, the vibrations that strike your ears, are merely signs of what you see or hear. It may also help to consider intermediate cases, such as seeing in the mirror, hearing over the telephone, recognizing in a video or through a telescope. These are all ways helping to funnel back to a single locus diverse pieces of information about the same thing, this person, that have been widely scattered through time and through space. They are input methods that you have acquired over time for putting all this information into just one particular mental "folder" (Strawson 1974, Lockwood 1971).

Our remarkable abilities to reidentify through diverse media under diverse conditions are not restricted to individual objects. We can recognize various properties, say, shapes or colors or distances, under various external conditions. Think of the variety of proximal visual stimulations — what actually hits the eye — to which a given shape may give rise when viewed from various angles, from different distances, under different lighting conditions, through various media such as mist or water, when colored different ways, when partially occluded. How shape constancy is achieved by the visual system, the capacity to recognize the same shape as the same under a wide range of proximal stimulation conditions, is a problem of enormous complexity on which psychologists of perception are still hard at work. And shape is coidentified by the haptic systems, feeling the shape of a small object in your hand in a variety of ways, with these fingers or those, when the object is turned this way or that way, perhaps by using two hands, by merely holding the object or by actively feeling or stroking it, by exploring with larger motions that involve your arms, body and perhaps legs, employing the touching surfaces of a wide variety of your body parts. This kind of perception of shape, which involves the coordination of information about the exact positions of one's body parts with information about what touches these parts, is of such a complex nature that psychologists have hardly begun to study it. Similarly, the variety of ways in which color constancy, texture constancy, size constancy, place constancy, distance constancy, sound constancy, phoneme constancy are achieved are enormously complicated matters. Recalling again that even the most direct perception is perception through signs, we can add information received about various properties through the use of all kinds of measuring instruments and scopes, and through the use of different kinds of inference. All of these are ways of bringing back to one focus the scattered bits and pieces of information about the disposition of a property that have been dispersed over space and time and through diverse media to impinge on our sensory surfaces.

In previous papers, I have argued that many and perhaps most of our words for empirically-known kinds correspond to what, following Mill, I have called "real kinds." Real kinds have a structure that separates them sharply from classes, and that makes clear why there both are and must be many alternative ways to recognize their members as such, none of them "definitional" of the kind. A real kind is recognized in much the same way that an individual is. There are very many different ways to recognize the presence of a dog or a cat, and many different ways to identify, for example, vitamin C.[10]

Above, I used Lockwood's metaphor (based on Strawson's lectures) of a file folder for the "place" that all the information gathered about the same individual is "put." This image is no longer helpful, however, when we must take into account collections of information involving kinds, properties and relations. One would have to model *thinking that Johnny is tall* as involving both putting *is tall* into the *Johnny* folder and putting *Johnny* into the *is tall* folder. The thought of Johnny and the thought of being tall would each take two forms, a mental word, say, and a mental folder, with no explanation of how these are bound together. But concentrate instead on what is supposed to be *accomplished* by putting information about the same thing "all in the same place." The purpose is that various pieces of information about the same should be enabled to *interact* with one another, one bit of information bearing on another or joining with another in the production of further thought or action. This requires only that information about the same be somehow *marked* as such, so that middle terms can be recognized for inference, the "marking" being such as to trigger the cognitive systems in appropriate ways.[11] Rather than proposing a physical model for this (my private image involves a neural network), I have recently coined the term "unicept" for the mental/neural marker or vehicle of such a focus *taken along with* the repertoire of input methods that the person harboring the unicept knows to employ.[12]

"Uni" is, of course, for *one*, and "cept" (as in "concept") is from Latin *capera*, *to take or to hold*. One's unicept of an object, or property, or kind, or relation etc., takes in many proximal stimulations and holds them as one distal entity. A developed unicept reaches through a radical diversity of sensory impressions to find the same distal thing again. (It may also have to sort through similar or identical sensory impressions to find diverse distal things behind them.) A unicept integrates identification methods, funneling information about the same into storage in a way that marks it as concerning the same, that is. marks it to interact in inference and action guidance in an appropriate way. A unicept could be thought of as a tiny developed *faculty*, designed for a very specific purpose, the purpose of collecting and integrating information about some particular thing. Note that a unicept is not a "concept" on any traditional reading of that word, but a capacity/achievement belonging to only one individual. It is a particular; no two people have the same unicept. Nor are similarities between different people's unicepts of the same thing to be taken for granted, but must be argued for separately or empirically determined.

Of special interest in regard to the matter of this essay, is the fact that should various people each possess a unicept of a certain thing, say of the kind *dog*, and should each possess an understanding the English word "dog" as one input method to their dog unicept, there is no necessary implication that they would possess any other common input methods for these unicepts, nor that they would possess common inference dispositions or uses for these unicepts. (It is well always to keep Helen Keller in mind, who actually spoke as well as writing English.) Children are almost never taught input methods nor inferential connections for the words they learn. They have to figure out on their own how to fill out their unicepts, learning to agree in judgment both with themselves and with others as they come to recognize over time when information is again likely to concern the same thing.[13] Understanding a word for something in one's home language or in a new language is merely one more way of feeding one's unicept of that thing with information. Typically, extensional terms *themselves* do not impart anything more than extension. The rest is filled in with whatever the interpreter's corresponding unicept happens to contain.

Gaining information by seeing or hearing or feeling a thing and gaining information by reading or hearing about it are not, in this respect, fundamentally different.[14] What is different, of course, is that unlike the information gained through ordinary perception, information though language very seldom concerns the current relation of the things learned about to oneself, as would be needed to guide immediate action on these things. What is nearly unique about observing the world through language is that conventional languages, even languages of the deaf, always exhibit a categorical or "digital" vehicular structure, for example, phonological or alphabetic, the words all being composed of recombinations of a quite limited number of recombined elements, or being at least highly conventionalized. For a sign system to be used reliably, the aspects that compose its syntactic structures and its words should be easily reidentifiable. It should be easy to tell when one is encountering the same sign again. Because each word is made up of some recombination of phoneme-like elements taken always from the same small pool, proficiency in reidentifying each of the elements yields proficiency in reidentifying every complete sign in the language. Indeed, words can generally be reidentified readily after only one hearing/sighting. A clear linear order and/or inflections composed also of repeating parts makes syntax equally clear.

Where self signs are used instead of words, and where syntactic conventions fade into less conventional forms that sometimes demand more of a hearer's discernment, nothing about the unicepts employed changes. Language does not determine the *form* of thought that is expressed or understood through it. It alters only the input means. Whether I say or understand that I am taller than Aino through the words "Ruth is taller than Aino," or the words "Ruth is taller than she is," or the words "Ruth is taller than you are" or the words " I am taller than you are," exactly the same thought is expressed. Of course it is true that I may know to identify a person in one way but not in another, by one name or description but not by another. And it is true that knowing about something, even oneself, does not imply either knowing its name or being able to recognize all of its traces. I can know that Mark Twain wrote *Tom Sawyer* without knowing that Samuel Clemens wrote *Tom Sawyer*, that is, without associating the names "Mark Twain" and "Samuel Clemens" with the same unicept.

Similarly — and relevant especially to Perry's claims in "The Problem of the Essential Indexical" (1979) — I can see that someone must be trailing sugar from a broken bag in their grocery basket without knowing it is Jane, hence without trying to inform her. And I can see that someone must be trailing sugar from their grocery cart without knowing it is I, hence without fixing my own sugar bag. These are entirely parallel. The indexicality of the word "I" has nothing to do with it. And when I am inclined to utter "A bear is chasing Perry" I will of course behave entirely differently from the way Perry will behave when he is inclined to utter "A bear is chasing me." We would need to do entirely different things to avoid the impending disaster. Similarly, having heard "A Bear is chasing Perry," Jane, standing on one side of Perry, will need to do something different from me, standing on the other, perhaps throwing sticks from the west while I throw rocks from the east. These differences have nothing to do with indexicality.

4. Parallels for indexicals and demonstratives in thought

Indexicals and demonstratives in thought are not then thoughts of a peculiar kind that is expressed or transmitted when one uses or properly understands a linguistic indexical or demonstrative, for there no such thoughts. We are left then with the question whether there is in thought anything that is *analogous* in any interesting way to a linguistic indexical or a linguistic demonstrative.

At first we might think the answer pretty negative. If thoughts are mental representations of some kind, and if indexicals and demonstratives always involve, at root, self signs, given that external objects and properties cannot literally be in the mind, it might seem that indexical or demonstrative thoughts could at most be thoughts about perceptions or thoughts. Perhaps there are such thoughts. But if so, they are not anything like what indexical and demonstrative thoughts have traditionally been taken to be.

Leaving this possibility aside, however, recall that both time and place are components of linguistic signs that sometimes serve indexically, standing for themselves. Is it possible, perhaps, that the time or the place of a thought might serve indexically as a sign of the time or place of that which the thought represents? When I suddenly realize that it's raining, does the time that I realize this represent the time that it's raining? Does the place represent the place?

Let me argue for that possibility. The key question here is surely what would *constitute*, say, that the time of a representation was, as such, the time that it represented. The answer is that the representation would have normally to be *used* in the guidance of action or inference, in accordance with design by evolution or by learning, in the following way. It would have to be used such that the correspondence of the representation time to the represented time served as a causally relevant factor in controlling the actions or inferences produced, controlling them such that these actions or inferences would suit the time of the represented.[15] Now it seems to me perfectly reasonable that that is exactly what the time of thinking that it's raining normally does. Further, in the typical case, ordinary perceptions of what is temporally present work in exactly the same way. The time of the perception represents the time of the represented.

Not all ordinary perception, however, is of what is temporally present. The outfielder, for example, immediately perceives not merely where the ball is but where it is going to land. (There is no mystery in this, of course, since all perception is mediated by proximal signs and signs can be signs of the future.) In such cases, the time of what is perceptually represented would seem to be determined as a direct function of the time of the representation. Similarly, ordinary perception generally tells of the places of things perceived *relative to various parts of the the perceiver,* hence relative, it would seem, to the representation itself. It appears then that the bulk representations that are in use when we are engaged in external activity indexicals in that they work through self-signing, or through identity determining functions that take themselves as arguments.

The question whether there are mental demonstratives seems to be rather different. Also whether there are indexicals corresponding to "I" and to "you," which have as values people rather than times or places. The strict answer has, I think, to be negative. To figure as referents of literal mental demonstratives, people, objects, demonstrated properties, kinds and so forth would have literally to be inside of our minds. But the impulse to *suppose* that there are mental demonstratives can be explained, I think, and the explanation is interesting.

There is one use of linguistic demonstratives that stands out as central and peculiar. Demonstratives can be used anaphorically to indicate items that are present but for which we have not only no ready words, but no prior or permanent unicepts. They can be used, for example, to designate passing objects that we have no need to or could not keep track of for long, or to designate momentary things such as sounds, or to designate colors so precise that we could only reidentify them concurrently, not by memory over time. Then we have to use demontratives to express the contents of our thoughts in words. Because these transitory ways of thinking of things force us into the use of linguistic demonstrtatives, these ways of thinking are considered "demonstrative." If you are thinking of something that you cannot reidentify and collect information about otherwise than by currently tracking it in perception, it is natural to call the thought itself demonstrative.

On the other hand, however, lots of the things that get called "this" or "that" are things that both speaker and hearer are quite able to identify otherwise, objects, kinds, properties, relations and so forth of which they know very well "what they are." The thoughts expressed with these uses of "this" and "that" are different in no way from thoughts that would be expressed using names for these things.

Notes

1. See Millikan 1984 Ch 4 and Kaplan 1990.
2. One can, of course, complete the sentence with "in Oshkosh" rather than letting the place stand for itself. One might even omit the "in Oshkosh" when it is clear that the information about the rain has just been directly transmitted from

Oshkosh, or that it is Oshkosh everyone is waiting to hear about. But it is of the essence of natural languages that *which* among a variety of different common conventions is the exact one being employed on a given occasion is typically left up to context. Knowing which kind of "bank" is being talked about is generally left up to context. Whether "Could you reach the hammer?" is a request for information or for a hammer is generally left up to context. In neither case does the existence of homonymous conventions require reduction of one convention to the other or an inference from knowledge of one convention to the other (Millikan 2001 para. 11, 2005 Chs. 3 and 10, 2008a).

3. In his (2001 Ch. 5.4 ff., 2006) John Perry suggests that we take parts of signs (and also signs the significance of which one doesn't understand) as having truth conditions of a deeper sort which he calls "reflexive," because if they were completed in certain ways or if they had certain conventional meanings they would be true or would be false. This seems to confuse the conventional truth conditions of a sign with what it may serve as a natural sign of. The conventional function of saying "It's raining" is to cause the belief that it's raining, but when someone says "It's raining" we may sensibly use that also as a natural sign that he believes it's raining. Similarly, we may use pieces of conventional signs as natural signs, or we may use utterances of sentences that we don't understand as natural signs. We figure that the person who has said something in an assertive manner has uttered a sentence having some conventional propositional content and that if this content is true then they have said something true. We figure that the postcard saying "I am having a good time" with the illegible signature was signed by someone who, if they wrote down the truth, was having a good time when they wrote it. Observing part of a sign may serve one as a natural sign that there is or was another sign part there for which we should look or about which we can sensibly speculate. Even though one does not know who is being addressed, hearing someone say "Please leave!" may serve one as a natural sign that someone is being addressed and that if the satisfaction conditions of that sentence are to be met that person must leave. But it is not part of the conventional functions of the these language forms to produce these inferences. It is not because they have been producing inferences of this kind that their forms have survived in the language community. (For this interpretation of the conventional functions of linguistic forms, see, most easily, my 2005.)

4. To parody Kaplan in "Dthat" (1978) *That's right, John himself, right there, trapped in a representation!*

5. For an analysis of the kind of "conventions" that are involved in language use, see my (1998).

6. On Gricean intentions, see my (1984 Ch. 3, 2005 Ch. 10)

7. Other statements of this proposal appear in my (2012a, forthcoming a, b). Precursors, but using the misleading term "empirical concept" in place of the present term "unicept," were in Millikan 1984 Chs. 15 and 18–19, 1993, 2000 entire, 2010, 2011.

8. The next few paragraphs are adapted from my (2012a).

9. In (2012b, 2013) I have argued that the sense of "information" involved in these various cases is univocal.

10. See, in particular, Millikan 2010. Also Millikan 1984 Ch. 16, 1999, 2000.
11. The kind of "marking" required is discussed at some length in (Millikan 2000, Chs. 10–11).
12. The predecessors of unicepts in my writing were called "empirical concepts." The next paragraphs make clear why I have withdrawn that term in favor of "unicepts."
13. Millikan 1984 Ch. 10, 2004 Chs.18–19, 2010, forthcoming a.
14. Millikan 2000, Ch. 6, 2004 Ch. 9, 2005 Ch.10.
15. This is a reference to the biosemantic theory of intentional content, articulated first in my (1984), defended and amplified in various papers since. Particularly useful may be my (2008 b).

References

Almog, J., J. Perry and H. Wettstein 1989. *Themes from Kaplan.* Oxford: Oxford University Press.

García-Carpentero, M. 2000. "A presuppositional account of reference fixing." *Journal of Philosophy* 97.3:109–147.

Kaplan, D. 1978. "Dthat." In P. Cole, ed., *Syntax and Semantics.* New York: Academic Press.

——— 1989a. "Demonstratives." In Almog, Perry, and Wettstein 1989, pp. 481–563.

——— 1989b. "Afterthoughts." In Almog, Perry, and Wettstein 1989, pp. 565–614.

——— 1990. "Words." *Aristotelian Society Proceedings, Supplementary volume* 1990: 93–119.

Lockwood, M. 1971. "Identity and Reference." In M. K. Munitz ed., *Identity and Individuation*, New York: New York University Press, pp. 199–211.

Millikan, R.G. 1984. *Language Thought and Other Biological Categories.* Cambridge MA: The MIT Press.

——— 1993. "Knowing What I'm Thinking Of." *The Aristotelian Society, Supplementary volume* 67, pp. 109–124.

——— 1998. Language Conventions Made Simple." *Journal of Philosophy* 95.4: 161–180. Reprinted in *Linguistic and Philosophical Investigations*, 7, 2008 and in Millikan 2005.

——— 1999. "Historical kinds and the special sciences." *Philosophical Studies* 95: 45–65.

——— 2000. *On Clear and Confused Ideas.* Cambridge UK: Cambridge University Press.

——— 2001. "Purposes and Cross-purposes: On the Evolution of Language and Languages." *The Monist* 84.3: 392–416. Reprinted in *The Epidemiology of Ideas*, ed. Dan Sperber (Open Court, 2003).

——— 2005. *Language: A Biological Model.* Oxford: Oxford University Press.

——— 2008a. "A Difference of Some Consequence between Conventions and Rules." In *Convention: an Interdisciplinary Study*, ed. Luca Tummolini ed., *Topoi* 27:87–99.

——— 2008b. "Biosemantics." In Brian McLaughlin ed., *The Oxford Handbook in the Philosophy of Mind*. Oxford: Oxford University Press, 394–406.

——— 2010. "On Knowing the Meaning; With a Coda on Swampman." *Mind* 119.473: 43–81.

——— 2011. "Loosing the Word-Concept Tie." *Proceedings of the Aristotelian Society, Supplementary Volume* 85: 125–143.

——— 2012a. "Accidents." The John Dewey lecture for the Central Division APA 2012, *Proceedings and Addresses of the American Philosophical Association*, November 2012.

——— 2012b. "Natural Signs." In S. Barry Cooper, Anuj Dawar, Benedikt Loewe eds., *Computability in Europe 2012, Lecture Notes in Computer Science.* Springer 2012, pp. 496–506.

—— 2013. "Natural Information, Intentional Signs and Animal Communication" In Ulric Stegmann ed., *Animal Communication Theory: Information and Influence*. Cambridge University Press, April 2013.

—— forthcoming a. "Confessions of Rengade Daughter." In James Shea, ed., TBA Oxford University Press.

—— forthcoming b. "An Epistemology for Phenomenology?," In Richard Brown ed., *Phenomenology and the Neurophilosophy of Consciousness*. Springer.

Perry, J. 1979. "The Problem of the Essential Indexical." Nous 13.1: 3–21.

—— 2001. *Reference and Reflexitity*. Stanford: CSLI Publications.

—— 2006. "Using Indexicals." In Michael Devitt and Richard Hanley eds., *The Blackwell Guide to the Philosophy of Language*. Oxford: Blackwell, pp. 314–334.

Strawson, P.F. 1974. *Subject and Predicate in Logic and Grammar*. London: Methuen and Co.

Philosophical Perspectives, 26, Philosophy of Mind, 2012

PERCEPTUAL PHENOMENOLOGY

Bence Nanay
University of Antwerp and Cambridge University

1. Introduction

I am looking at an apple. The apple has a lot of properties and some, but not all, of these are part of my phenomenology at this moment: I am aware of these properties. And some, but not all, of these properties that I am aware of are part of my perceptual (or sensory) phenomenology. If I am attending to the apple's color, this property will be part of my perceptual phenomenology. The property of being a granny smith apple from Chile is unlikely to be part of my perceptual phenomenology.

Here are two problems for anyone who is interested in conscious experience in general, and perceptual experience in particular:

(a) How can we tell which properties are part of our phenomenology and which ones are not?
(b) How can we tell which properties are part of our perceptual phenomenology and which ones are part of our non-perceptual phenomenology?

I will focus on (b) in this paper. My aim is twofold: I propose a methodology for answering the question of which properties are part of our perceptual phenomenology and I provide an example for how this methodology could be applied.

2. The Methodology of Contrast Cases

Both (a) and (b) have been widely discussed (Siegel 2006, Masrour 2011, Pitt 2004, Robinson 2005, Bayne and Montague 2011) and it is universally assumed that the right methodology for deciding how to answer (a) and (b) is by appealing to contrast cases (see Masrour 2011, Siegel 2007, Kriegel 2007 and Bayne 2009 on the methodology of settling these questions). In the case of (a), this means that if we find two token experiences, E1 and E2, that only differ in that property P is represented in E1 but not in E2 and if E1 and E2 are phenomenologically different, then property P is part of our phenomenology. Similarly, in the case of (b), if we find two token experiences that only differ in that property P is represented in one but not the other and if the two experiences differ in their perceptual phenomenology, then property P is part of our perceptual phenomenology.

An example for how this might work in the case of problem (a) above: I am looking at a page written in Arabic script before and after taking an intensive Arabic language class. These experiences are E1 and E2, respectively. My sensory stimulations in E1 and E2 are the same, since I am looking at the very same page, but there is a kind of property that is represented in E2, but not in E1: the property of being meaningful Arabic words (and not merely nicely curving lines). If E1 and E2 differ in their phenomenal character, then this property is part of my phenomenology.

Problem (b): At a dinner party, I'm eating a piece of meat that I take to be chicken, when my host tells me that it is in fact a piece of rat meat (or pigeon, etc; use your favorite disgusting animal). My experience before she told me this is E1; my experience after that is E2. The only difference between E1 and E2 is that there is one property, the property of being a rat, that is represented in E2 but not in E1 — in all other respects, E1 and E2 are the same. If I am really disgusted by rats, then the point can be made that the perceptual phenomenology of E1 and E2 are different: the meat will *taste* different.

3. Doing Without Contrast Cases

The problem with the contrast case methodology for deciding (a) and (b) is that it is difficult to settle disagreements about phenomenology. If I say that E1 and E2 differ in their phenomenal character (or in their perceptual phenomenology) and you deny this, it is not clear how the issue can be decided. This is even more problematic in the case of (b), where intuitions wildly differ with regards to what phenomenal character counts as perceptual. Does the rat meat example really show that the property of being rat meat is part of our *perceptual* phenomenology? If someone were to claim that this property is part of our non-perceptual phenomenology, it is difficult to see how we could settle this disagreement.

As a result, I propose a methodology for settling (b), at least in the case of some kinds of properties, that does not appeal to contrast cases. The methodology involves close attention to patients with brain lesions.

I take my lead here from Tim Bayne, who used such cases in order to decide (a). He argues that associative agnosia patients lose their ability to recognize objects as belonging to certain sortals (to recognize them as bicycles or stethoscopes) but not their ability to represent the shape, size and color properties of these objects. He concludes that as their phenomenology also changes, this change can only be explained with the change in the represented sortal property: hence, sortal properties are part of one's phenomenology (Bayne 2009).

We need to note two aspects of this argument. First, it is an argument about (a) and not about (b): it says nothing about whether sortals are part of our perceptual phenomenology. Second, and more importantly, in spite of Bayne's appeal to patients with brain lesions, the argument still uses the methodology of contrast cases. The patients' experience before the accident that caused the brain lesions is E1 and their experience after is E2. E1 and E2 differ only in that sortals are represented in E1 but not E2. If E1 and E2 differ in their phenomenal character, we can conclude that sortals are part of our phenomenology. But then we encounter the usual problems with the methodology of contrast cases. If one denied that E1 and E2 really differ in terms of their phenomenal character, it is not clear how Bayne could respond.

I want to keep Bayne's emphasis on patients with brain lesions but drop his contrast case methodology. My claim is that if we find patients who (a) consciously see object x, (b) experience property P of x, but (c) do not experience any lower level properties of x, such as shape, size or color, then we have good reason to conclude that property P is part of our perceptual phenomenology.

Here is why. Suppose, for *reductio*, that property P is part of the subjects' non-perceptual phenomenology. What about their perceptual phenomenology then? It follows from the claim for *reductio* that these patients lack any perceptual phenomenology of x's properties while they consciously see x. The only property they are aware of is property P, but this property is, by supposition, not part of their perceptual phenomenology. In other words, it follows from the claim for *reductio* that it is possible to consciously see an object and nonetheless lack visual phenomenology altogether.

This is the skeleton of the argument for keeping apart perceptual and non-perceptual phenomenology. I will now use a case study to show how this argument can be fleshed out.

4. Case Study: Unilateral Neglect and the Experience of Action-Properties

To give a case study of how this might work, I argue that a property that is even less obviously perceptual than sortal properties is part of our perceptual phenomenology: the property of being suitable to perform an action with (see also Nanay 2011a, forthcoming). I call properties of this kind action-properties.[1] My claim is that action-properties are part of our perceptual phenomenology.

The claim I am making is about perceptual *phenomenology*. It needs to be distinguished from a similar but importantly different question, namely, the question about whether a property is represented in perception (see Nanay 2011a, 2012, forthcoming). Perception can be conscious or unconscious and there may be properties that are perceptually represented but nonetheless fail to show up in our perceptual phenomenology. Further, depending on how we think about the relation between perceptual content and perceptual phenomenology, a property may be part of our phenomenology but nonetheless fail to be part of our perceptual content. The question I am addressing in this paper is about perceptual phenomenology, not perceptual content.

As promised, my argument is based on empirical findings about patients with brain malfunction. More specifically, some patients with symptoms of unilateral neglect are slow and sometimes even unable to find objects in the contralateral side of their visual field if they are defined by salient visual properties (such as their color). Yet, they are capable of, and relatively efficient in, finding objects defined by the action they can be used for – by what I called 'action-properties' (Humphreys and Riddoch 2001, Riddoch et al. 1998, esp. p. 678).

This experimental finding satisfies the conditions for the methodology I sketched at the end of the last section. Let us focus on the moment when the patients spot the object in the contralateral side of their visual field (in the course of those experiments where they are trying to identify the objects with the help of their action-properties).

The first thing to note is that the patients are unaware of the shape, size and color properties of the objects presented to them in the contralateral side of their visual field. This is not particularly surprising as it is held to be true of all unilateral neglect patients. In fact, unilateral neglect is often defined as the lack of awareness of visual details in the contralateral side of one's visual field (see Driver and Vuilleumier 2001 and Kinsbourne 2006 for summaries).[2]

Second, these patients do consciously experience the property of what an object can be used for. In fact, what alerted the experimenters to the possibility of this experiment is that the patients noticed and told the experimenters that when performing visual search tasks, they experience what the objects can be used for (see Humphreys and Riddoch 2001, p. 84). To use the terminology of feature-binding (Treisman 1996), at this moment, the action-property is bound to the object, but the shape and color properties are not.

But should we really accept the claim that unilateral neglect patients are aware of action-properties? Wouldn't it be possible that these patients are like blindsight patients: that they are not aware of any properties, but unconsciously represent some of them, which allows them to perform actions (in this case, the action of picking out objects in the contralateral field)? My answer is that unilateral neglect patients are very different from blindsight patients. We do not, of course, have fool-proof evidence that they are aware of action-properties. We never do, not even in the case of healthy human beings — this is the famous problem of other minds. The point is that we have no more reason to doubt that unilateral neglect patients are aware of action-properties than to doubt that a healthy human adult is. Remember that the experimenters were alerted to this phenomenon that they went on to test empirically because a patient told them that it is easier for him to find objects when he thinks about what the objects can be used for. Blindsight patients are not in the position to say any such things. The unilateral neglect patient says that he is aware of these properties of the objects and we have no *prima facie* reasons to think that he is lying — we have as much justification to conclude that he is aware of the action-properties as we ever do.

One may also have a general worry about the reliance of this argument on the subjects' introspective claims about their phenomenology. The grand aim of this paper is to use empirical findings and not introspection for drawing a distinction between perceptual and non-perceptual phenomenology. Nonetheless, I am accepting claims about the subjects' phenomenology without any further empirical support. Am I entitled to do so? My answer is that I am. Remember that the aim is to get clear about the difference between perceptual and non-perceptual phenomenology. And I use the subjects' introspective report in order to establish whether they are having an experience *per se* rather than whether they are having a *perceptual* experience. Thus, I do not use the introspective report of their perceptual phenomenology to support my claim about perceptual phenomenology. Rather, I use the introspective report of what they are aware of — perceptually or non-perceptually — to support my claim about perceptual phenomenology.

Now let us see why these experimental findings are relevant for the purposes of keeping perceptual and non-perceptual phenomenology apart.

It is important to clarify what does not follow from these findings. It does not follow that in the course of perceptual processing the representation of shape and color comes after, and is grounded in, the representation of action-properties. What follows from these findings is only that the phenomenology of action-properties comes before (hence, cannot be based on) the phenomenology of shape and color: the subjects experience action-properties before they experience shape and color properties.

Here we need to keep claims about representation and claims about phenomenology apart (see Nanay 2011b). Unilateral neglect is normally described as a disorder of visual attention. The general idea is that the patients are unaware of the contralateral side of their visual field because they cannot unlock their attention from the other side of their visual field. One reason to think so is the following (Mark et al. 1988). If a unilateral neglect patient is unaware of the left side of her visual field, then in a line crossing task, she will only cross the lines in the right side of her visual field. But if the task is not line crossing, but line erasing, that is, if the visual stimulus is slowly removed from the right side of her visual field, then she will eventually erase all the lines, including the ones on the left side of her visual field.

In other words, I take it to be the consensual view about unilateral neglect that these patients do have some kind of representation of the visual details on the contralateral side of their visual field, but, because of their attentional deficit, they are not aware of them.[3] So the general picture is this: there is a representation of shape and color, there is a representation of action-properties

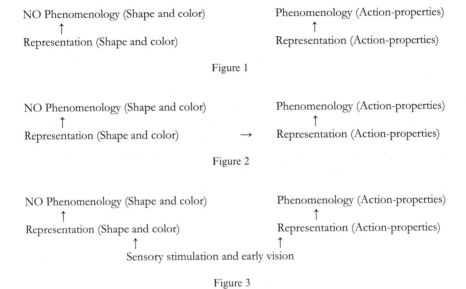

NO Phenomenology (Shape and color)   Phenomenology (Action-properties)

↑   ↑

Representation (Shape and color)   Representation (Action-properties)

Figure 1

NO Phenomenology (Shape and color)   Phenomenology (Action-properties)

↑   ↑

Representation (Shape and color)   →   Representation (Action-properties)

Figure 2

NO Phenomenology (Shape and color)   Phenomenology (Action-properties)

↑   ↑

Representation (Shape and color)   Representation (Action-properties)

↑   ↑

Sensory stimulation and early vision

Figure 3

and there is phenomenology of action-properties. But there is no (or there is delayed) phenomenology of shape and color.

This gives us the picture of figure 1.

One detail that is missing from this picture is the arrow (or lack thereof) between Representation (Shape and color) and Representation (Action-properties).

I'm assuming that it would be absurd to suggest that the representation of shape and color is based on, and grounded in, the representation of action-properties (in any case, if this were true, we could immediately conclude that action-properties are perceptually represented). This leaves us two options. The first is in figure 2, and the second in figure 3.

In the case of the first alternative, the representation of shape and color gives rise to the representation of action-properties, which, in turn, is responsible for the phenomenology of action-properties. But for the unilateral neglect patients the phenomenology of shape and color is missing — presumably because the representation of shape and color is not attended to.

The second alternative is that the representation of shape and color and the representation of action-properties are formed independently from one another — our early vision gives rise to both of them independently. According to this account, there are two separate visual subsystems, one responsible for the representation of shape and color and the other responsible for the representation of action-properties. And only the latter, but not the former is accompanied by phenomenology in the unilateral neglect patients.

This second alternative could be thought to be supported by empirical considerations and I need to say a couple of words about these. There is some important empirical evidence in favor of the double dissociation between the perceptual subsystem that is responsible for recognition and identification (ventral subsystem) and the one that is responsible for the perceptual guidance of actions (dorsal subsystem) (see Milner and Goodale 1995, Goodale and Milner 2004, Jeannerod 1997). If we apply this empirical evidence to the unilateral neglect case, we might conclude that the ventral subsystem is slow or malfunctioning in unilateral neglect patients, whereas the dorsal subsystem is intact, which is why these patients experience action-properties before (or even without) experiencing its shape or color.

I doubt that relying on the ventral/dorsal distinction is the best bet for the advocates of the second alternative. The double dissociation between the ventral and the dorsal visual subsystems has no immediate implications as to what is visually *experienced*. Importantly, the distinction is not between the *experience* of identifying and recognizing and the *experience* of action control. In fact, the main proponents of the two visual systems hypothesis, Milner and Goodale argue that while ventral processing is typically conscious, dorsal processing is unconscious. This view has been criticized both on empirical and on conceptual grounds (see for example Dehaene et al, 1998, Jeannerod 1997, see also Jacob and Jeannerod 2003, Briscoe 2009, Brogaard forthcoming for summaries): it seems that dorsal processing can also be conscious if it interacts with ventral processing under some special circumstances. There also seems to be evidence that the ventral and the dorsal stream are not as independent from each other as has been previously supposed: they routinely interact at various points of perceptual processing (see, again Jeannerod 1997 for a summary).

What is important for us is not the debate about whether and to what extent dorsal processing interacts with ventral processing and to what extent it can become conscious as a result. What matters from our point of view is that, regardless of whether we accept Milner and Goodale's strict separation of conscious ventral vision and unconscious dorsal vision or Jeannerod's more complex picture where dorsal processing can be made conscious, neither picture gives support to the claim that in the case of the unilateral neglect patients the conscious experience of shape and color is missing (or comes late) because of a breakdown in the ventral stream. The dorsal stream is either unconscious *per se* (as Milner and Goodale suggest) or can only be made conscious under special circumstances as a result of interaction with ventral processing (as Jeannerod suggests). But neither of these scenarios is consistent with the suggestion that the dorsal stream can give us conscious experience of action-properties in the complete absence of any conscious experience of shape and color.

These considerations do not show that the first alternative is to be preferred to the second one. All they show is that we should be careful in our attempt at fleshing out the second alternative with the help of the dorsal/ventral distinction. The argument I will present in the next section will apply in the case of both of these alternatives.

5. The Argument from Unilateral Neglect

The argument from unilateral neglect is a *reductio* argument. The claim that action-properties are not part of perceptual phenomenology yields some very implausible consequences when it comes to characterizing the phenomenal character of the experience of unilateral neglect patients when they are performing the visual search task.

The supposition for *reductio* is that action-properties are part of the patients' non-perceptual phenomenology. What about their perceptual phenomenology then? The objector is forced to conclude that these patients lack any perceptual phenomenology while they are performing this visual search task. The only properties they are aware of are action-properties, but these properties are, by supposition, not part of their perceptual phenomenology. This is an extremely problematic conclusion as these people are staring at objects, performing visual tasks with what they see, talking about what they see, manipulating what they see, and, importantly, claim to consciously experience what they see. Nonetheless, the objector needs to say that they lack *perceptual* phenomenology: that there is nothing it is like for them to see these objects.

In other words, the objector is forced to say that it is possible to consciously see an object and nonetheless lack visual phenomenology altogether. If we allow for unconscious perception, it is possible to perceive an object without any accompanying phenomenology, but the consequence of denying that action-properties are part of perceptual phenomenology is something much more radical: it amounts to saying that it is possible to *consciously* perceive an object without any accompanying perceptual phenomenology — a claim that comes dangerously close to a straight logical contradiction. If denying that action-properties are part of perceptual phenomenology forces us to postulate such empty perceptual phenomenology during conscious perception, then we have strong reasons to accept the claim that action-properties are indeed part of perceptual phenomenology.

The aim of the last two sections was to show that action-properties are part of our perceptual phenomenology and thereby providing a case study for the methodology of deciding whether a certain kind of property is part of our perceptual phenomenology. But the main aim of the paper was to provide an unproblematic methodology for deciding what properties are part of our perceptual phenomenology. The case study is supposed to help us to understand what would count as evidence for concluding that a property is part of our perceptual phenomenology. More specifically, we can generalize from the unilateral neglect case study: if we find patients who are capable of experiencing property P without being capable of experiencing the low-level properties of shape, size and color, then we have good reason to conclude that property P is part of our perceptual phenomenology. If we want to know which properties are part of our perceptual phenomenology, we need to look for empirical studies of patients with brain lesions.

6. Objections

I need to address some potential objections.

First, some may have a very general worry about my methodology of using findings about a very narrow subset of people, namely, those with unilateral neglect symptoms, in order to arrive at some general claim that would hold for all humans, not only unilateral neglect patients. The answer is simple: if action-properties were part of non-perceptual phenomenology (for humans in general, healthy or not), then we would get extremely implausible results for unilateral neglect patients.

Second, one could point out that I am not entitled to take action-properties to be part of our perceptual phenomenology without showing that they are not part of our action phenomenology.[4] It has been argued that action phenomenology is different from, and not reducible to, perceptual phenomenology (see, e.g., Pacherie 2008, Bayne and Levy 2006). Action phenomenology is the phenomenology that accompanies the performance of actions (opinions differ about whether such phenomenology is necessary for the performance of actions and we do not need this extra assumption here).

This proposal would imply that action-properties are part of the unilateral neglect patients' action phenomenology, not their perceptual phenomenology. But then I can run the very same argument I ran against the view that action-properties are part of the unilateral neglect patients' non-perceptual phenomenology. Both of these views lead to the consequence that the unilateral neglect patients' perceptual phenomenology during visual search is empty and I argued above that this consequence is extremely implausible. In short, if my argument against the claim that action-properties are part of our non-perceptual phenomenology is any good, then we can apply it directly against the proposal that action-properties are part of our action phenomenology.

Third, consider the possibility that what happens with the unilateral neglect patients in this visual search experiment is that the unconscious perception of action-properties gives rise directly to the non-perceptual awareness of action-properties. What rules out this explanation? My answer is that this proposal, just like the proposal about action phenomenology, leads to the implausible consequence that the perceptual phenomenology of these unilateral neglect patients during visual search is empty.

And this leads to the last and probably most important potential objection I need to address. Why is it such an implausible conclusion that the unilateral neglect patients have empty perceptual phenomenology? Couldn't my opponents simply bite the bullet and endorse the claim that these patients' perceptual phenomenology is indeed empty? Because of these considerations, I explicitly avoided saying in the last section that the assumption that action-properties are part of our non-perceptual phenomenology (or the assumption that they are part of our action phenomenology) leads to a straight contradiction. I am not sure that it is a straight contradiction to say that the unilateral neglect patients' perceptual phenomenology is empty.

But it comes very close to being a straight contradiction. Let us summarize what we know about the unilateral neglect patients when they are performing the visual search task. First, they have phenomenology: they are aware of action-properties. And remember that these are action-properties of the very objects that they perceive. Second, they are completing a visual search task: they are performing perceptually-guided actions on the objects that they perceive. If we put these two claims together with the supposition that they lack perceptual phenomenology, what we get is that these subjects consciously experience what they see but have no perceptual phenomenology. Again, not a straight logical contradiction, but a very radical claim indeed.

To demonstrate just how radical this claim is, consider the current debate about cognitive phenomenology. As we shall see in the next section, there is an important debate in philosophy of mind about whether there are conscious *non-perceptual* states, more specifically, thoughts, that lack any perceptual phenomenology. This divides the philosophical field: some philosophers accept and some deny the existence of conscious non-perceptual states that lack any perceptual phenomenology. But note how much more radical the claim we are considering here is. What we are considering here is not the possibility of conscious non-perceptual states without perceptual phenomenology, but the possibility of conscious *perceptual* states without perceptual phenomenology. If we want to refrain from embracing this claim, we need to conclude that action-properties are part of our perceptual phenomenology.

7. Conclusion: Perceptual versus Non-perceptual Phenomenology

The aim of this paper was to sketch the right methodology for drawing the distinction between perceptual and non-perceptual phenomenology. I conclude with some remarks on the relevance of this distinction for one of the most important debates in the philosophy of mind.

This debate is about whether all consciousness is perceptual (or quasi-perceptual). Some argue that phenomenology is necessarily perceptual phenomenology — that the phenomenal character of non-perceptual states, such as thoughts or beliefs, can be fully accounted for in terms of perceptual phenomenology (Carruthers 2005, Prinz 2007, Robinson 2005, Lormand 1996, Tye 1996, Nelkin 1996). Others deny this and argue that thoughts have distinctive phenomenology that is different from perceptual phenomenology (Pitt 2004, Siewert 1998, Strawson 1994, see also the majority of papers in Bayne and Montague 2011).

It is unlikely that this debate can be settled without having a clear distinction between perceptual and non-perceptual phenomenology. Further, depending on what range of properties one allows to be part of perceptual phenomenology, the plausibility of the two competing views may change. If only shape, size and color properties are part of perceptual phenomenology, then the view about the distinctive phenomenology of thoughts may be more tempting, whereas if we allow a wide range of properties to be part of perceptual phenomenology, the view that all consciousness is perceptual may seem more palatable. In other words, we need an unproblematic distinction between perceptual and non-perceptual phenomenology in order to even engage with this debate. The aim of this paper was to sketch a possible methodology for doing so.[5]

Notes

1. In Nanay forthcoming, I differentiate between thick and thin action-properties. For consistency: what I mean by 'action-property' in this paper is what I defined as 'thick action-properties' in Nanay forthcoming. I will leave off the 'thick' adjective for the sake of simplicity here.
2. The same goes for a variety of unilateral neglect that is known as 'extinction' (Driver and Vuillemmier 2001). Extinction patients can be aware of one stimulus on the contralateral side, but not two (not the one that is further away from the center). The contrast here is between awareness of the first stimulus and the lack of awareness of the second.
3. Note that it is taken for granted in this literature that attention is necessary for consciousness, something I am happy to go along with (see Cohen et al. 2012 for a summary, Prinz 2010 for a philosophical overview, but see also Lamme 2003 for a dissenting view).
4. Thanks to Elisabeth Pacherie for raising this objection.
5. This work was supported by the EU FP7 CIG grant PCIG09-GA-2011–293818 and the FWO Odysseus grant G.0020.12N. I gave earlier versions of this paper at the 2011 Online Consciousness Conference and at the University of Fribourg. I am grateful for my commentators, Kevin Connolly, Farid Masrour and Andrea Giananti as well as comments by Tim Bayne, Carolyn Dicey Jennings, Jordan Dodd, Peter King and Maja Spener.

References

Bayne, T. 2009. Perception and the reach of phenomenal content. *Philosophical Quarterly* 59: 385–404.

Bayne, T. & N. Levy. 2006. The feeling of doing: Deconstructing the phenomenology of agnecy. In Natalie Sebanz & Wolfgang Prinz (eds.), *Disorders of Volition*. MIT Press.

Bayne, T. & M. Montague. 2011. *Cognitive Phenomenology*. Oxford: Oxford University Press.

Briscoe, R. 2009. Egocentric spatial representation in action and perception. *Philosophy and Phenomenological Research* 79: 423–460.

Brogaard, B. forthcoming. Conscious vision for action versus unconscious vision for action? *Journal of Philosophy*.

Carruthers, P. 2005. Conscious experience versus conscious thought. In his *Consciousness: Essays from a Higher-Order Perspective*. Oxford: Clarendon Press, pp. 134–156.

Cohen, M. A., P. Cavanagh, M. M. Chun & K. Nakayama. 2012. The attentional requirements of consciousness. *Trends in Cognitive Sciences* 16: 411–417.

Dehaene, S., L. Naccache, G. Le Clec'H, E. Koechlin, M. Mueller, G. Dehaene-Lambertz, P.F. van de Moortele & D. Le Bihan. 1998. Imaging unconscious semantic priming. *Nature* 395: 597–600.

Driver, J. & P. Vuilleumier. 2001. Perceptual awareness and its loss in unilateral neglect and extinction. *Cognition* 79 (1):39–88.

Goodale, M. A. & A. D. Milner. 2004. *Sights Unseen.* Oxford: Oxford University Press.

Humphreys, G. W. & M. J. Riddoch. 2001. Detection by action: Neuropsychological evidence for action-defined templates in search. *Nature Neuroscience* 4: 84–88.

Jacob, P. & M. Jeannerod. 2003. *Ways of Seeing. The Scope and Limits of Visual Cognition.* Oxford: Oxford University Press.

Jeannerod, M. 1997. *The Cognitive Neuroscience of Action.* Oxford: Blackwell.

Kinsbourne, M. 2006. From unilateral neglect to the brain basis of consciousness. *Cortex* 42(6): 869–74.

Kriegel, U. 2007. The phenomenologically manifest. *Phenomenology and the Cognitive Sciences* 6: 115–136.

Lamme, V.A.F. 2003. Why visual attention and awareness are different. *Trends in Cognitive Sciences.* 7, 12–18.

Lormand, E. 1996. Nonphenomenal consciousness. *Nous* 30: 242–261.

Mark, V.W., C.A. Kooistra, & K. M. Heilman. 1988. Hemispatial neglect affected by non-neglected stimuli. *Neurology 38*, 1207–1211.

Masrour, F. 2011. Is perceptual phenomenology thin? *Philosophy and Phenomenological Research* 83: 366–397.

Milner, A. D., & M. A. Goodale. 1995. *The Visual Brain in Action.* Oxford: Oxford University Press.

Nanay, B. 2011a. Do we see apples as edible? *Pacific Philosophical Quarterly* 92: 305–322.

Nanay, B. 2011b. Do we sense modalities with our sense modalities? *Ratio* 24: 299–310.

Nanay, B. 2012. Action-oriented perception. *European Journal of Philosophy*, 20: 430–446.

Nanay, B. forthcoming. *Between Perception and Action.* Oxford: Oxford University Press.

Nelkin, N. 1996. *Consciousness and the Origins of Thought.* Cambridge: Cambridge University Press.

Pacherie, E. 2008. The phenomenology of action: A conceptual framework. *Cognition* 107: 179–217.

Pitt, D. 2004. The phenomenology of cognition. *Philosophy and Phenomenological Research* 59: 1–36.

Prinz, J. 2007. All consciousness is perceptual. In B. McLaughlin and J. Cohen (eds.): *Contemporary Debates in Philosophy of Mind.* Oxford: Blackwell, pp. 335–357.

Prinz, J. 2010. How do perceptual states become conscious? In B. Nanay (ed.): *Perceiving the World. New Essays on Perception.* New York: Oxford University Press.

Riddoch, M. J., M. G. Edwards, G. W. Humphreys, R. West, & T. Heafield. 1998. Visual affordances direct action: Neuropsychological evidence from manual interference. *Cognitive Neuropsychology* 15: 645–693.

Robinson, W. 2005. Thoughts without distinctive non-imagistic phenomenology. *Philosophy and Phenomenological Research* 70: 534–561.

Schwitzgebel, E. forthcoming *Perplexities of Consciousness.* Cambridge, MA: MIT Press.

Siegel, S. 2006. Which properties are represented in perception? In T. Gendler & J. Hawthorne (Eds.), *Perceptual Experience.* Oxford: Oxford University Press, 481–503.

Siegel, S. 2007. How can we discover the contents of experience? *Southern Journal of Philosophy* (Supp) 45: 127–142.

Siewert, C. 1998. *The Significance of Consciousness.* Princeton: Princeton University Press.

Strawson, G. 1994. *Mental Reality.* Cambridge, MA: The MIT Press.

Treisman, A. 1996. The binding problem. *Current Opinions in Neurobiology* 6: 171–178.

Tye, M. 1996. Mental reality. *Journal of Philosophy* 93: 421–424.

Philosophical Perspectives, 26, Philosophy of Mind, 2012

FIRST PERSON ILLUSIONS: ARE THEY DESCARTES', OR KANT'S?

Christopher Peacocke
Columbia University and University College, London

I am going to bring to bear a contemporary conception of the first person and of the self upon Kant's discussion of Descartes and other 'rational psychologists' in the *Critique of Pure Reason*. My aim in doing so is to understand better the nexus of relations between the first person concept, the self, and their epistemology and metaphysics, in the light of the contributions made by these two great philosophers. Kant accuses rational psychologists, amongst whom he cites Descartes as a representative, of a mistaken conception of this nexus of relations. I will be arguing that plausible theses in the philosophy of mind and the theory of intentional content imply that not all the problems lie on Descartes' side of the argument.

1. The Issues

Kant's treatment of rational psychology in the section entitled 'The Paralogisms of Pure Reason' in the *Critique of Pure Reason* is philosophical writing of such brilliance and depth, admired by successive generations of philosophers, that several disclaimers about my aims are required right at the outset. I have no dispute with Kant's critique of the idea that the subject of consciousness must be a simple, non-complex entity. Kant's writing on that topic looks extraordinarily prescient, even in an age of cognitive science. More than two centuries later it could hardly be bettered in so short a compass. Nor do I think that any of the other characteristic metaphysical doctrines of Descartes and the rational psychologists are true. Those doctrines hold that the subject of consciousness is immaterial and non-spatial, and not only persists over time, but also never ceases to exist. My dispute with Kant is not about many of his conclusions. The disagreement concerns rather some crucial points in his reasoning, and his corresponding diagnoses of Cartesian thought.

Kant's section on the Paralogisms has also been the focus of some important critical commentary in recent years, and I will at some points draw on some of this work in comparing his position with one that seems to me more defensible.[1] Kant's treatment of the Paralogisms involves the intertwining of many strands in his thought, and a full textual discussion would merit a book-length examination.

The contemporary position on which I want to draw in developing my argument can be specified by four theses: two in the philosophy of intentional content, one in the philosophy of mind, and one in the metaphysics of subjects. The first thesis in the philosophy of intentional content concerns the individuation of the first person concept, and it is itself twofold. Its first part states that

> What makes something the reference of the concept *I* in any particular event of thinking is that it is the agent, the producer, of that thinking.

Its second part states that the displayed condition is not merely a constitutive condition for something's being the reference of *I* in a particular thinking. The second part holds that the displayed condition, the fundamental reference rule for the first person concept, is also what makes something, what individuates, the first person concept (see further Campbell (1994) and Peacocke (2008, 2012)). This second part of the thesis can be seen as an instance of a broadly Fregean claim. It is an application of the idea that what individuates a sense is the fundamental condition for something to be the reference of the sense (Dummett 1981, Peacocke 2008).

The other thesis in the theory of intentional content applies to first person, or *de se*, contents more generally. These contents may occur in perception, in memory, in action awareness, or even in sensation (you may have a pain experienced as occurring in *your* arm). This second thesis states that

> For a mental state or event to have a *de se* content is simply for it to have a content that, *de jure*, concerns the subject who enjoys that state or event.

This applies both to conceptual and to nonconceptual contents. Again, it is plausible that this is what makes *de se* content the content it is, both in the conceptual and in the nonconceptual instances. In the special case in which the mental event is a mental action of making a judgement with a first person content, there is no conflict between this second thesis and the first thesis. In the case of a mental action that is the judging of a first person content, the agent making the judgement is identical with the conscious subject who enjoys the action awareness of making the judgement.

The contemporary thesis in the philosophy of mind states that

> A subject who possesses the first person concept has a mental file on himself, a file for the first person concept. When all is functioning properly, the present tense contents of this file are updated noninferentially, as time passes, to the appropriately corresponding past tense contents. So, for instance, if on one day the subject's file contains something with the content *Today I am in Oxford*, then

the next day the file will contain something with the content *Yesterday I was in Oxford*, without any personal-level inference on the subject's part.

The idea that mental files are important for understanding first person thought is found in several writers of rather different stripes (Perry 2002, Peacocke 2012). This thesis about mental files can also be applied to nonconceptual *de se* contents, in accounting for the way in which a present tense perception with a *de se* content can generate a later memory with a correspondingly appropriate past tense *de se* content (Peacocke 2012).

Lastly, the contemporary thesis in the metaphysics of subjects states that

> The identity of a conscious subject over time is constitutively dependent on the identity of an integrating apparatus that integrates the precursors of perceptions, sensations, thoughts and emotions.

This is not a conception on which identity of subject is dependent on a subject's having a body. The conception does, however, involve the identity of a material entity, the integrating apparatus (Peacocke 2012).

So much by way of very brief statement of a contemporary position. I now turn to the application to Kant's critique of Descartes and the other 'rational psychologists'. When Descartes presents his arguments about what he is, and his essential properties, it is overwhelmingly plausible that he is using the first person in its ordinary sense. Descartes' arguments simply employ the first person pronoun, or first person case, in natural language (Latin or French), without any stipulation of a special sense. The sense expressed by these uses of the first person is the way of thinking of himself employed in Descartes' ordinary first person thoughts. We are meant to assess his arguments as sound or otherwise taking them to involve this normal sense. When you adapt Descartes's arguments to your own case, as when you think through the *Cogito* and refer to yourself, you will be using the ordinary first person way of thinking that you employ in your other first person thoughts.

Kant himself relies on a series of highly substantive theses in the philosophy of mind, the philosophy of thought, and the theory of meaning and intentional content in his critique of a Cartesian-style position. Here is a selection of these theses:

> The rational psychologist is making a mistake that involves a failure to appreciate the importance of the point that "not the least intuition is bound up with" first person representations (A350). A genuine and non-empty singular concept of an object that can be given (or at least an object that is a substance) must be based on an intuition of that object (B412–3).

> There is a positive account to be given of the role of the first person in the rational psychologist's premise "I think", an account that involves the idea that the **I** in 'I think' is "rather purely intellectual, because it belongs to thinking in general"

(B423). Kant says that if he has called "I think" an empirical proposition, that is because "without any empirical representation, which provides the material for thinking, the act I think would not take place, and the empirical is only the condition of the application, or use, of the pure intellectual faculty" (B423).

"rational psychology has its origin in a mere misunderstanding. The unity of consciousness, which grounds the categories, is here taken for an intuition of the subject as object" (B421).

The rational psychologist's reasoning as captured in the First Paralogism "passes off the constant logical subject of thinking as the cognition of a real subject of inherence" (A350). "Meanwhile, one can quite well allow the proposition **The soul is substance** to be valid, if only one admits [...] it signifies a substance only in the idea but not in reality" (A350–1).

The apparent awareness of we have of our own identity over time should be given a construal that does not involve awareness of the genuine identity of anything over time (A362–4). "The identity of the consciousness of Myself in different times is therefore only a formal condition of my thoughts and their connection, but it does not prove at all the numerical identity of my subject" (A363).

What exactly these claims mean, and what they are targeted against, we will consider below. My general position is that while some of these points involve incisive and original insights, which is why Kant's discussion has been so admired, what is right in these points cannot be soundly applied against significant parts of Descartes' reasoning. Others of these theses I will be arguing to be untrue. Any case against Descartes' metaphysics of the mind needs to be differently organized, and in part differently based. I divide the relevant issues into three clusters.

(i) Kant's Complaints About the Cartesian Use of The First Person Concept:

The first cluster of questions concerns some plausible claims that Kant makes about the first person concept. Does what is right in Kant's points about the first person concept as it occurs in certain premises used by the rational psychologist really undermine the early stages of Descartes' argument? Kant seems to suggest that an appreciation of his points about the relevant occurrences of the first person concept, when taken together with other theses held by the rational psychologist, will show that the rational psychologist's position involves the violation of constraints on significance, or at least the violation of constraints required for a singular concept to refer to a 'substance'. What, if anything, is the connection between what is right in Kant's points about the first person, in its relevant uses, and the alleged violation of a principle of significance? Is Kant's target the transitions made in Descartes' thought from certain states of consciousness, or is it something else?

(ii) Kant's Positive Account:

The second cluster of questions centres on Kant's positive account or conception of how the 'I' in 'I think' operates. What is Kant's own positive account, and with which parts of Descartes' position is that positive account incompatible?

(iii) 'A Merely Logical Subject'

The third cluster of questions concerns Kant's frequently expressed idea that there is in first person ascriptions of conscious states a 'merely logical subject'.[2] Kant's oft-expressed idea is that the rational psychologist is mistaking this 'merely logical subject' for something more substantial. What is a 'merely logical subject'? How does this notion relate to the concerns in the question clusters (i) and (ii)? Is it really true that there are uses of the first person that are correctly described as involving 'merely logical subjects', and produce illusions of reference to something more substantial? If we question the idea of a 'merely logical subject', is there any good reason for a subject not to take her apparent awareness of her own identity over time at face value?

2. Some Replies to Kant's Objections

I will be arguing that a contemporary account of the first person and the self that endorses the theses displayed above suggests answers to some of the questions raised in these clusters (i)–(iii), answers that diverge from Kant's own position.

(i) Kant's Complaints About the Cartesian Transitions Involving the First Person Concept:

In developing his case against rational psychology, Kant makes the point that there is a use of the first person which does not involve its reference being given in an intuition: "For the I is, to be sure, in all thoughts; but not the least intuition is bound up with this representation, which would distinguish it from other objects of intuition. Therefore one can, to be sure, perceive that this representation continually recurs with every thought, but not that it is a standing and abiding intuition, in which thoughts (as variable) would change" (A350). That the first person 'representation' about which Kant is saying this is something he takes to be genuine, and not something illusory postulated by the rational psychologist, is evident in several other passages. In the following passage, from the B edition, he emphasizes that this representation is used in describing what the thinker can really become conscious of, and again it does not involve any intuition of the subject: "this identity of the subject, of which I can become conscious in every representation, does not concern the intuition of it, through which it is given as object" (B408). Later in the second edition he writes of "the empirical but in regard to all kinds of intuition indeterminate proposition 'I think'" (B421).

Kant emphasizes the absence of any intuition associated with this use of the first person, because the rational psychologist is concerned to establish the existence of purely mental, non-material substances. For Kant, any genuine thought about substance must involve an intuition of the substance. He writes of "the category of substance, which always presupposes a given intuition" (B422). He repeatedly asserts this link between substance and intuition. "The concept of substance is always related to intuitions, which in me cannot be other than sensible" (B408). We must "ground the persistence of a given object on experience if we would apply to that object the empirically usable concept of a substance" (A349). "Thus if that concept, by means of the term "substance", is to indicate an object that can be given, and if it is to become a cognition, then it must be grounded on a persisting intuition as the indispensable condition of the objective reality of a concept, namely, that through which alone an object is given" (B412–3). So the argument seems to be: the use of the first person in the rational psychologist's premise "I think" does not have the required connection with an intuition that it would have to have if the rational psychologist's reasoning is to establish what he wants it to establish. Kant summarizes his discussion of the paralogisms in the second edition discussion: "From all this one sees that rational psychology has its origin in a mere misunderstanding. The unity of consciousness, which grounds the categories, is here taken for an intuition of the subject as object, and the category of substance is applied to it" (B421–2).

Kant's starting point in this reasoning, that there is no intuition 'bound up with' the first person seems to me entirely correct. It is supported by everything in a good account of the first person concept. No demonstrative, either of the form 'that' or 'that F', in perception or sensation or any other form of consciousness, is equivalent to a representation of something as oneself. Even when a perceptual experience has a genuine first person content—as in the example of seeing something as coming towards oneself—there does not need to be an intuition of oneself in the experience which gives it that first person content. Kant's premise seems to be true and important. It is in part a Humean insight. The point is completely independent of Kant's phenomenal/noumenal distinction, and of other contentious theses in his theoretical thought. That is, dialectically, part of the strength of this premise.

The explanation of the truth of this point about the absence of any intuition "bound up with" the first person lies in the difference between the fundamental reference rule for any demonstrative and the fundamental reference rule for the first person (in both its conceptual and its nonconceptual forms). Any intuition-based demonstrative picks out the object experienced, either perceived or sensed.

That is, it refers to the object standing in a certain relation to what Kant would call the intuition. The first person by contrast always refers *de jure* to the subject of the experience or conscious event in question. These are utterly different conditions. The condition for the first person to refer does not even require an intuition of what is in fact the subject, for the first person may feature in the content of an experience in which the subject is not given in any intuition. The first person may also feature in an intuition-free thinking. This difference between any intuition-based demonstrative and the nature of the first person is brought out clearly by the first two theses above of the contemporary conception.

I pause the argument briefly to note that this account of what is arguably defensible in Kant's thought makes the point one that is quite specific to the first person concept, rather than something applicable to any singular concept that can feature in subject position in the content of a thought. In his highly illuminating article 'Kant's First Paralogism', Ian Proops (2010) gives a construal of Kant's treatment of that paralogism. On his construal, the rational psychologist rightly points out that the first person concept cannot feature in predicative position. Proops' point is that nothing follows from this about whether the subject referred to by the first person concept is something whose existence depends on the existence of other things. As Proops notes, a singular concept picking out something whose existence is obviously dependent upon the existence of other things, such as your right fist (Proops' example), is equally incapable of featuring in predicative position (2010: 475–7). I think that Proops is certainly identifying one strand in Kant's thought here. But this particular strand is not something unique to the first person, as the example of the fist shows. We need to cite something distinctive of the first person, amongst singular notions of persisting entities, if we are to contribute to an explanation of why there should be a special tendency to illusions about the self. The non-equivalence of *I* with any demonstrative concept of the form *that F*, where this demonstrative is some perceptual or sensorily-based singular concept, is certainly a feature of much more restricted application. The feature integrates well with some of Kant's adumbrations and analysis. In particular, if the *F* that occurs in a perceptual demonstrative is something true of material extended things, then if *I* were equivalent to such a demonstrative *that F*, then the subject would even be given as something material and extended; and in fact the subject is not so given.[3] In the first edition's treatment of the First Paralogism, the absence of any "intuition bound up with" the first person is certainly playing a role in the argument (A350). By contrast, there would, of course, be an intuition bound up with the perceptual demonstrative "this right fist".

To return to the main argument: I have argued that Kant is recognizing an important point about the distinctive nature of the first person concept *I*, viz. that its fundamental reference rule does not mention or require any relation of the reference of the concept, on a particular occasion, to any experience enjoyed by the thinker. This elaboration of the point on which I want to agree with Kant about the first person does, however, undermine part of the use Kant wants to make of the very same point. The explanation just given of what seems right in his point is entirely at the level of modes of presentation, at the level of intentional content rather than the level of reference. The explanation is quite neutral on the nature of the ontology of subjects. It does not advert to the metaphysics of subjects at all, but only to distinctions drawn between ways in which something can be represented.

It is, then, entirely consistent with acceptance of Kant's point about the first person to insist that in a thinking of 'I think', the first person concept does refer. It just does not refer by means of a relation to some particular intuition. It would even be consistent with such a position to hold that, if the first person is to refer, it must be to something that could be an object of intuition (though Kant would not agree, in this particular case). Such a constraint is not at odds with the explanation at the level of modes of presentation.

There are other genuinely indexical concepts that refer on particular occasions of their use, but do not do so via a relation to a perceptual intuition. If we prescind from Kant's own very special and complex views about time, the present tense concept *now* is plausibly a salient example. The present tense concept can feature in thoughts ("I wonder what is happening in Congress now") without there existing any perceptual intuition of which it is true that it is an intuition of the time referred to by *now* in the thought in question, and is an intuition whereby *now* as used on this occasion gains its reference. Perceptual experience represents events as occurring in the present, and one's thinkings are experienced as occurring in the present, but none of this means that the present is itself given in a perceptual intuition. Also, the way the present is given in experience is not something that makes the present time something that is available as an object of attention. A detailed discussion of time in experience is a topic for some other occasion, but still it should be clear a broad parallelism is present. The fundamental reference rule for *now* is that in any mental event in whose content it occurs, *now* in that event refers to the time of occurrence of that event. Since any event occurs time, its present tense component will refer to a particular time, even if there is no such thing as a perceptual intuition of a time. If it is equally in the nature of mental events that each such event must be enjoyed by a subject, then equally in any mental event with a first person content *I*, that use of *I* will refer, under the fundamental reference rule we have been discussing, and it will refer to the subject of that event.

We can now ask a pivotal question about Kant's intended target in the argument of the Paralogisms. When Kant makes what we have endorsed as the sound point that "no intuition is bound up with" the first person as it occurs in the rational psychologist's reasoning, what is his aim? Is his argument aimed

(a) against the transitions that lead the rational psychologist to his conclusion *I think*, as inadequate to ground knowledge about the thing that is the reference of *I*? This we can call "the inadequate-grounds interpretation". Or is his argument aimed

(b) to establish that the rational psychologist is presupposing an incorrect theory of the nature of the first person concept? This is the "misunderstood-concept interpretation". Or is his argument

(c) that if the rational psychologist's general metaphysics of the subject is to be correct, the first person concept together with its reference would have to have various properties that the rational psychologist's reasoning has in no way established that they have? This is the "missing properties" argument.

Kant might of course have had more than one of these aims simultaneously. But I will argue that the first two of these interpretations take as their target something to which a rational psychologist such as Descartes has a good defence, while the third interpretation, when considered in more detail in the light of Kant's text, has problems as an interpretation of Kant's intentions.

The inadequate-grounds interpretation, (a), has Kant as insisting that the transitions that, for example, Descartes makes from thinkings or experiencings or imaginings or willings to *I think* are fallacious. But there is a strong case to be made that such transitions, taken simply at face value, are not fallacious. What makes it the case that some event or state is a conscious event is that there is something it is like for the subject of that event (Nagel 1974, Peacocke 2012). If that is correct, then a transition in thought from enjoyment of a conscious state to self-ascription of a state, of the conscious kind it is, will always yield a true judgement. If the conscious kind is thought of in a way that has constitutive links to self-ascription when the subject enjoys the conscious state or event, then there is a good case to be made that the transition not only yields a true judgement, but one to which the thinker is entitled, and which can be knowledge (Peacocke 2012b). There is not required to be any intuition of the subject in the conscious state from which the transition to *I think* is made. Even if *per accidens* there is an intuition of the subject in the initial conscious state, that is not what makes the transition truth-yielding, entitled, and knowledge-yielding.

These points do not rest on or presuppose any questionable Cartesian metaphysics of subjects of consciousness. They stand independently of any such metaphysics. Nor do they presuppose some bleached-out or *ersatz* notion of reference for the concept *I* as it features in the conclusion *I think*. Whatever is wrong with a Cartesian metaphysics of subjects, it is not these transitions.

The misunderstood-concept interpretation, (b), has Kant protesting that the rational psychologist is presupposing an incorrect theory of the nature of the first person concept. I suspect this interpretation does an injustice to both Descartes and Kant. Of course neither Descartes nor Kant, to the best of my knowledge, formulated explicit semantic theses about the first person concept. A fortiori, neither connected semantic theses with the epistemology and metaphysics of subject. (Much as one may wish to the contrary: the question of what Kant might have said had he had Frege's sense/reference apparatus to hand is intriguing here as in other areas too.) The reason this interpretation (b) seems to be an injustice is that some of the most striking points that each of these philosophers makes about the first person is vindicated under the supposition of correctness of the first thesis in the philosophy of mind we mentioned at the outset: that what makes something the reference of the concept *I* in any particular event of thinking is that it is the agent, the producer, of the thinking. This reference rule contributes essentially to the validation, both semantic and epistemic, of the *Cogito* transitions in Descartes (again, see Peacocke 2012b). If Descartes had thought some intuition had to be associated with the first person for it to gain reference, he would never have accorded to the *Cogito* the status he actually gave it. Nor could the *Cogito* have turned back the doubt for him. Equally, there are comments in Kant that would seem to be best explained by his having some tacit appreciation of the above reference rule for *I*, or at least the independence of any correct rule from intuitions of the thing that is its reference. Kant acutely observes that "even if we supposed" "secure observation" of a soul (whatever that might involve), that would not establish the persistence of what is referred to by the first person, precisely because "not the least observation is bound up with this representation, which would distinguish it from other objects of intuition" (all quotes from A350). More generally, Kant comments: "I would not say by this that the **I** in this proposition [viz, **I think** – CP] is an empirical representation; for it is rather purely intellectual, for it belongs to thinking in general" (B426). If Kant had held that an intuition of an object were required for *I* to refer to the object, he would after all be holding that the **I** in **I think** is an empirical representation, which is precisely what he is denying.

Kant does repeatedly emphasize in his discussion of the Paralogisms that one cannot obtain from a concept alone "the usual conclusions of the rationalistic doctrine of the soul" (A350–1); "here as elsewhere we can have little hope of broadening our insight through mere concepts" (A361). His point here concerns what conclusions can be drawn from various phenomena involving the first person concept, not that Descartes or other rational psychologists have mistaken the nature or fundamental identity of that concept.

The missing-properties interpretation, (c), has Kant saying that the rational psychologist has failed to establish that the first person concept and its reference has certain properties they would have to have if the rational psychologist's conclusions are to be true. Certainly anyone who agrees that subjects do not exist for ever, and are not immaterial, is committed to saying that Descartes' arguments must be unsound somewhere. His arguments must either have false premises, or rely on invalid transitions. Now in the *Meditations*, the stage of Descartes' reasoning at which he concludes that he is purely a thinking thing, and not an extended thing, is to be found in Meditation VI. His reasoning there is complex and articulated. It involves the notion of a clear and distinct idea, it involves a conception of natures of things, the notion of a 'complete' thing, and his own supposed capacity to conceive of thought without extension. (For a particularly good discussion of the structure of Descartes' argument there, see Wilson 1978, Ch. VI, esp. p.197 ff.) So one might have expected Kant to address Descartes' reasoning involving these various notions in his section on the Paralogisms. In fact he does not. Rather, what Kant does is to imply that Descartes had already gone astray in his conception of conscious mental events and states, and of their relation to what contents we can know that contain the first person concept in their content. The implication is that he is under some illusion about the role of the first person and its relation to consciousness, and about what conscious states can justify.

Here are some of Kant's statements. One of his formulations is that the rational psychologist has confused a 'formal condition' of the identity of his thoughts with the numerical identity of a subject (A363). "I relate each and every one of my successive determinations to the numerically identical Self in all time, i.e. in the form of the inner intuition of my self. On this basis the personality of the soul must be regarded not as inferred by rather as a completely identical proposition of self-consciousness in time, and that is also the cause of its being valid *a priori*. For it really says no more than that in the whole time in which I am conscious of myself, I am conscious of this time as belonging to the unity of my Self" (A362). Most striking, in discussing the concept of personality, conceived of as applying to subjects who are aware of their identity over time, he writes that: "we can never boast of it [the concept of personality – CP] as an extension of our self-knowledge through pure reason, which dazzles us with the uninterrupted continuous duration of the subject drawn from the mere concept of the identical self, since this concept revolves in a circle around itself and brings us no farther in regard to even one single question about synthetic cognition" (A366). At the start of the B edition discussion of the Paralogisms, he emphasizes, clearly intending his remarks in opposition to the rational psychologist, "I cognize myself not by being conscious of myself as thinking" (B406). It is, on Kant's view, the philosophical scrutiny of consciousness, its nature, and its relations that reveals the errors in the rational psychologist's thought. Presumably that is why he thinks there is no need to go into the theory of clear and distinct ideas, complete natures, and the rest, in the case of Descartes. "Thus through the analysis of the consciousness of myself in thinking in general not the least is won in regard to the cognition of myself as object" (B409). Kant's summary diagnosis of the errors of rational psychology mentions a mistake about consciousness, and not anything about the (highly problematic) argumentative apparatus of Meditation VI. In his summary, Kant writes, "From all this one sees that rational psychology has its origin in a mere misunderstanding. The unity of consciousness, which grounds the categories, is here taken for an intuition of the subject as object, and the category of substance is applied to it. But this unity is only the unity of **thinking**, through which no object is given; and thus the category of substance, which always presupposes a given **intuition**, cannot be applied to it, and hence this subject cannot be cognized at all" (B421–2).

If Kant's arguments are indeed confined to the domain of the consciousness/thought relations, where does this leave him if we accept the positions in the philosophy of mind, thought, and metaphysics that I mentioned at the outset? As far as the first paralogism is concerned (I will return to the third), it looks as if an option has been overlooked. It is possible to maintain that the *Cogito* transitions are sound, that they yield knowledge, and that it is simply open to further investigation what other kind of properties are possessed by the entity to which the ordinary first person in the *I think* refers. It is consistent with the soundness and knowledge-yielding status of *Cogito* transitions that the first person refers to something, perhaps must refer to something, that could be an object of intuition. There is no obvious requirement that if *I* is to refer to something that could be an object of intuition, it must be an object of intuition in the very mental states or events that are the starting point of a *Cogito* transition. Under this overlooked option, there is no reason for saying that *I* is not being treated as fully referential in *I think* when that conclusion is reached by a *Cogito* transition. Attempts in the spirit of Lichtenberg to say that what is supported by the starting point of a *Cogito* transition can be explained in subject-free terms have proved difficult to sustain (see Williams 1978 Chapter 3, Peacocke 2012, 2012b). Though I have no brief for the full Cartesian metaphysics of the subject, it is not clear to me that Descartes has made any mistake within the sphere of consciousness/thought relations when he concludes that one can have knowledge of an entity in making a *Cogito*-like transition in thought.

This objection to an element of Kant's line of thought, like the other objections I will raise, does nothing to support a rational psychologist's conception of an ontology of purely mental subjects that never go out of existence. As I said, the objection in this case is to Kant's reasoning, not to his conclusion. Moreover, it is hard not to sympathize with Kant's view that a Cartesian conception of egos violates some form of a principle of significance. No possible experience has been associated, even indirectly, with the distinction between one Cartesian ego persisting and its replacement by another with the relevantly same mental states. That application of a principle of significance operates, however, at the level of reference and objects. It is an objection to the Cartesian conception of a certain kind of object, Cartesian egos. The objection does not fundamentally have to be formulated at the level of sense, at the level of the first person concept; though it will of course have ramifications for the truth-conditions of first person thoughts.

(ii) Kant's Positive Account:

The second cluster of questions asks whether Kant's own positive account of the 'I' in 'I think', or the underlying motivations for it, are incompatible with Descartes' position. The first task here is to say exactly what Kant's positive account is. On this, Béatrice Longuenesse (2008) has some important suggestions. Her view is that according to Kant, "In referring his thoughts to 'I', the thinker (perceiver, imaginer) is doing nothing more than committing himself to the unity and consistency of his thoughts, and committing himself to obtaining a unified standpoint that could be shared by all" (2008: 17). Following her description of the role of 'I' in relation to these unifying functions, Longuenesse writes that "There is nothing more to be known of 'I' in the context of this argument" (2008: 17); and "It is thus apparent that the function of 'I' in this argument is quite different from what it was in Descartes' *cogito* argument" (2008: 17). "'I' in "I think" does not refer to a permanent *object* whose properties *change*. 'I' is just the term to which we refer our thoughts in order to think of them as unified by one standpoint and bound by rules that commit us ("me") to bring about unity and consistency under a unifying standpoint" (2008: 22) "... of course what we refer to by 'I' has to be one and the same through the whole time of our experience. And of course this identity is prior to and different from the identity of any object identifiable and reidentifiable *in* time, although it may readily be mistaken for such an identity" (2008: 23). Of such a statement as that the reference of "I" in "I think" is a mind distinct from a body, on this reading of Kant, "when we make this kind of statement we make a category mistake. For we compare the certainty of the pre-categorial existence contained in "I think" and the certainty of the *actuality* of objects given, identified, and reidentified in space and time" (2008: 25).

There is considerable textual support for some aspects of this reading, even beyond the passages Longuenesse cites. One such passage is a note Kant made about "I think" in his own copy of the first edition of the *Critique of Pure Reason*: "[This] is a proposition *a priori*, is a mere category of the subject, intellectual representation without anywhere or at any time, hence not empirical. Whether the category of reality lies in it, whether objective inferences are to be drawn from it" (1998: 413 note *a*). The reading gives further significance to such passages as A346/B404: "consciousness in itself is not even a representation distinguishing a particular object", and to the idea of what Kant calls *modi* of self-consciousness, which he describes in the second edition as "mere functions, which provide thought with no object at all" (B407). There is further support in these passages: "I would not say by this that the **I** [in "**I think**" – CP] in this proposition is an empirical representation; for it is rather purely intellectual, because it belongs to thinking in general"; "I think of myself, in behalf of a possible experience..." (B426).

The first set of points I want to make about this interpretation is that, under this reading of Kant, the "I" in "I think" must still have a very close connection with the ordinary first person concept, for three reasons.

First, to engage with such a rationalist as Descartes, these Kantian points will be relevant to Descartes' reasoning only if they employ the same first person concept as Descartes was employing in reasoning. But it was the ordinary first person that Descartes was employing. This is consistent with Longuenesse's main points if we regard Kant as making a contribution to a constitutive account of what is involved in grasp of the first person. That account can be developed consistently with the first person being governed by the fundamental reference rule I have been defending. The Kantian account aims to say something philosophically informative about grasp of the same first person concept mentioned in the fundamental reference rule.[4]

Second, it is very plausible that the constraints of consistency and unity that Longuenesse very properly emphasizes must involve consistency and unity of predications about objects in the world. These predications will include both contents that are not about oneself, and also some that are about oneself (including one's spatial, temporal, and causal properties and relations). Having consistent and unified predications about the wrong thing would not be enough. How is the reference that is the target of these consistency and unity requirements determined when the contents involve the first person? The plausible answer is that the reference must be the thinker who is thinking the "I" in "I think". But that rule is precisely the rule that individuates the normal first person concept, on the contemporary account outlined at the start of this paper.

Third, Longuenesse emphasizes that " 'I think' is a *universal* form of thought, which can be attributed to *any* thinker; on the other hand, this universal form is necessary for *particular, empirically determined perceivers and thinkers* to come up with thoughts about the world that *are independent of their own particular standpoint in the world*" (2008: 17). I agree. This interplay between the general requirements that apply to an arbitrary thinker in the world, and those that apply to each one of us thinkers individually, is entirely consistent with taking the constraints with which Kant is concerned in the "I" in "I think" as applying to its normal sense when used by any one of us. The first person concept as employed by any one thinker is an instance of a general type instances of which are employed by other thinkers. This is the type labeled the '[self]' type in the kind of neo-Fregean terminology account I would favour myself (1981). The constraints of unity and consistency can be formulated for an arbitrary thinker, for anyone who is employing an instance of the [self] type; the constraints are then given for arbitrary instances of that type. That is consistent with use of any instance of the type, so constrained, being the ordinary first person concept as used by a particular thinker.

It would, however, be a mistake to think that Kant's points about 'I' apply only at the level of the type of concept. On the contrary, it is clear that in many passages, Kant is talking about his own uses of 'I'; and it is clear that anyone else is meant to appreciate that the same points apply to his own uses (involving that instance of the [self] type available to him). This point applies to many of the passages quoted or cited above. As we saw, Longuenesse wrote " "I" in "I think" does not refer to a permanent *object* whose properties *change*" (2008: 22). But if Kant's points apply at the level of instances of the first person type, those are instances that do refer—not indeed to a permanent object, but certainly to an object that changes. What is true is that in thinking of something in the first person way, one is not thereby thinking of it as an object identified in a particular way in relation to space, nor as something temporally reidentified in a certain way, nor as an object given in an intuition. These are all points at the level of sense, not of reference. As far as I can see, accepting these points and acknowledging their philosophical importance is consistent with the soundness and knowledge-yielding character of *Cogito*-like transitions, when taken at face value. The points elaborate constraints on what is involved in grasping the first person that features in the *Cogito*-like transitions. The constraints do not undermine those transitions, taken at face value. In particular, they do not undermine that part of Descartes' discussion that is confined to the nexus of consciousness/judgment relations involving the first person, as opposed to the further metaphysics of Meditation VI, and Descartes' views about the nature of the reference of the first person.

(iii) 'A Merely Logical Subject'

The third cluster of questions concerns Kant's idea that the rational psychologist mistakes what is a 'merely logical subject' for something more substantial, a mistake that involves confusing the unity of experience with an experience of unity. The first paralogism, he writes, "passes off the constant logical subject of thinking as the cognition of a real subject of inherence" (A350). Kant's view seems to be that all conscious states have a certain common form; this form is captured by the characterization "I think ….."; "consciousness in itself is not even a representation distinguishing a particular object" (A346/B404), but the "I" in "I think" is still a logical subject, and the fact that the "I think" can accompany all my representations may, according to Kant, lead to the mistaken thesis that from all this, with no other premises, one can conclude that some entity stands in a relation to all one's own conscious states.

I agree that there is a phenomenology of all of what Kant would call one's 'representations' being one's own. This is a feature of consciousness, of its form if you will. Nonetheless, Kant's argument as summarized in the preceding paragraph is open to objection if the points I made on the second cluster of questions are correct. If "I" in "I think" does not have a reference at all, then of course mental states with an intentional content "I think …." cannot be a source of knowledge about the normal reference of "I" in "I think", since it has no such normal reference. But if it does have its normal reference, the possibility is reopened that such mental states can, on occasion, be a source of knowledge about the thing that is its reference. That it does have a normal reference in Descartes' thought is implied by what I have been arguing. If Descartes' *I* has its normal sense, it must also have its normal reference, however mistaken Descartes may have been about the properties of that normal reference.

If a thinker, including a rational psychologist, is clear-sighted about how the reference rule for *I* works, then is it quite unfair to accuse him of mistaking the unity of experience for an experience of unity. The clear-sighted thinker will not hold that an experience of unity (as opposed to unity of experience) is in any way necessarily involved in a correct, referential use of *I*. Neither the rational psychologist, nor we, in judging "All these experiences are mine", need to be committed to thinking that, in making this attribution of common ownership of the experiences to a single subject, there needs to be an experience or intuition of that subject. According to the fundamental reference rule, a thinking "All these experiences are mine" is true iff all the experiences in question belong to the subject doing the thinking. The experiences can all seem to be the thinker's, and the thinker can be entitled to take this seeming as correct, without the thinker needing to have an intuition of himself. In its seeming to the thinker that all the experiences are his, he enjoys a seeming with a primitive first person content. The correctness condition for that content is as given in the thesis at the outset of this paper, that all the experiences do in fact belong to the subject enjoying that seeming. (Of course we also have to give an account of the entitlement to take the seeming at face value.) If Descartes did ever say that he has an experiential (Kantian-style) intuition of himself that is involved in such self-ascriptive uses of the first person, it is not something he ever needed to say. An easy acceptance of the stylish formulation "unity of experience, not experience of unity" should not lead us into thinking that this was a mistake Descartes had to make.

In his discussion of the third paralogism in the first edition, Kant makes a further point. He rightly and forcefully observes that it's seeming to oneself that one was thus-and-so in the past does not suffice to make it the case that one was thus-and-so in the past (A362–5). His discussion is cast in terms of consciousness of the identity of oneself at different times.

Now it cannot follow from Kant's true observation that there is a seems/is distinction in this area that there is no such thing as genuine awareness of one's identity over time. To argue from that premise alone would be to apply the fallacious argument from illusion to the case of apparent awareness of identity over time.

The thesis in the contemporary philosophy of mind displayed at the outset of this paper serves further to illustrate why a fallacy would be involved. A temporally sensitive mechanism that noninferentially updates a subject's file on itself, a file of the sort described in that thesis, can generate knowledge-sustaining awareness of identity over time. The mechanism will not be infallible, any more than perception needs to be infallible. But when the temporal updating mechanism is working properly, it can give a subject genuine awareness of its identity over time, an awareness that he did or was thus-and-so in the past, just as perception can give genuine awareness of physical objects and events. The operation of the updating mechanism also does not at all require that the subject who is aware that he was thus-and-so in the past have a current intuition of himself.

An adequate defence of the claim that such memories give genuine awareness of identity must involve an account of the kind of thing of whose identity over time the thinker is aware (even though of course a thinker may be unaware of his or her own kind in making ascriptions of individual identity over time). It is very plausible that Descartes, given the metaphysics of Meditation VI, has no good account of the matter. On the particular account I have been developing, the identity of the subject over time involves identity of integrating apparatus. The view that identity of subject in the most fundamental case involves identity of embodied subject also has an account, a different one, of the matter. Insofar as Kant's point was merely that the rational psychologist has no good account of the kind of entity the awareness of identity is awareness of, I am in agreement. But again, this is a point having to do with the level of reference, and the nature of the entities referred to, rather than one turning on the nature of the intentional content of mental states. It does not rule out genuine, knowledge-sustaining awareness of one's own identity with the person who was so-and-so in the past.

At this stage in the discussion, we reach a point at which I find myself in agreement with John McDowell in his book *Mind and World* (1994). Although a quick review of the literature will rapidly show that McDowell and I differ on the nature of subjects of consciousness, and differ on the correct account of the nature of the first person concept, we are nevertheless in agreement on a further point. McDowell writes that "we make room for supposing that the continuity of 'I think' involves a substantial persistence, without implying that the continuant in question is a Cartesian ego", once we discard a certain assumption (1994: 101). The assumption is "that when we provide for the content of this idea of persistence, we must confine ourselves within the flow of 'consciousness'" (1994: 101). If "confining ourselves to the flow of 'consciousness'" means confinement to what is common to both genuine and illusory experiences as of the identity of the subject over time, then I agree.[5] In good cases, there is no more obstacle to saying that a subject is genuinely aware of his having been so-and-so in the past than there is to saying that perceptual experience is, in good cases, of an external material object. If I have understood him aright, McDowell and I agree that there can be genuine awareness of one's own identity over time.

This general approach to Kant's treatment of the third paralogism is not at all a complete dismissal of his thought. What it suggests rather is that Kant's insights should be put in a conditional form, and regarded as part of a *reductio* argument against the Cartesian conception. If the first person refers to something like a Cartesian ego, then grasp of the (alleged) distinction between one continuing ego and the replacement of one by another similar ego is something that would not show up in the thinker's psychology. In those circumstances, we could not properly make the distinction between mere apparent awareness of one's own identity over time and illusions of identity. The argument could be elaborated within the non-verificationist framework I developed in 'The Limits of Intelligibility' (1988). The truth of this conditional formulation of Kant's insight is, however, entirely consistent with the distinction between apparent and genuine awareness of identity being applicable when subjects are something other than Cartesian egos. Further, on this construal of what is valuable in Kant's discussion of the third paralogism, the argument does not turn on any kind of misinterpretation of the first person concept, nor on misunderstanding of the consciousness/judgement nexus for first person contents. It turns rather on the consequences of the Cartesian metaphysics of the self for the intelligibility of certain distinctions in memory and awareness.

We can contrast this treatment of the Paralogisms with that of Peter Strawson in *The Bounds of Sense* (1966: 163–9). Strawson's position and my own agree that the 'I' in the Kantian 'I think' does in fact refer, and refers to an entity for which there are empirical conditions of identity. For Strawson, that entity is a person conceived of as fundamentally embodied: "our ordinary concept of *personal* identity does carry with it empirically applicable criteria for the numerical identity through time of a subject of experience (a man or human being) and that these criteria, though not the same as those for bodily identity, involve an essential reference to the human body" (1966: 164). " ... the notions of singularity and identity of souls or consciousnesses are conceptually dependent upon, conceptually derivative from, the notions of singularity and identity of men or people. The rule for deriving the criteria we need from the criteria we have is very simple. It is: *one* person, *one* consciousness; *same* person, *same* consciousness" (1966: 168–9). On an account endorsing the contemporary theses displayed above, the entity is a subject whose identity over time turns on the identity of an integrating apparatus. This produces several divergences from Strawson's position. In one direction, the integrating apparatus may or may not be embedded in a body which is the body of the subject in question (see further below). In the other direction, we can apparently, in certain conceivable split brain cases, make sense of there existing two subjects in the same body. In such cases there will, functionally, be two pieces of integrating apparatus. In those cases, Strawson's rule "*same* person, *same* consciousness" is incorrect if there is meant to be only one person per body at a given time. I acknowledge that this position has a commitment to, and an obligation to justify, the proposition that the nature and identity of an integrating apparatus over time can be explained independently of embodiment.[6]

Strawson usually formulates the conceptual issues in terms of language rather than thought. For the most part, this makes no substantive difference. Strawson regards part of Kant's crucial insight as the recognition that when someone "ascribes a current or directly remembered state of consciousness to himself, no use whatever of any criteria of personal identity is required to justify use of the pronoun "I" to refer" to the subject of that experience (1966: 165). That is, such ascriptions are, as we have come to say, immune to errors of misidentification. I agree that they are so immune, and that there is some more or less explicit recognition of the point in Kant. The immunity does, however, need some explanation. There are explanations of the immunity, explanations that go hand-in-hand with the contemporary conception outlined above (see Peacocke 2012a). A crucial part of such explanations is the account of the soundness of the transition, noninferentially, from a conscious event or state enjoyed by a subject to the subject's self-ascription of an event or state of the relevant kind. The account emphasizes that a subject who moves from a mental state or event to the judgement that he is enjoying a state of event of the relevant kind will not, for reasons in the nature of the case, thereby be led to a false judgement on the contemporary conception outlined above. That explanation does not, apparently, require that subjects are fundamentally Strawsonian persons. Nor does it require that they be subjects whose experience is in part as of a route through an objective spatial world.

Strawson also says, and I agree, that in the criterionless self-ascription of mental states, "reference to the empirically identifiable subject" is "not in practice lost" (1966: 165). On my account, a public utterance of "I have an experience as of a lawn in front of me" will be produced by a subject, and this subject's identity depends on the identity of an integrating apparatus whose persistence and identity over time is an empirical matter. The experience itself makes rational the self-ascription, when thought of under psychological concepts of experience. The experience could not exist without a subject, and its subject must be the subject for whom the ascription is thus made rational. For Strawson, such an utterance of "I" can still refer to a subject "because—perhaps—it issues publicly from the mouth of a man who is recognizable as the person he is by the application of empirical criteria of personal identity" (1966: 165). This indeed explains how the term refers, but it does not yet explain the immunity to error through misidentification.

Strawson could, of course, endorse the explanation of immunity to error through misidentification that I offered. It would then need much further argument that the subject for whom such self-ascriptions are thus made rational must also be fundamentally embodied, rather than meeting the weaker condition of having an identity dependent upon a continuing integrating apparatus. Strawson does give part of an argument for that view. He argues that subjects with a unified consciousness must have experiences that are unified, in being (in part) experiences having a certain relation to a path through an objective world. His argument is of great interest, given our present concerns, for it would question the adequacy of a contemporary conception based on the theses displayed above, and I turn now to consider Strawson's argument.

3. Strawson's Neo-Kantian Conception of Subjects

Nothing in the four contemporary theses displayed at the start of this paper implies that there are not also further true theses that equally constrain the properties and relations of conscious subjects. Nothing that has been argued so far rules out the possibility that further investigation of the nature of conscious subjects may not reveal that there are plausible principles implying that conscious subjects must in some central cases be embodied, and must have perceptions that involve a route through the spatio-temporal world. In *The Bounds of Sense*, Strawson argues precisely that there are such principles.

We can distinguish various strengths of a proposed requirement on conscious subjects concerning either embodiment or experienced spatio-temporal history. In the case of embodiment, the requirement might be

(B1) that the subject actually possess a body;

(B2) that the subject once had a body;

(B3) that it must be for the subject as if it has a body; or

(B4) that it must be for the subject as if it at least once had a body.

There is a similar range of possible proposals for a requirement of experienced spatio-temporal history. The requirement might be

(S-T1) that the subject has throughout its history a location the subject either perceives, or is capable of perceiving, as its own;

(S-T2) that the subject in an initial segment of its history had such a perceived or perceptible location;

(S-T3) that throughout the subject's history it is for the subject as if it has such a perceived or perceptible location; or

(S-T4) it is for the subject as if in some initial stage of its history it had such a perceived or perceptible location.

My own view is that not even the weakest of these proposed requirements is correct, either for embodiment, or for spatio-temporal location and history. There is in my view no conceptual or metaphysical obstacle to the possibility of a subject having only a sequence of monaural sound experiences, of a sort that do not represent objective events. This possibility is arguably that of Strawson's own sound world in *Individuals* (1959). Again, the subject may have a sequence of visual experiences with only what I called sensational properties in *Sense and Content* (Peacocke 1983), or olfactory experiences, or any combination of the preceding, non-representational experiences.

In *The Bounds of Sense*, Strawson sets out to expound a Kantian argument intended to prove the opposite. He considers "the thesis that for a series of diverse experiences to belong to a single consciousness it is necessary that they should be so connected as to constitute a temporally extended experience of a unified objective world" (1966: 97). This formulation seems to be of the form (S-T1) of the spatio-temporal view. Strawson writes "of a unified objective world", not "*as* of a unified objective world". The requirement is also stated for the whole sequence of experiences, not just for some initial segment thereof. Strawson, rightly in my view, takes this thesis to be in conflict with the view that there could be a subject of consciousness whose experiences consist solely of "a succession of items such that there was no distinction to be drawn between the order and arrangement of the objects (and of their particular features and characteristics) and the order and arrangement of the subject's experiences of awareness of them (1966: 98–99). "Such objects might be of the sort which the earlier sense-datum theorists spoke of—red, round patches, brown oblongs, flashes, whistles, tickling sensations, smells." (1966: 99).

Strawson's argument in support of his thesis can be divided into the following steps. I label them "Points", because they are set out here in not exactly the order in which he expounds them, to bring out the direction in which the argument is proceeding:

Point (1): "Unity of the consciousness to which a series of experiences belong implies, then, the *possibility* of self-ascription of experiences on the part of a subject of those experiences" (1966: 98).

Point (2): Nothing but "a form of words" is added to the hypothesis of a "succession of essentially disconnected impressions" by saying that they all belong to a single subject, or that a unitary consciousness is aware of them all (1966: 100).

The remainder of Strawson's argument from here on argues for a necessary condition for a series of experiences to belong to a single subject.

Point (3): There is a necessary condition for a series of experiences to belong to a single subject, a condition without which "even the basis of the idea of the referring of such experiences to an identical subject of a series of them by such a subject would be altogether lacking" (1966: 101).

The argument for the necessary condition proceeds from a claim about the nature of experience:

Point (4): "There can be no experience at all which does not involve the recognition of particular items *as* being of such and such general kind. It seems that it must be possible, even in the most fleeting and purely subjective of impressions, to distinguish a component of recognition, or judgement, which is not simply identical with, or wholly absorbed by, the particular item which is recognized, which forms the topic of the judgement." (1966: 100)

Strawson immediately goes on to say there is an apparent difficulty here:

Point (5): "Yet at the same time we seem forced to concede that there are particular subjective experiences (e.g. a momentary tickling sensation) of which the objects (accusatives) have no existence independently of the awareness of them." (1966: 101)

Strawson says the tension he sees between Points (4) and (5) can (actually, he writes "must") be regarded by Kant, or a Kantian, as resolved by this observation:

Point (6): "the recognitional component, necessary to experience, can be present in experience only because of the *possibility* of referring different experiences to one identical subject of them all. Recognition implies the *potential* acknowledgment of the experience into which recognition necessarily enters as one's own, as sharing with others this relation to the identical self." (1966: 101)

Point (7): The potentiality of such an acknowledgment implies that "some at least of the concepts under which particular experienced items are recognized as falling should be such that the experiences themselves contain the basis" (1966: 101) for a seems/is distinction; and "collectively, the distinction *between* the subjective order and arrangement of a series of such experiences on the one hand and the objective order and arrangement of the items of which they are experiences on the other" (1966: 101).

I am not at all sure, well over forty years after first reading it, that I understand the conception of the subject matter that generates this bold and fascinating argument. But I do think the argument as formulated here is vulnerable to the following objections.

(a) There is a fundamental distinction between giving a theory of the relation

experience *e* is owned by subject *s*

and giving a theory of the different relation

the subject *s* is capable of self-ascribing experience *e* in thought.

Having an experience *e* is one thing; having the mental capacities to be able to self-ascribe *e* is another. Prima face, many animals and young children have the former and lack the latter. Some passages from Strawson show him using now a thesis about ownership of experiences, now a thesis about using some form of first person representation and self-ascribing experiences. At the start of the argument, he is apparently writing about first relation, that of ownership: "First, we ask: how can we attach a sense to the notion of the single consciousness to which the successive "experiences" are supposed to belong?" (1966: 100). Yet the argument later mentions what's "in fact self-ascribed": "Not all the members of such a series [of "experiences which belong to a unitary consciousness" – CP] are in fact self-ascribed: a man may be more prone to forget himself in contemplation of the world.... than he is to be conscious of, or to think of, himself as perceiving" (1966: 104). If it is the relation of ownership itself that is in question, no 'in fact' qualification necessary. For self-ascription, the qualification surely is required. The starting point of the argument concerns the unity of the consciousness to which a series of successive experiences belongs. Any move from this to consideration of self-ascription needs justification.

Strawson almost certainly thought there is a connection between the two relations, a connection that can be formulated in two propositions. First, he likely thought that a subject enjoys a token experience only if the subject can self-ascribe it. Thus, "The notion of a single consciousness to which different experiences belong is linked to the notion of self-consciousness, of the ascription of an experience or state of consciousness to oneself" (1966: 98). It is not only the animals and young children that make this problematic. The passage also seems to imply that consciousness requires a certain kind of self-consciousness (a form that is sometimes called reflective self-consciousness). The second connecting proposition that Strawson likely accepted is that a subject can self-ascribe an experience only if he enjoys a sequence of interconnected experiences of an objective world—though this of course would have to be the conclusion of the argument, not its premise.

Even if we restrict our attention to the case of subjects who have the concepts required to self-ascribe experiences, we need to draw a further distinction. The fact that, for such subjects, when *s* owns *e*, it is possible for *s* to self-ascribe *e* does not imply that that fact is what *makes e* one of *s*'s experiences. For there may be some philosophical explanation of why that possibility always holds that traces the possibility to a quite different constitutive origin. That seems to me to be the case here. *e* as a conscious event is in an element of its subject's total subjective state. Thereby *e* can make rational for the subject various judgements, including a judgement of it, demonstratively given, to the effect "That's mine", or "I am having that experience of such-and-such kind". It is entirely consistent with this non-Strawsonian, non-Kantian direction of constitutive explanation that whenever there is ownership of a conscious event, there is the possibility of self-ascription. But this 'whenever' claim is true not because ownership consists in the possibility of such self-ascription. Rather, it is ownership that grounds the possibility of the self-ascription. In short, in the order of philosophical explanation, Strawson has not established that an "ascription-first" view of these matters is correct, rather than an "ownership-first" view.

An ownership-first view can be correct, and is a rival to such neo-Kantian views as Strawson's, only if there is a background account of the nature and identity over time of the subjects who are said to enjoy the experiences. But that is precisely what the contemporary conception, outlined in the earlier displayed theses, offers. It presents an account of conscious subjects capable of representing themselves that involves identity of integrating apparatus and the possession of files on themselves that does not involve the neo-Kantian materials.

(b) Points (4) through (6) of the argument raise other issues. Strawson says that in even the most fleeting of impressions there is a "component of recognition, or judgement" (1966: 100). Judgement has conceptualized content. Not every subject who has experiences or impressions has to possess mental states with conceptualized content. Even for a subject who possesses concepts, the occurrence of a mental event need not engage or involve the subject's concepts. Once we distinguish judgement from awareness, then even when a subject has a rich conceptual repertoire and conceptualizes his mental events under various kinds, there is no incompatibility between this conception of awareness and the fact that for pains, for instance, there is no distinction between the experience of the pain and the pain event itself. There certainly would be a problem if awareness were to consist in judgement; but it does not. So the "yet" that starts off the quotation in Point (5) ("Yet at the same time we seem forced to concede . . . . .") does not seem to be well motivated; there is no apparent need to see the acknowledgment of such subjective sensations as any kind of concession.

Why is the possibility of self-ascription thought to solve a problem that is alleged to exist for sensations, but which is apparently not thought to exist for objective perceptions of the spatio-temporal world? One can imagine an argument that is motivated as follows. If one fails properly to distinguish awareness and judgement, and one thinks, as apparently Strawson (or at least Strawson's Kant) does, that all awareness has to involve judgement, then it may indeed seem that in sensation we have collapsed the item/recognition distinction. Such a combination of views may lead one to think that a sensation being of a certain kind cannot come apart from the subject's thinking that it is. By contrast, it may be said, for objective perception, since it is always possible that some objective state of affairs exists without experience as of it, and conversely, there is no such (alleged) danger of the so-called item/recognition distinction collapsing. Then, this argument may continue, genuine recognition in the sensation case is secured because the possibility of self-ascription means that this is a subjective item. Presumably on this view that means that we can thereby have recognition of kinds without the kind of seems/is distinction that is present for experiences with objective content. The ascription of purely subjective experiences to a subject is not vacuous, on this view, only because the subject is an independent entity that traces a path through the spatio-temporal world.

I confess to being utterly unclear how the argument of this reading is meant to work. Recognition needs to be recognition of the subjective item as of a particular kind—as a pain, as a particular kind of smell or sound, and so forth. Consider the self-ascription to which appeal is made in this version of the argument: does that self-ascription specify the kind of the experience, or is it not? If the kind of the experience is not included, the argument has not provided for what is involved in recognition.

If the kind is included, how has the specific kind of the subjective experience been secured merely by the possibility of self-ascription of a particular experience? Isn't self-ascription of an experience of a specific kind, and ascription as that specific kind, possible, and made rational, by the experience's already being of the kind in question? Then it seems that the experience's being of the kind it is is causally and explanatorily prior to the possibility of proper self-ascription. Without that basis, it is not clear how a specific kind is available for self-ascription on the Strawsonian conception.

Perhaps the argument is meant to be that a conception of the experience and its properties as causally and explanatorily prior, as in the ownership-first view, is some kind of illusion. We say that the experience makes reasonable the self-ascription, but this is, it may be said, a way of speaking that should not be confused with constitutive or metaphysical priority in this area. The problem is that we have been given no real reason for taking these appearances as illusory. If we combine the conception of subjects outlined in the contemporary conception with an insistence on the awareness/judgement distinction, there will indeed always be the possibility of self-ascription of a sensation as being of a particular kind, when the sensation occurs to a conceptually competent subject. There is no obvious obstacle to the naïve view that the kind of the sensation, at an appropriate level of kind, contributes to the rational explanation of the subject's self-ascription of a sensation of that kind.

There is a parallelism here between this criticism and the earlier criticism of Strawson's discussion of the way links are not "in practice" severed with a bodily subject in 'criterionless' mental self-ascription (in language). In both cases, Strawson's argument aims to succeed in securing an embodied subject, as, respectively, owner or ascribee of the mental state; but in both cases, the rationality and entitlement to the transition involved in each case seems to be left unelucidated in his account.

(c) Point (2) of Strawson's argument, taken in the context of his reasoning, suggests that there is some vacuity in saying "all the experiences have the same owner" when the experiences are purely subjective, and that the vacuity disappears when some at least of the series are perceptions of an objective world, through which the subject traces a route. But having a continuous spatio-temporal route and point of view on an objective world is neither sufficient nor necessary for identity of subject over time or for identity of owner of the experiences. We can conceive of inserting a new brain, of a new subject, into one identical continuing body that traces a continuous path in space. This possibility shows that even if the perceptions of the new subject trace a continuous series of points of view with experiences of the previous subject on that route, that continuity is not sufficient for identity of subject over time. A further condition is needed: continuity of integrating apparatus over time.

This further condition is not vacuous. Moreover, this further condition can also hold without the condition of an experienced spatio-temporal route condition being met. The condition of an experienced spatio-temporal route is not met in Strawson's own sound world in *Individuals*, but the relevant auditory experiences could all be enjoyed by a subject with continuity of integrating apparatus over time.

I am inclined to think that what objective perceptions add to the purely subjective ones is not by itself enough to make sameness of subject intelligible if it were not so already. And when we add what is enough for identity of subject, viz. identity of integrating apparatus, then tracing a continuous spatio-temporal route through an objective world is not obviously required. Indeed it is not met in some cases even when there are objective perceptions. Such is the case of Daniel Dennett's subject in his paper "Where Am I?" (1978), in which a subject whose physical integrating apparatus is in Houston may control, and perceive from, different bodies at different times. The location of the body controlled by this subject does not need to possess spatio-temporal continuity over time. It may jump around as the subject controls different bodies at different times.

We can also add that if some split-brain cases are possible in which there are two conscious subjects in the same body at the same time, then it is possible that two subjects have exactly the same genuinely perceived spatio-temporal path through the world, yet remain distinct subjects. The two subjects could share a visual perceptual apparatus in such cases. A spatio-temporal path through the world does not fix identity of the subject of experience either at a given time, or over time.

There is, I agree, an important psychological and representational distinction between a subject whose experiences are interconnected because they are of an objective world, and a subject whose experiences are not so interconnected. The former subject, but not the latter, is able to locate itself as an element in the objective order of things and events. On my view, that is a difference between a subject that has an applicable conception of itself as having a location in the world, and a subject who does not have such a conception. That is a distinction in respect of the conception available to two subjects who differ in that respect. It is not a distinction in point of existence of the two subjects. There is further discussion of these points in Peacocke (2012).

(d) Strawson's argument relies upon an alleged experience/concepts connection: "Certainly concepts, recognition . . . would be necessary to a consciousness with any experience at all" (1966: 99). There is by now a fairly extensive literature detailing what would be involved in a notion of nonconceptual content of experience.[7] Perhaps Strawson's arguments should not be taken as required to dispute the possibility of nonconceptual content. Perhaps much or all of what he says should be translated to the level of nonconceptual content. There is a legitimate notion of nonconceptual recognition of shape, of nonconceptual correctness conditions, and, on my own views, a nonconceptual version of subject-representation that refers to a subject of consciousness. But I do not see how any such translation of Strawson's argument rules out the possibility of a subject of consciousness with a sequence of purely sound, visual-sensational, or olfactory experiences. The account of subjects with updateable subject-files on themselves helps to explain how such subjects could represent themselves as having been in certain states earlier, without having any conception of themselves as occupying spatial locations.

These points are all arguments that the conclusion of Strawson's argument is too strong. If the conclusion is too strong, then there is no point in trying to construct different arguments to the same conclusion (the reasoning is too strong however the conclusion is reached). It does not at all follow that there are not successor arguments to Strawson's that draw in interesting ways on the materials he deployed, to related, though different, conclusions. It would take us too far afield to develop successor arguments here. But I note that consideration of what is involved in having experiences that do have objective spatio-temporal content, and consideration of the nature of subjective properties and their relation to the public world may each have interesting interconnections and consequences for self-representation in an objective world. The light cast by neo-Kantian arguments may come not from a Strawsonian conclusion, but from what they illuminate in adjacent areas.

I also note a final point of agreement with Strawson, though it has a twist. Strawson writes, at the end of his section 'Unity and Objectivity' in *The Bounds of Sense*,

> memory is involved in experience, recognition, consciousness of identity of self through diversity of experience. But it is far too deeply and essentially involved to be capable of being safely handled as if it were a separable and detachable factor which can, say, be conveniently invoked to link up temporally successive or separated episodes into an experiential sequence. If experience is impossible without memory, memory is also impossible without experience. From whatever obscure levels they emerge they emerge together (1966: 111–12).

The non-Strawsonian view of subjects I have endorsed is committed to agreement with Strawson on his point in the final sentence of this most recent quotation. Part of what makes something a continuing and self-representing subject is its capacity for primitive self-representation in memory of its own earlier properties and relations. Self-representing subjecthood and memory really are essentially interdependent on the account I have been offering, and both involve the operation of the subject's file on itself. Neither self-representing subjecthood nor memory is something more primitive than the other: and so neither is available for reductive explication of the other. The twist in this point of agreement is, however, that on the treatment I propose, the way in which personal identity and memory emerge together, via identity of integrating apparatus and the subject's file on itself, is also a way that provides the materials for a non-Strawsonian, non-Kantian account of conscious subjects.[8]

Notes

1. In the past thirteen years, see especially Ameriks (2000), and the references therein to literature to that date, and more recently Longuenesse (2008) and Proops (2010).
2. A350, A363 (which speaks of the "the logical identity of the I"), B413 (which speaks of "a merely logically qualitative unity of self-consciousness in general"). Translations are from the Guyer and Wood edition (Kant 1998).
3. Of course, from the true premise that the subject is not so given in first person thought we should not move to the false conclusion that the subject is not in fact material and extended—the fallacy of moving from "not being given as having property P" to "not having property P". I do not in fact think that Descartes made any such fallacious inference. His arguments for the distinctness of mind and body involve other, further premises.

4. When Longuenesse writes, elaborating Kant, " "I" in "I think" does not refer to a permanent *object* whose properties *change*" (2008: 22), we have to agree with the proposition thereby attributed to Kant, because "I" does not refer to a permanent object. But it does refer to an impermanent object whose properties change. That is something we are committed to by our ordinary views, in combination with the thesis that both Kant and Descartes are using "I" with its ordinary sense. This observation does not, however, damage the point that there are consistency and unity constraints on the first person concept that contribute to its having the sense (and thereby the reference) it does.

5. If I have understood him correctly, the quoted formulation from McDowell superficially seems to endorse a "highest common factor" conception of consciousness, a conception he strongly rejects for perceptual experience in its role of ordinary justification of perceptual knowledge. On that rejection, see for instance McDowell (1994: 113) and the references on that page. But his point about awareness of identity over time could be reformulated without such apparent endorsement of something he rejects elsewhere.

6. For further discussion see Peacocke (2012), especially the discussion there of cases described as of "Degree 0", in which there are subjects who do not self-represent at all. The relation of such subjects to the physical object in which their integrating apparatus is housed is not at all the same as our relation to our own bodies.

7. Examples of my own efforts are in Peacocke (1992: Chapter 3) and Peacocke (2001). See also the important contributions in Burge (2003, 2010).

8. Earlier versions of this material were presented in one of my lectures in the 'Context and Content' series in 2010 at the Institut Jean Nicod, École Normale Supérieure, Paris, and in one of my Kohut Lectures at the University of Chicago in 2011, in addition to my regular seminars at Columbia University and University College London. I thank Jonathan Lear, Robert Pippin, François Recanati, and Georges Rey for valuable comments. I was stimulated to think about these issues again by a joint Columbia/NYU seminar 'Kant and Contemporary Issues' I gave with Béatrice Longuessse in the fall of 2007. I thank her not only for many discussions over the years on these and related topics, but for highly illuminating comments on a late draft of this paper, and for further discussion of her own published views on these issues. This final version is significantly different as a result.

References

Ameriks, K. (2000), *Kant's Theory of Mind: An Analysis of the Paralogisms of Pure Reason* (Oxford: Oxford University Press, second edition).

Burge, T. (2003), 'Perceptual Entitlement', *Philosophy and Phenomenological Research* 67: 503–548.

—— (2010), *Origins of Objectivity* (Oxford: Oxford University Press).

Campbell, J. (1994), *Past, Space, and Self* (Cambridge MA: MIT Press).

Dennett, D. (1978), "Where Am I?", in his *Brainstorms* (Montgomery, VT: Bradford Books).

Dummett, M. (1981), *The Interpretation of Frege's Philosophy* (London: Duckworth).

Kant, I. (1998), *Critique of Pure Reason* tr. P. Guyer and A. Wood (Cambridge: Cambridge University Press).

Longuenesse, B. (2008), 'Kant's "I think" versus Descartes' "I Am a Thing That Thinks"', in *Kant and the Early Moderns* ed. D. Garber and B. Longuenesse (Princeton: Princeton University Press).

McDowell, J. (1994), *Mind and World* (Cambridge, MA: Harvard University Press).

Nagel, T. (1974), 'What Is It Like to be a Bat?', *Philosophical Review* 83: 435–50.

Perry, J. (2002), 'The Self, Self-Knowledge, and Self-Notions', in his *Identity, Personal Identity and the Self* (Indianapolis: Hackett).

Peacocke, C. (1981), 'Demonstrative Thought and Psychological Explanation', *Synthese* 49: 187–217.

―――― (1983), *Sense and Content: Experience, Thought, and their Relations* (Oxford: Oxford University Press).

―――― (1988), 'The Limits of Intelligibility: A Post-Verificationist Proposal', *Philosophical Review* 97: 463–496.

―――― (1992), *A Study of Concepts* (Cambridge MA: MIT Press).

―――― (2001), 'Does Perception Have a Nonconceptual Content?', *The Journal of Philosophy* 98: 239–64.

―――― (2008), *Truly Understood* (Oxford: Oxford University Press).

―――― (2012), 'Subjects and Consciousness', in *The Self and Self-Knowledge* ed. A. Coliva (Oxford: Oxford University Press).

―――― (2012a), 'Explaining *De Se* Phenomena', in *Immunity to Error through Misidentification: New Essays*, ed. S. Prosser and F. Recanati (Cambridge: Cambridge University Press).

―――― (2012b), 'Descartes Defended', *Proceedings of the Aristotelian Society, Joint Session* 86: 109–125.

Proops, I. (2010), 'Kant's First Paralogism', *Philosophical Review* 119: 449–495.

Strawson, P. (1959), *Individuals* (London: Methuen).

―――― (1966), *The Bounds of Sense* (London: Methuen).

Wilson, M. (1978), *Descartes* (London: Routledge & Kegan Paul).

Philosophical Perspectives, 26, Philosophy of Mind, 2012

ATTENTION TO THE PASSAGE OF TIME

Ian Phillips
University College London

Time travels in diverse paces with diverse persons. I'll tell you who time ambles withal, who time trots withal, who time gallops withal, and who he stands still withal.

(Shakespeare, *As You Like It*, III, ii)

1. Overview

The idea of an intimate connection between attention and time is a traditional one, long embraced by scientists and philosophers, and firmly enshrined in folk wisdom.[1] In explaining variations in our experience of duration, contemporary cognitive scientists commonly make appeal not just to attention, but specifically to the concept of *attention to the passage of time*.[2] Time, we are told, trots when we attend to its passage, and gallops when we are distracted from it. A wealth of data is explained in these terms. Yet the central metaphor of attending to the passage of time provokes uneasiness. As the psychologist Richard Block demands, 'What...does it mean to attend to time itself?' (1990, 22) This paper proposes an answer to that question.

I proceed as follows. In the next section (§2), I set-out the standard story concerning attention to time found in the empirical literature, and the evidence that supports it. In the following two sections I consider and reject two natural interpretations of attention to time. In §3, I consider interpreting attention to time in terms of attention to perceptible change. I argue that such an interpretation cannot be right, since attention to perceptible change has almost the opposite effect on perceived duration to that explained in terms of attention to time. In §4, I consider interpreting attention to time as a form of selective perceptual attention to stimulus duration, analogous to other forms of feature-based attention, e.g., to colour, orientation, or movement. I argue that this interpretation is also unsustainable, since it cannot explain the finding that combining a timing task with a perceptual or motor task only interferes with the performance of the timing task, whereas combining a timing task with a cognitive (e.g., mental arithmetic) task shows bidirectional interference (Brown 1997; Brown 2010).

Both rejected interpretations share the assumption that time should be thought of as analogous to other perceptible stimulus features (an idea enshrined in Michon's 'equivalence postulate'). Both interpretations thus assume that attention to time should be treated as analogous to other forms of perceptual attention. The failure of both interpretations casts doubt on that assumption. In §5, I suggest an alternative way of understanding attention to time as a form of *internal* attention (Chun et al. 2011). In turn, I suggest that internal attention should be identified with mental activity within our non-perceptual stream of consciousness: conscious thinking in the broadest sense of the term. I propose that attention to time, so understood, increases perceived duration because the quantity of such conscious mental activity provides for us a key measure of perceived duration. In §6, I show how we can account for the data from dual-task paradigms given this interpretation of attention to time. Finally, in §7, I consider in more detail the nature of the hypothesised relationship between conscious mental activity and our awareness of the passage of time.

2. Attention to Time: the Standard Story

It is commonly held amongst contemporary theorists of time perception that time perception in influenced by *attention to time* — attention which is competed for by non-temporal processing. Thus, Dutke describes the hypothesis 'that directing attention to the "course of time" increase[s] the subjective duration of temporal intervals, whereas distracting attention from time decrease[s] subjective duration' as the 'most successful hypothesis about the cognitive factors that influence duration judgments' (2005, 1404).[3] Many make an even stronger claim: time perception—here meaning specifically *duration* perception—*requires* attention to time.[4]

The evidence which underlies the appeal to attention in relation to duration perception comes principally from an abundance of paradigms which exhibit a dual-task interference effect, said to be 'the most robust, well-replicated finding in the time perception literature' (Brown 2010, 111).[5] In essence the effect is that, relative to a single-task (i.e. timing only) condition, duration judgments made under dual-task (i.e. timing plus non-timing task) conditions are *shorter* and/or *more variable and less accurate*. Additionally: when the difficulty of the concurrent (non-timing) task increases, the strength of the interference effect typically increases (e.g., Zakay, Nitzan, and Glicksohn 1983; Brown 1985; Brown 1997); when subjects are instructed to pay more or less attention to the timing task, they produce relatively longer or shorter duration estimates (e.g., Macar et al. 1994, discussed below); and, finally, when subjects receive training on either the timing or non-timing task, the interference effect reduces (e.g., Brown and Bennett 2002).

Here are two examples of the effect. Macar et al. (1994) presented subjects with visual and auditory stimuli of varying intensities and durations (between 250–3000msec across experiments) under five different attentional sharing instructions: duration only (control), maximum duration/minimum intensity, half/half, maximum intensity/minimum duration, and intensity only (control). The more attention subjects were instructed to pay to intensity, the more likely they were to classify the stimulus as having a 'short' as opposed to 'long' duration. The authors interpret this as a direct result of the decrease in attention to time when attention to intensity is prioritised. More generally, the authors conclude that 'the amount of attention allocated to time is a key factor of a temporal performance. The allocation of attention to time determines the accuracy of timing as well as the subjective length of the internal duration' (1994, 684).

In a rather different paradigm, Hicks et al. (1976) compared estimates of a 42s period during which subjects dealt cards according to one of the three rules: into a single pile (0-bit condition), by colour (1-bit condition), or by suit (2-bit condition). Subjects, who knew in advance they would be asked to estimate the time they had spent sorting the cards, estimated on average that they had been counting for 53s in the 0-bit condition, 43s in the 1-bit condition, and 31s in the 2-bit condition. In other words, the increase in task difficulty led to a dramatic reduction in subjects' sense of elapsed time (in the 2-bit condition 42s 'felt' like only 31s). Again Hicks et al. interpret the findings in terms of the idea that 'the prospective judgment of time requires attention to time' (ibid., 725). The harder the task is made, the less the subject can attend to time, and the shorter her sense of elapsed duration becomes.

As this last remark indicates, Hicks et al. do not seem merely to be expressing the view that duration perception is affected by attention to time, but rather the view that attention to time is *necessary* for duration to be perceived at all. Macar et al. suggest much the same, holding that 'it is not only possible but also necessary to pay attention to time-in-passing to perform a timing task correctly' (1994, 683). Comparable results and interpretations are found across a very wide range of paradigms and timescales.[6]

Attention to time is typically modelled within a widely adopted (if highly controversial) internal-clock model of time perception. This model posits an internal-clock or pacemaker whose function is to generate 'pulses'.[7] Perceived duration is then understood as a monotonic function of the number of pulses collected in an accumulator/counter during the course of a given period or event.[8] The number of stored pulses is obviously affected by two factors: the *initiation and termination* of pulse collection, and the pulse *rate*. In order to accommodate the dual-task data noted above, it is proposed that the number of accumulated time units is affected by *attention to time*. This effect can be modelled in a variety of ways. One popular model due to Zakay and Block (1996, §4) introduces an 'attentional gate' between the pacemaker and accumulator. According to Zakay and Block, '[a]s an organism allocates more attention to time, the gate opens wider or more frequently' (1996, 154), thereby allowing

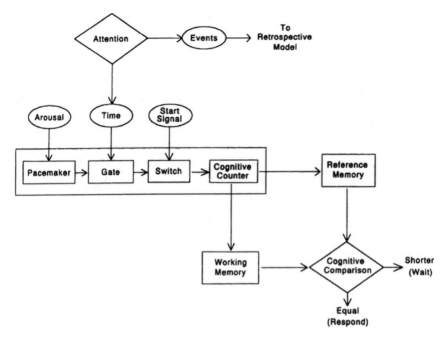

Figure 1. The attentional-gate model of prospective time perception. From Zakay and Block 1997, 14. Copyright © 1997 American Psychological Society. Reprinted by permission of SAGE Publications.

more pulses to reach the accumulator. They later suggest that attending to time is not merely facilitative of pulse transmission but 'necessary, for pulses to be transmitted to the cognitive counter' (ibid., 155).[9] This model can then be represented as in Figure 1 which shows the pacemaker and counter system embedded within a larger memory and decision system. Here, in effect, a gate controlled by attention to time has been grafted on to a more traditional pacemaker-counter system.

Much the same picture is sometimes expressed in terms of the idea that 'attention is needed to *activate* an internal timer that will accumulate units' such that 'pulses may be lost when attention is not focused on the elapsing time' (Macar et al. 2002, 244; my emphasis). But, however exactly one models the effect, the basic idea remains the same: increasing attention to time causes more pulses to be accumulated over a given period (Wittmann et al. 2010, 7). And on many such models the absence of attention simply leads to a failure to accumulate pulses at all: duration perception requires attention to time.[10]

Despite the consensus over the *involvement* of attention to time in duration perception, the *concept* of attention to time is liable to provoke unease. It is not uncommon for psychologists to recognize that further clarification is needed. For instance, Sawyer, Meyers, and Huser, although generally supportive of an attentional model, express concern that such models 'fall short of furnishing a clear explanation of the experimental results' and ask for greater clarification of 'the notion that subjects can devote attention to temporal processing' (1994, 656). Likewise, Dutke, again operating within an attentional framework, closes a paper by noting the need 'to further specify the cognitive processes addressed by the metaphor of *directing attention to time*' (2005, 1412; emphasis in original). This dissatisfaction goes back at least to Block (1979, 193; see also Block 1990, 21–2), who complains that previous explanations invoking attention to time are 'vacuous' and 'unacceptably vague', asking, 'What ... does it mean to attend to time itself?'[11]

Block's first response to his own question is to take 'attention to time to mean attention to temporal information' (Zakay and Block 1996, 152). However, this simply begs the question as to what is meant by 'temporal information'. Both Block and Zakay offer a number of different suggestions in this relation, and I will return to these in the course of the discussion below. However, I want to start by considering two very natural suggestions as to how we should understand the concept of attention to time (and so of temporal information), and show why they are inadequate as they stand. In the next section, I consider understanding attention to time as attention to perceptible change. In the subsequent section, I consider whether attention to time can be thought of as a kind of feature-based attention to stimulus duration. Having shown that neither interpretation is sustainable, I build on some suggestive but initially puzzling remarks of Block and Zakay's to argue that attention to time should not be thought of as a form of perceptual attention at all. Instead, I propose that attention to time, at least in the relevant experimental contexts, is a form of *internal* attention. Internal attention, I claim, should be identified with non-perceptual conscious activity: conscious thinking in its broadest sense. What explains the involvement of internal attention so construed in duration perception is the fact that for us a crucial measure of perceived duration is the quantity of concurrent non-perceptual activity which occurs during the interval to be timed.

3. Attention to Time as Attention to Change

Philosophers and psychologists alike have traditionally felt uncomfortable at the idea that we might literally be said to perceive time or its passage. Kant, for example, repeatedly proclaims throughout the *Analytic of Principles* that 'time cannot be perceived by itself' (2003, B233; see also A33/B49–50, B219, B225, B257, and A183). And later philosophers and psychologists have echoed this sentiment. Thus, Woodrow declares that 'time is not a thing that, like an apple, may be perceived' (1951, 1235); Gibson takes as his title the widely endorsed slogan that 'events are perceivable but time is not' (1975, 295; cf. Fraisse 1984, 2); and Block reminds us that 'time itself is not a stimulus' (1990, 9).

This traditional piece of negative wisdom is usually combined with the positive claim that we are nonetheless aware of time in virtue of our perception of change. As Shoemaker puts it, tracing the view back to book IV of Aristotle's

Physics: 'we measure time by observing changes' (1969, 366). In the same spirit, talk of our perceiving the 'passage of time' is modestly rendered in terms of our awareness of change. In James' phrase: 'awareness of change is the condition on which our perception of time's flow depends' (1890, 620). Likewise, Le Poidevin: 'We . . . see time passing in front of us, in the movement of a second hand around a clock, or the falling of sand through an hourglass, or indeed any motion or change at all' (2007, 76). In what follows I assume that any satisfactory account of attention to time ought to accord with these insights.

Given this, it is extremely tempting to think that attention to time or its passage should be understood in terms of attention to perceptible change. Fraisse takes this view, proposing that 'direct time judgments [are] founded immediately on the changes we experience' (1963, 234) and that 'attention to the lapse of time affects duration estimation only by changing the number of perceived changes' (Kojima and Matsuda 2000, 145). More recent glosses of attention to time or temporal information also place stimulus change centre stage. Thus, Block (citing Fraisse) writes that 'changes serve as referents, or cues, to use in experiencing, remembering, and judging time' (1990, 9). And when Brown holds that [a]ttention to time involves a heightening consciousness of temporal cues', stimulus changes are his first example (2008, 114).[12]

Natural as this view is, attention to time cannot be identified with attention to perceived change. To see this first consider a recent paper on the effect of music on perceived duration (Droit-Volet et al. 2010). Using a temporal bisection task, during which 'participants are instructed to pay attention to time' (ibid., 227), Droit-Volet and colleagues establish that the duration of a melody is perceived to be shorter than a non-melodic stimulus of the same objective duration. This finding is interpreted in terms of the idea that music is able to 'divert attention away from the passage of time' (ibid., 226), in line with the attentional-gate model discussed above.

Imagine being a participant in this experiment who is instructed to pay attention to time. As is standard in such experiments, you are explicitly told not to count (ibid., 227), and all watches and clocks are removed. So what do you do? As proposed above, it is natural to interpret the instruction as an instruction to attend to perceivable change. If you are to attend to change, what should you attend to? Surely the most obvious candidate is the music itself. After all, 'the notion "musical change" is a tautology. Music *is* change' (Kouwenhoven 2001, 54). Similarly, as Brown puts it, 'Western music consists of an organized set of pitch changes, rhythmical patterns, phrase structures and accents, and temporal hierarchies' (2008, 116).[13] Yet if attending to music is the most natural way of attending to the passage of time, how can music 'divert attention *away* from the passage of time', as Droit-Volet and colleagues propose? Assuming that attention to time should be understood as a form of perceptual attention to change, the idea that attention to music somehow competes with attention to time is hard to make sense of. Attending to music seems a paradigmatic way of attending to time on the present understanding.[14]

Droit-Volet et al. conclude that their 'results show that time flies in the presence of music because it distracts our attention away from the processing of time, probably due to music's rich structure or the pleasure produced by listening to it' (2010, 231). These additional and very different ideas do little to ease our puzzlement. First, as we have just seen, it is hard to understand why music's rich structure should distract us from attending to time, insofar as that structure is a *temporal* structure of pitch changes, rhythmical patterns, phrase structures, etc. Second, we might think that the pleasure we get from listening to music should increase our desire to listen. It is only if we already have assumed that listening to music is opposed to attending to time, that our pleasure in listening might help account for why music distracts us from attending to time.

Puzzlement is far from confined to the musical case. Many other tasks which are held to distract attention from time clearly involve an increase in attention to perceptible change. For example, Brown (1997) focuses on the effects of the non-temporal task of 'pursuit rotor tracking', a task which involves a subject manually following a continuously moving visual target. Here attention to a target that is continuously *changing* its position shortens perceived time. Likewise, many studies have used flight (Bortolussi, Kantowitz, and Hart 1986) or driving simulators as their primary task. For example, Baldauf, Burgard, and Wittmann (2009) manipulate primary task difficulty by shifting from a 'straight road' driving simulation with no curves or obstacles to a 'city drive' simulation in which 'there were many events demanding caution and appropriate reactions by the driver' including a person in a parked car suddenly opening their door, a child with a ball jumping out from behind a parked car, the need briefly to wait for a traffic light to turn green, and a pedestrian crossing the road (ibid., 3). They also use an 'oncoming traffic' simulation in which the driver has to negotiate a winding road against a dense stream of oncoming cars passing at varying speeds. On the face of it these increases in primary task demand appear to involve an *increase* in 'temporal cues', viz. environmental changes. They contain more changes, and a greater number of successive events with a richer temporal structure. Thus again, assuming that attention to time is a form of perceptual attention to change, it is puzzling that longer productions in the demanding primary tasks should be explained by proposing 'that under higher workload conditions a subject is distracted more from attending to time' and so the 'production of a certain time interval then takes longer because hypothesized time counts (or pulses) that represent that duration take longer to accumulate' (ibid., 6). Higher workload conditions are conditions where more changes are present and demanding of attention, so it is obscure how such conditions distract attention away from time on the present hypothesis.

Just as in these cases change appears to have the opposite effect to that which we might expect, we similarly find a large number of cases in which the *absence* of change appears to *increase* attention to time. Consider a set of experiments designed to test the adage that a watched pot never boils (Block, George, and Reed 1980; Cahoon and Edmonds 1980). In Block, George, and

Reed's experiment, observers were instructed to attend to a beaker filled with liquid, as it stood on an electric burner for 270 seconds. During the last 30 seconds in some conditions, the pot began to boil, or the subject was asked a series of task-unrelated questions. Roughly speaking, under *prospective* conditions (see fn.4), boiling and questioning led to a shortening of experienced duration, a finding which the authors interpret in terms of the resultant distraction of attention from time. In contrast, under *retrospective* conditions, 'the presence of changes in task-related content (boiling), task-unrelated content (questioning) or both causes a lengthening of remembered duration compared to a condition in which there are no changes in content (no boiling and no questioning)' (1980, 91–2).

In making sense of this retrospective data here, the authors take it to be intuitive that the boiling and questioning conditions involve *more change* than the no-boiling and no-questioning conditions. After all, 'in the no-boiling condition, the liquid did not change in appearance' (ibid., 85). Similarly, what distinguishes the no-questioning condition is simply that there is no sudden change for the subject from simply watching the pot, to answering the experimentalist's questions. This is said to support a hypothesis on which *retrospective* estimates of time are based on the number of remembered changes during the period. However, once again, if attention to time involves attention to change, how can it make sense to suggest that salient changes (changes which are obviously noticed since remembered), *distract* us from attending to time? Yet this is just what is proposed to explain the effect of questioning under prospective conditions: '[the task] interruption causes attention to shift from the passage of time to the interrupting content, and experienced duration is shortened' (ibid., 91). We must surely wonder what attending to time could be such that a subject can be distracted from it by change, despite all there seemingly being to attend to in the undistracted case is a beaker of water failing to change in appearance. How can watching a pot be attending to time?[15]

It is clear then that attention to time cannot be understood simply in terms of attention to perceptible change. I now turn to another suggestion, namely that attention to time is a form of feature-based perceptual attention to stimulus duration.

4. Attention to Time as Attention to Stimulus Duration

Recall now the findings of Macar et al. (1994) above demonstrating that when subjects preferentially attend to the intensity of visual (or auditory) stimuli as opposed to their durations, they perceive their durations as shorter. In these experiments it is not very natural to think of allocating attention to time in terms of allocating attention to perceptible change. The visual stimuli do not themselves change. Rather, it is more natural to think that attending to time involves attending to a stimulus' duration *as such*. As Macar et al. suggest,

[T]he terms *attention to time* or *temporal information* . . . are meant to stress the similarity between the mechanisms that are involved in temporal and in any other type of processing. They underline the fact that duration is one of the attributes of any stimulus, and, as such, is information and can plausibly be given either automatic or controlled attention. (1994, 674)[16]

In making sense of this idea, it is natural to appeal to what we already know about other forms of feature-based attention. We can deploy visual attention not just to locations and objects but also to particular feature-dimensions (at least: colour, orientation and motion), and specific features within these dimensions (e.g., blue, horizontal orientation, upwards motion). Such attention can operate throughout the visual field, and in principle independently of where spatial attention is deployed (for a review see Carrasco 2011, §6). The proposal above simply extends this model to duration. Coull is explicit: 'selectively attending to and estimating the passage of time itself' (2004, 224) involves 'selectively attending to temporal stimulus features . . . . if more attention is allocated to time rather than another stimulus feature (such as colour), estimation of duration is more accurate. This represents a process of temporal selective attention.' (ibid., 217) Conversely, 'The less we attend to the temporal properties of a stimulus, the more likely we are to misperceive its duration' (ibid., 222; see also Coull et al. 2004).[17]

It is clear from the data that subjects are able to adopt an 'attentional set' for time (cf. Correa and Nobre 2008). However, the more specific proposal that this set be thought of as a form of feature-based perceptual attention to stimulus duration is unsustainable. The problem emerges when we consider the full pattern of data concerning the interference effect, in particular data concerning the presence or absence of bidirectional interference depending on whether the competing, non-timing task is a perceptual/motor task, or an executive task. What emerges from such comparative studies (Brown 1997; Brown and Frieh 2000; Brown 2010) is that whilst manual tracking and visual search tasks interfere with a concurrent timing task, here the timing task has no (negative) effect on the tracking or search task.[18] In contrast, there is *bidirectional* interference with respect to executive tasks: these tasks interfere with timing, but timing also interferes with performance in these tasks.

This is hard to reconcile with the current proposal about attention to time (cf. Brown 1997, 1135). If attention to time is simply a form of perceptual attention to a stimulus attribute (viz. duration), we should expect it to compete with other forms of perceptual attention for a limited pool of shared resources. This competition is, after all, what is said to explain the effect of attention being distracted from time. But, if this were right, the pattern of interference in perceptual (e.g., visual search or intensity discrimination) and motor tasks ought to be bidirectional (cf. Brown 1997, 1120). Yet perceptual and motor tasks do not seem to be interfered with by timing. Consequently, we have reason to doubt that attention to time draws from the same attentional pool(s) as do motor and perceptual tasks. On the other hand, we do find bidirectional interference in relation to executive tasks (e.g., mental arithmetic, verbal reasoning, or memory updating). This supports Brown's view that 'time perception is closely related to the resources that supports these executive functions' (2010, 116). This contention is central to the positive proposal I develop below. For now I simply note that, if timing is an executive task, it is disanalogous to familiar feature-based perceptual attention.

In the time perception literature, it is common to assume that time be treated as analogous to other perceptible features, an attitude captured in Michon's 'equivalence postulate', the 'basic tenet of the psychophysics of time' that 'time behaves like any other psychological dimension such as brightness, loudness, itch, or sweetness' (Michon 1986, 62; see also Michon 1972; Michon 1985; and Michon and Jackson 1984), or as Brown glosses it, that 'time has the same status as any other stimulus attribute, such as size, loudness, or colour' (2008, 112). The pattern of bidirectional interference set-out above, together with the conclusion of our earlier discussion concerning attention and perceptible change, suggests that the equivalence postulate should be rejected.

Such a view is already implicit in the remarks of various authors.[19] For instance, consider this initially baffling passage from Zakay and Block, in which they describe the basic idea behind their attentional gate model of time perception described above.

> On each occasion on which an organism attends to time, as opposed to external stimulus events, the attentional gate opens more frequently, thereby allowing more pulses to be transferred from the pacemaker to the cognitive counter.... The attentional-gate model . . . includes and elaborates the notion that a subject may divide attentional resources between attending to external events and attending to time. (1996, 155)

Zakay and Block here contrast attention to time with attention to external stimulus events (cf. Figure 1 where attention to 'time' is contrasted with attention to 'events'). Yet, on the face of it, the durations to which attention is supposed to facilitate awareness simply are the durations of the external stimulus events. And as Le Poidevin puts it, in a different context, 'I cannot be aware *just* of the duration of an event, independently of my awareness of the event itself' (2007, 99). So how can external events distract from attending to the passage of time? The best way to make sense of the passage, I suggest, is to treat Zakay and Block as rejecting equivalence. Attending to time contrasts attending to external stimulus events because, at least in the relevant contexts, it is not a form of perceptual attention at all.[20]

Before developing my positive proposal concerning attention to time, let me summarise the discussion thus far. First, I showed that despite the presumptive fact that 'awareness of change is the condition on which our perception of time's flow depends' (James 1890, 620), it is not possible to understand attention to time simply as a form of attention to perceived change. Second, I claimed that, given the data concerning bidirectional interference, it is not possible to conceive of attention to time as a form of feature-based attention to stimulus duration. However, as Kant famously emphasised, time is the form of *inner* as well as outer sense. Pursuing this idea, I now suggest that we should conceive of attention to time as a form of *internal* attention. In particular, I claim that attention to time can be identified with conscious activity within non-perceptual consciousness: thought for short. The reason time perception involves attention so understood is because such non-perceptual activity provides for us an important measure of perceived duration. In §6, I show why a connection between activity in the stream of conscious thought and our sense of time's passage can explain the dual-task interference data outlined in §2. In §7, I conclude by exploring the relationship between conscious mental activity and our awareness of the passage of time in more detail.

5. Time Perception, Internal Attention, and the Stream of Conscious Thought

James tells us: 'Every one knows what attention is . . . . It is the possession by the mind, in clear and vivid form, of one out of what seems several possible objects or trains of thought' (1890, 403–4). Thus, the very first thing James has to say about our ordinary understanding of attention is that it can be a matter of the mind taking possession, not only of objects, but of *trains of thought*.[21] Recently, Chun et al. (2011) have emphasised James' distinction between what they call 'external' (or 'perceptual') and 'internal' (or 'central', or 'reflective') attention as the starting point for a taxonomy of attention.[22] Following James, Chun et al. distinguish between the two forms of attention in terms of their objects.

> Sitting at your desk, you can focus on the information on the computer screen, a conversation in the hallway, or the taste of the stale coffee brew in your cup. These examples of external attention can be distinguished from how you could instead be focusing your attention on your thoughts, contemplating a talk you just heard, trying to remember the author of a paper you want to find and cite, or trying to decide where to go to lunch, all while staring at your computer screen with conversations going on in the hallway. (2011, 76–7)

Straightaway, note two things about this non-technical characterisation of internal attention. First, although Chun et al. talk about focusing attention on *thoughts*, the examples they give make clear that they really mean focusing attention on the *subject matter* of those thoughts: the recent talk, the forgotten author, a possible lunch venue. In other words, internal attention is nothing different in these examples from thought itself: evaluating, trying to bring to mind, deliberating and so forth. This relates to an important *structural* contrast between internal and external attention which Martin points to.

> In general, whatever we are prepared to call an object of thought—be it the things thought about, what one thinks about them, or the proposition one thinks in thinking these things—we can also take to be an object of attention. Conscious, active thought is simply a mode of attending to the subject matter of such thoughts.... Arguably, it is part of the manifest image of the mind that we are aware of objects of sense experience in a different way from being aware of the objects of thought, and that this is reflected in the ways attention can relate to an object of sense as opposed to thought.... it is tempting to think of experience in terms of a whole array of items stretching beyond what I have focused my attention on at a time... There seems to be no corresponding array of items to shift one's attention over in thought: if we think of thoughts as determinations of attention, then there can be no way of thinking of something without thereby to some extent to be attending to it. (1997, 77–8)

This suggests that we might contrast internal and external attention not in terms of their objects—after all, can you not think about or imagine the very same object which just now you were visually attending to?—but rather in a *structural* way. Perceptual attention seems to range over an array of objects of which we are already aware. Internal attention does not range over contents, some of which were already objects of thought; internal attention just is that determination of attention which is conscious thought. The stream of perceptual consciousness is divided by attention; the stream of thought simply is a stream of attention. Of course, Martin's particular structural contrast will be rejected by someone convinced that there is no perceptual awareness outside attention. But such a theorist can still contrast internal and external attention insofar as they take there to be *some* structural difference between non-perceptual and perceptual modes of consciousness. And that is surely plausible.

The second thing to note about Chun et al.'s initial characterisation of internal attention is that their examples—assessing a talk, trying to recall an author, figuring out where to go to lunch—do little justice to the great variety within our streams of thought. Compare a recent discussion from Baars.

> The stream of spontaneous thought is remarkably rich and self-relevant, reflecting one's greatest personal concerns, interpersonal feelings, unfulfilled goals and unresolved challenges, worries and hopes, inner debates, self-monitoring, feelings of knowing, visual imagery, imaginary social interactions, recurrent beliefs, coping reactions, intrusive memories, daydreams and fantasies, future plans, and more—all of which are known to guide the stream of thought. Spontaneous ideation goes on during all of one's waking hours, according to randomly timed thought monitoring studies. (2010, 208)

Baars warns psychologists of the dangers of neglecting this aspect of our psychological lives. The stream of spontaneous thought, he suggests, may play a vital role in our cognitive economies, even if we are not always aware of its relevance, or even meta-cognitively aware of its contents.[23] Of course, given this concern, his quoted characterisation tends to neglect the ways in which spontaneous thought is often of no great concern at all, a barely smouldering hubbub of half-formed ideas, images and vague feelings, filling the passing time to no obvious end. Nonetheless, whether the contents of the stream of thought are of great concern or not, in my view Baars is absolutely right to emphasise its importance. As I now suggest, part of that importance lies in its connection to our perception of time.[24]

My suggestion is that our sense of how long a time has elapsed between one perceptual experience, or witnessed environmental event, and another, is importantly a matter of how much mental activity has occurred in the stream of non-perceptual consciousness between the two events. These events could be the onset and offset of a visual stimulus, the instruction to start a card sorting task and the instruction to stop, or simply the beginning of a tedious wait and its eventual end. In each case, an important aspect of one's sense of the lapse of time between the two events is the amount of activity that occurs within the stream of non-perceptual consciousness between them. We can think of the amount of activity in terms of the number of changes in the stream of thought, where thought is intended to cover all aspects of non-perceptual consciousness, including mental imagery and episodic memory.

This suggestion retains the basic insight that 'awareness of change is the condition on which our perception of time's flow depends' (James 1890, 620). It simply recognizes that our consciousness is replete with *internal* as well as *external* change. The suggestion also makes sense of the idea of there being an 'attentional set' for time. In particular, it makes sense of the basic idea that the more we attend to time, the slower time seems to run. Duration perception is influenced by how much we attend to time in this way because to attend to time is to generate conscious mental activity. Given that how much conscious mental activity occurs concurrently with a perceived event provides a key measure of the duration of that event, attending to time thus increases perceived duration. I explore this suggestion in more detail in §7. First, however, I explain how this basic idea that our sense of time's passage is significantly a matter of the amount of activity in the stream of conscious thought can help explain the dual-task interference data left unaccounted for above.

6. The Interference Effect Explained

Any understanding of attention to time must make sense (a) of the basic interference effect and (b) of the pattern of bidirectional interference discussed above. This section shows how the hypothesis that attention to time is internal attention or conscious thinking does so. On the face of it, dual-task effects where the concurrent non-timing task is an executive task are the hardest to account for on this proposal. Consequently, I take such cases first, before turning to the case of perceptual and motor-task interference.

6.1 Interference in Executive Tasks

Dual task situations in which the non-timing task is an executive (e.g., mental arithmetic) task, lead to an under-estimation of duration. On the current proposal, under-estimations of duration arise when there is less non-perceptual conscious mental activity ('thinking') per unit time. This might seem counter-intuitive because we might initially think that demanding mental arithmetic tasks would involve more thinking per unit time than, say, a simple number reading task. There is a sense in which this is right. Difficult mental arithmetic tasks are demanding of *cognitive processing*. However, this is fundamentally different from their demanding a greater degree of *conscious mental activity*. Let me illustrate the distinction and its role in relation to the interference effect by discussing a particular experiment.

Burnside (1971) contrasted reproductions of time for intervals where the subject had to *read* numbers on a series of cards, *add* numbers, *multiply* them, or *obey* an instruction to perform a more complex operation (add and multiply).[25] What Burnside found is that subjects produce increasingly shorter intervals, moving through these increasingly difficult conditions. To explain this he supposes that whilst subjects are 'processing at full capacity in each condition', they are 'performing different types of processing' (1971, 406). In particular, he suggests that 'estimates of duration...decrease as [the] amount of necessary information processing [to complete each individual problem, i.e. processing per card] increase[s]' (ibid.). Burnside thinks of this in terms of what is stored in memory relating to the interval. He suggests that the steps to each solution are discarded from memory, and only the solutions retained. Thus, duration is measured by the number of stored solutions (ibid., 404). However, we can arguably better understand the effect in terms of conscious versus unconscious processing. This is a more fundamental explanation than Burnside's insofar as only conscious processing (or the conscious products of processing) are eligible for storage in memory.

The processing by which we solve basic mental arithmetic problems is largely unconscious. As Sloman puts it, 'conclusions simply appear at some level of awareness, as if the mind goes off, does some work, and then comes back with a result' (1996, 3). Or as Abbott puts it more dramatically, 'In mental arithmetic...the processing is as hidden and mysterious as it is using a pocket calculator. Only the result flashes up on the little liquid crystal display screens of the mind' (1999, 74). Of course, more complicated problems involve the conscious structuring of the arithmetical procedure. But if we focus on each step of the process, the more difficult the individual step, the more processing will be required to reach a given result. If we think of the output of the process as a conscious product – a new element in the stream of thought – then the more difficult a step, the more processing it will demand, and so the longer it will take to produce a product at the level of consciousness (resources being limited). In general, then, the more difficult the task, the more unconscious processing will be required, and so the 'thinner' the stream of *conscious* thought will become. The harder the task, the less conscious activity.[26]

Burnside suggests that his memory-storage view helps 'clarify the familiar paradox that time seems to pass either very quickly or very slowly when one is exceptionally busy. Time may seem to pass quickly when a lot of processing is done to obtain a few solutions, but it may seem to pass slowly while one is performing a tedious task in which all the substeps are remembered' (ibid., 406). On the view suggested here, the paradox is resolved by noting that harder tasks demand a lot of unconscious processing and so yield fewer changes *within the stream of consciousness*; whereas a tedious task allows more to happen *within awareness*. This fits not just mental arithmetic data but other executive tasks used in dual task paradigms. Recall, for example, Hicks et al.'s card counting task described above. Here subjects simply counting cards into a single pile for 42s managed on average to count out 75 cards. They estimated the period as being 53s long on average. As response uncertainty increased because subjects had to sort the cards by colour or suit, the average number of cards dealt out decreased (to 46 and 35 cards respectively), and estimates of time's passage decreased also (roughly linearly, to 43s and 31s respectively). Again, we might suppose that increased processing associated with categorising and correctly sorting each card was largely unconscious, with only the decision ('red ... right pile', 'spade ... bottom left stack') being conscious.[27] As a result, the more demanding sorting task led to fewer conscious products (less conscious thought) per unit time.

Further data, including crucially the bidirectional data, associated with the interference effect is easily explained too. The instruction to pay (more) attention to timing, will incline a subject to pay (increasingly) less attention to the mental arithmetic task, and to engage in other forms of thinking in order to generate more change within the stream of thought. This will not only lead to increased estimates of time (as more occurs within the stream of thought) but lead to a reduced performance on the concurrent arithmetic task (as processing resources are drawn away from that task). Conversely, focused solely on a mental arithmetic task, we will often try to hold spontaneous thought in abeyance, thereby reducing our sense of the passage of time.

6.2 Interference in Non-Executive Tasks

We can now turn to the interference of perceptual and motor tasks on timing. Since these tasks do not obviously rely on executive resources, the current proposal raises a question as to how to explain their impact on timing. Brown offers an answer here: it is the *co-ordination* required for multi-tasking of *any* kind which creates executive resource demands (2010, 117; also Brown 1997). As Lavie puts it, 'Cognitive control functions are loaded when people have to switch back and forth between different tasks' (2010, 147). Plausibly, it is these demands of multi-tasking that interfere with timing.[28] There is no interference of timing on the perceptual or motor tasks because these tasks do not themselves draw on executive resources, and so are unaffected by the executive resource demands of multi-tasking. They will only be affected when the situation involves a concurrent task drawing on shared resources.

A similar hypothesis explains what is occurring in the other cases mentioned above. Listening to music and driving can be thought of as tasks which distract attention away from time (that is, reduce conscious thinking) in much the way that the more sterilised visual and motor tasks do. When either is combined with a timing task this leads to the same multi-tasking effect. As a result there is a shortening of perceived duration caused by a reduction in concurrent mental activity. In the watched pot experiment reported, the opposite occurs. The uninterrupted 'watching' condition leaves thought wholly undistracted by either the demands of multi-tasking, or executive processing. In contrast, the boiling and questioning conditions effectively create dual-task conditions, respectively of a perceptual or an executive kind.

Whether non-executive task interference effects are entirely due to multi-tasking, or whether in fact perceptual and motor tasks do at a certain level of difficulty draw on executive resources—and so introduce the potential for bidirectional effects—is unclear. If so, part of the effect of music, for instance, might be understood as reducing the number of changes in the stream of conscious thought independently of multi-tasking demands. Clearly, the explanations offered here are highly speculative. My aim is only to recommend a certain understanding of attention to time for further investigation in the light of a more fully worked-out theory of the resource structure of cognition.

Since the dual-task data here accounted for are the crucial data lying behind the appeal to attention to time, we have successfully answered Block's challenge to say what attention to time is. Attention to time is internal attention, which is to say non-perceptual conscious activity broadly classifiable as thinking. In the next and final section I explore the general hypothesis which underlies this claim, namely that a key measure of perceived duration is how much concurrent mental activity occurs within the stream of thought.

7. Mental Activity as Our Measure of Perceived Duration

I have thus far stated the general hypothesis that non-perceptual conscious activity is an 'important' or 'key' measure of time's passage with deliberate imprecision. How important a measure? Is our sense of perceived duration always a matter of how much mental activity has occurred during the relevant period or event? Or is such activity simply one amongst many potential measures of elapsed time? This question is closely related to the question whether attention to time is necessary for duration perception, or simply an important influence on it (see the ambivalence on this score within empirical discussion, noted in §2). Of course, both questions are largely empirical matters which cannot be settled conclusively by philosophical/conceptual analysis. Nonetheless, I want to end this paper by raising a number of considerations which might seem to tell against the idea that conscious mental activity is our sole measure of perceived duration, and ask how powerful they really are. I begin by discussing two broadly conceptual objections to the claim (§7.1). I then consider whether conscious thought can plausibly provide a measure of duration even at sub-second timescales (§7.2). Finally, I consider whether the hypothesis that conscious thinking is our measure of duration can be extended to account for effects usually considered to be a result of arousal (§7.3).

7.1 Conceptual Objections

The claim that mental activity is our measure of perceived duration might seem to entail that our thinking itself could never seem to run faster or slower, it being our sole measure of duration. Yet, as Reid objects to Locke in discussing his theory of duration perception: 'every man capable of reflection will be sensible, that at one time his thoughts come slowly and heavily and at another time have a much quicker and livelier motion' (1827, III, v, 171).[29] It is important to appreciate that the hypothesis under consideration does *not* claim that mental activity is our sole measure of duration, but only our measure of *perceived* duration. The idea is that environmental events are perceived as having durations relative to concurrent mental activity. But we can further add that the pace of thought can be measured by reference to the amount of concurrent apparent perceptual change in our environment.[30] As a result we can make sense of thoughts coming swiftly or slowly *relative to the pace of environmental change*; just as I am suggesting we think of environmental change as seeming to occur fast or slow *relative to the pace of our conscious mental activity*. It is true that a consequence of this picture is that there will be no difference from the inside between a situation in which one's speed of thought is decelerated and one in which change in one's environment is accelerated. In either case, the world will seem fast *relative to your mental speed*, and your mental speed slow *relative to the pace of worldly events*. But there is no reason to think that this consequence is unacceptable.[31]

A related objection is that it is perfectly possible to imagine awareness of the passage of time in the complete absence of perceptual experience, i.e. in a hypothetical total sensory deprivation tank. On the above account one might question how this could be possible, since in such a tank we will lack any measure of the pace of thought, viz. apparent perceptual change. This objection relies on a highly controversial empirical claim: not just that it is possible to lack all perceptual awareness but that it is possible to lack all apparent perceptual awareness (including hallucinatory awareness) and yet continue to think consciously. There is, of course, no reason to think that actual sensory deprivation tanks achieve this, and it does not strike me as unreasonable simply to doubt the possibility supposed here. A more concessive reply is available, however. This is to suggest that the possibility of being aware of the passage of time without perceptual awareness only arises because we can *remember* the kinds of perceptual changes that normally occur concurrent with our thinking. In full sensory deprivation, we can retain our sense of passing time only insofar as we retain a sense that our current thinking is of the kind that is usually matched by a certain amount of apparent change in our environment. What will not be possible in this situation, however, will be to have any sense of one's stream of thought *as a whole* being slowed down or sped up. Again I see no reason to think this consequence unacceptable.[32]

7.2 Clunkiness

Another natural objection to the suggestion that mental activity provides our sole measure of perceived duration is that thought is insufficiently fine grained, too 'clunky', to provide our measure of perceived duration at short timescales. Even if this is so and thought fails to provides our standard measure of sub-second durations, the story above may still be right concerning supra-second timescales. This connects to a large and ongoing empirical dispute as to whether timing operates differently at millisecond and second timescales, a leading hypothesis here being that supra-second timing relies on cognitive, attentional mechanisms, whereas sub-second timing is 'sensory' and independent of supra-second mechanisms.[33] Note that since the concept of attention to time which is the focus of this paper is typically invoked in the context of supra-second timing, the objection leaves untouched the interpretation of that concept above.

A distinct but related objection is that taking conscious thinking to be our measure of duration is simply a version of the view that duration perception involves counting. Yet, the objection continues, counting is inadequate as an account of perceived duration in general, and especially at short timescales. How powerful are these concerns?

Certainly, an obvious way in which duration perception might require a form of internal attention would be if duration perception required explicit chronometric counting.[34] Explicit counting can undoubtedly make a dramatic difference to the accuracy of our estimates of elapsed time, at least at intervals greater than about 1.2s (Grondin, Meilleur-Wells and Lachance 1999).[35] However, it seems implausible to claim that duration perception requires explicit counting. This is in part because experimentalists take steps to prevent subjects from counting, for example by demanding concurrent verbalization of temporally irregular random numbers (e.g., Nichelli, Alway, and Grafman 1996; Wearden, Rogers, and Thomas 1997; see also the discussion in Wearden, Denovan, et al. 1997, esp. Experiment 3), and yet this does not appear to prevent subjects from tracking the passage of time (even if their accuracy is diminished).[36] However, there is no reason to think that such experimental interventions eliminate the spontaneous stream of thought—indeed, arguably concurrent verbalization involves a form of thinking out loud. Thus, subjects prevented from explicit chronometric counting may nonetheless sustain the spontaneous mental activity characteristic of the stream of thought. As a result, it remains open to suggest that our measure of time's passage is change within the stream of thought.

Nonetheless, a common argument against treating all interval timing as involving counting is naturally redeployed against this more general proposal. The argument is that timing can occur at sub-second timescales, and that such sub-second timing is incompatible with the 'clunkiness' of counting or thought in general. Coull responds to prima facie neurological evidence of language areas being involved in timing tasks in just this way.

> [F]rontal operculum (ventral premotor cortex) is recruited ... in all ... aspects of temporal attention and timing behaviour. Frontal operculum, at least in the left hemisphere, is also intimately linked to language function. However, activation of frontal operculum during timing tasks is unlikely to simply represent a linguistic strategy, such as sub-vocal counting, since the time-frame involved in our tasks is only around 1500 ms or less. (2004, 224)

Likewise, Wearden, Denovan, et al. write that they use 'short-duration stimuli (usually tones) less than 1.0 s long ... to prevent chronometric counting' (1997, 502).

As mentioned, explicit counting only seems to *improve* performance at timescales above 1.2s (Grondin, Meilleur-Wells and Lachance 1999). But this finding does not show that counting never occurs at timescales below 1.2s. Moreover, even if over such timescales subjects are not motivated to count since they (rightly) see no benefit in doing so, the absence of explicit, sub-vocal counting must be distinguished from the absence of activity within the stream of thought. If all timing involves thought, then the fact that timing benefits from a chronometric counting strategy at 1.2s may only show that counting is a way of structuring thought in the service of more accurate timing for durations of 1.2s and above.

Counting aside, there is in fact positive reason to think that thought can provide a measure of duration down to the kinds of sub-second timescales over which duration perception occurs. As Papafragou notes, 'Humans can comfortably produce speech at the rate of four words per second, and comprehension follows the speech of production' (2009, 519). The rate of syllable and phoneme production is correspondingly higher: around six syllables and up to sixteen phonemes a second in English. Assuming these timescales are mirrored by inner speech, and making the (obviously extreme) over-simplification that the stream of thought is a stream of inner speech (i.e., inner speech provides our sole vehicle of thought), then we can think of perceived duration as measured in units of words (viz., ~250msec units), syllables (viz., ~167msec units) or phonemes (viz., ~62msec units). Thought then can in fact plausibly provide a measure of duration at the timescales over which we make perceptual duration judgments.[37] In consequence, the objection that thought is simply too coarse-grained or 'clunky' to provide our measure of perceived duration is much weaker than it might first appear.

7.3 Other Factors Affecting Duration Perception

Many other factors influence our judgments of elapsed time. The extent to which these too can be understood in terms of an increase or decrease in the amount of conscious mental activity engaged in during the period to be timed tests the *extent* to which mental activity provides our measure of the passage of time: whether at the extreme it is our sole measure of perceived duration, or whether it is simply one amongst many factors.

In §2, we encountered the idea that timing should be modelled in terms of an internal-clock. Such a view remains popular amongst theorists, despite a number of concerns about the hypothesis, not least the fact that the clock and its pulses remain elusive.[38] What attracts people to the model in the first place is the wealth of evidence that perceived duration is increased by factors associated with arousal, e.g., rises in body temperature, dopamine agonists, emotional (and especially fear-related) stimuli, and repetitive bursts of stimulation such as click or flicker trains. These effects are widely interpreted as due to an arousal-driven increase in the pulse rate of the internal clock, leading to more pulses being produced per unit time, and thus a greater number of accumulated pulses during the relevant interval, with a consequent increase in apparent duration. Again see Figure 1.[39]

Can the idea that mental activity provides our measure of perceived duration explain such data? It will be able to do so to the extent that interventions which lead to increased duration judgments lead to an increase in the amount of conscious activity within the stream of thought. A major barrier to testing this is the lack of a clear operational measure of such activity. But there is at least some suggestive evidence that various arousal effects do correlate with increased mental activity. I confine myself to three brief points here concerning what is an extremely complicated and developing literature.[40]

Firstly, there is a wealth of anecdotal evidence which connects reports of time seeming to slow down in extreme situations with an increase in conscious mental activity during the relevant events. For instance, in their investigation of the subjective effects of life threatening danger, Noyes and Kletti (1977) report 'altered passage of time' (with 'few exceptions' a slowing down) in 78% of subjects who believed they were about to die, and an 'increased speed of thoughts' in 68% of subjects, as well as 'unusually vivid thoughts' in 65% of these subjects. Further, in their collected anecdotal reports, a direct connection between the slowing of time and speed of thought is repeatedly drawn. One individual (a car-crash victim) recalls: 'My mind speeded up. Time seemed drawn out.' (ibid.: 376); another that as 'the time in which everything happening seemed to slow down, my thoughts speeded up' (ibid.: 378); and yet another that 'my thinking processes increased at an incredible [sic.] rapid rate so that my movements, in relation to them, seemed extremely slow' (ibid., 387).[41]

Secondly, the pharmacological interventions known to affect duration perception typically also affect mental function in broadly the way predicted by the mental activity hypothesis. Thus, dopamine antagonists (e.g., anti-psychotics such as haloperidol) lead to underestimates of perceived duration (Rammsayer 1989; Rammsayer 1999), as would be predicted given that they have a 'robust "tranquilizing" action', leading to a reduction in alertness and 'a blunting of cognition' (Nasrallah and Tandon 2009, 538–9). Conversely, dopamine agonists (e.g., traditional psychostimulants such as methamphetamine) lead to an over-estimation of intervals as might be predicted given that they increase alertness and 'enhance waking cognitive functions' by increasing cerebral blood flow (Ballas, Evans, and Dinges 2009, 846).[42]

Finally, it is well-known that stimuli preceded or accompanied by a train of repetitive stimulation (periodic clicks or flashes) are perceived as if their duration is increased compared to a control (Treisman et al. 1990; Penton-Voak et al. 1996; Wearden, Philpott, and Win 1999; and Droit-Volet and Wearden 2002). This effect is standardly understood in terms of an arousal-based increase in internal clock rate (see Wearden 2003 as well as the papers just cited). However, recent work by Jones, Allely and Wearden (2011) has established a connection between click trains and speed of information processing across a range of tasks, including a mental arithmetic task where responses were substantially speeded by clicks (yet unaffected by white noise which also has no effect on duration judgments). Of course, the established correlation is just that. But again the prospect of unifying the data by thinking of perceived duration as measured by concurrent mental activity remains tantalisingly open.

To the extent that mental activity is at the heart of these kinds of arousal effects, we can significantly simplify the attentional gate model in Figure 1 above, effectively identifying the arousal, pacemaker, and attentional gate system with conscious thought. Indeed, if attention to time just is mental activity, and mental activity is our internal clock, then there is no need to build attention to time into the model at all. To attend to time just is to generate pacemaker activity, viz. thought. Of course, this does not mean that we do not need to locate neural timing mechanisms at lower levels (either of explanation, or arguably timescale). Nonetheless, this unification provides a way of making sense of cryptic remarks made by Zakay when he suggests that 'attention to time is the energy that activates the counter' (1990, 61) and that "temporal information" is not external but rather an internal input to the time processor'. Understandably these remarks have met with some scepticism (e.g., Sawyer, Meyers, and Huser 1994, 656) but they can perhaps be understood as gesturing towards the way in which conscious thought is our basic measure of perceived duration. For, if what I have argued is right, attention to time is a matter of conscious thinking, and the quantity of such thinking provides for us a key measure of the passing of time.[43]

Notes

1. For instance: 'the time which we feel is probably due to the work of attention' (Mach, quoted in James 1890, 635); 'in periods of boredom or expectation we pay more attention to the passage of time than usual... in periods in which we are deeply interested in what we are experiencing, we have little attention to spare for the lapse of time' (McTaggart 1927, 277, §618); Stout: 'in general, temporal perception is bound up with the process of attention... What measures the lapse of time is the cumulative effect of the process of attending' (1932, 499–501). As for folk wisdom, witness sayings such as 'a watched pot never boils', 'time flies when you're having fun', or, most explicitly, 'when you're not paying attention'.
2. The relevant literature does not distinguish between 'attending to time', 'attending to the course/flow/passage of time', and 'attending to time-in-passing'. I follow suit. Note, however, that attention to time is different from attention *within* time, which is not the target of the present discussion. On the distinction see Coull 2004. I am also not concerned with the fact that both exogenous and endogenous *spatial* attention increase the perceived duration of a stimulus relative to an unattended stimulus (e.g., Mattes and Ulrich 1998; Enns, Brehaut, and Shore 1999; Yeshurun and Marom 2008; and Seifried and Ulrich 2011).
3. Dutke cites experimental evidence going back to Hülser 1924.
4. Cf. Tse who, surveying the literature, takes the claim that 'the prospective judgment of time requires attention to the passage of time' to be part of a "standard attentional model" of time perception' supported by '[t]he majority of work in the time literature' (2010, 138). Prospective judgments are judgments made by subjects who are aware during the interval to be timed that timing is a task-requirement. Such judgments contrast retrospective judgments, and are thought to track perceived duration as opposed to duration constructed via memory. The data in this paper solely concerns prospective judgments. For more on the distinction see, e.g., Block and Zakay 2004; and Block, Hancock, and Zakay 2010.
5. Likewise, Fortin and Couture 2002; for reviews see Brown 1997, 2008, and 2010; and Block, Hancock, and Zakay 2010.
6. Further examples from a large literature include the following. Curton and Lordhal: 'time estimates were reliably lower for Ss performing an attention-demanding task [alphabetically connecting a randomly ordered circle of 26 letters] during [a 5–19s] interval than for those engaged in a task designed to focus attention on the passage of time [connecting dots at a rate of 1 dot/sec]' (1974, 861); McKay: 'time estimation of a standard interval was significantly lower when subjects attended to the stimulus material than when attending to the interval of passing time' (1977, 584); Coull et al.: 'subjects attended to time and/or colour attributes of visual stimulus pairs' under five attentional conditions; results confirmed that 'the subjective duration of stimulus presentation is increasingly shortened the more subjects attend to nontemporal stimulus features' (2004, 1506); Grondin and Macar: 'Our data generally show... that decreasing attention

to time decreases subjective duration' (1992, 127). I discuss a variety of other tasks below.

7. The status of these pulses is obscure. Macar et al. describe the basic idea as follows: 'the pulses that are assumed to be stored . . . may be viewed as chemical changes at the cell level, as spikes within neural networks, or as any other physiological event; their nature remains quite speculative' (1994, 674).

8. Early clock models were developed in Creelman 1962 and Treisman 1963. The most influential model is the scalar timing (or expectancy) theory (SET) due to Gibbon (1977), developed in Gibbon et al. 1984, and applied to human timing in, e.g., Wearden 1991. For reviews of the development and controversies surrounding such models see, for instance, Wearden 2001 and 2003, and Buhusi and Meck 2005. In all these models, the clock-accumulator system is only one part of a more sophisticated cognitive system for producing time judgments, involving short- and long-term memory stores and decision mechanisms.

9. Likewise, Fortin et al.: 'Concurrent nontemporal processing would put the gate in an "off" state, and would temporarily interrupt the accumulation process' (1993, 536). See also, Thomas and Brown who suggest a rather different attentional model according to which during 'periods of inattention . . . the passage of time is not recorded' (1974, 456).

10. In addition to the experimental work already cited, important contributions to the development of attentional approaches to time perception include: Thomas and Weaver 1975; Hicks et al. 1977; Fraisse 1984; Brown 1985; Brown and West 1990; and Zakay 1989.

11. See also Underwood and Swain 1973, 105.

12. That said, Block and Brown both make clear that their understanding of 'attention to time' is broader than simply attention to perceived change. Later, Block mentions 'changes in events or cognitions' (1990, 22), and, in addition to stimulus changes, Brown also mentions 'the ordering or succession of events, and the organization of those events', and further that, in paying attention to time, a subject 'may engage in some type of timekeeping strategy such as chronometric counting, executing a series of repetitive movements (e.g., rhythmical tapping) or visualising the sweep of a second hand on a clock face' (2008, 114). Some of these ideas are of course much closer to the account developed below. My only claim here is that understanding attention to time as attention to perceptible change is a very natural view to take. That said merely broadening temporal information out from perceived change to include 'the ordering or succession of events, and the organization of those events' will not save the view from the critique below. The critique therefore applies to the view in Michon and Jackson 1984 that temporal information is entirely a matter of the 'simultaneity and order' relations amongst events.

13. Brown cites Jones and Boltz 1989. Cf. Large and Jones: 'we offer a theory about how people attend to events that change over time. Our theory begins with audition . . . because a most persuasive case for positing dynamic attending comes when we consider attending to speech and music. . . . We take the time structure of events as a point of departure by assuming that, in acoustic patterns, it can capture and maintain attending' (1999, 120).

14. Cf. Langer who declares: '*Music makes time audible, and its form and continuity sensible*' (1953, 110; emphasis in original).

15. Ornstein claims that we can explain the watched pot phenomenon in terms of our being 'more vigilant than usual', since '[a]n increase in vigilance should result in a greater amount of awareness to input, and consequently a lengthening of duration experience' (1969, 112). It is unclear what this amounts to. On a natural interpretation it implies that our awareness of change is heightened, returning us to the criticism in the text. Cf. Underwood and Swain who reject Ornstein's view of the watched pot phenomenon, preferring the view 'that the increase in attention itself is causing the increase in duration experience' (1973, 101). That said, if vigilance is understood in terms of an increase in non-perceptual conscious activity, then Ornstein's view can be brought in line with that suggested below.

16. Likewise, Coull: 'The less we attend to an event's duration, the shorter it seems to last' (2004, 1506). Also Tse et al.: 'paying more (less) attention to the duration of an event increases (decreases) its perceived duration' (2004, 1172). Underwood and Swain discuss attention to time in terms of selectivity but for them it is 'attention to a particular source of stimuli, to the exclusion of other stimuli available in the environment' (1973, 104). This kind of selectivity cannot be used to explain the results in the present context.

17. Coull explicitly invokes analogical reasoning (2004, 222f.), drawing on work on selective attention to specific stimulus features such as colour and motion to argue for a similar picture of attention to time. It is notable that the experimental cues (e.g., 'attend selectively to stimulus time more than colour') used in her experiments presume the equivalence.

18. Brown notes that performance in the more difficult version of his rotor tracking task was in fact *improved* with the addition of a timing task (1997, 1133). In other conditions, timing had no significant effect: 'Tracking and visual search were essentially unaffected by the addition of a timing task, whereas mental arithmetic was disrupted by concurrent timing' (ibid., 1118). In Macar et al.'s study discussed above, 'the effect of attention sharing was significant in the duration but not in the intensity task' (1994, 680; see data on p.679), again manifesting the lack of bidirectional interference in this perceptual task.

19. Indeed, Thomas and Weaver (who developed the first modern attentional model of timing) think of attention as divided between 'a visual information processor and a timer' (1975, 363). In doing so they evidently contrast timing and visual information processing, in clear tension with *equivalence*.

20. Cf. Block: 'temporal information probably also includes changes in internal attributes, including proprioceptive information, moods or emotions, kinds of cognitive processes, and so on' (1990, 22).

21. James later distinguishes 'sensorial attention' to 'objects of sense', from 'intellectual attention' to 'ideal or represented objects' (1890, 416).

22. For further discussion of the notion of internal attention see De Brigard 2012. De Brigard, and indeed Chun et al. (2011), is principally interested in internal attention understood at an informational processing level. My interest is principally in the personal level phenomenon.

23. Baars draws attention to the extraordinary amount of resource the brain commits to spontaneous thought, suggesting that it would extremely implausible if this resource were being spent to no end.

24. A connection of this kind, though developed in a very different way, is central to O'Shaughnessy's work. In particular, O'Shaughnessy claims that 'an active process of thinking must be going on continuously' (2000, 267) as 'a categorically necessary condition of consciousness' (ibid., 100), and further that ongoing mental activity is part of what guarantees that in 'experiencing anything one experiences the passage of time' (ibid., 272). For discussion of O'Shaughnessy here see Soteriou 2011.

25. See further: Hawkes and Sherman 1972; Wilsoncroft and Stone 1975; and Wilsoncroft et al. 1978.

26. A research programme suggests itself here, exploiting what is known about mathematical cognition to test this picture of time perception.

27. For further examples of interference effects of this kind see, for example, the mental rotation task in Fortin and Breton 1995, and the anagram and Stroop tasks in Sawyer, Meyers, and Huser 1994. For a review of the many similar studies see again Brown 1997.

28. See Dutke 2005 for evidence supporting this hypothesis.

29. Locke develops his theory in his *Essay* (1975, II, xiv). Locke's view is clearly an important precursor of the view developed in this paper.

30. An analogous reply is available in relation to the analogous (and equally flawed) objection to body-relative accounts of size-perception, namely that such accounts are committed to one's body always seeming to be the same size.

31. Cf. The false opposition that lies behind the opening remark of a recent paper on body-relative spatial perception by van der Hoort et al.: 'Imagine that during your sleep you shrank to the size of a Barbie doll. Upon awakening, would you feel your body to be small, or would you sense that you were normal in a gigantic world inhabited by giants?' (2011, 1). The analogous question in the temporal case presupposes an equally false opposition. Of course in both spatial and temporal cases our perceptual experience exploits the natural measure it does (i.e., our body/our thoughts) in part because that measure is reasonably stable over time. As Locke puts it, the 'appearance of [ideas] in train, tho' perhaps it may be sometimes faster, and sometimes slower, yet, I guess, varies not very much in a waking man' (1975, II, xiv, 9).

32. Of course, our stream of non-perceptual consciousness is far from homogeneous as the quotation from Baars' above brings out. Thus, in such a situation it might be that we could gain some sense of *aspects* of our stream of thought slowing down or speeding up relative to other aspects. For example, we might experience our stream of auditory imagery as slowed relative to our stream of visual imagery.

33. For neurological evidence here see, e.g., Kagerer et al. 2002; Gutyrchik et al. 2010; and the review in Coull et al. 2011. For psychophysical evidence see, e.g., Ulbrich et al. 2007; and Zélanti and Droit-Volet 2011.

34. Recall Brown's remarks that in attending to the passage of time a subject 'may engage in some type of timekeeping strategy such as chronometric counting, executing a series of repetitive movements (e.g., rhythmic tapping) or visualising the sweep of a second hand on a clock face' (2008, 114). Tellingly, Underwood writes, 'A watched pot or a boring lecture may take a subjectively long period to terminate because we are attending to and counting the passage of time' (1975, 291). Consider also this very suggestive passage describing the model developed

in his paper: 'This model assumes that we gain an impression of the passage of time by consideration of the events occupying an interval, and accounts for the phenomenon of the watched pot (which never boils) by assuming that the activity of considering the events occupying an interval is in itself an event which will contribute to the next judgement of the extent of the interval. The more such judgements of time there are, the greater will be successive estimations of that same interval.' (ibid., 295)

35. At even slightly longer timescales of 5s or so, subjects appear to engage in 'ancillary timekeeping strategies (such as finger tapping, rhythmical motions, and visualization of clock faces) to supplement counting' (Brown, Newcomb, and Kahrl 1995, 536).

36. Interestingly, Rattat and Droit-Volet (2011) suggest that simply instructing subjects not to count is the best method for preventing counting without distorting timing processes.

37. Note that these timescales are longer than timescales over which we are capable of judging order and succession, but as Fraisse argues, 'The perception of duration, *stricto sensu*, is situated at a level above 100 ms' (1984, 30).

38. See, e.g., Mauk and Buonomano 2004; Buhusi and Meck 2005; and Karmarkar and Buonomano 2007. See also the closing remarks in Droit-Volet and Gil 2009.

39. Internal clock models were in fact first developed in response to data concerning the influence of body-temperature on perceived duration (see Hoagland 1933). For a recent review of this data see Wearden and Penton-Voak 1995.

40. I discuss these ideas in much greater detail in my 'Perceiving the Passing of Time' (in preparation).

41. Many of the anecdotes also support the common place idea that one's life flashes before one's eyes in such situations (Noyes and Kletti 1977, 387–8; 380–1). For further anecdotal evidence see Flaherty 1999 which collects a vast number of accounts of temporal distortions in various situations, many of which highlight the intimate connection between increased mental activity and a sense of time being stretched out or slowed down (i.e. an increase in perceived duration). See also Hancock and Weaver 2005. For recent laboratory based studies of the effect of emotional stimuli on time perception see, e.g., Droit-Volet and Meck 2007; Droit-Volet and Gil 2009; and Tipples 2011.

42. Work on amphetamine and cocaine is largely confined to rat studies (e.g., Maricq et al. 1981) given ethical limitations. That said, it is fair to say that the presumption in the field is that such effects are to be found in humans. For an overview of the effect of pharmacological interventions on duration perception in humans and non-human animals see Meck 1996.

43. I presented versions of this paper at ASSC16 at the University of Sussex, and at a conference on Attention at the University of Antwerp. I am very grateful to the audiences on those occasions, and especially to my two commentators in Antwerp: Chris Mole and Chris Peacocke for their extremely thoughtful replies. Particular thanks to Ned Block, Brit Brogaard, John Campbell, Dave Chalmers, Tim Crane, Felipe De Brigard, Carolyn Dicey Jennings, Imogen Dickie, Katalin Farkas, Craig French, Angelica Kaufmann, Fiona Macpherson, Bence Nanay, Casey O'Callaghan, Adrienne Prettyman, Jesse Prinz, Susanna Siegel, Barry Smith, Maja Spener, James Stazicker, Michael Tye, Sebastian Watzl, Keith Wilson, and Wayne Wu, and many others. Finally, special thanks as always to Hanna Pickard for her invaluable advice and constant support.

References

Abbott, R. 1999. *The World as Information*. Exeter: Intellect Books.

Ayers, M. 1991. *Locke: Epistemology and Ontology*. London and New York: Routledge.

Baars, B. J. 2010. "Spontaneous repetitive thoughts can be adaptive: Postscript on 'mind wandering'" *Psychological Bulletin* 136(2): 208–210.

Baldauf, D., E. Burgard, and M. Wittmann. 2009. "Time perception as a workload measure in simulated car driving." *Applied Ergonomics* 40(5): 929–35.

Ballas, C. A., D. L. Evans, and D. F. Dinges. 2009. "Psychostimulants and Wakefulness-Promoting Agents." In *The American Psychiatric Publishing Textbook of Psychopharmacology*, edited by A. F. Schatzberg and C. B. Nemeroff, 843–860. Arlington, VA.: American Psychiatric Pub.

Block, R. A. 1979. "Time and consciousness." In *Aspects of consciousness*, edited by G. Underwood and R. Stevens. Vol. 1 of *Psychological issues*, 179–217. London: Academic Press.

Block, R. A. 1990. "Models of psychological time." In *Cognitive models of psychological time*, edited by R. A. Block, 1–35. Hillsdale, NJ.: Erlbaum.

Block, R. A., E. J. George, and M. A. Reed. 1980. "A watched pot sometimes boils: A study of duration experience." *Acta Psychologica* 46: 81–94.

Block, R., and D. Zakay. 2004. "Prospective and retrospective duration judgments: an executive control perspective." *Acta Neurobiologiae Experimentalis* 64: 319–328.

Block, R., P. Hancock, and D. Zakay. 2010. "How cognitive load affects duration judgments: a meta–analytic review." *Acta Psychologica* 134(3): 330–43.

Bortolussi, M. R., B. H. Kantowitz, and S. G. Hart. 1986. "Measuring pilot workload in a motion base trainer: A comparison of four techniques." *Applied Ergonomics* 17(4): 278–283.

Brown, S. W., and E. D. Bennett. 2002. "The role of practice and automaticity in temporal and non–temporal dual–task performance." *Psychological Research* 66: 80–89.

Brown, S. W., D. C. Newcomb, and K. G. Kahrl. 1995. "Temporal-signal detection and individual differences in timing." *Perception* 24: 525–538.

Brown, S. W, and A. N. West. 1990. "Multiple timing and the allocation of attention." *Acta Psychologica* 75: 103–121.

Brown, S. W. 1985. "Time perception and attention: The effects of prospective versus retrospective paradigms and task demands on perceived duration." *Perception and Psychophysics* 38: 115–124.

Brown, S. W. 1997. "Attentional resources in timing: Interference effects in concurrent temporal and nontemporal working memory tasks." *Perception and Psychophysics* 59(7): 1118–1140.

Brown, S. W. 2008. "Time and attention: review of the literature." In *Psychology of Time*, edited by S. Grondin, 111–38. Bingley: Emerald.

Brown, S. W. 2010. "Timing, resources, and interference: attentional modulation of time perception." In *Attention and Time*, edited by A. C. Nobre and J. T. Coull, 107–121. Oxford: OUP.

Brown, S. W., and C. T. Frieh. 2000. "Information processing in the central executive: Effects of concurrent temporal production and memory updating tasks." In *Rhythm perception and production*, edited by P. Desain and L. Windsor, 193–196. Lisse, The Netherlands: Swets & Zeitlinger.

Brown, S. W., and A. N. West. 1990. "Multiple timing and the allocation of attention." *Acta Psychologica* 75: 103–121.

Buhusi, C. V. and W. H. Meck. 2005. "What makes us tick? Functional and neural mechanisms of interval timing." *Nature Reviews Neuroscience* 6(10): 755–765.

Burnside, W. 1971. "Judgment of short time intervals while performing mathematical tasks." *Perception and Psychophysics* 9(5): 404–406.

Cahoon, D., and E. M. Edmonds. 1980. "The watched pot still won't boil: Expectancy as a variable in estimating the passage of time." *Bulletin of the Psychonomic Society* 16: 115–116.

Carrasco, M. 2011. "Visual Attention: The past 25 years." *Vision Research* 51: 1484–1525.

Chun, M. M., J. D. Golomb, and N. B. Turk-Browne. 2011. "A Taxonomy of External and Internal Attention." *Annual Review of Psychology* 62: 73–101.

Correa, A., and A. C. Nobre. 2008. "Spatial and temporal acuity of visual perception can be enhanced selectively by attentional set." *Experimental Brain Research* 189(3): 339–44.

Coull, J. T. 2004. "fMRI studies of temporal attention: allocating attention within, or towards, time." *Cognitive Brain Research* 21: 216–226.

Coull, J. T., R. K. Cheng, and W. H. Meck. 2011. "Neuroanatomical and neurochemical substrates of timing." *Neuropsychopharmacology* 36: 3–25.

Coull, J. T., F. Vidal, B. Nazarian, and F. Macar. 2004. "Functional anatomy of the attentional modulation of time estimation." *Science* 303: 1506–1508.

Creelman, C. D. 1962. "Human discrimination of auditory duration." *Journal of the Acoustical Society of America* 34: 582–593.

Curton, E. D., and D. S. Lordahl. 1974. "Effects of attentional focus and arousal on time estimation." *Journal of Experimental Psychology* 103: 861–867.

Droit–Volet, S., E. Bigand, D. Ramos, and J. L. O. Bueno. 2010. "Time flies with music whatever its emotional valence." *Acta Psychologica* 135: 226–236.

Droit–Volet, S., and S. Gil. 2009. "The time–emotion paradox." *Phil. Trans. R. Soc. B* 364: 1943–1953.

Droit–Volet, S., and W. H. Meck. 2007. "How emotions colour our perception of time." *Trends in Cognitive Sciences* 11(12): 504–513

Droit–Volet, S., and J. H. Wearden. 2002. "Speeding up an internal clock in children? Effects of visual flicker on subjective duration." *Quarterly Journal of Experimental Psychology* 55B: 193–211.

Dutke, S. 2005. "Remembered duration: Working memory and the reproduction of intervals." *Perception and Psychophysics* 67(8): 1404–1413.

Enns, J. T., J. C. Brehaut, and D. I. Shore. 1999. "The duration of a brief event in the mind's eye." *The Journal of General Psychology* 126: 355–372.

Flaherty, M. 1999. *A Watched Pot: How We Experience Time.* New York and London: NYU Press.

Fortin, C., and R. Breton. 1995. "Temporal interval production and processing in working memory." *Perception and Psychophysics* 57: 203–215.

Fortin, C., and E. Couture. 2002. "Short–term memory and time estimation: beyond the 2-second 'critical' value." *Canadian Journal of Experimental Psychology* 56: 120–127.

Fortin, C., R. Rousseau, P. Bourque, and E. Kirouac. 1993. "Time estimation and concurrent nontemporal processing: Specific interference from short–term–memory demands." *Perception and Psychophysics* 53(5): 536–548.

Fraisse, P. 1963. *Psychology of Time.* New York: Harper & Row.

Fraisse, P. 1984. "Perception and Estimation of Time." *Annual Review of Psychology* 35: 1–36.

Hancock, P. A., and J. L. Weaver. 2005. "On time under stress." *Theoretical Issues in Ergonomics Science* 6: 193–211.

Hoagland, H. 1933. "The physiological control of judgments of duration: evidence for a chemical clock." *Journal of General Psychology* 9: 267–287.

Gibbon, J. 1977. "Scalar expectancy theory of Weber's law in animal timing." *Psychological Review* 84: 279–325.

Gibbon, J., R. M. Church, and W. Meck. 1984. "Scalar timing in memory." In *Timing and time perception*, edited by J. Gibbon and L. G. Allan. Vol. 423 of *Annals of the New York Academy of Sciences*, 52–77. New York: New York Academy of Sciences.

Gibson, J. J. 1975. "Events Are Perceivable but Time Is Not." In *The Study of Time II. Proceedings of the Second Conference of the International Society for the Study of Time*, edited by J. T. Fraser and N. Lawrence, 295–301. Berlin: Springer-Verlag.

Grondin, S., and F. Macar. 1992. "Dividing attention between temporal and nontemporal tasks: a performance operating characteristic—POC—analysis." In *Time, action, cognition: towards bridging the gap*, edited by F. Macar, V. Pouthas and W. Friedman, 119–128. Dordrecht: Kluwer.

Grondin, S., G. Meilleur–Wells, and R. Lachance. 1999. "When to start explicit counting in a time–intervals discrimination task: A critical point in the timing process by humans." *Journal of Experimental Psychology: Human Perception and Performance* 25: 993–1004.

Gutyrchik, E., J. Churan, T. Meindl, A. L. W. Bodke, H. von Bernewitz, C. Born, et al. 2010. "Functional neuroimaging of duration discrimination on two different time scales." *Neuroscience Letters* 469: 411–415.

Hawkes, G. R., and S. J. Sherman. 1972. "Vigilance effects for duration judgments with two levels of task demand." *Perceptual and Motor Skills* 34: 351–356.

Hicks, R. E., G. W. Miller, and M. Kinsbourne. 1976. "Prospective and Retrospective Judgments of Time as a Function of Amount of Information Processed." *The American Journal of Psychology* 89(4): 719–730.

Hicks, R. E., G. W. Miller, G. Gaes, and K. Bierman. 1977. "Concurrent Processing Demands and the Experience of Time-in-Passing." *The American Journal of Psychology* 90(3): 431–446.

Hülser, C. 1924. "Zeitauffassung und Zeitschätzung verschieden ausgefüllter Intervalle unter besonderer Berücksichtigung der Aufmerksamkeitsablenkung." [Time perception and time estimation of differently filled intervals with respect to distracted attention.] *Archiv für die gesamte Psychologie* 49: 363–378.

Hume, D. 1978. *A Treatise of Human Nature*. Edited by L. A. Selby-Bigge, 2nd edition revised by P. H. Nidditch. Oxford: Clarendon Press.

James, W. 1890. *The Principles of Psychology*. New York: H. Holt and company.

Jones, L. A., C. Allely, and J. H. Wearden. 2011. "Click trains and the rate of information processing: Does 'speeding up' subjective time make other psychological processes run faster?" *Quarterly Journal of Experimental Psychology* 64(2): 363–380.

Jones, M. R., and M. G. Boltz. 1989. "Dynamic attending and responses to time." *Psychological Review* 96(3): 459–491.

Kagerer, F. A., M. Wittmann, E. Szelag, and N. von Steinbüchel. 2002. "Cortical involvement in temporal reproduction: Evidence for differential roles of the hemispheres." *Neuropsychologia* 40: 357–366.

Kant, I. 2003. *Critique of Pure Reason*. Translated by N. Kemp Smith. New York: Palgrave Macmillan.

Karmarkar, U. R., and D. V. Buonomano. 2007. "Timing in the absence of clocks: encoding time in neural network states." *Neuron* 53(3): 427–38.

Kojima, Y., and F. Matsuda. 2000. "Effects of attention and external stimuli on duration estimation under a prospective paradigm." *Japanese Psychological Research* 42: 144–154.

Kouwenhoven, F. 2001. "Meaning and Structure: The Case of Chinese qin (zither) Music." *British Journal of Ethnomusicology* 10(1): 39–62.

Langer, S. 1953. *Feeling and form*. New York: Charles Scribner.

Large, E. W., and M. R. Jones. 1999. "The dynamics of attending: How we track time-varying events." *Psychological Review* 106: 119–159.

Lavie, N. 2010. "Attention, Distraction, and Cognitive Control Under Load." *Current Directions in Psychological Science* 19(3): 143–148.

Le Poidevin, R. 2007. *The Images of Time*. Oxford: OUP.

Locke, J. 1975. *An Essay Concerning Human Understanding*. Edited by P. H. Nidditch. Oxford: OUP.

Macar F. 2002. "Expectancy, controlled attention and automatic attention in prospective temporal judgments." *Acta Psychologica* 111(2): 243–62.

Macar, F., S. Grondin, and L. Casini. 1994. "Controlled attention sharing influences time estimation." *Memory and Cognition* 22(6): 673–86.

Martin, M. G. F. 1997 "The shallows of the mind." *Proceedings of the Aristotelian Society* 74(1): 75–98.

Maricq, A. V., S. Roberts, and R. M. Church. 1981. "Methamphetamine and time estimation." *Journal of Experimental Psychology: Animal and Behavioral Processes* 7: 18–30.

Mattes, S., and R. Ulrich. 1998. "Directed attention prolongs the perceived duration of a brief stimulus." *Perception and Psychophysics* 60: 1305–1317.

Mauk, M. D., and D. V. Buonomano. 2004. "The Neural Basis of Temporal Processing." *Annual Review of Neuroscience* 27: 307–40

McKay, T. D. 1977. "Time estimation: effects of attentional focus and a comparison of interval conditions." *Perceptual and Motor Skills* 45: 584–586.

McTaggart, J. M. E. 1927. *The Nature of Existence II*. Edited by C. D. Broad. London: CUP.

Meck, W. H. 1996. "Neuropharmacology of timing and time perception." *Cognitive Brain Research* 3: 227–242.

Michon, J. A. 1985. "The compleat time experiencer." In *Time, Mind, and Behavior*, edited by J. A. Michon and J. L. Jackson, 20–52. New York: Springer.

Michon, J. A. 1986. "J. T. Fraser's 'Levels of Temporality' as Cognitive Representations." In *The Study of Time V: Time, Science, and Society in China and the West*, edited by J. T. Fraser, N. Lawrence, and F. C. Haber, 51–66. Amherst, MA.: University of Massachusetts Press.

Michon, J. A. 1972. "Processing of temporal information and the cognitive theory of time experience." In *The study of time*, edited by J. T. Fraser, F. C. Haber, and G. H. Müller, 242–258. Heidelberg: Springer-Verlag.

Michon, J. A., and J. L. Jackson. 1984. "Attentional effort and cognitive strategies in the processing of temporal information." In *Timing and time perception*, edited by J. Gibbon and L. G. Allan. Vol. 423 of *Annals of the New York Academy of Sciences*, 298–321. New York: New York Academy of Sciences.

Nasrallah, H. A., and R. Tandon. 2009. "Classic Antipsychotic Medications." In *The American Psychiatric Publishing Textbook of Psychopharmacology*, edited by A. F. Schatzberg and C. B. Nemeroff, 533–554. Arlington, VA.: American Psychiatric Pub.

Nichelli, P., D. Always, and J. Grafman. 1996. "Perceptual timing in cerebellar degeneration." *Neuropsychologia* 34(9): 863–71.

Noyes, R., and R. Kletti. 1977. "Depersonalization in Response to Life-Threatening Danger." *Comprehensive Psychiatry* 18(4): 375–384.

O'Shaughnessy, B. 2000. *Consciousness and the world*. Oxford: OUP.

Ornstein, R. E. 1969. *On the experience of time*. Harmondsworth: Penguin.

Papafragou, A. 2010. "Language" In *Encyclopedia of Perception*, edited by B. Goldstein, 519–522. Thousand Oaks: Sage.

Penton–Voak, I. S., H. Edwards, A. Percival, and J. H. Wearden. 1996. "Speeding up an internal clock in humans? Effects of clicks trains on subjective duration." *Journal of Experimental Psychology: Animal and Behavioural Processes* 22: 307–320.

Phillips, I. B. In preparation. "Perceiving the passing of time."

Rammsayer, T. 1989. "Is there a common dopaminergic basis of time perception and reaction time?" *Neuropsychobiology* 21: 37–42.

Rammsayer, T. 1999. "Neuropharmacological evidence for different timing mechanisms in humans." *Quarterly Journal of Experimental Psychology* 52: 273–286.

Rattat, A. C., and S. Droit-Volet. 2012. "What is the best and the easiest method of preventing counting in different temporal tasks?" *Behavior Research Methods* 44: 67–80.

Reid, T. 1827. *Essays on Powers of the Human Mind.* London: Thomas Tegg.

Sawyer, T. F., P. J. Meyers, and S. J. Huser. 1994. "Contrasting task demands alter the perceived duration of brief time intervals." *Perception and Psychophysics* 56: 649–657.

Seifried, T. and R. Ulrich. 2011. "Exogenous visual attention prolongs perceived duration." *Attention, Perception and Psychophysics* 73: 68–85.

Shoemaker, S. 1969. "Time Without Change." *Journal of Philosophy* 66: 363–81.

Sloman, S. A. 1996. "The empirical case for two systems of reasoning." *Psychological Bulletin* 119: 3–22.

Soteriou, M. J. 2011. "Occurrent Perceptual Knowledge." *Philosophical Issues* 21(1): 485–504.

Stout, G. F. 1932. *A Manual of Psychology.* London: W. B. Clive, University Tutorial Press Ltd.

Thomas, E. A. C., and T. I. Brown Jr. 1974. "Time perception and the filled–duration illusion." *Perception and Psychophysics* 16: 449–458.

Thomas, E. A. C., and W. B. Weaver. 1975. "Cognitive processing and time perception." *Perception and Psychophysics* 17: 363–367.

Tipples, J. 2011. "When time stands still: Fear–specific modulation of temporal bias due to threat." *Emotion* 11(1): 74–80.

Treisman, M. 1963. "Temporal discrimination and the indifference interval: Implications for a model of the 'internal clock'." *Psychological Monographs: General and Applied* 77: 1–31.

Treisman, M., A. Faulkner, P. L. N. Naish, and D. Brogan. 1990 "The internal clock: evidence for a temporal oscillator underlying time perception with some estimates of its characteristic frequency." *Perception* 19: 705–743.

Tse, P., J. Intriligator, J. Rivest, and P. Cavanagh. 2004 "Attention and the subjective expansion of time." *Perception and Psychophysics* 66(7): 1171–1189.

Tse, P. U. 2010. "Attention underlies subjective temporal expansion." In *Attention and Time*, edited by A. C. Nobre and J. T. Coull, 137–150. Oxford: OUP.

Ulbrich, P., J. Churan, M. Fink, and M. Wittmann. 2007. "Temporal reproduction: Further evidence for two processes." *Acta Psychologica* 125: 51–65.

Underwood, G. 1975. "Attention and the perception of duration during encoding and retrieval." *Perception* 4(3): 291–296.

Underwood, G., and R. A. Swain. 1973. "Selectivity of attention and the perception of duration." *Perception* 2(1): 101–105.

van der Hoort, B., A. Guterstam, and H. H. Ehrsson. 2011. "Being Barbie: The Size of One's Own Body Determines the Perceived Size of the World." *PLoS One* 6(5): 1–10.

Wearden, J. H., L. Denovan, M. Fakhri, and R. Haworth. 1997. "Scalar timing in temporal generalization in humans with longer stimulus durations." *Journal of Experimental Psychology: Animal Behavior Processes* 23: 502–511.

Wearden, J. H. 1991. "Do humans possess an internal clock with scalar timing properties?" *Learning and Motivation* 22: 59–83.

Wearden, J. H. 2001. "Internal Clocks and the Representation of Time." In *Time and Memory*, edited by C. Hoerl and T. McCormack, 37–58. Oxford: OUP.

Wearden, J. H. 2003. "Applying the scalar timing model to human time psychology: progress and challenges." In *Time and mind II*, edited by H. Helfrich, 21–39. Gottingen: Hogrefe & Huber.

Wearden, J. H., and I. S. Penton-Voak. 1995. "Feeling the heat: body temperature and the rate of subjective time, revisited." *Quarterly Journal of Experimental Psychology* 48B: 129–141.

Wearden, J. H., K. Philpott, and T. Win. 1999. "Speeding up and (... relatively...) slowing down and internal clock in humans." *Behavioural Processes* 46: 63–73.

Wearden, J. H., P. Rogers, and R. Thomas. 1997. "Temporal bisection in humans with longer stimulus durations." *Quarterly Journal of Experimental Psychology* 50B: 79–94.

Wilsoncroft, W. E., and J. D. Stone. 1975. "Information processing and estimation of short time intervals." *Perceptual and Motor Skills* 41: 192–194.

Wilsoncroft, W. E., J. D. Stone, and F. M. Bagrash. 1978. "Temporal estimates as a function of difficulty of mental arithmetic." *Perceptual and Motor Skills* 46: 1311–1317.

Wittmann, M., V. van Wassenhove, A. D. Craig, and M. P. Paulus. 2010. "The neural substrates of subjective time dilation." *Frontiers in Human Neuroscience* 4(2): 1–9.

Woodrow, H. 1951. "Time perception." In *Handbook of Experimental Psychology*, edited by S. Steven, 1224–1236. New York: Wiley.

Yeshurun, Y., and G. Marom. 2008. "Transient spatial attention and the perceived duration of brief visual events." *Visual Cognition* 16: 826–848.

Zakay, D. 1990. "The evasive art of subjective time measurement: Some methodological dilemmas." In *Cognitive Models of Psychological Time*, edited by R. A. Block, 59–84. Hillsdale, NJ: Erlbaum.

Zakay, D., and R. A. Block. 1997. "Temporal Cognition." *Current Directions in Psychological Science* 6: 12–16.

Zakay, D. 1989. "Subjective time and attentional resource allocation: An integrated model of time estimation." In *Time and Human Cognition: A Life Span Perspective*, edited by I. Levin and D. Zakay, 365–397. Amsterdam, The Netherlands: North Holland.

Zakay, D., and R. A. Block. 1996. "The role of attention in time estimation processes." In *Time, Internal Clocks and Movement*, edited by M. A. Pastor and J. Artieda, 143–164. Amsterdam, The Netherlands: Elsevier.

Zakay, D., D. Nitzan, and J. Glicksohn. 1983. "The influence of task difficulty and external tempo on subjective time estimation." *Perception & Psychophysics* 34: 451–456.

Zélanti, P., and S. Droit–Volet. 2011. "Cognitive abilities explaining age-related changes in time perception of short and long durations." *Journal of Experimental Child Psychology* 109: 143–157.

INDISCRIMINABILITY AND PHENOMENAL CONTINUA

Diana Raffman
University of Toronto

The relation of perceptual indiscriminability is widely thought to be non-transitive: there can be a series of objects (stimuli) $s_1 \ldots s_n$ in which s_1 is pairwise indiscriminable on some perceptual dimension from s_2, and s_2 is indiscriminable from s_3, and s_3 from s_4, and so forth, but s_n is discriminably different from s_1. For example, Timothy Williamson writes that

> [t]wo stimuli whose difference is below the threshold cannot be discriminated. Since many indiscriminable differences can add up to a discriminable difference, one can have a series of stimuli each indiscriminable from its successor, of which the first member is discriminable from the last. Indiscriminability is a non-transitive relation. (Williamson 1994, 69)

According to some theorists, the possibility (indeed, actuality) of a phenomenal continuum—*viz.*, a seemingly continuous progression from an instance of one color (pitch, loudness, etc.) to an instance of another, incompatible color—shows that perceptual indiscriminability *must* be nontransitive. Here is Crispin Wright, for example:

> It is familiar...that we may construct a series of suitable, homogeneously coloured patches, in such a way as to give the impression of a smooth transition from red to orange, where each patch is *indiscriminable* in colour from those immediately next to it; it is the non-transitivity of indiscriminability which generates this possibility. (Wright 1975, 338–9)

> Suppose that we are to construct a series of colour patches, ranging from red through to orange, among which indiscriminability is to behave transitively. We are given a supply of appropriate patches from which to make selections, an initial red patch *C1*, and the instruction that each successive patch must either match its predecessor or be more like it than is any other patch not matching it which we later use. Under these conditions it is plain that we cannot generate any change in colour by selecting successive matching patches; since indiscriminability is to be transitive, it will follow that if each *Ci* in the first *n* selections matches its

predecessor, [then] Cn matches $C1$. The only way to generate a change in colour will be to select a non-matching patch. (Wright 1976, 344–5)

The alleged nontransitivity seems to cause trouble wherever it goes, however. Just for example, it threatens the coherence of the ordinary idea of determinate perceptual qualities like shades, pitches, and intensities; and it helps to generate a particularly toxic version of the sorites paradox. In what follows I want to begin by illustrating the kinds of problems that are created by the alleged nontransitivity, and the lengths to which philosophers have often had to go in order to deal with them. Then I will suggest a way of thinking about phenomenal continua that may eliminate some of the difficulty.

I

Before going further, we need to draw two important distinctions. First, we need to distinguish between the statistical relation of indiscriminability and the phenomenal relation of appearing (looking, sounding, tasting, etc.) the same. The statistical relation, employed primarily in psychology and psychophysics, is expressed in terms of percentages of same/different comparisons in which two physically different stimuli appear the same. Thus understood, indiscriminability is clearly nontransitive: there can be a series of stimuli $s_1 \ldots s_n$ such that, under some constant viewing conditions (suppose even that $s_1 \ldots s_n$ are all in view simultaneously), s_1 appears the same as s_2 in (e.g.) 75 percent of same/different trials, s_2 appears the same as s_3 in 75 percent ... and s_{n-1} appears the same as s_n in 75 percent, but s_1 and s_n appear the same in only 30 percent of trials. (More intuitively, perhaps: there can be a series of stimuli such that s_1 and s_2 can be told apart 25 percent of the time, s_2 and s_3 can be told apart 25 percent of the time, and so forth, but s_1 and s_n can be told apart 70 percent of the time.)

In contrast, virtually all philosophical discussions of indiscriminability concern not the statistical psychophysical relation but rather the phenomenal relation of appearing (looking, sounding, etc.) the same, in terms of which the statistical relation is defined.[1] Philosophers tend to refer to stimuli as looking the same as if this were an invariant relation, i.e., as if stimuli that "look the same" under certain conditions *always* look the same under those conditions. But there are no stimuli that always look the same, so it can be hard to understand what the philosophers have in mind, and interpretative decisions may have to be made. In order to connect with the philosophical discussions, for the sake of argument, in what follows I will bracket this worry and go along with the idea that appearing the same is an invariant relation. I'll suppose that it's the latter relation whose nontransitivity is at issue.

The second distinction, observed by at least some philosophers working in the area (e.g., Graff 2001, 927, Mills 2002, 391), is between (in)discriminability construed as a relationship discernible in a single pairwise same/different comparison (often expressed by saying of two objects that we can or cannot "tell them apart"), and looking the same construed as a more demanding, epistemically laden relationship. Pierre Chuard explains:

> [F]allibilists about looks... argue that... indiscriminable adjacent patches may well look different, despite their perceptual indiscriminability; it's just that we cannot notice the relevant differences in the chromatic appearances of such patches....[V]ery small differences in chromatic appearances may be visually indiscriminable to normal perceivers because they cannot notice them, thus lacking perfect access to small differences in how things look to them. (2007, 162)

In what follows, I will sometimes speak inexactly to keep my discussion from becoming cumbersome; but where the differences are important or an author's usage is not clear from the context, I will do my best to distinguish these varying senses of 'indiscriminable' and 'looks the same'.

As I just mentioned, the alleged nontransitivity of indiscriminability appears to threaten the coherence of the ordinary idea of determinate perceptual ("phenomenal") qualities. Intuitively we want to say that objects have the same shade or pitch or loudness just in case they are indiscriminable, i.e., just in case they appear the same, in the relevant respect. But unlike indiscriminability, the identity relation is transitive; so this natural way of individuating determinate qualities is not available. Peacocke observes:

> [I]t is pretheoretically tempting to suppose that... perceived shades s and s' are identical if and only if s is not discriminably different from s'. The non-transitivity of nondiscriminable difference ("matching") entails that there is no way of dividing the spectrum into shades that meets that condition. Take an example in which, in respect of color, x matches, y matches z, but x does not match z. To conform to the above principle about shades, the shade of y would have to be identical with shades that are distinct from one another. (1981, 83)

Drawing a famously radical conclusion, Michael Dummett contends that the nontransitivity of indiscriminability renders the idea of phenomenal qualities, and the vague predicates that ostensibly express them, incoherent:

> What, then, of phenomenal qualities?... [W]e cannot take 'phenomenal quality' in a strict sense, as constituting the satisfaction of an observational predicate, that is, a predicate whose application can be decided merely by the employment of our sense-organs: at least, not in any arena in which non-discriminable difference is not transitive....[T]here are no phenomenal qualities, as these have been traditionally understood; and, while our language certainly contains observational predicates[, they] infect it with inconsistency. (1975, 324)[2]

Conceptualism about the representational content of perceptual experience (e.g., McDowell 1994, Brewer 2005) has also required treatment for difficulties caused by the alleged nontransitivity of the indiscriminability relation. According to the conceptualist, all experiential content is conceptual: we can experience, or perceptually represent, only what we can conceptualize upon inspection. An apparent counterexample is our experience of determinate phenomenal qualities: surely, opponents have argued, these shades, pitches, intensities, and the rest are too fine-grained for us to conceptualize in this way. Conceptualists reply that, on the contrary, we do have sufficiently fine-grained concepts—*viz.*, demonstrative concepts such as 'this shade' or 'that shade of magenta', or 'that flat leading tone'. For example, McDowell contends that you possess (and deploy) a demonstrative concept of a given determinate shade of red just in case you can tell, after your experience of the shade is over, whether a (closely) subsequent experience as of a shade of red is as of *that same shade.*

The nontransitivity problem rears its head when we try to say what representing that same shade consists in: how does your experience represent objects as having *the same shade?* The natural answer: by representing them in such a way that they are indiscriminable with respect to hue. But there the problem takes hold, for this natural answer attempts to define the transitive relation of sameness or identity with respect to hue, in terms of the nontransitive relation of indiscriminability with respect to hue.[3]

Disjunctivism in the philosophy of mind also runs into trouble in its appeal to the indiscriminability relation. Bucking tradition, the disjunctivist holds that veridical perceptions are essentially different in kind from illusions and hallucinations.[4] He thinks that the mind-independent entities that are the intentional objects of our experiences are *constituents* of the experiences that are veridical; and for obvious reasons, no such constituency can obtain in the case of illusions or hallucinations. The disjunctivist acknowledges that veridical perceptions, illusions, and hallucinations are all experiences, but he claims that what unites them as such is just their indiscriminability from veridical perceptions—not, as philosophical tradition would have it, their qualitative or intentional or adverbial properties. Specifically, a mental event is an experience as of Φ just in case it is indiscriminable from a veridical perception of Φ. M. G. F. Martin explains:

> Rather than appealing to a substantive condition which an event must meet to be an experience, and in addition ascribing to us cognitive powers to recognise the presence of this substantive condition, [disjunctivism] instead emphasizes the limits of our powers of discrimination and the limits of self-awareness: some event is an experience of a street scene just in case it couldn't be told apart through introspection from a veridical perception of the street as the street.... (2004, 48)

[A] challenge to the sufficiency of indiscriminability for identity of kind of experience comes from the alleged nontransitivity of indiscriminability for some observable properties. Certainly, given observers on particular occasions may fail to detect the difference in shade between sample A and sample B, and also fail to detect the difference between sample B and sample C, and yet be able to detect the difference between sample A and sample C. If this leads us to the conclusion that experiences of A are indiscriminable from experiences of B, and experiences of B are indiscriminable from experiences of C, then we face a problem supposing that there are kinds of event which are sensory experiences of colour shades on the disjunctivist proposal. The indiscriminability of experience of A and experience of B would require us to suppose that these are just the same kind of experience; likewise for the experience of B and of C. By transitivity of identity, this requires that the kind of experience one has of A is of the same kind as the experience one has of C, but this contradicts the observation that the experience of C is discriminable from the experience of A since kinds of experience are discriminable only where distinct. (2004, 76)

If I understand correctly, Martin reasons that if two stimuli are indiscriminable, then the experiences they occasion are indiscriminable, and experiences are indiscriminable just in case they are phenomenally identical.[5] Hence if indiscriminability is nontransitive, something has to give.

Now I want to consider some of the responses that defenders of these and other affected views have made to the alleged nontransitivity problem.

II

The most common response to the problem has been to argue that the relation of looking the same is transitive, or at least that there is no good reason to think it's nontransitive, because adjacent items in an ostensible phenomenal continuum are, after all, either discriminably different (Hardin 1988, Burns 1994, e.g.) or indiscriminable but phenomenally different (Graff 2001, Mills 2002, e.g.).[6] Proponents of the latter option claim that although we cannot tell adjacent items apart in a pairwise same/different comparison, they are nevertheless phenomenally different, i.e., they appear (look, sound, taste) different. Hence there can be no phenomenal continua after all.

I haven't yet said exactly what a phenomenal continuum is. As a first approximation, a phenomenal continuum is a series of stimuli in which neighboring items appear the same but the endpoints appear different, at a given time, to a perceiver who proceeds along the series, inspecting each pair of neighboring stimuli. Or better: a phenomenal continuum is a continuous progression in appearance that is *instantiated*, at a time, by a series of stimuli in which neighboring items appear the same but the endpoints appear different at that time, etc. The phenomenology of phenomenal continua is baffling because, even given perfectly constant viewing conditions, the first and last items appear different and yet nowhere between the two is any local difference in appearance discerned.

Why think adjacent items in a putative phenomenal continuum are phenomenally different? And why, if they are phenomenally different, are they indiscriminable, as "fallibilists" (Chuard 2007) have claimed? Typically, fallibilists construe indiscriminability as an epistemic (rather than purely perceptual) failing, but the details are unclear. They tend to cite factors—such as the small size of the relevant stimulus differences or the slow rate of the relevant change(s) of appearance, or failures of attention—that might explain the indiscriminability of neighboring items but do not obviously leave room for any phenomenal differences as these are usually understood. Eugene Mills writes:

> I deny first-person infallibility for the belief that two patches look as though they share all their color-appearance properties. But infallibility for this belief is silly anyway. Each patch has a vast array of color-appearance properties, nested and otherwise. It is fantastic to suppose that in comparing two patches, I could not fail to notice a slight difference with respect to one of these (at least) thousands of colors. (2002, 391)[7]

Delia Graff expresses her view this way:

> Another explanation, consistent with transitivity, is that when we look (say) at the hour-hand on a clock, although it does in fact look to change in position over the course of twenty-second intervals, the change in appearance is too slight, and too slow, for us to notice it. We judge the hour-hand to look still, but our judgement about the character of our experience is mistaken. (2001, 927)

According to the fallibilist, the relation of looking the same can be transitive because adjacent items do not in fact look the same.[8] Williamson suggests that phenomenal continua do not (cannot?) exist because physically different samples are always "impersonally" discriminable, i.e., because some observer in some context could tell that the samples are different. The trouble with this response is that all that's required for nontransitivity is that some series of stimuli instantiate the requisite sort of progression for some observer at some time. It's irrelevant whether some other observer could tell the stimuli in question apart. John Zeimbikis (2009) writes that a

> distinction between phenomenal indiscriminability and phenomenal identity is adopted by Austen Clark (1989) when he says that that there are phenomenal differences below the threshold of sensible discrimination, or 'a qualitative difference between the sensations engendered by indiscriminable things'. The difference could also be described as that between *looking* phenomenally identical and *being* phenomenally identical. (357–8)

The preceding are some examples of the strategies that philosophers have been forced to adopt in response to the alleged nontransitivity of indiscriminability. In my view, granting that stimuli that cannot be told apart in a pairwise comparison (under normal or standard conditions, whatever exactly these may be) may nevertheless be phenomenally different—in other words, may look different—or that stimuli that look phenomenally identical could fail to *be* phenomenally identical, is too high a price to pay for a resolution of the problem. In the remainder of this paper I will advance a different response to the nontransitivity problem, one that may allow us to resolve it in a less drastic way. Specifically, rather than postulating undetectable phenomenal differences between indiscriminable adjacent items, I will urge that some of the individual stimuli in (a series that instantiates) a phenomenal continuum change their appearance, change how they look, as an observer moves along the series. In other words, instead of a difference in appearance between adjacent items, I will propose that a change occurs in the appearance of one or more items individually. I'll call this proposal the 'instability hypothesis'.[9] Of course, for a claim of nontransitivity to hold good, the stimuli in a phenomenal continuum must remain constant in appearance throughout; the instability hypothesis must be false. A series in which the stimuli change their appearance doesn't show that appearing the same is nontransitive, any more than the fact that Tom and Dick weigh the same, and Dick and Harry weigh the same, but Tom and Harry have different weights, shows that identity is nontransitive if we've weighed Tom and Dick in 2001, and then Dick and Harry in 2002, and then Tom and Harry in 2003.

In the next section I am going to present some experimental results that seem to support the instability hypothesis. The conclusion we should draw, I'll suggest, is that neighboring stimuli in a phenomenal continuum appear (look, sound, etc.) the same, but such a continuum provides no evidence that appearing the same, in contrast to statistical indiscriminability, is nontransitive.

III

The experiment described below was designed and run in collaboration with Delwin Lindsey of the Psychology Department and Angela Brown of the School of Optometry at Ohio State University.[10]

The stimuli were a series of 41 patches of colored light that instantiated a phenomenal continuum (on almost all trials) between two slightly but clearly different shades of green. The stimuli were presented on a high-resolution color monitor in the circular arrangement shown in Figure 1. Nothing depended upon the locations of the endpoints. About half of the stimuli were redundant: roughly every other patch in the circle was physically identical to its predecessor.[11] Neighboring physically different patches differed by less than the discrimination threshold or just noticeable difference in hue of our most sensitive subject. (We had established the thresholds of our subjects in an earlier experiment, requiring correct detection on 75% of trials.) The subjects in the experiment were ten philosophy and psychology faculty, students, and staff at Ohio State University, including several faculty and graduate students in psychology of vision.

Each trial began with a same/different comparison of the hues of two neighboring of 'different' (which happened rarely), the next trial began immediately and she was cued to judge the next pair of patches. (If the patches are numbered #1–#41, the order of the pairs was #1/#2, #2/#3, #3/#4, etc. Consecutive pairs always shared a patch.) If the subject made a judgment of 'same', a disk

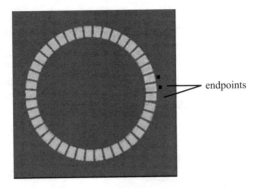

Figure 1. Stimuli as presented for the same/different task on each trial. Black dots cued the subject to judge the indicated pair. The patches marked 'endpoints' are clearly discriminable.

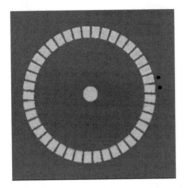

Figure 2. Stimuli as presented for the adjustment task on each trial. Subjects' task was to adjust the hue of the central disk to match the hue of the indicated pair.

of colored light appeared in the center of the circle, as pictured in Figure 2. The subject then adjusted the hue of the disk by moving the computer mouse back and forth until the disk matched the hue of the two patches. (The starting hue of the disk and the directionality of the mouse were randomized.) The disk then disappeared and the next trial began. In this way the subject was taken around the circle, judging each pair of patches *seriatim* and adjusting the hue of the disk accordingly. Subjects went around the circle twice. At the end of the experiment we asked roughly half of the subjects if they had noticed any changes in the colors of the patches during the experiment. All said 'no'.

What we found was that even though all of the patches were in view throughout, and the members of every pair were judged 'same' by every subject on almost every trial, subjects' settings of the disk progressed more or less systematically with the physical values (wavelengths) of the patches.[12] In other words, subjects matched the pair #2/#3 to a longer wavelength than the pair #1/#2, the pair #3/#4 to a longer wavelength than the pair #2/#3, and so on.

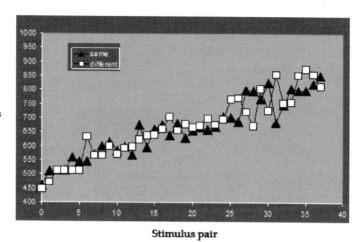

Disk setting in
arbitrary units

Stimulus pair

Figure 3. Data from an individual subject, showing a systematic progression of the setting of the disk on more or less every trial.

More to the point, patch #2 was matched to a different wavelength when it was compared to #1 than when it was compared to #3; patch #3 was matched to a different wavelength when compared to #2 than when compared to #4; and so on. Data from one subject, which are typical, are pictured in Figure 3. On the *y*-axis is the setting of the disk (in arbitrary units), and on the *x*-axis is the number of the stimulus pair to which the disk was being matched. Black triangles indicate redundant trials in which the stimuli in a pair were physically identical; white squares indicate trials in which stimuli were physically different. Since the graphs show the disk settings, the data points (squares and triangles) represent all and only trials in which the members of a pair were judged 'same'. (The graphs contain more than 41 data points because subjects went around the circle twice; hence pairs that were judged 'same' both times received two disk settings.) The curve shows fairly steady progression of the disk settings as subjects progressed through the pairs of patches, for both the physically identical and physically different pairs.[13]

No doubt our data admit of various interpretations. But I think that at the least they cast doubt upon the idea that neighboring patches are phenomenally different, i.e., that they look different. If anything, the data suggest that individual patches looked different in their different pairwise comparisons. We must proceed with caution here, though. It is overwhelmingly likely that our subjects could not have recognized, could not have noticed, any such change of hue. And this lack of recognition would not be analogous to (for example) change blindness, in which observers become aware of the change in question as soon as their attention is drawn to it or the relevant visual disruption is removed. (Subjects who experience change blindness fail to notice changes, often large ones, in visual scenes when the changes occur during a visual disruption such as a saccade or blink or a cut in a film.[14] For example, viewers in one experiment failed to notice that two people in a scene had exchanged heads (Grimes 1996.) Nor would it be analogous to attentional blindness, in which, again, subjects see a previously unnoticed aspect of the stimulus array as soon as they start paying attention to it. In contrast, in our experiment, making the same/different comparisons and setting the hue of the disk required sustained conscious attention, with no visual disruption.

Nevertheless, I do want to suggest that phenomenal changes occurred in the appearances of one or more of the patches as subjects proceeded around the circle. But why is a hypothesis of unrecognized phenomenal changes in individual patches more plausible than the fallibilists' hypothesis of unrecognized phenomenal differences between adjacent patches? I think there are at least three reasons. First, there are circumstances, different from the ones in the change and attentional blindness scenarios, in which these phenomenal changes could be recognized by the subject herself (or so I predict–more on this in a moment); second, recognition of such changes in appearance would defeat the nontransitivity claim but leave phenomenal continua intact; third, there will be no need to endorse the fallibilists' counterintuitive claim that stimuli judged the same in a pairwise comparison may nonetheless look different.

Let me illustrate what I have in mind. (I have not done an experiment to test the hypothesis I'm about to put forward; for now I can only make a prediction.)

IV

Consider a hypothetical version of the experiment using only 6 (non-redundant) patches, arranged in a straight line, progressing from one shade of green to another, slightly but perceptibly different one. Suppose that you perform the experimental tasks at some time t, and you reproduce our results: you judge adjacent patches the same and the endpoints #1 and #6 different, and your disk settings progress steadily. How then should we characterize the phenomenology: how do the patches look to you? Specifically, as against the fallibilists, can we characterize how the patches look, compatibly with preserving the intuition that objects judged the same in a pairwise comparison appear the same?

Perhaps, despite the systematic progression of your disk settings, until a patch that is pairwise clearly different from patch #1—*ex hypothesi* #6—becomes sufficiently prominent in your attentional field, all of the patches you have observed to that point (*viz.*, #1-#5) look the same, i.e., you have no experience of a *phenomenal* progression. (Plausibly, the same/different judgment of each successive pair of patches is made in a distinct attentional act, and you cannot attend to all 6 patches, a *fortiori* all 6 pairs, simultaneously.) However, when #6 enters your attentional field, you experience a phenomenal progression. The question is: if #1 and #5 look the same pairwise, how does #6 get to look different from #1 without #5 looking different from #6?

My thought is that #5 and #6 never need to look different because as soon as #6 looks different from #1, so does #5, and maybe also #4, depending upon how much attention #4 receives. Thus #5 (and possibly #4) undergoes a shift in its hue appearance as you shift your attention from the #4/#5 pair to the #5/#6 pair; #5 looks different in its two comparison pairings with #4 and #6.[15] And *you can notice this*. I predict that if you were to scan quickly back and forth along the series, from one end (#1) to the other (#6), you would see and notice, would recognize, at least some of the patches between #1 and #6 subtly (very subtly!) shifting their hues back and forth, together, now looking like #1, now like #6, now like #1, now like #6. The result would be that you never see a hue difference between adjacent patches. The fallibilist would contend that adjacent patches look different to you, but unrecognizably so; in effect, he asks us to take these phenomenal differences on faith. In contrast, on the view I am proposing, you can recognize the kind of phenomenal change that (e.g.) #5 undergoes.

I remarked earlier that our experimental subjects probably could not have noticed or recognized hue shifts of the kind that, if I am right, would be recognized in (e.g.) a shorter series like #1-#6. There may be various reasons why: for example, maybe the large number of stimuli used in the experiment, or their circular arrangement, or the slow and halting pace of subjects' progression through the series, or the demands of performing two different tasks, made the hue shifts unnoticeable. Whatever the reasons, they are compatible with the notion that one or more individual patches in the experimental series changed their appearance, changed how they looked, even if subjects could not notice that.

This changing of hue appearance is what makes a phenomenal continuum possible, enabling the first and last items to appear different although nowhere between the two is any local difference in appearance discerned. It makes possible the perception of an apparently smooth, *continuous* progression in hue. To put the point another way, these subtle changes, not any nontransitivity, are what make phenomenal continua possible. If this is correct, then neighboring items in a phenomenal continuum do indeed look—"really look" (*cf.* Graff, 2001)—the same in pairwise comparisons, but the instability of their appearances across different pairings defeats the nontransitivity claim.

The picture I am proposing requires letting go of the notion that shades of color are stable, mind-independent properties of objects, "out there" on their surfaces. Shades are neither stable nor mind-independent nor (simply) out there. Under normal or standard conditions (we leave open what these are), shades are informative about what's out there, in particular about the surfaces of objects and the light striking them. But they are also informative about what's "in here"– about the state of my visual system, what I have been looking at recently, what order I have been judging things in, and so forth.

Where then have we gotten to? I proposed the instability hypothesis as a way of undercutting the nontransitivity claim with respect to the relation of appearing the same, without being pushed into the counterintuitive strategies described earlier. To the extent that it succeeds, the hypothesis allows us to (1) reject the nontransitivity claim, (2) acknowledge the reality of phenomenal continua, and (3) preserve the intuition that stimuli judged the same in a pairwise comparison look the same. In addition, nothing in the proposed account stands in the way of claiming that whenever two or more stimuli look the same, they share a *look*—*viz.*, a determinate quality (shade, pitch, loudness, etc). This isn't yet to provide identity conditions for shades or looks; indeed, I don't think that such identity conditions can be formulated in terms of discriminatory or same/different judgments. I think there is a way to do it, in terms of a perceptual task called *magnitude estimation*, in which shades are identified by their percentages of different chromatic components. For example, unique blue is the shade containing 100% blue and 0% of any other hue; balanced orange is the shade containing 50% red and 50% yellow; balanced red-orange contains 75% red and 25% yellow; and so on. I cannot go into the details here, but see my 2013 for discussion.

Notes

1. As we'll see, not everyone would accept the idea that statistical indiscriminability is defined in terms of appearing the same.
2. See also Goodman 1951.
3. I don't mean to suggest that the conceptualist is without a response (though I think the present predicament is not easily escaped; see e.g. Pelling 2007 for discussion). My present goal is just to illustrate the kinds of difficulties posed by the alleged nontransitivity.
4. Here I ignore many significant differences among disjunctivist positions; see e.g. Haddock and Macpherson 2008 and Soteriou 2009 for detailed surveys.
5. The notion of (in)discriminability as a relation between *experiences* is probably not coherent; see Siegel 2004, 109, and my 2013.
6. Briefly, the trouble with Hardin's and Burns's ingenious proposals is that nontransitivity requires only that adjacent items appear the same and the endpoints appear different, to some individual observer on some single occasion.
7. Consider that in order for Mills' view here to undercut the nontransitivity claim, I must *invariably* fail to notice some such slight difference. Nontransitivity requires only the possibility of a single occasion on which adjacent items in the series look the same, to a single subject.
8. Adopting this view allows Graff (2001) to hold on to the principle that "if two samples really do look alike then they share a look".
9. An ancestor of the instability hypothesis is proposed, but not tested, in my 2000.
10. Lindsey.43@osu.edu, Brown.112@osu.edu. These experimental results are presented also in my 2011 and 2013, for different philosophical purposes.
11. There were 21 physically distinct stimulus values (wavelengths; but see note 9). If we label the 21 values as *a–u*, their order in the circle can be specified as *a, a, b, b, c, c,* and so on. Consecutive trials then involved the pairs *a/a, a/b, b/b, b/c, c/c,* and so on. (The "redundant" pairs [*a/a, b/b,* etc.] tested for false alarms,

viz., 'different' responses to identical stimuli. The latter data are irrelevant to the present discussion.)

12. For convenience I use the term 'wavelength', but strictly speaking it is incorrect. Rather, the stimuli were mixtures of broadband lights, and neither the primaries nor the mixtures had a defined wavelength.

13. This result suggests that subjects may have been matching the hue of the disk to the mean physical value of the two patches in each pair.

14. Though see Simons et al. 2000.

15. Note that I have said nothing about the related, difficult question of how an unattended patch looks at any given time. For example, when you are making a same/different judgment of the #5/#6 pair, how does #3 look? I am not certain of the answer. One possibility is that unless stimuli are attended to at least some significant degree, the contents of our experiences of them are merely "determinable", becoming determinate only when our attention focuses on them. For instance, maybe the content of our unattended experience of #3 could be expressed by something like 'on the way from the green of #5 and #6 to the slightly yellower green of #1'. I am not now in a position to develop the latter idea further, however. While this question about experiences of the unattended patches will need to be answered soon, I *think* it doesn't need to be answered immediately. (I will say more below about the nature of the determinate contents of our hue experiences of attended stimuli.)

References

Brewer, B., 2005. "Perceptual Experience Has Conceptual Content". In M. Steup and E. Sosa (Eds.), *Contemporary Debates in Epistemology* (Blackwell), pp. 217–230.

Burns, L., 1994. "Something to do with Vagueness", in *Spindel Conference* 1994: *Vagueness. Southern Journal of Philosophy* 33 [supplement], ed. T. Horgan, 23–48.

Chuard, P., 2007. "Indiscriminable Shades and Demonstrative Concepts". *Australasian Journal of Philosophy*, *85* (2): 277–306.

Clark, A., 1989. "The Particulate Instantiation of Homogeneous Pink". *Synthese*, *80* (2): 277–304.

Dummett, M., 1975. "Wang's Paradox". *Synthese*, *30*: 301–24.

Graff, D., 2001. "Phenomenal Continua and the Sorites". *Mind*, *110*, 440: 905–935.

Goodman, N., 1951. *The Structure of Appearance*. Harvard University Press.

Grimes, J. 1996. "On the failure to detect changes in scenes across saccades", in Akins, K. (Eds.), *Perception (Vancouver Studies in Cognitive Science)* 2, 89–110. Oxford University Press.

Haddock, A., and Macpherson, F., (Eds.) 2008. "Introduction" to Disjunctivism: Perception, Action, Knowledge. Oxford University Press.

Hardin, C., 1988. "Phenomenal Colors and Sorites". *Nous*, *22*: 213–34.

Martin, M. G. F., 2004. "The Limits of Self-Awareness". *Philosophical Studies*, *120*: 37–89.

McDowell, J., 1994. *Mind and World*. Harvard University Press.

Mills, E., 2002. "Fallibility and the Phenomenal Sorites". *Nous*, *36* (3): 384–407.

Peacocke, C., 1981. "Are Vague Predicates Incoherent?" *Synthese*, *46*: 121–141.

Pelling, C., 2007. "Conceptualism and the (Supposed) Non-transitivity of Colour Indiscriminability". *Philosophical Studies*, *134*: 211–234.

Raffman, D., 2000. "Is Phenomenal Indiscriminability Nontransitive?" (Eds.) C. Hill *Philosophical Topics* 28, 1, *Vagueness*, pp. 69–87.

Raffman, D., 2011. "Vagueness and Observationality". In Giuseppina Ronzitti (Eds.), *Vagueness: A Guide* (Springer)

Raffman, D., forthcoming 2013. "Indiscriminability, Discrimination, and Categorization". In Berit Brogaard (Eds.), *Does Perception Have Content?* Oxford University Press.

Siegel, S., 2004. "Indiscriminability and the Phenomenal". *Philosophical Studies*, *120* (1–3): 91–112.

Simons, D., Franconeri, S., and Reimer, R., 2000. "Change blindness in the absence of a visual disruption". *Perception*, *29*: 1143–1154.

Soteriou, M., 2009. "The Disjunctive Theory of Perception". *Stanford Encyclopedia of Philosophy*. Metaphysics Research Lab, CSLI, Stanford University.

Williamson, T., 1994. *Vagueness*. Routledge.

Wright, C., 1975. "On the Coherence of Vague Predicates". *Synthese*, *30*, 3/4: 325–65.

Wright, C., 1976. "Language Mastery and the Sorites Paradox". In G. Evans and J. McDowell (Eds.), *Truth and Meaning*, pp. 223–47. Clarendon Press.

Zeimbekis, J., 2009. "Phenomenal and Objective Size". *Nous*, *43*, 2: 346–362.

DON'T PANIC: SELF-AUTHORSHIP WITHOUT OBSCURE
METAPHYSICS[1]

Adina L. Roskies
Dartmouth College

Many people claim that the folk are intuitive Libertarians: they believe that
freedom is incompatible with the truth of determinism, and that determinism is
false (Ekstrom, 2002; Kane, 1999; Nichols, 2004, 2006). Others respond that the
folk are intuitive compatibilists (Nahmias, 2006; Nahmias, Coates, & Kvaran,
2007; Nahmias, Morris, Nadelhoffer, & Turner, 2005; Turner & Nahmias, 2006;
Vihvelin, in press). While it is difficult to map the folk views cleanly on to any
sophisticated philosophical position on free will, I think it is uncontestable that
the folk believe they at least sometimes have the ability to choose freely and
that they have a significant measure of control over their choices. They believe
in moral responsibility, in the idea that people's characters are relatively stable
and morally assessable, and that people's actions are often a reflection of those
characters. Moreover, they believe that people are in a sense responsible for their
characters, and that they are able to shape themselves in a way that is, in an
important sense, "up to them". It is this common intuition about malleability of
character and the link between character and action that underlies approaches to
morality as diverse as Aristotelian or virtue-centered approaches to ethics, and
Robert Kane's attempt to ground responsibility in indeterministic "self-forming
actions" (Kane, 1996, 1999). This is the intuition that I am particularly concerned
with in this paper.

Philosophical views that purport to capture and respond to the folk concepts
of freedom and responsibility are diverse. Incompatibilists — those who think
that determinism is incompatible with freedom — argue that certain critical
aspects of freedom are threatened by determinism. On one crude way of
slicing the pie, there are possibility incompatibilists[2] and source incompatibilists.
Possibility incompatibilists are particularly bothered by the alleged inability of
the compatibilist to make sense of the notion of real choice or "being able to
do otherwise" in a deterministic world, where the evolution of the universe is
entirely specified by the complete state of the universe at some time and the

laws of nature.[3] Source incompatibilists, in contrast, are more troubled by the inability of the compatibilist to give an account of authorship or autonomy of the agent in such a world.[4] The general worry of the source incompatibilist is that if every event — including events that are decisions and actions — is a result of the physical laws acting upon the state of the world, then there is no relevant sense in which the agent's action is really "up to him". Moreover, if determinism is true, the agent himself is merely a product of outside forces. And if an agent's actions and character are not up to him, if he lacks a measure of control, then it is difficult to justify holding that agent morally responsible for his actions, and it would be inappropriate to blame or praise him (except perhaps insofar as praise or blame could be justified on utilitarian grounds). It is the intuition that we can be held responsible for the people we are and for how that influences what we do that drives Libertarians like Kane to base his theory of freedom around "self-forming actions"(Kane, 1996, 1999), and Chisholm and O'Connor, to posit *sui generis* agent-causes (Chisholm, 1964, 1976; O'Connor, 2003).

In this paper I attempt to respond to the worries of the source incompatibilist, and try to sketch a naturalistically plausible, compatibilist notion of self-authorship and control that I believe captures important aspects of the folk intuitions regarding freedom and responsibility. It is my hope to thus offer those moved by source incompatibilist worries a reason not to adopt what P.F. Strawson called "the obscure and panicky metaphysics of Libertarianism" (P. F. Strawson, 1982) or the panic-inducing moral austerity of the hard incompatibilist (Pereboom, 2001). I am well aware that many great minds have sunk their teeth into this problem and have not prevailed, but at the very least, I hope to become clearer on where the sticking points are.

In what follows, I will draw upon philosophical resources developed to describe causal structures that rely upon the connection between causation and control. These approaches, developed by attending to the practices of experimental science, are aimed at both identifying and manipulating causal processes, and they eschew the heavy metaphysical commitments that characterize some approaches to causation. Interventionist theories of causation identify causes by finding pairs of variables that covary, and for which alterations or interventions in one lead to (or would lead to) concomitant changes in the other (Hitchcock & Woodward, 2003; Woodward, 2005; Woodward & Hitchcock, 2003). Interventionist approaches to causation thus provide a thoroughly naturalistic resource for understanding and identifying causal processes. They rely on the existence of rich counterfactual structure, yet are legitimately deployed even if determinism is true. They thus provide a promising model of causation and causal explanation for discussions of causation related to the debate between compatibilists and incompatibilists.

I also make use of a related framework for identifying loci of control, developed by John Campbell. Drawing inspiration from interventionist approaches to causation, Campbell elaborates the notion of a control variable, which is a causal factor that not only bears the right kind of covariation relation to a variable of interest to be a cause on the interventionist account, but also has other features, which make the covariation "systematic" and thus a potential locus of control (Campbell, 2010). Although a full explication of Campbell's framework is beyond the scope of this paper, two features are of particular interest to us: 1) control variables do not exhibit "gratuitous redundancy," and 2) they are "manipulable by local processes." The meaning and importance of these features will be explained in due course.

Campbell uses the notion of control variables to give an account of mental causation. His goal is to defend the notion of mental causation as it plays a role in interactions with other beings and objects in the world, and to provide an account of how both objects and others can causally affect and be affected by mental states. Our problem is not the problem of mental causation writ large, but more precisely the problem of self-causation. However, the kinds of considerations that Campbell musters to argue for the reality of mental causation in social interactions and in epistemology strike me as particularly helpful in explicating the kind of causation involved in self-causation.

The Problem(s)

As I see it, there are two primary problems to address when trying to offer a positive picture of what it is to have control over oneself and to be, in an important sense, the (or an) author of one's character.[5] On the one hand, there is a forward-looking problem: How can an agent shape his or her self in ways that legitimate notions of responsibility, even in the face of determinism? Secondly, there is a retrospective problem: When we assign responsibility we are typically looking for causes. But causes can be traced back to prior causes. Given that we are assuming that the agent is embedded in a causally closed world, what reason do we have to stop at the agent as the relevant cause, rather than tracing the agent's decision back to earlier causes having to do with, for example, the state of the universe at some time in the past and the laws of nature? Both problems point us toward the same underlying puzzle: why should we see the cause as the agent or self, rather than the forces or components that make up and influence that agent? And as we will see, both problems point us toward the same answer. I take for granted a fairly standard picture of rational behavior, in which agents exercise their rational capacities to deliberate about possible actions, and choose for reasons.

In this paper, I will be primarily concerned with giving an account of how an agent can have control over the kind of person she is. I leave aside the more often discussed point of being the source or author of individual actions, though a similar story can be told for control of actions. In any case, I take it that the shaping of oneself, or character, at least sometimes affects and is reflected in one's actions. The focus on character is an essential one for those who favor virtue-theoretic approaches to morality, but even those who doubt that people have stable characters (Doris, 2005; Harman, 2000) do not necessarily have to reject the basic insight of virtue theoretic notions (Kamtekar, 2004), nor need they deny that one can deliberately shape oneself in ways that matter to future behavior.

Looking Forward: Shaping Actions and High-Level Control

In one sense, there is no mystery regarding how an agent can have causal influence over its future states: My stepping into traffic caused the accident that led to my walking with a limp for the rest of my days. Had I not stepped in front of the car, the accident wouldn't have happened, and I wouldn't have broken my leg. This is true regardless of whether or not the accident was the inevitable result of the laws of nature and the state of the world. Determinism does not rob us of causal efficacy: the things that we do are part and parcel of the causal nexus of the world; we affect the world and the world has effects upon us. But this kind of causal efficacy is not sufficient to ground the self-causation that supports autonomy or responsibility. Non-agents are also causes in this sense: the acorn's falling from the tree was a cause of it growing into an oak.

Why is mere causal efficacy insufficient? For two reasons: on the one hand, agentive causes should be goal-directed and forward-looking, and on the other, those causes should in some sense be identified with the agent. In other words, we want the agent to exert control over those causes. Importantly, causation is not equivalent to control: control is an intentional notion, whereas causation is not. We can think of control as being goal-directed or teleological, and as assessable for efficacy according to whether the interventions aimed at controlling states or behaviors result in the system's parameters conforming to the intended or goal state. Although control is effected via causal relations, many causal processes are not control processes. If we are looking for a locus of control, then, merely identifying causal relations seems to miss the point. Instead, we should be looking at elements of the world that can properly be interpreted as intentional or goal-directed.

Our target should thus be intentional actions (construed broadly) resulting from choice or deliberation that are like interventions on one's current self. We thus have to look to a range of abilities that normal agents have, including the ability to formulate and evaluate options, to mentally project themselves into the future, to reason about how to have a desired effect on the self and the world, to plan and to execute those plans. What distinguishes agents from objects is that they exert a kind of control over the way in which they cause their future states: Through deliberation an agent can forecast the effect of various actions, and form an intention to act on the basis of the means that best accords with their goals. Via these intentions and subsequent actions they deliberately shape their future selves in virtue of their decisions.

On the view that intentions are often (if not always) the outcomes of decisions, we can see one reason that the acorns and agents are not causally on par: the acorn's falling was not the result of an intention to fall resulting from a decision. But what makes decisions special? Given what we know so far about the neuroscience of decision-making, decisions appear to be as much happenings as are acorn-fallings (Gold & Shadlen, 2007). On some accounts, it is the mechanistic view of physical causation, increasingly supported by neuroscientific understanding, that threatens our notion of agency (Nahmias, et al., 2007). As Nagel evocatively describes the predicament,

> The area of genuine agency, and therefore of legitimate moral judgment, seems to shrink under this scrutiny to an extensionless point. Everything seems to result from the combined influence of factors...that are not within the agent's control...The effect of concentrating on the influence of what is not under his control is to make this responsible self seem to disappear, swallowed up by the order of mere events. (Nagel, 1993, p. 66)

Causation and determinism both seem to rob us of agency or autonomy because we imagine that they make impossible relevant kinds of control. We become mere cogs in the wheel of the evolving universe, an acorn falling from a tree. The picture that supports this intuition is one in which low level physical processes such as brain states control our actions, while "we" passively or even helplessly look on from the sidelines, unable to intervene or alter the course of our own lives.[6] On this picture, we and our mental states are merely hitchhikers along for the ride.[7] This view should be combated. Mechanism does not entail mindlessness, and not all causes have the requisite structure to be considered loci of control.

In what follows I hope to make plausible the view that we exert control over ourselves by deliberately intervening on our future selves, thus effecting changes in the selves we come to be. It is part of our folk view that deliberation and choice, and the resultant formation of intentions are ways in which we can act as causes of ourselves. The notion is familiar from Kantian approaches. For instance, Korsgaard writes, "When you deliberate, when you determine your own causality, it is as if there is something over and above all of your incentives, something which is *you*, and which chooses which incentive to act on." Korsgaard, 2009, p. 72). The challenge is to show how can this be true, even if decision-making at the neural level is a purely mechanistic affair, the outcome of which depends upon the firing rates of various populations of neurons. In what sense can our decision-making be seen as deliberation, or even as an activity of the self? The answer lies in the relation between those decisions and the goals and reasons which we recognize.

Intervention on Oneself

So let us frame the problem as one of intervention on future states of oneself. An immediate problem confronts us: Intervention in the standard scientific methodological sense requires that we delineate a system and act upon it from the outside. We idealize by viewing the system of interest as a closed system. But if such idealization were necessary, self-intervention would require that a closed system acts upon itself. Intervention thus threatens to collapse into mere causal evolution. In order to understand how self-intervention is possible, it is important to conceptualize the system that is the agent in particular ways:

1) the agent is not a closed system: it is constantly being impinged upon by other influences from the environment (including social information such as moral norms and cultural expectations), as well as from its own intrinsic activity.
2) the agent is not a static system. It is a system with its own recurrent dynamics. Even if external conditions are held constant, internal variables can change.
3) the agent has limited and indirect access to its own physical substrate. The access it has is largely via mental content, which supervenes on, but is not identical with, the neurophysiological.
4) The agent's self-conception, as it figures into deliberation, projection, and decision, is constrained by that which is subjectively accessible, either directly, or through reflection, external information, and reason.
5) The agent can project her own current self-conception into the future (otherwise called mental time travel, or simulation) and thus establishes the baseline or non-interventional condition. By mentally simulating the effects of various hypothetical behaviors, actions, situations, etc., that are foreseeable outcomes of potential choices, the agent can form expectations about the consequences of potential interventions. From her perspective, all the options she recognizes as real options are open to her (see the digression on the agentive perspective).
6) The agent deliberates among her options, and chooses what to do based on reasons and desires, including second-order desires, or desires about the kind of person she would like to be.
7) Because the agent has access to the content of her mental states, as well as feedback from the external world, she has the ability to reflect and reconsider, and to modify courses of action over time.

Intervention on one's future self is the result of a self-reflective decision. But what legitimates thinking of it as an intervention of a causally efficacious agent who exerts control? I postulate that attention to the nature of control variables accomplishes this.

Recall that Campbell defines control variables as parameters which, when changed, lead to systematic changes in other variables of interest. For example, he points to the gear-shift and steering wheel as control variables for a car: interventions on these lead to systematic changes in the behavior of the car. Let us suppose that the variables of interest here (the effects) are certain types of intentional behavior. Campbell argues that the relevant control variables, at least for some instances of behaviors that matter to us, are at the psychological level (Campbell, 2010). That is, the correct identification of some putative causes of human behavior in terms of control variables will refer to psychological states, and not to physical ones.[8]

One reason that this is the case is that psychological states, and not physical ones, satisfy the manipulability constraint. The constraint can be thought of as restricting potential control loci to features of the world to which the system in question has the kind of access such that it can actually intervene to produce a desired outcome. For example, although there are potentially many physically possible interventions in the internal physical states of a radio that could produce alterations of volume, most of us cannot manipulate the radio's internal states directly: twiddling the volume knob is the one that is accessible to the user. The knob functions as the control variable for volume. Analogously, although the mental supervenes on the physical, agents cannot intentionally directly alter their brain states: we cannot control our brain states by forming intentions whose content makes reference to particular brain states.[9] (We can alter them indirectly, however, by taking drugs, for example). But normally, the control we have of both physical and some mental states is indirect, and effected via our psychological states (e.g. mental states to which we have introspective access). These are the control variables.[10]

Campbell argues that:

> (a) psychological variables function as control variables for the outcomes in which we are interested, (b) what is going on at a psychological level of description supervenes on what is going on at a physical level of description, but (c) at the physical level, there are no control variables for the outcomes in which we are interested. (Campbell, 2010, p.26)

The reason why this is so is that 1) the subject has access to the content of his or her mental states, and not to their physical nature, and indeed, it is in virtue of the content and not the physical realization that the agent makes her choice; and 2) systematic changes to the mental content of a state result in systematic changes to behavior. 1) conforms to the requirement that the control variable be manipulable by local processes; it restricts the control variables to those that are candidates for self-intervention. 2) expresses the importance of systematicity to the notion of prediction and control. It is by manipulating mental content in ways that have foreseeable consequences that we control our own behavior, and are accountable for how we do it.[11] What legitimates thinking of such manipulations as interventions of the agent is the fact that the relevant control variables are subjectively accessible intentional mental states, and not the physical states on which they supervene.[12]

Here I present a few examples of ways in which the mental can serve as control variables for both mental and physical states.

Examples of interventions:

1) Engineering the physical world:

It is a sad fact that I love potato chips. I know I love potato chips, and that once I start eating them, my desire to have just one more is virtually unconquerable. You might consider me a compulsive potato chip eater. But I also have a standing desire to not gain weight, and to eat a healthy diet. Based on those desires, which are my considered desires, and knowledge of my potato-chip-eating habits when in the presence of chips, I have developed a strategy for controlling potato-chip-eating behavior: I avoid putting myself in environments that are conducive to potato-chip-eating. I control my behavior by engineering my environment so that it elicits or makes manifest dispositions I value and does not realize those I disvalue.

Engineering my environment can be the result of forming intentions to be or not be in certain places (i.e. not to spend time in rooms at parties that have those snacks); to act in certain ways that I know may be easier for me than to refrain from eating chips when they are in front of me (I can relatively easily refrain from buying chips at a store, though I may not be able to resist eating them if they are in my house); to seek the company of people who value fitness. By doing these things I deliberately foster some aspects of my self and seek to alter others. Through normal processes of learning and association, these temporary interventions can lead to the alteration of some dispositions and have lasting effects. Pascal had a similar insight when he counseled nonbelievers how to come to believe in God (Pascal, 1670).

2) Influencing the mental

I can intervene on myself by intervening on my future mental states. Commitment, or forming an intention to do something in the future, is a way of intervening on my future self. I can pledge now to do something in the future, when certain conditions hold. I can avoid potato-chip-eating not just by manipulating my physical environment, but also by committing to a cognitive strategy: "I will, when faced with chips, think about x", where x may be my goals for performance in an upcoming race, or how I will look in a bathing suit this summer (see also Mele, 2009, Ch. 7). I may rehearse something so as to deliberately store it in memory, to ensure or increase the chance that it will play a role in future deliberation and action. In addition, and perhaps most importantly, I can set overarching policies ("value accuracy over speed"), or explicitly weight variables in deliberation, both of which can also be thought of as mental interventions (Shadlen & Roskies, 2012). By virtue of these kinds of decisions, I reconfigure neural circuits such that at a future time, a desired mental process unfolds. It is quite clear that I could not have achieved the same reconfiguration by operating or trying to operate directly on my brain states; neuroscientists do not even know what brain states would lead to the desired functional changes.

3) The plasticity of control

One important aspect of agentive control is that it is not static: control variables themselves can be learned, adjusted, and deliberately engineered. Consider the case of biofeedback. The heart is not a voluntary muscle, and I cannot directly intentionally manipulate my heart rate by willing it to go up or down. There is no innate psychological control variable for heart rate. However, there are other control variables for heart rate that I do have access to: I can voluntarily act in ways that modulate my heart rate, such as run, rest, or breathe deeply. I may think thoughts that may as a downstream consequence affect my heart rate, although I may not initially know that those mental contents have control powers over heart rate. However, with appropriate feedback, I can learn what thoughts (e.g. imagine floating in a warm sea, recall scenes from Scream II, etc.) will reliably modulate my heart rate in desired directions, and through these I can indirectly manipulate and exert control over my heart rate, despite the fact that I have no direct access to it. Over time and with training these psychological states or processes will become control variables for heart rate. In analogous ways we can exert control over aspects of our selves, including our behaviors and our dispositions. This example illustrates a number of important points: 1) The importance of feedback and continuous reciprocal interaction with the environment in establishing control; 2) that control skills can improve with practice; 3) that control variables need not (all) be innate; some can be acquired.

In sum, it is in virtue of the content, and via the appreciation, valuation, and weighing/prioritizing of reasons that we can affect our own decision-making. Intervening by affecting mental content corresponds to Campbell's desideratum that the control variables that delineate a cause be manipulable by local processes. In essence, the control panel for our own minds, or the toggles that we have for ourselves are in terms of the contents of our mental states and their rational relationships. Through deliberately thinking and acting in strategic ways we can exert control, modulate and intervene in our future states, both physical and mental. It is this that allows us to shape ourselves in ways that make it the case that we are in some very real sense responsible for who we are.

Digression: The Agentive Perspective

Decision looms large in the interventions described above. One might worry that if determinism were true, I could predict my choices by calculating them from the state of the world, and thus be freed from the necessity of making a choice. But this is impossible. From the position of the agent, the result of his deliberation in a choice is unknowable prior to choosing. This is true both for the hard decisions we typically think of as genuine or "torn" decisions (Balaguer, 2004; Kane, 1999), and for trivial ones. In order to choose, I must know what the options are to choose from, and have some access to reasons that bear upon the choiceworthiness of various options, but I cannot know with certainty prior to choosing what I will choose.

Suppose I believe that my choices are determined, and if they are so determined, they are ultimately determined by facts about the physical state of my brain. The physical state of my brain is objective, and thus at least in principle knowable. Could I, even in principle, employ this knowledge to guide my choices, and thus to make otiose the position of the chooser? No. First, I have no access to the state of my brain, other than indirectly, via the content that I have epistemic access to through thought and introspection, and the emotional responses that I can access via my perception of bodily changes that accompany or partly constitute those emotions. Though my physical state may determine my choice, it cannot do so by influencing my act of choosing through explicit adoption. Moreovoer, as MacKay so effectively argues, any measurements of my physical state that one might theoretically postulate would determine my behavior, if they were to become known to me, would nullify themselves (MacKay, 1960). Hilary Bok very lucidly makes a similar point when she argues that from the agentive perspective, a Pocket Oracle — an external device that could unfailingly predict your choices and actions — could do so only if you refused to consult it (Bok, 1998). In other words, although objective measurements of the brain might enable others to predict my actions,[13] they can reliably do so only if they cannot influence me. Epistemic access to such information is sufficient to negate its value, so that an agent cannot become predictive of itself.

This frames the problem in an important way: there is no sense, even in a deterministic world, in which the agent can opt out of the agentive role by relying on the physical world to tell him what to do. From the standpoint of the agent, there are choices — moments which require decisions, and any way of moving forward requires a decision, and the decision must be taken on the basis of the contents to which the agent has access (e.g. the agent's reasons).[14] This is one reason that the process of deciding is an active, not passive process. It requires the agent's attention, input, awareness, in ways that other kinds of happenings do not. Finally, its outcome is limited by, and thus causally influenced by, the epistemic position of the agent. So in what sense are decisions really decisions, if determinism is true? In a very real, lived sense. These are all reasons to think that decision (and subsequent intention-formation) are processes that, in an important sense, originate with the agent.[15]

So far I have tried to argue that the forward looking part of the problem can be addressed by recognizing that the intentional aspect of control is addressed by the agent's own awareness of her psychological states which constitute reasons for her decisions, and the effective aspect of control is accounted for by her ability to influence her future states by affecting changes via control variables, which are often mental states. However, an issue remains regarding the source of this control. Causal accounts tend to trace causation backward to ever earlier causes. If causal closure is true, then there is a sufficient cause for any physical event, including events we can identify as sources of agentive control. Isn't that another way that we lose agency in a mechanistic world?

Looking Backward: The Threat of the Causal Regress

When we attribute responsibility for something we look for its causes. The transitivity of causation encourages us to trace causes backwards in time. Because we are agents embedded in a causal world, for any event that is an agent's choice or action we quickly find this process leading us to causes that are outside, and not up to, the agent. It is this assumption that makes incompatibilist arguments like van Inwagen's Consequence Argument seem like a compelling challenge to moral responsibility (van Inwagen, 1983).

Recognizing this, Hilary Bok has noted that compatibilists must claim that "because we or our choices have some particular natural property, we have reason to disregard the general rule that responsibility flows backwards along the causal chain when we encounter the choice of an agent." (Bok, 1998, p. 33). This is precisely what I intend to do. When we look backwards to attribute responsibility, we are looking for a certain *kind* of explanation, a reason to say, "The buck stops here." Although all physical events can be traced backward to prior causes, not all causes have equal status in explaining a phenomenon. For example, we might explain the trajectory of a ball by citing the force with which it was thrown, its mass, and the acceleration due to gravity. But prior causes are responsible for those causes, including the birth of the person that threw it, her conception, the meeting of her parents, the coalescing of the rock and gas that now make up our planet, and the fabrication of the ball. Nonetheless, those causes are simply not relevant to an explanation of the ball's trajectory, not even that particular ball's trajectory, once the relevant physical parameters are specified. There are reasons, pragmatic and otherwise, to limit the backward progression in the causal chain when giving an account of events, even when giving a purely causal account. Similarly, there are reasons to pick out some causes as the relevant ones when giving an account of an agent's choice or action.

Why is the relevant cause identified with the agent? As I have argued, the kind of cause we are interested in is an intervention by the deliberative agent on a candidate locus of control, and the relevant control variables for behaviors and for the character they stem from are contentful mental states to which the agent has conscious access and upon which the agent can intervene (the manipulability constraint). The agent is the source of this intervention: she deliberates and chooses by considering her reasons, and not by considering or directly acting upon their physical basis.

The requirement for control variables of what Campbell terms "no gratuitous redundancy" provides another reason to look to the psychological level for causal explanations. It is generally recognized that mental states can be multiply realized, and neuroscience supports the view that physical states are more fine-grained than the mental states they realize. Thus, the same psychological state may supervene on different physical states. To give an account of mental causation in terms of the physical supervenience base would thus involve gratuitous redundancy: one would have to make reference to a disjunction of physical states. The same is not true if we take the control variables to be psychological: the grain of the psychological captures much more succinctly the relevant counterfactuals. This argument for locating the relevant level is similar in spirit to Yablo's argument using the determinable/determinate relation for identifying the psychological level, and not the physical, as the appropriate level for causal explanation of behavior (Yablo, 1992), and to Jackson and Pettit's argument for the causal relevance and efficacy of mental states (Jackson & Pettit, 1990). In other words, reasons-explanations or explanations at the level of psychological states capture the right level of generality to capture relevant counterfactuals; explanations invoking the subvenient brain states do not. This, I believe, is the strategy for addressing Kim's famous exclusion problem (Kim, 1998).[16]

Parfit worries that accounts of action in terms of reasons always give way to a question of physical determination by some event or other, deterministic or indeterministic. Since he believes that neither determinism nor indeterminism leaves room for free will, Parfit thinks freedom is impossible.

> When someone acts for some reason, however, we can ask why this person acted for this reason. In some cases, the answer is given by some further reason...But we shall soon reach the beginning of any such chain of motivating reasons. My ultimate reason for telling my lie may have been to avoid being punished for my crime. When we reach someone's ultimate reason for acting in some way, we can ask why this person acted for this reason, rather than acting in some other way for some other reason. If I had a self-interested reason to try to avoid being punished, and a moral reason not to tell this lie, why did one of these reasons weigh more heavily with me, so that I chose to act as I did? This event did not occur for some further motivating reason. So the suggested third alternative here disappears. This event was either fully caused or partly random. And there is always such an event at the start of any chain of motivating reasons. Since our decisions to act as we do all involve such events, there is no coherent third alternative. (Parfit, 2011, Ch. 11)

In a way, Parfit's problem is our solution. I am not denying that there will always be some kind of non-reason, physical explanation for the presence of a reason, but what I am suggesting is that that is not the place to look. Certainly, our reasons may be elements of us that are in some sense given. But they are not unchangeable. The agent, in appreciating the content of a reason, can intervene in the way in which that reason operates in his deliberation, in loops of agential control. If he or she did not, and by not doing so the agent accepted and endorsed that reason and its role in his deliberation, then for reasons discussed above, that is the appropriate place to stop. Agents control themselves via conscious access to mental content. We therefore have a convenient way of locating the source of the control: at the agentive, aware level.

I should emphasize that to fully understand the picture I sketch here one must be able to shift perspective fluidly between a purely naturalistic framework and the more commonsensical framework usually adopted by those concerned about such things as freedom and responsibility. The shift, however, is not a metaphysical one. Some naturalists will object that I reify a non-natural entity, "the agent", in an attempt to give a naturalistic compatibilist account of agency and responsibility, and that my account of self-intervention invokes the agent as a causal intervener into her own mind/brain processes. On the contrary: I do not mean to deny that an agent-in-control is metaphysically speaking anything over and above a certain kind of complex physical system with appropriate representational and metarepresentational resources, where some meta-representational processes play a role in modulating or regulating the way other processes unfold. But an account of such structure in terms of brute physical processes does little to illuminate the two problems I identify, and I think it is a mistake to do away with the language of the folk metaphysics of agency in this context. It is only by retaining the commonsense notions that inform our intuitions about freedom and responsibility and showing how these relate to a naturalistic account that the worries of those moved by source incompatibilism can begin to be alleviated.

How does this ground Responsibility?

Thus far, I have argued that we can innately use or learn to use psychological states as control variables for intervening on our future states. However, one might question whether the ability to control grounds responsibility. Clearly, how I act ultimately depends on the state of my brain; the state of my brain, as specified by the occurrent configuration of millions or billions of neurons, is not something I can know, and consequently it is not the kind of object that I can, as such, directly intentionally shape. But the previous argument about control variables suggests that it is not the case that I do not have any control over the state of my brain. I do, indirectly, via mental content. That is, just as I can voluntarily modulate my heart rate by thinking certain thoughts, I can have access to certain brain states by virtue of becoming introspectively aware of the content or representations instantiated by those brain states. Over the course of a lifetime, we can learn to intervene on our own brain states and to deliberately alter them. And insofar as we are able to manipulate or regulate our contentful states, we are able to affect, through choice, the people we come to be, to shape our diachronic selves, and to affect our future choices. It is this that Parfit seems to have in mind when he says,

> What we do often depends on our beliefs about what we ought to do. And if we come to believe that some act of ours was wrong, or irrational, because we ought to have acted differently, this belief may lead us to try to change ourselves, or our situation, so that we do not act wrongly, or irrationally, in this kind of way again. These changes in us or our situation may affect what we later do. It does not matter that, for us to have acted differently in the past, we would have had to perform some miracle. If we come to believe that we ought to have acted differently, this change in our beliefs may cause it to be true that in similar cases, without any miracle, we do in the future act differently. (Parfit, 2011, Ch. 11)

My argument has been that if we focus on control variables for behavior then the proper point to stop looking backward for prior causes is at the level of the mental. In virtue of exercising high-level control, or playing with the control variables available to the agent, he or she can be understood to be intervening in her self. Focus on control variables places attention on the appropriate level for identifying causes, via the "no redundancy constraint" in terms of the level of explanation for mental causation as intervention, and, via the "manipulability constraint", on the nature of the states that do the causing. Although we can legitimately ask questions about prior causes for reasons, and specifically for physical causes for reasons, we are not then asking about the kinds of causes that constitute viable control variables for human agents, or the kinds of behaviors we care about. Because of this, when thinking about the question of responsibility, we are not compelled to move beyond reasons to a purely physical event for which we cannot be held responsible.

Determinism Revisited

All this may seem to gain little traction if one hypothesizes that determinism is true. After all, isn't it the case that a person's reasons, values, and deliberation are determined if determinism is true? That even if an agent does exert this kind of control, she had no control over whether she would? This is certainly what lies at the foundation of all incompatibilist worries. But the desire for what might be called "ultimate" control is misplaced. Our concepts of freedom and responsibility are concepts whose function is to regulate human action and interaction. Determinism is not action-guiding, nor is it constraining in a way that impedes what most people mean by freedom. The causal laws merely provide the backdrop against which our lives are lived. In living them, as I argued in my digression on the agentive perspective, determinism has no special relevance.

In contrast, the potential for self-intervention and the necessity of deliberation and decision are paramount. It is because taking account of causal processes (deterministic or not) usually cannot obviate the need for deliberation that the agent is the source, and the proper locus of responsibility, of her decisions, character, or actions.

Being a *Causa Sui*

I hope to have provided a potential refuge for those tempted by source incompatibilism. In closing, I want to look back at alternative notions to the kind of self-causation that I propose that some incompatibilists have thought necessary to ground freedom and responsibility. I argue that nothing as metaphysically problematic as these notions is necessary to ground moral responsibility.

In "Free Agents" Galen Strawson outlines a kind of freedom that could ground desert, or as he says, "justify heaven and hell," which he calls "U-Freedom" (short for Ultimate freedom) (G. Strawson, 2004). He contends that his Basic Argument establishes that U-freedom is impossible because it requires that the agent be self-caused, self-created, or, as he terms it "*a causa sui*". But being a *causa sui*, he argues, is impossible. He continues:

> The notion CAUSA SUI has nothing hidden about it. If it feels obscure, that is only because it is so evidently paradoxical. The feeling of obscurity does not show that the concept CAUSA SUI does not come clear before the mind (the feeling may stem principally from the fact that the notion presents vividly as something impossible, but without the obvious visualizable impossibility of ROUND SQUARE). (G. Strawson, 2004, p. 362)

Strawson's claim that the concept CAUSA SUI is clear is surely mistaken. The unease we feel about the concept CAUSA SUI is due at least in part to the fact that it is not at all clear what precisely is meant by it, quite independent of the question of whether self-causing is possible. There are a variety of different candidate notions, some more paradoxical than others.

Strawson is not the first to argue against the possibility of self-causation. Nietzsche dismissed its coherence long before:

> The desire for 'freedom of the will' in the superlative metaphysical sense, which still holds sway, unfortunately, in the minds of the half-educated; the desire to bear the entire and ultimate responsibility for one's actions oneself, and to absolve God, the world, ancestors, chance, and society involves nothing less than to be precisely this causa sui and, with more than Baron Munchhausen's audacity, to pull oneself up into existence by the hair, out of the swamps of nothingness... (Nietzsche, 1886, Section 21)

One clearly paradoxical way to cash out what it is to be a *causa sui* is to cause oneself to exist or to bring oneself into existence *ex nihilo*. This is what Nietzsche alludes to when he ridicules those who want an account of free will that enables us "to pull oneself up into existence by the hair, out of the swamps of nothingness..." Indeed, if this is what were necessary for ultimate responsibility, the prospects seem very dim. Causes are rarely if ever forces that create something out of nothing. As I have argued above, however, it is not necessary to create oneself out of whole cloth. Continual shaping of the given over time establishes sufficient control of the agent to suffice as a grounding kind of self-causation.

A second way in which being a *causa sui* may be misunderstood is to imagine it requires a type of synchrony that is uncharacteristic of causal relations. That is, what it is to be a *causa sui* is to cause oneself now to do something now. But causation is a diachronic relation, with the causes temporally prior to effects. As I have argued, self-causation should not be expected to be a kind of synchronic causation, as having some effect on one's current self, but rather in terms of doing something at one time to affect oneself at a later time.

A third, common, way in which being a *causa sui* is (mis)understood, is as being an uncaused cause. It is this notion that is elaborated in the kind of agent causal accounts we see from, for example, Chisholm, who writes, "But if a man is responsible for the occurrence of a certain event, then there is some event that is caused, not by other events or states of affairs, but by the man himself, by the agent. If this is true, then each of us, when we really act, is a prime mover unmoved."(Chisholm, 1964). Agents are seen as entities which are in some important respect unbound from the laws of nature, such that in choice situations those laws fail to provide sufficient conditions to determine the agent's choice: the agent himself determines the outcome. Accounts of agent-causation either postulate *sui generis* kinds of causes unknown to science (Chisholm, 1964; O'Connor, 2003), an approach that I reject on naturalistic grounds[17], or they posit an indeterministic element in the agent, which threatens to collapse into an event-causal Libertarian account (i.e. not a source incompatibilist account) (Kane, 1999). Because on such views agents seem to lack control, but rather seem to be controlled by random events, this strategy seems unsuitable as an unpacking of CAUSA SUI. Again, my version of self-causation is in no way predicated on the agent being the first or uncaused cause.

One last way I'll consider in which one might think a *causa sui* must manifest is by contravening or nullifying all other causes, such that the causal influence of the agent trumps all other causal forces. But that is a much stronger criterion than is required: causes can be mere influences that lead to deviations in an already established path for already existent objects, yet they are causes nonetheless, with indisputable influence over future events. To act autonomously, I have suggested, does not require anything as drastic as negation of the causal influence of all or any of the other factors that undoubtedly play a role in shaping our behavior. Autonomous action is action that can coexist with partial determination by a myriad of other forces.

In my view, none of these traditional ways of unpacking the notion of *causa sui* accurately captures what is important for self-causation or authorship, and indeed their lack of plausibility is what may have led so many to jettison the notion of self-causation as impossible or incoherent. Instead, I have argued that there is a coherent and naturalistic notion that captures the essence of what people want in an account of self-origination that serves to ground freedom or responsibility. What it is to be self-caused is to use one's own mental states as control variables to affect one's future mental and physical states, and to intentionally take steps now to affect one's future self. Self-causation is thus less metaphysically demanding than has been previously noted. In brief, to be a *causa sui*, in any sense that we need it, is to be a self-conscious or deliberate shaper of one's character through time. This condition is rather frequently fulfilled by ordinary human beings, and it is sufficient to ground the kind of accountability that we humans are accustomed to bearing and attributing.

Notes

1. I thank Princeton University Center for Human Values for the support that made starting this project feasible. I am very grateful for the invaluable comments of Tori McGeer on an earlier and much inferior version of this paper. Discussions with Paul Benacerraf, Mario de Caro and George Sher were also extremely helpful. The paper has benefitted from the feedback of the 2011–12 LSR fellows at the Princeton University Center for Human Values, and from comments from Robert Kane, Mario de Caro, and Walter Sinnott-Armstrong.
2. Also called "leeway incompatibilists."
3. For the purposes of this paper, I ignore the problem of giving an account of being able to do otherwise, even though this too interacts with the problem of autonomy. Vivehlin does a nice job of this (Vihvelin, in press); It is just too much to bite off here.
4. Not all source incompatibilists are Libertarians. Galen Strawson, for example, we might consider a source impossibilist in that he thinks that our conception of agency is equally threatened by indeterminism. To be sure, the distinction between source and possibility incompatibilists is usually a matter of emphasis; some authors are both. Most source incompatibilists are so presumably because they think that lack of alternative possibilities makes self-authorship impossible, but their arguments focus primarily on the importance of authorship or autonomy.
5. This is roughly what I intend by "self-causation."
6. This problem is closely related to Kim's (1998) exclusion problem for mental causation, applied to higher-level constructs of agency more generally.
7. The notion that control comes from the bottom accords with much about our 21st century folk views of science, where altering the microscopic world can have massive effects on the macroscopic world, from the devastating explosions that can result from the fission of atomic nuclei, to the ravages of cancer that are generated by point mutations in the DNA. And indeed, by focusing on gaining

control of our microscopic world, we have altered the course of human history (or fulfilled it), and have ratified reductionist approaches.

8. I variously refer to events, states, and agents as causes. To say that some state S is a cause is shorthand for the obtaining of [physical or mental] state S being the cause. To say that an agent A is a cause is shorthand for saying that the obtaining of a [physical or mental] state S of A is the cause, where (1) A has subjective access to the content of S, and (2) where that access is important to the explanation of or identification of S as the cause. Also, I do not mean to intimate that psychological states are not also physical; rather, that when identifying control variables, the variable, properly picked out, will be a psychological state that may have multiple physical instantiations, and thus cannot be identified with a single physical state.

9. This is certainly the case now, though may be possible exceptions, such as in a case of supremely advanced brain science.

10. I pause briefly to flag a problem: The argument above seems to require not only that we access, but also directly manipulate our mental states. However, we often cannot directly control the contents of our mental states. I cannot, as a matter of course, choose to believe an arbitrary proposition, nor can I typically choose to desire one thing rather another. The dynamics of thought appears to be largely automatic. The extent to which we can intentionally direct the trajectory of our mental states is an important empirical question, and no doubt will be of intense interest for this and other philosophical projects. Nonetheless, I think we can grant that we often do not choose the content of our next thought without granting that we have no control over mental states. I can manipulate them diachronically, both by setting parameters for contents (choosing high level policies), and by acting in certain ways and engineering my environment so as to affect the future course of my desires and beliefs. These ways of thinking and acting can be thought of as ways to intervene in the course of one's own life. And even if we have no fine-grained forward control over mental content (which we may), I argue that we do have backward-looking, revisionary control that we can employ in forward-looking ways. Mental content can be regulated by training, association, learning. So even if we do not choose what our initial mental rough draft looks like, we are still editors of our selves (Pettit, 2007).

11. For another account of why it is mental content and not the physiological states the content supervenes on, see (Jackson & Pettit, 1990).

12. Some may argue that the only reason that we need to think of self-manipulation in mental terms is because of epistemic limitations, and that the argument so couched reveals nothing about the underlying causal relations or the metaphysics. This is too fast: even if we knew the nature of the brain states at issue, the causal levers that would operate would still be levers of mental content, only the contents would be neural-state contents rather than psychological-state contents. It is also not clear that the effective control relationships would come to rely on purely causal relations, rather than remain at a higher level.

13. This would not be so, of course if indeterminism were true (but here we are assuming determinism as we appeal to the incompatibilist intuitions about autonomy); it may also not be so, if, as many think, chaotic processes were to make prediction in principle impossible, even in a deterministic brain.

14. This is so even if you acknowledge that there are circumstances in which the agent might use a strategy of self-prediction in order to make a decision. To the extent that this is a hard strategy, the decision has already been made. As long as the agent truly considers the other option open, and sees it as a possibility, he cannot predict the outcome.
15. This perspectival aspect of the problem of agency also accounts for at least one other important aspect of agency: its phenomenology.
16. Kim's exclusion problem: Assume mental states supervene on physical states and causal closure is true (for every physical event there is a sufficient physical cause). These are basic tenets of physicalism. Then there is a sufficient physical causal explanation for any event, physical or mental, and the physical causal explanation excludes or makes otiose any reference to mental events as explananda. The upshot is that the mental is epiphenomenal.
17. O'Connor claims his view is naturalistic, but it hard to see why, since he postulates a new kind of event, an agent-causal event, not subject to causal laws.

References

Balaguer, M. (2004). A Coherent, Naturalistic, and Plausible Formulation of Libertarian Free Will. *Nous*, 38(3), 379–406.
Bok, H. (1998). *Freedom and Responsibility*. Princeton, NJ: Princeton University Press.
Campbell, J. (2010). Control Variables and Mental Causation. [Article]. *Proceedings of the Aristotelian Society* 110(1), 15–30.
Chisholm, R. M. (1964). Human Freedom and the Self. *The Lindley Lecture*, 438–445.
Chisholm, R. M. (1976). *Person and Object: A Metaphysical Study*. London: Allen & Unwin.
Doris, J. M. (2005). *Lack of Character: Personality and Moral Behavior*. Cambridge: Cambridge University Press.
Ekstrom, L. (2002). Libertarianism and Frankfurt-Style Cases. In R. Kane (Ed.), *The Oxford Handbook of Free Will* (pp. 309–322). New York: Oxford University Press.
Gold, J. I., & Shadlen, M. N. (2007). The Neural Basis of Decision Making. *Annual Review of Neuroscience*, 30(1), 535–574.
Harman, G. (2000). Moral Philosophy Meets Social Psychology: Virtue Ethics and the Fundamental Attribution Error. In *Explaining Value and Other Essays in Moral Philosophy* (pp. 165–178). Oxford: Oxford University Press.
Hitchcock, C., & Woodward, J. (2003). Explanatory Generalizations, Part II: Plumbing Explanatory Depth. *Nous*, 37(2), 181–199.
Jackson, F., & Pettit, P. (1990). Causation in the Philosophy of Mind. *Philosophy and Phenomenological Research*, 50(Supplement), 195–214.
Kamtekar, R. (2004). Situationism and Virtue Ethics on the Content of Our Character. *Ethics*, 114, 458–491.
Kane, R. (1996). *The Significance of Free Will*. New York: Oxford University Press.
Kane, R. (1999). Responsibility, Luck, and Chance: Reflections on Free Will and Indeterminism. *Journal of Philosophy*, 96, 217–240.
Kim, J. (1998). *Mind in a Physical World: An Essay on the Mind-Body Problem and Mental Causation*. Cambridge, MA: MIT Press.
Korsgaard, C. M. (2009). *Self-Constitution: Agency, Identity and Integrity*. Oxford: Oxford University Press.
MacKay, D. M. (1960). On the Logical Indeterminacy of a Free Choice. *Mind*, 69(273), 31–40.
Mele, A. (2009). *Effective Intentions: The Power of Conscious Will*. New York: Oxford University Press.

Nagel, T. (1993). Moral Luck. In D. Statman (Ed.), *Moral Luck*: State University of New York Press.

Nahmias, E. (2006). Folk Fears about Freedom and Responsibility: Determinism vs. Reductionism. *The Journal of Cognition and Culture*, 6(1–2), 215–237.

Nahmias, E., Coates, D. J., & Kvaran, T. (2007). Free Will, Moral Responsibility, and Mechanism: Experiments on Folk Intuitions. *Midwest Studies in Philosophy*, 31, 215–242.

Nahmias, E., Morris, S., Nadelhoffer, T., & Turner, J. (2005). Surveying Freedom: Folk Intuitions about Free Will and Responsibility. *Philosophical Psychology*, 18(5), 561–584.

Nichols, S. (2004). The Folk Psychology of Free Will: Fits and starts. *Mind and Language*, 19, 473–502.

Nichols, S. (2006). Folk Intuitions on Free Will. *Journal of Cognition and Culture*, 6(1–2), 57–86.

Nietzsche, F. W. (1886). *Beyond good and evil*.

O'Connor, T. (2003). Agent Causation. In G. Watson (Ed.), *Free Will* (2nd ed., pp. 257–284). Oxford: Oxford University Press.

Parfit, D. (2011). *On What Matters*. New York: Oxford University Press.

Pascal, B. (1670). *Pensees* (W. F. Trotter, Trans.).

Pereboom, D. (2001). *Living Without Free Will*. Cambridge: Cambridge University Press.

Pettit, P. (2007). Neuroscience and agent control. In D. Ross, D. Spurrett, H. Kincaid & G. L. Stephens (Eds.), *Distributed Cognition and the Will* (pp. 77–91). Cambridge, MA: MIT Press.

Shadlen, M. N., & Roskies, A. L. (2012). The Neurobiology of Decision-Making and Responsibility: Reconciling Mechanism and Mindedness. *Frontiers in Decision Sciences*, 6(56), 1–12.

Strawson, G. (2004). Free Agents. *Philosphical Topics*.

Strawson, P. F. (1982). Freedom and Resentment. In G. Watson (Ed.), *Free Will* (pp. 59–80). Oxford: Oxford University Press.

Turner, J., & Nahmias, E. (2006). Are the Folk Agent-Causationists? *Mind & Language*, 21(5), 597–609.

van Inwagen, P. (1983). *An Essay on Free Will*. Oxford: Clarendon Press.

Vihvelin, K. (in press). *Causes, Laws, and Free Will: An Essay on the Determinism Problem*: Oxford University Press.

Woodward, J. (2005). *Making Things Happen: A Theory of Causal Explanation*. New York: Oxford University Press.

Woodward, J., & Hitchcock, C. (2003). Explanatory Generalizations, Part I: A Counterfactual Account. *Nous*, 37(1), 1–24.

Yablo, S. (1992). Mental Causation. *The Philosophical Review*, 101(2), 245–280.

Philosophical Perspectives, 26, Philosophy of Mind, 2012

THE MENTAL LIVES OF ZOMBIES

Declan Smithies
The Ohio State University

1. Consciousness and Cognition

A *zombie* is a creature that is just like a conscious subject in all relevant physical, functional or behavioral respects, except that it has no conscious states — there is nothing it is like to be a zombie.[1] Zombies have figured prominently in metaphysical debates about the nature of consciousness, but they can also be usefully employed in raising questions about the relationship between consciousness and cognition. Could there be a *cognitive zombie* — that is, a creature with the capacity for cognition but with no capacity for consciousness? By definition, zombies cannot have conscious states, but can they nevertheless have cognitive states, such as beliefs, and cognitive processes, such as reasoning and other forms of rational belief revision?

In this paper, I am primarily concerned with conceptual questions about the relationship between consciousness and cognition. As far as possible, I want to remain neutral on empirical questions about the functional role of consciousness and metaphysical questions about the nature of consciousness and its place in the physical world. So, when I ask whether there could be cognitive zombies, the relevant modality is conceptual possibility, rather than physical possibility or metaphysical possibility. The question is whether cognitive zombies are conceptually possible or impossible — that is, whether they can be coherently conceived or whether this involves some kind of inherent conceptual confusion.[2]

Without attempting to provide an exhaustive taxonomy, I want to organize my discussion around three contrasting perspectives on the relationship between consciousness and cognition. Proponents of *bifurcationism* deny that there is any interesting conceptual connection between consciousness and cognition.[3] In contrast, proponents of *unificationism* agree that there is an interesting conceptual connection between consciousness and cognition, although they disagree about its nature. Some proponents of unificationism endorse a *cognitive*

344 / Declan Smithies

analysis of consciousness on which consciousness is analyzed in terms of its role in cognition.[4] Others endorse a *phenomenal analysis of cognition* on which cognition is analyzed in terms of its relations to consciousness.[5] Thus, proponents of unificationism agree that there is a conceptual connection between consciousness and cognition, although they disagree about whether consciousness is to be analyzed in terms of cognition, or vice versa.

Bifurcationism, which is perhaps the dominant view of the connection between consciousness and cognition, often takes the following form. The concept of consciousness is a *phenomenal* concept that defines consciousness in terms of "what it is like" for the subject. The concept of cognition, on the other hand, is a *functional* concept that defines cognition by its causal role. And crucially, according to proponents of bifurcationism, the phenomenal concept of consciousness is distinct from any functional concept that defines cognition by its causal role.[6]

One symptom of bifurcationism is the widespread view that the problem of explaining consciousness is a *hard problem*, whereas the problem of explaining cognition is an *easy problem*.[7] Explaining consciousness is viewed as a hard problem on the grounds that there is an *explanatory gap* between physical and functional facts on the one hand and phenomenal facts on the other: in other words, it is conceivable that the same physical or functional facts could give rise to different conscious states or none at all. Explaining cognition, by contrast, is viewed as an easy problem on the grounds that there is no such explanatory gap for cognition: it is inconceivable that the same physical or functional facts could give rise to different cognitive states or none at all. Indeed, it is widely held that cognition, unlike consciousness, can be explained in broadly functionalist terms by appealing to the causal properties of physical states. Therefore, proponents of bifurcationism tend to claim that cognition can be explained in functional terms, while denying that consciousness can be so explained.[8]

Unificationism, however, implies that the problem of explaining cognition is intertwined with the problem of explaining consciousness. In that case, the prospects for explaining cognition in physical or functional terms stand or fall with the prospects for explaining consciousness in physical or functional terms. These prospects may seem better or worse depending on the nature of the conceptual connections that are claimed to hold between consciousness and cognition. Given a cognitive analysis of consciousness, we can derive an explanation of consciousness from a prior explanation of cognition, and so the difficulty of explaining consciousness can be ameliorated by the ease of explaining cognition. Given a phenomenal analysis of cognition, on the other hand, an explanation of cognition depends upon a prior explanation of consciousness, and so the problem of explaining cognition inherits the difficulty of explaining consciousness.

Unificationism and bifurcationism have different implications for the question of whether cognitive zombies are coherently conceivable. Bifurcationism seems committed to the conceivability of cognitive zombies as a consequence

Table 1

	Functional zombies?	Cognitive zombies?
Cognitive Analysis of Consciousness	No	No
Phenomenal Analysis of Cognition	Yes	No
Bifurcationism	Yes	Yes

of the following two-step argument. First, it is conceivable that there could be a *functional zombie* — that is, a zombie that is a functional duplicate of some conscious creature that has a capacity for cognition. And second, it is inconceivable that a functional zombie, so defined, should lack the capacity for cognition. Therefore, we have the following simple argument for the conceivability of cognitive zombies:

(1) Functional zombies are conceivable.
(2) Functional zombies that lack cognition are inconceivable.
(3) Therefore, cognitive zombies are conceivable.

To illustrate, consider Block's (2002) example of Commander Data, who is functionally just like us, at least at the level of commonsense psychology, but who is physically unlike us insofar as his brain is silicon-based, rather than carbon-based. It seems conceivable that Data is conscious, but it also seems conceivable that he is a zombie; indeed, as Block puts the point, it is an open question whether or not Data is conscious and, moreover, it is a question that we have no conception of how to close. Nevertheless, Block would claim that Commander Data has cognition, since he has states that play the right kind of causal role in the production of behavior.

Unificationism, on the other hand, seems committed to denying that cognitive zombies are coherently conceivable, although the rationale for this will depend upon the nature of the conceptual connections that are claimed to hold between consciousness and cognition. On a cognitive analysis of consciousness, cognitive zombies are inconceivable because functional zombies are inconceivable. Any functional duplicate of a conscious creature with the capacity for cognition is thereby a conscious creature with the capacity for cognition. Therefore, proponents of a cognitive analysis of consciousness accept the second premise of the zombie argument, but they reject the first premise. On a phenomenal analysis of cognition, cognitive zombies are also inconceivable, but for different reasons. Functional zombies are conceivable, but since cognition is analyzed in terms of consciousness, it is inconceivable that any zombie (functional or otherwise) could have cognition. Thus, proponents of a phenomenal analysis of cognition accept the first premise of the zombie argument, but they reject the second premise.

All three perspectives are represented in Table 1.

With these options in mind, let me outline the goals of the paper. The main goal is to argue for the incoherence of cognitive zombies by appealing to a phenomenal analysis of cognition, as opposed to a cognitive analysis of consciousness. Indeed, for present purposes, I will set aside the cognitive analysis of consciousness and work on the assumption (in my view, a plausible one) that functional zombies are coherently conceivable. The task remains to argue against bifurcationism by articulating, defending and motivating a phenomenal analysis of cognition on which it is inconceivable that functional zombies have cognition.

Although I am not the first to propose a phenomenal analysis of cognition, my arguments are different from the familiar ones. The usual strategy is to argue that the connection between consciousness and cognition is a consequence of a more fundamental connection between consciousness and intentionality. As I will explain, however, there are good empirical reasons for rejecting the proposed connection between consciousness and intentionality. My strategy, in contrast, is to argue that the connection between consciousness and cognition can be derived from a more fundamental connection between consciousness and rationality. As such, this paper forms part of a much larger project of exploring the normative role of consciousness and its implications for our mental lives.[9]

2. Two Conceptions of Cognition

Could there be a cognitive zombie? Let us suppose, at least for the sake of the argument, that there could be a functional zombie — that is, an unconscious creature that is a functional duplicate of a conscious creature with a capacity for cognition. It is a further question whether functional zombies have cognition. Do functional zombies have cognitive states, such as beliefs, and cognitive processes, such as reasoning and rational belief revision? Perhaps not surprisingly, the answer to this question depends upon how we understand the concept of cognition. In this section, I draw a distinction between two conceptions of cognition — the *behavioral* analysis and the *phenomenal* analysis — that have different implications for the question of whether functional zombies have cognition.

2.1 The Behavioral Analysis

On the *behavioral analysis of cognition*, beliefs and other cognitive states are analyzed in terms of their dispositions to cause physical behavior. The behavioral analysis comes in simpler and more sophisticated versions. In particular, we can distinguish between *analytical behaviorism*, which is the earliest and simplest incarnation of the behavioral analysis of cognition, and *analytical functionalism*, which is a more sophisticated descendent of analytical behaviorism.[10]

According to analytical behaviorism, all psychological concepts, including the concept of belief, can be given a reductive analysis in terms of behavioral dispositions described in wholly non-psychological terms. On this view, there are conceptual truths of the form: one has a belief B if and only if one has a disposition D to engage in physical behavior P in circumstances C. The standard objection to this view is that the analysis is circular, since we cannot specify the circumstances in which beliefs manifest themselves in behavior without making reference to the presence or absence of background beliefs. Given the holistic relationship between beliefs and behavioral dispositions, we cannot analyze beliefs in terms of their behavioral dispositions alone.

Analytical functionalism retains the same ambition to give a reductive analysis of psychological concepts such as belief in terms of non-psychological concepts such as physical behavior. However, it avoids the circularity problem by giving an analysis of beliefs and other psychological states in terms of their place in a causal network that grounds behavioral dispositions holistically, rather than atomistically. As Lewis (1972) explains, we begin with an explicit statement of the causal relationships between psychological states, environmental inputs and behavioral outputs using the terms of our commonsense psychological theory. Next, we generate the *Ramsey sentence* for the theory by eliminating all the psychological terms in the theory and systematically replacing them with existentially quantified bound variables. The result is a complex definite description that specifies the causal role of beliefs and other psychological states in non-psychological terms.

Block (1978) and others have argued that analytical functionalism fails as an analysis of consciousness. There seems to be no incoherence in the idea that a zombie could satisfy the Ramsey sentence for commonsense psychology. All we need is a functional isomorphism that maps states of a conscious creature onto states of the zombie in a way that preserves causal relations between them. Nevertheless, Block does not reject functionalism altogether. Instead, he recommends the *containment response* — that is, to abandon the functionalist analysis of consciousness, while retaining the functionalist analysis of cognition.[11] On this proposal, there could be a cognitive zombie, since satisfying the Ramsey sentence for commonsense psychology is sufficient for cognition, although it is not sufficient for consciousness.[12]

Despite Block's recommendation, however, it is not clear that we should accept this containment response. Why should we suppose that the functional role of cognition can be specified without appealing to phenomenal consciousness? After all, beliefs are dispositional states that manifest themselves not only in physical behavior, but also in phenomenal consciousness. So why privilege behavioral dispositions, as opposed to phenomenal dispositions, in the analysis of cognition?

In historical terms, the behavioral analysis of psychological concepts seems to have been motivated primarily by verificationist assumptions about semantics together with a desire to avoid certain metaphysical and epistemological problems about consciousness, such as dualism and skepticism about other minds.[13] However, the containment response cannot be motivated in this way, since it eschews any behavioral or functional analysis of consciousness. If the metaphysical and epistemological problems of consciousness can be solved, then there is no need for containment, but if they cannot be solved, then containment will not be enough to make them go away. So, unless the containment response can be motivated on other grounds, the suspicion will remain that it is an ideological relic of a previous era.

2.2 The Phenomenal Analysis

On the *phenomenal analysis of cognition*, beliefs and other cognitive states are analyzed in terms of their dispositions to cause phenomenally conscious episodes of judgment, rather than their dispositions to cause physical behavior. Unlike the behavioral analysis, the phenomenal analysis makes no attempt to give a reduction of psychological concepts in non-psychological terms. This removes an obstacle that otherwise prevents one from appealing to phenomenal consciousness in an analysis of cognition. In this section, I will articulate a phenomenal analysis of cognition and defend it against some preliminary objections, but I will defer the task of motivating this analysis until later sections of the paper.

I begin with a distinction between belief and judgment. As I use the term, judgments are phenomenally conscious episodes that have phenomenal character: there is something it is like for a subject to judge that a proposition is true. Moreover, judgments are individuated by their phenomenal character: two judgments are judgments of the same kind if and only if they have the same phenomenal character. Beliefs, unlike judgments, have no phenomenal character: there need be nothing it is like for a subject to believe that a proposition is true. Nevertheless, beliefs are disposed to cause phenomenally conscious judgments; indeed, they are individuated by these dispositions: two beliefs are beliefs of the same kind if and only if they are disposed to cause judgments with the same phenomenal character.[14]

Just as there is a distinction between outright belief and outright judgment, so there is a distinction between degrees of belief and their manifestations in phenomenal consciousness as feelings of confidence in a given proposition. One's feelings of confidence are phenomenally conscious episodes that are individuated by their phenomenal character, whereas one's degrees of belief are individuated by their dispositions to cause the phenomenal character of feelings of confidence. In this way, the phenomenal analysis of outright belief can be plausibly extended to degrees of belief too.

Beliefs and judgments are *intentional* states — they are intentional attitudes towards intentional contents that specify the conditions under which they are true. Moreover, it is widely assumed that beliefs and judgments are individuated by their intentional properties — that is, by their intentional contents and their intentional attitude-types. However, we need not choose between individuating beliefs and judgments in terms of their intentional properties, as opposed to their phenomenal properties, or the phenomenal properties that they are disposed to cause. Given plausible assumptions, these are equivalent ways of individuating them.

The key assumption is that the phenomenal character of judgment is sufficient to determine its intentional content and its intentional attitude-type. On this assumption, the phenomenal character of judgment is *content-specific* and *attitude-specific* in the sense that what it is like to judge a proposition is different from what it is like to adopt the same attitude towards a different proposition and what it is like to judge a proposition is different from what it is like to adopt a different attitude towards the same proposition. This assumption is not uncontroversial, but it has been widely discussed elsewhere, and so for present purposes, I will simply take it for granted.[15]

One important objection to the assumption above is that the intentional contents of beliefs and judgments are externally individuated by their relations to the environment. On this view, there can be phenomenal duplicates whose beliefs and judgments have different intentional contents in virtue of their different relations to the environment. However, this is consistent with the claim that the beliefs and judgments of phenomenal duplicates also share intentional contents in virtue of their shared phenomenal character. Thus, we can distinguish between the *narrow* contents of belief and judgment that are individuated by their phenomenal character alone and the *wide* contents of belief and judgment that are individuated by their phenomenal character together with their relations to the environment.[16]

Another objection to the phenomenal analysis of cognition is that there are familiar cases of self-deception in which one's dispositions towards judgment come apart from one's dispositions to engage in physical behavior. Moreover, in such cases, there is some tendency to suppose that our beliefs are reflected in our actions, rather than our judgments. For instance, Peacocke (1998) gives the example of an academic on a hiring committee who is disposed to judge that foreign degrees are equal in standard to domestic degrees, although her votes in hiring decisions reveal that she does not really believe this; indeed, what she really believes is that foreign degrees are inferior, although this is not what she is disposed to judge. So described, the case presents a counterexample to the phenomenal analysis of belief.

My response is to dispute this description of the case. One possibility is that the academic has inconsistent beliefs. In some contexts, such as hiring decisions, she may be disposed to judge that foreign degrees are equal, while in other contexts, such as the local tavern, she may be disposed to judge that foreign degrees are inferior. We can explain away any lingering temptation to say that what she *really* believes is that foreign degrees are inferior, since this is the belief that is primarily operative in guiding her behavior in hiring decisions.

Alternatively, perhaps there are no suitable contexts in which the academic is disposed to judge that foreign degrees are inferior to domestic degrees. In that case, she does not believe that foreign degrees are inferior, although she behaves in many respects *as if* she does.[17] In that case, her rational defect is practical, rather than epistemic. We may assume that her beliefs and judgments are rationally formed in a way that is appropriately responsive to the evidence. Her problem is not that her beliefs are unjustified, but rather that her behavior is unjustified, since her justified beliefs fail to exert an appropriate influence on her behavior.

We can imagine cases in which one's behavioral dispositions are even more radically dissociated from one's dispositions towards judgment. For instance, Strawson (1994) gives the following example of the Weather Watchers:

> The Weather Watchers are a race of sentient, intelligent creatures. They are distributed about the surface of their planet, rooted to the ground, profoundly interested in the local weather. They have sensations, thoughts, emotions, beliefs, desires. They possess a conception of an objective, spatial world. But they are constitutionally incapable of any sort of behavior, as this is ordinarily understood. They lack the necessary physiology. Their mental lives have no other-observable effects. They are not even disposed to behave in any way. (1994: 251)

Strawson claims that the Weather Watchers have beliefs about the local weather, although their beliefs do not dispose them to engage in physical behavior at all. According to the behavioral analysis, of course, the case is incoherent as described, since beliefs are analyzed in terms of their behavioral dispositions. According to the phenomenal analysis, however, the case is perfectly coherent, since beliefs are analyzed in terms of their phenomenal dispositions, which are merely contingently associated with their behavioral dispositions.

These two conceptions of cognition — the behavioral analysis and the phenomenal analysis – also have different implications for the conceivability of cognitive zombies. If cognition is analyzed in terms of its phenomenal dispositions, as the phenomenal analysis claims, then cognitive zombies are incoherent. But if cognition is analyzed in terms of its behavioral dispositions, as the behavioral analysis claims, then cognitive zombies are perfectly coherent. What basis do we have, then, for deciding between these competing conceptions of cognition?

2.3 A Terminological Debate?

Our ordinary concept of belief is associated with a cluster of dispositions, including dispositions to make judgments, dispositions to engage in behavior, and perhaps other dispositions besides. These dispositions usually come together, but there are conceivable scenarios, such as zombie scenarios, in which they come apart. Do we have any principled reasons for privileging some of the dispositions in the cluster, rather than others, for purposes of analyzing the concept of belief?

Or is this merely to insist on a terminological stipulation about how to use the word 'belief'?

Schwitzgebel (2002, 2010) avoids the choice between the phenomenal analysis and the behavioral analysis by opting instead for a cluster analysis on which one has a belief just in case one has enough of the dispositions in the cluster that is associated with our ordinary use of the term 'belief'. On this view, there are cases of "in-between believing" in which it is indeterminate whether or not one has a belief because one has some but not all of the dispositions in the cluster. Presumably, for instance, it is indeterminate whether or not zombies have beliefs, since they have the behavioral dispositions, but not the phenomenal dispositions, that are associated with the concept of belief. Of course, we might sharpen the concept of belief in such a way as to deliver a determinate answer to the question of whether or not zombies have beliefs. However, the question remains whether there is any substantive question, as opposed to a merely terminological one, about whether we should precisify the concept of belief in one way rather than another.

Chalmers (1996) draws a distinction between two concepts of mind — the phenomenal concept of mind as conscious experience and the psychological concept of mind as the causal-explanatory basis of behavior. Moreover, Chalmers claims that there is no substantial question, as opposed to a merely terminological question, about which of these is the correct analysis of mind:

> On the phenomenal concept of mind, mind is characterized by the way it *feels*; on the psychological concept, mind is characterized by what it *does*. There should be no question of competition between these two notions of mind. Neither of them is *the* correct analysis of mind. They cover different phenomena, both of which are quite real. (1996: 11)

The distinction between phenomenal and behavioral (or psychological) conceptions of cognition is a special case of Chalmers' distinction between two concepts of mind. Accordingly, perhaps there is no substantial question, as opposed to a merely terminological question, about which is the correct analysis of cognition. Everyone can agree that zombies have beliefs in the behavioral sense, but not in the phenomenal sense. The only question that remains is whether we should use the term 'belief' to express the phenomenal concept or the behavioral concept of belief, but this seems like a merely terminological question, rather than a substantive one.

In more recent work, Chalmers (2011) makes a useful methodological proposal about how to avoid terminological debates of this kind. The proposal is that we should begin by clarifying the theoretical roles that we associate with the concept of belief, and then ask what belief must be like in order to play that role:

> On the picture I favor, instead of asking, 'What is X', one should focus on the roles one wants X to play, and see what can play that role. . . . [I]nstead of asking,

"What is a belief? What is it to believe?" and expecting a determinate answer, one can instead focus on the various roles one wants belief to play, and say, here are some interesting states: B_1 can play these roles, B_2 can play these roles, B_3 can play these roles. Not much hangs on the residual terminological question of which is really belief. (2011: 538)

I agree wholeheartedly with this proposal. We need not concern ourselves with questions about our ordinary use of the term 'belief', such as whether we use it in a way that expresses the phenomenal concept, the behavioral concept, or some cluster concept. Instead, we should ask which of these concepts are most useful for us to have because they pick out states that play an important theoretical role. Moreover, we should be open to a form of pluralism on which our ordinary concept of belief conflates a range of useful concepts, each of which picks out a unique kind of state that plays an important and distinctive theoretical role.

My goal in this paper is to argue that the phenomenal concept of belief picks out a kind of state that plays an important and distinctive theoretical role. I do not intend to deny that there are other concepts in the vicinity that pick out more generic or more specific kinds of states that also play an important and distinctive theoretical role. My claim is simply that there is an important theoretical distinction in the vicinity of our ordinary concept of belief that cannot be drawn except in terms of phenomenal consciousness. This is a substantive claim, and not merely a terminological one, which many philosophers are inclined to reject. Indeed, Chalmers himself claims that we can "subtract out" the phenomenal component of belief without thereby sacrificing anything of theoretical importance:

The most substantial requirements for having a specific belief will lie elsewhere than in the phenomenal. One could even subtract any phenomenal component out, leaving a concept of pseudobelief that resembles belief in most important respects except that it does not involve the concept of consciousness. Indeed, it is plausible that pseudobelief could do most of the explanatory work that is done by the concept of belief. (1996: 20)

Chalmers' claim here is that the phenomenal concept of belief does not correspond to any theoretically interesting kind of state and so, for theoretical purposes, it is the behavioral (or psychological) concept, rather than the phenomenal concept, that we should be interested in. The challenge for proponents of the phenomenal analysis is to show that there is some theoretically important role that a belief can play if and only if it is individuated by its relations to phenomenal consciousness.

In what follows, I consider two ways of arguing for the theoretical significance of phenomenal consciousness in an analysis of cognition. The first strategy is to argue that the connection between consciousness and cognition is a consequence of a more fundamental connection between consciousness and intentionality. However, I argue that there are good empirical reasons for rejecting the proposed connection between consciousness and intentionality. Instead, I propose an alternative strategy on which the connection between consciousness and cognition is explained as a consequence of a more fundamental connection between consciousness and rationality.

3. Consciousness and Intentionality

What is the relationship between consciousness and intentionality? Many contemporary philosophers endorse a weak version of *intentionalism*, according to which all conscious states are intentional states:

> Intentionalism: all conscious states are intentional states.

Some philosophers also endorse the converse of intentionalism, which we might call the *intentional connection thesis*.[18] In its strongest version, the intentional connection thesis says that all intentional states are conscious states. But there is also a weaker version, which says that all intentional states are either conscious states or they are individuated by their relations to conscious states:

> The intentional connection thesis: all intentional states are either conscious states or they are individuated by their relations to conscious states.

If the intentional connection thesis is true, then all intentional states are states of conscious creatures and so there cannot be an *intentional zombie*.[19] Moreover, assuming that all cognitive states are intentional states, it follows that all cognitive states are states of conscious creatures and so there cannot be a *cognitive zombie*. In this way, the connection between consciousness and cognition can be derived from a more fundamental connection between consciousness and intentionality:

(1) All cognitive states are intentional states.
(2) All intentional states are either conscious states or individuated by their relations to conscious states.
(3) So, all cognitive states are either conscious states or individuated by their relations to conscious states.

The first premise seems uncontroversial, but the second premise stands in need of further argument. Why should we accept the proposed connection between intentionality and consciousness?

Perhaps the most influential line of argument is that the intentional connection thesis is needed in order to explain the intentionality of cognition in a way that avoids the problem of radical indeterminacy.[20] There are well known attempts to explain the intentionality of cognition in broadly causal terms by appealing to the functional role of intentional states in cognition together with their causal relations to environmental inputs and behavioral outputs. However, these causal theories of intentionality face equally well known problems explaining how the intentionality of cognition is not radically indeterminate.[21]

Some argue that the problem of radical indeterminacy arises because of a failure to appreciate the role that consciousness plays in securing the determinate intentionality of cognition. The suggestion is that conscious states have determinate intentionality in virtue of their determinate phenomenal character, while unconscious states have determinate intentionality in virtue of their relations to the determinate phenomenal character of phenomenally conscious states. This yields the following argument for the intentional connection thesis:

(1) All intentional states have determinate intentional properties in virtue of being conscious or individuated by their relations to conscious states.

(2) So, all intentional states are either conscious states or individuated by their relations to conscious states.

I will argue, however, that the argument rests on a false premise: we have good empirical reasons to suppose that some intentional states have determinate intentional properties, although they are neither conscious nor individuated by their relations to consciousness.

In rejecting the premise, of course, one takes on the burden of explaining intentionality in a way that solves the problem of radical indeterminacy, while avoiding any appeal to consciousness. This is a heavy burden. After all, it is not an attractive option to take intentionality as a primitive and irreducible feature of the world.[22] And yet nobody has succeeded in showing how intentionality can be reductively explained in purely causal terms in such a way as to avoid the problem of radical indeterminacy. Following Lewis (1983), it may be that we can give a reductive explanation of intentionality that avoids radical indeterminacy if we supplement the appeal to causation with further assumptions about the eligibility of objects in the world to serve as the objects of our intentional states. In any case, I assume that one of these options must be viable, since we have good empirical reasons to reject the intentional connection thesis.

Let us begin with the strongest version of the intentional connection thesis, which states that all intentional states are conscious states. This version of the intentional connection thesis conflicts with the explanatory role that unconscious intentional states play in commonsense psychology and scientific psychology alike. For instance, commonsense explanations of action appeal to unconscious beliefs, desires and intentions of the agent, while computational explanations in cognitive science appeal to computational processes defined over unconscious mental representations, such as Chomsky's (1965) tacit knowledge of syntax and Marr's (1982) primal, 2.5D, and 3D sketch.

Some proponents of the intentional connection thesis claim that, strictly speaking, there is no unconscious intentionality, although it can be useful to speak metaphorically as if there were.[23] However, unconscious intentionality seems to play an indispensable role in psychological explanation in common sense and cognitive science. Moreover, we have good reasons to believe in existence of these states, rather than regarding them as useful fictions, insofar as they play an indispensable role in explanation. After all, it is a widely accepted methodological precept that we ought to believe in the entities posited by our best theories. Therefore, we should endorse realism, rather than eliminativism or instrumentalism, about the existence of unconscious intentional states.

Others weaken the intentional connection thesis in an attempt to make it consistent with the existence of unconscious intentionality. The general idea is that all unconscious intentionality is individuated by its relations to consciousness. Consider Searle's (1990) connection principle:

> The ascription of an unconscious intentional phenomenon to a system implies that the phenomenon is in principle accessible to consciousness. (1990: 333)

According to Searle, an unconscious intentional phenomenon is "accessible to consciousness" just in case it is "potentially conscious" in the sense that it is "a possible conscious thought or experience" (1990: 336). This prompts the objection that beliefs are not accessible to consciousness, since they are distinct from the potentially conscious manifestations that they cause. However, there is a more plausible variation on Searle's proposal, according to which the *contents* of beliefs are accessible to consciousness as the contents of conscious judgments. This proposal is best understood as a consequence of the claim that beliefs are individuated wholly by their dispositions to cause judgments with a certain content-specific phenomenal character. As Searle acknowledges, however, this proposal cannot be extended to the "subdoxastic" mental representations that figure in computational explanations in cognitive science.[24]

Subdoxastic states, unlike beliefs, are not individuated wholly by their disposition to cause phenomenally conscious states. On the contrary, they are individuated at least in part by their dispositions to play a role in computational processes that occur below the level of phenomenal consciousness. To illustrate the point, consider Davies' (1989) hypothetical example of states of tacit knowledge of language that are disposed to cause phenomenally conscious itches or tickles. Presumably, what makes it the case that these states embody tacit knowledge of language is not their disposition to cause itches and tickles, but rather their roles in linguistic processing.

Consider Quine's (1970) challenge to Chomsky's notion of tacit knowledge. Quine's challenge is to explain what constitutes tacit knowledge of a rule if it is less demanding than explicit knowledge of the rule, but more demanding than merely exhibiting linguistic behavior that conforms to the rule. The standard account is that tacit knowledge of a rule is a matter of the causal structure in the psychological processes that underpin one's linguistic behavior.[25] More specifically, one has tacit knowledge of a rule if and only if the causal structure

356 / Declan Smithies

of one's psychology mirrors the logical structure of a theory that includes that rule. There could be two subjects that exhibit the same linguistic behavior, although their behavior is explained by psychological processes that embody tacit knowledge of different linguistic rules. Thus, tacit knowledge is individuated not merely by its disposition to cause linguistic behavior, but also by its role in psychological processes that occur beneath the level of phenomenal consciousness.

This point can be generalized to other subdoxastic mental representations, including those involved in vision. There could be two subjects that have the same visual experiences, although their visual experiences are explained by different kinds of visual processing involving different representations and rules. Thus, visual representations and rules are individuated not just by their role in explaining conscious experience, but also by their role in psychological processing that occurs beneath the level of phenomenal consciousness.

One reaction would be to weaken the intentional connection thesis even further so as to allow for subdoxastic mental representations that are individuated in part by their role in unconscious computational processes, but also in part by their relations to conscious states. After all, this weakened version of the intentional connection thesis is strong enough to sustain the claim that all intentional states are states of conscious subjects and hence that there cannot be an intentional zombie. For instance, Horgan and Graham (2012) claim that consciousness is an "anchor point" for intentionality in the sense that all unconscious intentional states are causally integrated within a network that includes conscious intentional states. This seems plausible for some, but not all, unconscious intentional states. Some visual representations are constrained by their role in explaining the intentional properties of conscious visual experience, but there are others that play no role in explaining the intentional properties of conscious visual experience and which are individuated wholly by their role in explaining behavior.

To illustrate the point, consider Milner and Goodale's (1995) distinction between two visual streams: the ventral stream processes visual information for the conscious identification and recognition of objects, while the dorsal stream processes visual information for the unconscious control of action. This hypothesis is designed to explain a range of empirical data, including cases in which one's experience of an object conflicts with the way in which one acts upon the object. In the Titchener illusion, for example, subjects whose experience misrepresents the size of a coin are able to accurately proportion the size of their grip in reaching for the coin. In such a case, one's experience of the coin is explained by representations in the ventral stream that misrepresent the size of the coin, while the spatial parameters of one's visually guided action are explained by representations in the dorsal stream that accurately represent the size of the coin.

If this hypothesis is correct, then visual representations in the ventral stream are individuated in part by their role in explaining the conscious identification and recognition of objects, whereas visual representations in the dorsal stream are individuated wholly by their role in the unconscious control of action. Of course, there are some functional connections between the dorsal stream and the ventral stream, but these connections are highly circumscribed. Moreover, if vision evolved in response to motor demands, as Milner and Goodale claim, then we should expect to find phylogenetically more ancient creatures that have some analogue of the dorsal stream, but no analogue of the ventral stream. Presumably, for instance, honey bees and desert ants have perceptual systems that explain the complex, relational properties of their behavior, although it is an open question whether or not these creatures are conscious.[26]

I conclude that the intentional connection thesis is probably not true and, in any case, it is certainly not conceptually true. It is conceivable that some intentional states are neither conscious nor individuated by their relations to consciousness. Indeed, it is conceivable that some intentional states are states of unconscious creatures. Zombies, like the zombie systems within us, are best construed as having unconscious intentional states that explain the relational properties of behavior. Therefore, we must conclude that there can be intentional zombies after all.

4. Consciousness and Rationality

If intentionalism is true, then all conscious states are intentional states, but if the intentional connection thesis is false, as I argued in the previous section, then not all intentional states are conscious or individuated by their relations to conscious states. Nevertheless, there may be an important theoretical distinction to be drawn between intentional states depending on their relations to consciousness. Various philosophers have endorsed the idea that consciousness is the basis of an important theoretical distinction between intentional states, including Davies (1995) and Campbell (2002), who summarizes the point like this:

> The cautious view. . .is that we have (at least) two different types of representation (Davies 1995). On the one hand, there are the conceptual contents of ordinary beliefs and desires, to which consciousness may constitutively attach. On the other hand, there are the non-conceptual contents of information-processing states. (2002: 12)

Meanwhile, others remain highly skeptical about the theoretical significance of any distinction between intentional states that is drawn in terms of consciousness. Thus, for instance, Chomsky (1975) writes:

> It may be expected that conscious beliefs will form a scattered and probably uninteresting subpart of the full cognitive structure. (1975: 163)

Meanwhile, Fodor (1975) issues the following challenge for proponents of the theoretical significance of consciousness:

> That will depend upon whether there *are* generalizations which hold (just) for conscious mental states, and that depends in turn on whether the conscious states of an organism have more in common with one another than with the *un*conscious states of the nervous system of the organism. It is, in this sense, an open question whether conscious psychological states provide a natural domain for a theory. (1975: 52, n.19)

The challenge is to find some important theoretical generalizations that hold just for intentional states that are either conscious or individuated by their relations to consciousness. Fodor himself remains unconvinced that this can be done.

In this section, I respond to Fodor's challenge by proposing that there is an important theoretical connection between consciousness and rationality. More specifically, I propose to replace the intentional connection thesis with the following rational connection thesis:

> The rational connection thesis: an intentional state plays a rational role if and only if it is either conscious or individuated in such a way that its content is accessible to consciousness as the content of a conscious state.

If the intentional connection thesis is false, then not all intentional states are conscious or individuated by their relations to conscious states. But if the rational connection thesis is true, then there is an important theoretical distinction to be drawn between those intentional states that satisfy this criterion and those that do not. More importantly, for current purposes, the rational connection thesis can be used as a premise in arguing for the phenomenal analysis of cognition:

(1) All cognitive states are intentional states that play a rational role.
(2) All intentional states that play a rational role are either conscious or individuated by their relations to conscious states.
(3) So, all cognitive states are either conscious or individuated by their relations to conscious states.

This argument derives the connection between consciousness and cognition from a more fundamental connection between consciousness and rationality together with rational constraints on cognition. According to this argument, there cannot be a *cognitive zombie* because there cannot be a *rational zombie*.

The rationale for the first premise is that cognition is the domain of beliefs, which unlike subdoxastic mental representations, play a rational role in reasoning. Some, like Chomsky (1975), use the term 'cognition' in a broader sense on which all intentional states and processes count as cognitive states and processes. As I use the term, by contrast, cognitive states and processes are distinguished from merely computational states and processes by virtue of their rational role in reasoning. What is crucial here is not the terminological issue of whether the term 'cognition' should be used in a broad sense or a narrow sense, but rather the substantive claim that there is a theoretically important distinction to be drawn between intentional states and processes that play a rational role and those that do not.

What does it mean to say that all cognitive states play a rational role? We can distinguish between weak and strong versions of this rationality constraint on cognition. The strong version of the rationality constraint says that all cognitive states figure in cognitive processes that are either rational or approximately rational. However, this version is too strong to be plausible: there is substantial empirical evidence to suggest that many of our cognitive processes are neither rational nor even approximately rational.[27] Nevertheless, there is a weak version of the rationality constraint that is perfectly consistent with the empirical evidence. This version says that all cognitive states provide a source of reasons (or perhaps rational requirements) to engage in some cognitive processes, rather than others. The weak version of the rationality constraint does not entail that all cognitive processes are rational, or even approximately rational, but only that they are subject to rational assessment.

Cognitive processes and computational processes are in many ways alike. Many computational processes, like cognitive processes, are intentional processes that involve causal transitions between intentional states that are causally sensitive to their intentional properties.[28] The difference is that computational processes, unlike cognitive processes, are not subject to rational assessment: it makes no sense to ask whether they are reasonable or rational. This point is best illustrated by means of examples.

Chomsky (1965) explains our ability to understand syntactically well-formed sentences of our native language in terms of our tacit knowledge of a syntactic theory for the language. For instance, when we understand the syntactic structure of a sentence, this is explained as the result of an inference-like computational process defined over representational states that mirror the steps in a logical derivation of the syntactic structure of the sentence.

Similarly, Marr (1982) explains visual experience of the environment in terms of inference-like computations defined over a series of representational states, including the primal sketch, the 2.5D sketch, and the 3D sketch. These computations take as input the representation of light intensity in a pair of two-dimensional retinal images and yield as output a three-dimensional representation of shapes and their spatial organization in an object-centered frame of references.

These computational processes are *inference-like* in the sense that they are transitions between intentional states that are sensitive to the intentional properties of those states. Unlike genuine inferences, however, they are not subject to rational assessment. It makes no sense to ask whether it is reasonable or rational for the syntactic system to compute the syntactic structure of a sentence. Likewise, it makes no sense to ask whether it is reasonable or rational for the visual system to compute a representation of the distal environment from a pair of retinal images. These intentional processes are simply not subject to rational assessment at all.

That is not to say that these intentional processes are not subject to any other kinds of normative assessment. The point is rather that the normative standards that are relevant to the assessment of computational processes are distinct from the normative standards that are relevant to the assessment of cognitive processes. For current purposes, the distinction can be left at a more or less intuitive level. Ultimately, of course, it would be desirable to give a more theoretical account of the distinction between computational and rational norms. This is beyond the scope of the present paper, but I have argued elsewhere that rational norms are subject to structural principles of accessibility that need not apply in the computational domain.[29]

Assuming that there is a theoretically important distinction to be drawn between the norms that govern our cognitive processes and the norms that govern our computational processes, we can ask what explains this distinction. Why are cognitive and computational processes subject to different kinds of normative assessment? Presumably, the normative distinction between these intentional processes cannot simply be taken as primitive; rather, it should be explained in terms of some non-normative distinction between the intentional states that figure in those intentional processes. In particular, the normative distinction between cognition and computation should be explained in terms of some non-normative distinction between cognitive states and computational states — that is, between beliefs and subdoxastic states. But what is the nature of this distinction?

One tempting avenue is to appeal to Dennett's (1969) distinction between personal and subpersonal levels. On this proposal, beliefs are intentional states of the person, whereas subdoxastic states are intentional states of parts of the person — namely, their computational subsystems. The problem with this proposal is that we need a more fundamental account of what makes it the case that an intentional state is properly attributed to the person as opposed to one of the person's subsystems. Bermudez (1995) makes the point effectively:

> Either personal level states have further features in virtue of which they are properly attributable to persons rather than parts of persons, or they do not. If they do not then the distinction is doomed. But if they do have such further features then it makes more sense to state the distinction in terms of these further features. (1995: 353)

Broadly speaking, there are two options for cashing out the distinction between personal-level and subpersonal-level intentional states: one can appeal either to facts about consciousness or to facts about functional role.

The problem with appealing to consciousness is that not all of our cognition occurs within the stream of consciousness. On the contrary, much of our reasoning and rational belief revision draws on background information that is represented unconsciously in the belief system. For instance, inductive reasoning is causally sensitive to vast amounts of background information, not all of which can be brought to consciousness in the process of drawing a conclusion from observed evidence. Indeed, there may be inferential processes that occur entirely below the level of consciousness — as when one realizes that one has discovered the solution to a problem without consciously thinking about it. So how can we explain the normative distinction between unconscious cognitive processes and computational processes by appealing to consciousness alone?

The answer is that we can explain the normative distinction between cognition and computation by appealing to the rational connection thesis in combination with a phenomenal analysis of cognition. According to the rational connection thesis, an intentional state plays a rational role only if it is either conscious or individuated by its relations to conscious states in such a way that its content is accessible to consciousness as the content of a conscious state. Moreover, according to the phenomenal analysis of cognition, cognitive states are either conscious or individuated in the right way by their relations to conscious states, whereas computational states are individuated at least in part by their role in unconscious computational processes. Together, these two claims explain the datum that cognitive states play a rational role, whereas computational states do not. Thus, we have an argument by inference to the best explanation for a package that explains the rationality of cognition in terms of a phenomenal analysis of cognition together with a connection between rationality and consciousness.

5. Consciousness and Functional Role

In the previous section, I argued that the normative distinction between cognition and computation is explained by a phenomenal analysis of cognition together with a connection between rationality and consciousness. But this argument, like any inference to the best explanation, is vulnerable to the objection that there are alternative, and superior, explanations of the datum to be explained. In this context, the obvious alternative is to explain the normative distinction between cognition and computation by appealing to some functional analysis of cognition together with a connection between rationality and functional role. So, the challenge for proponents of the functional analysis of cognition is to develop a plausible explanation of the normative distinction between cognition and computation in purely functional terms. In this section, I consider what is, in my view, the most promising version of a functional explanation of this kind and I argue that it fails. I conclude, pending further proposals, that the phenomenal analysis of cognition is to be preferred to a functional analysis of cognition on the grounds that it provides a better explanation of the rationality of cognition.[30]

One influential proposal associated with Stich (1978) and Fodor (1983) is that the distinction between computation and cognition can be explained in terms of modularity. According to this proposal, computation is functionally isolated within a series of distinct, modular subsystems, whereas cognition is functionally integrated within a unified, nonmodular system.

For instance, Stich (1978) claims that beliefs are functionally integrated with one another by means of their inferential connections, whereas subdoxastic states are functionally isolated from beliefs and from other subdoxastic states.[31] There are several points to be made here: first, beliefs do not combine with subdoxastic states to yield further beliefs; second, subdoxastic states do not combine with beliefs to yield other subdoxastic states; and third, subdoxastic states do not combine with subdoxastic states in other subsystems to yield further subdoxastic states. Stich sums up the proposal as follows:

> If we think in terms of a cognitive simulation model, the view I am urging is that beliefs form a consciously accessible, inferentially integrated cognitive subsystem. Subdoxastic states occur in a variety of separate, special purpose subsystems. And even when the subdoxastic states within a specialized subsystem generate one another via a process of inference, their inferential interactions with the integrated body of accessible beliefs is severely limited. Similarly, in all likelihood, the potential inferential connections among subdoxastic states in different specialized subsystems are extremely limited or non-existent. (1978: 507–8)

Fodor (1983) draws a closely related distinction between modular and non-modular systems. According to Fodor, modular systems are domain specific and informationally encapsulated in the sense that they take a specific domain of information as input and use a specific domain of information in processing this input.[32] A non-modular system, on the other hand, is domain general and informationally integrated in the sense that it takes inputs from various different modules and processes these inputs in a way that is sensitive to all of the information that is represented in the central system. In Fodor's terminology, the proposal under consideration is that computational processes are modular, whereas cognitive processes are non-modular.

Fodor's distinction between modular and non-modular processes is clearly an important one. However, it is a further question whether this functional distinction provides a basis for explaining the normative distinction between computation and cognition. In order to explain the normative distinction, we would need to invoke a *functional connection thesis* of the following kind:

> The functional connection thesis: an intentional state plays a rational role if and only if it is functionally integrated with other intentional states within a unified nonmodular system.

However, the functional connection thesis is not plausible. On the one hand, not all nonmodular states and processes are cognitive, rather than computational, in the sense that they are subject to rational assessment. For instance, if perception is cognitively penetrable in the sense that it is influenced by background cognition, then some perceptual processes are nonmodular, but they are not thereby subject to rational assessment.[33] On the other hand, not all modular states and processes are computational, rather than cognitive, in the sense that they are immune from rational assessment. For instance, Spelke (2000) argues that infant cognition is subserved by "core knowledge systems" that are domain specific and informationally encapsulated, while Cosmides and Tooby (1992) argue that adult cognition involves the operation of a series of domain specific and informationally encapsulated modules, such as a "cheater detection" module. Nonetheless, the cognitive processes that are subserved by these specialized modules, including the reasoning involved in detecting cheaters, may be subject to rational assessment.

Similarly, Stich's functional distinction between inferentially integrated and isolated states is an important one, but it cannot explain the normative distinction between beliefs and subdoxastic states. Stich gives the following example to illustrate the proposed functional distinction between beliefs and subdoxastic states:

> As another example, suppose that, for some putative rule r, you have come to believe that if r then Chomsky is seriously mistaken. Suppose further that, as it happens, r is in fact among the rules stored by your language processing mechanism. That belief along with the subdoxastic state will not lead to the belief that Chomsky is seriously mistaken. By contrast, if you believe (perhaps even mistakenly) that r, then the belief that Chomsky is seriously mistaken is likely to be inferred. (1978: 508–9)

The descriptive point that Stich is making in this example has an obvious normative counterpart. If I believe that if r, then Chomsky is mistaken, and I also believe that r, then I am rationally committed to believing that Chomsky is mistaken. By contrast, if I merely subdoxastically represent that r, then I am not rationally committed to believing that Chomsky is mistaken. More generally, there is a normative distinction between beliefs and subdoxastic states such that one's beliefs are subject to rational assessment in terms of ideals of logical consistency and closure, whereas subdoxastic states are not subject to the same ideals. But what is the basis of this normative distinction between beliefs and subdoxastic states?

Broadly speaking, there are two options for explaining the normative distinction between beliefs and subdoxastic states. On the one hand, we can appeal to a phenomenal distinction on which the contents of beliefs, unlike subdoxastic states, are accessible to consciousness as the contents of conscious judgments. On the other hand, we can appeal to a functional distinction on which beliefs, unlike subdoxastic states, are inferentially integrated with other beliefs. In order to decide between these options, we need to consider cases in which the relevant phenomenal and functional properties are dissociated.

First, let us consider a variation on Stich's example in which the content of one's representation that r is accessible to consciousness as the content of a conscious judgment, although it is not functionally integrated with one's other beliefs and judgments. In that case, one is disposed to judge that r, but one is not disposed to infer that Chomsky is mistaken. This seems rationally defective: if one believes the conditional, and one is disposed to judge the antecedent, then one has a rational commitment to infer the consequent. But if the representation grounds a rational commitment to make an inference, then it is a belief, rather than a subdoxastic state.

Next, let us consider another variation in which the content of one's representation that r is functionally integrated with one's other beliefs and judgments, although it is not accessible to consciousness as the content of a conscious judgment. In that case, one is disposed to infer that Chomsky is mistaken, but one is not disposed to judge that r. Again, this seems rationally defective: if one believes the conditional, but one is not disposed to judge that the antecedent is true, then one has no rational commitment to infer the consequent; indeed, one has a rational commitment not to infer the consequent on those grounds alone. But if the representation does not ground a rational commitment to draw the inference, then it is a subdoxastic state, rather than a belief.

The upshot of this discussion is that it doesn't matter how much we elaborate the functional role of a subdoxastic state to mimic the functional role of belief: it cannot play a rational role unless it is individuated in such a way that its content is accessible to consciousness as the content of a phenomenally conscious judgment. Therefore, I conclude that the functional connection thesis should be rejected and replaced with the rational connection thesis: an intentional state plays a rational role if and only if it is conscious or individuated by its relations to consciousness. Furthermore, given rational constraints on cognition, the rational connection thesis entails the phenomenal analysis of cognition.

A further question remains. What explains this connection between consciousness and rationality? In my view, the connection is fundamental and so we cannot explain it by deriving it from anything more fundamental in the order of explanation. Nevertheless, I claim that we can acquire some reflective understanding of the connection by recognizing how it explains a connection between rationality and critical reflection. My remarks here will be brief, since I explore these issues in more detail elsewhere.[34]

The concept of rationality is essentially tied to the practice of critical reflection. To a first approximation, a belief is rational if and only if it is based in such a way that it would survive an idealized process of critical reflection. On this conception, the rationality of one's beliefs depends solely upon facts that are accessible to one by means of introspection and a priori reasoning, since these are the methods that constitute the practice of critical reflection.

Given this connection between rationality and critical reflection, we can say that an intentional state plays a role in determining which beliefs it is rational for one to hold only if it is accessible to one by means of introspection. Moreover, it is plausible that an intentional state is accessible to one by means of introspection only if it is either conscious or individuated by its relations to consciousness. Thus, we can argue for the rational connection thesis as follows:

(1) All intentional states that play a rational role are introspectively accessible.

(2) All introspectively accessible states are either conscious or individuated by their relations to consciousness.

(3) So, all intentional states that play a rational role are either conscious or individuated by their relations to consciousness.

This argument provides a theoretical rationale for the rational connection thesis by linking the concept of rationality with the practice of critical reflection. Intentional states that are neither conscious nor individuated by their relations to conscious states do not play a rational role because they are not accessible by means of introspection for use in critical reflection about what to believe. Thus, the connection between rationality and consciousness can be understood by taking into consideration the connection between rationality and critical reflection.

6. Summary and Conclusions

My main goal in this paper has been to argue for a phenomenal analysis of cognition on which all cognitive states are either conscious or individuated by their relations to consciousness. The main argument is that the phenomenal analysis of cognition is indispensable for explaining why cognitive states play a rational role. The general strategy is to explain the connection between consciousness and cognition as a consequence of a more fundamental connection between consciousness and rationality together with rational constraints on cognition.

6.1 Zombies

Can there be a cognitive zombie? Some argue that there cannot be a cognitive zombie because there cannot be an intentional zombie. In opposition, I have argued that zombies (like the zombie systems within us) have intentional states and processes that are indispensable for explaining the relational properties of their behavior. Nevertheless, their intentional states and processes are not cognitive states and processes, since they do not play a rational role. In picturesque terms, zombies are excluded from the space of reasons and so they cannot have cognitive states and processes, since these are positions and movements within the space of reasons. In sum, there can be an intentional zombie, but there cannot be a cognitive zombie, since there cannot be a rational zombie.

6.2 The Unity of the Mental

Do we have any unitary conception of the mental? One historically influential view is that our concept of the mental is fundamentally disjunctive: all mental states are either conscious or intentional. Some mental states, such as pains, are conscious but not intentional, while other mental states, such as beliefs, are intentional but not conscious. However, there is no further property that mental states such as pains and beliefs have in common in virtue of which they all count as mental states.[35]

More recently, some philosophers have sought to restore the unity in our concept of the mental by arguing for tighter connections between consciousness and intentionality. Some argue for intentionalism, according to which all conscious states (including pains) are intentional states. Others argue for the intentional connection thesis, according to which all intentional states (including beliefs) are either conscious or individuated by their relations to conscious states. If these claims can be sustained, they promise to salvage the unity in our concept of the mental.

However, I have argued that the intentional connection thesis is false: not all intentional states are either conscious or individuated by their relations to consciousness. Moreover, there is a theoretically important distinction between intentional states that can be drawn in terms of consciousness. In particular, cognitive states are distinguished from computational states by the fact that they play a rational role in virtue of their relations to consciousness. If intentionality is the mark of the mental, then the mental is divided between cognition and computation, but cognition is unified by its relations to consciousness.

6.3 Causal and Normative Functionalism

Given a phenomenal analysis of cognition, the prospects for a functional analysis of cognition stand or fall with the prospects for a functional analysis of consciousness. Neither consciousness nor cognition is subject to a reductive style of functional analysis in terms of its causal role. Nevertheless, both consciousness and cognition are subject to a non-reductive style of functional analysis in terms of its normative role. According to a weak version of the rationality constraint on cognition, all cognitive states play a rational role in the sense that they provide reasons or rational requirements to engage in some cognitive processes, rather than others. Moreover, according to the rational connection thesis, all intentional states that play a rational role in this sense are either conscious or individuated by their relations to consciousness. Thus, consciousness and cognition alike can be analyzed in terms of their normative, rather than their causal, functional roles.

6.4 The Hard Problem of Consciousness

If there is a conceptual connection between consciousness and cognition, then the problem of explaining cognition is intertwined with the problem of explaining consciousness. If consciousness is analyzed in terms of cognition, then the problem of explaining consciousness can be ameliorated by independently solving the problem of explaining cognition. But if cognition is analyzed in terms of consciousness, then the problem of explaining cognition cannot be solved without independently solving the problem of explaining consciousness. So, if the problem of explaining consciousness is a hard problem, then the problem of explaining cognition is a hard problem too.[36]

Notes

1. See Chalmers (1996) for an influential discussion of zombies in the context of metaphysical debates about the nature of consciousness.
2. See the introduction and essays in Gendler and Hawthorne (2002) for more on the distinctions between physical, metaphysical, and conceptual possibility. To a first approximation, it is conceptually possible that *p* if and only if it is not a priori that *p* is false. For present purposes, I assume that metaphysical possibility entails conceptual possibility, but not vice versa.
3. Bifurcationist themes can be found in the work of Block (1978), Chalmers (1996), and Kim (2005), although in more recent work, Chalmers (2003) has moved away from bifurcationism.
4. The project of giving a conceptual analysis of consciousness in terms of its role in cognition is closely associated with proponents of analytical functionalism, such as Armstrong (1968), Lewis (1972) and Shoemaker (1975). Others, including Dennett (1978, 1991), endorse cognitive theories of consciousness that are proposed as empirical theories, rather than as conceptual analysis.
5. Proponents include McGinn (1988), Searle (1990, 1992), Strawson (1994, 2004), Davies (1995), Campbell (2002), Chalmers (2003), Kriegel (2011), Smithies (2011), Horgan and Graham (2012).
6. Compare Block's (1995) distinction between the phenomenal concept of consciousness and various functional concepts of consciousness, including access consciousness and monitoring consciousness; see also Chalmers (1996: 25–31) for a related distinction. Both Block (2002) and Chalmers (2003) endorse *phenomenal realism* — that is, the thesis that the phenomenal concept of consciousness cannot be defined or analyzed in terms of any functional concept.

7. See Chalmers (1996: xi-xiii) on the hard problem of consciousness. See also Nagel (1974) and Levine (1983) for two influential discussions of the explanatory gap.

8. Thus, Chalmers (1996: 172) writes, "Cognition can be explained functionally; consciousness resists such explanation." See also Block (1990: 53–4) and Kim (2005: 161–70).

9. Smithies (forthcoming a) provides an overview of my position on the normative role of consciousness, while Smithies (2011, 2012a) explores applications to demonstrative concepts and introspection.

10. Ryle (1949) and Wittgenstein (1953) are often interpreted as proponents of analytical behaviorism, although this interpretation is controversial. Analytical functionalism has many influential proponents, including Armstrong (1968), Lewis (1972) and Shoemaker (1975). Others, including Fodor (1975), endorse functionalism as an empirical theory, rather than a conceptual analysis, of cognition.

11. Thus Block (1990: 53–4) writes, "The 'containment response'...would be to give up on functionalism as a theory of experience (or at least of its qualitative aspect), retaining functionalism as a theory of the cognitive aspect of the mind."

12. Block (1990: 54) acknowledges that "the containment response...arguably commits its proponents to the possibility of a 'zombie', a being that is like us in cognitive states but totally lacking in qualia."

13. These considerations loom large in Ryle's (1949: Ch. 1) discussion of Descartes' Myth.

14. This dispositional analysis of belief is consistent with Audi's (1994) distinction between dispositional beliefs and mere dispositions to believe, since we can distinguish between first-order dispositions towards judgment and second-order dispositions to acquire those dispositions.

15. For detailed discussion and defence of this assumption, see Smithies (forthcoming b). See also Strawson (1994), Siewert (1998), Horgan and Tienson (2002), and Pitt (2004). The terminology of 'content-specific' and 'attitude-specific' phenomenal character is borrowed from Ole Koksvik (2011); see also Horgan and Tienson (2002) for a related distinction between the phenomenology of intentional content and the phenomenology of attitude-type.

16. See Horgan and Tienson (2002) and Chalmers (2004) for related proposals.

17. See Zimmerman (2007) and Gendler (2008) for additional cases of absent-mindedness, phobia, and prejudice, in which a subject is disposed to behave as if she believes a proposition, although it seems wrong to say that she believes it. According to Gendler, the subject's behavioral dispositions do not reflect her beliefs, but rather a distinctively practical attitude, which she dubs 'alief'.

18. Strawson (1994, 2004) endorses the strong version of the intentional connection thesis, while Searle (1990, 1992), Kriegel (2011) and Horgan and Graham (2012) endorse weaker versions.

19. Here, I set aside Kriegel's (2011) interpretationist theory on which unconscious intentionality depends on a conscious act of interpretation.

20. See Horgan and Graham (2012) for the most sustained development of this line of argument.

21. See the essays in Stich and Warfield (1994) for a representative sample of causal theories of intentionality. See Quine (1960), Davidson (1973), Putnam (1981), and Kripke (1982) for classic discussions of the problem of radical indeterminacy. See Boghossian (1989) and Loewer (1997) for discussion of these problems in connection with causal theories of intentionality.
22. See Boghossian (1989) for sympathetic discussion of anti-reductionism about mental content.
23. Searle (1990) and McDowell (1994) endorse instrumentalism about the role of content in computational explanation, whereas Strawson (2008) endorses a more extreme form of eliminativism about all unconscious intentionality. See Peacocke (1995) for a defence of the claim that content plays an indispensable role in computational explanation.
24. Stich (1978: 499) defines subdoxastic states as "psychological states that play a role in the proximate causal history of beliefs, though they are not beliefs themselves." For current purposes, we can assume that subdoxastic states are intentional states, but not phenomenally conscious states.
25. See Evans (1981) and Davies (1987) for this account of tacit knowledge.
26. Compare Burge's (2010: 374–6) discussion of unconscious perception.
27. See Bortolotti (2009) for an overview and discussion of the empirical evidence on irrational cognition.
28. See Peacocke (1995) for arguments that we need to recognize a semantic conception of computation in addition to a purely syntactic conception of computation.
29. See Smithies (2012b, forthcoming c) for arguments that epistemic rationality or justification is accessible in the sense that one has justification to believe a proposition if and only if one has justification to believe that one does and, equally, one lacks justification to believe a proposition if and only if one has justification to believe that one does.
30. See Smithies (2011, 2012a) for discussion of attempts to undercut the rational role of consciousness by appealing to functional properties of accessibility or metacognition. Here, I focus instead on the functional property of inferential integration, which I take to be closely related to the functional property of systematicity, since a representational system is inferentially integrated only if it is systematic. I plan to discuss systematicity in more detail elsewhere.
31. Stich (1978: 517) claims that beliefs are distinguished from subdoxastic states not only by their inferential integration, but also by their accessibility to consciousness, although he does not explain why these properties come together or argue that they cannot be dissociated.
32. Fodor (1983: 71) claims that informational encapsulation is "the essence of...modularity", although he also claims that modules typically exhibit a cluster of related symptoms, including inaccessibility to consciousness, fast and mandatory operation, shallow outputs, fixed neural architecture and characteristic patterns of breakdown and development.
33. Pylyshyn (1999) argues that early vision is cognitively impenetrable, but this view is consistent with the claim that higher-level vision is cognitively penetrated.
34. See Smithies (2012a, Forthcoming a & c).
35. Rorty (1979: 22) gives a very clear statement of this view.

36. More or less distant ancestors of this paper were presented at the CUNY Graduate Center in 2005, the Australian National University in 2007, the Australasian Association of Philosophy in 2009, my epistemology seminar at the Ohio State University in 2009, the Columbia-Barnard Perception Workshop in 2012 and Oberlin College in 2012. Many thanks to audiences on all those occasions and especially to Ned Block, Paul Boghossian, David Chalmers, Benj Hellie, Uriah Kriegel, Geoff Lee, Christopher Peacocke, Abe Roth, Richard Samuels, Eric Schwitzgebel, Nico Silins, and Jeremy Weiss.

References

Armstrong, David. 1968. *A Materialist Theory of the Mind*. London: Routledge.

Audi, Robert. 1994. "Dispositional Beliefs and Dispositions to Believe." *Nous* 28 (4): 419–34.

Bermudez, Jose Luis. 1995. "Nonconceptual Content: From Perceptual Experience to Subpersonal Computational States." *Mind and Language* 10 (4): 333–69.

Block, Ned. 1978. "Troubles with Functionalism." *Minnesota Studies in the Philosophy of Science* 9: 261–325.

Block, Ned. 1990. "Inverted Earth." *Philosophical Perspectives* 4: 53–79.

Block, Ned. 1995. "On a Confusion About a Function of Consciousness." *Behavioral and Brain Sciences* 18: 227–47.

Block, Ned. 2002. "The Harder Problem of Consciousness." *The Journal of Philosophy* 99 (8): 1–35.

Boghossian, Paul. 1989. "The Rule-Following Considerations." *Mind* 98: 507–49.

Bortolotti, Lisa. 2009. *Delusions and Other Irrational Beliefs*. New York: Oxford University Press.

Burge, Tyler. 2010. *Origins of Objectivity*. New York: Oxford University Press.

Campbell, John. 2002. *Reference and Consciousness*. New York: Oxford University Press.

Chalmers, David. 1996. *The Conscious Mind: In Search of a Fundamental Theory*. New York: Oxford University Press.

Chalmers, David. 2003. "The Content and Epistemology of Phenomenal Belief." In *Consciousness: New Philosophical Perspectives*, edited by Q. Smith and A. Jokic. New York: Oxford University Press.

Chalmers, David. 2004. "The Representational Character of Experience." In *The Future for Philosophy*, edited by B. Leiter. New York: Oxford University Press.

Chalmers, David. 2011. "Verbal Disputes." *Philosophical Review* 120 (4): 515–66.

Chomsky, Noam. 1965. *Aspects of the Theory of Syntax*. Cambridge: MIT Press.

Chomsky, Noam. 1975. *Reflections on Language*. New York: Pantheon.

Cosmides, Leda and Tooby, John. 1992. "Cognitive Adaptations for Social Exchange." In *The Adapted Mind: Evolutionary Psychology and the Generation of Culture*, edited by J. Barkow, L. Cosmides, and J. Tooby. New York: Oxford University Press.

Davidson, Donald. 1973 "Radical Interpretation." *Dialectica* 27: 313–28.

Davies, Martin. 1987. "Tacit Knowledge and Semantic Theory: Does a Five Percent Difference Matter?" *Mind* 96: 441–62.

Davies, Martin. 1989. "Tacit Knowledge and Subdoxastic States." In *Reflections on Chomsky*, edited by A. George. Oxford: Blackwell.

Davies, Martin. 1995. "Consciousness and the Varieties of Aboutness." In *Philosophy of Psychology: Debates on Psychological Explanation*, edited by C. MacDonald and G. MacDonald. Oxford: Blackwell.

Dennett, Daniel. 1969. *Content and Consciousness*. New York: Routledge.

Dennett, Daniel. 1978. "Toward A Cognitive Theory of Consciousness." *Minnesota Studies in the Philosophy of Science* 9: 201–28.

Dennett, Daniel. 1991. *Consciousness Explained*. Boston: Little, Brown and Co.

Evans, Gareth. 1981. "Semantic Structure and Tacit Knowledge." In *Wittgenstein: To Follow a Rule*, edited by S. Holtzmann and C. Leich. London: Routledge and Kegan Paul.

Fodor, Jerry. 1975. *The Language of Thought*. Cambridge: Harvard University Press.

Fodor, Jerry. 1983. *The Modularity of Mind*, Cambridge: MIT Press.

Gendler, Tamar. 2008. "Alief and Belief." *Journal of Philosophy* 105: 634–63.

Gendler, Tamar and Hawthorne, John. 2002. *Conceivability and Possibility*. New York: Oxford University Press.

Horgan, Terry and Graham, George. 2012. "Phenomenal Intentionality and Content Determinacy." In *Prospects for Meaning*, edited by R. Schantz. Berlin: De Gruyter.

Horgan, Terry and Tienson, John. 2002. "The Intentionality of Phenomenology and the Phenomenology of Intentionality." In *Philosophy of Mind: Classical and Contemporary Readings*, edited by D. Chalmers. New York: Oxford University Press.

Kim, Jaegwon. 2005. *Physicalism, or Something Near Enough*. Princeton: Princeton University Press.

Koksvik, Ole. 2011. *Intuition*. Ph.D. Dissertation, Australian National University.

Kriegel, Uriah. 2011. *The Sources of Intentionality*. New York: Oxford University Press.

Kripke, Saul. 1982. *Wittgenstein on Rules and Private Language*. Cambridge: Harvard University Press.

Levine, Joe. 1983. "Materialism and Qualia: the Explanatory Gap." *Pacific Philosophical Quarterly* 64: 354–61.

Lewis, David. 1972. "Psychophysical and Theoretical Identifications." *Australasian Journal of Philosophy* 50: 249–58.

Lewis, David. 1983. "New Work for a Theory of Universals." *Australasian Journal of Philosophy* 61: 343–77.

Loewer, Barry. 1997. "A Guide to Naturalizing Semantics." In *A Companion to the Philosophy of Language*, edited by B. Hale and C. Wright. Oxford: Blackwell.

Marr, David. 1982. *Vision: A Computational Investigation into the Human Representation and Processing of Visual Information*. New York: Freeman.

McDowell, John. 1994. "The Content of Perceptual Experience." *Philosophical Quarterly* 44: 190–205.

McGinn, Colin. 1988. "Consciousness and Content." *Proceedings of the British Academy* 74: 219–39.

Milner, David and Goodale, Melvyn. 1995. *The Visual Brain in Action*, New York: Oxford University Press.

Nagel, Thomas. 1974. "What is it Like to Be a Bat?" *The Philosophical Review* 83 (4): 435–50.

Peacocke, Christopher. 1995. "Content, Computation and Externalism." *Philosophical Issues* 6: 227–64.

Peacocke, Christopher. 1998. "Conscious Attitudes, Attention, and Self-Knowledge." In *Knowing Our Own Minds*, edited by C. Wright, B. Smith, and C. MacDonald. New York: Oxford University Press.

Pitt, David. 2004. "The Phenomenology of Cognition, Or, What is it Like to Think that P?" *Philosophy and Phenomenological Research* 69: 1–36.

Putnam, Hilary. 1981. *Reason, Truth and History*. Cambridge: Cambridge University Press.

Pylyshyn, Zenon. 1999. "Is Vision Continuous with Cognition? The Case for Cognitive Impenetrability of Visual Perception." *Behavioral and Brain Sciences* 22: 341–423.

Quine, Willard van Orman. 1960. *Word and Object*. Cambridge: MIT Press.

Quine, Willard van Orman. 1970. "Methodological Reflections on Current Linguistic Theory." *Synthese* 21: 386–98.

Rorty, Richard. 1979. *Philosophy and the Mirror of Nature*. Princeton: Princeton University Press.

Ryle, Gilbert. 1949. *The Concept of Mind*. Chicago: Chicago University Press.

Schwitzgebel, Eric. 2002. "A Phenomenal, Dispositional Account of Belief." *Nous* 36: 249–75.

Schwitzgebel, Eric. 2010. "Acting Contrary to Our Professed Beliefs, or the Gulf Between Occurrent Judgment and Dispositional Belief." *Pacific Philosophical Quarterly* 91: 531–53.

Searle, John. 1990. "Consciousness, Explanatory Inversion and Cognitive Science." *Behavioral and Brain Sciences* 13: 585–96.

Searle, John. 1992. *The Rediscovery of the Mind*. Cambridge: MIT Press.

Shoemaker, Sydney. 1975. "Functionalism and Qualia." *Philosophical Studies* 27: 291–315.

Siewert, Charles. 1998. *The Significance of Consciousness*. Princeton: Princeton University Press.

Smithies, Declan. 2011. "What is the Role of Consciousness in Demonstrative Thought?" *The Journal of Philosophy* 108 (1): 5–34.

Smithies, Declan. 2012a. "Introspection and Consciousness." In *Introspection and Consciousness*, edited by D. Smithies and D. Stoljar. New York: Oxford University Press.

Smithies, Declan. 2012b. "Moore's Paradox and the Accessibility of Justification." *Philosophy and Phenomenological Research* 85 (2): 273–300.

Smithies, Declan. Forthcoming a. "The Phenomenal Basis of Epistemic Justification." In *New Waves in Philosophy of Mind*, edited by J. Kallestrup and M. Sprevak. Basingstoke: Palgrave Macmillan.

Smithies, Declan. Forthcoming b. "The Nature of Cognitive Phenomenology." *Philosophy Compass*.

Smithies, Declan. Forthcoming c. "Why Care About Justification?" In *Epistemic Evaluation: Point and Purpose in Epistemology*, edited by J. Greco and D. Henderson. New York: Oxford University Press.

Spelke, Elizabeth. 2000. "Core Knowledge." *American Psychologist* 55: 1233–43.

Stich, Stephen. 1978. "Beliefs and Subdoxastic States." *Philosophy of Science* 45: 499–518.

Stich, Stephen and Warfield, Ted. 1994. *Mental Representation: A Reader*. Oxford: Blackwell.

Strawson, Galen. 1994. *Mental Reality*. Cambridge: MIT Press.

Strawson, Galen. 2004. "Real Intentionality." *Phenomenology and the Cognitive Sciences* 3: 287–313.

Wittgenstein, Ludwig. 1953. *Philosophical Investigations*. Oxford: Blackwell.

Zimmerman, Aaron. 2007. "The Nature of Belief." *Journal of Consciousness Studies* 14: 61–82.

Philosophical Perspectives, 26, Philosophy of Mind, 2012

ACTIONS AS PROCESSES

Helen Steward
The University of Leeds

In this paper, I want to argue that actions are processes, and not events. The view that actions are processes has, of course, been mooted before.[1] But despite what I regard as its immense plausibility, the suggestion has never really caught on. Debates in the philosophy of action and the free will area continue to be framed largely in terms of an event ontology[2]—or else 'events and processes' are both mentioned, but in one breath, and without further clarification, so that the reader is left with the impression that nothing significant could possibly hang on the distinction. No serious concessions have really ever been made to the view that actions should be conceived of as processes *rather than* events. My suspicion is that this has been because no sufficiently radical understanding of the nature of processes and their distinctness from events has really been made available by the philosophers who have proffered the suggestion, so that the insistence that we think of actions as processes has appeared merely to be a minor tweak to the standard event-based view which could make no real difference to the philosophical issues at stake. Processes are often thought of, roughly speaking, as mere chains of events—and on this conception, it can indeed be hard to see why the distinction would make any serious difference to anything. The issue, if there is one, can sometimes seem to be about no more than temporal extension[3]— and of course, if processes were no more than *long* events (perhaps composed of a multiplicity of shorter ones), it might be right to suppose that nothing much could hang on the insistence that actions be thought of as processes. But there is a much better way to understand the event-process distinction, which is capable of grounding a more serious change to the ontology of philosophy of action. In this paper, I want to try to explain how to arrive at this more radical understanding, to show why the new ontology is needed in the philosophy of action and to say a little, at the very end, about what sort of work it might conceivably do.

Roughly speaking, the paper will have two halves, one negative, and one positive. I shall begin, in section (i), by offering some reasons for thinking that the things that it is most plausible to suppose we are trying to cotton on to with the generic talk of 'actions' in which philosophy indulges cannot be events. Then, in section (ii), I shall try to present a framework for thinking about the event-process distinction which I believe can help us understand how we ought to think about the ontology we need instead. Building on some excellent work already done by philosophers working at the intersection of philosophy and linguistics, I shall try to explain how to arrive at the more radical understanding of the nature of processes that I think we need—and will try to show what might need to be added to the ideas already in existence in this literature to help the resulting ontology serve the purposes of the philosopher of action.

1. Why Actions Cannot Be Events

It may be that the view that actions are best thought of as particular events is of older provenance than its explicit formulation; but whatever its roots, there is no doubt that it received an enormous boost to its prominence in the 1960s and 70s in the light of the detailed work carried out by Donald Davidson, both on the ontology of events in general, and on the claim that actions form a sub-class of the class of events, in particular. Until then, a number of distinctions of great importance to the formulation of a coherent ontology of events had not been clearly presented within a unified framework—e.g. that between type and token event; that between particular cause and necessary and sufficient conditions; that between an event and its description. And although the claim that actions are events doubtless has attractions that make it appealing even to those sceptical that ontology is best done on the back of detailed work in semantics, it cannot be doubted that Davidson's arguments for the view that the semantics of action sentences required the recognition of an underlying ontology of individual events had an enormous impact. How, he asked, are we to understand the inferential relationships between adverbially qualified action sentences without recognition of such an ontology? From the sentence 'Jones buttered a piece of toast, slowly, deliberately, in the bathroom, with a knife, at midnight' we can infer that Jones buttered a piece of toast, that Jones buttered a piece of toast slowly, that Jones buttered a piece of toast with a knife, etc. But if these inferences are to be made in virtue of logical form alone, it is very tempting to suppose that the simplest and neatest explanation is that the sentences in question quantify over *butterings* which are then available to be described in various different ways. As Davidson writes:

> Much of our talk of action suggests . . . that there are such *things* as actions, and that a sentence like . . . ['Jones buttered the toast in the bathroom with a knife at midnight'] describes the action in a number of ways. 'Jones did it with a knife'. 'Please tell me more about it'. The 'it' here doesn't refer to Jones or the knife but to what Jones did – or so it seems.[4]

I do not want here to undertake a general defence of the usefulness of the idea that many sentences contain an underlying ontological commitment to actions which can be conceived of as described in various ways by the adverbs which qualify the main sentence. That suggestion can certainly be questioned, and for all I shall say here, it may well be that in the end, it will turn out that the best account we can give of the relevant sentences requires no ontological commitment to anything other than the subject and object (if there is one) of the action verb; or, if to events at all, perhaps only to the events which are the *results* of actions, rather than to actions themselves—to arm-risings, but not to arm-raisings, for example.[5] It might also be questioned whether semantics and ontology are really connected together in the way presupposed by the Davidsonian programme, and so whether there is any easy way to move from the suggestion that an ontology of individual actions is needed for semantics, to the idea that we should give them full-blooded metaphysical recognition. But for present purposes, I wish to leave these more general issues to one side. What I want to ask is whether, even if one accepts, in outline, both the Davidsonian conception of ontological commitment in general, and the Davidsonian argument for the existence of actions in particular, one should agree with Davidson that the correct category in which to place the entities found to be quantified over is really the category of e*vent*. My central claim is, then, that *thus understood*, as an ontological commitment thought of as deriving from what is required for the semantics of adverbs, the commitment to actions cannot be a commitment to events.

Davidson, as is well-known, has trouble with a couple of the adverbs in his original example sentence, and suggests they may be special in ways which require exceptional handling. 'Slowly' turns out to create difficulties, given Davidson's ideas about action-individuation, since (for instance) a swimming of the Channel that was also a crossing of the Channel may be fast for a swimming but slow for a crossing. Davidson notes, though, that in this respect, 'slow' looks as though its behaviour needs the same treatment as 'tall', 'good' and other attributive adjectives, and may be set aside to be covered by whatever treatment turns out to work for those recalcitrant modifiers in more uncontroversially predicative usages. And 'deliberately' is also singled out by Davidson for special treatment. It cannot be allowed simply that Jones' action was 'deliberate' – since, for example, Jones' midnight buttering may have awoken his brother. And though the buttering was deliberate, Jones' awakening of his brother may not have been. But if, as Davidson supposes, the buttering simply *was* the awakening, this creates a contradiction. Davidson's solution is to insist that 'deliberately' cannot be treated on a par with the other modifying clauses – since (he claims) to do something deliberately is not a manner of doing it.[6]

By implication, though, Davidson suggests that adverbs which *do* speak to the manner in which an action is done ought to be straightforwardly transformable into predicates of events; and those who have attempted to develop and refine Davidson's suggestions have generally restricted the domain of application of his proposal to such adverbs.[7] But it is in fact not at all easy to maintain this idea. Surely 'with a knife', for example, is a prepositional phrase which speaks to the manner in which the buttering was done. But suppose Jones buttered the toast by moving his knife back and forth across the surface of the bread. Then, since the buttering was 'with a knife', and since the moving of the knife back and forth across the surface of the bread just *was* the buttering (according to Davidson), then it looks as though Jones must have moved his knife back and forth across the surface of the bread with a knife. And surely we would not want to accept that implication.[8] Modifiers of time and place have proved no more amenable to easy treatment. Suppose, for example, that Jones intended, by buttering the toast, to cause the depression of a button cleverly concealed on the plate beneath it, and thereby to initiate the countdown of a timing device connected to a bomb. After 24 hours, the bomb will (let us suppose) cause an aeroplane to explode. The buttering occurred at midnight. But did Jones' destroying of the plane (which he did by buttering the toast) also occur at midnight? Many people have found it implausible to think so; but that claim is entailed by Davidson's view that when one ϕs by ψ-ing, the ϕ-ing and the ψ-ing are normally identical.[9] Nor is it obviously any more natural to think that Jones' destroying of the plane was an event that took place wholly in the bathroom. Perhaps it *started* there. But many have found it quite natural to suppose that some parts of the destroying event occurred outside the bathroom too— and notably, that the eventual explosion of the plane must have been amongst them.

Of course, Davidson (and others) have made attempts to deal with some of these difficulties.[10] One obvious solution, having surveyed these various problems, is to suggest that the problem really stems from Davidson's account of event-individuation and that it might be best simply to jettison that account.[11] But I want here to raise another concern, which I think is connected to some of these original difficulties, and which is plainly not solved either by the adoption of a more fine-grained account of the individuation of events, nor by the variety of special measures proposed by Davidson and others for dealing with supposed attributives, purportedly intensional contexts, causal relations, etc. The difficulty is a very basic one which so far as I know has been noted only rather rarely,[12] and it is simply this: that it is most unnatural to think of most of the adjectives which can be obtained by grammatical modification (in English, usually deletion of the terminating 'ly') from qualifying adverbs of manner as adjectives which are straightforwardly applicable to *events*. Here is a list of 'adverbs of manner' taken from a grammar website: 'angrily, naughtily, prettily, slowly, proudly, happily, easily, loudly, carefully'. Clearly, we can do many of the things we do in all or some of these ways—and perhaps there is nothing obviously wrong with the idea of an angry or a naughty or even a pretty action.[13] But are there really *events* which are angry or naughty or careful? I hope the suggestion seems at least a little peculiar—although I hasten to note that it is important not to rest much weight on the sheer oddness simply of *saying* that there are e.g. angry or careful events. The oddness might simply be a superficial awkwardness due to the combination of relatively specific and personal predicate with relatively abstract and impersonal noun. And it might with justice be pointed out that it is not evidently any less peculiar to speak of angry or careful processes than it is to speak of angry or careful events. But it is possible to do much better than this by way of justifying the insistence that events make uncomfortable bedfellows for properties like angriness and carefulness.

Consider the following sentences:

(i) Smith waved more and more frenetically in the attempt to attract Jones' attention.
(ii) I rowed vigorously at first, but less vigorously as I began to tire.
(iii) Alice protested increasingly stridently as she realised what the consequences of the pronouncement would be.

In these sentences, the adverbial modifiers are comparative phrases ('more and more frenetically', 'less vigorously', 'increasingly stridently', etc.), instead of the basic adverbial modifiers considered by Davidson. But surely it is natural to think that if the basic sentence, 'Smith waved frenetically' quantifies over wavings, then the somewhat more complex sentence 'Smith waved more and more frenetically' must do so too—and that, in this case, there is said to be a waving that is not merely frenetic, but which *became more frenetic* as time went by. In other words, if these sentences of the form 'S ϕ-ed more and more/ less and less F-ly' are to be represented as quantifications over actions, the action in each case has to be represented as *changing* over time in respect of the degree to which it is F. But there are very good reasons, which have been often rehearsed and carefully defended, for thinking that events do not change—or at any rate, not in respect of their *intrinsic* properties.[14] They *are* changes—and there are good grounds for supposing that changes do not themselves change.

The argument for supposing that events do not change in respect of their intrinsic properties usually goes roughly as follows. True change (as opposed to mere succession) implies the persistence of an individual entity over a period of time during which the persisting thing first has one property and then loses it to gain another from the same quality space. But where events are concerned, this is not what we have. Suppose an event takes place from t_1 to t_3—a stone rolls down a hill, say. It may begin by rolling smoothly until t_2 and end by rolling bumpily between t_2 and t_3 as the ground becomes more uneven. Was the whole event which was the stone's rolling down the hill first smooth and then bumpy? No. The whole event was never smooth at any time (not even at the beginning), and the whole event was never bumpy either. The whole event—the entity which took place between t_1 and t_3—is in a certain important sense *static*—it has the nature it has, and that is that. The stone rolled smoothly between t_1 and t_2, and then bumpily between t_2 and t_3—and the event which was its (completed) rolling just consists of an episode of smooth rolling followed by an episode of bumpy rolling. And the event always has this property. No change in respect of it is possible. The event itself does not change.

What, then, are we to make of the fact that we appear to speak of walks which get faster, rollings which get bumpier, wavings which get more frenetic, etc? The natural response is to suggest that when we appear to predicate change of events, what we are really speaking of is a kind of progression within the event from one phase to another. It might be plausibly suggested, for instance, that what we really *mean* when we speak (inaccurately) of the rolling of a stone getting bumpier, for instance, is just that its later phases are bumpier than its earlier ones; what we mean when we speak (inaccurately) of a battle's growing noisier is that its later phases are noisier than its earlier ones; and so on. But this is not *real* change in the rolling or the battle, any more than the fact that a poker is redder at the tip than at the handle is change—it is merely that certain temporal parts of the event have properties different from those possessed by other temporal parts of that same event. This is to suggest that so far as events are concerned, talk of change is to be understood as a mere *façon de parler*. Change for events turns out, in fact, to be mere succession.

But this suggestion, which is, so far as I can see, the *only* plausible recourse for the event theorist in the face of examples like (i)–(iii), is problematic in a number of respects. There is, to begin with, the too-little-remarked-upon unsatisfactoriness of adopting a view which will not allow us to take straightforwardly, at face value, what looks like a *prima facie* commitment to ϕ-ings that change (at any rate, if the Davidsonian view of the semantics of adverbially qualified sentences is even roughly correct). It is extremely natural to think that an angry ϕ-ing should be able (quite literally) to get angrier, that a gentle ϕ-ing should have the potential to become less gentle, and so on—and that such transformations, where they occur, represent genuine changes in the properties of the ϕ-ings in question. A view which cannot strictly allow for these transformations to be changes in a direct and straightforward sense is, to that extent, less plausible. Secondly, there is a problem about predications made in the present tense progressive. Suppose, watching Jones butter some toast, I say that he is buttering it angrily. Presumably, then, if I am right about Jones, and if an event-based semantics for action sentences is correct, there must have been a buttering of some toast by Jones, which was angry. But what is it that I am implicitly predicating 'angry' of, exactly? Surely it cannot be the whole buttering event, conceived of as an event which lasts for as long as Jones butters. For then my claim would have to be judged false if the whole buttering turned out, in the end, to be mainly a calm affair, in which there was merely a short and angry phase which I happened to witness. One might try suggesting that perhaps I am predicating angriness of some shorter event. But what would be the bounds of this event, precisely? Not the bounds represented by the extent of the period during which I watch Jones—for that might perfectly well extend in such a way as to encompass the whole of a largely calm buttering. And there seems to be no other event with naturally well-defined beginning and end points to suggest. One might, of course, suggest any one of a number of candidate artificially delimited events to be the target of my predication—but how could any one of these really

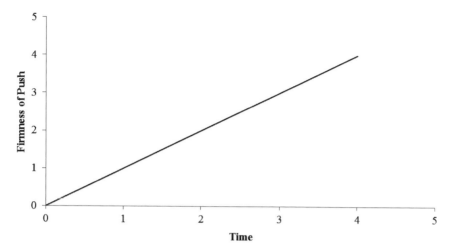

Figure 1. A Smooth Push Profile

make out its case to be the unique object of my thought when there seems to be nothing to elevate its candidacy above that of any of the others?

A third problem is that the change-as-succession view appears to rule out the existence of actions with what one might call a smooth change profile. Consider for example the sentence: 'Brown pushed increasingly firmly at the door'. It is natural to think that it should be possible for the profile of Brown's increasingly firm push to look as it does in Figure 1 (though of course this is not the only profile consistent with the truth of the sentence). In other words, it is natural to think that it should be possible in principle for Brown's pushing to increase steadily in firmness as time goes by. But this cannot truly represent the profile of a changing event, according to the view under consideration. For each event-phase is itself, presumably, a shorter event—and so the argument for the view that events cannot change will apply equally to each phase—no individual phase can change in respect of its degree of F-ness, except by consisting itself of phases which have differing degrees of F-ness. In other words, the profile has ultimately to be as in Figure 2, if we are to make sense of the idea of change for events via the concept of succession.

But this seems unattractive. Why shouldn't Brown's increasingly firm pushing genuinely have the profile represented by Figure 1? If our understanding of the nature of the change involved as Brown pushes increasingly firmly at the door seems to rule out this profile, that is surely a strike against it.

A final unappealing consequence of this suggestion relates to what might be supposed to be the modal properties of actions. We might want to say that Brown's pushing of the door could have lasted longer than it did, for instance. (If it had lasted longer, perhaps he would have succeeded in opening the door). But the same sorts of worries which attend the question whether events can change

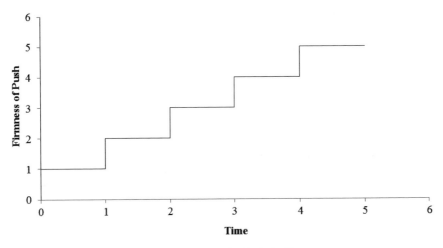

Figure 2. A Stepwise Push Profile

attend the question whether they could have had properties other than those they in fact have. Of Brown's pushing, conceived of as a complete event, one feels a powerful temptation to say that *it*—that very event—could *not* have lasted longer than it did. If Brown had pushed for longer, that is, it is tempting to think, a *different* pushing event would have occurred. Perhaps this is not an unassailable position, but it should be noted that many theorists who have considered the question have defended mereological essentialism for events—i.e. the view that events have all their temporal parts essentially.[15] But it is hard to see how this mereological essentialism is to be rendered consistent with our inclination to say such things as that Brown's pushing could have lasted longer. There is, of course, considerable room for doubt about how secure are our intuitions about the essential properties of events, and faced with the evidence of ordinary claims such as that Brown's pushing could have lasted longer than it did, one might simply think that it is the mereological essentialism which has to go. But we need to choose between these two views only if the pushing that could have lasted longer is the same thing as the pushing event which began when Brown began pushing and finished when he stopped. And that this is so might be questioned.

How might it be questioned? In the next section of the paper, I shall try to answer that question, by making out the case for the view that as well as events, we must recognise a second category of occurrent entity that I call *processes*. And processes, unlike events, I shall suggest, *can* change; and they do not have all their temporal parts essentially.[16] They are therefore, I claim, much better candidates than events to be the entities that are quantified over by action sentences, and which are implicitly described by adverbs of manner—in short, if we are at all Davidsonian in inclination, they are much better candidates than events to be actions.

2. Event and Process: A Positive Account of the Distinction

A useful starting point for the development of the needed distinction between events and processes can, I think, be found in some valuable work which has been done at the intersection of philosophy and linguistics on the ontological implications of the phenomenon of *aspect*. An important strand of thinking in that literature has already suggested a conception of process such that processual activity is to be conceived of as the 'stuff of' events, standing in the same sort of relation to them as that in which, for example, stuffs like gold and milk stand to the rings, puddles, etc. which might be composed of them.[17] For ease of reference, I shall call this the Count-Mass view of the event-process distinction. The Count-Mass view is dependent on the idea that the nominalisations obtained from sentences having imperfective aspect seem better thought of as mass-quantified than as count-quantified. Consider, for instance, the sentence 'Jones was swimming yesterday'. Nominalising, it is argued, it is better to suppose that what we obtain is 'There was (some) swimming by Jones yesterday' rather than 'there was *a* swimming by Jones yesterday'—since, for all the sentence tells us, Jones might be swimming still. The imperfective construction, the idea is, does not make available to us the idea of an end-point to the swimming which concludes it, and makes it appropriate to consider the swimming as a kind of completed whole—an event. Only a sentence with perfective aspect, such as 'Jones swam the Channel yesterday' permits us to think of Jones' swimming as a true *unit*—a swimming of the Channel by Jones, a thing of a type of which there might have been one or two or several, rather than simply some. Of course, Jones' swimming (of which the first sentence tells us there was some yesterday) might in fact have constituted the swimming of the Channel which the second sentence tells us also occurred. But if we are ontological pluralists, this need not be to say that the swimming of which there was some, and the swimming of which there was one, are to be identified with one another. Just as it is often argued that we must make an ontological distinction between, for example, a statue and the clay of which it is made, so it might be argued that we need an ontological distinction between swimming event and swimming process/activity—that we must recognise both, in spite of their being co-occupants of the same space-time region. Reasons for doing so might include, for example, the recognition that there seem to be predicates which are applicable to the swimming of which there was *some* which are not applicable to the swimming event. The swimming of which there was some, for example, might have been intermittent, Jones having paused several times to float on his back to catch his breath. But can an *event* be intermittent? It does not seem to me to make proper sense to say of an individual event that it was intermittent. Something which is intermittent has to be first happening and then not happening and then happening again. But the event of Jones's swimming which took place, let us say, between 8am and 4pm yesterday was happening throughout the whole of that time—we have to think so if we are to think of it as a single event, rather than a multitude of separate events, at all.

What may have ceased to happen for a while was something else—something to refer to which we need a mass noun, and which we might therefore call swimming *activity*.

I have argued elsewhere for the importance of this distinction between actions and activity.[18] I continue to think it important—and that it is certainly *one* distinction—perhaps that it is ultimately even the most important distinction—that needs to be recognised within this area of ontology of action. But I shall not spend more time defending it here.[19] What I want to insist upon is rather that we need (in addition to the distinction made by the Count-Mass view, and partly based upon it) a related new understanding of what the *particulars* are that fall on the 'count' side of the 'count-mass' distinction as here applied in the realm of happenings, and more specifically, in the realm of action. My suggestion will be that the relevant particulars, the actions, the things which are qualified by adverbs when these occur in sentences with *perfective* aspect, are not best thought of as events.

The Count-Mass view will, admittedly, serve to solve some of the problems that appeared to beset the unmodified Davidsonian view, all by itself. It will solve, for example, the difficulty about Jones' angry buttering which I raised earlier. If Jones was buttering angrily, and I report this, we can take my report to be made true by the occurrence not of any particular angry buttering *event,* but rather simply to some angry buttering activity. The truth of my claim that Jones was buttering angrily is now not hostage to fortune—it will remain true even if Jones suddenly becomes calm as he butters, so that it would be inaccurate to report the occurrence of *an* angry buttering. But other problems remain. For some of the claims I have made in the previous section apply to the nominalisations of many perfective no less than to those of imperfective action sentences. The aspectual character of a predication can admittedly be hard to determine—but 'Jones buttered the toast' looks, on the face of it, to be perfective, or at any rate we can elaborate so as to make it unambiguously so (e.g. 'Jones buttered the toast yesterday, so I am going to do it today—that's only fair')—and hence its nominalisation should be count-quantified—'there was *a* buttering of the toast by Jones'. And yet this buttering, when considered as a thing which might be, for instance, slow, or aggressive, or careful, seems to me not to be an event for the reasons I have given above. What is aggressive should be able to get more or less aggressive; what is slow should be able to speed up, etc.—and moreover, we should be able to think of these alterations as things which it is conceivable might go on smoothly and continuously with respect to time. But these sorts of changes, as I have already argued, cannot happen to events. Jones' buttering thought of as a thing which accepts such predicates as these cannot be an event, then, but must be something else—something in which Jones was engaged, which progressed through time and whose properties changed as it did so. Since we can speak of *a* buttering, in this case, we are not talking about mere activity, the stuff of action, so the Count-Mass view cannot be wheeled in to help us out. In speaking of Jones' buttering, here, it seems that we must be talking about an occurrent individual, but about an occurrent individual which is not the event, since it is the sort of thing which can change.

Is there an occurrent individual here that is not the event, though? I think there is, but in order to see what it might be, what is usually a central presupposition of the Count-Mass view needs to be challenged. In drawing parallels between the occurrents of which we are attempting to give an account, and various types of entity in the realm of continuants, the Count-Mass view relies on the idea that events stand to processual activity roughly as substances stand to the matter which composes them. But in fact, the events of which we have been speaking are in many ways not at all like substances. They are more like what might be called Lockean masses of matter. Locke writes in Book 2 Chapter xxvii of his *Essay Concerning Human Understanding* that:

> if two or more Atoms be joined together into the same Mass ...whilst they exist united together, the Mass, consisting of the same Atoms, must be the same Mass or the same Body, let the parts be never so differently jumbled: But if one of these Atoms be taken away, or one new one added, it is no longer the same Mass or the same Body' (Locke, 1975, 330).

What Locke here calls masses of matter are particulars ('bodies'). But they are particulars which are both mereologically and modally fragile—the addition or subtraction of even one atom from a Lockean mass destroys its identity; and *this* mass of matter could not have been composed of atoms other than those of which it is actually composed. And all this is entirely parallel to what we have so far said of events, thought of as completed changes. They cannot grow— because the addition of further temporal parts simply creates a new event; and if mereological essentialism is correct, they are also modally fragile with respect to their temporal parts, just as Lockean masses are modally fragile with respect to their spatial parts, for an event could not have lasted longer than it actually did without becoming a new event.

Substances, though, at any rate on one very powerful and traditional conception of what they are, are very different from masses of matter in this regard.[20] Substances—like horses and trees, for instance—can change, they can gain and lose parts without losing their identities, and they could have been other than they are in a great many different ways. They are what one might call *robust*—both mereologically and modally. And what I should like to suggest is that our ways of thinking and speaking about occurrent entities suggest that we are implicitly committed to the existence of entities which are parallel to substances in these respects—which are also mereologically and modally robust. But these are not the events. They are what might be called *individual processes*— and actions are a most important species of the genus.

Individual processes, unlike events, are not changes. They are what might be called *changings*—bringings about of results by things or collections of things. In the case of human actions, they are of course bringings about of results by us.

And though it does not make sense to think of *changes* as themselves capable of change, there is no reason to suppose that *changings* cannot change—my raising of my arm, for example, can perfectly well become more or less quick or careful or smooth as I raise it. The argument for the conclusion that *events* cannot change depends on the thought that an event simply consists of the temporal parts of which it consists and that variation in some quality amongst those parts does not constitute a change in the event itself, any more than a pole's being red on top and blue on the bottom constitutes a change in the pole. But an individual process—a changing—can *grow*. At t_1, for example, it may consist of a certain set of temporal parts; but by t_2 it may consist of another, larger set, because further things have happened in the ongoing changing which is under way. And this is real change in the process itself—the process now has properties it did not have before. We can of course think about the whole set of temporal parts which has occurred by the time the process is complete. But to think of *that* is to think of an event—to think of the whole change, conceived of as a unit which is now over and done, a completed whole. But our immersion in the flow of time means that we require in addition to this, another way of thinking of occurrents—as things which are ongoing, which might turn out one way or another, which might end sooner or rather later, depending on what happens. A process, like a substance, is singled out in thought by way of what might reasonably be called its *form*, which frees it up for participation in such things as growth and change. Just as, in thinking of a horse, say, we lock onto a creature whose principle of individuation has to do with continued life and not with continuation of the very same matter, so in thinking of a process, we lock onto an entity which we conceive of as having a principle of individuation which has to do with what one might call norms of development—or, in the case specifically of human action, with such things as intentions and goals. This means that we are thinking of it as a thing that e.g. may come to have extra parts, in addition to those it has already—and as a thing that might easily have had other parts. But these thoughts make no sense with respect to events.

My suggestion, then, is that the things we quantify over (if indeed there are any such) when we adverbially qualify an action sentence which has perfective aspect, such as 'Jones swam the Channel cautiously yesterday', say, are individual processes and not events. They are the analogues (in certain respects, anyhow) not of Lockean masses of matter, but of Aristotelian substances. Swimmings cannot be cautious unless they are swimmings of the sort in which human beings or other animals might engage cautiously—which means they cannot be swimmings of the sort that might be constituted by a completed episode of engagement—for we do not engage in *those*. The completed episodes are, to be sure, constituted by our having engaged in activities—but they are not what we engage *in*, for they are not *there* to be engaged in until the engagement is over. We engage in changings and not in changes, in movings and not in completed motions. The things we engage in are things which are themselves susceptible of change—and this means they cannot be events.

In fact, just to reemphasise the fundamentality of the distinction insisted upon by the Count-Mass view, it might be very plausibly insisted that our engagement in (countable) changings is frequently parasitic upon our engagement in uncountable, massy changing—our engagement in swimmings is rooted in engagement in swimming, pure and simple, and the predications appropriate to countable swimmings are in many cases based on predications appropriate to massy activity. To see how, it may be useful to revert once again to an analogy from the realm of continuants. Consider the predicate 'dense'. One can make perfectly good sense of an individual mass of matter's having a given density. But masses of matter need not be homogeneous—and so there is a sense in which we have to think of the density of a mass of matter as a kind of average, recognising the possibility that some parts of the mass may be denser—perhaps considerably denser—than others. The idea of density pure and simple—the idea of the feature of which we are trying to arrive at an average measure when we attribute density to an individual—seems to me best understood in the first instance as a property of *stuff*, not of things—a property which relates to the way in which that stuff fills space. The idea of average density is derivative from this more basic idea of density itself, conceived of as a property of stuffs. And likewise, we can make sense of (countable) swimmings which are cautious or frenetic or gentle. But we can only do so by understanding these predications as averagings over a period of time of properties which belong primarily not to particulars of any kind, but rather to processual stuff—properties which characterise the way in which processual stuff is distributed through time.

The things I have been calling individual processes share with the masses from which they are constituted what I have elsewhere called a certain 'temporal shape'. They *go on*, so to speak, in time, just as massy processes do. As Jones swims, (some) swimming by Jones goes on, and if Jones eventually swims the Channel, a swimming by him of the Channel, a swimming in which he engaged, and which changed throughout in various respects throughout its length can likewise be said to have gone on—a swimming which may have begun cautiously, for instance, and become frenetic, a swimming which might have taken longer than it did, if Jones, for example, had become more tired. But events—changes—do not go on, at least not in the same way—and they therefore do not change throughout their length. They come to exist in virtue of other things having gone on. But that, as I have been at pains to emphasise, is different.

I hope, then, to have shown that we have reason to be doubtful about making events the basis of the ontology of action. Those inclined, as I am, towards ontological pluralism will not want to deny the existence of events whose occurrence consists in a person's having brought something about intentionally. But these are not the things which are implicitly modified by adverbs of manner—and an ontological pluralist will want to insist that the 'fait accompli' perspective which the event ontology brings with it makes invisible the things we should truly be interested in when we are interested in action. To see *those* things, she will think, we need standpoints which make prominent such things as imperfective aspect, the role of the agent not only as instigator but also as controller and ongoing adjuster of change—standpoints which properly represent the positioning of agents in time, attempting to get things done by one means or another, in the midst of all the contingencies and uncertainties which that positioning brings with it. These things, the development of which we have an enormous interest in perceiving and tracking—and indeed, in our own case, in executing—are not events—and we should resist the pressures to identify and collapse the one ontology (of changings) into the other (of changes). It has not been possible in the course of such a short paper as this properly to show why the distinction might matter to philosophy of action. My suspicion, though, is, that the so-called 'disappearance of the agent'[21] in what is often called the standard story of human action is connected to the failure to recognise the character of actions as processes and not events. Individual processes, in my sense, must be *carried out* – if there is a changing, something or someone must be changing something. Whereas changes simply happen and our role (such as it may be) in their having happened is utterly hidden and disguised. If agents are going to reappear in action theory, we are going have to conceive properly of the nature of their doings. If I am right, that means conceiving of them as processes, and not events.

Notes

1. See especially Dretske (1988)—though Dretske speaks mainly not of 'actions' but of 'behavior' as the thing for which a processual understanding is recommended.
2. Thus, for example, the type of libertarianism which is standardly opposed to agent-causal libertarianism is called 'event-causal libertarianism', the crucial assumption which distinguishes event-from agent-causalist being that actions are events.
3. See e.g. Salmon (1984), p.139: "The main difference between events and processes is that events are relatively localized in space and time, while processes have much greater temporal duration...In space-time diagrams, events are represented by points, while processes are represented by lines".
4. Though many would now incline to the view (as I myself incline) that Davidson was wrong to identify 'what Jones did' with the individual action that is quantified over by the sentence. 'Things done' are better understood as *kinds* of thing—thus, some of the things Jones did were: butter the toast, butter the toast slowly, butter the toast in the bathroom, etc. It is his *doing* each of these things that is best regarded as the action. See especially Hornsby (1980: 3).
5. For the former suggestion, see e.g. Ralf Stoecker (1993); for the latter, Maria Alvarez (1999).
6. Strictly speaking, this claim is false—for of course 'deliberately' *can* be used as an adverb of manner, not merely as a general synonym for 'on purpose'. Taylor (1985), p. 21 also makes this point, calling the general phenomenon of which this is an instance 'Austinian ambiguity', in recognition of Austin's discussion

in 'A Plea for Excuses' (Austin, 1970). The general phenomenon consists in the fact that many adverbs can be used either as adverbs of manner (or 'mode', to use Taylor's terminology) or as what Taylor calls 'phrase adverbs'. Phrase adverbs are those which permit rephrasing of the structures in which they occur in the form 'It was M of x that x ϕ-ed'. Austin's example is 'He clumsily trod on a snail' which may mean either: 'It was clumsy of him that he trod on a snail' (phrase adverb) or 'He trod, in a clumsy manner, on a snail' (mode adverb).

7. See e.g. Taylor (1985), 20–1; Parsons (1990), 62–4.
8. This objection is raised by Parsons (1985) and (1990), who attributes it originally to an unpublished paper, 'On What's Happening', by John Wallace; and also by Taylor (1985), p. 26, who attributes it to Christopher Arnold.
9. See e.g. Thomson (1971).
10. See, in particular, Davidson (1985), Taylor (1985), Parsons (1990).
11. This is Parsons' solution in many of these awkward cases—see his (1990), p.158.
12. It is noted by McCann (1979, 138), though he is commenting on a view of Vendler's rather than of Davidson's: '... suppose John's singing of the Marseillaise was suave and graceful, that his playing of the poker hand was deft, and his killing of Smith sloppy and unprofessional. Are we then to have suave and graceful events, deft events, sloppy events?'"
13. Although one can hardly fail to notice that in at least some of these cases, the thing which would most naturally said to be angry, naughty, etc. is the *agent* – and it may well be that *some* of these cases might be best dealt with by interpreting the sentence as incorporating a conjunct pertaining to the agent, such as 'The agent was F to ϕ' (e.g. the agent was naughty to laugh'). But this will clearly not work everywhere—there are at least some cases where the adverb is clearly intended specifically to characterise the manner of the action and not (except indirectly) the agent. An agent can arguably laugh naughtily, for instance, in circumstances in which we would not want to accept that she was naughty to laugh.
14. It might be arguable that we must accept that they can undergo relational change—e.g. an avalanche might *become* the event which killed Hans, who was unfortunately buried beneath the snow and died a week later of his injuries. For the view that events cannot change in respect of intrinsic properties, see e.g Dretske (1967), Mellor (1981), Hacker (1982), Simons (1987), Galton and Mizoguchi (2009).
15. See e.g. Simons (1987); Lombard (1986); Neale (1993).
16. See Galton and Mizoguchi (2009) for a similar view that we cannot make sense of the sorts of changes that occur within the category of happening without recognising types of happening that are not events, but processes.
17. For views of this sort see e.g. Mourelatos (1978); Galton and Mizoguchi (2009); Hornsby (2012, forthcoming). Strictly speaking, these views are not all identical by any means—in particular, Hornsby criticises Mourelatos for continuing to operate with a count-based notion of process, in spite of his comparison between mass and process. Her view is that to continue to speak as Mourelatos does of 'processes' (plural), at any rate if we imagine we are singling out particulars rather than types by this means, is to perpetuate a mistake which the comparison with stuffs ought to have eradicated. She means, I think, also to criticise me for the

same mistake (and the criticism is fair—I think I had not in my (1997) clearly understood what the mass-process comparison really implied).

18. Steward (1997), Ch 3.

19. One reason not to do so is that Hornsby's 2012 already offers such a defence—one that I think much improves on my (1997).

20. See e.g. Wiggins (2001), Fine (2003) for the development and defence of what is basically an Aristotelian conception of an individual substance.

21. See Velleman (1992) for this phrase.

References

Austin, J.L. (1970), 'A Plea for Excuses' in his *Philosophical Papers*, second edition (Oxford: Oxford University Press): 175–204.

Davidson, D. (1985), 'Adverbs of Action' in Vermazen, B., and Hintikka, M.B., *Essays on Davidson: Actions and Events* (Oxford: Oxford University Press): 230–41.

Dretske, F., (1967), 'Can Events Move?', *Mind* 76: 479–92.

Dretske, F. (1988), *Explaining Behavior: Reasons in a World of Causes* (Cambridge MA: MIT Press).

Fine, K. (2003), 'The Non-Identity of a Material Thing and its Matter', *Mind* 112: 195–234.

Galton, A., and Mizoguchi, R., (2009), 'The Water Falls but the Waterfall Does Not Fall: new Perspectives on Objects, Processes and Events", *Applied Ontology*, 4: 71–107.

Gibbard, A., (1975) 'Contingent Identity', *Journal of Philosophical Logic* 4: 187–221.

Hacker, P.M.S., (1982), 'Events and Objects in Space and Time', *Mind* 91: 1–19.

Hornsby, J., (1980), *Actions* (London: Routledge and Kegan Paul).

Hornsby, J., (2012), 'Actions and Activity', forthcoming in *Philosophical Issues*.

Locke, J., (1975), *An Essay Concerning Human Understanding* ed. P. Nidditch (Oxford: Oxford University Press).

Lombard, L.B., (1986), *Events: A Metaphysical Study*, (London: Routledge and Kegan Paul).

McCann, H.J., (1979), 'Nominals, Facts and Two Conceptions of Events', *Philosophical Studies* 35: 129–49.

Mellor, D.H., (1981), *Real Time* (Cambridge: Cambridge University Press).

Mourelatos, A., (1978), 'Events, Processes and States', *Linguistics in Philosophy* 2: 415–34.

Neale, S., (1993), *Descriptions* (Harvard, MA: MIT Press).

Salmon, W.C., (1985), *Scientific Explanation and the Causal Structure of the World*, (Princeton NJ: Princeton University Press).

Simons, P., (1987), *Parts: A Study in Ontology* (Oxford: Oxford University Press).

Steward, H., (1997), *The Ontology of Mind: Events, Processes and States* (Oxford: Oxford University Press).

Stoecker, R., (1993), 'Reasons, Actions and their Relationship' in R. Stoecker (ed.) *Reflecting Davidson* (Berlin: de Gruyter): 265–86.

Taylor, B., (1985), *Modes of Occurrence: Verbs, Adverbs and Events* (Oxford: Blackwell).

Thomson, J.J., (1971), 'The Time of a Killing', *Journal of Philosophy* 68: 115–32.

Velleman, D., (1992), 'What Happens when Someone Acts?' *Mind* 101: 461–81.

Wiggins, D., (2001), *Sameness and Substance Renewed* (Cambridge: Cambridge University Press).

Philosophical Perspectives, 26, Philosophy of Mind, 2012

INTROSPECTIVE KNOWLEDGE OF NEGATIVE FACTS*

Daniel Stoljar
ANU

1.

According to Ernest Sosa, there is a "gaping deficiency" in a number of popular approaches to introspective knowledge and justified belief. "The gap", he says,

> concerns our knowledge that we do *not* believe such and such and our knowledge that we do *not* intend such and such and our knowledge that we do *not* seem to see anything red or any triangle. In no such case can our knowledge derive from first-order inquiry or deliberation of any sort; nor can it flow from some conscious state that rationalizes it. On the contrary, it is precisely the *absence* of a relevant belief or intention or experience that makes it a case of knowledge. Moreover, our belief that the state is absent seems clearly *not* to be based on any conscious state to which it is appropriately responsive (2003, 257).

Sosa has two approaches to the epistemology of introspection in mind here. The first—the *transparency-based account*, as I will call it—is at issue when he talks of "first-order deliberation". According to this account, if I am justified in believing that some arbitrary proposition *p* is true as a result of deliberating on whether it is true, I will thereby have justification to believe a further proposition, viz., *that I believe that p*. So for example, if I am justified in believing that it is garbage night, as result of deliberating on whether it is, I am thereby justified in believing something further, viz., that I believe that it is garbage night. The second—*the consciousness-based account*, as I will call it—is at issue when he talks of knowledge that flows "from some conscious state that rationalizes it". According to this account, if I am in a conscious state, I thereby have justification

*I am very grateful to audiences at ANU (Kioloa) and Lingnan University, Hong Kong, where previous versions of this paper were read. I am also grateful for discussion with David Chalmers, Adam Pautz, and Declan Smithies.

for believing that I am in that state. So, for example, if I feel a tingle in my elbow—a paradigmatically conscious state—I thereby have justification for believing that I feel a tingle in my elbow.

The transparency-based account is popular in recent philosophy, and raises a number of interesting issues.[1] But my focus here will be on the consciousness-based account, and in particular on the objection that Sosa raises for it, viz., the objection that the account founders on introspective knowledge of, or justified belief in, negative facts such as *not* believing that it is garbage night or *not* having a tingle. As will emerge, I am sympathetic to the attitude expressed here by Sosa; my aim is to bring out, in a paper rather than a paragraph, why this is so.

2.

We may begin by stating more explicitly what the consciousness-based account ('CBA', henceforth) is. No doubt the general idea that introspective knowledge "flows from some conscious state that rationalizes it" may be understood in various ways, but in what follows my focus will be on the following:

(CBA)

If S is in conscious state C, then, and because of this, S has justification of a certain kind to form the belief that s/he is in C.

Here are some comments designed to bring out what this involves.

First, CBA is put in terms of justification rather than knowledge, and indeed so far I have talked in terms of justification rather than knowledge. This is a departure from Sosa's passage, which focuses on knowledge. But it seems to me that putting things in terms of justification is, first, more in the spirit of those philosophers who hold CBA,[2] and, second, does not alter the underlying issues I will concentrate on substantially; so that will be my policy here. (My title is to that extent misleading but I will leave it as is.)

Second, CBA speaks, not only of justification, but of justification 'of a certain kind'—what kind? What I have in mind is *prima facie, direct, propositional* justification. (a) The justification is *prima facie* (rather than all things considered) in the sense that while being in C means that S has justification to believe that she is in C, it does not follow from CBA that there are no defeaters for that justification. Perhaps for example, someone trustworthy has just informed S that she is not in C. (b) The justification is *direct* (rather than indirect) because it does not depend on any other justification that S might have. This is not to deny that the justification depends on something; on the contrary, it depends on C if CBA is right. (c) The justification is *propositional* (rather than doxastic) in the sense that we are not supposing that S has formed the belief that she is in C. According to proponents of CBA, being in C confers on S a certain kind of epistemic status—whether S takes advantage of that status by believing something is another matter.

Third, CBA is not simply a statement of a metaphysically sufficient condition for having justification of a certain kind—though I will assume that it is at least that—it is in addition a statement about explanation. According to it S bears the epistemic relation to the relevant belief *in virtue of* S's being in the conscious state, i.e. the consciousness explains the epistemic relation.

Fourth, CBA speaks of a 'conscious' state, but of course states can be conscious in several senses (e.g. Block 1995)—which sense is at issue? I will assume that what is at issue here is *phenomenal* consciousness since philosophers who have been interested in CBA have themselves been mostly interested in phenomenal consciousness. This is not to deny that one might try to develop a version of CBA against the background of a different notion of consciousness, but I will set that aside here.

3.

If that is CBA, what can be said in a preliminary way either for or against it? On the positive side, CBA may seem obvious. When you have a sharp pain, doesn't it seem obvious that you are justified in believing that you have sharp pain, and aren't you justified because you have that sharp pain? Likewise, when you are consciously seeing a lemon, doesn't it seem obvious to that you are justified in believing that you are seeing a lemon, and moreover aren't you justified because you are consciously seeing a lemon? On the face of it, CBA is just a generalization of these obvious truths, and that is part of what makes it plausible.

A further positive feature of CBA is that it provides a way to solve various puzzles about introspection that have emerged in the literature. One example is the evidence puzzle recently formulated by Fred Dretske.[3] Suppose you consciously see a lemon, and suppose (as is sometimes the case) that you know that you are doing so. How is it that you know? On the one hand, there must be some answer to this question; that you know it is not a miracle after all. On the other hand, it is hard to know what the answer to this question is. For the question 'how do you know?' is usually a request for evidence, and if evidence is something that (a) you are aware of and (b) which supports what you know, there seems to be nothing here that meets these conditions. Certainly when you see a lemon you are aware of a lemon, and perhaps too of the fact that there is a lemon. But this does not entail, and does not make probable or confirm, that you are seeing a lemon. How then do you know you are seeing a lemon?

As against this, a proponent of CBA can argue plausibly that are two legitimate things one might have in mind by 'evidence', and that the evidence puzzle arises only from neglecting the second of these. The first is the one at issue in Dretske's discussion, i.e. the one according to which evidence is something which you are aware of and which supports what you know. The second is the idea of a fact that makes it appropriate for you to believe something, or provides justification for you to believe something.[4] On the assumption that the second notion of evidence is legitimate, the proponent of the CBA may say that seeing a lemon does provide you evidence, i.e. because if CBA is true, then if you see a lemon you have justification of a certain kind to believe that you do. Hence the evidence puzzle is solved—and this too is a reason to endorse CBA.

Finally, CBA can seem attractive if we place it in some (recent) historical context. One thing that has happened in the parts of philosophy of mind and epistemology that discuss introspection is a general disenchantment with two sorts of view that for a long time have been dominant. The first of these views is a sort of reliabilism which says (to put it roughly) that the belief that one is in a conscious state is reliably connected to the fact that one is, and that its status as justified is founded on this fact. It is natural, for example, to read a view like this into David Armstrong's discussion of introspection (1968, 1973; Armstrong and Malcolm 1984). But this sort of view has come to seem unsatisfactory for a number of reasons, which I will mention here rather than work through. One is a general dissatisfaction with reliabilism brought to the topic of introspection (Peacocke 1998, Zimmerman 2006). Another is the apparent plausibility of specific arguments against Armstrong's position such as Shoemaker's self-blindness argument (see Shoemaker 1996).

The second view that has come to seem unsatisfactory is the sort of inner sense view that Shoemaker (1996) calls the 'object-perception' account. (Shoemaker contrasts an 'object-perception' view with a 'broad-perception' view—the latter is in effect Armstrong's reliabilism.) The object perception view tries to explain the relation I bear to the fact that I have a sharp pain on the model of the relation I bear to the pain itself. The main problem here is that these relations seem about as different as two relations could be. For one thing, I *feel* the pain, but I do not feel the fact that I have a pain in my foot. Moreover, when I have a pain in my foot, the pain is something I may attend to and to refer to, and in particular I seem to be able to attend to it, and refer to it, *in advance* of coming to know or believe that I feel it. But the *fact* that I feel the pain is not something I may attend to in this way. Of course, *if* I know or believe this fact, then I can attend to what I know or believe; knowing or believing something makes it a possible object of attention and reference just as feeling it does. But this point assumes that I already know or believe the facts in question, and the manner and nature of this knowledge is precisely what is at issue in discussions of introspection.

Now proponents of CBA can reasonably point out that their position is neither of the two views just mentioned. As against the reliabilist/broad perception view, CBA denies the mere existence of a law-like or reliable connection between a conscious state and a belief to the effect that one is in the state is sufficient to provide one with justification to form the relevant belief. As against the object-perception/inner sense view, CBA denies that the relation between the conscious state and the belief is be modelled on the sort of perceptual relation I bear to pains when I feel them. The fact that it is neither of these increasingly unpopular views constitutes a third way that CBA is attractive.

4.

While CBA is attractive in these ways, it also raises some difficult questions. To maintain equilibrium, I will mention three. The first is *the truth question*. Normally, the truth of a belief does not *by itself* justify one in having it. For example, if I weigh N kilos, I do not *thereby* have justification of any kind to believe that I do. So why should it be the case, as CBA implies, that if I am in a conscious state C, I am thereby justified in believing that I am? Of course a proponent of CBA will say that conscious states are special in this regard. But saying this doesn't really answer the question; it only raises the further question of *why* they are special. Why is it the case that conscious states have the property, which other states do not, that by themselves they put their bearers in a certain sort of epistemic state?

The second difficult question for CBA is *the selection question*. Any situation in which the (de se) belief that I have a sharp pain is true is also a situation in which other beliefs are true (e.g. the (de dicto) belief that Stoljar has a sharp pain, or the (philosophically sophisticated) belief that I am presented with, or represent, such and such a condition in my body). But having a sharp pain does not provide me with justification to form these further beliefs, or least not in the way that it provides me with justification to form the belief that I am in pain. For example, no-body thinks that if I feel a sharp pain then I have justification of a certain kind to believe that *Stoljar* feels a sharp pain. Presumably therefore the conscious state provides me with justification to hold some beliefs and not others, even when the beliefs are necessarily equivalent. But why is this the case?

The third is *the scope question*. As stated CBA makes a claim about a sufficient condition for being justified in believing that I am in a conscious state, a claim that is most plausible when what we have in mind are paradigmatic examples of conscious states like having a tingle, consciously seeing a lemon and so forth. But we have introspective access to many facts that do not concern paradigmatic conscious states. For one thing, we can come to know via introspection that we are in standing states, such as standing beliefs or knowledge or desire. Likewise, we can come to know via introspection various general facts about our psychology, e.g. the fact that itches are less unpleasant than pains. Finally, we can come to know negative facts, which is precisely the sort of case raised by Sosa, and which I will concentrate on. So from this point of view the problem about negative facts is an instance—though just one instance—of the scope question.[5]

5.

So what *is* the negation problem exactly? Well, when asked by the doctor 'Are you in much pain?' you can reply 'no I am not in pain' and your answer seems to be an expression of introspective knowledge or belief just as much as if you had answered 'yes I am in agony'. Likewise if you know that you are not in pain, there must be a way that you came to know this—it is not a miracle after all—but it is plain that you did not come to know it by perception or inference (at least not in any obvious sense of perception or inference). And this feature—ability to know a fact about oneself but not via any obvious form of perception or inference—is a common marker of introspection.

Observations like this suggest a Pari Passu principle something like this:

Pari Passu: Any adequate approach to the epistemology of introspection of positive facts should apply pari passu to negative facts.[6]

The problem is that CBA apparently violates this principle. For the obvious way to adjust CBA so that it applies to negative facts is to advance this:

(CBA-neg)

If S is not in C, then and because of this, S has justification of a certain kind to form the belief that s/he is not in C.

But (CBA-neg) is objectionable for two reasons. First, it is open to obvious counterexamples:

- My left sock is not feeling a sharp pain, and yet nor is it true that my left sock has some justification to believe that s/he (it?) is not feeling a sharp pain.
- Henry VIII is not feeling a sharp pain (i.e. because he is dead), and yet nor is it true that Henry VIII is justified in believing that he is feeling a sharp pain.
- Reggie the goldfish is not wondering whether Camus had a more noble war record than Sartre (i.e. because he is too stupid), and yet nor is Reggie justified in believing that he is not wondering whether Camus had a more noble war record than Sartre.

Second, and more generally, while it is initially plausible to go along with CBA in supposing that being in a conscious state provides you with justification, it is hard to see that *not* being in a conscious state can do likewise. The underlying reason is that the class of states that constitute states of (phenomenal) consciousness is not closed under negation. For example, having a tingle in the elbow might be a state that constitutes a state of consciousness, but *not* having a tingle does not. This is not to deny that it is a state; it may be. It is rather to deny that it is a state that constitutes a state of consciousness. But if it is not, it is hard to see how it remains in the spirit of CBA to say that not having a tingle provides justification just as having a tingle does.

It is important to see that the problem here is distinct from the general metaphysical problem about negative facts, states or properties, i.e. the problem of whether such privative entities exist and if so, what explanatory or causal role they play in the world.[7] This is a major topic in metaphysics, but it is not our topic. To see this, suppose we agree both that there is such a fact as that my left sock is not conscious (or that it is not the case that my sock is conscious) and that this fact may explain certain things, e.g. that I am unfazed about attempting to trade my sock on e-bay. Even so it remains implausible that a fact of this sort confers on it (i.e. the sock) any sort of epistemic status—but this is precisely what would be the case if CBA-neg were true. More generally, the objectionable thing about CBA-neg is not that it is committed to the existence of, and an explanatory role for, negative facts; it is rather the particular explanatory role it says that such facts have.

6.

How then might a friend of CBA respond to the problem? I want first to consider a suggestion that may initially seem unexpected; my reason for doing so is that it permits us to introduce some material that will be required later. The suggestion I have in mind appeals to a doctrine in philosophy of mind that I will call *holism* (as opposed to atomism) about mental states.

To illustrate the general idea, consider first the case of belief. Some philosophers—atomists—assume that it is possible for a person to have just one belief. So, from this point of view, it is possible, say, for Tom to believe that he has an older brother in Cleveland, *and nothing else*.[8] For other philosophers—holists—this is not possible. From their point of view, if Tom believes he has an older brother in Cleveland, then he must also have a system of beliefs of which this belief is just one. (It is not assumed that Tom has just one system of beliefs; he may have more than one.) We might put this by saying that, for the holist, the unit of analysis for philosophy of mind—and for the abstract parts of psychology that overlap philosophy of mind—is the system of beliefs rather than individual beliefs; for the atomist, by contrast, the unit of analysis is the individual belief.

This point about beliefs may be extended to other mental states too. According to atomists about perception, for example, it would be possible for you to have just one perception, for example, to see the color of the lemon and that is all. According to holists, this is not possible, and if you see a lemon, then you must have a system of perceptual states of which the state of seeing a lemon is just one. So for example, perhaps you also see the shape of the lemon, its position relative to you, features of the surrounding environment, and perhaps other things too.

Now some ways of describing this distinction in the literature seem to me to be misleading. For example, David Lewis expresses sympathy for the holistic view when he says that 'beliefs' is a *bogus plural*, i.e. a word that bears the superficial marks of a plural but which is not semantically plural (see Lewis 1994). In particular, Lewis says, you have beliefs in the way that you have the blues, where 'blues' in the intended sense certainly *is* a bogus plural. However, if Lewis is making a claim about English, what he says is implausible. In ordinary English, 'belief' is not a bogus plural, if only because it so often picks out things believed, i.e. propositions (see Stalnaker 2004). Moreover, Lewis's way of stating the issue encourages the suggestion that there are no individual belief states. But this seems implausible because there is surely a sense in which if Tom believes that he has a brother in Cleveland, then he is in the state of believing that he has a brother in Cleveland. A better option for the holist is to say, not that there are no individual states but rather that a person has these states *in virtue of* having a system of beliefs—if you like, it is the system of beliefs, rather than the individual belief, that is explanatorily or metaphysically prior.

Somewhat similar remarks apply to Michael Tye's (2004) discussion in *Consciousness and Persons*. Tye is concerned in that book not with beliefs but with experiences, and he appeals to (what I call) holism to provide an attractive explanation of the unity of consciousness, i.e., of the sense in which when you have a beer *and* eat a ham sandwich *and* sit in the sun, you intuitively have a single overarching experience here, rather than three separate experiences. Tye describes his view by saying that, at any one time, a person has a single experience; his is a 'one experience' view, as he says. This suggests, in turn, that it is literally false in the circumstances that one has the experience of tasting the beer. But again, this is implausible: if one tastes the beer at all, there is surely a sense in which one has the experience of tasting the beer. As before, a better option for the holist is not to deny the existence of individual experiences but to claim that what is prior here from an explanatory or metaphysical point of view is the system of experiences.[9]

Suppose now we concentrate, not on the particular way that Lewis and Tye describe their view, but on the view itself—on the view, as I put it, that the basic unit of analysis is the system of beliefs or experiences. What has this to do with the negation problem? Well, holism of this sort permits us to draw a distinction between:

- not being in an individual conscious state – e.g. not having a sharp pain; and
- being in a system of conscious states which does not include some individual conscious state—e.g., being in a system of conscious states which does not include having a sharp pain.

On the face of it, these are different. It is true that my sock does not feel a sharp pain, but it is not true that my sock is in a system of conscious states that does not include having a sharp pain. Likewise, 'Henry VIII is not feeling a sharp pain' is true, but 'Henry VIII is in a system of conscious state that does not include feeling a sharp pain' is false.

With this distinction in hand, we now have a reply to the negation problem on behalf of CBA. The first part of the reply is to advance, not CBA-neg, but CBA-sys:

(CBA-sys)

If S is in a system of conscious states C, then, and because of this, S has justification of certain kind to form the belief that s/he is in C.

The second part is to argue that if CBA-sys is true, then S may have *in*direct justification to believe that some negative fact obtains, so long as S is justified in believing that he or she is in the system of conscious states C. Perhaps, if one were being fully explicit about the reasoning it would go something like this: I am in a system of conscious states C; if I am in C, then I am not having a sharp pain; hence, I am not having a sharp pain.

Does this two-part reply compromise Pari Passu? It does not. First, one might treat the positive case similarly. Second, Pari Passu need not be interpreted as requiring direct justification in both cases, what it requires is only introspective justification flowing from consciousness in both cases.

7.

The response I have outlined to the negation problem is attractive because holism is independently motivated; so far as I know no one who holds holism does so because of *this* problem. But is the response plausible? Of course an atomist will object that holism is false. For example Fodor (1987) argues that holism about belief has the terrible consequence that people can never agree or disagree with each other (or with previous or future versions of themselves). A similar objection would be that, according to holism, no two people could ever feel the same way (i.e. agree in feeling rather than belief). It seems to me that holism can be defended against these objections, but I will not try to make that point here.[10] What is of greater interest at present is whether, assuming it is correct, holism provides an answer to the negation problem.

Well, this depends on whether CBA-sys is true, and unfortunately, it seems to me it is not. Take the system of conscious perceptual and sensory states that you are currently in and call it 'S'. Clearly S is going to be very complicated, containing as parts a number of distinct individual conscious states. In view of its complicated nature, it is very plausible to suppose that, while it may be true that you are in S, it is also true that you could easily fail to be; not because you could easily fail to be in any conscious state at all, but rather because you could very easily be in some state which is *almost but not quite* exactly like S—S*, as it might be. However, if you are in S but could easily not be, we have a straightforward argument against CBA-sys. CBA-sys says that if you are in S, then and because of this, you are justified in believing that you are in S. But what we have just seen is that if you are in S, you could very easily be wrong if you formed the belief that you are in S—for if you formed that belief, it remains the case that you could very easily be in S*, rather than S, in which case the belief would be false. But the fact that you could very easily be wrong in holding some belief is a good indicator that you are not justified in holding that belief. The conclusion is that it is not true that if you are in S, you are justified in believing that you are; more generally, CBA-sys is false, and we have no response here to the negation problem.

Admittedly, this line of argument against CBA-sys depends on an epistemological idea that might be challenged, in particular, that if you could easily be wrong about some proposition then you are not justified in believing it. I won't try to defend that idea here. Instead I will merely note that the problem I have just mentioned for CBA-sys is precisely analogous to a distinct problem raised by Sosa elsewhere in his discussion of the epistemology of introspection, viz., the problem of the speckled hen.[11] Construed as an argument against CBA, the speckled hen problem is as follows. Take a case in which you see a hen with 3 speckles, and assume that this is a phenomenally conscious state. If so, CBA predicts that you are thereby justified in believing that you are seeing a hen with 3 speckles. But now take a case in which you see a hen with 43 speckles, and assume that this too is a phenomenally conscious state. If so, CBA predicts that you are thereby justified in believing that you are seeing a hen with 43 speckles. But this prediction, Sosa argues, seems to be false. You are not justified in believing that you are seeing a hen with 43 speckles—the reason is that you could very easily be wrong. So a pleasing aspect of this point in our discussion of Sosa's negation problem is that it links up with his discussion of the speckled hen.

8.

The holism response to the problem about negative facts is attractive because it appeals to an idea that is independently motivated. But as I mentioned it is not the most straightforward response. Perhaps the 'most straightforward response' award goes (if at all) to any response founded on a classic distinction between consciousness of negation and negation of consciousness. For example, one might say that, in addition to there being such a thing as the experience of being in pain, and the experience of wondering whether Camus has a more noble war record than Sartre, there is also the experience of *not* being in pain, the experience of *not* wondering whether Camus had a more noble war record than Sartre, and so on. More generally, we might insist on a distinction between:

- not being in an conscious state—e.g. not having a sharp pain; and
- the experience of not being in a conscious state—e.g. the experience of not having a sharp pain.

Once again, these are different. It is true that my sock does not feel a sharp pain, but it is not true that my sock has the experience of not having a sharp pain.

Likewise, 'Henry VIII is not feeling a sharp pain'—true; 'Henry VIII has the experience of not feeling a sharp pain'—false.

With this distinction in hand, we now have a different reply to the negation problem. The first part of the reply is to advance, not CBA-neg, but CBA-con-neg:

(CBA-con-neg)

If S is has the experience of not being in C, then, and because of this, S has justification of certain kind to form the belief that s/he has the experience of not being in C.

The second part of the reply is to argue that if CBA-con-neg is true, then S is justified in believing some negative facts obtains. Perhaps, if one were being fully explicit about the reasoning it would go like this: I am have the experience of not being C; if I have that experience, then I am not in C; hence, I am not in C. Does this two-part reply compromise Pari Passu? For the reasons mentioned earlier, it does not.

9.

But how plausible is this second response? I think the main problem with it comes in saying what the experience of not having a sharp pain *is*. There would seem to be four possibilities here, but all of them are implausible in one way or another.[12]

The first possibility is to appeal to the notion of a system of experience, and advance something like this:

System: S has the experience of not being in C iff S has some system of experiences that does not include being in C.

However, the problem with this proposal has already emerged in our discussion. In particular, if *System* is right, then CBA-neg-con recapitulates CBA-sys, and likewise recapitulates its problems.

The second possibility is to appeal to the notion of a totality state, i.e. a state, roughly, which is the conjunction of all the individual states you are in together with the (higher-order) state of not being in any further state:

Total: S has the experience of not being in C iff S is in a total conscious state C# (where C# does not include C).

However, the problem with this proposal is analogous to the problem with *System*. For take C#, your total conscious state. On the face of it, this state will be very complicated, and moreover it is very easy for you to fail to be in it and instead be in one very similar to it. But this raises an analogous problem to that we already raised for *System*.

The third possibility is to appeal to the idea that conscious states are incompatible with each other.

> *Incompatibility:*   S has the experience of not being C iff S is in some conscious state C# (where C# is incompatible with C)

However, this proposal is insufficiently general. It is true that in some cases mental states are incompatible with each other. For example suppose I feel relaxed and comfortable. It is incompatible with feeling this way that I also suffer unbearable pain; you can't very well be both relaxed and comfortable *and* suffer unbearable pain. So in this sort of case the incompatibility proposal works well. But in other cases it is implausible. For example it is not incompatible with my being relaxed and comfortable that I develop a mild itch in the knee; that would not make me any *less* relaxed and comfortable. On the other hand, nor would *not* developing a mild itch in the knee. More generally: both the presence and the absence of a mild itch are compatible with being relaxed and comfortable. Nevertheless, suppose as a matter of fact I do *not* develop and so do not have a mild itch. How do I know this? Knowing that I am relaxed and comfortable is clearly no help, since that knowledge leaves open whether I have the itch or I do not.

The final possibility is to appeal to the notion of an absence:

> *Absence:*   S has the experience of not being in C iff S has an experience of the absence of C.

However, this proposal seems to trade in one difficult question for another. Our main question in this section is: what is for someone to have an experience of not being in pain? *Absence* answers that it is for the person to experience an absence of pain. But what's that? It is natural to feel that no advance has been made here.

It might be objected that sense can be make of the idea of experiencing the absence of a state by pointing out that experiences, and conscious states generally, very often represent things, and there does not seem to be any problem in general with representing the absence of things. Entering the café, one might see that Pierre is absent, and so represent that he is absent. Isn't this fairly described as the experience of the absence of Pierre?[13]

However, while this might be true, it has no any application to the case at hand. For it is one thing to represent the absence of Pierre, another thing to represent the absence of a conscious state. For one to represent the absence of Pierre is presumably either for one to believe that Pierre is absent or for it to seem to one in perception that Pierre is absent. By analogy, to represent the absence of a conscious state would be either to believe that one is not in the state or for it to seem to one in perception that one is not in that state. But neither option is helpful to the CBA. The problem with the belief option is that we are interested here in what happens *prior* to belief—that was the point of emphasizing propositional justification in the initial statement of CBA. The problem with the perception option is that if we adopt it we seem to have backed into the inner sense account. But as we noted above, part of the point of CBA is that it is distinct from that account. Hence it is very hard to see how CBA can appeal to the idea that the experience of not being in pain is or entails a representation that one is not in pain.

10.

The discussion so far has set out the negation problem for CBA, and considered and rejected two ways to deal with it: the appeal to holism, and the appeal to the distinction between consciousness of negation and negation of consciousness. What unites these suggestions is that they stay close to the spirit of CBA; indeed it is natural to read both as attempting of find a proxy mental state that might 'act up' for the negative fact that one is not in a particular conscious state.

In the next part of the discussion, I want to consider two further ways in which CBA might be defended. What unites these further suggestions is the thought that the versions of CBA I have been concentrating on are too simple, and that a more complicated proposal will do better. Both of these suggestions raise a number of complicated issues that go well beyond the scope of this paper, so it is important to be aware of the limits of the discussion to follow. I will be interested in these proposals to the extent that (and *only* to the extent that) they may help CBA solve the negation problem.

The first of the options I have in mind is to appeal to acquaintance. We noted in §3 that the framework for contemporary discussions of introspection is very largely set by the disenchantment many philosophers feel with both reliabilism and the inner sense theory. Now for some philosophers the proper response to this situation is not to look forward to some new theory, but to look back to the notion of acquaintance in something like the sense developed in defended by Bertrand Russell roughly a hundred years ago.[14] This idea—the *acquaintance-based account*, I will call it—need not be thought of as inconsistent with the basic impulse behind CBA. Rather it can be understood as elaborating the basic idea. A natural elaboration, for example, might go as follows:

(ABA):

(a) If S is in conscious state C, then S is acquainted with S's being in C; and
(b) If S is acquainted with S's being in C, then, and because of this, S has justification of certain kind to form the belief that S is in C.

402 / Daniel Stoljar

So understood ABA entails CBA but not vice versa. Someone might agree with CBA and yet disagree with ABA, precisely because they disagree with the notion of acquaintance with which it operates. Hence ABA is genuinely different to anything we have seen before.

Now one objection to ABA is that the notion of acquaintance it employs is awfully close to the sort of relation postulated by the object perception account described by Shoemaker, and so the basic position here is awfully close to the inner sense view. Acquaintance theorists typically insist in reply that that acquaintance is not a kind of perception. For example, it is common to assert that the state of perceiving something is in some sense metaphysically distinct from the thing perceived; acquaintance, they say, is not like that, or at least is not in the intended sense. I am doubtful that this answers the problem, but I don't want to pursue that here.[15] Rather I want to concentrate on whether ABA represents a development of CBA that does better as regards the negation problem than anything we have met before.

On the face of it, the answer is no. For if it is adjusted to handle negation, the proposal would become:

(ABA-neg):

(a) If S is not in conscious state C, then S is acquainted with her/his not being in C; and
(b) If S is acquainted with her/his not being in C, then, and because of this, S has justification of certain kind to form the belief that s/he is not in C.

And the problem with this is that its first part faces the same counterexamples as CBA-neg. After all, my left sock is not feeling a sharp pain but nor is it true that my left sock is acquainted with its not feeling a sharp plain; *mutatis mutandis* for Henry VIII and Reggie the goldfish.

Might one suggest that this problem is generated by the particular way in which I have connected CBA to ABA? A feature of the proposal so far is that it entails that *if* one is in (or not in) a conscious state, *then* one is acquainted with one's being (or not being) in that state. An alternative might be to trade in this conditional for a conjunction. From this point of view, ABA becomes:

(ABA*)

If (a) S is in conscious state C and (b) S is acquainted with S's being in C, then, and because of this, S has justification of certain kind to form the belief that S is in C.

Developing the proposal in this direction (and adjusting it so as to deal with the negation case; I will pass over the details of how to do this) would indeed result in a view that avoids the left-sock counterexamples but it nevertheless seems to face problems, at least if it is interpreted as a development of CBA. First, one might wonder whether anything is left of the CBA on this account. For one thing, in order for S to be justified in the specific way at issue, we require now, not simply that S is in a conscious state but two things: the conscious state and the acquaintance relation. This by itself is not a problem of course, but it is if we are out to find some elaboration of the CBA. Second, it is now more mysterious than it might otherwise be what the relevant notion of acquaintance is. If a conscious state bears only a contingent connection to acquaintance as ABA* implies, then the latter notion cannot be understood as the proponent of ABA wants. Indeed, as noted a moment ago, that was precisely supposed to be the difference between the approach to introspection that looked back to acquaintance and the discredited inner sense view.

11.

I said before that there are two ways in which one might seek to elaborate the basic thought behind CBA in order to handle the negation problem. Appealing to acquaintance is the first way; the other is to appeal to the notion of understanding, and so adopt what I will call the *understanding-based account*. As in the case of the ABA, the understanding based-account need not be understood as inimical to the basic thrust behind the CBA; rather it can be understood as an elaboration on it.[16]

A natural elaboration proceeds on the model of the acquaintance-based account:

(UBA):

(a) If S is in conscious state C, then S understands the proposition that S is in C; and

(b) If S is understands the proposition that S is in C, then, and because of this, S has justification of certain kind to form the belief that S is in C.

However, the problem with UBA is that it brings us no closer to solving the negation problem. Applied to that problem it would entail:

(UBA-neg):

(a) If S is not in conscious state C, then S understands the proposition that S is not in C; and

(b) If S is understands the proposition that S is not in C, then, and because of this, S has justification of certain kind to form the belief that S is not in C.

But this faces the same problems that CBA-neg faces. After all, my left sock is not feeling a sharp pain but nor is it true that my left sock understands what it is for it to not feel a sharp pain; *mutatis mutandis* for Henry VIII and Reggie the goldfish.[17]

Could one respond as we did in the case of the acquaintance-based view, and suggest that the problem comes from the conditional structure of the first clause of this account? Well if we mimic the structure of ABA* we would arrive at UBA*

(UBA*)

If S is in conscious state C and S understands the proposition that s/he is in C then, and because of this, S has justification of certain kind to form the belief that s/he is in C.

Developing the proposal in this direction (and adjusting it so as to deal with the negation case; I will as before pass over the details of how to do this) would indeed result in a view that avoids the left-sock counterexamples. But, as in the case of ABA*, it is now not clear what is left of the motivating idea of CBA, namely the idea that self-knowledge flows from some conscious state that rationalizes it.

We may bring this out by recalling again the widespread disenchantment we have mentioned a number of times with both the reliabilist and the inner-sense approaches. As we noted, CBA represents one reaction to this disenchantment. A completely different reaction is to try to explain introspective belief on the model of analytic or conceptual truths. For some propositions—e.g. the proposition that if Ed kills Fred, then Fred is dead—it is plausible that merely understanding them puts one in a position to know (or provides one with justification to believe) that they are true. It is natural to read UBA* as trying to bring this idea to the topic of introspection, not by saying that the propositions we come to know by introspection are analytic or conceptual—which they clearly are not—but by supposing that they are, if you like, conditionally analytic or conceptual. So the thought is that just as understanding the proposition that if Ed kills Fred, then Fred is dead provides one with justification to believe that it is true, so does understanding the proposition that I am in pain provide one with justification of a certain kind to believe that it is true—at least on the condition that it is true. This sort of account is controversial—for one thing, it puts considerable pressure on the notion of understanding—but I don't want to assess it here. The main point is that it looks to have a very different shape from CBA.

12.

The natural conclusion to draw from the discussion so far is the following. There is no way to accommodate the phenomenon of introspective knowledge of, or justified belief in, negative facts within the framework provided by CBA. On the one hand, a proponent of that view cannot plausibly find a proxy state that plays the role of not being in a conscious state. On the other hand, a proponent of that view cannot plausibly elaborate the view so as to avoid the problem, and remain with in the spirit of the view. It is for this reason that I agree with Sosa that there is a gaping deficiency in views that say that introspective knowledge flows from a conscious state that rationalizes it.

What is to be done? The obvious move is to stop trying to defend or elaborate CBA but rather to capture whatever the truth lies behind in it in a different framework. There might be a number of ways to do this. Indeed, both ABA and UBA provide hints; it might be best for proponents of those views to drop the connection to CBA entirely. But in what remains of the paper I want briefly to set out a different way in which this might be done.

The proposal is to adopt what I will call the *rationality-based account*.[18]

(RBA)

If (a) S is in a conscious state C and (b) S has a rational disposition to form the justified belief that s/he is in C if certain conditions are met (e.g. S is in C, it matters to S whether s/he is in C, and S understands the proposition that s/he is in C), then and because of this, S has a justification of certain kind to form the belief that s/he is in C.

Here are some comments designed to bring out what this involves:

First, RBA takes over some of the ideas from CBA: 'justification of a certain kind', 'because', 'conscious'. We can assume that these are to be interpreted in the same way as was set out previously.

Second, RBA talks of a 'rational disposition'—what is this? Roughly, S has a rational disposition to F if and only if (a) there is a requirement or requirements of rationality R1, R2...RN that entail that you should F in such and such circumstances and (b) S abides by R1, R2...RN. (Analogy: S has a natural disposition to F if and only if (a) there are various empirical laws L1, L2...LN that entail that you should F in such and such circumstance and (b) S is governed by those laws.)

Third, RBA talks of a disposition to form a justified belief. Here the relevant notion is a doxastic justification rather than propositional justification. So in effect RBA is explaining propositional justification in terms of a rational route to doxastic justification, rather than the other way around.[19]

Fourth, as against the acquaintance-based view, RBA makes no appeal to a Russellian notion of acquaintance, and as against the understanding-based view, while it makes some claim about understanding, it does not place anything like as much weight on that notion as UBA does.

13.

What are the points of comparison between RBA and CBA? As regards the three positive points about CBA I mentioned in §2, these points do not discriminate between CBA and RBA, and to that extent provide no support for RBA *as opposed to* CBA. First, CBA can certainly accommodate the apparently obvious fact that when you have a sharp pain you are justified in believing that you do, but so can RBA. RBA may say that claims of this sort are perfectly true and obviously so; it is simply that they treat the relevant rational disposition as an enabling factor. Second, CBA has the resources to respond to Dretske's evidence problem, but so does RBA. RBA too can say that being in a conscious state and being rational in a particular sort of way can provide one with evidence—in one sense of 'evidence'—that one is in the state (see Stoljar 2012). Finally, it is true that CBA has the advantage that it is neither reliabilism nor the inner sense view, but the same is true of RBA.

How does this view fair with respect to the truth, selection and scope problems, which I mentioned in §4? First, RBA avoids the truth problem because it does not entail that merely being in a conscious state provides one with justification to form the belief that one is in it; what is required in addition is that you have a certain sort of rational disposition.[20] Second, RBA avoids the selection problem because being rationally disposed to form the belief that I am in a conscious state is distinct from being rationally disposed to form the belief that Stoljar is. More abstractly, what is required to solve this problem is some sort of hyper-intensional filter, something that takes the belief that I am in a conscious state, and separates it from the belief that Stoljar is in that state. The notion of a rational disposition is such a filter, though it is not the only one—for example, both the acquaintance-based and the understanding-based accounts likewise postulate such a filter so the selection problem is not a problem for them.

Finally, as regards the scope problem, the most important aspect of this for our purposes is of course the issue about negation, and here too RBA avoids the problem. We saw above that the natural way to respond to the problem from the point of view of CBA is to advance CBA-neg, and that this faces some serious problems. By contrast, the obvious way to adjust RBA so that it applies to negative facts is to advance this:

(RBA-neg)

If S is not in C, and if S has a rational disposition to form a justified belief that s/he is not in C if certain conditions are met, then and because of this, S has justification of a certain kind to form the belief that s/he is not in C.

But this does not face the same sort of problems. After all, my left sock is not feeling a sharp pain but nor is it true that my left sock has the relevant rational disposition; *mutatis mutandis* for Henry VIII and Reggie the goldfish.

Of course I am not suggesting here and now that RBA is true. For one thing, as noted in §4, there are other aspects of the scope problem apart from the issue of negation. Moreover, there are lots of questions about the requirements of rationality and other paraphernalia that RBA is committed to, some of which we have mentioned (Cf. fn. 20). Finally, there is the matter of comparing RBA with UBA or ABA or developments thereof, which is something I have not gone into. So I present RBA here not as a completed view but as a program for research. On the other hand, I am able to offer the introspective report that I am *not* aware of any approach distinct from RBA that is more attractive than it when it comes to the epistemology of introspection.

Notes

1. See, e.g., Evans 1982, Moran 2001, Byrne 2005, 2012, and Silins 2012.
2. For writings that seem to me sympathetic with CBA, see, e.g, Peacocke 1998, Conee and Feldman, 2004 Smithies 2012, forthcoming.
3. See Dretske 2003, 2012. For my own response to this problem, see Stoljar 2012; for a different response, see Byrne 2005, 2012.
4. For this notion of evidence, see Pryor 2005. For some discussion of how this notion relates to Dretske's puzzle see Stoljar 2012.
5. For some discussion of the problem about standing states, see Smithies 2012; for some discussion about the problem of general facts, see Pautz 2011.
6. The general idea behind Pari Passu is noted in a number of places in the literature, apart from the Sosa passage. See, e.g. Shoemaker's discussion of not believing something in his 2009.
7. The literature on this problem is large. For some recent discussion of the general issue, see Bjornsson 2007, Schaffer 2010 and Barker and Jago 2012.
8. This example is from Dennett 1981, 251.
9. For a suggestion that holism might be understood in something like this way (at least in the case of experiences) see Chalmers 2010, 502 (fn.1). The appeal to explanatory priority rather than existence is obviously reminiscent of recent debates about monism, e.g. in Schaffer 2010. I won't try to elaborate the connection here in any detail however.
10. My reasons have to do partly with those mentioned in Stalnaker 2004, 207–10, and partly with the distinction emphasized in the text between approaches to holism that deny the existence of individual belief states or experience states, and those which admit their existence but insist that one has those states in virtue of being in a system of belief or experience states. If one does not deny the existence of such states then there is no reason to deny that two people cannot literally share the state in question.
11. See Sosa 2003, and also Bonjour and Sosa 2003, ch.7. As Sosa notes, the example goes back to Chisholm 1942. For more background and references, see Gertler 2012. For an interesting discussion of the speckled hen from the point of view of CBA, see Smithies forthcoming; I will not try to deal with issues raised in Smithies' paper here.
12. Aficionados of the general problem of negative facts might notice that the options I am discussing here parallel the options often mentioned there. (See the papers mentioned in fn.7). I noted above that the general problem is not ours—that is consistent with its being a source of example.

408 / Daniel Stoljar

13. This example is from Sartre 1956, 9–10.
14. A recent defence of the acquaintance view is Gertler 2010, 2012. See also Chalmers 2010.
15. My scepticism in part derives from the thought that what similarities you discern between introspection and perception depends on what theory of perception is salient. For these points see Shoemaker 1996.
16. Some strands in Peacocke 1998 seem to me to suggest the understanding-based account. Appealing to understanding has also been suggested to me a lot in conversation as the main way in which the CBA account can respond to the negative fact problem. My comments in the text will be confined to this topic, viz. whether a proponent of CBA can appeal to understanding to avoid the negation problem—dealing with the UBA in detail is something that I hope to do in on a different occasion.
17. UBA-neg (and UBA) faces the further problem that (b) is of a form that is not generally true. From the mere fact that I understand p, it does not follow that I am justified in believing it—e.g. if I understand the proposition that it is garbage night, this does not make me justified in believing it. So a friend of UBA-neg (and UBA) is committed to the idea that there is something special about understanding this proposition; but what? (This is related to the truth problem mentioned in §4.)
18. The rationality-based account I am about to sketch is similar in some ways to Shoemaker's (e.g. 1996, 2009) view and Sosa's (e.g. 2012) view; certainly I have arrived at the view in part by thinking about theirs. I will not try to present a discussion of the pros and cons of these suggestions here but perhaps two comments are in order. First, Sosa embeds his account within a virtue epistemology, which I do not. Second, it is part of Shoemaker's account as I understand it that an introspective belief, e.g. the belief that I am in a particular conscious state, is nothing over and above the fact that I am in the state, and am rational and have reflected on the matter. This account in the text is not committed to this view of introspective belief, which seems to me to be implausible.
19. In this sense, RBA follows the suggestion of Turri 2010.
20. It might be objected that the RBA faces a version of the truth problem of its own. After all, the rational necessities at issue here will presumably entail that if one is in a state, and if various background conditions obtain, then one should believe that one is in the state. But we do not think in general it is rationally necessary that if p is true, the one should believe that p—why here? This is a topic too big to deal with here. In brief, though, my response is two fold. First, rational necessities tell us about the permissible and impermissible ways of bringing together mental states. Hence if we suppose only that it is rationally necessary that if p is true then one should believe that p, we already know something about what p is or concerns, viz., it is a proposition about mental states. In this way, rational necessities are quite unlike natural or metaphysical necessities. If it is metaphysically or naturally necessary that if p then you should believe p, this by itself tells us nothing about what p is or concerns. Second, to say what the precise scope is of the rational necessity in question here is part of the job of spelling out RBA, so the objection raises a project not a problem. Presumably, for example, it is not true that for any mental state, or even for any

conscious mental state, it is rationally necessary that if one is in it one should believe that one is. For some further, but still too brief, discussion of this matter see Stoljar 2012.

References

Armstrong, D.M. 1968. *A Materialist Theory of the Mind*. London: Routledge and Kegan Paul.

Armstrong, D.M. 1973. *Belief Truth and Knowledge*. Cambridge University Press.

Armstrong, D.M and Malcolm, N. 1984. *Consciousness and Causality*. Oxford: Blackwell.

Barker, S and Jago, M. 2012. 'Being Positive about Negative Facts', *Philosophy and Phenomenological Research* 85(1): 117–138.

Bjornsson, G. 2007 'If you believe in positive facts, you should believe in negative facts', in Toni Rønnow-Rasmussen, Björn Petersson, Jonas Josefsson and Dan Egonsson (eds), *Hommage à Wlodek: Philosophical Papers Dedicated to Wlodek Rabinowicz*. Lund University 2007. Available at http://www.fil.lu.se/hommageawlodek/.

Block, N. 1995. 'On a confusion about a function of consciousness', *Behavioral and Brain Sciences* 18: 225–47.

Bonjour, L and Sosa, E. 2003. *Epistemic Justification*. Oxford: Blackwell.

Byrne, A. 2005. "Introspection", *Philosophical Topics* 33: 79–104.

Byrne, A. 2012. "Knowing that I See", in Smithies, D and Stoljar, D. (eds), *Consciousness and Introspection*. New York: Oxford University Press.

Chalmers, D. 2010. *The Character of Consciousness*. New York: Oxford University Press.

Chisholm, R. 1942. "The Problem of the Speckled Hen", *Mind* 51:368–373.

Conee, E and Feldman R. 2004. *Evidentialism: Essays in Epistemology*. New York: Oxford University Press.

Dennett, D. 1981. *Brainstorms: Philosophical Essays on Mind and Psychology*. Cambridge, MA: MIT Press.

Dretske, F. 2003. "How do you know you are not a Zombie?" in B. Gertler (ed.), *Privileged Access: Philosophical Accounts of Self-Knowledge*, 1–14. Burlington: Ashgate Publishing.

Dretske, F 2012. "Awareness and Authority: Skeptical Doubts about Self-knowledge", in Smithies, D and Stoljar, D. (eds) *Consciousness and Introspection*, 93–128. New York: Oxford University Press.

Evans, G. 1982. *Varieties of Reference* (ed. John McDowell). Oxford: Oxford University Press.

Fodor, J. 1987. *Psychosemantics*. Cambridge, MA: MIT Press.

Gertler, B. 2010. *Self-Knowledge*. London: Routledge.

Gertler, B. 2012. "Renewed Acquaintance", in Smithies, D and Stoljar, D (eds.) *Consciousness and Introspection*, 93–128. New York: Oxford University Press.

Lewis, D. 1994. 'Reduction of Mind', in S. Guttenplan ed., *A Companion to the Philosophy of Mind* 412–31. Oxford: Blackwell. Repr. in his *Papers in Metaphysics and Epistemology* (Cambridge: Cambridge University Press, 1999), 291–324. All references are to the reprinted version.

Moran, R. 2001. *Authority and Estrangement*. Princeton: Princeton University Press.

Pautz, A. 2011. "Can disjunctivists explain our access to the sensible world?". *Philosophical Issues, The Epistemology of Perception*, 21: 384–433.

Peacocke, C. 1998/ "Conscious attitudes, attention, and self-knowledge" in C. Wright, B. Smith & C. Macdonald (eds.), *Knowing Our Own Minds*. Oxford University Press.

Pryor, J. 2005. "There is Immediate Justification", In Sosa, E and Setup, M (eds.), *Contemporary Debates in Epistemology*, 181–201. Oxford: Blackwell.

Sartre JP. 1956. *Being and Nothingness*, trans. Hazel Barnes. New York: Philosophical Library.

Schaffer, J. 2010. "The Least Discerning and Most Promiscuous Truth-Maker,' *The Philosophical Quarterly* 60(239): 307–324.

Silins, N. 2012 "Judgment as a Guide to Belief" in Smithies, D and Stoljar, D. (eds) *Consciousness and Introspection*, 295–328. New York: Oxford University Press.

Sosa, E. 2003 "Privileged Access", in Gertler, B (ed.), *Privileged Access: Philosophical Accounts of Self-Knowledge*. Burlington: Ashgate Publishing.

Sosa, E. 2012. "The Epistemology of Introspection", in Smithies, D and Stoljar, D. (eds) *Consciousness and Introspection*, 169–182. New York: Oxford University Press.

Shoemaker, S. 1996. *The First-Person Perspective and Other Essays*. Cambridge: Cambridge University Press.

Shoemaker, S. 2009. "Self Intimation and Second Order Belief", *Erkenntnis* 71: 35–51. Reprinted in Smithies, D and Stoljar, D. (eds) 2012 *Consciousness and Introspection*, 239–258. New York: Oxford University Press.

Smithes, D. 2012 "A Simple Theory of Introspection", in D. Smithies and D. Stoljar (eds.), *Introspection and Consciousness*, 259–93. Oxford: Oxford University Press.

Smithies, D. forthcoming "Mentalism and Epistemic Transparency", *Australasian Journal of Philosophy*.

Stalnaker, R. 2004. "Lewis on Intentionality", *Australasian Journal of Philosophy*, 82(1): 199–212.

Stoljar, D. 2012 "Knowledge of Perception", In Smithies, D and Stoljar, D. (eds) *Consciousness and Introspection*, 65–92. New York: Oxford University Press.

Turri, J. 2010. "On the Relationship Between Propositional and Doxastic Justification," *Philosophy and Phenomenological Research* 80(2).

Tye, M. 2004. *Consciousness and Persons*. Cambridge, MA: MIT Press.

Zimmerman, A. 2006. "Basic Self-Knowledge: Answering Peacocke's Criticisms of Constitutivism", *Philosophical Studies*. 128(2): 337–379.

Philosophical Perspectives, 26, Philosophy of Mind, 2012

DEFINING AND DEFENDING NONCONCEPTUAL CONTENTS AND STATES

James Van Cleve
The University of Southern California

Discussions of whether perceptual states have nonconceptual content typically define the issue in a way that is bound to be confusing to anyone entering the debate for the first time—they conflate questions about the nature of contents *per se* with questions about the requirements on perceivers if they are to be in states with those contents. My principal aim in what follows is to provide a more perspicuous way of setting up the issue, building on work by Speaks, Byrne, and Crowther. My secondary aim is to sharpen and endorse one of the arguments for the nonconceptuality of perceptual states—the argument from experience as a source of concepts.

I.

I begin with a sampling of definitions of nonconceptual content:

To say that a mental content is nonconceptual is to say that its subject need not possess any of the concepts that we, as theorists, exercise when we state the correctness conditions for that content. (Tye 2000, 62)

Those who hold that there is non-conceptual content maintain that there are mental states which represent the world, even though their subject lacks the concepts that would enable her to specify that content. (Gendler and Hawthorne 2006, 14)

The central idea behind the theory of nonconceptual mental content is that some mental states can represent the world even though the bearer of those mental states need not possess the concepts required to specify their content. (Bermudez 2008)

The content of a state is nonconceptual if "an individual does not or cannot exercise the concepts involved in its articulation." (Gunther 2003, 14)[1]

> For any state with content, S, S has a nonconceptual content, P, iff a subject
> X's being in S does not entail that X possesses the concepts that canonically
> characterize P. (Crane 1992, 143)...(T)o say that concepts are not components
> of contents is to say that the subject does not have to possess the concepts used
> to characterize the content in order for his or her state to have such a content.
> (Crane 1992, 155)

> A mental state has [non]conceptual content iff [it is not the case that] "it has
> a representational content which is characterizable only in terms of concepts
> which the subject himself possesses" and which has a form enabling it to serve
> as an inference. (Brewer 2005, 217–18)[2]

I mention one feature of these definitions only to set it aside for now. All of
the definitions make mention in their definientia of the concepts that *characterize*
a certain content or that would enable one to *specify* the content or the like;
they do not make mention of the concepts that *figure in* or are *constituents of*
the content. Is a distinction intended here? Not necessarily; many writers on
nonconceptual content, including some of those quoted above, explicitly identify
the concepts that characterize a content with the concepts that compose it or
are constituents of it.[3] I shall return below to the possibility of distinguishing
characterizing concepts from constituent concepts.

The feature of the definitions on which I wish to concentrate is something
else. All of them purport to define nonconceptuality as a property of *contents,*
yet in their definientia, they seem to formulate what is more properly (at least in
the first instance) a feature of a *state* of a subject or of a subject's *relation* to a
content. The linguistic marker of this apparent disconnect between definiendum
and definiens is that all of the definitions make mention on the right side of a
subject of experience, but this subject is nowhere in evidence on the left.

That something is askew with the standard definitions has been noted by
several recent writers, all of whom have suggested that the definitions conflate two
distinct notions of conceptuality and nonconceptuality. To rectify this situation,
Byrne (2005, following Heck 2000) distinguishes between the conceptuality or
nonconceptuality of *states* and that of *contents*; Speaks (2005) distinguishes
between *relatively* and *absolutely* conceptual or nonconceptual content; and
Crowther (2006) distinguishes between *possessional* and *compositional* conceptual
or nonconceptual content.[4] Each of these three writers observes that definitions
like those quoted above mash together the two sides of his distinction—they use
in their definienda language apt for the expression of a notion on one side of the
distinction, but in their definientia language more suited for a notion on the other
side, making a muddle of the issue. Byrne, Speaks, and Crowther also note that
typical arguments purporting to establish conclusions about nonconceptuality in
the content, absolute, or compositional sense may in fact only reach conclusions
about nonconceptuality in the state, relativized, or possessional sense. If they are
right about this, their distinctions certainly matter.

As I noted above, the standard definitions all make mention of a subject on the right that is nowhere in evidence on the left. To see why this is a problem (and to make it stand out more starkly), let us note that there would be a *logical* defect in a definition of the following form:

> State M with content p has nonconceptual content iff S can be in M even though S does not possess the concepts in p.

The defect is that the variable 'S' has free occurrences on the right, but no occurrences at all on the left.[5] The same defect is present in the definition 'n is a superior number iff n is greater than m', where 'm' is a free variable.

There are three ways to rectify this situation. We could (1) *remove* the variable S on the right, (2) *add* a corresponding variable on the left, or (3) do neither of these things, but *quantify* the variable on the right. The attempts of the authors I have cited to bring further clarity to the notion of nonconceptual content may all be viewed (though none of them is explicit about it) as employing one or another of these three strategies.

The "remove on the right" strategy has been employed by all three of the reformers in characterizing one pole of the distinction they wish to draw. Thus Speaks defines what he calls *absolutely* nonconceptual content as follows:

> A mental state has *absolutely nonconceptual content* iff that mental state has a different kind of content than do beliefs, thoughts, and so on. (2005, 360)

Byrne does something similar; he says that for a content to be nonconceptual in the sense in which nonconceptuality is a property of contents themselves is for it to be a content of the kind other than that possessed by beliefs (2005, 233).

Crowther offers something potentially different, but equivalent for anyone who thinks belief contents are Fregean:

> p is a (compositionally) conceptual content iff p is composed exclusively of concepts. (2006, 250).[6] [Correlatively, p is a (compositionally) nonconceptual content iff it is not the case that p is composed exclusively of concepts.]

Crowther explains further that concepts are Fregean senses, individuated in such a way that C is a sense iff for some concept D coextensive with C, it is possible for someone in whom the question arises to believe that . . . C . . . while doubting or disbelieving the corresponding proposition that . . . D . . .[7] His definition is more committal than those of Speaks and Byrne, but it would come to the same thing as theirs for anyone who held that the contents of belief are Fregean propositions, built up from Fregean concepts—an assumption that Crowther says is common ground for most parties to the conceptual-nonconceptual debate.

What happens to the debate about nonconceptual content if the objects of belief are held to be either Russellian propositions (structures consisting of individuals and properties) or Stalnakerian propositions (sets of possible worlds)? Stalnakerian propositions, if held to be not merely determined by sets of worlds but identical with them, are composed of worlds rather than concepts. Russellian propositions are not composed *exclusively* of concepts, since they have individuals as constituents, and perhaps they are not composed even *partly* of concepts, if concepts are individuated more finely than properties. How, then, should we classify perceptual contents in the view of someone who takes perceptual contents and belief contents alike to be Russellian propositions, or who takes both alike to be Stalnakerian propositions? Are such perceptual contents conceptual or nonconceptual? Byrne and Speaks would classify them as conceptual, since they have the same type of content as beliefs. Crowther would classify them as nonconceptual, since they are not composed exclusively of concepts.

For the purposes of this paper, I am going to side with Crowther. It is desirable to have an intrinsic characterization of what it is for a content to be conceptual or nonconceptual—one we can apply independently of what we have antecedently decided about the contents of beliefs.[8]

By getting rid of the reference to a subject on the right, the definitions of Byrne, Speaks, and Crowther do define a property that is a property of contents themselves. However, the same is not true of the definitions one typically sees. If we retain a reference to a subject on the right (as the typical definitions do), we need to use one of the other strategies for avoiding the logical defect.

The "add on the left" strategy has been employed by Speaks in formulating what he calls the *relativized* notion of nonconceptual content:

A mental state has *nonconceptual content relative to agent A* at a time t iff the content of that mental state includes concepts not grasped (possessed) by A at t. (2005, 360)[9]

Here we do not speak of nonconceptual content *simpliciter*, but only of nonconceptual content relative to this or that agent, now explicitly mentioned on the left.[10]

For an application of the distinction between the absolute and the relativized notions, we may look at what Speaks has to say about one of the arguments for holding that perceptual states have nonconceptual content—the argument from animal perception, which runs as follows:

1. Some animals possess no concepts at all (or hardly any).
2. They nonetheless enjoy some perceptual states with the same contents as some of our own perceptual states.
3. Therefore, some perceptual states of humans have nonconceptual content.

Speaks rightly notes that it does not follow from these premises that any human perceptual states have nonconceptual content in the absolute sense. For all that has been said, it could be that the content of the states in question is absolutely conceptual, even though animals need not grasp the concepts in the content to be in states having that content. In that case, the premises would be true and the conclusion false (if taken to be about absolutely nonconceptual content). We could nonetheless allow, says Speaks, that the following argument for *relatively* nonconceptual content is valid:

1. Animals can be in state M without grasping the concepts included in its content.
2. Humans cannot be in state M without grasping those concepts.
3. Therefore, M has nonconceptual content for animals, but not for humans.[11]

Speaks's distinction is certainly of value in enabling us to see what does and does not follow from the premises of the argument from animal perception. However, it seems to me that the terminology he uses to express his distinction is horribly misleading. It suggests (what Speaks by no means wishes to say) that the content of a given state can be of one sort (the conceptual kind) for some subjects while the same content is of another kind (the nonconceptual kind) for other subjects. How odd!

The 1–2–3 argument in the previous paragraph (which is valid given the way Speaks defines the relativized sense of nonconceptual content) may be compared with the following argument (whose formal parallelism with the original does not at all depend on whether grasping concepts is anything like grasping handlebars):

1. Tommy can ride his bike without grasping its handlebars.
2. His grandmother cannot ride Tommy's bike without grasping its handlebars.
3. Therefore, the bike has nonhandlebar content for Tommy, but not for his grandmother.

Surely Tommy's bike does not have one kind of content for Tommy and a different kind for Grandmother—it is the same bike with the same parts no matter who rides it.[12] What is true is simply that Tommy and his grandmother have different requirements for riding the bicycle. Similarly, perceptual states do not have contents of one kind for animals and of another kind for humans. The entire issue is misleadingly framed when framed as an issue about a subject-relative kind of content.

For the foregoing reason, I prefer the quantificational strategy to the relativizing strategy for dealing with the problem of the variable that occurs only on the right. This strategy is implicitly employed by Byrne. He gives a preliminary definition of one notion of nonconceptuality as follows:

> Mental state M has nonconceptual content p iff it is possible to be in M without possessing all the concepts that characterize p. (2005, 233)

He then rightly notes that the definiens does not seem to define a kind of content but rather a kind of state one can be in with regard to a content. So he alters the definiendum to suit:

> State M with content p is a *nonconceptual state* iff it is possible to be in M without possessing all the concepts that characterize p.

'It is possible to be in M' is presumably elliptical for 'it is possible for *someone* to be in M', so we may expand Byrne's definition of a nonconceptual state as follows:

> State M with content p is a *nonconceptual state* iff it is possible for someone to be in M without possessing all the concepts that characterize p.

This is Byrne's definition of nonconceptuality for states (as opposed to contents).

In this definition, there is no stray variable on the right; the variable has been lassoed by a quantifier. In symbols, the definiens may be rendered as '◊∃S(S is in M & it is not the case that S possesses all the concepts that characterize p)'. We could also have remedied the problem of the stray variable by using a *universal* quantifier: it is possible for *anyone* to be in M without possessing all the concepts that characterize p. Perhaps that would define a notion of nonconceptuality worth exploring. Yet another option, if we take seriously such phrases as '*the* subject' as they occur on the right sides of some definitions of nonconceptual content, would be to use an iota operator or definite description-forming operator rather than a quantifier as our variable-binding operator. Our definition would then read 'state M with content p is a nonconceptual state iff *the S* such that S is the subject of M need not have all the concepts that characterize p'. This definition would not be apposite, of course, if we mean to be talking about state types, for there is not just one subject of a given state type.[13]

The Byrne definiens for state conceptuality, unlike the Speaks definiens for relativized conceptual content, formulates a monadic property—a property that can be ascribed to a state by itself and not simply to a state in relation to a subject. It may be compared with the formula '∃y(x is the father of y)', which expresses a monadic property of x even though the formula 'x is the father of y' expresses a relation between x and y. It is therefore inaccurate for Speaks to distinguish the absolute sense from the state sense by saying that only the former expresses a monadic property.[14] The property of being a nonconceptual state in Byrne's sense is monadic, though not absolute in the Speaks sense.

Finally, let us look at Crowther's definition of nonconceptual content in the possessional sense—his counterpart of Speaks's nonconceptual content in the relativized sense and Byrne's nonconceptuality in the state sense. Crowther's definition does not quite fit any of my three molds for dealing with the problem of the extra variable; perhaps it should be accounted a fourth strategy. Here is his definition of conceptual content in the possessional sense:

> If [subject] S has [experience] e with content p, p is a (possessionally) conceptual content iff in order for S to be undergoing e, S must possess all the concepts that characterize p. (2006, 252)[15]

The complementary definition would be

> If subject S has experience e with content p, p is a (possessionally) *non*conceptual content iff it is *not* the case that in order for S to be undergoing e, S must possess all the concepts that characterize p.

This is a conditional definition, having the overall form 'If P, then Q iff R', as in a Carnapian reduction sentence. There is a free variable, 'S', in the definiens that does not occur in the definiendum, but one cannot complain that it comes out of nowhere, since it is introduced in the antecedent clause prefixed to the definition.

I have a mild complaint about Crowther's definition. Although his intent is to define a property that is not a property of contents themselves, he backslides by using the misleading locution 'p is a nonconceptual content' in formulating his definiendum. It would have been more perspicuous for him to use 'e' rather than 'p' as the variable in his definiendum, as follows:

> If subject S has experience e with content p, then e is a possessionally nonconceptual experience iff in order for S to be undergoing e, S need not possess all the concepts that characterize p.

That would emphasize that what is nonconceptual is the *state* the subject is in; the content itself (so far as the definiens goes) might be composed of concepts.

I also have a potentially more serious complaint. What if we instantiate the conditional definition twice, once to Joe and again to his dog Fido? Joe might not be able to undergo his experience without possessing all the concepts characterizing p, whereas Fido can undergo an experience with the same content without having those concepts. We would then have two experiences of the same type one of which is possessionally conceptual and the other of which is possessionally nonconceptual, which sounds odd if not contradictory.

To summarize the discussion so far, we should distinguish two issues. One is about perceptual contents proper: Are they like belief contents? More fundamentally, are they composed of concepts? The other is about the relations of subjects to those contents or about the states of subjects that incorporate the contents: Does standing in the relation or being in the state require the subject to have whatever concepts characterize the content? The standard definitions of nonconceptual content muddy this distinction; they make it look as though an answer of 'no' to the latter question would *automatically* amount to an answer of 'no' to the former question. Worse, insofar as the standard definitions mention a subject of contentful states on the right that is not mentioned on the left, they run the risk of being logically defective. The best way to deal with this situation is to define one notion of nonconceptuality that applies to contents proper (without reference to subjects) and another definition of nonconceptuality that applies to states of subjects or their relations to contents. Moreover, the state sense is better captured by quantifying the subject variable in the definiens (à la Byrne) than it is by making the notion defined relative to subjects (à la Speaks) or going conditional (à la Crowther).

II.

Having distinguished between styles of definition apt for defining non-conceptuality as a property of contents proper and styles apt for defining nonconceptuality as a property of states (or of subject-content relations), we may now ask how the two types of nonconceptuality are related. Do they always go hand in hand, or can they come apart? Is it possible for a state to be conceptual despite having nonconceptual content or, conversely, for a state to be *non*conceptual despite having a conceptual content? Crowther has argued that each of these mixed combinations is indeed possible. In this section, I examine and cast doubt on his reasons for thinking so.

Take first the question whether a state could be nonconceptual despite having a conceptual content or, in Crowther's terms, whether we could have compositional conceptuality together with possessional nonconceptuality—the combination he calls P4.

Let M be a perceptual state with content p. If p is a conceptual content, we have

(1) p is composed of concepts (there are concepts in p).

If M is a nonconceptual state, then by either Byrne's or Crowther's account, it is possible for someone to be in M without possessing all the concepts in p. So there is a possible world w in which someone, call him S, is such that

(2) S is in M & S does not possess all the concepts in p.

Now I am going to bring into the discussion a principle once propounded (though later abandoned) by Peacocke:

Peacocke's Principle: It is a conceptual truth that no one can have an experience with a given representational content unless he possesses the concepts from which the content is built up. (1983, 19)[16]

If this principle is correct, we can apply it to world w to obtain

(3) If S is in M, S possesses all the concepts in p.

We have now reached a contradiction. (2) and (3) cannot be true together, except perhaps vacuously for want of concepts in p, but (1) assures that there *are* concepts in p. Crowther's P4 combination is not possible if Peacocke's Principle is true.

So what is the status of Peacocke's Principle—*is* it true? There is a principle in its neighborhood that would be difficult to deny, namely:

If S has a propositional attitude with content p, then S possesses all the concepts involved in p.[17]

This principle has fair claim to being regarded as an analytic truth. Going at it from one end, Chisholm once defined what it is for a proposition p to *involve* a concept F (that is, to have it as a constituent) as follows: p involves F iff necessarily, whoever entertains p entertains or grasps F. Obviously, you cannot entertain or grasp a concept you do not possess. Going at it from the other end, Speaks defines what it is to *possess* a concept as follows: S possesses F iff S is capable of thoughts involving F. Either of these definitions would make it analytic that if p involves F, then whoever entertains p possesses F—for Chisholm it would be analytic of involvement, and for Speaks it would be analytic of possession.[18] Since entertaining is the common core of all propositional attitudes, it follows that whoever has any propositional attitude toward p possesses all the concepts involved in p.

The principle I have just derived is not quite tantamount to Peacocke's Principle, however. It would yield Peacocke's Principle only when supplemented by the following assumption: having an experience with a given representational content *is having a propositional attitude toward that content*. So one could deny Peacocke's Principle if one also denied that having an experience that p is a propositional attitude—even though its content is a proposition, and even though "experiencing that" sounds like an attitude.

What is emerging, then, is that perception can be a nonconceptual state with conceptual contents *provided* that perceptual states are not propositional attitudes.[19] Experiencing is not an attitude; it's an ain't-a-tude.

The natural question to ask at this point is the following: in what sense can an experience have a certain proposition as its content if the experience is not an attitude toward that propositional content? One possible suggestion is that it is a matter of the experience's having that proposition as its *informational* content, which might be analyzed further as follows: the experience is a nomologically reliable indicator of p's being the case.[20] However, this suggestion makes it obscure how one Fregean proposition rather than another can be the content of the experience. An experience that indicates that p also indicates that q, where q is any proposition nomologically equivalent to p, even if q is not the same Fregean proposition as p and does not involve the same concepts as p. So the possibility of states that are possessionally nonconceptual but compositionally conceptual as Crowther understands the latter phrase—in terms of having a Fregean proposition as content—has not been fully made out.[21]

Let us turn now to the other mixed combination—being conceptual in the state sense, but nonconceptual in the content sense. To assume a case fitting this description as envisioned by Crowther, we must assume a subject S in a state M with a content p that is not a conceptual content—so whatever sort of thing p is, it is not composed of concepts—yet S must nonetheless possess certain concepts. But *which* concepts? We cannot say "the concepts in p," because there are no concepts in p!

The problem that is now emerging can be set out as a dilemma concerning how we are to understand the definition of state conceptuality. The definition from Byrne I have been using runs thus: state M with content p is state conceptual iff it is not possible for someone to be in M without possessing all the concepts that characterize p. The first horn of the dilemma threatens if we understand the definiens as implying that there are concepts in p, as though the definite description had been placed out front: the concepts in p are such that it is not possible for someone to be in M without possessing those concepts. In that case, the combination of content nonconceptuality with state conceptuality would be contradictory: there would and would not be concepts in p. The second horn threatens if we understand the definiens as *not* implying that there are concepts in p, as though it had been written as a universal generalization: whatever concepts are in p are such that it is not possible for someone to be in M without possessing those concepts. In that case, if there are no concepts in p, the definiens will be true vacuously—any subject of the state will need to have whatever concepts are in p, namely, none. If a state has *non*conceptual content, it will therefore follow trivially that it is a *con*ceptual state. This is an odd result and no doubt an unintended one.

To avoid this unintended result, Byrne redefines state nonconceptuality as follows:

State M with content p is state nonconceptual iff (i) either p contains concepts, but it is possible for someone to be in M without possessing those concepts, or (ii) p is a nonconceptual content (2005, 234).

Under this definition, a state with nonconceptual content no longer qualifies trivially as a conceptual state. Instead, it automatically counts as a *non*conceptual state by virtue of the second disjunct in the definiens. The combination of content nonconceptuality with state conceptuality is excluded by definition.[22]

Yet Crowther defends the possibility of precisely this combination (his P3). Obviously, then, he must not be using Byrne's definition. Here again are his own definitions of the two notions that make up the P3 combination:

> If S has experience e with content p, p is a (possessionally) conceptual content iff in order for S to be undergoing e, S must possess all the concepts that characterize p. (252)

> p is a (compositionally) nonconceptual content iff it is not the case that p is composed exclusively of concepts.

The distinction mooted earlier between a content's being *composed* of concepts and its being *characterized* by concepts now becomes significant. Crowther never highlights this distinction, but if I am right, it is crucial for upholding the possibility of the P3 combination. If a content can be characterized by certain concepts without being composed of any concepts, there is room for a nonvacuous requirement that a subject having an experience e with content p must possess certain concepts—those that *characterize* p—even though p is not *composed* of any concepts at all. That would give us the P3 combination.

What is it for a concept to characterize a content? Crowther offers no definition, but he does give us an example:

> The concepts that characterize the content of the belief that grass is green, for example, are the concept *grass* and the concept *green*. (2006, 251)

This is in line with the more general definition given by Byrne:

> F characterizes p iff p = the proposition that ... F ... (2005, 233)[23]

What would be an illustrative case of the P3 combination? Crowther says we would get this combination if a perceptual state had a Russellian proposition *a is F* as its content (a nonconceptual content by his Fregean lights) and if there were a requirement à la Evans that you do not perceive p unless you possess the concepts that characterize p.[24] *Voila!*—a state that is compositionally nonconceptual, but possessionally conceptual.

But which concepts characterize the Russellian proposition *a is F*? Trouble arises here given the coarse-grained way in which Crowther takes Russellian propositions and their constituents to be individuated. He says the constituents of Russellian propositions are not Fregean senses, but "items at the level of reference" (2006, 253). Apparently, the Russellian proposition *a is F* is identical with the Russellian proposition *b is G* if 'a' is coextensive with 'b' and 'G' with 'F'. By the Byrne criterion, *a is F* will therefore be characterized by *G*.[25] That makes for an awful lot of concepts the subject needs to possess![26]

Perhaps the perplexities I have raised about the P3 and P4 combinations can be resolved. However that may be, there is a further criticism that may be leveled against Crowther: his arguments cannot be used to establish the possibility of *both* mixed combinations, since one of them uses a premise that is the contradictory of a premise used in the other.

In his illustration of the P4 possibility (compositional conceptuality without possessional conceptuality), Crowther supposes that animals without concepts might have a mode of access to conceptually composed facts that counts as perceiving them—they might undergo perceptual events with the content *a is F* as the result of capacities to respond differentially to *a* and *F*. To get this possibility, he must suppose that perception does *not* require the possession of any concepts.

In his illustration of the P3 possibility (possessional conceptuality without compositional conceptuality), Crowther supposes that a state with the content *a is F* does not count as a perceptual state unless the subject is able to have the thought that a is F. To get this possibility, he must suppose that perception *does* require the possession of concepts.

So we cannot, by Crowther's assumptions and examples, show that the two mixed combinations are *both* possible. We can show at best that one or the other of them is possible.

I am inclined to think myself that a state is nonconceptual in the possessional or state sense if and only if its content is nonconceptual in the compositional or content sense. So why did I urge in section I that the nonconceptuality of contents not be defined in terms appropriate to the nonconceptuality of states? The answer is that if there is an equivalence between the two notions, it ought to be established by argument rather than by definition.[27]

III.

In this section I present an argument I find convincing for the thesis that some perceptual states have nonconceptual content—the argument from perceptual experience as a source of concepts.[28]

Not very long ago (in the writings of Sellars, for instance, who was continuing a tradition going back to Kant), the expressions 'having conceptual content' and 'having propositional content' were used more or less interchangeably.[29] This is not true today; there are many who affirm that perception has propositional content, but then go on to debate whether it has conceptual content. Being somewhat nonplussed by the notion of a propositional content that is not conceptual, I take the argument I present as an argument for the nonpropositionality of some perceptual states. But others may take it if they like merely as an argument for the nonconceptual character of some perceptual contents or of the states incorporating those contents.

My argument consists in setting forth an inconsistent tetrad of statements, one of which must of course be rejected, and then contending that the best strategy for avoiding the inconsistency lands us in a nonpropositional view of the contents of perception. Here is the tetrad:

A. All experience, including perceptual experience, has propositional content; it is experience that p.
B. No one can have any propositional attitude (or any other experiential relation) toward a propositional content who does not already grasp whatever concepts are involved in the articulation of that content. (You cannot entertain or be experientially related to the proposition that *a is F* unless you grasp the concept of an F thing.)
C. As Locke taught, there are many concepts that are first acquired through perceptual experience; it is experience that makes it possible for you subsequently to entertain contents involving the concept.
D. If concept F is acquired through experience E and E has propositional content, then F is a constituent of that content.

To see that these four statements are indeed inconsistent, assume (as C says we may) that concept F is acquired through experience E. According to A, E has a propositional content. According to D, F is a constituent of that content. According to B, no one can undergo E who does not already possess or grasp F. But that contradicts our initial assumption that F is first acquired through E.

There are four possible responses to the tetrad.

Reject A: This is what I recommend. There is such a thing as seeing an expanse of red or a shiny apple or a vista of the Grand Canyon without thereby being experientially related to any proposition. You may, of course, entertain or believe various propositions in response to your experience, but your experience is not constituted by relations to those propositions. In holding this view, I am rejecting not just content conceptualism, but the position nowadays often known as intentionalism (Byrne 2001).

Reject B: This response would be available if the combination of state nonconceptuality with content conceptuality were possible. That, however, is one of the combinations I raised doubts about in section II.

Reject C: This is what Sellars (1963) and McDowell (1994) do; they reject empiricist-abstractionist theories of concept formation along with their rejection of the so-called Myth of the Given. I think the Myth is no myth, but that is too large a matter to be argued here.[30]

Reject D: This alternative may seem strange at first, but I shall mention two reasons that might be given for questioning D.

First, it might be suggested that a complex concept can be acquired from a sequence of experiences no one of which has that concept as a constituent, as when one constructs the concept Unicorn from the concepts Horse and Horn, each acquired separately from experience. That, of course, was explicitly allowed for in Hume's version of concept empiricism. However, this consideration only shows that it would be false to say that if concept F is acquired from experiences E_1 through E_n, then F is a constituent of one of E_{1-} E_n. It does not show that D is false as stated. Moreover, we could avoid this objection altogether simply by stipulating in C that some *simple* concepts are acquired through experience, which is what concept empiricists typically assert.

Second, it might be suggested that besides having propositional content, an experience has a surrounding phenomenal halo or aura from which a concept could be abstracted even if the content did not contain that concept. However, it is clear that this suggestion runs contrary to the spirit of intentionalism and could hardly be used in defense of it. A properly formulated intentionalism goes beyond A to A': all perceptual experience has its phenomenal features *exhaustively determined* by its propositional content. Under this assumption, it is plausible that a phenomenal feature of an experience could permit the acquisition of concept F from the experience only if F were a constituent of the propositional content of that experience.[31]

Of course, if A is strengthened to A' in this way, the conclusion I obtain from my favored way of eliminating the inconsistency will have to be correspondingly weakened. The conclusion will now be that not all experience has a propositional content that determines its phenomenal character. The weaker conclusion is good enough for me, as perceptual contents would still have a nonconceptual aspect.

Going back to the original A-D tetrad, perhaps some will say that a better response than mine is to hold that some experiences have (i) propositional contents with no concepts as constituents or else (ii) contents composed of concepts, but such that the perceiver need not possess those concepts to take those propositions as contents. To go for (i) would be to embrace content nonconceptualism;[32] to go for (ii) would be to embrace state nonconceptualism. Either way, we would arrive at some form of nonconceptualism about perceptual content.[33]

Appendix: Terminology and Taxonomy of Positions

Table 1 lists the terms employed by the authors I have discussed to express their respective distinctions.

Table 1

	Notion that applies to contents themselves	Notion that applies to states of subjects or their relation to contents
Speaks	Absolutely nonconceptual content	Relatively nonconceptual content or conceptual content relative to subject A
Byrne	Nonconceptual content	Nonconceptual state
Crowther	Compositionally nonconceptual content	Possessionally nonconceptual content

With definitions in hand of what it is to have conceptual content or nonconceptual content, one may go on to distinguish a number of possible positions or "isms." Some of the possible positions in regard to what Byrne calls conceptual or nonconceptual content arranged are listed in Table 2, in a modified square of opposition.

Table 2

Total content conceptualism: every perceptual state has conceptual content exclusively.	Total content nonconceptualism: every perceptual state is devoid of conceptual content; it has nonconceptual content exclusively.
Moderate content conceptualism: every perceptual state has some conceptual content.	Moderate content nonconceptualism: every perceptual state has some nonconceptual content.
Minimal content conceptualism: some perceptual states have some conceptual content.	Minimal content nonconceptualism: some perceptual states have some nonconceptual content.

The top two positions are contraries (assuming there are perceptual states). The bottom two positions are subcontraries (assuming there are perceptual states and that at least some of them have content). Each position entails all the positions below it (again assuming there are perceptual states). Each position in a corner is the contradictory of the position in the diagonally opposite corner.

If we combine the left middle with the bottom right position, we get the view Byrne calls "partial content conceptualism." If we combine right middle with bottom left, we get the view he calls "partial content nonconceptualism,"

The chart presupposes a notion that has not actually been defined: that of having *some* conceptual content. That notion sounds reasonable enough; after all, a soft drink can have some sugar content and some nonsugar content. It is strange, then, that many definitions on offer of 'having conceptual content' and 'having nonconceptual content' (including those discussed in this article) make those notions mutually exclusive. This is so even in cases in which the author employing the definition goes on to discuss the possibility of a state's having some conceptual content and some nonconceptual content.[34] Here is a place where further refinement of notions is in order.

A chart for parallel positions regarding state conceptuality or nonconceptuality may also be drawn up. Table 3 presupposes that there are perceptual states, that total content conceptualism is true, and that Crowther combinations of state nonconceptuality with content conceptuality are possible.

Of course, there are yet further positions in logical space if we consider intersections of positions regarding state conceptuality or nonconceptuality with

Table 3

Total state conceptualism: every perceptual state is such that the subject must possess all the concepts involved in its content.	Total state nonconceptualism: every perceptual state is such that the subject need not possess *any* of the concepts involved in its content.
Moderate state conceptualism: every perceptual state is such that the subject must possess some of the concepts involved in its content.	Moderate state nonconceptualism: every perceptual state is such that the subject need not possess *all* of the concepts involved in its content.
Minimal state conceptualism: some perceptual states are such that the subject must possess some of the concepts involved in their contents.	Minimal state nonconceptualism: some perceptual states are such that the subject need not possess all of the concepts involved in their contents.

moderate or minimal content conceptualism or (as countenanced by Crowther) total content nonconceptualism.[35]

Notes

1. This is actually one of three possible conditions listed by Gunther. One of the others—"it cannot be represented conceptually"—does not have the confusing feature I focus on here.
2. As the brackets indicate, I have replaced Brewer's definition of conceptual content by the definition of its complement.
3. I believe this is true of Crane 1992 and Byrne 2005.
4. Some of these authors make their distinctions in regard to the *doctrines* of conceptualism or nonconceptualism. I think it is more perspicuous to make them first for the *properties* of being conceptual or nonconceptual; one may then go on to explain the doctrines in terms of the properties. I suggest one way of doing this in the appendix.
5. A definition with exactly this defect occurs on p. 149 in Crane 1992. There may be tacit quantifiers binding his subject variable, but he does not say what they are or how they are to be placed.
6. Crowther's actual words are 'Where S has an experience, e, with the content p, p is a [compositionally] conceptual content if p is composed of concepts'. I presume that his 'if' is a typo for 'iff', since his definition of the complementary concept uses an 'iff'. The 'where' clause is inessential, as what follows does not depend on it. It is clear from Crowther's surrounding commentary that the word 'exclusively' should be inserted after 'composed'.
7. What he actually says is "someone in whom the question arises may believe (where F is some completing content) that C is F, while rationally doubting or disbelieving that D is F, though 'C' and 'D' are co-referring terms" (2006, 250). It is clear, however, that he wants his characterization of senses to apply whether they occur in subject or predicate place in a proposition, so I have used a more general formulation.

8. It is a peculiarity of the Byrne-Speaks definition of conceptuality that if someone held that the contents of perception are composed of Fregean concepts while the contents of belief are Stalnakerian propositions, the perceptual contents would count as nonconceptual despite being composed of concepts.

9. I have made two changes from Speaks's own formulation, which is this: "A mental state of an agent A (at a time t) has relatively nonconceptual content iff the content of that mental state includes contents not grasped (possessed) by A at t." I have rearranged the terms in his definiendum to highlight the relativized character of the definition. I have also replaced the third occurrence of his 'content' by 'concept'. I presume he uses 'content' instead of 'concept' because he wants to count some nonFregean propositions as conceptual contents, but they do not contain any concepts to be grasped or not by a subject.

10. A relativized notion of nonconceptual content is also presupposed in the following sentence from Tye 2006, even though the definition he uses in that article does not make any relativization explicit: "For what makes the content nonconceptual for subject S is simply the fact that S need not herself have the relevant concepts and thus need not herself be in a position to form the relevant thought" (207). The definition he uses runs thus: "a visual experience E has a nonconceptual content if and only if (i) E has correctness conditions; (ii) the subject of E need not possess the concepts used in a canonical specification of E's correctness conditions" (207). Though he recognizes that the definiens does not really tell us anything about the conceptuality or nonconceptuality of the content itself, he nonetheless retains the old misleading language of nonconceptual content in the definiendum.

11. See Speaks 2005, 362 and 366. I have not employed precisely his formulation of the argument, but it is clear from his discussion that he would agree that the premises imply that M has nonconceptual content relative to animals while lacking nonconceptual content relative to humans.

12. Even if we can attach sense to the notion of nonhandlebar content (e.g., the bike must have pedals or a seat for Tommy to ride it without using the handlebars), the bike has that same content for Grandmother.

13. Actually, when phrases like 'the subject' occur in the definiens, they are more charitably taken as being symbolizable by a universal quantifier, as with 'the whale is a mammal'. The idea would be that *whoever* is in the state could be in it without possessing the concepts that characterize p, as in the previous suggestion in the text.

14. See his 2005, 359–60, where Speaks says the absolute sense expresses a monadic property whereas the relative sense does not, and note 5, in which he equates his relative sense with the state sense of Heck and Byrne.

15. I have made two changes from Crowther's actual wording. First, I have replaced Crowther's 'where' clause, "Where S has an experience, e, with the content p," by an equivalent 'if' clause. Second, I have inserted 'all' before 'the concepts', which is probably redundant, but in any case indicated by the context.

16. Crane says Peacocke changed his mind about this by 1986.

17. Compare Bermudez 2008: "It is hard to see how one can have a propositional attitude whose content is a complex of concepts without possessing each of them."

18. Proof for the Speaks case: Assume that p involves F (the left side of the theorem) and that S entertains p (the antecedent of the right side of the theorem). We must now show that S possesses F (the consequent of the right side of the theorem). The two assumptions imply that S is capable of a thought involving F, which in turn implies (in accordance with the Speaks definition of concept possession) that S possesses F. Q.E.D.

19. This point is noted in Bermudez 2008, section 3.
It was after he abandoned the principle I have named after him that Peacocke began defending the idea that experiences have nonconceptual content. This makes his use of the term 'nonconceptual content' misleading, since once you abandon the principle, you can believe that experience is nonconceptual in the state or possessional sense without believing that its *contents* are nonconceptual in any good sense at all.

20. I take this analysis of informational content from Dretske 1981. Crowther uses the phrase 'informational content' without committing himself to any particular analysis of it, but I doubt that he would object to Dretske's.

21. A similar problem arises if perceptual contents are Stalnakerian or Russellian, since these, too, may differ even when they are nomologically equivalent.

22. This is the same result as under the first horn above, though not reached from the same case assumption, as Byrne's revised definiens does not imply that there are concepts in p.

23. I am not sure that Byrne himself intends any distinction between composing and characterizing; he seems to use the phrases 'contains concepts' and 'is characterized by concepts' interchangeably.

24. The Evans requirement stems from two other requirements: (i) that you do not perceive a content *a is F* carried by your visual system unless that content can serve as an input to your reasoning system, and (ii) that the content *a is F* cannot serve as such an input unless you have the concepts *a* and *F*.

25. The Byrne definition of characterizing, though perhaps intended to be applied to non-Fregean propositions, does not in fact comport very well with them. Take, for example, the Stalnakerian proposition *all cats are cats*. This proposition is characterized by the concept *cat*. Moreover, it is identical with the proposition *all dogs are dogs*, since the cat proposition and the dog proposition are true in precisely the same worlds (namely, all of them). So the proposition *all dogs are dogs* is characterized by the concept *cat*.

26. If you say, "Not at all, because *F* and *G* are the same concept," you have gone from making possessing all the requisite concepts too difficult to making it too easy. Get hold of the concept *creature with a heart* and you will thereby get hold of the concept *creature with a kidney*.

27. Here is an example illustrating the dialectical point I am trying to make. The positivists believed that there is no such thing as the synthetic a priori—that the notions of the synthetic and the empirical were necessarily coextensive. Believing this to be so, Ayer defined an analytic statement as one whose truth depends only on the meanings of its constituent symbols; he then proceeded to define a synthetic statement not simply as a nonanalytic one (which would have been the neutral definition), but as one whose truth can be ascertained only by experience (Ayer [1946] 1952, 78–79). That is an objectionable tactic. Even if the synthetic and the empirical are necessarily coextensive, one should not secure that result

directly by definition. Ayer closed a question that should have been left open to further investigation.

28. Versions of this argument are given by Heck (2000) and Roskies (2008) among others. In the scheme suggested in the appendix, its conclusion is minimal content nonconceptualism. .

29. "The only use the understanding can make of these concepts," Kant says, "is to judge by means of them" ([1787] 1965, A68/B93). The content of a judgment is, of course, a proposition.

30. See Van Cleve 1985 for a limited defense of the Myth of the Given. See Roskies 2008 for an argument that those who deny that concepts are learned from experience must endorse either an implausible nativism about concepts or an implausible theory of concept acquisition through brute-causal processes occurring at some sub-personal level.

31. In effect, I am suggesting that if the second challenge to D is taken seriously, one should rewrite D as D′: If concept F is acquired through experience E and E has a propositional content that determines its phenomenal character, then F is a constituent of that content.

32. Here I am using Crowther's characterization of what it is for a content to be nonconceptual and embedding it in Byrne's form of definition for content nonconceptualism.

33. The leading argument on the other side of the debate is the epistemic argument of McDowell and others, which may be formulated as follows: (1) experiences are capable of justifying beliefs; (2) experiences justify beliefs only if they transmit justification to the beliefs; (3) experiences are capable of transmitting justification to beliefs only if they have the same sort of content as beliefs, namely, conceptual content; therefore (4) experiences have conceptual content. In this formulation, I would deny premise (2). For a critique of the transmission model of justification, see Van Cleve 1985.

34. Typical in this regard is Nöe 2004. On p. 181, Nöe defines the notion of a content's being conceptual in an all-or-nothing way. On p. 183, he discusses arguments for the view that perception is not "thoroughly conceptual."

35. I wish to thank Bryan Blackwell, Janet Levin, Michael Pace, and David Bennett for comments on earlier drafts.

References

Ayer, A.J. (1946) 1952. *Language, Truth, and Logic*. New York: Dover (reprint of 1946 edition).

Bermudez, Jose. 2008. "Nonconceptual Mental Content." *The Stanford Encyclopedia of Philosophy* (Summer 2008 Edition), Edward N. Zalta (ed.), forthcoming URL = <http://plato.stanford.edu/archives/sum2008/entries/content-nonconceptual/>.

Brewer, Bill. 2005. "Perceptual Experience has Conceptual Content." In *Contemporary Debates in Epistemology*, edited by Matthias Steup and Ernest Sosa, 217–30. Oxford: Blackwell.

Byrne, Alex. 2001. "Intentionalism Defended." *The Philosophical Review*, 110:199–240.

———. 2005. "Perception and Conceptual Content." In *Contemporary Debates in Epistemology*, edited by Matthias Steup and Ernest Sosa, 231–50. Oxford: Blackwell.

Crane, Tim. 1992. "The Nonconceptual Content of Experience." In *The Contents of Experience*, edited by Tim Crane, 136–57. Cambridge: Cambridge University Press.

Crowther, T.M. 2006. "Two Conceptions of Conceptualism and Nonconceptualism." *Erkenntnis* 65:245–76.

Dretske, Fred. 1981. *Knowledge and the Flow of Information*. Cambridge: MIT Press.

Gendler, Tamar, and John Hawthorne, eds. 2006. *Perceptual Experience*. Oxford: Clarendon Press.

Gunther, York, ed. 2003. *Essays on Nonconceptual Content*. Cambridge, Mass: MIT Press.

Heck, Richard. 2000. "Nonconceptual Content and the 'Space of Reasons.'" *The Philosophical Review*, 109:483–523.

Kant, Immanuel. (1787) 1965. *Critique of Pure Reason*. Translated by Norman Kemp Smith. New York: St. Martin's Press.

McDowell, John. 1994. *Mind and World*. Cambridge: Harvard University Press.

Nöe, Alva. 2004. *Action in Experience*. Cambridge, Mass.: MIT Press.

Peacocke, Christopher: 1983. *Sense and Content*. Oxford: Oxford University Press.

Roskies, Adina. 2008. "A New Argument for Nonconceptual Content." *Philosophy and Phenomenological Research*, 76:633–59.

Sellars, Wilfrid. 1963. "Empiricism and the Philosophy of Mind." In *Science, Perception, and Reality*, 127–96. London: Routledge and Kegan Paul.

Speaks, Jeff. 2005. "Is There a Problem about Non-conceptual Content?" *The Philosophical Review*, 114:359–98.

Tye, Michael. 2000. *Consciousness, Color, and Content*. Cambridge, Mass.: MIT Press.

———. 2006. "Nonconceptual Content, Richness, and Fineness of Grain." In Gendler and Hawthorne 2006, 504–30.

Van Cleve, James: 1985. "Epistemic Supervenience and the Circle of Belief." *The Monist* 68: 90–104.

Philosophical Perspectives, 26, Philosophy of Mind, 2012

BELIEF, INFORMATION AND REASONING

Bruno Whittle
Yale University

Here are two plausible ideas about belief. First: beliefs are our means of storing information about the world. Second: if we believe something, then we are willing to use it in reasoning. But in this paper I will introduce a puzzle that will show that these cannot both be right. The solution, I will argue, is a new picture of belief, on which there are two different kinds of belief — one for each idea.

The puzzle is based on a certain sort of example that is familiar from discussions of knowledge: in particular, the main example will involve someone first thinking about what they are going to do next summer, and then about whether to buy a lottery ticket. But I will argue that we have been thinking about these examples in the wrong way: rather than focussing exclusively on knowledge, we should *also* have been asking what they tell us about belief. Only once we do that, I will argue, will we be able to see what is really going on in these examples.

The structure of the paper is as follows. In §1 I will introduce the puzzle. In §2 I will outline the new picture of belief, and explain how it solves the puzzle. But in §3 I will consider whether one might not be able to solve the puzzle in a less radical way (i.e., without giving a new picture of belief). I will argue, however, that no such solution would seem to be available. In §4 I will then return to the proposed picture, and try to go some way towards filling in, and refining, the outline that I initially gave. Finally, in §5, I will try to give an alternative argument for the new picture, using considerations from desire.

1. The Puzzle

The puzzle that I will raise, then, stems from two apparently plausible ideas about belief. The first of these is:

(I) Beliefs are our means of storing information.

Thus — the idea is — the way in which we store information about what the world is like is by having beliefs about it. For example, the way in which we store information about what snow is like is by having beliefs about it (such as the belief that snow is white).

The second idea is: if we believe something, then we are willing to use it in reasoning. I.e.:

(R) If S believes that p then she is willing to use p in reasoning.

For example, suppose that Rachel wants to build a snowman, and that the ground to her left is green, while that to her right is white. And suppose also that she believes that snow is white: then (the idea is) she will use this proposition in her reasoning (and as a result will head right).[1]

(I) and (R), then, would seem to be very plausible ideas about belief. We will see, however, that they cannot both be true. To see why, suppose that they are, and consider the following example.[2] To begin with, suppose that Rachel is thinking about what she is going to do next summer. And suppose that what she really wants to do is go on safari. *But*, after checking her bank balance, and thinking about how much she is going to earn between now and then, she reluctantly concludes that she is going to have to stay in the US. That is, she comes to believe that she will be in the US next summer.

But suppose next that she goes to a deli to buy a sandwich. And suppose that while she is there she thinks about buying a lottery ticket. She thinks: if I win, then I will be on safari next summer; and she decides to buy the ticket. Now, in this new situation, Rachel is *not* willing to use the proposition that she will be in the US next summer in her reasoning: because if she was, she would conclude that there is no point in buying the ticket (for she would reason that if she buys the ticket and it wins, then she will be on safari, and not in the US, next summer; thus, since she *will* be in the US, if she buys the ticket it won't win). Thus it follows from (R) that she no longer believes that she will be in the US next summer. But then it follows from (I) that she has lost the information she acquired at the start of the example: for if our store of information is simply our beliefs, and Rachel has lost the belief she acquired, then it follows that she has lost the information she acquired.

But of course that is not right. For suppose that when Rachel gets home she takes a call from a friend who wants to know if she is going to be around next summer. Rachel will be able to answer 'Yes' immediately. But that means that she still has the information she acquired at the start of the example: because it is still available for her to use to guide her answer; after all, it is not as if she has to revisit the facts about her bank balance and so on; rather, she simply uses the result of her earlier deliberations. Thus, as promised, (I) and (R) cannot both be true.

And this is far from an isolated counterexample: rather, others are easy to come by. For one such, suppose that David is thinking about when to buy a new computer. And suppose that he decides to keep his current machine until next year. That is, he comes to believe that he will keep his computer until next year. But suppose now that he moves on to thinking about insurance. He will not, in this new situation, be willing to use in his reasoning the proposition that he will keep his computer until next year: for example, he will not be willing to reason that since he is going to keep it until next year, it is not going to be stolen before then, and so there is no need to insure it. Thus, as before, it follows from (R) and (I) that he has now lost the information he acquired at the start of the example. But, again, this isn't right: for if, after he has finished thinking about insurance, a colleague calls and asks if he is going to have his computer later in the year, he will be able to answer 'Yes' immediately; so it follows that he has *not* lost the information after all. Thus, again it follows that (I) and (R) cannot both be true. And many other examples, which can be used to make the same point, are easy to find.

2. A New Picture

The solution, I want to argue, is a new picture of belief. On this picture, there are two distinct components: on the one hand, there is our information; and, on the other, there are the things that we are taking seriously at any given point. Each of these can be thought of as a set of worlds.[3] Thus, on the one hand, we have an 'information set': consisting, intuitively, of those worlds that our information leaves in play. But, on the other hand, the idea is that at any given point we are only taking *some* worlds seriously; that is, we are only taking some worlds seriously as candidates for how the world is. For example, in a typical situation in which Rachel is thinking about what she is going to do this weekend, she might take seriously (typical) worlds where she goes to visit her parents, and (typical) worlds where she stays at home; but she will *not* take seriously worlds at which she is hit by a bus on Friday morning, or at which there is a nuclear holocaust on Friday afternoon. Thus, in addition to an information set, we also have a 'relevance set': consisting of those worlds that we are (at that point) taking seriously. Thus, the worlds that are not in S's relevance set are those that she is not taking seriously, but it will be useful to have a similar term for the worlds that are not in her information set; so I will say that S has 'ruled out' a world if it is not in this latter set.

These two sets then give rise to two distinct kinds of belief, as follows. For example, consider again Rachel's deliberations about what she is going to do this weekend. And suppose that Rachel decides to visit her parents. What is going on in this sort of case — according to the picture I am proposing — is that Rachel is ruling out (i.e., eliminating from her information set) the *relevant* worlds at which she does not visit her parents this weekend. Thus, the only relevant worlds *left* are those at which she does visit them. However, it is not that she rules out absolutely *every* world at which she does not visit them (for example, she does not rule out the far-fetched world at which she is hit by a bus on Friday morning). Thus, in one sense, Rachel believes that she will visit her parents this weekend: i.e., in the sense that this proposition is true at every *relevant* world that is left in her information set. However, in another sense, she does *not* believe this: because there are still *some* worlds in this set where this is not true (such as the hit-by-a-bus-on-Friday-morning world). Thus, on this picture, there are these two distinct kinds of belief. On the one hand, there are *R-beliefs* that are determined by our information together with what we are taking seriously; that is, we R-believe something if it is true at every *relevant* world in our information set; thus, in the example, Rachel *does* R-believe that she will visit her parents this weekend. But, on the other hand, there are also *I-beliefs* that are determined by our information alone; that is, we I-believe something if it is true at *every* world in our information set; so, in the example, Rachel does *not* I-believe that she will visit her parents.[4]

The idea is then that (I) is true of our I-beliefs (i.e., it is *these* that are our means of storing information) while (R) is true of our R-beliefs (it is *these* that are connected to reasoning). Thus:

(I*) I-beliefs are our means of storing information.

(R*) If S R-believes that p then she is willing to use p in reasoning.

Thus, in the example that we have been considering, it is *not* part of Rachel's information that she will visit her parents this weekend; nevertheless — despite this — this proposition *is* something that she is willing to use in reasoning (for example, if a friend calls and asks what she is going to be doing this weekend, she will use it in her reasoning about how to answer). And the idea is that, quite generally, this is how things go: we store information by having I-beliefs; but we are nevertheless willing to use in our reasoning anything that we merely R-believe.[5]

That, then, is the picture of belief that I want to propose; in a moment I will explain how it solves the puzzle; but first I want to say something about my decision to call both I-beliefs and R-beliefs kinds of *belief*. For while it does seem to be natural to think of each of these as a variety of belief, all that I *really* want to claim here is that we have these two distinct kinds of mental states, one of which is tied to information, and the other of which is tied to reasoning; and it is then a further matter which of these should really count as beliefs (or which of these the English word 'belief' really applies to). Thus, one view (the one which my presentation has so far assumed) is that *both* I-beliefs and R-beliefs are beliefs. But one might also take the view that only I-beliefs are, or that only R-beliefs are (and so on). Thus, although in this paper I will, in my terminology and more generally, assume the first of these views, this is simply for the purposes of presentation, and everything that I say could very easily be rephrased so as to be compatible with any of the alternative views about this.

I will now explain how the proposed picture solves the puzzle. Thus, consider again the main example of §1, starting with the part in which Rachel is thinking about what she is going to do next summer (and checking her bank balance and so on). The idea is that, at this point, Rachel is taking seriously worlds at which she has saved enough from her salary to be able to go on safari; and she is also taking seriously worlds at which she has not saved enough, and at which she instead spends the summer in the US. But she is *not* taking seriously worlds at which she is kidnapped and forced to work as a safari guide; or worlds at which she wins the lottery and uses the winnings to go on safari. What Rachel does (in this part of the example) is then to rule out those worlds that she is taking seriously and at which she is not in the US next summer. On the other hand, she does *not* rule out any of the more far-fetched worlds that she is not taking seriously (and so these remain in her information set). Thus, at the end of this part of the example, Rachel R-believes that she will be in the US next summer (even though she does not I-believe it).

In the next part of the example — when Rachel is in the deli and considering whether to buy the lottery ticket — what happens is simply that certain worlds that *were ir*relevant become relevant: for example, worlds at which she wins the lottery and uses her winnings to go on safari next summer. Thus, since she has not ruled out these worlds, she no longer counts as R-believing that she will be in the US next summer: and so (R*) no longer gives the result that she is willing to use this proposition in her reasoning. But — crucially — we get this change despite the fact that her information remains the same (in particular, the worlds that she ruled out in the first part of the example *remain* ruled out). Thus, unlike when we had (I) and (R), we can now have a change in what Rachel is willing to use in reasoning *without* a subsequent change in her information (because (I*) and (R*) tie reasoning to R-beliefs, while information is instead tied to I-beliefs).

Consequently, on the proposed picture, the information that Rachel acquired in the first part of the example *is* still available for her to use in the third part: meaning that we no longer have a puzzle. More precisely, what happens in the third part of the example — on this picture — is simply that the worlds that became relevant in the second part go back to being *ir*relevant. As a result, Rachel goes back to R-believing that she will be in the US next summer, and so by (R*) we get the desired result that Rachel will once again be willing to use this proposition in her reasoning. But, crucially, we get this *without* having to say that Rachel must have 'reacquired' the information she acquired in the first part.

Thus, on the proposed picture, we get all the right results about when Rachel acquires and loses information, and about what she is willing to use in her reasoning — while retaining versions of (I) and (R). So the puzzle would seem to be solved.

Now, as I said in the introduction, the sort of example that we have been considering has been much discussed in connection with knowledge. However, if what I have said so far is on the right track, then it would *seem* that we have been thinking about such examples in the wrong way. For, even before we get to questions about what Rachel *knows*, there is a puzzle relating purely to what she believes. And, further, it is hard to imagine that what we ultimately want to say about knowledge in such cases will not to a large extent be affected by what we say about belief. Thus, to focus principally on what these examples tell us about knowledge, as we have been, would seem to be the wrong way of going about things.[6]

I will return to the proposed picture of belief later in the paper. First, however, I want to consider whether one might not be able to solve the puzzle in a less radical way: i.e., without introducing a new picture of belief.

3. Solving the Puzzle without the New Picture?

Specifically, I want to consider whether one might not be able to solve the puzzle simply by appealing to *degrees* of belief: i.e., something which people typically think we have anyway; so if we *could* solve the puzzle this way, that would seem to be more economical. Thus, one might think that degrees of belief would allow a relatively straightforward solution, as follows. The basic idea would be to understand binary belief in terms of degrees in something like the following way: in any given situation, there would be some number x (with $0 \leq x \leq 1$) such that S counts as believing p (in that situation) iff she believes p to degree at least as great as x. Thus the idea would be that something about S's situation determines a certain threshold x, and S counts as believing something just in case her degree of belief in that thing is at least as great as x.[7] Further, the idea would be that what we are willing to use in reasoning is also tied to this threshold x: so, in particular, we are willing to use in reasoning anything that we believe to degree at least as great as x. But — the idea would continue — different situations determine different thresholds, and so S can go from believing to not believing (for example), without changing her underlying degrees of belief. The hope would then be that this would be enough to solve the puzzle. More precisely, since binary belief is now being understood in terms of degrees, one would replace (I) with:

(I′) Degrees of belief are our means of storing information.

And the hope would then be that the threshold account of belief would allow us to hold onto (R) unchanged.

To see how this is supposed to work, consider again the main example we have been discussing. The idea would be that in the first part of the example, when Rachel comes to believe that she will be in the US next summer, she in fact comes to believe this to some degree y (which is sufficient in this situation for her to count as binary believing it). But (the idea would continue) in the second part of the example what happens is simply that the threshold for belief rises: and so, even though Rachel's degree of belief in the proposition in question remains unchanged, she no longer counts as believing it; and so (R) no longer commits us to saying that she will be willing to use this proposition in her reasoning. But, crucially, we get this change in what Rachel is willing to use in her reasoning *without* saying that her information changes, and so we do *not* get the puzzling result that the information she acquired in the first part of the example is no longer available for her to use in the third part. Thus perhaps degrees of belief (together with this account of binary belief in terms of them) are all that we need to solve the puzzle after all?

Unfortunately, however, it is easy to vary the example so as to reintroduce the problem (i.e., to give a puzzle that this proposed solution cannot be extended to). Thus, suppose that a few years ago a friend of Rachel's went on safari. And suppose that she was driven around by a wonderful guide called Miriam. Suppose, further, that Rachel does not *just* want to go on safari: she wants to go with Miriam. And suppose, finally, that when Rachel is in the deli, rather than thinking, 'if I win, then I will be on safari next summer', she instead thinks: if I win, then I will able to go on safari with any guide I like this summer; Miriam is a safari guide; so if I win, then I will be able to go on safari with Miriam this summer. (But suppose that everything else in the example is unchanged.)

Now, we are presumably going to want to say that, when Rachel is in the deli, she believes that Miriam is a safari guide: after all, she is willing to use this proposition in her reasoning in just the way that she is willing to use her beliefs, and she would presumably also be willing to assert it (along with the other premises of her reasoning) if she was asked why she decided to buy the ticket. Thus, if x is the degree to which Rachel believes that Miriam is a safari guide (in this part of the example), then the threshold for belief here is no greater than x. The problem for the proposed solution, however, is that we can also plausibly assume that, if y is the degree to which Rachel comes to believe that she will be in the US next summer, in the first part of the example, then $x \leq y$: for, she is really pretty sure that she will be in the US next summer, whereas she is well aware that Miriam could have changed careers, or been taken ill, or moved to New York, etc. But then the puzzle is back — and in a way that the proposed solution is powerless to solve. For Rachel is *not*, in this part of the example, willing to use in her reasoning that she will be in the US next summer. Thus, by (R), together with the fact that the threshold for belief in this situation is $\leq x \leq y$, it follows that she no longer believes this proposition to degree y. That is, we are once again forced to say that Rachel has lost the information she acquired in the first part of the example (since, by (I′), our store of information is now identified with our degrees of belief; and Rachel no longer has the degree of belief she acquired). Thus, it seems that degrees of belief are not enough to solve the problem, after all.[8,9]

4. Back to the New Picture

In this section I will return to the new picture, and try to go some way towards filling in and refining the outline that I gave above.

4.1 Information Sets vs Relevance Sets

The first thing that I want to discuss is the division of labour between information sets and relevance sets. For, on the picture that I have proposed, what one is willing to use in reasoning is determined by the intersection of these (by (R*), one is willing to use p in reasoning if one R-believes it, and one R-believes it iff it is true at every world in the intersection of these two sets). But the upshot is that even if we know exactly which propositions S is willing to use in her reasoning (at a particular moment), this will not necessarily allow us to determine what her information set is and what her relevance set is (because, of course, distinct pairs of sets can have the same intersection); and if one cannot determine what her information and relevance sets are, then neither can one determine which of the propositions she is willing to use in reasoning she I-believes, and which she merely R-believes.

Now, the question of how exactly these sets divide the labour is presumably an empirical one. One simple hypothesis might be that one only ever rules out (i.e., excludes from one's information set) worlds at which one's course of experience is different from its actual course. Thus, every world at which my experiences are as they actually are would be in my information set: including worlds where I am a brain in a vat, or where the universe is about to cease to exist, etc. On this hypothesis, then, all of the work of getting from this basis to the things that we actually use in reasoning (e.g., that there is a computer in front of me, that it is raining outside, etc.) would be the job of our various relevance sets.

So that is one hypothesis that one might make about the division of labour. But alternatives, with less austere accounts of our information, are also possible. Thus, one might think that we *also* rule out worlds in the following ways, for example: (i) sense perception (e.g., if I see a computer in front of me, then I would exclude from my information set worlds at which there is *not* a computer in front of me); (ii) a combination of others' sense perception and testimony (e.g., if you see an elephant outside, and tell me about it, then I will exclude from my information set worlds at which there is *not* an elephant outside); and (iii) basic inductive inference (e.g., I might rule out from my information set worlds at which you drop that vase but at which it doesn't break).

Thus, a range of hypotheses would seem to be available. Those with less austere accounts of our information seem to me to be the most plausible. But I will content myself here with these descriptions of some of the alternatives; arguing for one in particular will have to wait for future work.

4.2 More than One Relevance Set at a Time?

In talking about the new picture, I have implicitly assumed that subjects will at any given moment have no more than one relevance set. This is surely an oversimplification, however. For example, suppose that Rachel is walking to the deli to buy a lottery ticket while at the same time talking on her cell phone about how she is going to spend her next summer in the US.[10] Then, relative to one of her tasks (i.e., walking to buy the ticket), she is *not* willing to use in her reasoning that she will be in the US next summer (for, if she was, then she would conclude that the ticket would be a waste of money, and thus that she should turn around and walk in the opposite direction). But, relative to the other (i.e., her phone conversation), she *is* willing to use this proposition in her reasoning. It would seem that the proposed picture can straightforwardly be extended to cover such multi-tasking, however. One must simply say that relevance sets (and, in turn, R-beliefs) are relative not simply to subjects and times, but, rather, to subjects, times and activities (so if a subject is engaged in n activities, she will have n relevance sets). So extended, the picture would seem to apply happily to multi-tasking Rachel just as it applied to her earlier incarnation.

4.3 Less than One Relevance Set at a Time?

But there is also the opposite issue: the idea behind relevance sets is that in different situations I will take different worlds seriously (depending on the sort of cognitive activity I am engaged in); but what about times at which I am not engaged in *any* conscious cognitive activity, and where I would thus not seem to be taking *any* worlds seriously? For example, when I am in a dreamless sleep? Now, it is presumably true that at such times I will *not* have a relevance set; and thus that I will *not*, strictly speaking, have R-beliefs.[11] Nevertheless, we could surely make perfectly good sense of a practice of ascribing R-beliefs to people at such times: such talk would simply have to be understood as making implicit reference to a certain sort of cognitive activity, and thus to a certain sort of relevance set.

4.4 There is Nothing We are Always Willing to Use in Reasoning!

A worry one might have about the proposed picture stems from the fact that there does not seem to be *anything* that we are *always* willing to use in reasoning. For example, suppose that I am offered a bet that pays a penny if p is true, and that offers an eternity of torture otherwise. Then it would seem that, whatever p is, I will *not* in such a situation be willing to use it in my reasoning (to conclude, for example, that I would be better off taking the bet than passing on it). But how is this to be handled on the proposed picture, without saying that in such a case I must have lost the information that p? For, on the proposed picture, we are *always* willing to use in our reasoning anything that is true throughout our information set (by (R*) together with the definition of R-belief). Thus, there would seem to be little alternative to saying that, if p is something that is so true, then: if I am offered such a bet, I must lose the information that p. But this conclusion is surely just as unacceptable here as it was in the original puzzle case involving Rachel. Hence the concern!

What I want to suggest, however, is that there is a very natural generalization of the proposed picture that can handle even such cases.[12] For, the basic idea behind this picture is that there are two distinct components to belief: on the one hand, there is our information; and, on the other, there is what we are willing to use in reasoning. In particular, I have thought of our store of information as a set of worlds, and then I have said that, to get at what we are willing to use in reasoning, you have to *remove* from this set any worlds that we are not taking seriously. Perhaps, however, the correct moral of the bet example is that this is an oversimplification: it is not simply that in certain situations we *remove* worlds from our information set; rather, we also sometimes *add* them. Thus, in the bet situation, the idea would be that we temporarily add to our information set some worlds at which p is false. More generally, one would generalize the notion of a relevance *set* to that of a relevance *pair* of (disjoint) sets, $\langle R^-, R^+ \rangle$: thus, if I is our information set, then—the idea would be—we are willing to use in our reasoning anything that is true throughout $(I \cap R^-) \cup R^+$ (the case in which one *only* has a relevance set R would then simply be a case in which $R^- = R$ and $R^+ = \emptyset$). But the basic idea behind the picture would be preserved: for we would still have two components—a stable store of information, together with something more variable—and what we are willing to use in reasoning would still be determined by modifying the former using the latter. Thus, I hope that even the sort of problematic case considered can be handled by a natural generalization of the proposed picture.[13]

I hope in this section, then, to have gone at least some way towards filling in, and refining, the outline that I gave in §2.

5. Desire

In this final section, however, I want to consider a different way in which one might try to argue for the proposed picture of belief. In particular, I want to do this via considerations from desire. More precisely, the idea is as follows. I will argue that there are independent reasons for giving an account of desire that is, in important respects, very similar to the proposed picture of belief. Thus, since one would presumably like to give a unified account of propositional attitudes in general—and so of belief and desire in particular—this will amount to a new argument for the picture of belief. The thought behind this last point is simply this: the whole idea behind the general notion of a propositional attitude is that there is something important that a whole range of mental states have in common; and it would thus seem to be theoretically virtuous to take this unity as far as it is possible to.

I want to start, then, by asking some basic questions about desire. The first of these is simply: what exactly does it *mean* to desire that p (for a proposition p)? For example, suppose that I want a ham sandwich (that is, suppose that I desire that I have a ham sandwich): what exactly does this amount to? And the first *point* that I want to make is just this: in general, this seems to be a very intricate matter. For there are all sorts of ways in which this proposition (i.e., the proposition that I have a ham sandwich) could be made true: for example, I could have a delicious, freshly prepared sandwich from the best restaurant in town; or I could have one that is completely tasteless, or rotten, or poisoned, or ... Now, to count as desiring this proposition I presumably have to like the idea of at least *some* of these ways it could be made true—but exactly *which* is, prima facie, unclear.

However, if one *instead* considers desire-like attitudes to whole worlds (for example, preferences between these) then there would seem to be no comparable intricacy. For there are *not* multiple ways for a world to be actual, in the way in which there *are* multiple ways for a proposition to be true. As a result, while it is hard to say what exactly desiring that p amounts to (or preferring p to q, for that matter), there is no comparable unclarity when it comes to the question of what preferring one *world* to another amounts to.

But this then suggests that a very natural strategy for giving an account of desire would seem to be this: take desire-like attitudes to worlds as basic, and give an account of desiring that p in terms of these. But this is then already to say that we should give an account of desire that is in a fundamental respect similar to the proposed picture of belief: for, in each case, we would be taking attitudes to worlds as basic, and giving an account of the propositional attitude in question in terms of these (in the belief case the attitudes to worlds we took as basic were of course ruling out and taking seriously, and we gave an account of (two sorts of) propositional belief in terms of these). What I now want to argue, however, is that once one thinks in a bit more depth about what one's account of desire should look like, then even greater similarities with the proposed picture of belief will emerge.

Thus, I now want to try to think in a bit more detail about how exactly one's account of desire might go. So suppose that one takes preferences between whole worlds as basic: how might one give an account of desiring that p in terms of these?

Since desiring that p presumably in *some* sense involves preferring p-worlds to not-p-worlds (i.e., preferring worlds at which p is true to worlds at which it is not), a very natural first thought is that desiring that p amounts simply to preferring *any* p-world to *any* not-p-world. Unfortunately, though, this cannot quite be right (and for, essentially, reasons we have already considered). For I can surely desire a ham sandwich without its being the case that I prefer *all* worlds

442 / Bruno Whittle

at which I have a poisoned ham sandwich to *all* worlds at which I do not have a ham sandwich at all. But that means that the proposed account of desire is not right.

But a very natural *second* thought is then that desiring that p amounts to one's 'most preferred' worlds all being p-worlds: thus—the idea would be—it is not required that one prefer *every* p-world to *every* not-p-world; but there must be some group of 'most preferred' worlds, all of which must be p-worlds. Thus, the account of desire would look something like this: S desires that p iff there is some world w such that every world that S likes at least as much as w is a p-world; so, intuitively, the idea would be that there is some point in S's preference ranking (represented by w) such that every world at or above that point is a p-world.

Unfortunately, though, this *still* isn't quite right. For suppose that I am in a deli choosing which sort of sandwich to order. Surely I can truthfully say 'I want a ham sandwich'—and surely I can count as desiring that I have a ham sandwich—even if I would much prefer to have caviar; i.e., even if there are caviar-worlds that I prefer to *all* ham-sandwich-worlds.

A natural diagnosis of what has gone wrong is this: the reason that you count as desiring a ham sandwich, in such a situation, despite your preference for caviar-worlds, is that caviar-worlds are *irrelevant* here (i.e., you are not taking them seriously). A natural *third* thought is thus this: S desires that p iff there is some world w such that every *relevant* world that S likes at least as much as w is a p-world. This would then seem to get around the 'caviar problem': for, in the deli, I am not taking caviar-worlds seriously, and so they do not give a counterexample to the proposed account. And I would suggest that, more generally, what we have arrived at would seem to be a very plausible account of desire.[14, 15]

But, if this account of desire is on the right track, then we are going to end up with something that looks a lot like the proposed picture of belief. For in each case there is both a stable component and a more variable relevance set (thus, in the belief case the stable component is our information set, while in the desire case it is our preference ranking of worlds). Further, in each case this pair of components will give rise to a pair of species of the attitude in question— a stable and a variable one. Thus, in the belief case, the two species arise as follows: one stably (i.e., I-)believes something iff it is true at every member of one's information set; whereas one variably (i.e., R-)believes it iff it is true merely at every *relevant* world in one's information set. Similarly, in the desire case, one will get two species of the attitude as follows.[16] On the one hand, there will be 'stable desires': where S 'stably desires' that p iff her most preferred worlds are all p-worlds (i.e., iff there is some w such that p is true at every world that she likes at least as much as w). But, on the other hand, there will also be 'variable desires': where S 'variably desires' that p iff her most preferred *relevant* worlds are all p-worlds (i.e., iff there is some world w such that p is true at all of the *relevant* worlds that she likes at least as much as w). Thus, to return to our example: while I might variably desire a ham sandwich, I will typically *not* stably desire one (because there is always *something* that I would prefer; if not caviar then . . .).

Thus, there would seem to be independent reasons for giving an account of desire that is, in important respects, similar to that which I proposed for belief. And this would then seem to constitute a further argument for the account of belief itself: for one would surely like to give a unified account of these attitudes, as opposed to saying that we have two very different cognitive capacities, one of which is responsible for belief, and the other for desire.

Thus, I hope to have a made a strong case for a new picture of belief: a picture on which information and reasoning each get their own kind.[17,18]

Notes

1. (R) would ultimately have to be qualified to take account of (what one might call) 'overriding factors'. For example, suppose that S is very lazy, or that she believes that reasoning is evil: in such cases, she may believe something, but be unwilling to use it in reasoning. Thus (R) would have to be qualified so as to make a claim only about what happens in the absence of such factors. But I will not try to state this qualification precisely here, since the issue is orthogonal to the concerns of the paper (and, further, any account of what we are willing to use in reasoning would seem to face a similar problem).

2. For discussions of this sort of example in connection with knowledge see, e.g., Cohen 1988, Harman 1973, Hawthorne 2004 and Vogel 1990.

3. In this paper, by a 'world' I will mean a metaphysically possible world, i.e., a metaphysically possible way the world might have been. And I will state the proposed picture of belief in terms of these. Ultimately, one might very well want to replace this notion of a world with a more liberal one. However, I will not, in this paper, consider how exactly one might do this. Rather, I will stick with the notion of a metaphysically possible world because it is both familiar and sufficient for my purposes here. However, it should be clear that there is nothing about the general approach that I am proposing that requires using this as opposed to a more liberal notion.

4. This picture of belief is structurally similar to the account of *knowledge* proposed in Lewis 1996 (on that account, 'S knows that p' is true in context C iff S has eliminated all of the not-p-worlds that are relevant in C). Thus one might think of the present paper as arguing that this basic structure goes deeper than Lewis realized: applying not merely to knowledge, but to the apparently more fundamental state of belief itself. (However, I should note that a further difference between the two proposals is that, on Lewis's account, knowledge-ascriptions are *speaker*-relative; whereas, on the proposal of this paper, the corresponding notion of belief (R-belief) is *subject*-relative; but on this see §4.3.)

5. Note that R-believing is entailed by I-believing (because if something is true at absolutely every world in our information set, then, a fortiori, it is true at every *relevant* world in that set).

6. I should at this point perhaps mention a distinction that is familiar from the literature, and that one *might* think is similar to that which I have proposed between I- and R-beliefs: namely, the belief-acceptance distinction; for which see, e.g., Bratman 1992, Cohen 1992, Stalnaker 1984 and van Fraassen 1980. Now, there does not seem to be any very widely accepted understanding of this distinction, and so one possibility might seem to be to think of this paper as giving a new account of, and a new argument for, *it*. This is probably *not* a helpful way of thinking about things, however: for the proposed distinction between I- and R-beliefs would in fact seem to be quite different from those that have been proposed under this guise. For example, proponents of the belief-acceptance distinction have not given any indication that they would exclude from the belief-category anything like Rachel's attitude to her plans for next summer. Thus—for this reason among others—it would seem best not to try to construe the proposed distinction as a version of the belief-acceptance one.

7. For accounts of belief along these lines see, e.g., Foley 2009, Hawthorne 2009 and Weintraub 2001; see also Christensen 2004 for a sympathetic presentation of such an account.

8. Note that the account proposed in §2 does not have any problem with this variant example: because, in the deli (in the variant example), Rachel *is* taking seriously worlds where she wins the lottery; whereas she is *not* taking seriously worlds where Miriam is no longer a safari guide. As a result, the variant example is handled just as the original was.

9. An alternative account of binary belief in terms of degrees has been proposed by Brian Weatherson (see 2005 and 2012; similar proposals are made in Ganson 2008 and Fantl and McGrath 2010). The basic idea is that S believes that p iff her degree of belief in p is sufficiently high that changing it to 1 would not change her answer to any relevant question. This account is specifically developed to handle (among other things) beliefs about lotteries, and it should be able to handle the variant example just described. Thus, a fuller presentation of the proposal of this paper would contain a detailed discussion of Weatherson's account. One problem with this account, however, is that (in its simple form) it gives the result that people (almost always) have inconsistent beliefs: for if neither p nor not-p bear on any relevant question, then (on this account) I will count as believing both. Now, Weatherson is well aware of this problem, and he has a patch to propose (see 2005 and 2012; and note that the proponents of similar proposals would *also* seem to require such patches). However, this patch makes the account significantly more complicated, and, thus, less attractive. Further, I would argue that (even independently of this issue) the picture that I have proposed gives a much more straightforward treatment of the examples that generate the puzzle. For a thorough critique of Weatherson's (and similar) proposals, see Ross and Schroeder, forthcoming.

10. This case is inspired by one presented in DeRose 2009, 269–72.

11. Thus, the principle that I-belief entails R-belief (see footnote 5) strictly speaking only holds at times at which I actually *have* R-beliefs (i.e., at which I actually *have* a relevance set).

12. Thanks to John Hawthorne here.

13. A further reason for wanting to generalize the proposed picture along the lines suggested would be so as to account for things such as reasoning under a

hypothesis (for, on the proposed generalization, this could be thought of in terms of temporary additions to our information set). However, for reasons of space I will not try to develop this idea here.

14. This account of desire is similar in structure to accounts of various modal terms that have been proposed by Angelika Kratzer (see, e.g., 1991). Insofar as Kratzer's proposals have been successful, that perhaps offers *some* support for the proposed account of desire.

15. An alternative account of desire in terms of possible worlds has been proposed by Irene Heim (see 1992). The proposal is essentially this: S desires (or wants) that p iff for every doxastically possible world w, (i) if w is a p-world then S prefers w to its nearest not-p-alternatives; and (ii) if w is a not-p-world then S prefers w's nearest not-p-alternatives to w. Unfortunately, however, this account seems prone to counterexamples. For example, suppose that I am at a wedding and I have to choose ice cream or cheese. If I choose ice cream, then I will randomly be assigned one of ten varieties, and similarly if I choose cheese. Suppose, further, that I prefer nine of the flavours of ice cream to all of the types of cheese, but that I prefer all of the types of cheese to the other flavour (coffee, say, which I detest). (And suppose that I know all of this about the set-up.) It is then very natural for me to say, 'I want ice cream, but I don't want coffee flavour (and so I'm not sure what to do)'. But, on Heim's proposal, I do *not* count as wanting ice cream, because there are doxastically possible ice-cream-worlds that I do *not* prefer to their nearest not-ice-cream-alternatives (because I do not prefer coffee-flavour-worlds to their nearest not-ice-cream-alternatives, i.e., worlds at which I have one of the varieties of cheese).

16. In my initial presentation in this section, I have only made the case for thinking of desire as the variable attitude here; whereas, in the belief case, the puzzle made cases both for the identification of belief with I-belief, and *also* for the conflicting identification with R-belief. A fuller discussion of desire, however, would argue that there is a similar tension in this case (using examples similar to those that generated the puzzle for belief).

17. I would like to close by just mentioning an alternative way in which this paper might have been written; i.e., an alternative way in which the basic ideas might have been presented. What this would have emphasized is what these ideas tell us about the way in which our minds store information. Now, the prima facie natural view about this would seem to be that we store information in the form of propositions (where these are understood in *something like* the Fregean or Russellian mould): for, it would seem that we store information by having beliefs; and thus that our store of information amounts to the set of propositions we believe. But what this version of the paper would argue is that we in fact store information in the form of worlds. For, the main example of §1 above would seem to show that the propositional account cannot be right: for, given the plausible principle that we are willing to use in reasoning what we believe, it would give the (unacceptable!) result that Rachel loses the information about what she is going to do next summer as soon as she starts thinking about lottery tickets. The solution, I would then argue, is a new picture of mental information on which our store of information is not a set of propositions, but a set of worlds (i.e., the picture of §2 above). Of course, the idea that we store information in the form of worlds has (in effect) been argued for before (e.g., by Stalnaker 1984). However,

this alternative version of the paper would seem to give a new, and very simple, argument for this position. But I leave it to the reader to decide which version would have been better!

18. For comments and discussion I am extremely grateful to David Chalmers, Keith DeRose, Adam Elga, Katrina Elliott, Branden Fitelson, Elizabeth Harman, John Hawthorne, Josh Knobe, John Morrison, Ted Sider, Zoltán Gendler Szabó, Tim Williamson, and the members of a seminar at Yale.

References

Bratman, M. 1992. 'Practical Reasoning and Acceptance in a Context'. *Mind* 101: 1–15.

Christensen, D. 2004. *Putting Logic in its Place: Formal Constraints on Rational Belief*. Oxford: Oxford University Press.

Cohen, J. L. 1992. *An Essay on Belief and Acceptance*. Oxford: Oxford University Press.

Cohen, S. 1988. 'How to be a Fallibilist'. *Philosophical Perspectives* 2: 91–123.

DeRose, K. 2009. *The Case for Contextualism: Knowledge, Skepticism, and Context, Vol. 1*. Oxford: Oxford University Press.

Fantl, J. and M. McGrath. 2010. *Knowledge in an Uncertain World*. Oxford: Oxford University Press.

Foley, R. 2009. 'Beliefs, Degrees of Belief, and the Lockean Thesis'. In *Degrees of Belief*, edited by F. Huber and C. Schmidt-Petri, 37–47. Berlin: Springer.

Ganson, D. 2008. 'Evidentialism and Pragmatic Constraints on Outright Belief'. *Philosophical Studies* 139: 441–58.

Harman, G. 1973. *Thought*. Princeton: Princeton University Press.

Hawthorne, J. 2009. 'The Lockean Thesis and the Logic of Belief'. In *Degrees of Belief*, edited by F. Huber and C. Schmidt-Petri, 49–74. Berlin: Springer.

Hawthorne, J. 2004. *Knowledge and Lotteries*. Oxford: Oxford University Press.

Heim, I. 1992. 'Presupposition Projection and the Semantics of Attitude Verbs'. *Journal of Semantics* 9: 183–221.

Kratzer, A. 1991. Modality. In *Semantics: An International Handbook of Contemporary Research*, edited by A. von Stechow and D. Wunderlich, 639–50. Berlin: de Gruyter.

Lewis, D. 1996. 'Elusive Knowledge'. *Australasian Journal of Philosophy* 74: 549–67.

Ross, J. and M. Schroeder. Forthcoming. Belief, Credence, and Pragmatic Encroachment. *Philosophy and Phenomenological Research*.

Stalnaker. R. C. 1984. *Inquiry*. Cambridge, MA: MIT Press.

van Fraassen, B. C. 1980. *The Scientific Image*. Oxford: Oxford University Press.

Vogel, J. 1990. Are there Counterexamples to the Closure Principle? In *Doubting: Contemporary Perspectives on Skepticism*, edited by M. Roth and G. Ross, 13–27. Dordrecht: Kluwer.

Weatherson, B. 2005. 'Can We Do without Pragmatic Encroachment?' *Philosophical Perspectives* 19: 417–43.

Weatherson, B. 2012. Knowledge, Bets, and Interests. In *Knowledge Ascriptions*, edited by J. Brown and M. Gerken, 75–103. Oxford: Oxford University Press.

Weintraub. R. 2001. 'The Lottery: A Paradox Regained and Resolved'. *Synthese* 129: 439–49.

0 1341 1526166 8

RECEIVED

SEP 1 0 2013

GUELPH HUMBER LIBRARY
205 Humber College Blvd
Toronto, ON   M9W 5L7